LANDSCAPE ARCHITECTURE IN CANADA

Landscape Architecture in Canada

RON WILLIAMS

McGill-Queen's University Press
Montreal & Kingston · London · Ithaca

© McGill-Queen's University Press 2014
ISBN 978-0-7735-4206-8

Legal deposit second quarter 2014
Bibliothèque nationale du Québec

Printed in Canada on acid-free paper

This book has been published with the help of a grant from the
Canadian Federation for the Humanities and Social Sciences,
through the Awards to Scholarly Publications Program, using funds
provided by the Social Sciences and Humanities Research Council of
Canada. Funding has also been provided by the Visual Arts Section
of the Canada Council for the Arts (Assistance for the Promotion of
Architecture Program) and by the Landscape Architecture Foundation
of Canada.

McGill-Queen's University Press acknowledges the support of the
Canada Council for the Arts for our publishing program. We also
acknowledge the financial support of the Government of Canada
through the Canada Book Fund for our publishing activities.

Library and Archives Canada Cataloguing in Publication

Williams, Ron, 1942–, author
Landscape architecture in Canada / Ron Williams.

Includes bibliographical references and index.
ISBN 978-0-7735-4206-8 (bound)

1. Landscape architecture – Canada – History.   I. Title.

SB470.55.C3W54 2014   712.0971   C2013-908036-8

Set in 10.5/13.25 Sina Nova with Calluna Sans
Book design and typesetting by Garet Markvoort, zijn digital

CONTENTS

Introduction   3

Part I   Landscape Heritage of the First Nations and Colonists

1   The Oldest Land in the World: The Natural Landscapes of Canada   13

2   Turtle Island: Landscapes of Canada's First Nations   23

3   Maritime Approaches: The First Europeans   37

4   Sacred Land in the New World: The Colonial Heritage of New France   49

5   Dreams of Empire: The British Colonial Tradition   77

6   Promised Lands in the West   103

Part II   The Nineteenth Century: Challenges of an Urban and Industrial Landscape

7   The Making of Canada's Rural Landscape   133

8   The Greening of the Urban Landscape   152

9   Public and Private Gardens of the Nineteenth Century   170

10   Taming the Industrial City: City Parks and Rural Cemeteries   195

11   Taming the Industrial City: The Great Public Parks   216

12   Natural Monuments: The Creation of the National and Provincial Parks   236

13 New Ideals in Urban Design: Garden City and City Beautiful   263

14 Landscapes of the "Belle Époque"   292

Part III   Years of Challenge, 1914–1945: Landscape Innovations in Times of War and Depression

15 Landscapes of Memory: Memorials of the First World War   311

16 Private Gardens of the Twenties and Thirties   328

17 "The City Efficient": Changing Currents of Urban Development   344

18 Embers in the Shadows: Remarkable Landscape Projects of the 1930s   362

Part IV   Birth of the Modern Landscape, from 1945 to the Present Day

19 Brave New Landscapes: The Postwar Era   389

 20 Urban Renaissance 416

 21 Birth of an Environmental Conscience 452

 22 Beyond Modernism: New Currents in Landscape, 1975–2000 475

 23 Landscapes for a Multicultural Society 503

 24 The Twenty-first Century: Canadian Landscapes in a Time of Rapid Change 527

Epilogue: The Conservation of Historic and Significant Landscapes 555

Acknowledgments 561

Landscape Architecture Canada Foundation and Corporate Supporters 567

Illustrations 569

Appendix: Glossary of Plants Mentioned in the Text 579

Notes 585

Bibliography 627

Index 653

LANDSCAPE ARCHITECTURE IN CANADA

INTRODUCTION

This book is a history of landscape architecture in Canada, seen from a broad geographical and cultural perspective. Its principal objective is to provide the Canadian landscape architect, members of related professions, and the public with an overview of the development of "designed landscapes" in Canada. While a wealth of existing published material covers various aspects and periods within the field, no book has yet examined the full range of projects, people, and ideas that animate and have created the landscape architecture of Canada. Landscape has been a powerful influence on Canadian life and thought, and it is the author's belief that the art and science of modifying the landscape to accommodate the life of human beings in all its aspects, spiritual as well as physical, are worthy of exploration and explanation, from the extensive but little-known interventions of the First Nations to the diverse creations that reflect the many cultural currents of today's Canada.

Landscape architecture involves the design, planning, management, and conservation of exterior spaces. It is defined by its practitioners as a social art, focusing on the creation of places for people to "circulate, to relax, to develop, and to undertake various activities both workaday and recreational." It is also an environmental art; landscape architects aspire to be "stewards of the environment" and to apply their creative abilities to designing "outdoor places and systems of open spaces that are useful, imaginative, enjoyable, and environmentally appropriate."[1] The ultimate goal of landscape architects, as expressed by one of the associations that represent them, is to help integrate people into their environment.[2]

For some 150 years, landscape architecture has existed as a profession in Canada, but long before professional practitioners earned their living designing landscapes, the Canadian landscape was shaped and modified by human hands in a deliberate and conscious manner. In fact, the landscape is constantly changing as successive generations manipulate and rework the lines and forms they have inherited, creating a sort of palimpsest, not unlike the pages of a book that have been written over many times. "Le paysage se tricote dans le temps," as Danièle

Routaboule has suggested – the landscape weaves itself together over time.[3] The familiar urban or rural landscape where we live has almost always been consciously planned, either by professionals – we may call this "the designed landscape" – or according to the traditions of a particular community – the "cultural" or "vernacular" landscape, sometimes described in French as *le paysage humanisé*. Whether designed or vernacular, the landscape we see today has been overlaid on a whole series of previous landscapes: fields have replaced forests, new buildings have replaced old, freeways have replaced railways. But despite this constant process of obliteration and renewal, some of the earliest man-made patterns on the land remain as deep structures within all that has followed, like the old farm layout systems that have defined the street patterns of today's cities. And somehow unique vestiges of a vanished past survive, inexplicably, in an entirely new landscape, like the *chemin de croix* that long persevered in the centre of a bustling commercial area on Jean Talon Avenue in Montreal.

All of our human patterns are superimposed on pre-existing natural landscapes. The two may be closely integrated – a road that follows a river, for example – or they may be in sharp contrast – a checkerboard town or a farmland survey that has imposed a predetermined image or geometry with no regard for the natural forms and features of the land. Sometimes great sensitivity has been shown in this overlay of human and natural patterns; sometimes the opposite. And when we look more closely at natural landscapes, we again see the present state of an almost infinite series of previous landscapes. The land changes with every season, and indeed with every day, as plants grow and wind and water erode soil and rock from one place and deposit it in another. Over decades and centuries, forests seed in and expand, grow and prosper, experience fire and undergo the gradual change in species composition that we call "succession." Over thousands and millions of years, glaciers and geological forces shape and scour mountain ranges and plains, forming complex alternating sequences of "landscapes of erosion" and "landscapes of deposition."

Cultural Significance of Landscapes

"Landscapes are visual records of human response to the environment."[4] Vernacular and designed landscapes of past and present have responded not only to their natural and man-made settings and to a variety of functional concerns, but also to the ideas and ideals of the times and places in which they were created. Landscapes are the largest, most visible, and most pervasive things we make. Once we have made them, we live in them. Thus they are both a form of cultural expression and an environment that shapes our every action. They express what we are – our values, beliefs, and thoughts about the universe, the essential character of our civilization. They are linked to other forms of artistic expression: obviously to architecture, which exists physically within the landscape, but also to literature and painting, which both influence landscape design and explore landscape as a subject, and to sculpture, film, and music, which gradually unfold as we move through them, just as landscapes do.

When we live within these landscapes, either natural or man-made, they become invested with meaning and significance for us. They become *paysages identitaires* that are a part of us and that contribute to our identity. The meanings we ascribe to landscapes may be based on their intrinsic character and qualities as well-defined and well-proportioned spaces, sensitively organized in sequences, displaying colours, materials, textures, and rhythms. Their meanings may also work through association with the events, traditions, or people of our own personal lives or of society in general. Thus the old neighbourhood street or the country schoolhouse of childhood elicits a personal and individual response to landscape, while a walk through the ruins of an ancient battlefield affects everyone who knows the story or shares a particular background.

A corollary: since they are cultural phenomena, landscapes of the past can only be fully understood in terms of the events and values of the times and places in which they were created. Of course, we each respond to past landscapes in our own way and modulate them according to our own values, but we should do this after we have tried to see them on their own terms. If we *can* decipher them, historic landscapes recount essential messages about the past and thereby help us to understand our own culture. Landscape offers a prism through which we can view Canadian history unobscured by arbitrary boundaries or official interpretations.

The Canadian Landscape

The landscape has had a powerful effect on Canadian life. In fact, the self-image of Canadians seems to be inexorably tied up with the natural landscape of the country. Almost all our national symbols – the maple leaf flag, the engravings on our coins, banknotes, and stamps – come from the natural environment,[5] and the ways in which Canada has been defined by its artists and writers have been profoundly linked to the landscape.

This is particularly true of the visual arts. Landscape paintings and drawings (from Canada and abroad) have exerted a profound influence on the design of Canadian landscapes, and the reverse has also been the case. The picturesque vision of seventeenth-century European painters informed the villa gardens of the eighteenth and nineteenth centuries, and later, rural cemeteries and urban parks adopted a similar landscape vocabulary. Romantic painters of the mid- to late-1900s prepared the way for the creation of our national and provincial parks, and these parks, in turn, provided both locale and inspiration for a further generation of painters who were to become national icons. The modern movement in painting and sculpture preceded and prefigured modernism in architecture and landscape architecture. Long before these developments, much of the graphic art of the First Nations had been painted onto or carved into powerful elements of the landscape, both stone and wood, and during the first century of European exploration and settlement, Canada's striking natural features called forth dramatic expressions of representational art.

The landscape has also been a central object of observation and a catalyst for reflection in Canadian literature, from the awestruck or despairing comments of early explorers rounding inhospitable capes to the paeans of praise lavished by later residents on its sea-like expanses of prolific farmland. The power and omnipresence of Canada's natural environment have inspired one school of thought that suggests that the Canadian landscape is too much for us, that its age and immensity overwhelm our meagre efforts to understand it, let alone impose our will on it. Margaret Atwood notes the overwhelming presence of natural images and allusions in Canadian literature.[6] In her interpretation, these images reflect a variety of perceptions of and attitudes towards nature, ascribing to it alternate roles of an implacable and indifferent presence, a hostile and menacing enemy, or a welcoming milieu, gentle but somehow unreal. According to this view, the Canadian landscape often imposes a sense of powerlessness on human initiative, limiting our capacity to come to terms with it.

The thesis of the present book opposes this view. It considers that Canadians have, in general, successfully integrated themselves into the natural landscape and that many of the human landscapes of Canada, vernacular and designed, are as fascinating and interesting as the country's natural features. Although the landscape can indeed be intimidating, as Atwood and others suggest, it has also inspired impressive realizations, sometimes complementing its own majestic scale, as the following pages hope to demonstrate.

Of course, many of our natural landscapes are famous and impressive – the Rockies, the Great Lakes, the gates of the Saguenay in Quebec; they don't need our design efforts to be magnificent. Few works of Canadian landscape architecture are as well known internationally as our natural heritage. Many of our best works are brilliant exploitations of already outstanding natural landscapes – the whole complex of fortifications and parks on the heights of Quebec City, the unique fusion of dolomite cliffs and Gothic spires of the Parliament Building complex in Ottawa, the castle-style hotels and spectacular golf courses of the Rocky Mountain parks, the University of Lethbridge, Vancouver's Stanley Park. Many designed landscapes in less spectacular milieus are less striking, but achieve nonetheless a high level of aesthetic and social quality through refinement of traditional elements, originality of design, or thoughtful response to specific circumstances. And some man-made Canadian landscapes are truly remarkable: Halifax Public Gardens, perhaps the outstanding Victorian garden in North America; the strikingly original urban landscapes of the 1960s and 1970s, highlighted by Expo 67; the dramatic City Beautiful landscape environments created for the provincial universities and legislative assemblies of Western Canada; and the evocative monuments and settings of First World War memorials across the country.

We should be proud of the landscapes Canadians have created, and we should do more to understand them, protect them, and bring them to public attention. For too long, Canada's designed and vernacular landscapes have been overlooked and undervalued. Somehow, the orderly and elegant town plans of colonial Philadelphia, Pennsylvania, and Savannah, Georgia, are widely known and celebrated in town-planning circles, while the equally ingenious and efficient plans of Charlottetown, Prince Edward Island; Halifax, Nova Scotia; and Saint John, New

Brunswick, are unknown and unappreciated, even by many of their own residents. Why this is so might be explained by the above-mentioned dominance of our natural environment; or perhaps by Canada's legendary tradition of self-deprecation, combined with our location next to a spectacularly overachieving nation that has no hesitation in announcing its merits; or simply by a lack of education and publicity concerning Canadian achievements in this field.[7]

The Canadian Experience

The Canadian landscapes explored in this book express and recount a unique national experience, one based on a social experiment that began with the collision and subsequent integration of three cultural currents – those of the French, the British, and the First Nations or Native Canadians. This complex interaction, which gave birth to our principal institutions and customs, was then modulated and enriched by the cultural impact of several waves of immigration, by the constant exchange of ideas between Canada and other countries,[8] and by the continuing presence of the frontier, still very much a part of the Canadian reality.[9]

Has this experience led to a uniquely Canadian approach to landscape design? It is clear that most of our work in this field has been based on ideas and practices from abroad, mostly but not exclusively occidental, adapted to the Canadian climate and evolving culture. Some of these adaptations were in themselves highly original or even brilliant, but they were explorations of existing themes. In more recent years, several original approaches have emerged, both regional and pan-Canadian, approaches that may permit us to speak of "Canadian landscape architecture" rather than of "landscape architecture in Canada."

A further precision: while the landscape architectural profession has had an extensive and profound positive influence on the designed environment of Canada, fine landscapes have also been created by professional and amateur gardeners; by architects and city planners; by civil, forestry, and railroad engineers; and by private citizens of many callings. For the purposes of this book, all such work is considered to be landscape architecture.

General Trends

As we look at the broad sweep of landscape development in Canada, several striking trends seem to emerge. First, as a society, we have often started by desecrating the landscape, and then coming back to fix things up. We have not often achieved intelligent or beautiful landscape design the first time around. Hence, landscape architecture has often been a countervailing force in reaction to the overall movement of events, an attempt to tame and civilize what people have done to the landscape through industrialization, urbanization, and pollution. Landscape architecture is not fully congruent with "economic development" as commonly defined; it tries to limit and modulate the impact of humans' often debilitating presence on the land. Second and perhaps consequently, some of our best landscape architecture was achieved at the most difficult times, under the most unlikely circumstances. The finest hours of landscape architecture in Canada were seen in the urban parks of the nineteenth century, in an explosion of creative projects during the Depression of the 1930s, and in response to the *crise urbaine* of the 1960s.

Sources of Information

Despite fears to the contrary, mountains of good-quality documentation are available to the student of Canadian landscape history: maps, nineteenth-century almanacs and postcards, municipal archives, graduate student theses, and specific articles in architectural and horticultural periodicals since the 1800s. The 1970s and 1980s saw a rich outpouring of magazine articles by landscape architecture professors at Canadian universities, shortly after the first schools were established. The publication of such articles has continued steadily since that time, both in national landscape architectural magazines (e.g., *Landscapes/Paysages*) and in province-based publications (e.g., the Quebec *Annuel du paysage* series, *Ground* from Ontario, and *Site Lines* from British Columbia). Professors and practitioners in related disciplines have also written many pertinent articles in a variety of professional and scholarly reviews, including *Urban History Review* and *Architecture in/au Canada*.

These efforts were supplemented by national and international conferences on landscape history, including two conferences in Montreal in the 1990s that provided inspiration for this book: the ICOMOS/CSLA Congress of 1993 and the CSLA/AAPQ Congress of 1998,[10] held at the University of Montreal. The proceedings of these two conferences are valuable resource materials, as are a remarkable collection of published interviews with senior contemporary landscape architects by Linda Legeyt of Alberta and Cecelia Paine's publication of the *compte rendu* of the CSLA's fiftieth anniversary congress in Ottawa in 1984. Many documents have been preserved and much research has been carried out at Canadian universities and by various government bodies, including Parks Canada and the Historic Sites and Monuments Board of Canada; the "Agenda Papers" regularly prepared by the latter organization are an invaluable resource. A great deal of information about Canadian landscapes is thus available, but much of it is little known outside its region of origin. It is hoped that this book will permit us to connect the dots and recognize pan-Canadian trends and patterns where we previously only saw isolated incidents.

While such documentary evidence is vital, I have tried to follow the dictum of John Brinckerhoff Jackson, the dean of American work in this field, to the effect that, in landscape studies, the primary source is the landscape itself.[11] I have therefore visited almost all of the places and projects cited in this book, throughout the country's many provinces and territories. I found that viewing a man-made landscape in its full natural and human context often makes clear why its authors, famous or obscure, designed it in a particular way. This research became a personal journey of discovery, a lengthy pilgrimage across the country that allowed me to comprehend and appreciate its remarkable biophysical and human variety.

Structure and Organization of the Book

The book is written from the point of view of a practising landscape architect with a passion for history and not from that of a historian interested in the landscape.[12] It does not attempt to be encyclopaedic or to offer a brief vignette of every significant project, but rather to describe the overall evolution of the designed landscape in Canada, illustrated by detailed discussion of a few key examples from each period, movement, or trend. To place the projects studied within their natural and cultural contexts, the text begins with a description of the natural and vernacular landscapes of Canada as established since the first eras of settlement. Chapters in this and subsequent sections are generally (but not rigidly) chronological. Each is based on a coherent theme reflecting a specific place, a specific time, or the impact of a specific revolutionary idea, such as that of the great urban parks of the late nineteenth and early twentieth centuries.

As a consequence of this thematic and chronological structure, the contributions of individual designers and the evolution of particular landscapes over long periods of time are necessarily described in a discontinuous manner, in various chapters of the book. I have inserted references within the text to tie the elements of their stories together.

Technical Notes and Corrections

Areas given for parks and open spaces are approximate; maps are meant to be indicative of general trends and do not aim for precision. There may be some uncertainty in dates, since many projects were realized some time after their design, the process having required several years or having been carried out in an intermittent manner. There are undoubtedly a number of errors in the text, for which the author apologizes; corrections will be happily received and I will try to integrate them into future versions of the book. Every attempt has been made to gain approval of copyright holders for images and extensive quotations used in the book, but difficulties in tracing ownership have prevented this process from being carried out completely. Again, precise information would be appreciated and will be included in future editions.

Most translations of other authors' work for the purpose of direct or indirect citation have been carried out by Ron Williams and Sachi Williams unless otherwise noted. Opinions are those of the author unless otherwise attributed; it is hoped that they will help to stimulate discussion and dialogue on landscape architecture in Canada. They do not reflect the opinions of McGill-Queen's University Press, the Presses de l'Université de Montréal, or the organizations that have contributed to the publication of the book.

Landscape Heritage of the First Nations and Colonists

1.1 The Canadian Shield

1

The Oldest Land in the World:
The Natural Landscapes of Canada

From west to east, the territory of Canada traverses some 6,500 kilometres, almost a quarter of the globe's circumference at these northern latitudes. This broad territory encompasses five of the world's time zones, which were invented, not surprisingly, by a Canadian engineer. This vast surface of land and water is composed of a great variety of physiographic forms and geological structures; these support a remarkable range of plant and animal communities, a multiplicity of human cultures, and the diverse landscapes that these cultures have created.

Old Land, Young Countenance

The age of this land is as difficult to grasp as its size. In his wartime history of Canada, Stephen Leacock described Canada as "the oldest country in the world."[1] From one point of view, this is indeed true. The granitic rocks that form the basis of the North American continent were created from molten magma at the very beginning of the solidification of the Earth's crust. They exist at the surface today as the Laurentian, or Canadian, Shield, that vast area of eroded hills that wraps around Hudson and James bays, the last vestiges of an ancient mountain massif that long preceded animal life, or even plant life, on the Earth. The mountains of the Shield are, along with similar formations in central Australia and Scandinavia, among the oldest on the planet. Their most ancient rocks, uninhabited by fossils, have witnessed the development of the Earth throughout the last 2.5 billion years, including all the subsequent processes of creation and erosion that formed the Canadian landscapes we know today.

Paradoxically, this Canada that is so old in geological terms is also one of the youngest countries in the world. Virtually all that is visible of its present form – its everyday appearance and most visible lineaments – is a consequence of the glacial era that began 2 million years in the past and only ended some 12,000 years ago. During that era, immense sheets of ice covered almost all of Canada. Their accumulation, displacement, and subsequent melting completely redrew the Canadian landscape, sculpting lakes, waterways, and mountains; modifying watershed limits and the courses of rivers; and redistributing soils, rocks, and sediments. This rejuvenation of the landscape revised fundamentally the plant regimes of the country, directed the paths of colonization, and, finally, made a central contribution to the definition of the national territory and its internal regions.

Canada's Physiographic Regions and Drainage Network

The territory of Canada is composed of several distinct regions, defined essentially by topography. Relatively young mountain ranges form its eastern, western, and northern bastions: the parallel ranges of the *Appalachian chain* constitute its eastern rampart against the Atlantic; on its western margin is an immense cordillera, also characterized by parallel mountain ranges that enclose a series of narrow valleys and a vast interior plateau, the *coastal ranges* and *Rocky Mountains*, backbone of North America; and in the far north the *Innuitian massif* is its northern fortress. In the centre of this mountainous framework is the *Canadian Shield*, its

14 LANDSCAPE HERITAGE OF THE FIRST NATIONS AND COLONISTS

1.2 Physiographic regions of Canada. Unless otherwise noted, in this map and subsequently, light green backgrounds indicate lowlands and valleys, while darker green indicates higher elevations and mountainous terrain.

ancient peaks long eroded to their foundations, disposed in an open circle around Hudson Bay. The Shield extends to the west, north, and south, where it is overlain by a series of broad plains: a great interior plain that extends from the Arctic Ocean to the Gulf of Mexico, a crescent that neighbours Hudson Bay, an Arctic archipelago to the northwest, and the St. Lawrence Lowlands, a broad valley bordered by the Shield and the Appalachians and traversed by the St. Lawrence River, which drains the Great Lakes to the Atlantic. Finally, all three coasts terminate in extensive coastal plains, largely submerged, the margins of the continent.

Impact of the Glaciers

The boundaries of Canada were not created by a series of more or less arbitrary historical accidents, as is sometimes suggested.[2] Instead, the territories they define share an important heritage – virtually all are lands that have only recently emerged from the grip of the Pleistocene-epoch glaciers, described above, which began to recede some 12,000 years ago. The maximum extent of the glaciers' reach

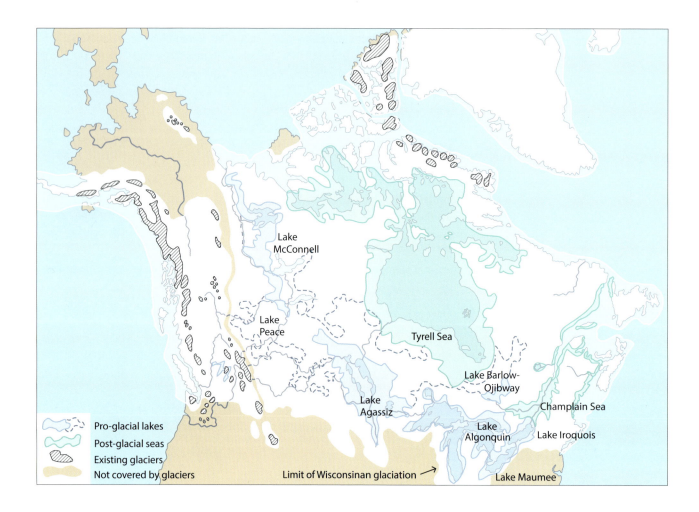

1.3 The glaciers and their aftermath

provides a fairly close definition of the Canadian territory. And everywhere within this limit, the glaciers left a sort of topographic signature that has endowed the many regions of Canada with a family resemblance, despite the distances that separate them and their varying geological origins. J.A. Kraulis, the well-known Canadian landscape photographer, expresses it well: "Before there was a Canada, there was a 'Canadian landscape.'"[3]

From their points of origin in the valleys of the high mountains of the West, in the centre of the Shield, and on Baffin Island, the glaciers spread out across the landscape in at least four successive waves. The last of these glaciations, the Wisconsinan – named for the American state where it reached its furthest extent – obliterated most of the traces of preceding glaciations and profoundly marked the Canadian landscape. Its legacy includes U-shaped river valleys gouged out by the ice and the bodies of water we call the "Great Lakes." The deep fjords that indent our coasts with magnificent harbours, the coves, bays, and "arms of the sea" on western, eastern, and northern coasts, were also sculpted by moving ice. Glaciers scratched out and transported soil and rock from higher elevations and, when they began to melt and disappear, deposited these materials as rocky *moraines*, *eskers*, and *drumlins*; as plains of sand, clay, rocks, and gravel; and as the indiscriminate mixture we call *glacial till*. Most of our best agricultural lands and many of our cities – including Toronto, Montreal, Winnipeg, and Vancouver – are located on lowlands or plateaux that owe their origins to the glaciers. Their constituents generally provide robust support for urban structures and good drainage capacity, but they are, unfortunately, subject to erosion. Moraines, visible today as linear networks of hills, have often become the limits of drainage basins and thus the boundaries between different areas of settlement and culture.[4]

As they accumulated and expanded, glaciers often blocked established drainage networks, forcing water to find new escape routes to the sea. During the thousands of years that it took for their ice to melt, glacier dams flooded vast areas, creating lakes that were much larger than those we know today. Meltwater from the glaciers also raised the level of the seas, which moved up to a thousand kilometres inland, practically to the centre of the continent, temporarily invading lands that had been compressed by the great weight of the ice they had borne.

Periodic changes in the levels of lakes and inland seas left a series of distinct terraces, recalling the evolution of their shores. Thus, the irregular path of Davenport Road in Toronto, which contrasts so markedly with the regular grid that informs the overall street pattern of that city, follows the former shoreline of Lake Iroquois, the larger ancestor of the present Lake Ontario. Similarly, in Montreal, Sherbrooke Street follows an ancient margin of the Champlain Sea.

The glacial era redefined surface drainage regimes everywhere in Canada and in the northern part of the United States. Over large areas of the Shield, ice excavated thousands of lakes and connected them with a chaotic river system, punctuated by abundant peat bogs and marshes. It has always been difficult to pass through this challenging and unpredictable landscape. Elsewhere, ice barriers that prevented the waters of the Great Lakes from following their usual route to the sea forced them to seek a new route to the south via the Mississippi, whose major tributaries, the Missouri and the Ohio, generally follow the southern limit of the last glacial invasion.

Following the retreat of the glaciers, the land began to rise from the depressed levels imposed on it by the weight of a kilometre or more of ice. Rapid at first, this "rebound" then proceeded more slowly, continuing up until the present day. During this long and gradual process, existing streams cut their channels more and more deeply, creating the ravines that are a feature of much of southern Ontario and Quebec. Similar deepening of channels eroded the glacial deposits and sedimentary rocks of the West, creating the deep *coulees* and "badlands" that are such familiar elements of the prairie landscape.

In the mountainous regions of East, West, and North, the force of the glaciers ripped out immense blocks of stone, creating steep cliffs as well as the majestic *cirques* of the Rockies. The ice then dragged the "erratic" rocks it had seized over considerable distances, often hundreds of kilometres, finally scattering them around at lower elevations or, sometimes, lining them up, as at Okotoks in

Alberta, where the forms of the deposited rocks seem like strange sentinels from a distant past.

Climatic and Vegetation Regions

Several of the physiographic phenomena we have seen exert a profound influence on climatic and vegetation regimes. The mountains of the West Coast intercept prevailing winds coming in from the Pacific, causing copious rainfall and moderate temperatures on west-facing slopes. In contrast, the valleys and plateaux situated between mountain ranges, in the "rain shadow" of the coastal mountains, are dry and even semi-desert environments. The central plains, in the shadow of the Rockies, are relatively arid in the southwest, becoming more and more humid towards the north and east. They are also subject to great seasonal variations in temperature. The eastern half of the country, at southern latitudes where the population is concentrated, receives abundant precipitation in all seasons; temperatures vary considerably from season to season, though in a less extreme manner than

1.4   Climatic regions of Canada

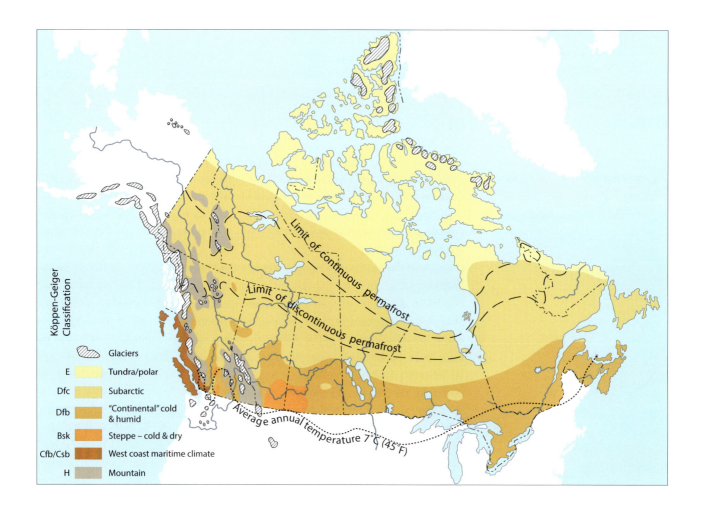

18   LANDSCAPE HERITAGE OF THE FIRST NATIONS AND COLONISTS

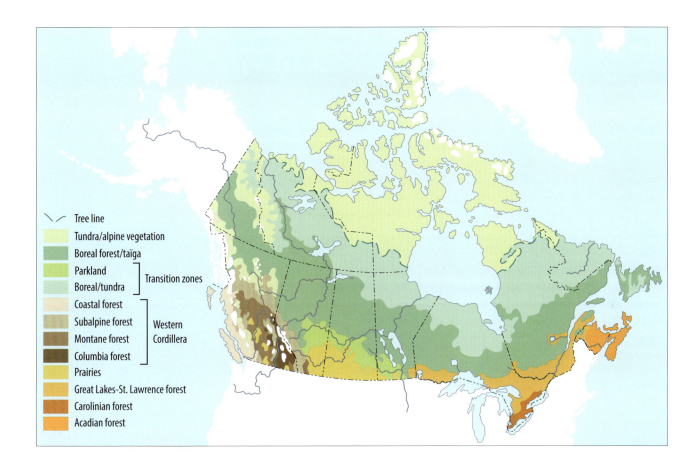

1.5 Vegetation regions of Canada

those on the prairies. These variations diminish further as one approaches the East Coast, where a maritime climate – humid and temperate – prevails.

Almost everywhere in Canada, there are four seasons and the winter is long and difficult. And in areas of milder temperatures, residents face the different challenge posed by long, dreary rainy seasons – harsh climate does not always mean cold. These demanding conditions have profoundly marked the Canadian personality and character, and have certainly helped forge the "garrison mentality" that scholar Northrop Frye has identified as a major feature of the Canadian character.[5] They have greatly contributed to the definition of Quebec, as affirmed by *chansonnier* Gilles Vigneault in his memorable song "Mon pays, ce n'est pas un pays, c'est l'hiver."[6] Further north, winter becomes longer and more severe. The average annual temperature diminishes rapidly, and since cold air retains less moisture, there is less total precipitation, so the climate becomes increasingly cold and dry. Here one encounters *permafrost* – permanently frozen ground – first, discontinuous and close to the surface, then continuous; and, finally, one reaches the glacial ice caps – *les glaces éternelles* – that are the last vestiges of the ancient glaciers that have vanished from the rest of the continent.

THE OLDEST LAND IN THE WORLD   19

During the slow retreat of the glaciers, the country donned a dense green mantle that accommodated a considerable diversity of plant and animal life. In general, the distribution of plant communities corresponds closely to the climatic regimes described above. There are seven major vegetation regions in Canada.[7] The most extensive, the *boreal forest* or *taïga*, extends from Newfoundland to British Columbia and beyond, across the Eurasian continent. It has been called "Earth's green crown."[8] Dominated by conifers, this forest region occupies more than 50 per cent of Canada, principally in cold and humid climate zones. To its north are the "barren lands" or *tundra*, where low temperatures, wind, and lack of moisture conspire to create "cold deserts" in which trees cannot flourish and vegetation is limited to low-growing – but often colourful and luxuriant – shrubs and ground covers.

Four distinct forest regions, all dominated by conifers, occupy most of the western highlands. The heavy rains that come in off the Pacific support the growth of the giant evergreens of the *coastal forest*. Further east, the *subalpine forest* occupies higher mountain elevations in British Columbia and the Rockies. In the drier climate of British Columbia's central plateau, the *montane forest*, featuring the Ponderosa pine, flourishes. And finally, the *Columbia forest region* follows the valleys of the great rivers that pass through the southeast sector of the province, its plant composition still essentially evergreen yet significantly different from those of the neighbouring regions.

The southern third of the country's central plain is covered by vast *prairies* dominated by herbaceous and perennial plants; within this region, local variations in rainfall and soil depth create several specialized plant communities. East of the prairies, mixed forests composed of both conifers and broadleaf trees extend from the edge of the Shield all the way to the Atlantic Ocean. These include the *Great Lakes–St. Lawrence forest region*, where maples, oaks, and yellow birches mingle with hemlocks and several species of pine; and the *Acadian forest*, occupying almost all of the Maritime provinces, noted for the frequent presence of red and white spruce. Finally, the rich soils and mild climate of Ontario's "peninsula," between lakes Ontario, Erie, and Huron, support the *Carolinian forest*, where conifers disappear almost entirely in favour of a variety of deciduous trees, including some not seen elsewhere in Canada.

Impacts of the Natural Landscape

Whether they are indigenous or "newcomers" from Europe or elsewhere, the people of Canada experience and interpret their country through a lens that is strongly refracted by its natural landscape and climate. Beyond their essential influence on the Canadian character and personality, landscape and climate have also exerted a powerful effect on Canadian history, much of which can be seen as "design responses" to natural systems. Historically, the river network and mountain barriers directed and defined the exploration and colonization of the country. In economic terms, climatic considerations have greatly influenced the location and configuration of human settlements, in both town and country. Even the limits of administrative authority reflect natural factors: for example, much of the boundary between British Columbia and Alberta follows the ridgeline separating the waters that run to the Pacific from those that run to the Arctic, and the treeline – the northern limit of arboreal vegetation – defines the southern boundary of the recently established territory of Nunavut.

The natural landscape also plays an important symbolic and cultural role. As in all human societies, Canadians consider certain areas within the landscape to be places of personal identification and healing, places of collective meaning and gathering, or even sacred places. We design these landscapes in particular ways to reinforce these roles, and sometimes, as a mark of respect, we choose *not* to design them, to preserve their unique qualities. An example is the Monteregian Hills, a series of rocky protuberances that punctuate the St. Lawrence Lowlands in southern Quebec, terminating within the Appalachians. These hills are igneous intrusions created as the continent moved across a "hot spot" in the Earth's mantle, like the Hawaiian Islands (which they resemble). Scattered for a distance of some 250 kilometres along an irregular line roughly oriented east-west, they are visible from all directions, contrasting sharply with the near-flatness of the plain. And almost every hill has been singled out to play some kind of special role, social or symbolic. No less than five of the ten hills contain provincial parks, conservation or recreation areas; at least three accommodate *calvaire*, or pilgrimage, routes; and one is the gem of the city of Montreal, Canada's first great urban park: Mount Royal.

2.1 Head-Smashed-In Buffalo Jump, Porcupine Hills, AB. For thousands of years, First Nations of western Canada took advantage of abrupt cliffs like these, located in southern Alberta, in their buffalo hunts.

2

Turtle Island: Landscapes of Canada's First Nations

The land that would become Canada began to be populated well before the disappearance of the glaciers. Although there is some controversy regarding their arrival dates and the precise routes they followed, there is a consensus that the ancestors of today's Canadian Indians and Inuit came from northeast Asia in successive waves, beginning when the level of the sea was considerably lower than it is now and glaciers covered most of Canada.[1] These First Nations, in adapting to the diverse milieus and climates of North America, developed many different cultures and ways of life that evolved continuously over thousands of years, benefiting from exchanges of goods and ideas with their counterparts throughout the continent. Beginning as skilful hunters of "big game" – most species of which have long since disappeared – the Amerindians subsequently expanded their economies in highly specialized ways, successfully exploiting diverse ecosystems. Residents of the boreal forest lived by hunting, fishing, and gathering of plants, while those who lived on the coasts specialized in fishing for salmon and hunting marine animals. Other Native Canadians became experts in exploiting the buffalo on the western grasslands, and many practised agriculture – without abandoning traditional hunting and gathering activities – in the rich soils and milder climates of the southern areas of the country.[2]

Aboriginal peoples developed an impressive detailed knowledge of the natural environment. Canada's First Nations used hundreds of different plants for dietary, medical, and ritual purposes, as well as for making clothing and tools.[3] The wild plants in Native larders included fiddleheads (young ferns), berries of all sorts, bulbs (e.g., the blue camas lily of Vancouver Island), bulrushes, and wild rice that grew in the lakes of the southern Canadian Shield. The First Nations contributed many elements of their culinary heritage to the general culture of Canada. Maple syrup and maple sugar are among their gifts, and one may recall that in

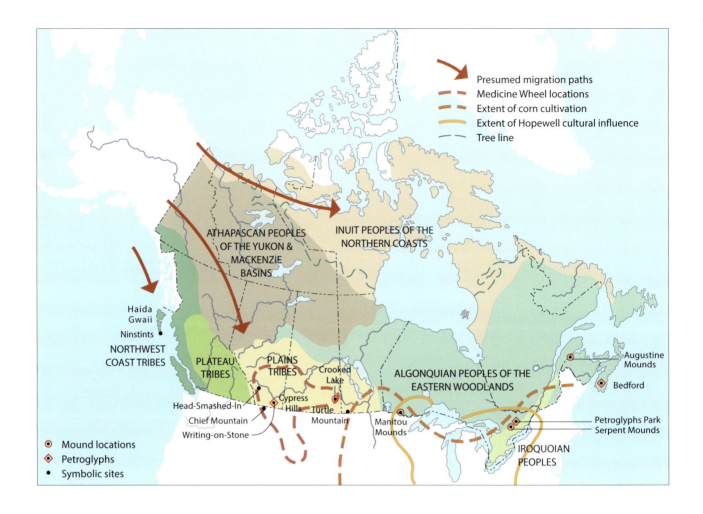

2.2 First Nations homelands and cultural sites

the sixteenth century the St. Lawrence Iroquois protected Jacques Cartier and his crew from scurvy by providing them with a beverage made from the needles of the eastern cedar, an excellent source of vitamin C. Native Canadians also invented diverse strategies to preserve food over long periods. The most celebrated of these strategies was *pemmican*, the staple nourishment of the fur trade, a mixture of dried buffalo meat, fat, and Saskatoon berries from the western serviceberry tree.

Far from simply gathering plants and hunting animals in an improvised or opportunistic manner, Amerindians cared for, nurtured, and controlled wild plants and animals assiduously to maintain their production in sufficient quantities. The Ojibways and other Anishinabe peoples, for example, weeded the marshes where wild rice grew, and reseeded the lakes every year.[4] In what are now the Maritime provinces and on the Gaspé Peninsula, the Mi'kmaq people established systems of ponds and weirs of such sophistication that it is more appropriate to speak of the management, and not just the gathering, of a resource.[5] And on the West Coast, as well as building rock walls to capture fish moving seaward with the tides, the Haida also developed elaborate systems of seines and nets.[6]

24 LANDSCAPE HERITAGE OF THE FIRST NATIONS AND COLONISTS

Agriculture and Cultural Exchange

In the St. Lawrence Valley and the Great Lakes region, Iroquoian peoples practised intensive agriculture, cultivating primarily corn, squashes, and beans – sometimes called the "Three Sisters." The women of these tribes – for agriculture was principally a feminine occupation once the men had finished logging and clearing the land – often sowed the three species together in the same hills to take advantage of their complementary and symbiotic relationships.[7] Thus, the large, prostrate leaves of the squashes kept down weeds and retained moisture in the earth, while cornstalks served as stakes for the growth of bean vines, which in turn helped transfer nitrogen from the air to the soil for the benefit of all three species.

The availability of these plants in areas north of the Great Lakes demonstrates the importance of trade networks for the exchange of goods, technologies, and ideas among different Native peoples, since all three of the "sisters" originated and were first domesticated in Central America. Native agriculture was both varied and systematic and was practised on a wide scale. The Iroquoian peoples cultivated several other plants, including sunflowers to produce oil,[8] and the Hurons grew a tremendous number of different varieties of the Three Sisters, including at least 15 types of corn, 27 of beans, and 12 types of squash.[9] Virtually all the current ways of eating corn – even popcorn – were already known by First Nations peoples before Europeans arrived on the continent.[10] In terms of the scale of operations, sources cited by the ethnologist Frederick Waugh speak of fields that extended over hundreds of hectares, with annual harvests measured in hundreds of thousands of bushels.[11] The agricultural techniques used by Iroquoian peoples were also practised by their Algonquian neighbours, including the Mi'kmaqs, Maliseets, and Abenakis of the Maritime provinces and southeastern Quebec, as well as by the residents of the Lake Michigan area in what is now the Midwest region of the United States, and in areas extending north from the Dakotas and Minnesota into southern Manitoba, as far as today's Lockport on the Red River.[12] Even today, the long agricultural heritage of the First Nations is hard to escape. The traveller who passes through the rich farmlands between lakes Erie and Huron still finds vast fields of corn and beans – mostly soybeans nowadays – sometimes planted in alternate rows to take advantage of their complementary qualities. And worldwide, roughly half of all the food crops cultivated anywhere on our planet – peppers, peanuts, potatoes, vanilla, and many others – were first grown in the Americas, long before the arrival of Europeans.[13]

Cultures Based on Nature

Outside the domain of economics, Nature pervaded the First Nations' ways of life and ways of thinking; the personification of cultivated plants seen in the expression "the Three Sisters" provides a striking example of this. Virtually all Native communities shared a spiritual conception of Nature in which the natural world and all its manifestations – animals, plants, mountains, rocks – were the concrete and palpable expressions of invisible yet powerful spirits.[14] The idea of a Great

Spirit that provides an overarching order to the universe – the "Gitchi Manitou" of some Algonquian peoples – is not far from the idea of God in the great monotheistic religions.[15] In the Native Canadian world, however, Manitou was usually a member of a larger pantheon in which real and mythical animals and humans also played important roles.

Some of the philosophies and practices that such a spiritual approach inspired among Native peoples were radically different from the European practices with which these peoples would soon be confronted. Their attitude towards the Earth, which they held sacred, is an example. It was to be shared by everyone, and even though a band or a family might exploit some part of it for farming or hunting, it was unthinkable that an individual could be its permanent owner. The idea that human beings were fully a part of Nature and that they could therefore not be in opposition to it, was another fundamental belief of virtually all Native peoples. Such a principle led easily to the conviction that human beings were close kin to animals and that, not far in the past, humans could become animals and vice-versa. Almost all Aboriginal cultures have featured legends in which animals intervene in human affairs, sometimes beneficially and sometimes for the worse, or even both at the same time when the Raven, a sort of clever rascal, was involved.

One of the most widely shared legends of the First Nations is that of the creation of the Earth. In one version of this story, the world was covered with water and several animals found refuge on the back of a turtle, an animal often seen as a respected emissary and communicator. After several unsuccessful attempts by the animals to find ground below the water, the beaver dove in and succeeded in bringing up a bit of mud from the bottom of the vast sea. He continued to do this, placing mud here and there, until the turtle's back grew immense, becoming the North American continent or "Turtle Island."[16] This story seems to refer to the great floods that occurred at the end of the glacial period, and it strangely prefigures our contemporary understanding of tectonic plates.

Most of the symbolic images that are important to people of the First Nations are inspired by Nature. The symbol most closely identified with the Mi'kmaqs, for example, is an eight-pointed star that represents the sun as a mysterious and magical object, to be venerated during traditional ceremonies that take place at dawn and dusk. The circle, an almost universal symbol, also represents the sun and the heavens and human society; the cross symbolizes the four cardinal directions and the four winds.[17]

Impacts on the Natural Landscape

This close relationship between the First Nations and the natural environment should not be exaggerated. Native Canadians have never had an attitude of non-intervention towards Nature. While one might recognize the profoundly spiritual approach that Aboriginal tradition has borne for the environment, it would be erroneous and patronizing to conflate this idea with the stereotypical "state of nature" imagined by Jean-Jacques Rousseau and to believe that Native peoples have always lived in perfect harmony with an environment upon which they have had no impact. In reality, they have considerably modified the North American landscape in order to remould it to their advantage. One example among many: in the absence of fertilization and crop rotation, the growing of corn rapidly exhausts the land's mineral resources. In consequence, agricultural communities had to abandon their fields and relocate frequently, at intervals of from four to a dozen years.[18] The progressive deforestation that this engendered was but one of the important impacts – often underestimated – of Native Canadians on their environment.

In addition to this deforestation for agricultural purposes, the imperatives of the hunt incited First Nations communities to set fire to forests in eastern regions of the continent in order to remove underbrush, thus improving grazing conditions for wild game.[19] This created an open forest where it was easy to travel, a condition noted by the first colonists of New England; but new vegetation filled in this forest within the space of a generation after the colonists' arrival. Some observers consider the open prairies of the West to be, at least partially, a cultural artefact, since they too had been enlarged and maintained by "controlled fires" set by First Nations to favour the regeneration of the prairie grasses that nourish the buffalo.[20]

Marks and Signs in the Landscape

The First Nations also marked the landscapes of today through the creation of numerous constructions and artefacts, as much ceremonial and artistic as practical and down-to-earth. Throughout southern Ontario, a long-established system of "Indian paths" continued to be used as main routes until 1825, well after the

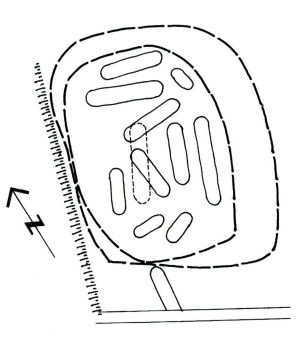

2.3   Plan of Iroquoian village, Ontario. This is a schematic drawing of the "Nodwell" site at Port Elgin in Bruce County, ON, a fourteenth-century village rediscovered around 1900. The village accommodated some 500 residents, ancestors of the Huron and Petun peoples, who lived in twelve longhouses varying in length from 13 to 42 metres, protected by a double palisade. The dotted line indicates the location of a previous longhouse that was removed.

2.4   Longhouse at the Sainte-Marie among the Hurons reconstruction, Midland, ON, near Georgian Bay

TURTLE ISLAND   27

building of new colonial roads. The Iroquois path that followed the foot of the escarpment across the Niagara Peninsula and the Lakeshore Road that ran along the north side of Lake Ontario are two examples of such indelible marks on the land.[21] Today, both routes have been transformed into modern highways.

The Long House

In their choice of sites and the design of their settlements, Native peoples demonstrated their close attention to the natural environment, at both symbolic and practical levels. The Hurons selected their village sites so as to ensure the close proximity of a water source, the availability of a hinterland of arable soil, sources of wood for fuel, the presence of a relatively young forest to provide wood for construction, and an easily defended location.[22] Like other members of the Iroquoian family, this people built large villages enclosed by palisades, each one sheltering some two thousand inhabitants who lived, in groups of five or six related families, in *long houses* framed in wood and covered with the bark of elm or other easily available trees.[23] These structures were essentially functional and practical, but symbolic and ceremonial aspects were also present. Thus, in the Iroquois Federation of the Five (later Six) Nations who lived south of Lake Ontario, the Mohawks were the "keepers of the eastern door," the Senecas protected the western door, while the Onondagas, who occupied the central territory, were the "keepers of the fire." In this way, the territory of the confederation was symbolically regarded as a sort of large-scale long house.[24]

Circles on the Prairie

In other Native cultures, the opposite was true: the house or the camp was created in the image of the territory or the cosmos. This was the case on the open prairies of western Canada, where the circle of the horizon is an inescapable presence. Among the Blackfoot and other peoples of the plains, a symbolic language of "circles within circles" developed. The family home was the famous *tipi*, a conical tent made of buffalo skins attached to a framework of wooden poles. When components of the band began one of the periodic migrations dictated by their habitual seasonal itinerary, the tipi left its mark on the prairie, a circular *tipi ring* defined by the stones used to hold down the sides of the tent. When the whole band reassembled in summer, tipis were set out in a great circle that opened – like the individual tipi – towards the east, to face the rising sun and the morning star, turning its back on the prevailing winds that came from the west. During the celebrations of the sun dance and other semi-religious ceremonies involving large numbers of people, the Plains nations, organized by band, erected their tipis in a series of smaller circles that, together, formed a vast circle, opening once again towards the morning star.[25]

The circle theme was repeated in the creation of *medicine wheels*, located at significant places in the landscapes of the west, over an immense territory that extended from southern Alberta and Saskatchewan to Montana and Wyoming.

Successive cultural groups who occupied this land over several millennia have elaborated these enigmatic compositions of circles, lines, and stone cairns.[26] Archaeologists have identified some eight typical wheel configurations.[27] In the most common arrangement, a central stone cairn is surrounded by several concentric circles. To this general pattern several lines might have been added, sometimes forming an "entrance corridor" made of two parallel lines; in other cases, radial lines or crosses were added to the basic structure. Other patterns, less common, consist only of lines with no circles. Where lines are included, they are often oriented to the cardinal directions: north, south, east, west. Finally, various other elements may be found inside medicine wheel circles, including human and animal effigies.

These constructions, dating back centuries or millennia, were most commonly built on hilltops and ridgelines or adjacent to river valleys.[28] An example of the latter is the Tipperary Creek medicine wheel, located close to the South Saskatchewan River at the Wanuskewin interpretation centre in the northern suburbs of Saskatoon. Composed of a large central cairn enclosed by a single circle, several irregularly positioned stones, and a number of smaller circles, this artefact was

2.5 Aerial view of medicine wheel at the Ellis Site in southern Alberta. This photo, taken during an archaeological dig, shows a central stone circle about 5 metres in diameter, with 10 stone "spokes" radiating outwards to distances of 14 to 19 metres.

created by a long process of gradual accretion, as attested by the large number of tipi rings roundabout. Another striking example of such constructions is found at Sundial Hill, near Lethbridge in Alberta. Here a large central cairn, 6 metres in diameter, is enclosed by two stone circles, of which the one on the exterior is irregular in form, varying in diameter from 25 to 30 metres. A north-south passage crosses the circles, and a small cairn and several depressions, located inside and outside the main circle, complete the composition.

These wheels have given rise to a great many interpretations. Some see them as ceremonial sites, others as observatories and solar or astronomical calendars, and still others as representations of the cosmos. Many recent medicine wheels (created up to about 1940) are memorials to a significant event, a battle, or an important chief. In the latter case, the central circle may be the location of a burial tipi where, beneath the stones, the chief's remains lie buried.[29]

Messengers of the Arctic

Like the First Nations of the Prairies, the Inuit of the Far North were not sedentary; their movements through the landscape were adapted to the seasons and to the habits of the animals they hunted. Living in tents in the summer, they also left stone circles as marks of their previous encampments, which they would subsequently reoccupy according to the rhythms of their migrations. As aids to orientation, they built stone sentinels in various forms. These are called *inuksuit* (from the Inuktitut word *inuk*, meaning "man"); a representation of such a structure in human form, its arms extended horizontally, may be seen on the flag of the recently constituted Nunavut Territory. These stone structures can take other forms and fulfil other purposes. Norman Hallendy regards them as metaphors whose function, today, is to help elders recall past times when traps for fish and animals were distributed over the land; traditionally, though, previous generations erected the imposing structures as a means of communication.[30] In their treeless territory, with few obvious landmarks, the Inuit thus created a visual system of orientation and, in parallel, a sophisticated method of mapping their territory, based on paths of seasonal movement and traditional hunting grounds.

Totems of the West Coast

In contrast, the natural bounty of sea and forest on the west coast of British Columbia, Washington, Oregon, and Alaska permitted several peoples to establish a sedentary way of life in villages that have prospered since the end of the Ice Age, more than seven thousand years ago.[31] These nations developed maritime cultures that allowed them to benefit from the abundant salmon, halibut, and other fish and mammals that the ocean provided. In the forests, some of the largest trees of the planet – western red cedar, Sitka spruce, western hemlock, and yellow (Port Orford) cedar – were able to thrive in the mild oceanic climate. These giant trees, along with the rich and varied flora they sheltered, provided food, medicine, and raw materials for useful products and works of art.[32] An active trade network with

2.6 Inuksuk at Kuujjuaq, in Nunavik (northern Quebec), located on a commanding hilltop site along the Koksoak River

other peoples, near and far, furnished additional goods to the wealthy and stable cultures of the Coast.

One could say that this civilization lived between land and sea. This was literally true in the villages of the Haida people of Haida Gwaii (formerly known as the Queen Charlotte Islands). The Haida built their villages in coves and bays that were well protected from winter storms.[33] A nineteenth-century visitor described these villages as being "beautifully situated, facing the south from cozy sheltered nooks, with splendid beaches, and abundant supplies of food conveniently near."[34] The village of Nan Sdins, or Ninstints, in the south of the archipelago, occupies such a site, separated from the sea by promontories and islands that frame a narrow entrance channel. Along the beach spread two rows of "big houses," rectangular structures with shallow peaked roofs, constructed of gigantic cedar posts and planks. Each house sheltered some thirty to seventy-five members of a large family; the largest house, located at the centre of the village, was that of the chief.[35]

TURTLE ISLAND   31

2.7 Totems at Ninstints, Gwaii Haanas National Park, BC. This sheltered village is located on Anthony Island near the southern extremity of the Haida Gwaii island chain. The village was abandoned in the late nineteenth century when villagers died or were relocated owing to disease brought by Europeans.

Integrated into the architecture of the houses and distributed throughout the space that separated them from the beach, a forest of totem poles dominated the scene and told the story of the Haida people.[36] These works of art, sculpted in red cedar, played a role similar to that of European coats of arms.[37] Their visual language included a panoply of about seventy emblematic figures belonging to different families and clans. Through a complex symbolic language, the totems also recounted the stories of each family.[38]

Sacred Places

Some locations and landscapes were recognized as sacred places that played particularly strong roles in Aboriginal cosmology or legend.[39] Such places might reflect creation myths, commemorate sites where important historical events took place, or, like Chief Mountain at the edge of the Rockies, be the residence of an important spiritual entity such as Thunderbird, who brings the rains.[40]

Mound Builders

The investment of some sites with religious meaning led to the creation of important structures, the oldest and most impressive of which are without doubt a series of earth mounds distributed through the southern part of the country, from the Prairies to the Maritime provinces. Built primarily between 200 BCE and 1,000 CE, these mounds bear witness to links with other cultural centres located hundreds of kilometres to the south. The Adena culture that flourished in the Ohio River valley (700–400 BCE) and the later Hopewell civilization in the Mississippi valley (100 BCE to 400 CE) built two types of mounds: cone-shaped tumuli for the burial of important leaders and more complex "effigy mounds" – often of great size – in the shape of animals such as serpents, birds, and panthers.[41]

This cultural practice extended to Canada, following the river networks that were the established trade routes of the times. Mounds were built across a wide sweep of Canada, from a hilltop at Moose Bay in Saskatchewan, looking out over a striking view of the Crooked Lake valley,[42] to Red Bank in New Brunswick, 3,000 kilometres to the east, where Mi'kmaq researchers discovered and studied the Augustine Mound at Metepenagiag, at the junction of the two branches of the Miramichi River. Both of these mounds contain prehistoric artefacts, ceremonial objects, and bones, the latter painted with red ochre to ensure the departed a peaceful passage to a future life. Many mound complexes have been discovered in Ontario; the site of Manitou Mounds (Kay-Nah-Chi-Wha-Nung) near Rainy River in the northwest of the province is particularly striking.

But the most unique of these many sacred places is found near Peterborough in Ontario at Serpent Mounds Park, on a peaceful promontory sheltered by tall oaks, enjoying a majestic view towards Rice Lake, an important link in an ancient trade route that preceded the present Trent-Severn canal network. At the place where they gathered yearly to harvest wild rice and freshwater clams, in exactly the sort of environment that we would choose today for a cemetery, the ancestors of the

TURTLE ISLAND 33

First Nations buried their dead for several hundred years (from about 200 BCE to 200 CE) in eight round burial mounds and a serpentine effigy mound 8 metres wide and almost 60 metres long. This remarkable feature has been described in the picturesque imagery of archaeologist W.A. Kenyon: "[T]he harsh climate of the northern latitudes is not suitable for tropical serpents. And so the last surviving member of that strange breed came to rest in Ontario, on the flank of the Precambrian Shield."[43]

Gathering Places

Other sacred places acted as sanctuaries, neutral areas in natural settings where people from diverse nations could gather in peace. The Cypress Hills on the Alberta-Saskatchewan border, as well as Turtle Mountain in southern Manitoba and North Dakota, were sites of this type. At the latter site, considered to be a sort of epicentre of the world, the members of up to seven Aboriginal nations camped at the same time. The highest points of both these sites had survived the glacial era as unglaciated islands, while all the land around them was submerged by ice or by the proglacial lakes that followed. This may explain some of the significance these places held for the First Nations.

2.8 Serpent Mounds, Rice Lake, ON

Petroglyphs and Pictographs

Certain sacred places served both as sites for communicating with the spirit world and as repositories of collective memory. Exchanges with the spirits were expressed permanently in stone in the form of engravings (petroglyphs) or as surface paintings (pictographs), often executed in red ochre. Such "stories in stone" are found in many parts of Canada, from one coast to the other and in the Far North. Near Bedford, Nova Scotia, an eight-pointed star incised in rock bears witness to the presence of the Mi'kmaq people some five centuries ago.[44] Elsewhere in Nova Scotia, petroglyphs found in Kejimkujik National Park recount many stories and legends of the Mi'kmaq. Examples of both kinds of images are found in the parks and historic sites of Ontario, most remarkably at Petroglyphs Park (Kinomagewapkong) near Peterborough. In this park, 600 to 1,100 years ago, ancestors of today's Algonquian peoples inscribed hundreds of images in an unusual outcrop of white marble, created through the metamorphosis of limestone. These "teaching rocks" occupy a forested site where, according to legend, spirits communicate with human beings.[45]

One of the most remarkable sites of First Nations spiritual communication is found in southeast Alberta, in the canyon of the Milk River. At Writing-on-Stone (Aisinaipi) Provincial Park, in a strange and spectacular landscape created by the erosion of sandstone pillars into forms called "hoodoos," local peoples created petroglyphs and pictographs over a period measured in thousands of years, telling their stories and describing their ways of life in a graphic vocabulary rich in

2.9 Horse petroglyph, Writing-on-Stone Provincial Park, AB. The relatively soft sandstone of this part of Alberta lent itself to large-scale erosion by the Milk River, creating steep canyon walls that could be easily carved. The warm-coloured sandstone takes on a pink coloration in the afternoon sun that illuminates the carvings.

TURTLE ISLAND 35

symbolism and representation. More recent images explain clearly the cultural evolution of the Blackfoot and other peoples from the "dog era" through the revolutionary changes brought by the "horse era," which began around 1730. Legendary personages such as Naapi, the creator of the world, and Thunderbird share wall space in this splendid gallery with images of warriors, originally on foot, carrying enormous shields made of buffalo humps, then later astride horses – animals whose movement is skilfully portrayed through deft and minimalist line drawings engraved in sandstone. Legend has it that these images were the work of the spirit world.[46]

Impact of European Colonization

When Europeans first arrived in the Gulf of St. Lawrence, the Native population of Canada numbered between 500,000 and 2 million people, most of whom lived in the region drained by the Great Lakes and the St. Lawrence River, as well as in what are now the Maritime provinces and on the West Coast. Three hundred years later, at the dawn of the twentieth century, this population had greatly diminished and the cultures we have just examined were everywhere in decline, following the colonization of this part of the "New World" by Europeans.[47]

That colonization, beginning in 1604, had set loose several waves of change and destruction that proceeded westward before the physical arrival of the colonists: a wave of new technologies and artefacts – metal tools, horses, firearms; a wave of diseases; and a succession of intertribal conflicts.[48] Later, much of the habitat of Native peoples was destroyed: changes in water levels led to the disappearance of wild rice from Rice Lake, and the almost complete extinction of buffalo from the Prairies removed the main food source of that region's First Nations. Native villages in many parts of the country were gradually abandoned, even Ninstints in Haida Gwaii, which is today classed as a World Heritage Site by UNESCO (United Nations Educational, Scientific, and Cultural Organization). Other Native lands were taken over through often-questionable treaty arrangements or by preemption with little legal basis, such that the vast territories once occupied by Canada's First Nations were compressed to a number of small reserves. This forced removal of long-time residents from their ancestral lands was to become a continuing theme – a sombre and recurring undertone – to the Canadian experience during the following centuries.

Renaissance

Yet the last forty years have seen a remarkable renaissance in the First Nations cultures of Canada, together with the development of a strong and growing interest in the traditional ways of living practised by Native Canadians. This revitalization cannot bring back all that has been lost, but the current resurgence of interest, shared by both indigenous peoples and newcomers, promises both to heal long-lasting wounds and to provide many helpful lessons to a contemporary society preoccupied with its relationship to the environment.[49]

3.1 Photo from Thaddeus Holownia's series *St. John's, NL, 1981–2006*. View across the Narrows to the Battery and Signal Hill. Even in a large city, buildings along the shore are located in an apparently irregular fashion that is nonetheless carefully related to views and to variations in terrain. They stand in stark contrast to the landscape, without modulation by extensive planting.

3

Maritime Approaches: The First Europeans

The Atlantic region was the first part of today's Canada to be explored, exploited, and settled by Europeans. A dynamic landscape awaited these newcomers; in this region where the continent meets the sea, the movements of the Earth's crust have left their most visible traces. The influence of the sea and its currents – both warm (the Gulf Stream) and cold (the Labrador Current) – has spawned a climate of transitions and contrasts along with great variations in vegetation regimes and in agricultural potential. From a few precarious early bases, the first Europeans in Canada gradually adapted themselves to the rugged coasts and bountiful valleys of this complex region, creating a variety of distinctive cultural landscapes.

The Atlantic provinces are, essentially, the northeastern extremity of the Appalachian mountain chain, created by the collision of continental plates, eroded by glaciers, then invaded by the sea, creating an infinity of indentations, bays, fjords, islands, and peninsulas.[1] The sea is as much a part of this region as is the land: beneath the Gulf of St. Lawrence lies a great plain of sedimentary rock, continuing beyond the edges of the land to form the Grand Banks and other shallow undersea plateaux, before falling into the oceanic abyss. An extremely rich community of aquatic life flourishes on these broad banks. It was, in fact, the promise of their almost miraculous fisheries that attracted Europeans to this region in the first place.

Temporary Bridgeheads: The Fisheries

Viking fishermen and farmers briefly occupied the northwestern extremity of Newfoundland in the eleventh century, but they failed to maintain a permanent foothold in North America.[2] The first official announcement of the abundance of fish in the Atlantic Region of Canada came from the Italian navigator John Cabot, who, searching for a passage to India in 1497 under the British flag, came upon Newfoundland or Cape Breton Island. Thousands of fishermen from western Europe – Portuguese and English sailors and Bretons, Normans, and Basques from France and Spain – responded to the news. Each summer, they organized expeditions to take part in the harvest of seemingly inexhaustible stocks of cod, which they dried out or preserved in salt for the return trip to Europe. Over a period of a hundred years, these treasure hunters moved west and south throughout the fishing grounds, gradually tracing the visage of the coast, the gulf, and the many islands and peninsulas that compose it.[3]

During his three voyages to Canada between 1534 and 1541, the Breton captain Jacques Cartier sailed into the gulf and continued up the St. Lawrence River. "The land God gave to Cain" was how he saw the first landscapes he encountered, on the north shore of the Gulf of St. Lawrence.[4] Despite these discouraging words, Basque fishermen set up shop on the Gaspé Peninsula during the same period, and a few years later, French entrepreneurs began to trade for furs on the north shore of the estuary, based at Tadoussac at the mouth of the Saguenay River.[5] And as Cartier sailed further up the St. Lawrence on his second voyage, his harsh verdict on the Canadian landscape reversed itself.[6]

In the estuary of the St. Lawrence as well as on the coasts of the future Atlantic provinces, these seasonal or temporary visitors established improvised settlements not meant to last for long and having little impact on the landscape. This practice was established even when it would have been desirable to create permanent villages, as on Newfoundland. In fact, the English merchants who controlled the fisheries did not have the slightest interest in encouraging their employees to winter over on the island; this would have distracted them from the principal objective of their voyage, which was to return to England each fall with the greatest possible number of fish.[7] Thus the fishermen built, at the edge of the sea, simple wooden platforms supported on posts, on which perched hastily built cabins, or

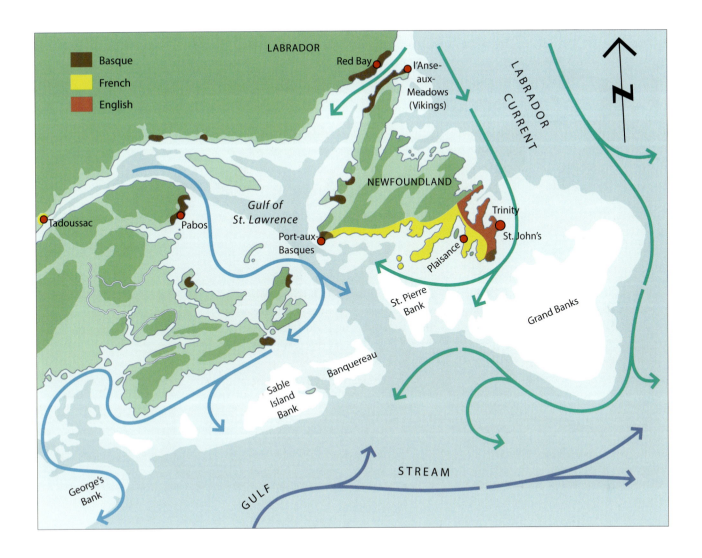

3.2 Fisheries and early settlements of the Atlantic region. Light-green backgrounds indicate lowlands and valleys, while darker green indicates higher elevations and mountainous terrain.

tilts, almost as simple and rude as the neighbouring *flakes* (scaffoldings erected for drying fish) and *stages* (rough cabins for splitting and preparing fish). This tradition of scaffoldings and simple buildings continues to the present day, as evidenced by the structures that can still be seen in Quidi Vidi village, a twenty-minute walk from St. John's.

When English and Irish fishermen finally began to build permanent villages on these rocky coasts,[8] the relationship between building and landscape remained – and still remains – adaptive and opportunist. At first glance, the houses seem to be spread out casually, almost randomly, over the site, but a more careful study shows that they have instead been carefully adjusted to the vicissitudes of an irregular terrain and to changing visual perspectives. Even when houses are aligned with each other along geometrically organized streets and share a common orientation, the changes of level typical of these rugged coastal landscapes give the impression that the buildings were erected in an irregular manner. The urban landscape is

3.3 Street scene, St. John's, NL. The city's colourful street environment is a jaunty contrast to its official buildings and its formal role as the province's capital.

particularly open and stark. Everywhere in the region, whether in the Acadian village of Chéticamp on Cape Breton or in the little town of Trinity in Newfoundland, the buildings renounce the softening effects that planting or grading might offer, preferring to address the landscape directly and implacably,[9] adopting simple profiles – squares, triangles, one-way slopes – sometimes with the roof corners cut off to diminish wind pressure. But there is a touch of gaiety in this austere decor: almost all the houses and outbuildings have been painted, most often white, but there is also plenty of dark green, pastel pink, blue, brick red/cranberry, as well as a cheerful wheat-toned yellow. Corner bargeboards and window and door frames are often picked out in a colour that contrasts strikingly with that of the main clapboard façades.

Through the combination of these factors, the towns and villages of the Atlantic Region go beyond the picturesque, achieving an appealing and charming simplicity. This is even true of such a large urban centre as St. John's, a city that is located in a sublime natural setting. Harold Kalman, the eminent historian of Canadian architecture, cites the remarkable irregularity of the plan of this city, where

40 LANDSCAPE HERITAGE OF THE FIRST NATIONS AND COLONISTS

long-ago paths between buildings "perched randomly on the hilly landscape" were transformed into the narrow and crooked main streets of today.[10] This unique urban quality of the towns and villages of the region has since become a central promotional feature in tourist brochures and television advertisements.

Acadian Odyssey

The first Europeans to establish permanent settlements in Canada were French-speaking Acadians who practised agriculture in the Atlantic region on lands expertly reclaimed from the sea. The story of these people also includes one of the darkest chapters in Canadian history. Even today, in the landscapes created by the Acadians – landscapes heavy with memory – this story can be read.

Champlain and Port-Royal: The Foundations of Acadia[11]

The first French colony in the New World was founded by the experienced Tadoussac fur trader Pierre Dugua, Sieur de Monts, on the shores of the "baie Française," known today as the Bay of Fundy, which borders the present provinces of Nova

3.4   Reconstruction of the *habitation* at Port-Royal National Historic Site, NS

Scotia and New Brunswick and the American state of Maine. Following a first catastrophic winter spent on Sainte-Croix Island on the north side of the bay, de Monts's colonists moved in 1605 to the south side, settling on the shores of the Port-Royal basin. This body of water, already mapped by Samuel de Champlain, lieutenant and navigator in the service of de Monts,[12] drains the waters of the Annapolis River (then known as the "rivière Dauphin") into the Bay of Fundy.

De Monts and Champlain made a judicious choice of site. The Annapolis Valley, protected from strong winds by two parallel mountain crests, benefits from rich, well-drained soils and from its location in the most equable climate zone of the Maritime provinces, permitting a diversified and productive agriculture.[13] Following Champlain's plans, the colonists first built a *habitation* close to the waters of the Annapolis Basin. This was a fortified village, based on the farm layouts of Normandy, constructed of wood and organized around a central protected courtyard.[14] Over the following years, overcoming such major stumbling blocks as the ravages of scurvy, attacks by the British, the abandonment of Port-Royal, and the replacement of Sieur de Monts, the little colony gradually expanded around the Annapolis Basin and upstream along the river. A map drawn by Champlain shows the first settlement in context: his garden outside the habitation, a cultivated field for growing wheat, a mill, and a road, as well as various elements of the natural environment and a site used by the Native people for fishing.[15]

Farming the Sea

In Champlain's map, the long-term development strategy of the colony was already prefigured by an indication of "prairies flooded by the sea at high tide."[16] The unique character of these *salt marshes*, which extended around the Annapolis Valley and occurred at many locations on the Bay of Fundy, provided settlers throughout Acadia with a rich agricultural resource. The marshes were inundated twice daily by saltwater tides that had long brought them rich deposits of sediment, materials that the sea had eroded from the floor and the cliffs of the bay.[17] By enclosing the marshlands with earthen dikes and employing the ingenious technique

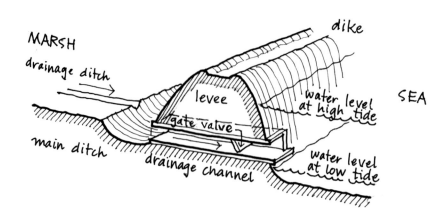

3.5 Dike and *aboiteaux* system used to drain salt marshes in early Acadia

3.6 Areas of Acadian settlement before and after the *Grand dérangement* of 1755. Many Acadians also resettled in Quebec, on both shores of the St. Lawrence and further inland.

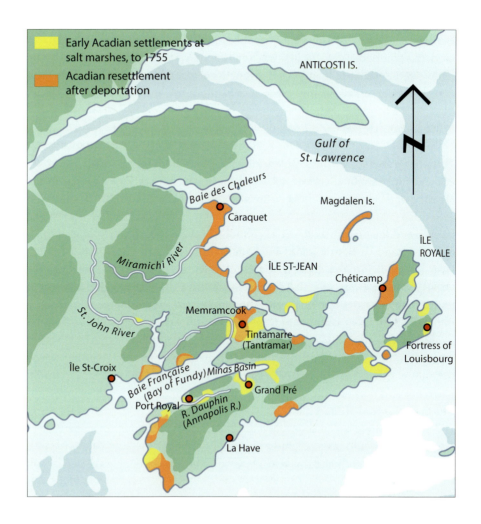

of *aboiteaux* (tunnels equipped with simple backwater valves or *clapets*), Acadian farmers were able to harness the great agricultural potential of the land, bringing into production vast fields that had previously been regularly submerged by the sea. The aboiteaux allowed fresh water to pass seaward from inside the dikes, while preventing the invasion of salt water from the sea. This gradually reduced the salinity of the fields so that, after two years, the marshlands were ready for ploughing, sowing wheat and barley, and pasturing livestock.[18]

Building the dikes required a laborious collective effort but was less demanding than cutting down the forests. It permitted the Acadians to extend their territory throughout the watershed of the Bay of Fundy during the seventeenth century, around the Minas Basin to the east (the location of the town of Grand Pré), to the northeast at Beaubassin and Tintamarre (the latter thus named in reference to the cacophony of bird calls over the marshes), and into the valley of the Petitcodiac, where the modern city of Moncton is situated. In 1699, a French observer was struck by the productivity of the region's farms, their prodigious harvests of wheat, apples, and vegetables such as cabbages, turnips, beans, peas, and corn.[19] A modern author notes that "Acadia was a culture based on the technology of dyking … the people's sense of identity and distinctiveness was derived largely from their dependence upon, and shared experience of, the Fundy marshlands."[20]

In the Shadow of Two Great Powers

This prosperous society, peaceable and egalitarian – building the dikes and aboiteaux was a communal endeavour – had the misfortune of being caught in the crossfire of the great wars of the eighteenth century, whose battlefields spread out over three continents. In 1713, Acadia and Newfoundland were taken over by the British, and the maritime territories controlled by the French were reduced to Île Saint-Jean and Île Royale (today Prince Edward Island and Cape Breton Island). Over the following four decades, the Acadians were spectators at a cold war between the two powers, punctuated by conflagrations. The most spectacular event of this long arms race that ravaged the Atlantic region was undoubtedly the building of the Fortress of Louisbourg close to the southeast extremity of Cape Breton by the French authorities, preoccupied with the defence of their remaining possessions. This immense fortified city, situated on an excellent natural harbour whose deep water offered ease of access in all seasons, controlled the entrance to the St. Lawrence and thus provided a protective umbrella for all the French colonies.[21] It was the Singapore of America.

A point of interest: Louisbourg saw the first example in Canada of a new type of structure that would later become a universal symbol of these maritime regions: the Louisbourg lighthouse, built in 1732,[22] of which a contemporary version remains even today.

"Le Grand Dérangement": Exile and Return

In a sombre prelude to the tragic "ethnic cleansing" that disfigured the twentieth century, eighteenth-century Acadian families suffered the assembly and deportation of their entire population. Some 10,000 Acadians were deported between 1755 and 1763; a few escaped expulsion by taking refuge with the Mi'kmaqs or hiding out elsewhere in the region.[23]

But as soon as it was possible, the Acadians began to return to the Atlantic region from their places of exile in such large numbers that, at the beginning of the nineteenth century, more than 70 per cent of the Acadian population of 23,400 lived in the Maritime provinces or Quebec. But they could not reclaim their ancestral lands around Port-Royal and Grand Pré: these had been rapidly distributed to "Planters," recent arrivals from New England.[24] The Acadian returnees settled instead on the north and east coasts of New Brunswick, on the west coast of Nova Scotia, at Chéticamp and St. Pierre on Cape Breton Island, as well as at Malpeque Bay and in the environs of Summerside on Prince Edward Island. Farmers by tradition, the Acadians were forced by events to become primarily fishermen, oriented to the sea rather than the land.

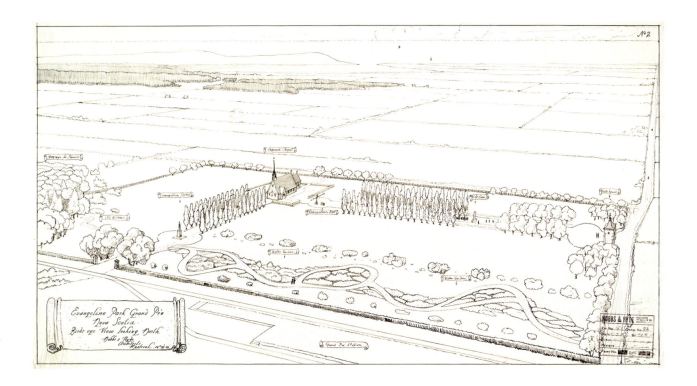

3.7 Drawing for Evangeline Memorial Park, Grand Pré, NS. Bird's-eye view looking north towards the Bay of Fundy. Percy Nobbs, architect.

As remarked by Georges Arsenault and the Capuchin fathers who contributed so much to collecting and preserving the rich heritage of Acadian folk songs, none of these traditional songs speak of the Great Expulsion or *Grand dérangement*.[25] It was the celebrated New England poet Henry Wadsworth Longfellow who immortalized the tragic fate of the Acadians in his epic poem *Evangeline: A Tale of Acadie*, published in 1847. A friend of his, fellow writer Nathaniel Hawthorne, had told him the dramatic story of the expulsion, which had been transmitted orally from generation to generation.[26]

The symbolic landscape of the Grand Pré National Historic Site, located close to the Minas Basin in Nova Scotia, also recounts in vivid terms the history of the Acadian people through the Evangeline legend. On a plateau overlooking vast fields that extend to far-off dikes and islands on the horizon, an Acadian association built, in the 1920s, a "memorial church" on the site of the Église Saint-Charles, where, on that sombre day in 1755, the men and boys of the parish were assembled before the deportation. In front of the church stands a statue of Evangeline, conceived by the Quebec sculptor Louis-Philippe Hébert and carried out, after his death, by his son Henri.[27] An orchard and a kitchen garden surround the church, designed, like the commemorative park in which it stands, by Montreal architect Percy Nobbs, as reminders of the agriculture of the time. Ancient willows frame and define the spatial ensemble. On walking the far-off dikes and contemplating the immense marshland prairie on one side and the vast bay on the other, one has the sense of being cut off from the world and returned to the eighteenth century.

3.8 St. Thomas Church, Memramcook, NB, seen from the approach road that runs across the Memramcook Valley

Memramcook, the Renaissance

Moving steadily towards St. Thomas Church across the Memramcook valley, situated in the southeast corner of New Brunswick, visitors find themselves on a pilgrimage, somewhat like going to Chartres. The great height of the church tower, the location of the church and its related buildings on top of a long ridge perpendicular to the perfectly straight approach road, laid out across a perfectly flat prairie – all these aspects of the landscape reinforce the meaning and importance of the slow ceremonial journey. Similar to Grand Pré, it is a landscape charged with memory, for Memramcook is the "Cradle of the New Acadia," the place of origin of a renaissance that rediscovered and advanced the Acadian language and culture. Resettled since 1766, this village was, in 1781, the site of the first post-deportation parish in the region. It was also here, in 1864, that Father Camille Lefebvre, of the Quebec teaching order the Congrégation des pères de Sainte-Croix, founded the Collège Saint-Joseph, the first French-language institution of higher education in the Maritime provinces. Finally, it was here that the first National Convention of

Acadians assembled in 1881, an event that served as the point of departure for a series of cultural, economic, and political movements that have contributed enormously to the development and the recognition of Acadian community.[28]

On arrival at the destination, nothing is spectacular except the sheer size of the church, the tallest in Acadia. Otherwise, visitors are in the familiar and comfortable confines of a rural French institution, which is the same anywhere in the world: rows of tall trees; symmetrical axes; statues of dignitaries, of Mary, and of the Calvary; a playground for the students at the convent that stands just beyond an elegant garden shelter. To this ensemble was added the Monument Lefebvre (a building that houses an auditorium famous for its almost magical acoustics), erected in 1895 in honour of the founder of the college. The institution later attained university standing and is now an important component of the University of Moncton.

3.9   Tantramar Marshes, NB

MARITIME APPROACHES   47

Return to Tantramar

One hundred and thirty years after the Great Expulsion, the celebrated Canadian poet Sir Charles G.D. Roberts (1860–1943), a native of New Brunswick who had grown up near the Tintamarre Marshlands, composed *The Tantramar Revisited*, a poem filled with nostalgia, written as by a man of advancing years who seeks, within his childhood memories, for the sense of permanence that he can no longer find as the years pass. Roberts was a man of broad culture who had mastered the French language; indeed, it was he who translated into English the novel *Les Anciens Canadiens* by Aubert de Gaspé.[29] He undoubtedly knew the origins of the wide prairies that inspired his reverie: "Miles on miles they extend, level, and grassy, and dim, / Clear from the long red sweep of flats to the sky in the distance, /... Miles on miles outrolled, and the river-channels divide them, – / Miles on miles of green, barred by the hurtling gusts." No poetry of the creators of the aboiteaux has come down to us, but Roberts's work shows how these landscapes inspired and even obsessed those of another century and another culture. The poet is stricken by the fact that "the hands of chance and change" have destroyed all that he adored, and he approaches the fields of Tintamarre in the hope that they have escaped such an unhappy destiny. But finally he doesn't go down to the marshlands; he turns about, preferring the memory to the sight, wary of the ravages that "the hands of chance and change" might have wrought, even here.[30]

He was right. Over the centuries and despite their apparent permanence, the meadows of Tantramar have constantly evolved in rhythm with great natural and cultural cycles, from the rebound and gradual subsidence of the Fundy Basin that followed the melting of the glaciers, to the diking of the marshlands by the Acadians, "the biggest ecological assault on the Bay of Fundy in the historic period."[31] By 1900, 90 per cent of the original 20,000 hectares of salt marsh had been harnessed for agriculture: farms that furnished industrial quantities of hay, the essential "fuel" for horses, the principal means of transportation at the time.[32] The end of the era of the horse marked the beginning of a long economic decline for the Tantramar. Over the years, much of the former farmland area was abandoned. Where four hundred hay barns flourished in 1900, only a few dozen can be counted today. The landscape is being transformed in new directions, which include an important trend towards "renaturalization." The marshlands are being reconverted – by such organizations as Ducks Unlimited and the Canadian Wildlife Service – into protected wetlands for waterfowl and other aquatic fauna.[33] Many of these had long departed; perhaps their return will allow the raucous *tintamarre* – for which these marshes were named – to be heard again in a land that today is strangely silent.

4.1   Sketch of Saint-Siméon on the St. Lawrence River, Charlevoix Region, QC

4

Sacred Land in the New World: The Colonial Heritage of New France

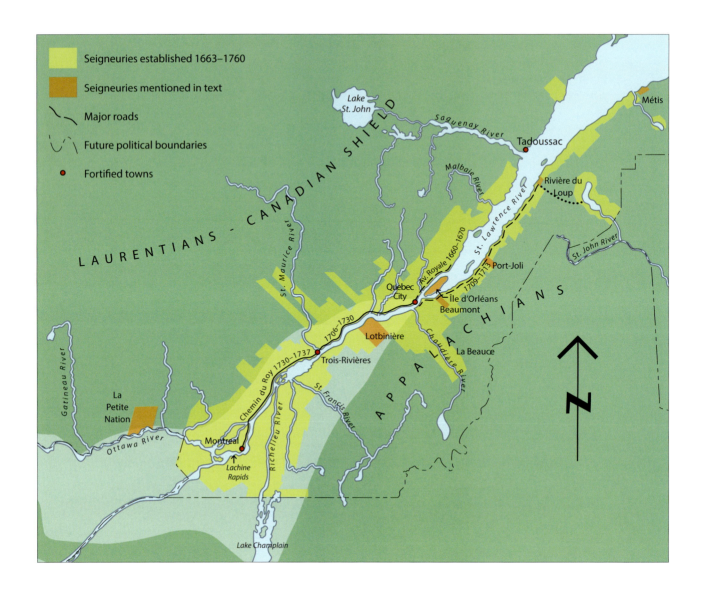

4.2 Seigneuries and settlements of New France, 1663–1760

On its 1,200-kilometre journey from the Great Lakes to the gulf, the St. Lawrence River flows across a broad and fertile alluvial plain – the St. Lawrence Lowlands – bounded by the Laurentian Mountains to the north and the Appalachians to the south, twin sources of major tributaries that flow down into the great river. At the end of the Ice Age, the Champlain Sea flooded this plain as far as the present site of Ottawa; its step-by-step retreat later created a succession of terraces extending from east to west parallel to the river.

The river and its valley have long served as the natural gateway to the interior of the North American continent. For a century and a half, from 1608 to 1760, generations of French-speaking voyageurs, bound for the forests and plains of the American heartland and beyond to the Rocky Mountains and the Gulf of Mexico, along with navigators, missionaries, soldiers, and fur traders, passed through its portals. But these explorers never truly occupied the interior of the continent, establishing only a few trading posts and the little farms needed to provision them, dispersed throughout an immense territory. The valleys and adjacent terraces of the St. Lawrence and its principal tributaries became the main *foyer* of a permanent French-speaking community with a prosperous and stable culture, its presence marked in the landscape by the patterns of farmers' fields and the streets of towns and villages. Here, in the heart of New France, the inhabitants of these farms and villages created a remarkable synthesis of natural and cultural landscapes. They also "sanctified" the landscapes beyond their villages by extending into field and forest the signs and symbols of their civilization and their Catholic religion.[1]

Towns of New France

The first establishments of the new colony were small fortified towns located at strategic, easily defended sites along the great river. Thus New France was urban before it was rural. These first establishments included Quebec City, founded in 1608 by Samuel de Champlain at the point where the river narrows; Trois-Rivières, founded in 1634 at the delta of the Saint-Maurice River, a major tributary which enters the river near the mouth of Lake Saint-Pierre; and Montreal, established in 1642 just below the impassable barrier of the Lachine Rapids and close to the mouth of the Ottawa River, the largest tributary of the St. Lawrence.

During colonial times, these fortified towns were dense and compact, like Port-Royal in Acadia. At first, they consisted of small assembly places surrounded by a series of contiguous buildings – quarters for officers, artisans, and workers; storage buildings for trade goods; and a kitchen – the whole complex enclosed by a protective wooden palisade. The towns were constructed beside the river, which was to remain for many years their only means of access. The first colonists were preoccupied with simple survival, confronted as they were by a difficult climate, a lack of resources and of experience in this new milieu, and the hostility of the Iroquois whom they had displaced. Even so, a little garden *à la française* – a decorative parterre – is shown, just outside the walls, in a celebrated engraving of the 1608 *Abitation de Québec*, based on a plan drawn by Champlain. We may conclude that there already existed, even during the first days of the colony, an interest in horticulture and beautification.[2]

These fortified towns served not only as depots for trade with First Nations peoples, but also as bases for their conversion to the Christian religion. The religious missions launched from New France extended well beyond the St. Lawrence Valley; already in the 1640s, Recollet and Jesuit fathers established distant missions among the Hurons or Wendats, allies of the French and their major suppliers of furs. The best known of these seventeenth-century missions, Sainte-Marie among the Hurons, near the present town of Midland in Ontario, was reconstructed in the twentieth century on the foundations of the original establishment, which had been burned by the Jesuits when war between Hurons and Iroquois forced the evacuation of Huronia in 1649.[3]

SACRED LAND IN THE NEW WORLD 51

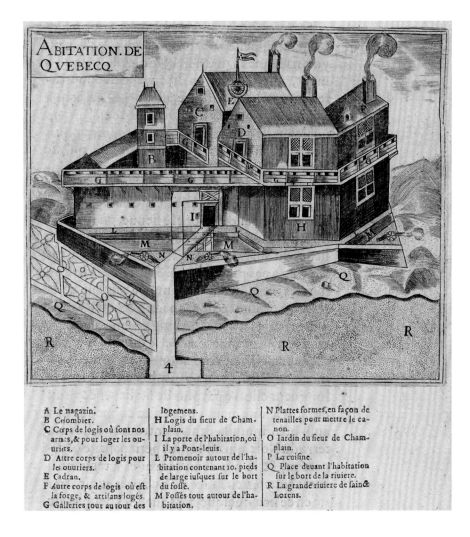

4.3 Champlain's *"abitation"* at Quebec City, 1608. Champlain himself made the original drawing on which this engraving was based. The governor's garden is seen at lower left outside the palisade walls.

French traders continued their explorations towards the interior of the continent as they pursued commercial exchanges with Native peoples. Despite the excessive trapping that this sometimes entailed (even leading to the local extinction of some animal species, particularly the beaver), the fur trade did not have a major impact on forest landscapes. The French habitually maintained excellent relations with the First Nations; it was clearly not in their interest to destroy the forest, which was both the source of their wealth and the living space of their business associates. The main long-term intervention of the French traders and missionaries as they moved west was the establishment of a network of fortified villages like that at Sainte-Marie, all around the Great Lakes and at intervals along the western rivers, located, as always, at strategic and easily defendable sites. The good sense of their choice of sites is still apparent today, as witnessed by the survival of the old French Quarter of New Orleans despite the widespread flooding caused by Hurricane

4.4   Typical vegetable garden at the Sainte-Marie among the Hurons reconstruction. The fortified settlement was a sort of hybrid between the habitations at Quebec and Port-Royal and an Iroquoian village. It consisted of a stone fort and a central complex of buildings. An interior courtyard was located within the double palisade. The garden shown here is located in the outer walled sector. The outer palisade is on the left; the inner palisade in on the right. Part of the stone fort is visible at rear.

Katrina in 2005. Throughout the centre of the continent, a significant number of modern cities, large and small, owe their origins to the villages founded by French traders. This is true of Toronto, which consisted originally of two forts located close to the mouth of the Humber River, at the best-protected site on the north shore of Lake Ontario; and of Detroit, situated on the river that links Lake Huron to Lake Michigan. Similarly, the French founded the first settlement at Winnipeg, gateway to the Prairies, located at the forks of the Assiniboine and Red rivers. And from the Great Lakes, they moved west and south into the drainage basin of the Mississippi through such river connections as Green Bay and Chicago that led to convenient portages between the two watersheds. Halfway down this great river, at its confluence with the Missouri, the French established the city of Saint Louis and finally, where the Mississippi enters the Gulf of Mexico, the port of New Orleans.[4]

Growth and Development of Cities

By the mid-1600s, the little towns of the St. Lawrence Valley had become relatively stable and were experiencing a gradual expansion in population. Much of this

new growth was due to the arrival in the colony of several religious orders that put in place much-needed hospitals and educational institutions. Augustine and Ursuline sisters came ashore at Quebec City in 1639, and 1657 saw the arrival of the Congrégation Notre-Dame and the Sulpician order in Montreal. These and several other religious communities created a strong institutional structure that formed the basis for New France's civic culture; the essential elements of this structure remained in place well into the twentieth century and, in some cases, have survived to the present day.

This consolidation and expansion inspired the leaders of the colonial society to replan their cities in a more systematic and orderly manner. In his classic *Montreal in Evolution*, Jean-Claude Marsan places this process in context.[5] Since the Middle Ages, he states, a standard model had guided the planning of new cities in territories recently acquired or conquered: the *ville-bastide*. This town design included several archetypal motifs: a rectangular overall outline; a surrounding wall for purposes of defence, pierced at several locations by fortified gates; inside the wall, a series of regular residential blocks defined by an orthogonal street grid. Some of these blocks were not built upon, but instead left open to serve as public spaces, enclosed by the important public buildings of the town. The social, civic, and commercial activities of the city were mainly carried out in these public spaces, each of which had its own specific vocation, either sacred – such as the *parvis*, a small square at the entrance to the church – or profane, such as the marketplace.[6]

While it was normal for the governor of New France and his associates to adopt this simple and traditional model, of medieval and even Roman tradition, other preoccupations also influenced the design of the colony's cities. Designers of city plans showed great concern for local topography and did not always follow the traditional sacred/profane division of public spaces. Finally, they integrated to city plans some of the new ideas of the French Renaissance concerning urban organization and fortification.[7]

Besides public plazas, the cities of New France boasted other types of open space. In his analysis of the plans of Montreal and Quebec City towards the end of the French régime, Benoît Bégin remarks that "in each city, there is a preponderance of green space: kitchen gardens, orchards, decorative gardens, esplanades, squares, woods and second-growth forest occupy the majority of the area within the walls."[8] This is evident in the plans prepared between 1710 and 1750 by Gaspard-Joseph Chaussegros de Léry (1682–1756), a remarkable engineer sent by Louis XV to direct the fortification of the cities of New France.[9] These drawings show that many of these green spaces were situated within the grounds of religious institutions – secret gardens, surrounded by walls, within cities themselves enclosed by walls.

Quebec City, 1640–1760

Quebec City comprised two distinct districts: "Lower Town" next to the river and "Upper Town," on the plateau atop the cliffs of Cape Diamond. Lower Town, laid out in the humble rectangular grid typical of new settlements, accommodated the city's port, along with commercial and residential activities. Its social and spiritual heart was the marketplace, Place du Marché, renamed Place Royale in 1686 in honour of Louis XIV. In contrast, Upper Town was the foyer of the city's institutions, its military installations, and the colonial administration (except for the Intendant's Palace, since that official's responsibilities for the direction of all economic and financial activity of the colony required his presence close to the port, in an extension of Lower Town along the valley of the Saint Charles River). Many people also lived in Upper Town. The arrangement of its main streets, seemingly random at first glance, is in fact a very sophisticated layout. These streets radiate in pinwheel fashion from major public spaces – Place d'Armes (the parade square) and Place de la Cathédrale (now City Hall Square), both spaces carefully integrated into the irregular topography of the plateau – towards the gates that traverse the city's fortifications.[10] Within the areas defined by these diagonal main thoroughfares, secondary streets are content to follow relatively conventional grid arrangements.

Between these two very different towns stand the cliffs of Cape Diamond, reinforced by stone ramparts built between 1720 and 1749 according to the drawings of Chaussegros de Léry. This distinguished engineer made many other contributions to the colony, including designs for the fortifications of Montreal and the forts at Niagara and Chambly, as well as the façade of the old Notre-Dame Church in Montreal and the Governor's Palace in Quebec City.[11] In the eighteenth century – as today – a handful of staircases and steeply sloping roadways descended the cliffs, connecting the two levels of the city. In both sectors, the street landscape was essentially mineral, "hardly softened by greenery, except where branches overflowed side or rear gardens, or extended from inside a courtyard."[12] On the other hand, the architecture of the two levels was marked by contrast: that of Lower Town sober, simple, robust, and utilitarian, while Upper Town's spires and the gates of its administrative buildings – and indeed this had already been the case in the seventeenth century – were characterized by elegance and refinement, and Grande-Allée – its extension to the west – was already lined with street trees.[13]

Montreal, 1670–1760

Following its first establishment at the Pointe-à-Callière, just to the southwest of today's "Vieux Montréal," the village of Montreal expanded eastward to the Coteau Saint-Louis, a modest hill parallel to the river, enclosed on each side by smaller streams. This was an easily defendable site, well protected from flooding. Without much planning, the first colonists laid out several streets and constructed several buildings, enclosing their little settlement inside a rough palisade of cedar logs. This primitive village was to change drastically in 1672 when Father Dollier de Casson (1636–1701), superior of the Sulpician order, prepared a plan that was to direct the growth of the town through its subsequent stages of development.[14] Father Dollier, who had been a captain of cavalry before taking up the priesthood, also wrote one of the first histories of Montreal – a true "Renaissance man" well prepared for his role as a city planner.

SACRED LAND IN THE NEW WORLD 55

In the Sulpician plan, the form of the town and the limits of its new fortifications followed, in general, the form of the hill: a long and somewhat irregular rectangle, oriented from southwest to northeast, roughly parallel to the river. Its streets were arranged in an approximately rectilinear grid. Similar to Quebec City but in less striking fashion, colonial Montreal consisted of two distinct urban districts defined by topography: a commercial and mercantile "Lower Town" along St. Paul Street, oriented towards the port, and an "Upper Town," religious, administrative, and institutional, centred on Notre-Dame Street, which followed the crest of the hill. On one of the summits of this crest, the colonists built the parish church of Notre-Dame, spiritual centre of the town, right in the middle of the street and oriented from west to east so that the sanctuary would be oriented towards the Holy Land. The street opened up to the north of the church, providing a parvis or church square. At the other extremity of the Notre-Dame Street axis, the residence of Governor Claude de Ramezay crowned the eastern summit of the hill. The Lower Town was deployed around its marketplace, Place Royale, located at the southern limit of the settlement, facing a gate cut into the enclosing wall. Outside the walls and along the riverbank, a long open space, the "common," served

4.5 Plan of Montreal, 1725, Chaussegros de Léry. De Léry's plan shows the city walls he designed to enclose the orderly plan laid out earlier by Father Dollier de Casson. Saint Paul Street and Notre Dame to its north run parallel along the length of the town. The parish church is located in the centre of Notre Dame next to Place d'Armes, shown as a white square in the upper centre of the town plan. Other open spaces are similarly marked. The future St. Lawrence Boulevard leads north beyond the city walls from the centre of town.

as a shared pastureland for the colonists' animals and a meeting place for trade between Frenchmen and Natives.

As at Quebec City, vegetation played a major role in the town, though without contributing greatly to the public streetscape, which was dominated by hard surfaces. This greenery – including orchards, geometric planting beds, and kitchen gardens – was concentrated behind the walls of institutions that provided all the social services for the colonists. Thus, the open-space pattern of the cities of New France combined hard-surfaced squares, which structured the public realm of the city, with a parallel network of hidden gardens in the private realm.[15]

Louisbourg, 1713–1760

The fortress of Louisbourg on Cape Breton Island, Nova Scotia, represents the apotheosis of the fortified city of the eighteenth century. Built almost at one stroke according to a precise overall design, this city of more than four thousand inhabitants, civilian and military, stood in great contrast to Quebec City and Montreal, which developed gradually over centuries and in which each reconstruction had to

4.6 Reconstruction of the King's Bastion barracks, Fortress of Louisbourg National Historic Site, NS

accommodate previous structures. The orderly and rational organization of Louis-bourg bears witness to the art of fortification, which reached its apogee in France during this period, following the innovations of the brilliant engineer Sébastien le Prestre, Marquis de Vauban (1633–1707). Four protective bastions and several batteries surrounded the city, whose streets and squares were laid out according to a perfectly regular grid following the cardinal directions. As always, the city was graced by a large number of gardens, formal and elegant for high officials, simple and functional for commoners.

The destruction and subsequent renaissance of the fortress of Louisbourg are legendary. After its capture and demolition by British forces during the 1750s and 1760s, Louisbourg, in ruins, was then utterly neglected for almost two centuries. The American historian Francis Parkman was astonished by the endless solitude of shapeless green mounds that had been a city.[16] Then, beginning in 1961, Parks Canada rebuilt a large part of the fortress and the city on their original founda-tions, according to the original drawings that had been carefully preserved all the while in France. The history of this reconstruction is an epic in itself. The sense of detail and the concern for authenticity that are evident in this reconstruction enable us to see and to explore – as much as this is possible after the passage of 250 years – a real eighteenth-century city of New France.[17]

Public Spaces

New France's public spaces reflected those created in Europe in the late Middle Ages and at the beginning of the Renaissance: restrained in dimensions, fairly regular in geometric form, strongly enclosed by the façades of buildings. All these properties combined to create intimate and coherent spaces, essentially "outdoor rooms." Each space provided the setting for an important building: church, offi-cial residence, public market, or customs house.[18] Their ground surfaces, often sloping and originally consisting of compacted earth, were eventually paved with stone, and they were gradually enriched with focal elements such as fountains and sculptures.[19] These spaces accommodated all the public activities of the time: the weekly sale of foodstuffs, announcements by the public crier, the social assem-bly of all classes, the exchange of information and gossip, and the punishment of criminals. They were "truly public places, animated by the lively public theatre of popular culture."[20]

Place Royale in Quebec City, often considered the most important historic site in New France,[21] is in Lower Town, adjacent to the very site where Champlain built his first *abitation* in 1608. Created in about 1640 to serve as a public market,[22] this space was defined by parallel streets of the urban grid; entry was at the cor-ners (a common theme), from the city and the port. The historic Notre-Dame-des-Victoires Church, erected in 1688, dominated the square in colonial times as it does today; merchants' houses provided its three other enclosing façades. As was often the case in New France, the square was both sacred and profane, fulfilling a dual role as both marketplace and parvis of a historic church.[23] In the early years

4.7   Place Royale, Quebec City

of the colony, before the present Place d'Armes was established on top of the escarpment, Place Royale even served as the locale for the assembly and practice of the militia. Its uniform paving of greystone blocks, begun in 1799, and the total absence of vegetation in the square gave it a rather severe aspect – but all this changed on market day, when the square was filled with lined-up horses and carriages and animated by buyers and sellers alike.[24] Worn out by centuries of use, the square and its district were restored and refurbished by the Quebec government in the years following 1960. Once enlivened by a three-level fountain, the square now features a bust of Louis XIV placed on a pedestal, just as was the case in the seventeenth century, as its only decorative element.[25]

In Upper Town on top of the cliff, Place de la Cathédrale has occupied, since the colonial period, a strategic site surrounded by important buildings: the Quebec Basilica to the east, the Jesuit College opposite, and, at its northwest corner, the courtyard and principal entry of the Old Seminary, founded in 1663 by Monsignor Laval, first bishop of New France.[26] In the seventeenth and eighteenth centuries, this public space housed the Upper Town market; a little stream passed across it, then trickled down the middle of the Rue de la Fabrique, before traversing the garden of the Hôtel-Dieu Hospital and losing itself in the Saint-Charles River below.[27] After having served as a barracks for the British garrison, the Jesuit College on the west side of the square was demolished in 1877 and replaced by the present city hall. The little stream disappeared long ago; today, the square consists primarily of a small garden on a steep slope, disposed around a statue of Elzéar-Alexandre Taschereau, first cardinal to be born in Canada and one of the founders of Quebec City's Laval University.[28]

SACRED LAND IN THE NEW WORLD   59

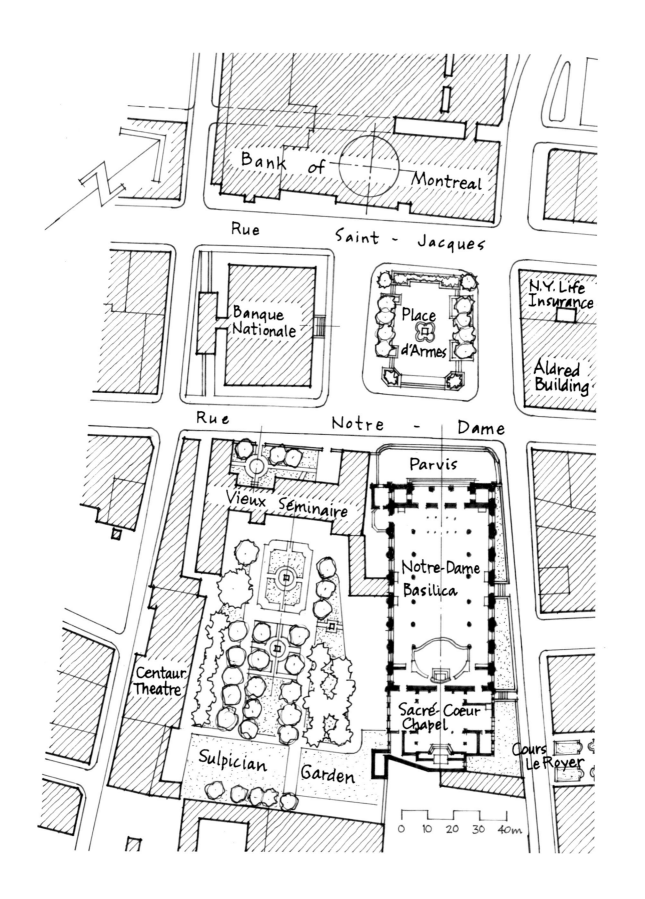

4.8 Plan of the Sulpician "Vieux Séminaire" and garden, Montreal, and the adjacent Place d'Armes. The Notre-Dame Basilica on the right, giving on to Place d'Armes square, is shown with its interior floor plan.

Montreal's Place d'Armes is the city's most impressive urban space. Once again combining the functions of church square, market (nineteenth century), and place for troops to assemble,[29] this space recounts the whole story of architecture in Montreal. On its south side, Notre-Dame Basilica and the Old Seminary of the Sulpicians (including the oldest garden in Montreal) bear witness to the important role played by the Catholic religion in the foundation and development of the city. To the north, the elegant façade of the Bank of Montreal (1848) recalls, in symbolic fashion, the French-English rivalries and the commercial success of Canada's metropolis of the nineteenth century. Office buildings on the east side of the square are excellent examples of the architecture of the 1880s and 1930s, and the black tower of the Banque Nationale on the west side, despite the heavy shadows it casts on the square, is nonetheless a classic example of modern architecture. Several aspects of the design of Place d'Armes – the quality and diversity of the façades that enclose it, the intimacy provided by its spatial configuration, the strong sense of centrality provided by Louis-Philippe Hébert's 1895 statue of the Sieur de Maisonneuve, Montreal's founder – merit its placement among the most significant public squares in North America.

Gardens

Public affairs in New France depended on a delicate equilibrium among three powerful forces: the military and executive authority, represented by the governor; the financial administration, directed by the intendant; and the church, within which the bishop was titular head of a large family of relatively autonomous orders and congregations. Each of these establishments had its own sphere of influence, physical as well as moral; and gardens played an important role in the physical milieus of all three. In this distant colony, every garden had to provide food, but the gardens of the governor and the intendant also served as symbols of power and prestige, while the gardens of the bishop and the religious orders had to respond to the spiritual needs of their communities as well as to the recreational needs of students and patients, among others. These varying demands led to the development of three principal types of garden, all of which followed the same precepts of structure and organization, although they differed considerably in detail and ambiance.

The Functional Garden

During the reconstruction of Fort Louisbourg, the team of archeologists, historians, and other professionals responsible for the work carried out extensive research on the gardens of the fortress city. Their research provided many insights into the horticultural and gardening practices of the colonial period. There had been more than a hundred gardens within the city, most of them bounded by picket fences and laid out in square or rectangular planting beds bordered with shrubs or flowers. Of variable dimensions (20 m × 15 m on average), these gardens were essentially functional, as suggested by such common inscriptions as "fruit garden" (*jardin fruitier*) and "kitchen garden" (*jardin potager*) on the original plans and maps. This can be easily understood, given the limited area within the city walls and the constant shortage of foodstuffs at Louisbourg.[30]

Since no detailed plan for a specific garden has ever been found, the team responsible for garden reconstruction at Louisbourg created "representative gardens," using plants and techniques harvested from a variety of sources: cookbooks and gardening books from the period in question (in particular *La nouvelle maison rustique* by Louis Léger, published in France in 1755), letters and documents of all kinds, and archaeological research on seeds and pollens.[31] Included among the plants identified, from Native sources as well as sources from the mother country, were cabbages, beans, onions, carrots, and squashes, usually placed in the middle of planting beds; anise-seed (caraway), hyssop, lavender, and spearmint at various locations; and blue iris along with carnations, bellflowers, and pansies as borders. Vertical planks were used to raise the level of beds, and wood was used for staking and supporting plants according to several traditional techniques.

The Official Garden

At Louisbourg, the governor's garden, along with those of the general store and the hospital, was more elaborate than those cultivated by merchants, artisans, and other residents. Similar distinctions could be observed in the other cities and towns of New France. On every plan of Quebec City from 1685 to 1760, the Jardin des Gouverneurs (Governors' Garden) is indicated on the cliff edge some 30 metres to the west of the Château St-Louis, the governor's residence (now the site of the Château Frontenac Hotel). This walled garden, laid out in the customary rectangular planting bed system, provided vegetables, fruits, herbs, and cut flowers to the governor's household. It served primarily, however, for purposes of recreation and as a promenade garden. Still existing but much diminished in size, the Governors' Garden is now a green square, its steep slope occupied by a simple grass lawn shaded by immense trees. The garden enjoys a spectacular view towards the river; an obelisk dedicated to the memory of the fallen generals Wolfe and Montcalm occupies a place of honour.[32]

The extensive Intendant's Garden, situated beside that official's "palace" (residence and offices) in Lower Town, followed once again the typical checkerboard plan. In 1739, the royal engineer Chaussegros de Léry prepared a plan for its enlargement, proposing the linkage of garden and palace by a mall featuring three parallel rows of trees. The garden seems to have been realized, but without the mall.[33] Though no vestige of this once splendid garden remains today, its presence is recalled in the name of Quebec City's railroad station, the Gare du Palais, which has long occupied the site.

Nor does anything remain of New France's other "official gardens," which were often embellished with fountains, water basins, and barrel vaults.[34] Nevertheless, it is still possible to visit a garden typical of the period. In the spring of 2000, the Château Ramezay Museum, which is housed in the historic residence of the governor of Montreal, created a Governor's Garden inspired by the official gardens of colonial times. Such a garden existed on the site during that period – and the recent discovery of its long-lost plan in the archives of France has provided clear indications of its location and overall design[35] – but the boundaries and the topography of the site have been greatly modified over the years, reinforcing the museum's earlier decision to create a more generic eighteenth-century official garden that "does not attempt the strict reproduction of historic reality."[36] The resulting garden comprises three distinct sectors: kitchen garden, orchard, and pleasure garden, all within an enclosing stone wall that nevertheless permits views of the surrounding city through openings fenced in wrought-iron. Plant choices reflect a great concern for authenticity; they include vegetables, aromatic herbs, and medicinal plants, or *simples*, along with fruit-bearing trees and shrubs and some purely decorative plants. The city of Montreal's Parks Service designed and built the Château Ramezay garden, with Robert Desjardins as landscape architect responsible for the project.

The Institutional/Convent Garden

The Upper Town of Quebec City was host to a panoply of institutions: the Seminary, Hôtel-Dieu Hospital, and several monasteries, including those of the Ursulines, the Jesuits, and the Recollets. Each establishment consisted of one or a series of buildings in the form of a quadrilateral, enclosing one or more interior courtyards.[37] All of these institutions were clustered about Quebec's Notre-Dame Basilica, creating a remarkable ensemble of towers, gates, spires, and masonry walls.

Inside the walls of these institutions, one may still see gardens that recall the regularity and discipline of the monastic tradition of the Middle Ages and the European Renaissance: tranquil spaces, calm and orderly. Chaussegros de Léry's plans show formal gardens divided into regular planting beds – as in the functional and official gardens we have seen – bordered by low hedges, perhaps yew or box. Within these beds grew vegetables, herbs for the table, flowers for the altar, and medicinal plants for treating members of the community. Orchards also provided a necessary contribution to the self-sufficient economies of these institutions. Elsewhere within these establishments, cloister gardens invited residents to spend time in contemplation. In these areas, the network of paths between planting beds often converged towards a focal element such as a fountain, a statue, or a particularly striking flowerbed.

This general structure and character of convent gardens has been maintained, in its essentials, right up until our own time, although the gardens have been somewhat simplified from those shown in the plans of Chaussegros de Léry. The present gardens of the religious orders are elegant and comforting but not elaborate. They exhibit a predominance of grass, usually shaded by rows or clumps of large deciduous trees – sugar maples, lindens, elms. A wide and straight main path, almost universal in such gardens, usually leads to a series of secondary paths and perpendicular vistas oriented towards objects of veneration. These generally include a statue of the Virgin Mary surrounded by benches for meditation and rosary; a dramatic "Calvary" with a central effigy of Jesus Christ, sometimes

SACRED LAND IN THE NEW WORLD 63

accompanied by the two thieves crucified by his side; and a representation of Saint Joseph or some other holy personage, chosen to coincide with the particular mission of the institution. Many such gardens also included cemeteries for their members, a practice now discontinued.

The tradition of self-sufficiency, once widespread among the religious orders (and virtually essential in the early years of the colony), has not entirely disappeared. Thus, all the flowers for the altar of the Ursuline Monastery in Quebec City are still provided by the order's own garden. The sisters still cultivate beautiful roses, and their apple and plum orchards remain highly productive. The horticultural *tour de force* of this garden is a veritable wall of peonies, a hundred metres long, well located to benefit from the sun and to offer a breathtaking visual spectacle when in flower.

A principal objective of all such institutional gardens, today as in the past, is to invite contemplation and reflection, and it is clear that this objective is still being more than satisfied. In order to sustain a sense of repose among community members, the gardens are often furnished with a number of small structures and pavilions. Thus, in the grounds of the Ursulines, one finds a traditional gazebo similar

4.9   Garden of the Ursuline Monastery, Quebec City

4.10 (facing page)   Domaine de Maizerets, Quebec City

64   LANDSCAPE HERITAGE OF THE FIRST NATIONS AND COLONISTS

to those seen in Victorian parks. In the garden of the Augustines at the Hôtel-Dieu de Québec, a rustic cottage affectionately called the "Tower of London" (there are Augustines in England, as well as in many other countries) provides a place for hard-working hospital workers to relax,[38] and at Quebec's Hôpital général, a small pavilion and garden swings serve the same purpose.

Besides their central-city locations, most religious communities also owned one or more country properties, with buildings located in natural, garden-like settings. Such a property might have been a *métairie*, a suburban farm that provided food for the community (the Maison Saint-Gabriel, founded by Marguerite Bourgeoys in 1662 in the Pointe-Saint-Charles district on the island of Montreal, is an excellent example); or a *retraite* that allowed brothers, sisters, or seminarians to take a vacation and recharge themselves (the Domaine de Maizerets in Quebec City's Limoilou district, affiliated with the Quebec Seminary, played exactly this role); or perhaps a *mission* built to provide Christian instruction to the Native people at a site located midway between their home grounds and the city. Fort de la Montagne, established by the Sulpicians in 1675 on what is now Sherbrooke Street in Montreal, corresponds to this third type of establishment.

The gardens associated with these suburban milieus were often more naturalistic and spontaneous than those in the cities. Thus, the hemicycle ring of water (or ice) and the small cupola of the Domaine de Maizerets, all but hidden in the forest, are true landscape treasures. The same is true of the long, mysterious reflecting basins of the Fort de la Montagne, framed by giant silver maples, and of the old Villa Maria Convent, both properties nestled into the flanks of Mount Royal.

As we look today at these convent gardens, which have existed for hundreds of years, it is clear that they have not become "museum gardens," frozen in the image of a past time. They are, instead, living gardens that respond to the needs of very active communities that still participate every day in the running of some of Quebec's most advanced hospitals and most respected schools. These gardens have evolved and continue to evolve with the passing of time. Some important components – such as the kitchen garden of the Ursulines at Quebec City – have disappeared owing to lack of time and resources for maintenance operations combined with the easy availability of market vegetables. In the same garden, recreational facilities (tennis courts, play structures for small children) have evolved according to student needs and the extent to which the city has furnished equipment for public parks.[39] Some gardens are going through repairs and refurbishing at present. Despite all this, their general composition, ambiance, and character have not been lost, and they still transmit faithfully a tradition that is more than three and a half centuries old. And since, in France, institutions of this nature were largely destroyed during the revolution of the late eighteenth century, some of these gardens may be among the best examples of this tradition in the world.

Pioneers of Botany and Gardening in Canada

From the beginning of colonization, several individuals were entranced with the native vegetation of Canada, and they lost no time in sending samples back to

France. This was true of apothecary Louis Hébert, the first farmer in New France, who had already benefited from the opportunity to experiment with medicinal plants at Port-Royal in Acadia when that colony had just begun. It has been speculated that the first book concerning Canadian flora, published in Paris in 1635 by Jacques-Philippe Cornut, was based on samples sent to the Jardin Royal des Plantes in Paris by Hébert, who also cultivated the first orchard in New France, initiated by Champlain with the use of apple trees from Normandy.[40] The surgeon-botanist Michel Sarrazin (1659–1734), named "King's doctor" in Canada in 1697, created a detailed herbarium and sent plant specimens to the Jardin des Plantes over a thirty-year period. Sarrazin, who, among other achievements, carried out the first surgical operation (successfully) at the Hôtel-Dieu in Quebec City, also collaborated on a book describing Canadian flora.[41] During his 1749 visit to New France, the Finno-Swedish botanist Peter Kalm was guided by Sarrazin's successor as King's doctor, Jean-François Gaultier. Kalm collected and identified many native plants while in Canada, including *Gaultheria procumbens* (mountain tea or wintergreen), which he named in honour of his colleague.[42] In turn, Kalm's famous patron, Linnaeus, named the laurel genus *Kalmia* after his envoy.

The Rural Milieu

Establishment of the Seigneurial System

Until the 1660s, New France had two principal *raisons d'être*: the fur trade and the conversion of the Native peoples. Agriculture and settlement were of little interest to the mother country. Certainly, Louis Hébert established Quebec's first farm in 1617 and the religious orders relied on their suburban *métairies* to ensure their own subsistence, but agriculture was still very limited in extent and the population remained very low, particularly when compared to the rapidly expanding British colonies to the south. Almost everything was imported from France, and the companies involved in the fur trade regarded agriculture as a dangerous threat to their business.[43]

Louis XIV had other objectives, however, and these included the systematic occupation of his territories in New France and their partial economic self-sufficiency. Thus his new colonial policy, adopted in 1663, reorganized New France as a network of fiefs and seigneuries, based on the traditional system of land tenure used in medieval Europe. This new measure authorized his representative, the governor, to concede territories along the St. Lawrence and other major rivers to *seigneurs*. In return, the seigneurs were to ensure the settlement of the lands given them by populating them with colonists or *censitaires*. The success of this system depended on a judicious equilibrium among diverse parties – governor, seigneur, censitaire – each with particular rights and responsibilities. The seigneurs were not necessarily members of the nobility, as in France; often of humble origin, many of them lived in houses that were hardly different from those of their censitaires. They were, ideally, good organizers with a talent for persuading people to take up farming; one might call them "entrepreneurs of settlement."[44]

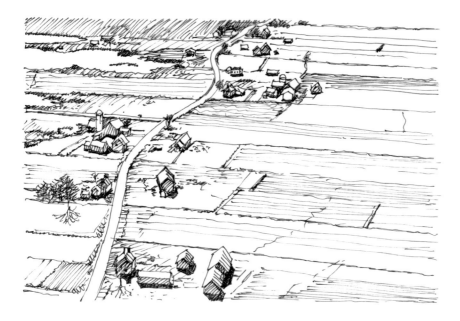

4.11 *Le rang*: linear settlement pattern in rural Quebec

By 1700, the first wave of seigneuries was in place in the region of Quebec City, along both the southern and the northern shores of the St. Lawrence. Generally rectangular in shape, the seigneuries were quite variable in dimensions, averaging approximately one league in depth (3.3 km, later increasing to about 3.9 km) by several leagues in width along the riverfront. The system expanded slowly throughout the French regime and, after 1760, during the British regime. Abolished in Canada in 1854, many decades after its abolition in France, the seigneurial system has left us a legacy of well-established cultural landscapes, efficient and humane, that are still present in the landscape of Quebec and of several other provinces.

Land Division

The seigneuries were divided into individual farms, and most of the land was distributed to the censitaires. Each farm was a long, narrow rectangle, its short side facing the St. Lawrence River or one of its tributaries; sometimes a triangular lot interrupted the rhythm in order to adjust the farms to a curve in the watercourse.[45] In this manner, each farm was assured of direct access to the river network, which was the "main street" of the colony, accessible by boat in summer or on the ice in winter. Since the principal topographic features of the landscape were disposed parallel to the river, this system of land division also offered each farmer a variety of land types and economic opportunities: access to fishing grounds; rich bottomlands along the riverfront, ideal for growing grains and vegetables; pasture for livestock on higher lands (where soils were often more rocky and less fertile); forested woodlots on hilly terrain and more distant plateaus, sources for firewood and maple syrup.

The censitaires, or *habitants*, usually built their houses at the extremity of their land, facing onto the river. While visiting Canada in 1749, the Swedish botanist Peter Kalm described this riverside settlement in memorable fashion: "The farmhouses hereabouts are generally built all along the rising banks of the river, either close to the water or at some distance from it ... It [the river] could really be called a village, beginning at Montreal, and ending at Quebec ... The prospect is exceedingly beautiful, when the river goes on for some miles together in a straight line, because it then shortens the distances between the houses, and makes them form exactly one continued village."[46]

Later, the colonial authorities built roads, called *côtes* or *rangs*, parallel to the rivers, to serve the farms and connect the towns. A plaque on the Porte St-Jean gate at Quebec City recounts that the "chemin du Roy" linking Quebec and Montreal was only completed in 1734. The *chemins*, located slightly above the normal level of spring floods, complemented and, eventually, largely replaced the river access system. As riverside lands came to be fully occupied, these single roads along the water became part of a more elaborate and extensive network of roads. Beyond the area already occupied by farms, a new settlement zone took form, according to the original template, along a new road parallel to the first; one spoke of the *premier rang* and the *deuxième rang* of settlement. The *montée*, a transverse road perpendicular to the rangs and to the river, linked each parallel road to its predecessors. This process repeated itself through generations along river valleys and their adjacent lands, creating the typical agricultural landscape of Quebec and of every part of North America where the first colonists were of French heritage.[47]

There were, in fact, other models for the division of agricultural land. During the 1660s, Jean Talon, the first intendant of New France, established several settlements based on a concentric plan, grouping houses in the centre around a parish church. His goal was to create the kind of dense village found in parts of France, with fields radiating out from the centre "like the blades of a fan with their extremities cut at right angles."[48] The intendant's efforts were in vain; the system of rangs and "long-lot" farms was victorious due to the force of the natural landscape to which it was so sensibly integrated. Today, only a few vestiges of the concentric pattern remain, at Charlesbourg, Bourg-Royal, and Petite Auvergne in the Quebec City metropolitan region.[49]

The long-lot system had another marked advantage over its rivals: the short distance between farmhouses encouraged contact and mutual support between neighbours, perhaps contributing, in the long term, to the sense of community that was and is such a tangible characteristic of francophone society in Canada.[50] The river-lot configuration of New France represents an interesting compromise between a common European system of land division, in which farmers live in villages and go out to their fields each day, and the system that occupies the majority of land in North America, in which each family lives on its own autonomous farm, at a considerable distance from its neighbours. One may speculate that the idealization of self-sufficiency and individualism that characterizes much of the culture of the western United States and, in some ways, that of western Canada is at least partly a consequence of the system of land division established in those areas (see chapter 6), in contrast to that of New France.[51]

Seigneury and Parish

The seigneury was essentially a practical economic system. Censitaires produced wheat and other grains and ground them at the seigneur's mill, which the seigneur provided as part of his legal obligations. Many of these old mills – which were also noted by Peter Kalm during his visit – still exist, located either at the point where a stream descends the riverbank, where rushing water provided the motive force, or out on a point or promontory where the mill depended on wind.[52] There are dozens of "windmill points" (*pointes-au-moulin*) in Quebec, and mills were social as well as economic centres. Besides its mill, each seigneury had a second landmark: the *manoir* or *domaine seigneurial*, where the seigneur and his family lived and to which, each year, the censitaires brought some of their produce and saluted their patron in symbolic fashion. The manoir was often substantial – that of St-Roch-des-Aulnaies on the south shore of the St. Lawrence is a good example – consisting of the main house with added wings; a dairy, laundry, orchards, and kitchen garden; sheds, barns, and stables, and several smaller pavilions.

In his historical novel *Les Anciens Canadiens* (translated as *The Canadians of Old*), Philippe Aubert de Gaspé (1786–1871), who had grown up in the seigneurial manor of Saint-Jean-Port-Joli, describes the landscape scene that the fictional "manoir d'Haberville" presented to the view of his characters, looking down from the top of a nearby promontory: "Immediately below, the little village, dazzlingly white, appeared to spring from the green bosom of the meadows. On all sides a panorama of splendid magnificence unrolled itself. There was the sovereign of streams, already seven leagues in width, confined on the north by the ancient barrier of the Laurentians, whose feet it washes, and whose peopled slopes are in view from Cape Tourmente to Malbaie ... and lastly, the hamlets of L'islet and St. Jean Port Joli, crowned with their gleaming spires."[53]

The parish soon added civic, cultural, and religious dimensions to the economic and social organization of the seigneury. In a typical municipality such as Beaumont, situated on the south shore of the St. Lawrence a few kilometres east of Quebec City and Lévis, the intendant Jean Talon conceded the seigneury of Beaumont and Vincennes to Charles-Thomas Couillard, Louis Hébert's grandson, in 1672. The parish registers were first opened in 1692, and the first church was built between 1704 and 1718. Finally, the municipality of Saint-Étienne de Beaumont – of which the first mayors were direct descendants of the original seigneur – was established in 1845.[54]

The Village

Humphrey Carver, a founding member of the Canadian Society of Landscape Architects and an unrivalled observer of the Canadian urban landscape, considered the typical Quebec village to be "perhaps the most successful Canadian

4.12 Cemetery, Grandes-Piles, QC

expression of a community."⁵⁵ He admired "its water-front communications and the spire of each parish church visible across the fields and the water, as a sign of authority and friendship in a lonely country." Carver was not alone in recognizing the charm and environmental quality of the village legacy of New France. However, these remarkable places were not actually planned by anyone; in fact, the village began as a "simple densification of population, originally unpremeditated, along a *chemin de rang*, on which the houses were a little more closely spaced."⁵⁶ Indeed, the village had little or no legal status until 1854, when the seigneurial system came to an end.

Villages consisting at first of small clusters of houses, tradesmen's ateliers, and commercial buildings were a response to a gradual growth in population and an increasingly diversified economy.⁵⁷ They naturally took on a linear form, following

SACRED LAND IN THE NEW WORLD 71

4.13 Town of Grandes-Piles seen from the west side of the Saint-Maurice River. The church – and virtually every other building in town – faces towards the river, which is the town's lifeline and *raison d'être*.

the chemin or rang, which became the main street, or rue Principale, that is found almost everywhere in Quebec. Within the village, each house tended to hold fast to its front property line, reducing its front yard to a minimum (which simplified snow clearance). The village house was essentially an urbanized farmhouse, maintaining the elegant proportions such buildings had developed over long evolution and keeping the traditional open gallery. The result was felicitous: a clearly and continuously defined street space, intimate and urbane, its form – straight or curved, often sloping – well adapted to local site conditions. The variety and richness of these village streetscapes have inspired innumerable artists, including, notably, Clarence Gagnon and A.Y. Jackson.

Religious Precinct and Village Nucleus

At the core of each village, usually located at the crossing of a rang or chemin and a perpendicular montée, is a complex of institutional buildings and open spaces, public and private, combined in an orderly and coherent overall composition. The buildings typically include the parish church and presbytery (the *curé*'s residence), primary and secondary schools for boys and girls, a convent, perhaps a seniors' residence. Open spaces include a parvis adjacent to the church, the cemetery, and the schoolyard, a public square or market square providing a link between sacred and profane, and private gardens within the religious institutions.

4.14 Wayside cross, Saint-Mathieu-du-Parc, QC. The inscription recalls the heavenly message seen by Roman Emperor Constantine before a victorious battle in AD 316 – *In hoc signo vinces* (In this sign you shall conquer) – which led to his conversion.

Though their various components were built at different times and to differing levels of finesse and detail, the overall compositions created by these buildings and open spaces are often remarkably harmonious and distinguished. This is as much the case in small and obscure villages in distant locations as it is with famous downtown monuments or in the neighbourhood centres of large cities. The village of Beaumont, mentioned above, is a striking example; fortunately, although located very close to a large urban centre, it has survived virtually intact – against all odds – to the present day.[58] On the island of Montreal, the old institutional

SACRED LAND IN THE NEW WORLD 73

nucleus of Lachine, situated along the Lachine Canal close to the point where it diverges from the St. Lawrence, is also a masterpiece of this genre.

In his novel *Les Anciens Canadiens*, Aubert de Gaspé rightly identifies the church spire as the essential landmark in the landscape of New France. In forest or plain everywhere in French Canada, it is the sign of habitation and the symbol of civilization. The location and orientation of these churches with respect to the landscape are, in themselves, fascinating objects of reflection. Although traditionally located in the village centre and often oriented so that the altar is situated to the east (towards the Holy Land) and the entrance to the west, churches have also responded to a series of other influences, subtle or obvious, in integrating with their natural milieus. Thus, a church located on the shore of a river or lake, like that of Pointe-Claire near Montreal, often turns its face to the water. In the mountains, it regularly occupies the highest point, overlooking the village below (Saint-Sauveur, Saint-Jean-de-Matha). In other towns located on flat ground, the church faces the main public square (Saint-Jérôme, Trois-Rivières) or terminates the perspective of a major artery (Saint-Norbert, Charlesbourg).

Croix de Chemin and Chemin de Croix

In addition to public squares, gardens, and village centres, several other traditions of intervention in the environment and integration with the landscape evolved

4.15   *Calvaire*, Saint-Élie-de-Caxton, QC

74   LANDSCAPE HERITAGE OF THE FIRST NATIONS AND COLONISTS

4.16 View from the *calvaire* overlooking Saint-Élie-de-Caxton, QC. This panoramic view of his hometown and its surrounding area is one of the landscapes that have inspired Fred Pellerin, Quebec's "raconteur extraordinaire."

in New France. The limits of the parish were frequently signalled by wayside crosses – *croix de chemin*, points of reference in space as simple and clear as the marking of time by the Angelus at noon. Wooden crosses have played an important role in New France since the first voyages of Jacques Cartier in 1534–36. Their presence along the St. Lawrence attracted the attention of voyager Peter Kalm in 1749; his detailed description of the appearance of such crosses corresponds precisely to that of those standing today.[59] Wayside crosses often bear a strong symbolic message through the display of the instruments of the crucifixion of Christ, the cock that recalls the apostle Peter's denial of his association with Jesus, and a central niche incorporating an effigy of Jesus, Mary, or one of the saints. A second type of structure was also commonly erected on the village outskirts: the *chapelle*

SACRED LAND IN THE NEW WORLD 75

de procession, a tiny church that "brought God into the street."[60] During the *Fête-Dieu*, or Corpus Christi festival, usually celebrated each June, such chapels served as destinations for the procession of the holy sacrament, which passed through the whole village, starting from the parish church and following a path strewn with flowers and garlands. The chapels of Beaumont, built in 1733 and 1738, are outstanding examples.[61]

Landscapes featuring abrupt changes of level provided perfect locations for the creation of a *chemin de croix* (way of the cross) or a *calvaire*, as pilgrimage sites. The exceptional hilltop landscapes of Oka and Rigaud west of Montreal are cases in point. A considerable number of such landscape elements are found in the Mauricie region, including the chemin de croix of Saint-Élie-de-Caxton, and in the Laurentian Mountains north of Montreal, where, at the village of Huberdeau in the valley of the Rouge River, the forested and hilly landscape shelters a profoundly moving sculptural depiction of Calvary.

Cultural Framework and Escape Route

This institutional and physical environment – school, hospital, seminary, church and chapel, wayside cross and way of the cross – provided a coherent and continuing cultural framework for all the physical requirements and processes of life, as well as a constant reminder of things eternal. One does not have to be a Catholic to feel the spiritual comfort offered by what was, for a while, the eternal and universal church.

This harmony extended to the landscape. In his description of the imaginary seigneury d'Haberville, Aubert de Gaspé painted in words that which many artists have recounted on canvas: a landscape of vast spaces, focused on river and mountain, but within which people had made a place for themselves in a particularly propitious manner. Reinterpreted as an ideal landscape inhabited by noble and generous seigneurs and loyal, hard-working peasants, such an image would later play a central part in an agrarian myth that would long provide a supportive structure for the French culture of Canada.

The relationship of this civilization to the forest was equivocal. On the one hand, the forest was the enemy: it had to be destroyed to "create land" (*faire de la terre*),[62] and in the early years, it could hide Natives hostile to the colony. On the other hand, the forest offered an escape route for those who felt stifled by the stable and structured society of the St. Lawrence Valley and did not want their lives to be planned out in advance. From the very beginnings of New France, there existed a parallel society oriented to the frontier. In 1685, almost all the young men born in the colony took part in a drastic "demographic hemorrhage" towards the forest.[63] The fur trade, always in competition with farm and village – and the principal source of exports from the colony – offered adventure and the possibility of getting rich to those young people who rejected the stability of the continuously settled territory – the *oecumène* – of New France.

5

Dreams of Empire: The British Colonial Tradition

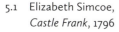

5.1   Elizabeth Simcoe, *Castle Frank*, 1796

The imperial rivalries of the eighteenth century, described in chapter 3, led the British government to establish a series of fortified towns on the Atlantic coast of Canada to protect and populate their newly won territories. This first wave of British colonization was followed by several others, bringing new residents from both the American colonies and the British Isles. The new arrivals built an economy based on fishing, lumber, and agriculture, while merchants and soldiers of the British Empire, then in its period of most rapid expansion, set up shop in the region's many natural river ports and seaports.

The Atlantic landscape was profoundly marked by this immigration. The towns, farms, and "townships" that the newcomers created between 1749 and the 1840s, integrated with the long-established Acadian cultural landscape already in place, still define the visual character of Nova Scotia, New Brunswick, and Prince Edward Island today. Many of the urban and rural environments created in the Maritime provinces during that period are still recognized as admirable examples of successful city planning, well integrated with the natural milieu.

The waves of immigration of this period also brought great change to the population, culture, and landscape of the old cities and rural areas of Lower Canada, or Quebec. Imperial expansion subsequently pressed on into Upper Canada, or Ontario, which was, until that time, a vast forest. In all these regions, the new immigrants redrew the landscape according to the lines and forms typical of the British colonial era: geometric patterns of land division, compact commercial towns integrating public squares and green spaces, "commons," and cemetery.

Planned Cities of the Maritime Provinces

In 1749, when he received the command to establish a fortified town on the southern coast of Nova Scotia, Colonel Edward Cornwallis of the British Army had to give military considerations first priority, since hostilities between the two great empires of Britain and France were only temporarily suspended. He chose as his site Chebucto Bay, a magnificent natural harbour, well protected from sea winds by a rocky peninsula and easily defended. In his choice of an urban model, he relied both on guidelines provided by the Board of Trade and Plantations in London and on the 140 years of town-planning experience gained by the British colonists along the Atlantic coast to the south. The township of New England was an excellent model, based on a central village organized around a *village green*,

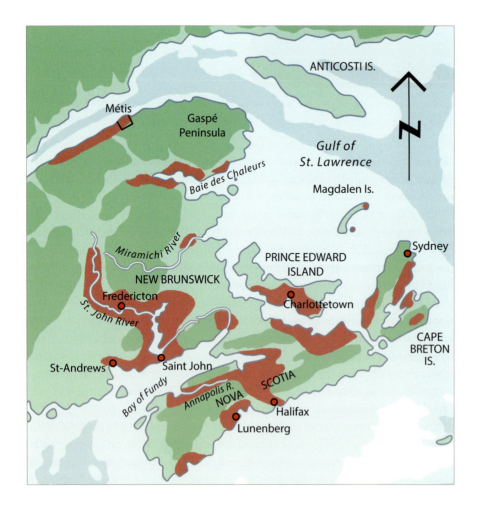

5.2 Areas of British colonization in Maritime Canada, 1749–1820. Colonized regions are shown in red, light green indicates lowlands and valleys, and darker green indicates higher elevations.

78 LANDSCAPE HERITAGE OF THE FIRST NATIONS AND COLONISTS

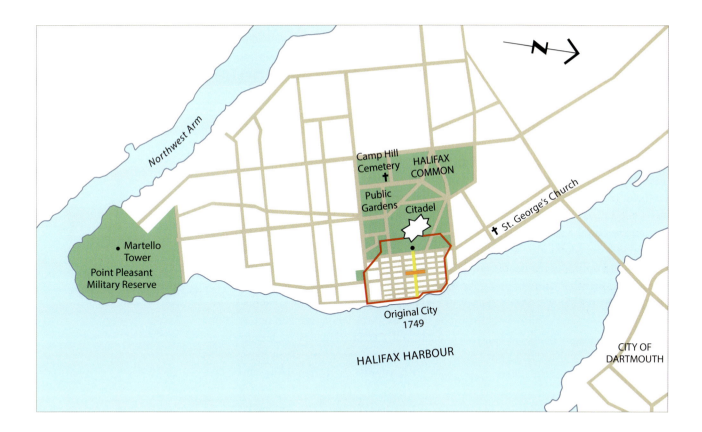

5.3 Plan of eighteenth- and nineteenth-century Halifax. Within the original city (outlined in red), George Street is yellow; the location of the "Grand Parade" is in orange. Open spaces owned in common or by governments are shown in green. The location of future roads and bridges is shown in grey.

surrounded by agricultural fields and common pasturelands, or *commons*, on less productive land.[1] The towns of the middle Atlantic and southern colonies also offered interesting lessons: Philadelphia, founded in 1683, and Savannah, in 1733, were rectangular in shape, their streets laid out in orthogonal grids regularly punctuated by green islands, or *squares*.[2]

The plan of Halifax, the city founded by Cornwallis and planned by the mission's engineer, John Bruce, and its surveyor, Charles Morris, owes much to military imperatives, as well as to the two American urban traditions. It superimposed a highly regular urban grid on a site that sloped distinctly down towards the port. At the grid's centre, on the axis of the main thoroughfare, George Street, two central blocks were left open; this was the "Grand Parade," a great open space, its original slope later graded flat to serve as a parade ground for the militia and as a site for major public buildings. The Anglican Church of St. Paul, which recalls the simple and elegant churches of New England, was built at the southern extremity of the space, beginning in 1750, and the city hall eventually took its place at its northern antipode. The centre was left open, preserving splendid views between the port and the Citadel (rebuilt several times between 1749 and 1856), located at the top of the slope. Colonists constructed a wooden palisade around the periphery of the town.[3] Extending over hills and marshes beyond the fortifications, common lands provided pasturelands for livestock, while the southern extremity of the peninsula, Point Pleasant, served as a military reserve and a source of wood.[4] These two

DREAMS OF EMPIRE 79

undeveloped areas, the commons and the point, became the city's treasured sites for public institutions and parks.

Halifax established the leitmotif for a series of other military and colonial settlements founded between 1750 and about 1840, all of which shared four characteristics identified by historian Brian Cuthbertson: a defensible location on a peninsula, protected by fortifications; a compact plan organized in a rectangular grid, with streets parallel and perpendicular to the shore; a central space for the assembly of the militia and the construction of public buildings, serving as the central focus of civic life, both as church square and market; and the allocation of lands for common use and farmland, beyond the fortifications.[5]

In 1753, the British government established a second new town, Lunenburg, further west on the south coast of Nova Scotia. Charles Morris, now the surveyor-general of Nova Scotia, also laid out its plan, which greatly resembled that of Halifax. A future centre for the fishing and boat-building industries, this town was settled by non-British Protestant immigrants, primarily of German and Swiss origin.[6] Its "Grand Parade" is still a central oasis of grass and large trees, enclosed by historic houses and churches, as steeply sloping today as it was when first laid out. A replica of an antique bandstand and a war memorial, a fixture in every important public space in Canada, find their homes here. At the bottom of the slope, business is concentrated at the waterside, opposite great wooden sheds that shelter the activities of the fishing industry. This classic arrangement, reinforced by a unique vernacular architecture, has won Lunenburg the rare distinction of being named a World Heritage Site by UNESCO.

The site of Charlottetown on Île Saint-Jean was identified in 1765 by naval captain Samuel Holland, the royal surveyor. His choice of site was most judicious: on a peninsula as always, enclosed by arms of the sea and interior rivers that formed a natural harbour, its entry narrow and easily controlled. The city was planned in 1768, once again by Charles Morris; the first British governor, Walter Patterson, and his surveyor, Thomas Wright, made several adjustments to the plan when it was implemented in 1770. Charlottetown descends a gradual slope, oriented to the southeast, towards a deep channel of the Hillsborough River that permits the anchoring of large boats a short distance from downtown. Common lands and pasture lands originally surrounded the city; the waterfront has always been reserved for public activities.[7] The plan of the city is an almost precise replica of that of Philadelphia, at a reduced scale: a regular grid divided by major roads into four quadrants, each structured around a central green square. These squares still exist and – just like the four squares of Philadelphia, as analysed by Jane Jacobs[8] – each has its own unique personality. Thus, Rochford Square, in the northwest quadrant adjacent to provincial government office buildings, features bright flower beds on a central mound, while Connaught Square, in the southwest sector, is more sober but no less elegant. All share a diagonal circulation pattern and have been framed since 1872 by immense elms and lindens.

At the centre of the city is a larger two-block space that provides a central urban and ceremonial focus. Queen Square was reserved for public buildings and activities that eventually included St. Paul's Anglican Church, a public market, the

5.4 British colonial town layouts in the United States and Canada. Central axes and main thoroughfares are identified in yellow and central market and assembly spaces in orange. Squares, common lands, and outlying farmland are in green. Contour lines are approximate only, to provide a general indication of landform.

provincial law courts, and the provincial legislature of 1843, designed by Isaac Smith (1795–1871) and now known as "Province House." This last is constructed in a formal and symmetrical Palladian style; its splendid arches, columns, and central pediment provide a majestic termination to the main street, Great George Street, a broad avenue, bordered by gigantic elm trees, that connects the heart of the city to the port.[9]

Loyalist Refuge

In the decade of the 1780s, a great wave of immigrants fleeing the American Revolution (1776–83) broke on the shores of the Maritime provinces. Wishing to remain British subjects or banished from their homeland, some 35,000 Loyalists – army veterans, civilians of all social levels, and slaves (freed or still in bondage) – arrived between 1782 and 1784 in Nova Scotia.[10] This demographic influx led to the creation of two new provinces within the former territory of Nova Scotia: New

DREAMS OF EMPIRE 81

Brunswick and, temporarily, Cape Breton. To accommodate these refugees and to establish capitals for the new provinces, the colonial government again created a series of new towns, their plans closely linked to those of the previous settlements. Some of these towns, however, took advantage of local conditions and creative innovations to go beyond the qualities of order and clear structure, which were already in evidence, to become outstanding examples of town planning.

Such was the case of Fredericton, founded in 1785 to serve as the capital of New Brunswick, located at the limit of navigation of the Saint John River in an area of rich farmland. The surveyor of Fredericton, Lieutenant Dugald Campbell, reserved the lands along the river as green space, providing a magnificent legacy to the city. These lands constitute a linear riverside park several kilometres in length, called "the Greens"; they have served as a verdant forecourt for such institutions and monuments as the lieutenant governor's residence, the Anglican cathedral, the provincial legislative assembly, and the war memorial, among others.[11] Also integrated to this pleasant linear space was Officers' Square, a parade ground framed by the headquarters of the old British garrison, a remarkable example of colonial architecture that still features military band concerts on its balcony.[12] Green spaces also define the other three boundaries of the city, creating a sort of "green belt" of parks and institutions.

The capital of the temporary province of Cape Breton, Sydney, established in 1876 in a coal-mining region, nearly broke with the traditional Maritime town plan by adopting a radio-concentric configuration, but the final plan as built followed the Halifax model quite faithfully.[13] Among its remarkable urban features are Great George Street, its main boulevard along the crest of the peninsula, and a park created on a Crown reserve around Wentworth Basin.

St. Andrews, located on a peninsula within Passamaquoddy Bay, close to Champlain and de Monts's first settlement on Île Sainte-Croix, was founded in 1783 on an old summer campground of the Abenaki. The new town continued to welcome seasonal visitors, including wealthy industrialists, who appreciated its colonial grid, its main street bordered by public buildings and historic churches, and the old marketplace situated by the port; these visitors built holiday villas and the magnificent Algonquin Hotel towards the end of the nineteenth and early twentieth centuries.[14]

The masterpiece among these colonial town plans is perhaps that of Saint John in New Brunswick, an important port and commercial city founded in 1783 on two rocky peninsulas at the mouth of the Saint John River. The town's central district was perfectly integrated with the topography of the site. Surveyor Paul Bedell laid out the customary orthogonal grid to create a "virtual" central axis along the crest of the peninsula.[15] Along this axis, he located two open spaces, King's Square and Queen Square, which are, respectively, the focal points of the commercial and residential districts of the city. At right angles to this axis, King's Square is linked via King Street, a grand avenue that descends the steep side-slope of the peninsula, to a third open space, Market Square, located right beside the port. This masterful spatial sequence provides the downtown of Saint John with a sense of elegance and equilibrium that persists to this day.

5.5   King's Square, Saint John, NB

The commercial pole, King's Square, typifies an open-space model that later became a normal component of Canadian cities: a fusion of two spatial archetypes of the eighteenth century, the *place* (located in a commercial milieu and usually paved) and the square (situated in a residential milieu and typically a green space, featuring broad lawns shaded by large trees). Today, the main character of King's Square is defined by its grass surface, its large trees (primarily maples, walnuts, and lindens), disposed in rows or standing alone, and its small flowering trees such as hawthorns and crabapples. Paths in the form of orthogonal and diagonal crosses (a standard motif, reminiscent of the Union Jack but more likely to have been a functional response to circulation requirements rather than a symbolic gesture) converge on a central circle dominated by the focal element of the park, a two-storey bandstand crowned by a flamboyant roof,[16] built in 1908 according to the design of local architect Neil Brodie. Beneath the second-storey band platform (to which there is no apparent means of access), a pool and fountain create movement and sound. The square is almost always filled with people, the benches fully occupied. Those out for a stroll, students, people using the park as a shortcut, tourists accompanied by their guide – all share the space comfortably. The important buildings of the city line the edges of the square – the old public market (built in 1876, where one can buy real dulse seaweed), the Imperial Theatre (both the market building and the theatre have been recently restored), the provincial court,

DREAMS OF EMPIRE   83

5.6 The Old Burying Ground (St. Paul's Church Cemetery), Halifax. The arched gateway with the lion on top is Canada's only monument to the Crimean War, honouring two Canadian soldiers who perished during that conflagration. St. Matthew's United Church is visible behind the cemetery.

the Bank of Nova Scotia, and the Admiral Beatty Hotel. King's Square, typical of the genre, is also the focus of its society's collective memory. Various monuments recount the stories of the province's founding, of its political leaders and its civil and military heroes. Overall, this is one of the most memorable urban squares in Canada.

Calm and reposeful, Queen Square is a world away from the lively and stimulating King's Square, enclosed as it is by residential buildings and composed of a gently sloping green lawn and a single monument, erected in honour of Champlain, the first European to explore the Saint John River. Back downtown, at kitty-corner to King's Square, is the municipal cemetery, or "Old Burying Ground," another classic component of the eighteenth-century provincial city. The cemetery, also included in Bedell's original plan,[17] is a quiet garden enclosed within a wrought-iron fence. Rows of burial stones descend a grassy slope traversed by brick paths and bordered by tall trees. Here and there, islands of flowers punctuate the lawn.

Usually located close to downtown and not in a churchyard, the municipal cemetery of a Maritime town is often one of its most important and impressive public spaces. St. Paul's Burial Ground in Halifax, established outside the palisades at the founding of the city, was called into immediate use to receive the bodies of one-third of the first colonists, killed by an epidemic during the winter of 1749–50.[18] Similar in character to the cemetery of Saint John, its irregular site is enclosed by stone walls and elegant wrought-iron fences, culminating in a magnificent entry via a stone arch built as a memorial of the Crimean War.[19] The fictional heroine of Prince Edward Island, Anne of Green Gables, created by author L.M. Montgomery, often passed through the gate "surmounted by the great lion of England" during her college years at "Kingsport," which resembled Halifax like two peas in a pod. The Burying Ground, under the name of "Old St. John's," became one of her favourite places. She gave herself to reveries and encounters in the old cemetery, "surrounded and intersected by rows of elms and willows, beneath whose shade the sleepers must lie very dreamlessly, forever crooned to by the winds and leaves over them, and quite undisturbed by the clamor of traffic just beyond."[20]

Symbolism and Landmarks

Many observers feel that the central areas of these Georgian cities (built during the reigns of Georges I to IV, between 1710 and 1830) constitute a series of urban jewels that are equally as impressive, in terms of orderly planning and civic character, as the older and more celebrated cities established during the colonial period in the future United States. The old squares, public spaces, and cemeteries of several Maritime cities have benefited from many dedicated efforts at preservation throughout the past two centuries. They are the pride of the local citizens and sources of literary inspiration. It should be noted that the regularity of their plans meant more than simple ease of implementation or straightforward functionality. Without a doubt, the symmetry and balance of both architecture and city planning during this period were seen as important values in themselves, values that reflected the orderly cosmos postulated by Newton, Descartes, and Galileo, expressing the broad humanism of the Renaissance.[21]

Certain physical realizations became symbols and landmarks in the towns and along the coasts. This was certainly true of churches. Unlike the planning of towns in New France, where each village revolved around a single religious and institutional pole, the Protestant revolution and its aftermath led to a multiplicity of different churches in the villages of the Maritime provinces and of other British colonies in Canada – Methodist, Congregationalist, Anglican, Presbyterian, Catholic. These churches were distributed throughout the urban fabric, in public spaces or on hilltops, according to the demographic organization of citizens. The juxtaposition of church buildings and their elegant wooden architecture, largely inspired by that of New England, often gave rise to urban compositions of great charm. The "three sisters" in the village of Mahone Bay on the south coast of Nova Scotia are a classic example. Such phenomena are part of a larger cultural continuity between Canada's Maritime provinces and the neighbouring American states, traditionally referred to as "the Boston States."[22] In many ways, the rural and urban arrangements of New England were simply transplanted further north.

A second inescapable landmark of the region is the lighthouse. Since its beginnings at Louisbourg, this essential aid to navigation on the perilous coasts of

5.7 The "three sisters," Mahone Bay, NS, seen looking west across the head of the bay. The churches – St. James' Anglican, St. John's Lutheran, and Trinity United, from left to right – took their places along Edgewater Street between 1869 and 1885.

86 LANDSCAPE HERITAGE OF THE FIRST NATIONS AND COLONISTS

5.8 Lighthouse, Louisbourg, NS. Built in 1923, this concrete lighthouse is located on the same site as Canada's first lighthouse, constructed across the harbour from the Fortress of Louisbourg in 1734.

Canada has become a universal emblem of the Maritimes, practically a cliché, widely emblazoned on posters promoting tourism. Lighthouses were very numerous; in 1950, more than 350 could be found in Nova Scotia alone,[23] including the oldest lighthouse still operating in North America, that of Sambro Island, constructed in 1758 at the entrance to Halifax Harbour. As they entered Canada through its largest east coast port, the first image of the New World for hundreds of thousands of immigrants would have been the red and white bands of this lighthouse – they "viewed Sambro Island lighthouse in much the same way that others like them looked upon the Statue of Liberty" in New York.[24]

The Rural Landscape: Field and Forest

The Maritime Provinces

The New England farmers who moved into former Acadian lands in the Annapolis Valley and elsewhere – the Planters – constituted the first wave of agricultural immigrants under the new British regime established in 1759. Each head of a family received 40 hectares of land, to which 20 additional hectares could be added for other household members and servants. Each family received a portion of the excellent alluvial soils in the valley floor, some of which had already been cultivated for many decades, as well as a larger area of land on the adjacent higher ground. In Europe, such a configuration of lands had led to the creation of dense, concentrated villages, but here, the owners of these concessions exchanged, sold, and bought properties to consolidate self-contained farms where they could live autonomously.[25] Situated in the mildest climate zone of the Maritimes, these mixed-produce farms – apples, milk products, grains, vegetables – have long been prosperous and stable.[26]

Prince Edward Island (then still known as Île Saint-Jean) had to overcome a major obstacle before agriculture could be practised in a coherent manner. Almost all of the sixty-seven regular lots surveyed by Samuel Holland in 1764 had been given to favourites of the British court, who were supposed to recruit colonists themselves. The unfortunate consequence was a long period of underdevelopment of the province owing to the lack of interest of its absentee landlords, of whom only a handful made any efforts at colonization.[27] In any case, prospects of working as a tenant farmer offered little attraction to candidates from England or, even more, New England, where the tradition of the independent farmer, owner of his own lands, had long taken root.[28] As soon as this stumbling block was removed, the island became an agricultural paradise, famous for its milk products as well as for the oats and potatoes cultivated in its sandy red soils. Its landscape of hill and vale, its small multicoloured fields separated by hedgerows of red or "pasture spruce," make the island one of Canada's most beautiful cultural landscapes.[29]

The arrival of the Loyalists at the end of the American Revolution rapidly and profoundly reshaped the rural landscapes of the Maritime provinces, particularly those of New Brunswick, an autonomous province since 1784. Settling these people on the land challenged the colonial authorities to undertake an immense surveying program. They had to plan new farm and garden lots, towns, and government reserves for purposes of defence, religion, education, and maritime transport – all to be done with virtually no previous documentation. Under the direction of the surveyors-general, Charles Morris Jr. in Nova Scotia (the second of four generations of the same family to occupy this post) and military engineer and surveyor George Sproule in New Brunswick, the task was rapidly accomplished by an army of surveyors who overcame the many obstacles that confronted them: mountains, forest, cold, heat, and mosquitoes. Besides creating the cadastral plans that were their primary goal, the surveyors also mapped information concerning topography, lakes and rivers, wetlands, and soil quality.[30]

A favourite site for new farms was the land along the Saint John River Valley, which drains a great proportion of New Brunswick towards the Bay of Fundy. The lowlands along the river – "island and interval" lands – were fertile, placid, and beautiful, an earthly paradise like the Loire Valley in France. These rich meadows were fertilized each spring with silts newly transported by temporary flooding. In contrast to the nearby uplands, densely forested with conifers, the valley floor was treeless, except for a riparian band along the river itself,[31] providing ideal conditions for the Maliseet and Acadians who had previously farmed the land.[32] Their Loyalist successors divided the territory in the same way that we have seen in New France (and for the same reasons): narrow strips of land, perpendicular to the river and its tributaries (since navigable waterways were the sole means of access), traversing a variety of different land types. The typical farm followed proportions of about 1 to 5, that is, 400 by 2,000 metres for a surface area of 80 hectares (200 acres). A supplement of 10 per cent was added in the case of poorly drained or otherwise difficult soils. When all lands along the water had been distributed, the government opened a second concession parallel to the first, assuring water access through perpendicular service roads. Farmers constructed their buildings close to the water or to the concession road, creating linear settlements where the regular succession of houses and barns was occasionally interrupted by a school, a church, or a general store.[33]

In New Brunswick as on Île Saint-Jean, influential settlers tried to create a patrician landscape. The Committee of 55, a group of formerly wealthy Loyalists from New York State, asked the governor to provide them with 2,000-hectare farms (5,000 acres) that would be cultivated by tenant farmers as in England's extensive domains. The refusal of the authorities to accede to these demands ensured that, during the first centuries of its history, Canadian agriculture would be dominated by small, independent family farms.[34] It should be remembered that the farmers who arrived in the Maritime provinces and in other British colonies were almost all refugees, driven from their former homes by the American Revolution, by the *enclosure* movement – displacements of peasants to expand pasturelands in Scotland and in Yorkshire, England – or, later, by famines in Ireland. It was not surprising that these people wanted to own the land they farmed.[35]

Lower Canada (Quebec)

After the fall of Quebec in 1759–60 and the transfer of New France to Great Britain by the Treaty of Versailles, a gradual transition from the French to the British regime took place. English, Scottish, and American merchants took control of commerce and the western fur trade step by step,[36] while British officers and merchants bought and developed several existing seigneuries. In 1802, for example, a family of Scottish lumber merchants from Quebec City acquired the seigneury of Métis on the Gaspé Peninsula.[37]

Following the passage of the Constitutional Act of 1791 that divided New France into two provinces, Upper and Lower Canada, provincial authorities opened up for colonization the southeastern sectors of Lower Canada between the seigneuries along the St. Lawrence and Richelieu rivers and the American frontier. Settled by Loyalist and British newcomers between 1794 and 1812, this territory was planned and surveyed according to a system that was completely different from that which preceded it.[38] In this new system, the land was divided into *townships,* quadrangular in shape; the townships were then divided into individual farms that were also quadrangular in form, unlike the elongated linear farms of the seigneurial tradition.[39] Farmsteads were usually located in the centre of each property, isolated

5.9 Twelve-sided barn at the Walbridge family farm in Mystic, QC, built in 1878–82. The barn has recently been rebuilt with major funding from Quebec's Ministère de la Culture and members of the Walbridge family, with support from other charitable foundations. It is now operated as a museum of agricultural artifacts by the Missisquoi Historical Society.

from their neighbours, creating a physical community that, according to Jacobs and Fortin, perfectly mirrored the Protestant individualism of the new anglophone settlers, in strong contrast to the communal solidarity of the previously established francophone society.[40] Still known as the "Eastern Townships" (translated into French as "Cantons de l'Est"), this pastoral region has kept many architectural and cultural traces of its English, Scottish, and Irish origins (including old Protestant churches of neoclassical inspiration, much-appreciated covered bridges, and round barns), despite a gradual demographic transformation, begun as early as 1825, towards a majority francophone population.[41]

Among the many Quebec towns founded by colonists of British origin, a faithful witness of this era of settlement can be found in the old city of Sorel, situated at the mouth of the Richelieu River on the southern shore of the St. Lawrence. The colonial grid of the "Town of William-Henry," thus named from 1787 to 1860 in honour of the prince who would later become King William IV, and the elegant Carré Royal (Royal Square) at its centre (a heavily wooded square, symmetrically laid out around a classic bandstand) preserve the simplicity and discipline of the Georgian era.

Upper Canada (Ontario)

As the British regime began, the only European establishments in Upper Canada were a chain of French fortified villages, strategically located at Fort Frontenac (today's Kingston), Niagara, and Detroit. Almost everywhere else in the province, dense forest clothed the complex topography that divided southern Ontario into several distinct regions. East of Kingston, the Canadian Shield extends south to the St. Lawrence, isolating the Ottawa plain from the lowlands along Lake Ontario. These lands are bounded on the north by the Oak Ridges Moraine, oriented east-west. Between lakes Ontario and Erie runs the dolomite wall of the Niagara Escarpment; this sudden change of level, following its long trajectory towards the northwest, demarks the lowlands to the east from the plateau of southwestern Ontario.

At the close of the American Revolution, the British government bought the territories adjacent to Kingston and Niagara from the First Nations to provide land for Loyalist refugees. The configuration adopted for the farms of these new arrivals followed the familiar model of the French river-lot system, long established in these regions.[42] The Six Nations of the Iroquois, allies of Great Britain during the revolution and subsequently dispossessed of their ancestral lands in New York State, received new lands near Kingston as well as a large grant further west along the Grand River, whose waters drain into Lake Erie. Since all these territories remained extremely vulnerable to American attack across the Great Lakes, the first governor of Upper Canada, John Graves Simcoe, proposed an ambitious plan for the occupation and development of areas further inland. In 1793, he located the provincial capital at York (previously and subsequently known as Toronto), the best natural port on the northern shore of Lake Ontario, well protected from the

5.10   Areas of British settlement in Upper Canada, 1760–1840. Colonial development expanded from former French bases at Kingston (Fort Frontenac), Toronto (Fort Rouillé), Niagara, and Detroit.

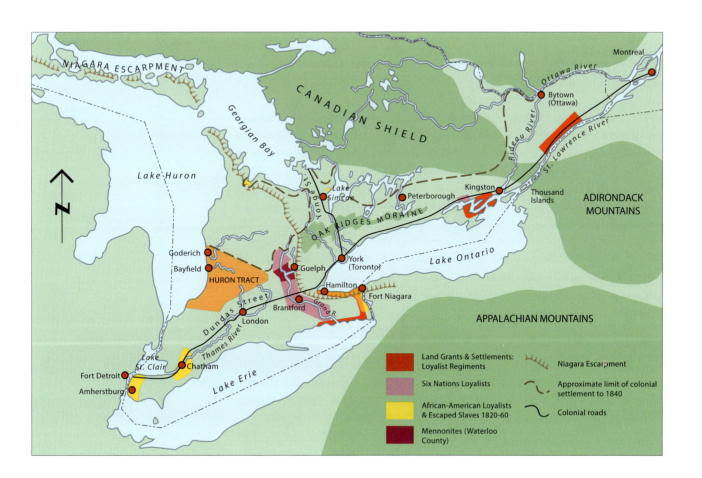

DREAMS OF EMPIRE   91

waves by a luminous crescent of islands and peninsulas. From this central point, Simcoe directed the construction of two military roads: "Yonge Street" to the north, running parallel to an ancient canoe route all the way to the lake that now bears his name; and " Dundas Street," extending to the west as far as the American frontier. The latter road passed through the site of the future city of London, at the confluence of two branches of the Thames River and the limit of navigation of this strategic waterway.[43]

The construction of these roads provided a vital catalyst for the agricultural exploitation of the territory. As in the Eastern Townships of Quebec, the *township system* of land division was adopted as the means of structuring the rural landscape. A vast empire of forest was surveyed and divided into lots according to an abstract geometry that virtually ignored the vicissitudes of topography and the complexity of the stream and river network.[44] The basic unit of the township system was a square of 100 "chains" of 66 feet (20 m) on each side, adding up to an area 1.25 miles by 1.25 miles (1,000 acres), bordered by "concession roads."[45] This area was then subdivided to provide for standard farms of about 200 acres (80 hectares). A study of the map of southern Ontario indicates that this normal pattern lent itself to considerable variation; townships were organized in large gridded blocks, oriented according to the cardinal directions or parallel to lakes or escarpments, the blocks often bumping into each other along diagonal lines. Visiting these landscapes today, one senses the validity of Owen Scott's comments: "This planned subdivision of land remains today and gives the landscape of Southern Ontario its major character and form. Future development, landscape form, building location, tree planting and smaller-scale subdivision of land have been greatly influenced by the early gridiron surveys."[46]

There were, inevitably, some exceptions to this implacable geometry. Scott notes that the lots and roads established in part of Waterloo County by the Mennonites, who arrived from Pennsylvania in 1800, were far more harmoniously integrated into the natural landscape than was the norm in Ontario.[47] Within the gridiron areas, the colonial authorities set up a major obstacle to colonization by reserving almost 30 per cent of all lands for Crown and clergy. The setting aside of these properties, which were to provide for the construction of government facilities and churches and to serve as land reserves to finance these institutions, discouraged the sale and the efficient occupation of the land. On the other hand, the *glebe lands* reserved for church use did facilitate the construction of religious buildings and the later development of residential districts such as the Glebe neighbourhood in Ottawa.

Entrepreneurs and Land Development Companies

A variety of strategies were brought into play to hasten colonization, including land development schemes operated by private entrepreneurs. Colonel Thomas Talbot, one of Governor Simcoe's lieutenants in 1793, became the promoter of a large sector of southwestern Ontario, in the Thames Valley.[48] In 1823 and 1825, Peter Robinson, a member of the provincial assembly, organized a large-scale program of Irish immigration destined for the environs of the future city of Peterborough.[49] The most ambitious enterprise of this nature was undoubtedly that of the Canada Company, a private company founded in Britain in 1824 with the aim of buying and colonizing unoccupied blocks of Crown land as well as the Huron Tract, an immense territory of 440,000 hectares situated in western Ontario. Led by its founder and director, Scottish novelist John Galt, the company made large investments in the infrastructure of these regions and succeeded in attracting colonists from Germany and the Netherlands, as well as from the British Isles. They founded many towns, including Guelph, Galt, and Goderich on Lake Huron.[50]

Impacts on the Natural Environment

The rapid expansion of agriculture in the Maritime provinces and Upper Canada was accomplished by decimating the forests that had occupied these lands for thousands of years. To set up his homestead, the new farmer first cut and burned the underbrush (often starting forest fires in the process), then cut the trees, of which the trunks provided the material for his first log house. He let the stumps rot in place before removing them. Contemporary observers noted the brutal ugliness of the new rural and village landscapes of the time, with their rotting stumps and burned-over soils.[51]

At the beginning of the nineteenth century, the Napoleonic Wars added a second motivation for the cutting down of the forests. France imposed a blockade on the export of products bound for England from Scandinavia, including the wood required for the British navy. Britain quickly turned to Canada for an alternative supply of this essential resource, putting in place a system of colonial trade preferences.[52] The Admiralty sought the long straight trunks of the white pine – monarch of the forest, easily capable of reaching 35 metres in height – as masts for their tall ships and oak trees for planks for their decks. A great lumber industry grew up, beginning in Nova Scotia and New Brunswick, then expanding into the watersheds of the St. Maurice and Ottawa rivers in Lower and Upper Canada, finally reaching the limits of the lands that drained into the St. Lawrence from the Canadian Shield. Every year, great rafts of squared timbers, lashed together, floated down the rivers from the *chantiers*, or logging camps, to the port of Quebec City, where the precious cargo was loaded into ships for transport to Europe.[53] The inspiration for countless images, songs, and legends, the lumber industry and its landscape of perpetual transformation have become ever-present components of the Canadian economy and culture.

Under this dual pressure of agricultural expansion and timber exploitation – and despite the relatively slow pace of manual work supported by oxen and horses – the dizzying scale and rapidity of the destruction of the eastern forests were nothing less than astonishing. By 1850, virtually all of southern Ontario had been denuded of its trees.[54] Colonel Samuel Strickland (1805–1867) witnessed this transformation of the Ontario landscape throughout this stage of colonization. Arriving from England in 1825, Strickland established two farms in the Peterborough area and worked for several years with the Canada Company at Guelph and Goderich, in collaboration with John Galt. In his book of 1853, *Twenty-seven Years in Canada West*, Strickland describes his first impressions of the Canadian landscape and its many riches. He tells of the beauty of the autumn foliage, the abundance of the salmon that swam up all the rivers, the innumerable passenger pigeons that abounded at the time, a species now extinct. He tells how easy it was to get lost in the dense forests, and recounts the gigantic dimensions of old-growth trees, including a cherry tree with a circumference of 3.2 metres, its lowest branch at a height of 15 metres. He also speaks of an oak 3.3 metres in diameter, its lowest branch 18–21 metres above the ground.[55] But despite his observations concerning the elimination of species, the smaller dimensions of the remaining trees, and the destabilizing effects of deforestation on temperatures and on the water regime, Strickland could not see these radical changes as anything but manifestations of an inevitable and desirable progress. With respect to the Huron Tract, he writes: "[O]nly twenty-four years ago [t]his vast and fertile tract of more than one million acres … did not contain a population of three hundred souls; no teeming fields of golden grain, no manufactories, no mills, no roads; the rivers were unbridged, and one vast solitude reigned around, unbroken."[56] Today Huron County, which occupies approximately the same territory, surpasses all other Ontario counties in agricultural production, as well as each of the four Atlantic provinces.[57]

Town and Villa

The planning of new towns in Upper and Lower Canada followed, in general, the rectangular gridiron model that had already been perfected in the Maritime provinces. Exceptionally, the plan of Toronto, designed in 1793 by Alexander Aitkin, did not include a central public square. It consisted of a rectangle of ten urban blocks, enclosed on the west, the east, and the south side facing the lake by a reserve set aside for public and military purposes. To the north of the urban grid, Governor Simcoe proposed that a range of "park lots," each 100 acres in area (40 hectares), be established for officials of the colonial government.[58] From this simple beginning grew the vast metropolis that we know today.

More typically, the town of Brantford, founded in 1830 in the Grand River territory given by the British government to the Six Nations, was laid out around a central public space, now known as Victoria Park, that exemplified the elegance and simplicity of the traditional squares of the time. Surveyor Lewis Burwell included this square as an open, undeveloped space in his original plan for the town; and in 1861, the space was transformed into a park according to the plans of local architect John Turner, who integrated the customary straight and diagonal paths into his symmetrical design for the park.[59] The square is framed by public buildings that tell the story of Brantford; these buildings include the county courthouse and Zion and Park Baptist churches (three buildings designed by Turner), as well as Central Presbyterian and Saint Andrew's United. The classical temple of the Bank of Montreal also borders on the square, as does the public library (imposing and miniature at the same time), a new concrete city hall dating from the postwar period, and, finally, the charming Art Deco building of the Bell Telephone

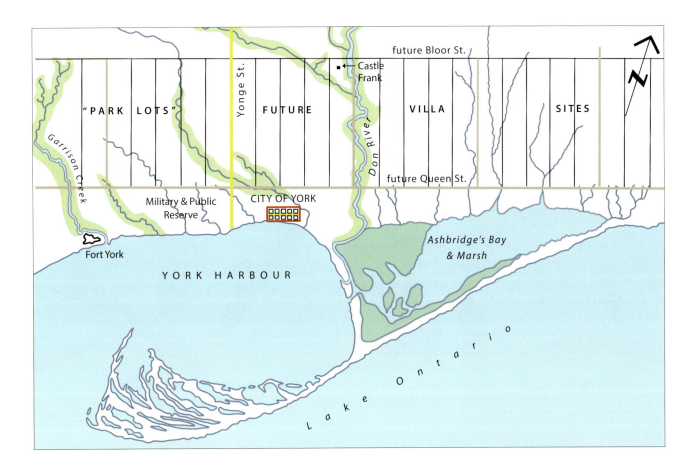

5.11 Toronto (York), Upper Canada: original site and early settlement, 1793. The harbour was originally sheltered by a continuous peninsula and island chain.

Company, its entrance porch sheltering a statue of Alexander Graham Bell, who had conceived the idea of the telephone in Brantford. The design of the park itself is equally strong and simple, with its grass surfaces, many large maples, several free-standing spruce trees, and rectilinear flower beds. The square is also, like that of Saint John, the guardian of the city's heritage. A water source calls attention to the important farm implement company Massey-Harris, and at the park's central point, a magnificent bronze monument executed in 1886 by sculptor Percy Wood commemorates Thayendanagea (Joseph Brant), the Mohawk chief and Loyalist leader during the American Revolution for whom the town was named. All that is missing is a monument to Wayne Gretzky, hockey player extraordinaire, a native of Brantford.

Town Planning Innovations in Upper Canada

Public spaces conceived within this tradition abound in the medium-sized towns of Ontario and Quebec. But in settlements founded by the Canada Company and in the Huron Tract generally, they also formed a part of highly original town plans in which a radial geometry replaced the traditional gridiron. At Goderich,

5.12 (facing page) Victoria Park, Brantford, ON. The courthouse is visible in the background.

5.13 Radial plan of Goderich, ON

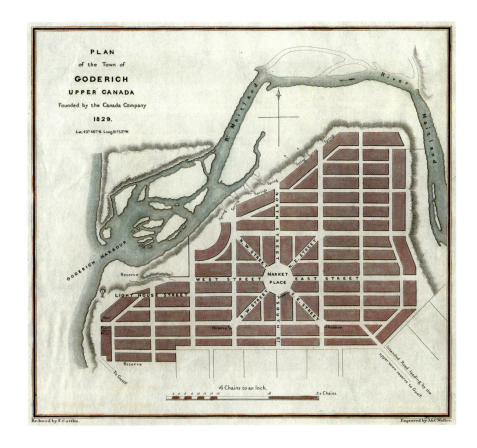

established in 1827 on the shores of Lake Huron, eight broad and imposing avenues, bordered by rows of trees, converge on an octagonal park in the centre of town, surrounded by commercial buildings. At the centre of the park, following the "court-house square"[60] pattern widely practised in the United States but little seen in Canada, is the Huron County courthouse. A few kilometres to the south is the small lake port of Bayfield, founded in 1832 by the Baron de Tuyll, a Dutch aristocrat. Here, the broad Clan Gregor Square follows a more classic model, enframed by several village churches and the historic town hall. A remarkably wide main street, reinforced by parallel rows of immense deciduous trees, leads to the square. The refined proportions of this avenue endow what is really a small community with a monumental character.[61] Established in 1827 by John Galt himself, the city of Guelph, the Canada Company's first realization, also followed a highly original plan.[62] In the town centre, built of stone like a town in Scotland, several radial streets converged on public spaces, including a great central space nestled in a meander of the River Speed and a grand marketplace that is now occupied by the railroad station and tracks. Here also, as seen in the Georgian towns of the Maritimes, the design of Guelph exploits the pronounced topography of the site, locating the Catholic church, in full theatrical fashion, at the summit of a natural promontory, its façade oriented to the axis of the main street.

DREAMS OF EMPIRE 97

5.14 Macdonnell Street, terminated by the Church of Our Lady Immaculate, Guelph, ON

Palladian Villas on Arcadian Sites: The First Generation

The placing of a public building on an imposing natural site was a relatively new phenomenon in the planning of Canadian towns of British tradition at that time, but dramatic topography and spectacular views had already been exploited for some time in the residential domain. In this land of small independent farmers, a few individuals, via their success in business or their high position in military or civic affairs, were able to gain access to larger properties, situated on elevated sites that benefited from splendid views towards wild or rural landscapes.[63] On these sites, they erected *villas*: country houses and gardens, their architecture inspired by British classicism (which was based on the principles of the great master of the Italian Renaissance, Andrea Palladio) and their landscapes influenced by the naturalist and picturesque movement that had revolutionized the rural domains of the English aristocracy since the early years of the eighteenth century.[64]

France Gagnon Pratte has brilliantly described the construction of the first domains of this genre in Quebec, built on breathtaking sites along the cliffsides around Quebec City from about 1780.[65] One of the first examples of this movement was the Manoir Montmorency, built on top of the cliff beside Montmorency Falls, to the east of Quebec City on the north shore of the St. Lawrence. In 1781, the third British governor of Quebec, Sir Frederick Haldimand (1718–1791), built himself a country residence in a colonial version of the Palladian style, grouping two wings with upper-floor galleries around a central two-storey pavilion, taking advantage of majestic perspectives towards the falls. Even closer to the gorge, the

5.15 Manoir Montmorency (Kent House), Montmorency Falls, QC. View to the west across the Montmorency River and Falls. Kent House is at top; viewing platform is below. Typical of the dramatic locations sought by the builders of eighteenth- and nineteenth-century villas in Canada.

governor built a small pavilion and lookout right above the cataract, exploiting the views of a chasm deeper than that at Niagara. Several years after Haldimand's departure, the house and its environs welcomed a distinguished resident: Prince Edward Augustus, Duke of Kent (1767–1820), the youngest son of King George III and future father of Queen Victoria. From 1791 to 1793, the duke and his companion, Madame Julie de Saint-Laurent, occupied the villa, where they regularly hosted prominent members of the francophone and anglophone bourgeoisie of Quebec City.[66] The duke was later posted to Halifax, where he directed the defence of all British territories in North America from 1794 to 1800. He nonetheless found the time to dedicate himself, along with Madame Saint-Laurent, to the design and construction of a superb country house and beautiful garden on Bedford Basin, on the wooded slopes to the north of the city. At Prince's Lodge, their Italian-style

DREAMS OF EMPIRE 99

villa, the couple enjoyed attractive views towards an immense protected harbour. A naturalistic park, freed of undergrowth by the troops, featured sinuous paths tracing the letters of Julie's name, as well as a garden pond in the shape of a heart. Several playfully composed pavilions completed the composition. One of these pavilions, the striking Music Room situated on a small promontory close to the water, still exists. It is a circular space for chamber music, its walls encircled by a colonnade, surmounted by a dome and crowned with a gigantic wooden sphere, originally gilded.[67]

The duke's influence on the physical fabric of Halifax was not confined to Prince's Lodge. His interest in an architecture of pure geometrical forms also made itself visible in three other circular buildings with which he was associated: the clock tower at the Citadel, which terminates the axis of George Street; the Martello Tower on Point Pleasant, the defensive peninsula situated at the southern extremity of the city; and St. George's Church, just north of the downtown area. Finally, it was he who directed the levelling of the Grand Parade and the construction of the walls and balustrades that contribute so much to the unique ceremonial character of that key public space of the old city.[68] The duke left another trace in the region: Île Saint-Jean was renamed Prince Edward Island in his honour.

Several other leading figures of the Maritime provinces created villas, gardens, and experimental farms during the period 1783–1813, particularly in the Saint John and Annapolis valleys.[69] The most well-known is Uniacke House, situated halfway between Halifax and Annapolis in Nova Scotia. Built in 1813 by Richard John Uniacke, a lawyer of Irish origin who reached the highest levels of the Nova Scotian establishment, this Palladian residence is oriented, across a simple sloping lawn, towards the diminutive Lake Martha. Native coniferous forest provides a

5.16   James Woolford, *Uniacke House, Mount Uniacke*, NS, c. 1830. The main house and Lake Martha are seen from the east in this romantic view. This may be a studio painting based on an 1817 watercolour sketch by Woolford. A similar view was painted by Maria Morris in 1828.

dramatic backdrop for the house: its principal façade is distinguished by a gracious gallery that continues around the sides of the building and a well-proportioned colonnade, crowned by a triangular central pediment.[70]

From the early days of its colonization, about 1790, the ideal of the Palladian villa inspired Upper Canada's governmental, military, and commercial elites. Southern Ontario's characteristic topography provided these enthusiasts with a multitude of potential sites, many benefiting from spectacular views. The lake-formed terraces and ravines typical of the landscapes around Toronto permitted the first governor, John Graves Simcoe, and his wife Elizabeth Posthuma Simcoe, to build Castle Frank (1795) on the heights above the western bank of the Don River, profiting from views of the valley. A celebrated drawing by Mrs. Simcoe indicates a sort of Greek temple with sturdy wooden columns 5 metres in height, in an Acropolis-like cliff-top setting.[71] Mrs. Simcoe's drawing, one of some five hundred that she executed during her five-year stay in Canada, represents two popular artistic traditions of the colonial era. First, the drawing itself was typical of numerous Canadian landscape scenes – from the Maritimes, the Heights of Quebec, the Great Lakes, and elsewhere – that were expertly delineated in ink wash and watercolour by professional military draughtsmen[72] and skilful female amateurs from aristocratic or professional families. And second, the landscape it depicted – the villa she and her husband built[73] and its dramatic landscape setting – was informed by the work of seventeenth-century European painters such as Claude Lorraine, Nicolas Poussin, and Salvator Rosa, whose picturesque and sublime compositions had inspired landscape gardens in England for much of the eighteenth century. The dramatic verticality of the cliffs and their rugged, forested character clearly place this particular landscape composition, and the drawing that represents it, on the sublime side of that stylistic dichotomy. One writer, Susan Glickman, has postulated that the prominence of the sublime view of the natural world, at a time when Canadian settlement by Europeans was proceeding rapidly, resulted in a permanent "imprinting of this view on Canadian poetry."[74] Perhaps the same was true of Canadian landscape painting and design.

Imperial Symbols

The colonization of the Canadian landscape permitted the world empire of Britain to regain its momentum following the catastrophic loss (from its viewpoint) of its American provinces, transformed into the United States. In the aftermath of this loss there flourished a desire for a new imperial culture that would not be corrupted by republican ideas and an intention among the Loyalist refugees to recreate the world they had lost. In the hybrid civilization that was in process of development, certain elements – such as the preponderance of the independent family farm and the social levelling typical of a frontier society – followed the North American model. But an opposing tendency also came to the fore, involving the ubiquitous display of imperial expressions and symbols. Thus, during the reign of the four Georges (1710–1830), there was an astounding proliferation of main streets named "George," "King," or "Great George." The names of towns, streets, rivers, and lakes rendered homage to various other members of the royal family (Prince Edward Island, Charlottetown), the British government (Sydney, Halifax), or the colonial service (Lake Simcoe). Indeed, according to Thomas Raddall, the names "Prince" and "Duke" were also widely used as a precaution against the possibility of leaving out someone of importance.[75] Architectural symbols of the Empire were much in evidence, and the construction of residences for British-appointed governors almost always preceded the building of structures to house provincial assemblies or parliaments. In the choice of their sites (usually on an elevated or riverside location just outside the limits of the original town, as in St. John's, Newfoundland, or at Halifax) and the gravity of their official Palladian architecture, the governors' residences clearly expressed the force and the permanence of the Empire.

In Canada around 1820, the British Empire was the pride of its elite and of many citizens, and despite the obvious chauvinism of imperial patriotism, sometimes excessive, its institutions offered stability, opportunity, and a considerable degree of liberty to those who were more distant from the sources of power, including francophones, Irish, Dutch, and German immigrants, and Methodists. With the exception of the rebellions of 1837–38, most of those outside the establishment accepted and participated in British institutions without conflict. In this sense, the British Empire resembled its predecessor, the Roman Empire of antiquity, which had also been a complex, constantly evolving political assemblage that nonetheless assured several centuries of peace and prosperity to a heterogeneous society comprising millions of people. These similarities went deep. The systems of land division in the British colonies, for example, closely resembled the Roman system of *centuriation*, and rectangular colonial towns centred on public spaces and civic buildings recalled the Roman *castrum* and its central *forum*, while the villas of aristocrats, built outside the urban areas on majestic sites with views of the natural environment, remind us of the similar estates of Roman patricians.

This Roman inspiration was certainly deliberate, at least for the dominant class. References to the "age of Augustus" figured prominently in the literature of the English garden.[76] In politics, the members of the powerful Whig party, part of the coalition that had brought about the "Glorious Revolution" of 1688, identified themselves with the great patricians who, at the founding of the Roman Republic, deposed an arbitrary monarch in favour of a state ruled by law, one that balanced the interests of the various classes of society. At its best, colonial civilization in Canada exalted the Roman virtues,[77] both in its physical realizations, its rural and urban landscapes, and its political and economic life. Its physical realizations were solid, logical, and ordered, and often elegant and well proportioned, largely through the inspiration the British tradition sought in France or Italy (just as the Romans were inspired by Greece). Today, urban and rural landscapes informed by the British colonial heritage constitute the everyday physical background of many regions of Canada, but the very familiarity of this rich tradition often makes it easy to overlook.

6.1　CPR poster promoting immigration to Manitoba, c. 1883

6

Promised Lands in the West

During the six decades that followed the United States' purchase of Louisiana in 1803, American settlers moved rapidly into the Middle West and other territories, opening up twenty new states. In the same period, the immense territory of the Canadian West, from Lake Huron to the Arctic and Pacific coasts, remained inaccessible to prospective colonists and was sparsely settled by Europeans, until dramatic changes began in 1870.

Landscapes of the West

The greatest barrier to settlement was the *Canadian Shield*. This vast zone of ancient eroded mountains, punctuated by countless rivers, lakes, and wetlands, extends for a thousand kilometres to the north and west of southern Ontario's rich farmlands. Its mixed forest cover changes gradually into a forest of small conifers, sombre and seemingly endless for the visitor who traverses it. This hardy soul finds no easy passage: the glaciers have created a complex and discontinuous drainage system that defies navigation, and innumerable cold lakes fill every hollow in the rocky landscape.

Beyond the Shield, the *Prairies* occupy the centre of the continent. This region is divided naturally into three levels, from east to west.[1] The first level is the ancient bed of Lake Agassiz, greatest of Canada's proglacial lakes, of which the Manitoba great lakes of today are the final vestiges. This

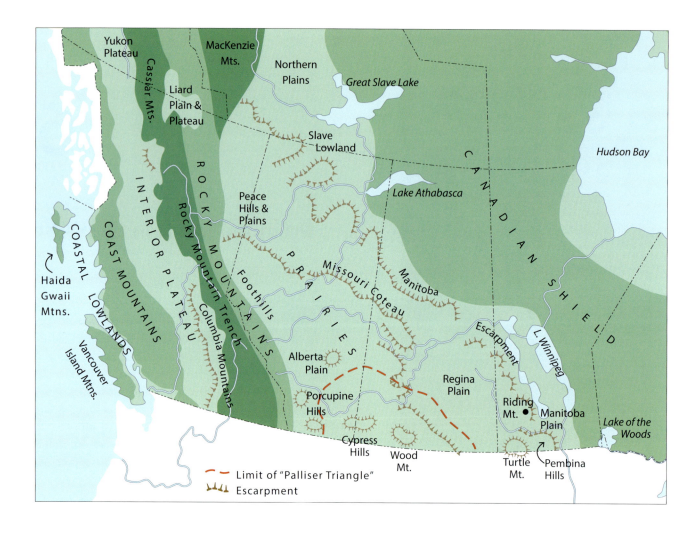

6.2 Physiography of western Canada

lake created, in southern Manitoba, an immense fertile plain, unbelievably flat, its slopes of only 1 or 2 per cent imperceptible to the untrained eye. A range of hills and mountains – the Manitoba Escarpment, a long, brooding, forested mass as seen from the neat and orderly fields of the plain – defines the western limit of the prehistoric lake. The escarpment marks the beginning of the second prairie level, which comprises the Regina Plain and other highly productive grasslands. Further west, the Missouri Coteau traverses the prairies along a northwestern alignment, announcing the third prairie level: drier lands of more complex topography, rolling westward until they meet the Rocky Mountains. Each level receives less precipitation than its neighbour to the east: from the tall-grass prairie around Winnipeg, one passes through several subtly graduated plant zones to the short drought-tolerant grasses of southern Alberta. The Prairies are thus divided by topography and water regimes into three natural provinces. To the north of the grasslands, stands of trembling aspen and white spruce – "parklands" – are succeeded by the boreal forest, both zones disposed in east-west bands perpendicular to the north-south patterns of landform.

The topography of the Prairies is often "negative," characterized not by hills but by valleys that are recessed into the broad horizontal plains. Great rivers – the North and South branches of the Saskatchewan, and their tributaries – the Bow, the Assiniboine, and the Qu'Appelle – all proceed majestically along the floors of these wide and deep valleys, often called "coulees." These valleys, carved by the sudden release of huge volumes of water from proglacial lakes, seem "too large for their rivers." Enclosed by steep, often forested slopes, these long, thin oases[2] frequently harbour the only native trees in their entire regions. In a landscape that is relatively arid, the valleys furnish excellent conditions for specialized agriculture and for parks. The waters from these river systems are eventually discharged into Lake Winnipeg, from which they find their way – through an amazing accident of geological history – across the Shield into Hudson Bay.

Among the infinity of remarkable landscapes in the West, the noblest are those of the *Rocky Mountains*, which rise abruptly from the prairies to heights of more than 3,000 metres on an almost linear north-south front, continuing as far as the eye can see in both directions. The origins of these mountains go back 200 million years, when horizontal sedimentary rocks of the North American plate, moving to the west, collided with the Pacific plate, moving eastward. In this struggle of titans, layers of rock from the two plates were torn off along fault lines and folded into tortuous wavelike forms.[3] Sandstone, limestone, dolomite, and shale, containing minerals that had accumulated over eons at the bottom of the sea, became the bedrock of mountain summits, displaying their courses of stratification in a spectacular panoply of patterns and colours. Water and wind – the forces of erosion – then sculpted steep-sided river valleys between and across the mountain ranges, depositing the eroded materials as *talus* slopes at lower elevations. Finally, very recently in the geological story, snow accumulations in the highlands began the process of glaciation described in the first chapter, scraping and tearing great chunks of stone from the mountains, leaving them with ragged, fanglike silhouettes and reworking the valleys into U-shaped profiles with flat valley floors, excavating lakes and depositing gravel, rocks, and finer materials everywhere in the valleys and on the plains. Coniferous and mixed forests rapidly established themselves on the newly created landscape during the brief period of about 10,000 years that have elapsed since the glaciers relinquished their grip.

Further west, similar processes of collision and folding built other *cordilleras*, parallel to the Rockies, creating a sequence of plateaux, mountains, and valleys all the way to the west coast and beyond, ending in parallel chains of offshore islands. Here the forces of wave and current, as well as dramatic variations in ocean levels over time, sculpted fjords, promontories, and deep bays, complex and mysterious. In this already out-of-scale environment, heavy rains engendered by the meeting of humid ocean air masses and high coastal mountains nourished an equally colossal stratum of vegetation, dominated by conifers that attained heights of up to 70 metres.

Exploration and Exploitation of the West

The Fur Trade

Europeans gradually surmounted these geographical obstacles, mounting a double invasion on eastern and western fronts along the networks of lakes and rivers that were the only practicable routes of the time. This invasion had a precise goal: furs. Trading for furs with Native peoples was as old as the first European incursions into the St. Lawrence valley. In the sixteenth century, before the foundation of Port-Royal, French and Basque sailors maintained seasonal trading posts on the lower river, bartering for furs with the Innu or Montagnais, who provided them with a commercial link to peoples further north.

Little by little, the frontier of the fur trade extended west and north, up the great river and its tributaries, passing through the Great Lakes to Huronia and the inland empire of the Mississippi, then up the Ottawa River and across Georgian Bay to the fur-rich forests of the Northwest. The next goal was the watershed of Hudson Bay, where the cold climate made for high-quality furs. This immense territory included most of the Canadian Shield and the western plains all the way

6.3   Fur-trading posts and missions in western Canada. The rivers of western Canada provided natural routes for the exploitation of the fur-bearing animals of the northern forests and, later, the buffalo of the plains. These waterways were complemented by overland trails and portages that linked them together. Beige indicates prairie and parkland vegetation; bright green the Great Lakes and St. Lawrence forest, dark green the boreal and western coniferous forests. Light green to the north of Churchill shows the start of the northern tundra.

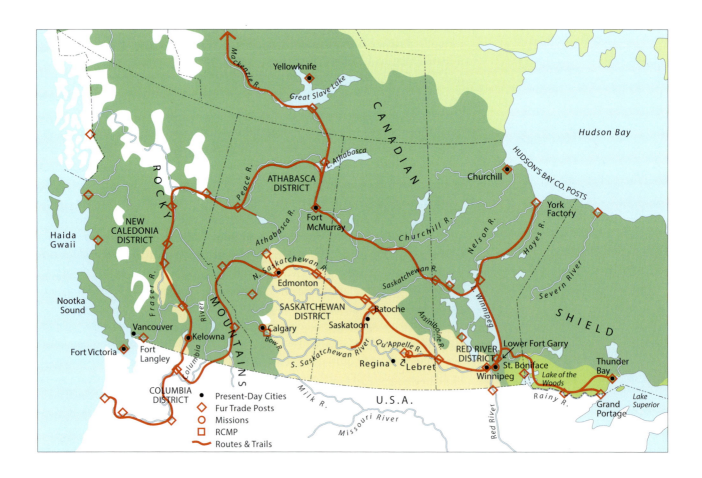

106   LANDSCAPE HERITAGE OF THE FIRST NATIONS AND COLONISTS

to the summits of the Rockies.[4] While British traders from the Hudson's Bay Company (HBC) waited to receive furs at ports on the bay at the mouths of the western rivers, French traders from Montreal continued their inexorable westward expansion, building a chain of forts on the great rivers, strategically located so as to intercept the furs moving to the coast.[5]

Finally, the mysterious North Pacific opened its doors to voyages of scientific exploration; these were organized by maritime nations that established close contacts with the peoples of the "last coast,"[6] contacts that rapidly led to the exchange of furs and other goods.[7] At the same time, companies from the other side of the continent – including the new North West Company, based in Montreal – continued their conquests through the interior, adopting intensive hunting strategies that made sustained yield impossible, using up, one after another, the northern forest regions of the continent.[8] Between 1770 and 1820, they overcame the last frontiers – the watershed of the Athabasca River,[9] the Rocky Mountains, and the New Caledonia and Columbia River regions on the Pacific slope, following trade routes used by the First Nations for thousands of years.[10]

Fur-Trading Posts

Each trading post was a small, isolated, yet surprisingly cosmopolitan village,[11] surrounded by a world that belonged to the First Nations, "an isolated dot in an Aboriginal sea."[12] Fort Langley, founded in 1827, is a typical example. The Hudson's Bay Company built this fort near the limit of navigation of the Fraser River in British Columbia, on elevated terrain near a waterway, as usual – access by boat was always a prerequisite. Located on a gradual slope, the post was a rectangle some 200 by 75 metres, oriented at right angles to the river, enclosed by a wooden palisade reinforced with bastions. Inside these rustic fortifications, a number of wooden buildings were distributed about a large central open space. The buildings included lodgings for artisans and clerks; storehouses for furs, trade goods, food, and various other equipment and materials; and workshops for the blacksmith and barrel maker. At the top of the slope stood the "big house" of the factor or chief trader, its gallery and central door placed on the axis of the central space to emphasize the importance of the factor and the company he represented. In a corner of the enclosure was a kitchen garden, to provide fresh vegetables for his table.[13] North of Winnipeg on the Red River, Lower Fort Garry, begun in 1831 as the home base of the governor of the HBC, followed a similar defensive configuration, but as the nerve centre of company operations in the North and West, it was distinguished by the stone construction of its walls and of some buildings and the unusual aesthetic concern shown in its structures and garden layout.

The companies planted gardens and established full-fledged farms in the neighbourhood of the trading posts, along with pasturelands for their cows and horses. At Fort Langley, a farm located several kilometres from the post supplied hay for the animals and grain (including wheat, barley, and oats), peas, and potatoes for the residents of the fort.[14] Many of the traders and voyageurs stayed for years at these remote posts, in constant contact with members of the First Nations, who

6.4 Lower Fort Garry, located on the Red River north of Winnipeg

established villages nearby and provided all the furs. The traders often established temporary or permanent marriages with Native women from the tribes of their trading partners.[15] When they retired, they and their descendants, the Métis, often established farms – on the linear river-lot pattern, for exactly the same reasons as in Quebec – near the trading posts.

These farms were not intended to be the first phase of a broad-scale colonization – quite the contrary. The fur-trading companies saw that the growth of agriculture would bring deforestation, with its inevitable consequence, the disappearance of the animals on which their industry depended. But nevertheless, with their kitchen gardens and local farms, the fur-trading companies did bring agriculture to the West. They also laid the first foundations of the forest industry, the fish export business, and the mining industry, and they were largely responsible for the first religious and educational institutions.[16] Their initiatives opened the gates to any number of subsequent developments in the West.

Ocean of Grass

The incursions of the fur trade into western Canada were soon matched by explorations for other purposes – scientific, political, and economic. The opening of new frontiers to various newcomers of European background exposed the visitors to a succession of stunning new landscapes; their writings bear witness to their reactions when confronted with them. From 1857 to 1860, John Palliser, a British officer of Irish origin, directed a scientific expedition sponsored by the British government in an effort to learn more about the Canadian West. Ably assisted by a Scottish geologist, Dr James Hector, and a French biologist, Eugène Bourgeau, Palliser analysed the diverse western regions visited during the expedition, from Lake Superior to the Pacific coast, and judged their capacity to accommodate agriculture. He considered a large zone in the southwest of the Prairies, located mostly in Alberta and in part of Saskatchewan, to be too dry for agriculture. The region still bears his name: the Palliser Triangle. He found the broad swath of country to the north and east of the Triangle to be more propitious for farming – the "fertile belt." Palliser's report, submitted in 1862, is a remarkable compendium of observations of the landscape and society of the West, including the first scientific analyses of the geology and botany of the Canadian Prairies and the Rockies.[17]

Several years later, in 1870, a second expedition, again led by a British officer, William Francis Butler, retraced the steps of the Palliser expedition. In his book, *The Great Lone Land*, Butler saw the landscape as an enormous ocean of grass, without a past or a sign of history, silent and solitary, offering an "infinite variety" of visual impressions.[18] The Canadian writer Gabrielle Roy (1909–1983), born in St. Boniface, Manitoba, pursued this ocean metaphor: "[T]he prairie stretched away as far as you could see; in one immense, rolling plain it unfolded in a series of long, fluid waves sweeping unendingly to the horizon."[19]

A Sublime Nature

The first explorers to encounter the cliffs and giant forests of the Pacific coast also left records of their reactions to these often unbelievable landscapes. Between 1750 and 1800, many maritime countries sent scientific expeditions to study the sea, the land, the plants, the animals, and the peoples of the coast.[20] In 1792, the British navy undertook a scientific and strategic voyage to the west coast, under the command of Captain George Vancouver. This experienced sailor had been a member of the crew of the illustrious Captain James Cook, the acme of explorers, who led three scientific expeditions around the world.[21] A Scottish surgeon and naturalist, Archibald Menzies (1754–1846), accompanied Vancouver on the *HMS Discovery*. Menzies (who was a plant collector at the Royal Gardens at Kew) identified, drew, and prepared specimens of a broad range of plants native to the west coast of Canada, including tall conifers and deciduous trees, numerous shrubs, and an impressive collection of orchids, ferns, grasses, and perennials.[22] A considerable number of these plants were named in his honour. Other botanists were to follow Menzies, including fellow Scot David Douglas (1799–1835), who travelled the West from 1825 to 1834 in search of plants for Britain's Royal Horticultural Society.[23]

These explorers often expressed their ambivalence in the face of the magnificent but frightening landscapes of the coast through such names as "Desolation Sound" (Vancouver). The French explorer de Galaup de Lapérouse called the Northwest Coast "an abominable land,"[24] yet spoke with awe of Lituya Bay in Alaska: "Perhaps the most extraordinary place on earth ... a vast basin, whose depth in the centre is impossible to estimate, edged by great, steep, snow-covered mountains ... The air is so clear and the silence so deep that the voice of one man can be heard half a league away, as can the sound of birds which have laid their eggs in the hollows formed by the rocks."[25] Menzies, as poetic as he was technical, described "a beautiful Waterfall ... its wild romantic appearance aided by its rugged situation & the gloomy forests which surrounded it."[26]

Artists who confronted the vast western landscapes reacted much like their literary counterparts. Groping to comprehend and convey their impressions of landscapes and cultures entirely new to them, such artists as painter Paul Kane on the Prairies, photographer Benjamin Baltzly in the Rockies and Selkirks, and John Webber and William Ellis, who made sketches and drawings on Captain Cook's 1778 expedition to the west coast, portrayed the landscape as both hostile and welcoming, and provided a remarkable record of the First Nations peoples who inhabited them.[27]

Colonization of the Prairies

From the seventeenth to the nineteenth centuries, the voyageurs concentrated their activities in the forested regions that provided ideal habitats for the animals they sought, paying little attention to the immense open prairie to the south, which extended from the Shield to the Rockies. The Prairies long remained the uncontested homeland of First Nations whose livelihood was based on the herds of buffalo, virtually uncountable, that roamed the grasslands.

The Red River

Little by little, however, Canadian and European influences extended into the Prairies. These influences were first evident at the forks of the Red and Assiniboine rivers, where the great city of Winnipeg would later be built. A favoured campground for First Nations for some 6,000 years, this site had often served as a peaceful meeting place for rival tribes.[28] Its strategic situation at a major confluence of the river network helped it become an important transfer and distribution centre for the fur trade. In 1738, Pierre de La Vérendrye chose this location to build Fort Rouge, precursor to many trading posts built at the beginning of the nineteenth century by the two largest companies, to provide their voyageurs with meat. In 1812, the first farmers were established on the site; they were Scottish peasants, displaced from their ancestral lands by feudal proprietors. Lord Selkirk, a member of the governing board of the Hudson's Bay Company, convinced his colleagues to provide these settlers with an extensive territory on the Red River. The new farmers settled on the west bank of the river, to the north of the forks of the Red and Assiniboine, on farms laid out in the familiar Quebec pattern of long lots, perpendicular to the river.[29] Each settler received a 100-acre farm (40.5 hectares) on the west bank, a neighbouring lot for haying, and a woodlot on the forested east side of the river.

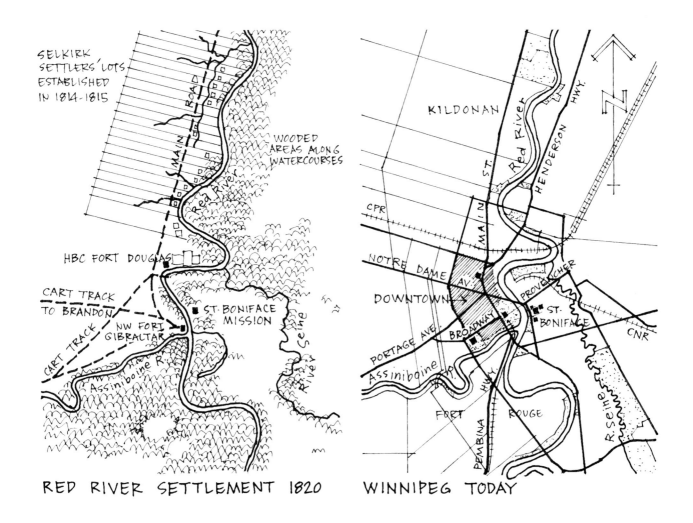

6.5 Comparison of the Red River Settlement in 1820, on left, and Winnipeg's configuration today. The modern street layout follows the lines of the original long-lot land division pattern, while Winnipeg's two principal thoroughfares, Portage Avenue and Main Street, mirror the routes of the original cross-country trail to the West along the Assiniboine River and the meandering Red River to the North, respectively.

The new settlement amplified what was already a fierce competition between the two major rivals, the Hudson's Bay and North West companies. Confrontations between the two, often culminating in bloodshed,[30] ended only with their fusion under the Hudson's Bay Company name in 1821. The merger was followed by an aggressive program of rationalization. Many downsized fur trade employees – Métis voyageurs and their families – were given farms along the Red River and the Assiniboine, laid out once again according to the traditional long-lot pattern.[31]

The Role of the Church

Lord Selkirk invited missionaries from Quebec to establish institutions for the fledgling colony. In 1818, two men arrived, one of whom was the young Father (and future Bishop) Joseph-Norbert Provencher (1788–1855). The two emissaries received land for their mission on the east side of the Red River at a place

PROMISED LANDS IN THE WEST 111

they called Saint-Boniface, where they quickly built a little log-cabin church. This simple mission marked the beginning of the central role that the church would play in the colonization of the West and the shaping of its landscapes. Innumerable schools, colleges, and hospitals founded by religious communities – mainly Catholic, but also Methodist and Anglican – eventually dotted the landscape of western Canada. Several religious orders responded to an appeal launched by Provencher, including the Sisters of Charity, commonly known as the "Grey Nuns," founded in Montreal in 1737 by Marguerite d'Youville; and the Oblate Fathers, or Oblats de Marie Immaculée, established in France in 1826, who included among their members the colourful Father Albert Lacombe (1827–1916), who provided inspiration and support to the francophone settlers of northern Alberta.[32] Other Oblate missionaries carried the gospel to Native people living around Fort Langley, BC, in 1840,[33] and in 1859, Father Charles Pandosy founded the Mission de l'Immaculée Conception in the Okanagan Valley, near the HBC fort. The mission served as the original nucleus of the village that has become the prosperous city of Kelowna. Father Pandosy, noticing the agricultural potential of that fertile valley, blessed with an ideal climate, planted the first apple trees and grapevines of the Okanagan, now famous for its fruit and wines.[34] In 1858, the sisters of Sainte-Anne (whose *maison mère*, coincidentally, is at Lachine, Quebec, directly across a narrow

6.6 Father Pandosy's Mission, Kelowna, BC. Several original buildings were preserved and repaired by the Okanagan Historical Society and other charitable organizations. Other historical buildings have since been moved to the site.

waterway from the main warehouse of the HBC, from which the giant canoes departed for the frontier) accepted a call to the West Coast. In their new home near the HBC's Fort Victoria, they created a masterpiece of architecture and landscape at St. Ann's Academy, which became the administrative centre for their many missions throughout the islands and rivers of the coast.

Saint-Boniface, Centre of French civilization in the West

Saint-Boniface rapidly became the great religious and cultural centre of the Canadian West. Along the right bank of the river, a whole series of structures, spaces, and monuments would be built, all oriented to the old river road. That thoroughfare, which recalls the traditional *chemin du roi* of Quebec, was named for Archbishop Alexandre Taché (1823–1894), and a second boulevard, perpendicular to the first – equivalent to a *montée* back in New France – bears the name of his predecessor, Joseph-Norbert Provencher, first bishop of the diocese.

At the southern limit of the old institutional complex stands what is considered to be the oldest building in Manitoba, erected in 1847 and now a museum: the *couvent des Sœurs Grises*, or Grey Nuns Convent.[35] North of the convent, on the opposite side of a historic wooded area, is a broad open space: the cemetery of Saint-Boniface, a great formal rectangle laid out in classical New France symmetrical style, with rows of headstones parallel and perpendicular to a central axis. Lilacs and honeysuckles soften somewhat the austere composition. The traditional emblems of the church – the *calvaire* and a statue of the Virgin Mary – are given places of honour, as are memorials to those who built or defended the French culture on the Prairies: the tombs of Provencher and Taché, who presided over the

6.7 Cemetery and façade of cathedral, Saint-Boniface, MB. Designed by Montreal architect Jean-Omer Marchand.

PROMISED LANDS IN THE WEST 113

development of the whole region from 1818 to 1894; and the *monument des Braves*, dedicated to the "Français de l'Ouest, morts pour leur patrie 1914–1918." And finally, the tomb of Louis Riel, martyr to the cause of French, Métis, and Catholic peoples of the West and now, increasingly, the symbol of resistance and affirmation for all residents of the Prairies.

The axis of the cemetery continues east and passes through the façade of Saint-Boniface Cathedral, the fourth church built on the site. Designed by the eminent Manitoba architect Étienne Gaboury, it is a modern church, deliberately understated and self-effacing, framed by the ruins of the baroque façade of the third cathedral, begun in 1906 and destroyed by fire in 1968.[36] The overall composition is subtle and evocative. Looking back towards the river, the visitor can see that the open façade of the old cathedral frames an axial view that continues across the river, terminating at the dome of the former Union Station, almost right on the axis. The linking of these two buildings juxtaposes symbols of the two principal forces in the Canadian settlement of the West.

Finally, the Archbishop's Palace is located at the northern extremity of this remarkable linear sequence, set back from the road by a formal and axial ceremonial driveway framed by a double row of elms and spruces. From the gallery of this elegant building, constructed in 1864–65,[37] the visitor looks out on a beautiful circular garden in which junipers, peonies, irises, and other perennials surround the customary statue of the Virgin Mary, welcoming and accessible rather than imposing and impressive. Beyond the garden, a shaft of space opens up to the Red River. Here, as at the cathedral, the fine workmanship of wrought-iron gates adds to the impact of the overall composition.

As a civic design ensemble, this grouping of buildings and spaces strongly recalls, in its character and organization, many such arrangements in Quebec. The linear assembly of buildings and spaces along a body of water, the crest of a hill, or an important road is one of the classic urban compositions of Quebec, as seen in the complex of institutions of the Sœurs de Sainte-Anne and their neighbours at Lachine, or the cathedral of Rimouski and its companions, or Saint-Laurent College in the northern suburbs of Montreal.

Lebret, Saskatchewan

Far from the comfortable confines of Saint-Boniface, the Métis people established villages and long-lot farms along many of the less-populated river valleys of the Prairies, including those of the Bow River west of Calgary, the Qu'Appelle River in Saskatchewan, and the North Saskatchewan near Edmonton. According to historian Graham MacDonald of Parks Canada, "The hand of the early French explorers and settlers is visible everywhere in the country, from the Atlantic to the Rocky Mountains, in the long-lot system that follows every river."[38] Lebret, a small village situated on the Qu'Appelle River northeast of Regina, is a typical example. It was founded by Bishop Taché in 1865 as the first mission in Saskatchewan, and its first chapel was built the following year. Its first school, directed by the Oblate Fathers, opened in 1884 – one of the industrial and residential schools for First Nations

6.8 Way of the Cross and church, Lebret, SK, in the Qu'Appelle River Valley

children, the many wounds from which may only now be starting to heal. A convent and a seminary followed. Finally, in 1929, a striking *chemin de la croix* was built, very simple and austere but perhaps closer in feeling to the original Way of the Cross in the Holy Land, an arid place like Saskatchewan, where agriculture is always a struggle. The view from the hilltop, after completing one's short pilgrimage, discloses a parish church built foursquare to the river, just like those seen in innumerable locations along the St. Lawrence and its tributaries.

Batoche, Saskatchewan – Last Refuge of the Bois-Brûlés

By a strange sequence of tragic coincidences and blunders, the river-lot agricultural system in the West – so sensible and effective – became the focus of controversy and eventually a contributory factor in two armed struggles. Although the physical expressions of that system in the West were almost identical to those in Quebec, the legal system of tenure supporting them was infinitely more fragile. There were no *seigneurs* or *seigneuries* in the West, and while many land claims were filed, the rights of farmers to the land they tilled were vague and uncertain. A conflict over such property rights touched off the 1870 resistance in the Red River, and despite the successful conclusion of that struggle (the creation of the new province of Manitoba), a considerable number of Métis – the *bois-brûlés* – pulled

PROMISED LANDS IN THE WEST 115

6.9 Church and presbytery, Batoche, SK

up stakes and moved northwest. Many moved to a place called Batoche, where the cart track from the Red River Settlement to Fort Edmonton forded the South Saskatchewan River. Here, Métis settlers established the agricultural colony of Saint-Laurent. Following models familiar since the time of New France, the colonists built their church and its presbytery on top of the plateau that encloses the river valley, carefully siting it with respect to topography, and laid out their long, narrow farms in the lowlands, perpendicular to the river and separated from one another by dense hedgerows.

The church and the hedgerows are still there, but the farmhouses and barns have long since disappeared. The abandoned valley reminds us that Batoche was the site of the last battle fought on Canadian soil, in 1885. As at the Red River, the Northwest conflict was a confrontation between two philosophies of land division and two ways of understanding property rights, a confrontation that, in retrospect, seems to have been completely avoidable. The open, unembellished landscape of Batoche powerfully evokes the story of the tragic events that occurred there. On the Plains of Abraham, in Quebec City – now a great urban park filled with thousands of people enjoying a remarkable variety of activities – it is easy to forget that you are on a battlefield, despite the presence of forts and cannons. But at Batoche, the battlefield is always there. Also located on the plateau, some distance away from the church, the graveyard is laid out in traditional formal arrangement with a fenced boundary.

Lines and Squares: Revolutionary Changes to the Western Landscape

New political developments were underway in eastern Canada, developments that responded to a multitude of local and international circumstances. A new strategy envisioned the confederation of the existing British provinces of North America, creating a transcontinental economic and political structure that would integrate the communities and territories of the West into Canadian political space.[39] These developments led to a series of interrelated events, all of which occurred between the two conflicts of 1870 and 1885, that drastically transformed western landscapes and ways of life.

The disappearance of the buffalo from the Prairies was the first of these occurrences. Gigantic herds of these animals (estimates vary between 30 million and 100 million animals)[40] had furnished the First Nations of the western plains with almost all the necessities of life – food, shelter, tools – and had once given the impression that "the prairie seemed to be moving."[41] But in the years from 1870 to 1885, these huge herds were reduced to a mere handful of animals. Trains and steamboats provided easy access to the territory, and modern weapons, which could kill with terrible efficiency, did their work.[42] In the face of this developing catastrophe and already decimated by European diseases, the Native peoples of the Prairies signed, between 1871 and 1877, a series of seven peace treaties that transferred their hunting grounds to the federal government in exchange for land

6.10 High Level Bridge, Lethbridge, AB: one of many ambitious engineering works built to bring railways to the West

reserves, payments, and other support programs. This permitted these vast lands, from northwestern Ontario to the Rockies, to be opened up to agriculture. In 1869, the Hudson's Bay Company sold its far-flung properties to the government of Canada. Two years later, when British Columbia entered Confederation, the Canadian government promised its new province that a transcontinental railroad would be built all the way to the West Coast, through Canadian territory.[43] Despite financial crises, scandals, and almost unimaginable technical challenges, within fifteen years the construction of the Canadian Pacific Railroad was completed, an epic celebrated in song and story.[44]

The Implacable Grid

These three events were closely linked to the opening of the Prairies to settlement and agriculture. But before settlers could be brought in, the land had to be quickly and efficiently measured, surveyed, and divided up. To do this, the federal government adopted, in 1871, the Dominion Land Survey Act, inspired by similar systems that were established by the United States in 1784 and 1787, during the first period of expansion of the young republic beyond the thirteen original colonies.[45] In contrast to the proven system of surveying and allocation of farmlands of New France, which was founded on the hydrographic network, topography, and agricultural potential, the survey system adopted in the West ignored all natural elements, favouring an implacable and universal geometric continuity.

In the new system, the lands of western Canada that were thought to be suitable for agriculture – including the southern sections of the Prairies, the more northerly Peace River region, a band of land through British Columbia along the rail line, and large sectors of the inland plateau and lower mainland – were divided and subdivided like an immense patchwork quilt oriented to the cardinal points of the compass. Several north-south *meridians* served as reference lines for east-west measurement, beginning with the *prime meridian* a few kilometres west of the Red River and continuing to the 7th meridian near Vancouver. East-west *base lines* began at the American frontier, repeating at regular intervals to the north. The spaces between these principal lines were divided into *ranges* and *townships*, the latter square in shape, measuring 6 miles (~ 9.65 km) on a side. Finally, each township was divided into 36 *sections* of a mile square, and each section into four *quarter-sections*, each with an area of 160 acres (64.8 ha), the amount of land generally considered sufficient for a viable family farm. In every township, sections were reserved for schools, churches, and the Canadian Pacific Railroad. Finally, the Hudson's Bay Company retained ownership of good farmlands and strategically located sites throughout all regions.

Template for a Social Ideal

This system of land division was more than a strategy to promote rapid colonization. It also provided the genetic code for a particular model of human society. As with our southern neighbours, the regular pattern of land division in Canada

6.11 Typical township layout in western Canada, late nineteenth century

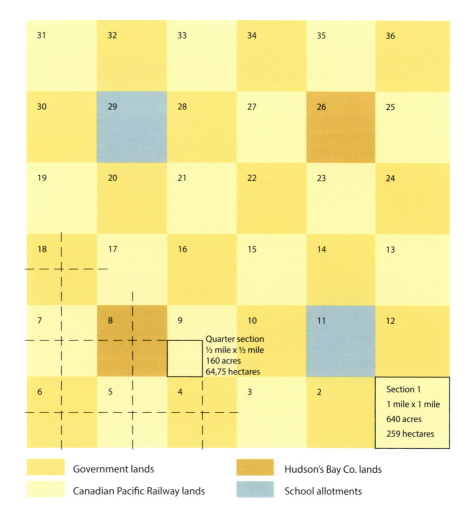

created a physical structure appropriate to a society of free farmers, living on their own farms and not in villages, each family separated from their counterparts, independent of seigneurs or other outside proprietors. In the United States, the establishment of such a system in the eighteenth century expressed an agrarian philosophy extolled by several of the founding fathers, particularly Thomas Jefferson.[46] The idealization of agriculture – and a belief in the nobility of the men and women who practise it – has a long history in the United States; and although Canada's fathers of Confederation did not formally announce their attachment to such principles, a strong agrarian myth soon took root on the Canadian Prairies. On this subject one might cite Clifford Sifton, who, as minister of Immigration in Laurier's government during the years 1896–1905, promoted the Canadian Prairies in Europe as a destination for potential immigrants, presenting agriculture as a desirable way of life and a means of achieving financial independence. We can hear Jefferson in the words of Sifton: "[A]griculture ... is the most valuable resource we have, because it raises a virile population which is the backbone of a nation."[47]

PROMISED LANDS IN THE WEST 119

The colonization plan was far from ideal; as the American observer John Brinkerhoff Jackson has stated, the grid consecrated the "triumph of geometry over topography."[48] By neglecting the natural elements of the landscape, including water, a key ingredient for agriculture in every environment (and particularly in the drought-prone lands of the southern Prairies), the universal grid created immense variations in the agricultural potential of farms. The system of land division was equally indifferent to local variations in climate and soil, and the isolation it imposed on farm families added to the challenges that the pioneers had to face.[49] Yet despite its limitations, the land division system achieved its goal of opening the West to rapid colonization and at least partially inspired the egalitarian spirit that has long characterized the culture of Prairie Canada.[50]

Landscapes of the Prairies: A Multicultural Mosaic

The new system of land division furnished a unifying backdrop for the colonization of the West, but colonists brought with them their own customs, agricultural practices, and rural and urban cultural traditions. Groups of newcomers often succeeded in modifying the rigidity of the grid to adapt it to their own traditions. And since their origins were extremely diverse, the configurations and spatial signatures of the West's cultural landscapes also demonstrate a great diversity.[51]

6.12 *Strattendorf* ("street village"), Neubergthal, MB

6.13   Shelterbelt, Neubergthal, MB

Refugees from across the Seas

Many of the immigrants were fleeing religious or political persecution in their home countries. This was true of the Mennonites, people of German descent who had left their farms and villages in Russia after 1874 to settle in two sectors of southern Manitoba, one located east and the other west of the Red River, that had been assigned to them. The landscapes of this region reminded them of the Russian steppes that they had left behind. In the East and West reserves, as their land grants were called, they built agricultural villages that followed a distinct spatial pattern, the *strattendorf*, or "street village." These settlements were composed of parallel lots, long and narrow, each harbouring a family residence oriented parallel or perpendicular to the main street. Behind each house and attached to it were the summer kitchen and barn; in front, the orchard. The vegetable garden and fields of each family extended out behind the "house-barn" complex. A church, cemetery, and school were customarily located at the crossroads in the centre of the village.[52] At Neubergthal in the West Reserve, the main road is bordered by two rows of immense cottonwood poplars. Lines of trees of the same species are deployed at regular intervals between fields, forming one of the classic components of the western landscape, the *shelterbelt*. These green barriers prevent the wind from eroding soil and protect farm buildings from the prevailing north and west winds.

Canada is the home of the largest Ukrainian community outside the original homeland and its Russian neighbour – over a million people.[53] Ukrainian

PROMISED LANDS IN THE WEST   121

6.14 St. Michael's Ukrainian Orthodox Church and cemetery, Tolstoi, MB

immigrants arrived at the beginning of the 1890s, settling lands in various parts of the Prairies, including a large territory in southeastern Manitoba, adjoining the Mennonites' East Reserve. Having similar glacial-till soil regimes, these Manitoba lands resemble those in the Austro-Hungarian Empire that the newcomers had come from.[54] The country boasts a rich heritage of Ukrainian institutions, of which a striking example is Saint Michael's Church and cemetery close to the village of Tolstoi. This fascinating complex of buildings comprises the church itself, its sanctuary oriented to the East like all Orthodox churches, an open pavilion to accommodate summer religious services, a kitchen building, and two free-standing elements, the cross and the church tower. In the cemetery, three-branched crosses ending in cloverleaf trefoils – signature of the Trinity – and a diagonal fourth arm, typical of the Orthodox religion, are much in evidence. Sometimes these colonists built their houses and barns at the corners of their quarter-sections, close to their neighbours, so as to create "mini-villages" that were closer to their traditions than were the isolated farms envisioned by the land division system.[55]

Many other immigrant groups sought to establish themselves in landscapes that resembled those of their homelands, as much for reasons of practical experience as for reasons of nostalgia. Natives of Iceland, for example, settled in 1875 in the autonomous territory of New Iceland, centred on the town of Gimli, west of Lake Winnipeg. In her short story "La vallée Houdou," the writer Gabrielle Roy tells the

122 LANDSCAPE HERITAGE OF THE FIRST NATIONS AND COLONISTS

story of Doukhobor immigrants, refugees from Russia, who sought a new land in the West where they could freely practise their religion of peace and non-violence. Day after day, they continued their quest – although "the plain had set about rebuffing them with its flat immensity" – ceaselessly looking for a country that resembled the Humid Mountains of their native Caucasus. Finally, against the advice of their guides, they chose the "exotic splendour" of the Hoodoo Valley, bewitched by the "fugitive beauty" of its water-eroded forms, shining brilliantly in the last rays of the sun.[56]

Migrants from within North America

Many migrants came not from overseas, but from within the North American continent, and they, too, left unique traces on the western landscape. Between 1887 and 1910, numerous Mormon communities, members of the Church of Jesus Christ of Latter-Day Saints, migrated from Utah in the American West into the southwestern sector of Alberta, in the heart of the Palliser Triangle. They founded seventeen agricultural villages in this region, following an original town-planning model known as the *Plat of Zion*. Towns built on this model recall the "City of Zion" proposed in 1833 by Joseph Smith, founder of the Mormon Church.[57] This was an arrangement of three concentric zones, each in the form of a square: the *social zone*, harbouring the institutions of government, religion, and education; the *residential zone*, composed of lots one hectare in area, large enough to permit subsistence agriculture and the raising of a few farm animals beside the house and barn; and, finally, the *agricultural zone*, for the growing of grains and other field crops. The village of Stirling in Alberta, now recognized as a National Historic Site, is a living example of this tradition. There, one can observe several particularities

6.15   Mormon temple in hilltop park setting, Cardston, AB

PROMISED LANDS IN THE WEST   123

of the Plat of Zion: streets 30.5 metres wide – "broad enough to turn right around with a team of oxen at full speed" according to the specifications of the prophet Brigham Young – and irrigation canals parallel to the streets.[58] The spiritual centre for the Mormons of this region is the magnificent Cardston Alberta Temple, designed by architects Hyrum Pope and Harold Burton. This building, consecrated in 1923 and reminiscent of architect Frank Lloyd Wright's 1908 Unity Temple at Oak Park, Illinois, is surrounded by a park and located at the highest point of the town.[59]

There was also considerable migration from the eastern provinces of Canada to the West. Between 1891 and 1914, approximately 35,400 inhabitants of the Maritime provinces and 36,700 Quebec residents moved to the West.[60] Together with francophone immigrants from New England and France, newcomers from Quebec settled in places where the French language and culture had already taken root: the valleys of the Red River in Manitoba and of the Qu'Appelle in Saskatchewan, the "historic corridor" north and east of Edmonton in Alberta, and a sector in the south of that province, around Pincher Creek.[61]

The majority of Canadian settlers, however, came from Ontario, some 232,600 during the period 1891–1914.[62] These migrants, along with many immigrants from the British Isles, established what would long remain the dominant culture of the Prairies and of British Columbia, eclipsing the freewheeling and picturesque traditional culture of the voyageurs, trading posts, and Métis. A remarkable example of a farm establishment of the period, typical of the new anglophone and largely Protestant culture, has been preserved at Abernethy, Saskatchewan, to the northeast of Regina. This is the Motherwell Homestead, "Lanark Place," founded in 1882 by William R. Motherwell (1860–1943), a young graduate of the Ontario Agricultural College at Guelph. Beyond his role as a pioneer, Motherwell was also very involved in politics, serving as commissioner of agriculture in the first government of Saskatchewan (1905–18) and then as Canada's minister of agriculture (1921–30), positions through which he made important contributions to the development of scientific agriculture. On achieving a certain level of prosperity, Motherwell began to invest in the transformation of his property into a "model farm" (see chapter 7).[63]

Eldorado on the Prairies

These successive immigrant waves from many countries, along with those from eastern Canada, established the physical and cultural mosaic of the Canadian Prairies. Almost all settlers faced a hard apprenticeship in this demanding milieu. But they were drawn by the golden Eldorado that the Prairies appeared to be. The West seemed like a promised land, a green country of hope that was waiting to be developed, where their sacrifice and efforts would surely be rewarded with prosperity. This faith in the future, this promise of prosperity, became an essential element in the agrarian myth of the West. And for several decades during which climate and international demand were relatively favourable, the golden sheaves of wheat on the provincial flag of Saskatchewan symbolized this promise fulfilled.[64]

Home on the Range

The southwestern part of the Prairies witnessed the birth of another kind of cultural landscape and a different way of life. The rolling hills of this corner of Alberta, too dry to grow wheat, could not sustain more than short-grass prairie – red fescue, western wheat grass, and a multitude of other grasses and herbs. These plants had nourished the immense herds of buffalo; they could also nourish other livestock, bulls and cows, leading to the establishment of the cattle-raising industry and to a culture of ranches and cowboys in the foothills of the Rockies. Similar conditions of topography and climate promoted similar developments on the interior plateaux of British Columbia and in the valleys of the Fraser, the Thompson, and the Okanagan. This was agriculture at an entirely different scale – at 7.3 hectares for a "bovine unit" of cow and calf, a ranch that accommodated 8,000 animals needed an area of at least 29,000 hectares – a long way from the standard quarter-section of 160 acres (64 ha).[65] In 1894, Mormons who were already experienced in the livestock industry in Texas and Utah founded a typical establishment of this genre, the McIntyre Ranch near Magrath in Alberta. Through the purchase of several adjacent farms, founder William H. McIntyre created a ranch of 64,000 acres (25,900 ha). Locating his *home ranch* on a relatively flat site well protected by the

6.16   Present-day McIntyre Ranch, Magrath, AB

Milk River Ridge, McIntyre erected a cluster of buildings for his family and hired hands, a corral, and a horse barn, all constructed of logs cut some 96 kilometres to the west, for there were not many trees in this dry land.[66] In these semi-arid conditions, he succeeded in raising Herefords and Aberdeen Angus, breeds developed in Britain and much less capable of withstanding western climatic conditions than the native buffalo. Other breeds of cattle are hardier, but one way or another, the long hard winters of the ranching country have always made the life of the cowboy and his charges a gamble, its results unpredictable from one year to the next.

Industrial Production on Land and Sea

On the coasts and in the mountains of British Columbia, another kind of Eldorado had already made its appearance during the final decades of the fur trade. In contrast to the planned conquest of the Prairies, with its clear goal of creating a stable and coherent landscape and society, the coastal province seems to have favoured the rapid discovery and exploitation of pre-existing resources. There were few, if any, treaties with the First Nations, and the new territories had not been planned before the arrival of the pioneers, except for a band of terrain along the railroad.

The mineral riches of the West contributed to what New Zealand historian Jim McAloon has called the "Pacific Rim Gold Rush."[67] Some 200 million years ago, collisions between oceanic and continental plates created a series of mountain ranges all around the Pacific Basin and projected minerals rich in gold, silver, lead, zinc, copper, and several other metals towards the surface. Throughout the latter half of the nineteenth century, a second series of collisions, between Europeans and the lands that fell within their influence, brought these minerals to the market, setting off a gold rush in all the lands that opened onto the Pacific Ocean – California in 1848, New Zealand and Australia in the 1850s and 1860s, and finally the Klondike, in Canada's Yukon Territory, in 1898. In British Columbia, this headlong race began in 1858 in the Fraser Valley, moved north and east to the Cariboo region, and then expanded broadly into the mountains. First harvested by painstaking manual procedures, gold was soon torn from its mountain fortresses by a broad range of industrial techniques. When precious metals ran out, prospectors targeted the new treasures essential to industry itself – lead, zinc, copper, and coal.[68]

Other industries of coast and mountain followed the same rhythm: discovery, extraction, and exhaustion. The first contacts with Native peoples led immediately to the exchange of furs and, between 1785 and 1825, to the rapid exploitation and exhaustion of sea otter stocks. Whales faced a similar fate between the 1840s and 1890s, under the intense pressure of industrialized hunting.[69] The lumber industry had begun on a small scale during the fur trade era; a hundred years later, in the early twentieth century, almost the entire site of the present city of Vancouver had been deforested and there were thirty sawmills on the Pacific coast.[70] Pacific salmon were next to experience a devastating confrontation with the industrial revolution.[71] The first salmon cannery on the West Coast was established in 1864; thirty years later, there was at least one such establishment on every river from Alaska to California.[72]

6.17 Haida Gwaii, BC, formerly the Queen Charlotte Islands. View of islands and mountains in Juan Perez Sound.

The extraction industries left permanent traces on the landscape and – one might say – on the soul of British Columbia. Recognizing the ecological and spiritual values of their unique environment, yet always depending on its riches to assure their livelihood, the province's residents have often been torn between the exploitation and the conservation of their natural milieu. Today, two versions of Eldorado collide: the economic gold rush and the quest for a natural paradise.

Cities and Towns of the West

Almost all the cities of western Canada were built beside its great rivers – the inescapable routes of the fur trade – or on natural saltwater harbours. Their founding reflects the influence of great economic actors. Former trading-post sites of the Hudson's Bay Company and its rivals grew to become Winnipeg, Edmonton, and Victoria; railroad companies created Regina, Saskatchewan, and Medicine Hat, Alberta, as depots or branching points. Government agencies founded several cities, either directly as in the case of New Westminster, the first city on the mainland of British Columbia, established in 1859 as the capital of the new territory,[73] or indirectly, like Calgary, its location chosen by Inspector Ephrem-A. Brisebois as a

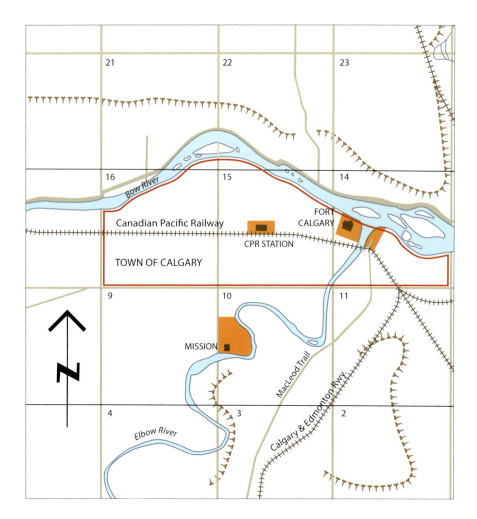

6.18 Original city limits and founding institutions, Calgary, 1875–90, located in Township No. 24, Range 1, west of the 5th Meridian. Natural landscape features of waterways and topography combined with the implacable survey grid as major influences on the urban landscape that Calgary would become.

base for the Royal Northwest Mounted Police (now the RCMP) in 1875. Calgary's strategic location at the confluence of the Bow and Elbow rivers had already attracted a Catholic mission and would soon help the town become a key link in the railroad. A constellation of institutions and organizations assured Calgary's growth into a major centre. Colonization societies, often motivated by a religious or utopian mission, also created several cities; examples include Saskatoon, founded in 1883 by the Temperance Societies of Ontario; several towns established by Father Lacombe near Edmonton; and still others built by the Mormons in southwestern Alberta and the Doukhobors in the mountains of British Columbia.

The Planning of Cities and Towns

City plans betray their origins. For example, the pattern of long, narrow river lots, perpendicular to the Red and Assiniboine rivers, can still be easily seen in the streets and blocks of the older quarters of Winnipeg. Edmonton is much the same;

its downtown streets follow the lines set by the original river lots. In the centre of these historic lots, the site of the provincial legislative assembly, high on a plateau near the original emplacement of Fort Edmonton, recalls the heritage of the Hudson's Bay Company. The cities of the West were often built on high ground, astride the great valleys and coulees that run through them, to minimize the impact of the periodic floods that pass through them and to preserve their riparian zones, which have now become magnificent linear parks at the heart of their metropolitan areas.

Where there were no traditional river lots, western cities were laid out according to a regular geometric grid like that of the Dominion Land Survey, punctuated by occasional public squares or, often, by one great central square, as at Regina. These arrangements recall the military and loyalist towns of the Maritime provinces and Ontario. Some cities were more ambitious, their plans including diagonal avenues, circles, and other green spaces of varying geometry. New Westminster is a remarkable example of this approach. The chief of the Royal Engineers, Colonel Richard Moody, located his town on the north side of the Fraser River, on an easily defended site similar to those of the eighteenth-century new towns of eastern Canada.[74] The town of Raymond in Alberta, founded in 1901 by Mormons from Utah, follows an equally complex and original plan.[75] In both cases, with the passage of time, practical considerations have gradually eliminated almost all of the geometrical particularities of these towns.

Since valuable minerals were to be found primarily in mountainous regions or in remote valleys enclosed by near-vertical slopes, mining towns were built on the only practicable sites: the deltas of rivers and streams that formed peninsulas jutting out into mountain lakes. The towns of southeastern British Columbia on the shores of lakes Kootenay and Slocan are a case in point.[76] These include Kaslo, Slocan City, and several towns that bear names recalling the search for mineral

6.19   Sandon, an abandoned mining town in southeastern British Columbia

PROMISED LANDS IN THE WEST   129

6.20 Lund, a small, sheltered village at the northern limit of the Sunshine Coast Highway along the coast of mainland British Columbia

riches – Eldorado (later changed to New Denver, in honour of a famous mining town) and Silverton. All of these towns applied a standard grid plan to their irregular sites.[77] Certain resource settlements, built on rocky sites on the coast or in the mountains, showed a greater talent for improvisation than for planning. The town of Sandon, in the Selkirk Mountains, built on both sides of a torrential river beside the richest lode of lead, silver, and zinc in the world, evolved in typical fashion. Founded in the 1890s and housing a population of 8,000 inhabitants after only a few years, it soon fell into a rapid decline and is today nothing more than a ghost town. Proceeding up the coast to the north of Vancouver, the traveller discovers little fishing villages – Madeira Park, Pender Harbour, Lund – that seem more and more detached from urban civilization, having integrated themselves into the rugged landscapes at the end of the road, like their homologues of the East Coast (see chapter 3). But, where every building on the Atlantic coast stands foursquare and solitary in a wide-open landscape, in a sort of heroic isolation, those of the West Coast merge with the forest, hiding themselves among its gigantic trees. And as the years pass by, every day seems to make them look more and more like integral components of Nature herself.

II The Nineteenth Century: Challenges of an Urban and Industrial Landscape

7

The Making of Canada's Rural Landscape

7.1 William Kurelek, *Prairie Farm*, 1976. This painting was featured on the cover of W.O. Mitchell's 1947 book *Who Has Seen the Wind*. It depicts a brief vignette from that classic story of a small agricultural town in western Canada.

In his famous 1893 speech "The Significance of the Frontier in American History," the American historian Frederick Jackson Turner described the process by which the American frontier had moved gradually westward from the beginning of the seventeenth to the end of the nineteenth century.[1] By "frontier," he meant the line of demarcation between the territory occupied by the farms and villages of new settlers and the landscape inhabited by Native Americans and a handful of explorers and adventurers involved in the fur trade. From this gradual evolution Turner drew several conclusions – some controversial – on the nature of American civilization. His description applied equally well to Canada, where each region, in its turn, had witnessed the arrival and the passing of the dynamic boundary of the frontier.[2] In each region, a similar process of action and reaction marked the passage of the frontier. A first stage might be called "the conquest of the landscape," during which new arrivals exploited the landscape for economic benefit as quickly as possible, with no regard for the aesthetic effects or the environmental consequences of their actions. Subsequently, another generation became aware of the damage done and hastened to repair it, aspiring to create a landscape of long-term productivity and beauty instead of one of ugliness. In short, to "civilize the frontier."

The Transformation of the Rural Landscape: Ontario

The evolution of the rural landscape of southern Ontario during the nineteenth century provides a fascinating view of this process of transformation. This landscape passed through three distinct stages, each of which expressed a specific relationship between people and the land and was marked by specific agricultural practices.[3]

The Pioneer Landscape

The first of these landscapes began to take form in the 1780s and lasted until the 1830s. As described in chapter 5, new immigrants set up their farms on land that seemed fertile (using the character of the forest cover as an index of soil quality) and was easily accessible via an existing road. They cut down the trees, cleared the undergrowth, and erected rudimentary shelters, literally log cabins. Among the stumps and rocks that remained in the fields, these farmers sowed or transplanted plants for their own consumption and raised a few animals. They were practising *subsistence agriculture*, a difficult proposition even at the best of times, in small clearings in the forest. Clearings were linked to each other by primitive roads, often impassable, that were like tunnels cut through the dark woods.[4] It was easier to get around in winter, when everything was frozen; in summertime, the roads resembled rivers of mud.

This first stage of development furnished plenty of disappointments, but it also had its charms, as attested to by the writings of "sisters in the wilderness" Susanna Moodie and Catharine Parr Traill, who had come out from England in response to the invitation of their brother Samuel Strickland, author of *Twenty-seven Years in Canada West*, to join him in the New World (see chapter 5). As soon as they arrived with their families near Peterborough, Ontario, in 1832, both women began to put on paper their ambivalent experiences on the frontier, writing fascinating books on their lives in Canada.[5]

Endless Fields of Wheat

This pioneer phase was followed by a "second landscape" – a new agricultural pattern based on the production of staples for market. All of southern Ontario was rapidly deforested as the settlers opened up land for farming and produced wood for fuel and construction,[6] leaving only marshes and steep cliffs uncut. In this denuded landscape, on large open fields of 16 hectares (40 acres) or more, farmers

7.2 A first-generation farm in the Eastern Townships of Quebec, 1881

grew great quantities of wheat,[7] which they sent to the markets of Europe via the newly established railroad lines of the times. The resulting prosperity allowed them to replace their rough cabins of the pioneer era with more elaborate wooden ("frame") houses and barns.

This "no holds barred" approach to agriculture had unforeseen and negative consequences. The elimination of vegetation along streams promoted the rapid erosion of forest soils[8] and led to the disappearance of fish species that required clear, cold water, like the salmon that once flourished in the rivers of southern Ontario. Without the protection of the forests, soils were also vulnerable to wind erosion. Once the forest soils had been depleted, nothing was available to ensure the gradual absorption of water from the melting of winter snows; the resulting increase in the spring runoff caused both further soil erosion and downstream flooding. These early-season phenomena were soon followed by drier, hotter summers and lower water levels.[9] The widespread construction of dams to facilitate navigation also brought dramatic changes in the water levels of lakes and rivers, causing the elimination of native plants in some environments,[10] including the wild rice that had been harvested for centuries by First Nations at Rice Lake. In winter, deforestation allowed the wind to blow away fallen snow that would otherwise have protected farmers' fields, and left houses and barns at the mercy of its glacial gusts. Finally, the monoculture of wheat or other grain crops, repeated year after year without benefit of crop rotation, contributed to the progressive diminution of soil fertility.[11]

Towards Specialized Agriculture and the Remaking of the Rural Landscape

Between 1860 and 1880, a "third landscape" would take form in Ontario, a landscape tempered by the planting of trees and shrubs and by the division of farms into smaller and more sheltered fields. Moving away from monoculture towards the cultivation of a great variety of specialized crops, well adapted to local soils and climates, farmers were able to sell their produce at a premium while contributing to the regeneration of the landscape.[12] Market gardening, the growing of various grains, oils, and vegetables, as well as tobacco and potatoes – all figured among the new practices of Ontario farmers. Better informed than their predecessors, they often rotated their crops so as to renew the soil. In propitious locations, the large-scale planting of fruit-bearing trees and shrubs was also begun, accompanied by the expansion of livestock rearing for meat production and the establishment of dairies and creameries for milk products and cheese.[13] To each of these types of agriculture there corresponded a characteristic "visual landscape," comprising particular forms, motifs, and rhythms. To accommodate their new crops, farmers divided the extensive 16-hectare wheat fields of the second landscape into much smaller fields of 3 or 4 hectares. They surrounded these with dense wind-break plantings, composed of native trees and shrubs: maples, lindens, hawthorns, and many species of wild cherry and apple, occasionally set off by an acacia.[14]

Farmers also planted parallel rows of trees along rural routes and farm entrance roads. They created rectangles of verdure around their *farmsteads* – clusters of houses, barns, and ancillary buildings – to protect them from sun and wind.[15] One tree surpassed all others – the sugar maple. Its hardiness, its universal availability, its capacity to adapt itself to varied soils, its handsome form and rich red-orange fall colour – all contributed to make it the favourite tree of rural areas. It is not surprising that the sugar maple became the common symbol of Canada. But it was not without rivals. The silver maple played an important role as a substitute in moist environments, where it often created natural hybrids with the sugar maple. In some areas, according to local soil and climatic conditions, the American elm, black walnut, or chestnut was preferred.[16]

In this third landscape, everything was ordered and regular, in tune with the regularity of the surveys and the land-division regime that had been gradually implanted since the first days of colonization. Even the streams had been realigned to conform to the regular geometry of the *township*. On the positive side, this realignment was often accompanied by the replanting of stream banks so as to prevent erosion.[17]

The patchwork quilt of family farms that characterized this third-generation landscape, with its small square and rectangular fields and orderly and regular clusters of houses, barns, and round silos, became the normal and familiar motif of rural Ontario for a whole era, until about 1950, and some sectors of the province have remained largely intact up until the present day. The devastated and unsustainable landscape of the second evolutionary stage had been succeeded by a landscape that was infinitely more beautiful, intelligent, and durable. In the perception of those who grew up in the towns and villages of southern Ontario towards the end of this period – including the author – this third rural landscape seemed profoundly stable and coherent. For such people, it appeared to have always existed and would without doubt continue to exist for centuries to come.

Agricultural Landscapes in the West

Similar cycles repeated themselves elsewhere in Canada. The coming of agriculture involved great changes to the original landscape; then first-generation subsistence farming gave way to large-scale grain growing and often to specialized crops, and natural forms and features were increasingly replaced with new human-generated geometries. As in Ontario, this transformation often involved a period of damaging exploitation, followed by mitigation and correction.

On the Prairies and in the *parklands* of the West, the subsistence farming of the fur trade era represented the first stage of agriculture. The needs of the trading companies were provided for by vegetable gardens within the forts and by local farms and livestock grazing in rich bottomlands near the trading posts or on adjacent plateaus. These farms and gardens were established by the companies themselves or by retired employees and their Métis descendants.[18] As settlers flooded into the West towards the end of the nineteenth century, a second stage of subsistence agriculture, of short duration, succeeded the first. The colonists, or homesteaders, came out by train as far as possible and then travelled by ox cart or horse-drawn wagon to their quarter-sections. There, each family built its own primitive log hut, surmounted by a sod roof,[19] dug a well by hand, and planted a small vegetable garden to sustain life.

The first years on these isolated sites were hard, even heroic. Settlers ploughed and seeded larger fields as required by government regulations, built new frame houses and fences, and eventually raised barns for livestock. Neighbours often helped each other out.[20] The move from subsistence farming to commercial agriculture proceeded rapidly. A key event in this transition was the arrival of a train line in the vicinity, allowing the colonists to participate in the market economy and to put more fields into cultivation, thus augmenting their production.[21] To encourage this process, railroad companies provided expertise and technical help; the ubiquitous Canadian Pacific Railway (CPR) established some twenty-six demonstration farms across the West, at such locations as Strathmore (farm opened in 1905) near Calgary, Alberta. These farms provided a model for new settlers, many of whom had not previously been involved in agriculture or who came from very different climate zones.[22]

7.3 Canadian Pacific Railway demonstration farm, c. 1910, Strathmore, AB

The coming of large-scale agriculture completed the geometrical transformation of the prairie landscape, in concert with the national survey system. As mentioned in the previous chapter, this transformation largely ignored the topography and water regime of the region. The complex web of herbs and grasses that composed the native vegetation could not withstand the elimination of the prairie fires that had influenced the vegetation pattern since time immemorial. Local monocultures replaced those rich plant compositions. The original vegetation of the Prairies had comprised perennial grasses well adapted to drought, tuberous plants and bulbs such as the prairie crocus, and many members of the broad family of the *Compositae*, including black-eyed Susan and purple coneflower, staples of our perennial gardens of today.[23] The "mixed-grass prairie," stretching from southwestern Manitoba to southeast Alberta, included some 150 plant species of great diversity, well adapted to an equivalent diversity of microclimates and local soil conditions. Of the 24 million hectares occupied by mixed-grass prairie before the colonization of the West, only 25 per cent remained in 2002.[24] The great majority of the original vegetation was replaced by a handful of annual grasses and legumes of European or Asiatic origin: wheat, oats, rye, barley, and alfalfa. Wheat was king; in 1877–81, it was sown on some 12.4 million hectares.[25] Thanks to the insatiable demand of Europeans, who depended on it for their daily bread, this grain swiftly became the staple product of the Prairies – and its symbol. It is no accident that a wheat field

138 CHALLENGES OF AN URBAN AND INDUSTRIAL LANDSCAPE

graces the flag of Alberta and that three golden sheaves appear on that of Saskatchewan, as well as on the coat of arms of the latter's provincial university.

Prairie Sentinels

The growing of grain gave birth to a powerful visual symbol of the Canadian Prairies, the *grain elevator*. Beginning in the 1880s, companies and cooperatives erected these structures in every community of the West as a means of storing grain for transport by train.[26] All along the railroad lines, whether major trunk routes or local spur lines, *country elevators* were massively built of solid wood, following only two standard designs in order to rationalize operations.[27] Their vertical format (20 to 25 m high) took advantage of the natural tendency of grains to flow like a liquid under the force of gravity. Various grains were lifted by a small motor to separate bins at the top of the structure, from which they were later emptied out into the appropriate railroad cars. A second type of silo, the *terminal elevator* – much larger and constructed of concrete, but equally destined to play an iconic role in the landscape – grew up in port cities like Vancouver, Fort William–Thunder Bay, and Montreal, transhipment destinations for the trains charged with grain from the interior.[28]

7.4 Country grain elevators, Medicine Hat, AB

Country elevators became the most visible elements on the prairie, standing either in isolation or in twos and threes in small towns and villages, seen for miles across the flat, open prairie, or in majestic phalanxes at the entrances to major cities like Calgary. A superb means of orientation, each elevator bore the name of the town where it stood in giant letters written on the side, along with the name of the company or cooperative (an important system of economic organization on the Prairies) that operated it: Pioneer, Paterson, ATL (Alberta Terminals Limited), Saskatchewan Pool, Agricore, UGG (United Grain Growers). Their bright colours – brick red, white, shiny metal – and their simple sculptural forms gave them a powerful aesthetic impact. They also served as markers of the human presence in a landscape that was mostly empty, and they represented economic vitality in the most direct manner. For all these reasons, grain elevators became the principal landmarks and signature elements of the Canadian Prairies, memorialized in innumerable drawings and photos, as well as on stamps and banknotes. They are prairie icons, the equivalent of such important and typical symbols as the lighthouses on maritime coasts and the silver spires of Quebec's village churches.

Although it has evolved over time, the second landscape still characterizes the greater portion of the Canadian Prairies. The difficult climate discouraged the development of a third landscape of specialized crops, as happened elsewhere in the country. There was nonetheless some specialization in response to market demand or technical innovation. The 1918 introduction of hard durum wheat for the production of semolina and pasta is an example.[29]

The gradual mechanization of agriculture played an important role, progressively increasing the scale of fields and farms. The landscape of the West also bears witness to the adoption of "scientific agriculture" and the development of a more sophisticated regional culture in such sites as the Motherwell Homestead at Abernethy in Saskatchewan (see chapter 6).[30] The *homestead*, or the central part of Motherwell's 8.7-hectare farm, was entirely enclosed by shelterbelts. Other green windbreaks, consisting of Russian and cottonwood poplars, chokecherry, caragana, white spruce, and American elm,[31] divided this central zone into quadrants, one of which contained the kitchen garden, situated in a slight hollow to capture as much water as possible. In a second quadrant, Motherwell had a large reservoir pit, or *dugout*, excavated; this depression filled with snow in winter, and the resulting meltwater was used to furnish water for both livestock and garden in summer. The third quadrant was devoted to farm animals and included an imposing two-storey barn, built in the Ontario style, and a granary. Residences for the family and the hired hands were located in the fourth and final quadrant, along with ornamental gardens (part of the Victorian heritage) and even a tennis court, creating an attractive ensemble that would later be complemented by an orchard. The family home, constructed of fieldstone and elegantly detailed in wood and metal, recalls the houses one finds in Lanark County, Ontario, where Motherwell started out. Like colonists from other heritages, this farmer from Ontario attempted to recreate on the Prairies the ambiance of his place of origin.[32] But outside his front door, just beyond the garden gate, the prairie held sway, endless and horizontal, punctuated here and there by silent shelterbelts.

7.5 Barn and house, Motherwell Homestead, Abernethy, SK

Transformation of the Water Regime

Bringing Water to Parched Lands

Irrigation provided the most effective means of support for specialized agriculture. In the West, as everywhere, water was a key resource. Natural rainfall usually sufficed for *dryland farming* on the mixed-grass prairie and its northern neighbour, the transitional forest zone. But the situation was entirely different in the short-grass prairie zone, particularly within the semi-arid Palliser Triangle, in the golden hills of the southwestern Prairies. Without much improvement, this territory supported extensive uses, such as the raising of livestock (see chapter 6), but its sparse and irregular rainfall did not permit the growing of non-indigenous

7.6 View through main gate to fields, Motherwell Homestead, Abernethy, SK

grains or other commercial plants. However, abundant water did flow through this region, in the great rivers that found their sources in the verdant and snowy Rockies and made their way to Hudson Bay and the Mississippi. Only a little time was to elapse between the first colonization of the region and the first proposal to capture these waters and harness them for agriculture.

William Pearce (1848–1930), a young Ontario surveyor who moved to the West in 1874, was among the first to see the potential offered by this resource. Shortly after his 1882 appointment to the Dominion Lands Board, the agency responsible for guiding government decisions on the improvement and administration of western lands, Pearce pressed the government to consider irrigation as a strategy to encourage the development of agriculture in southwestern Alberta.[33] He studied the irrigation techniques that the Mormon farmers of Utah, across the US border, had mastered. Fortified with this knowledge, he installed an irrigation system in the garden at his large property on the Bow River in Calgary. This garden soon became a local legend for its many high-quality plants.[34]

142 CHALLENGES OF AN URBAN AND INDUSTRIAL LANDSCAPE

Eventually, Pearce's energy and patience bore fruit. In 1894, the federal government asked him to collaborate on the drawing up of the new North-west Irrigation Act. This law, adopted in 1895, called into question traditional water rights by removing the "property and right of use" of surface waters from that minority of landowners lucky enough to have a watercourse on their property, and transferring it to the Crown – that is, the state – for general redistribution. This innovative strategy allowed all settlers to share the available water resources.

The first concrete project carried out according to the new law brought together Pearce, the Mormons, and private enterprise. They collaborated on a system of dams, reservoirs, and canals to bring water from the St. Mary River, in the south of Alberta, to lands that could employ it. In 1900, to the great joy of its residents, water arrived in Lethbridge, a city that is today filled with greenery but which was originally an open prairie without a single tree.[35] In agricultural areas, water from irrigation was used for forage crops (to nourish livestock), cereals, and sugar beets. The beet industry, which could not have functioned at all without the redistribution of water, attracted specialized workers, often of Japanese origin or descent – the first representatives of a community that would play an important role in this region.[36]

Elsewhere in southern Alberta and in the interior valleys of British Columbia, blocked from humid ocean winds by the high mountains of the West Coast, the implementation of other irrigation projects quickly followed. Since the gold rush years of the 1850s, the province of British Columbia had defined water as a public

7.7   William Pearce, c. 1880s

7.8   Vineyard, Okanagan Lake, BC

THE MAKING OF CANADA'S RURAL LANDSCAPE   143

resource rather than as private property.[37] Other laws established the corollary doctrines of *beneficial use* (which placed a limit on the amount of water furnished to users, based on their ability to put it to use) and the *interdiction of speculation* in water. In 1892, two irrigation projects were inaugurated in the Okanagan Lake region, at the Guisachan Ranch in Kelowna and the Coldstream Ranch near Vernon.[38] Later, between 1904 and 1914, several private companies, including the Kelowna Land and Orchard Company (or KLO, which still exists), radically transformed the lacustrine terraces that overlook the valley. Occupied until that time by ranches, these *benchlands* metamorphosed into "one huge orchard," thanks to the construction of dams, canals, channels, and siphons.[39] Some thirty-five varieties of apples, pears, cherries, crabapples, and plums flourished on these irrigated lands, a grand tribute to the legacy of Father Pandosy (chapter 6), who had introduced apples and grapes to the region in 1859–62.[40] His original grapevines represented the first steps towards the impressive wine-growing industry that is such a notable feature of the region today.

Drainage of Low-Lying Lands

While the semi-arid lands of the West lacked water, there seemed to be an over-abundance of this resource in some of the central and eastern parts of the country. These regions abounded in lowland soils rich in organic matter, swamps, fresh-water marshes, fens, peat bogs – wetlands of all kinds. The irrigation of the dry-lands of the West was mirrored by a dramatic campaign to drain wetlands across the country, with a similar goal of promoting specialized agriculture.

In the Manitoba Lowlands, once the bed of gigantic glacial Lake Agassiz, the incredible flatness of the land (sloping at 0.2 to 0.9 m per km) and the impervious clay subsoil of the Red River Plain combined to cause extensive ponding and swamping. Demands for artificial drainage through the excavation of ditches swiftly followed the establishment of farms, and response was quick.[41] As early as 1895, the province passed the Land Drainage Act, and by 1926, some 4,000 kilometres of drainage ditches had been dug, changing forever the water regime of a vast area and eliminating countless wetlands. Drainage problems in this agricultural land had always been exacerbated by the irregular and massive runoff from the highlands of the Manitoba Escarpment to the west, a chain of uplands running from the Pembina Hills north to Riding Mountain National Park. But as settlers cleared lands along the escarpment for agriculture and much-valued timber production, runoff was both dramatically increased and more concentrated. The flooding that inevitably followed led to further demand for drainage ditches; eventually, over a million hectares were artificially drained.[42]

Similar drainage systems had been put in place in Ontario since the mid-nineteenth century, through the excavation of networks of parallel ditches and the installation of *french drains*, drainage tiles laid in place on a gentle slope and connected up in hierarchical fashion. This process continued over a long period at constantly increasing scale. At the beginning of the twentieth century, the counties of southern Ontario had already lost at least 20 per cent, and in some areas up to

144　CHALLENGES OF AN URBAN AND INDUSTRIAL LANDSCAPE

80 per cent, of their original wetlands.[43] In 1918, the total area of drained lands in Ontario reached approximately 56,800 hectares.[44]

The largest project of this kind was the draining of the immense Holland Marsh, a wild area filled with uncountable ecological riches, located to the north of Toronto at the southern limit of Lake Simcoe. The marsh was a paradise for naturalists. John Muir, future founder of the Sierra Club (the world's first and still its most important conservation organization), spent some of his youthful years in its environs, from 1864 to 1866. He was fascinated by this milieu and dedicated much of his time there to botanizing. During his researches on plants and animals, he discovered a rare orchid specimen, *Calypso borealis*, the Northern calypso or Venus's slipper.[45] The work of draining the marsh – involving ditches, pipes, and pumping station – began in 1904 and was finished in 1930. Following its completion, the Holland Marsh became Ontario's premier area for market gardening, providing carrots, onions (50 per cent of the Canadian harvest of these two products), spinach, lettuce, and a variety of other vegetables to the dense urban areas of southern Ontario and to other parts of Canada. In contrast, neighbouring agricultural districts grew mainly corn and other grain crops or provided pasture for livestock and dairy industries, activities that generated less revenue. Thus this immense drainage project contributed inestimably to the prosperity and self-sufficiency of Ontario. But unfortunately for John Muir, *Calypso borealis* is no longer there.[46]

Catalysts for Change

Although it was largely accomplished by autonomous farmers and private companies, the transformation of the rural landscape of Canada would never have happened without the participation of powerful public and parapublic organizations who provided the knowledge, the research, and often the specific plants that led to a prosperous agricultural system, even in difficult milieus. Agricultural colleges and experimental farms were among the most important of these organizations.

Agricultural Colleges: Education, Research, and "Extension"

In Quebec, the teaching of agriculture had a long heritage. Monsignor Laval, bishop of Quebec, founded the first school in this discipline at Saint-Joachim, east of the old capital, in 1670. This school, like others founded in subsequent years, flourished for a relatively short time. Of all such institutions, only the École d'agriculture, established in 1859 by Abbot François Pilote at the Collège de la Pocatière, on the south shore of the St. Lawrence, is still active. It is now affiliated with Laval University, as is the other advanced-level French-language school of agriculture in Quebec, founded at Oka in 1898 by Trappist fathers from the well-known monastery near Montreal.[47]

In Ontario, education in this field was inspired by an American model. In 1862, the US federal government passed legislation to authorize the creation of *land-grant colleges*, institutions that were to provide specialized education in agricultural and mechanical sciences to students of all social levels. To help these colleges

establish campuses and to assure their long-term financing, the central government ceded large areas of land to each state. In their egalitarian and secular values, these state colleges[48] contrasted with the long-established universities of the East Coast, which were often affiliated with religious communities and had already become relatively elitist.[49] Following the confederation of the Canadian provinces in 1867, the newly formed province of Ontario was faced with many of the same problems as the American states of the West and Midwest. In emulation of the American approach, it created the Ontario Agricultural College, with emphasis on both scientific learning and practical farm work (including a model farm). In 1874, the OAC opened its doors at Guelph, northwest of Toronto.[50] Both landscape gardener H.A. Engelhardt (see chapter 9) and landscape architect Charles Miller of Philadelphia prepared layout and landscape plans for the campus.[51]

The Maritime provinces were quick to follow. In 1885, Nova Scotia established, at Truro, a school of agriculture that was soon to be united with the provincial farm and a school of horticulture to create the Nova Scotia Agricultural College.[52] Rapid agricultural and population expansion in western Canada in the late nineteenth

7.9 Main building and central oval of Macdonald College of McGill University, 1925, Sainte-Anne-de-Bellevue, QC. The building has an axial view south towards the St. Lawrence River; experimental fields are located to the north. East and west sides of the oval include two other original building clusters. Only final-year students were allowed to set foot on the central lawn within the oval. The original campus now houses John Abbott College; Macdonald has moved to an adjoining site.

146 CHALLENGES OF AN URBAN AND INDUSTRIAL LANDSCAPE

and early twentieth centuries soon created a demand for agricultural education in that region. To satisfy this need, the Manitoba Agricultural College was established in 1906 on a large campus located west of downtown Winnipeg. It would later move to a new facility south of Winnipeg, on the Red River, where it eventually became a faculty of the University of Manitoba.[53] In 1907, Macdonald College opened its doors in Sainte-Anne-de-Bellevue at the western extremity of Montreal Island, to provide education in agriculture, household science, and teacher training for Quebec's anglophone population. Benefiting from the financial support of Montreal tobacco magnate Sir William Macdonald, this co-educational college was later integrated with Montreal's McGill University.[54]

These schools and others that followed placed emphasis on technical and scientific knowledge. Their research mission was principally focused on the improvement of local agricultural productivity through applied research across a broad spectrum of fields, including weed control, the replenishment of depleted soils, and drainage techniques. OAC nurseries contributed to the reforestation of southern Ontario's often denuded farmlands, and genetics research, carried out in collaboration with the Ontario Veterinary College (also at Guelph), helped with livestock breeding.[55] The third component of the college triad, "extension," focused on the dissemination of up-to-date information on plants, farming methods, and equipment to practising farmers through publications, part-time classes, short courses, and direct fieldwork.[56] Such programs complemented visits to farms by government agricultural officers, or "agricultural representatives," most of whom were also graduates of the agricultural colleges or faculties.[57]

The Experimental Farms

Towards the end of the nineteenth century, it was obvious that the individual Canadian farmer had neither the knowledge nor the resources to develop the plants, the methods, and the equipment necessary for agriculture to progress in the various regions of the country. Of course, farmers had long organized agricultural societies to provide mutual help, share knowledge, and exercise political pressure; and agriculture colleges had begun to provide solid training in standard agricultural practices.[58] Private companies, such as Massey Manufacturing and Harris and Sons of Ontario, had taken the initiative in manufacturing a range of useful farm machinery. But in situations where tradition could not provide a clear guide to the future, new knowledge was sorely needed. The federal government was the only organization in the country with the resources to undertake the research work necessary to provide this knowledge. And fortunately, it also had the will and the vision to do so.

In 1884, the government created, under the chairmanship of Member of Parliament Georges-Auguste Gigault, a Select Committee on Agriculture. This committee recommended the establishment of a *network of experimental farms*, to be charged with the mission of testing different varieties of plants and fertilizers, studying various breeds of farm animals, exploring methods of controlling insects and other pests, and collecting and distributing information on all aspects of

7.10 Central Experimental Farm, Ottawa

agriculture. The network was established in 1886 under the guidance of John Carling, federal minister of agriculture.[59] The Central Experimental Farm in Ottawa, keystone of the system, was responsible for directing and coordinating the overall network, while supplying specific expertise to Ontario and Quebec. Four other regional experimental farms complemented the central establishment. The first director of the system, Dr William Saunders (1836–1914), who was born in England and arrived in Canada in 1848, chose the sites and organized the work.[60] Under Saunders and his successors, other generations of agricultural stations and laboratories were added to the original network. Little by little, one or more such facilities were implanted in all the agricultural regions of the country, responding to the specific challenges that each location presented.[61]

In their early years, the experimental farms explored various ways of maximizing production and diminishing loss of plants: crop rotation (including the use of nitrogen-fixing legumes), irrigation, letting land lie fallow after harvest, fertilization, weed control, water conservation, and variations in quantity of seed.[62] The selection of trees for use in shelterbelts was also a major preoccupation of the scientists: Saunders planted *Caragana*, or Russian pea shrub, on the Prairies, while the station at Indian Head in Saskatchewan evaluated a number of trees of diverse origins, including the native Manitoba maple. In order to supply the enormous demand for shelterbelt trees across the Prairies, the government established *forest nursery stations* at the Indian Head farm and at Sutherland, in Saskatchewan. Each of these two stations provided prodigious numbers of ash, Manitoba maple, and caragana to the farmers of the West. By 1963, more than 300 million trees had been supplied for windbreak planting throughout the Prairies.[63]

The greatest victory of the experimental farms was undoubtedly the development of the wheat varieties that opened the Prairies for settlement. The climate of eastern Canada permitted the use of *winter wheat*, seeded at the end of summer so as to germinate in fall and be ready for harvest in the middle of the following summer. But the more rigorous climate of the Prairies obliged the use of *spring wheat*, seeded in spring in order to be ready for harvest in the fall of the same year.[64] In 1888, William Saunders, with the help of his son Charles Saunders, began a series of cross-breeding experiments, using various wheat cultivars. Finally, it was Charles who selected the new variety *Marquis*, a spring wheat that matured early (to overcome the shortness of the growing season in the centre of the country),

7.11   Apple orchard in flower in the Annapolis Valley, near Wolfville, NS, c. 1956

THE MAKING OF CANADA'S RURAL LANDSCAPE   149

grew rapidly, was resistant to rust (a devastating disease), was highly productive, and offered excellent culinary qualities. After tests at Indian Head and elsewhere in the West around 1907, the Marquis variety was widely adopted; in 1920, it was sown on 90 per cent of the 6.9 million hectares of wheat grown on the Prairies.[65]

The experimental farms also had a decisive impact on the growing of fruit trees. William Saunders and his successors set up *agricultural research stations* in almost every area where orchards might prosper. There were many such locations, distributed across the southern part of the country: the Niagara Peninsula in Ontario, the Annapolis Valley in Nova Scotia, southern Quebec, and the Okanagan Valley in British Columbia. Even on the Prairies, where the climate makes fruit growing a difficult proposition, Manitoba's Morden station developed apple varieties well adapted for use in local farm gardens.[66] The experimental farms planted and tested hundreds of varieties of apples, cherries, peaches, and grapes from North American sources and abroad. They also crossed these varieties in search of improved qualities such as early or late maturity, hardiness, and disease resistance.[67] As a starting point for their experiments with apples, they relied principally on the McIntosh variety, the legendary apple found by accident in 1811 on the farm of John McIntosh, near Ottawa.[68] This versatile plant may be a descendant of the Fameuse (or Snow) apples, whose seeds were brought to Canada by early French settlers.

Mature Agricultural Landscapes

As a result of these transformations and innovations, almost all of the arable land areas of Canada – what we today consider the *Canadian ecumene* – had been ploughed and cultivated by the late nineteenth or early twentieth century. And generally, after overcoming some initial stumbling blocks, each sector of the country had developed a coherent set of farming methods, plant and animal selections, and spatial configurations. These arrangements, in combination with the remaining elements of the original environments, created a series of quite distinct rural landscapes, what one might call *mature agricultural landscapes*, productive, attractive, and reasonably stable. These landscapes were almost entirely occupied by family farms, supported by corporate and cooperative mechanisms and by the expertise of a sophisticated scientific establishment. They provided verdant and attractive backgrounds of everyday life for many generations of local residents, for whom they also became the objects of identification and even veneration. And they attracted numerous visitors. Crowds of tourists flocked to the Charlevoix region of Quebec from the 1830s on, to appreciate the seamless integration of man-made farms and villages into the natural panorama,[69] and the fruit lands of the Niagara peninsula long attracted throngs of train- or car-borne visitors from Hamilton and Toronto to see the white and pink apple, cherry, and peach blossoms each May.[70]

Finally, many rural landscapes, celebrated by several generations of renowned Canadian artists, have become widely recognized archetypes. From the mid-nineteenth century, in contrast to the earlier "topographical" artists who had expressed themselves in watercolour (chapter 5), a new generation of professional painters interpreted rural Canada primarily in oil on canvas, following the graphic

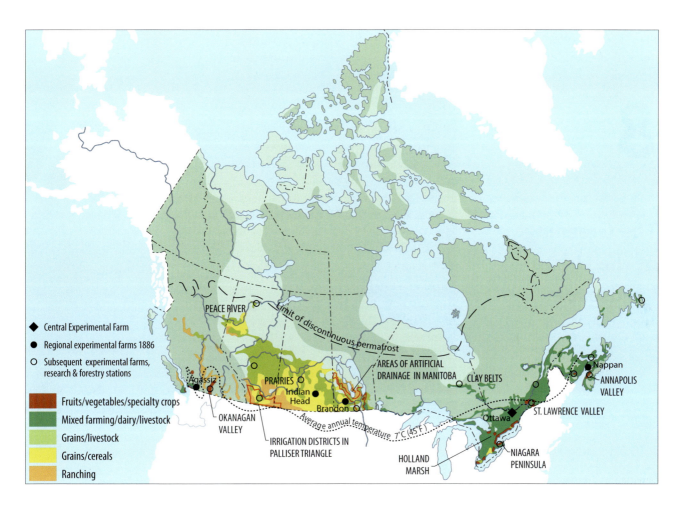

7.12 Distribution of agricultural lands in Canada. It is obvious that a very small percentage of the country's vast territory is suitable for agriculture, and much of that is quite limited in what can be grown. Plant and animal research, education, and land improvements, including irrigation and drainage, have created a productive agricultural system with several areas of highly specialized farming. Many of Canada's large urban areas are located within these areas, and competition between the two activities is intense.

languages of romantic naturalism as defined by such British masters as Turner and Constable and by various continental schools.[71] In rural Quebec, Joseph Légaré and Cornelius Krieghoff portrayed an archetypal land of fields and villages, long inhabited by peasant – *habitant* – families responding to a traditional and conservative image of New France.[72] As forests were cleared across the country to create second- and third-stage rural landscapes, images of bustling commercial towns set in wooded surroundings gave way to an Arcadian interpretation of agricultural life.[73] Through remarkable paintings executed over more than a century – Homer Watson's iconic images of the Grand River of rural Ontario, Horatio Walker's peaceful scenes on the Île d'Orléans, the idealized Charlevoix of Clarence Gagnon, and William Kurelek's stark and evocative visions of the rural Prairies – artists expressed the evolution of deep and persistent agrarian myths across Canada's diverse regions.[74]

THE MAKING OF CANADA'S RURAL LANDSCAPE 151

8

The Greening of the Urban Landscape

8.1   Victoria Square, Montreal, c. 1887

During the nineteenth century, the urban landscape of Canada, like the rural landscape, was to pass through a period of degradation, then to be markedly improved through concerted efforts at mitigation, of which the principal objective was the *greening* of the urban milieu.

In tandem with the expansion of agriculture in the various parts of Canada, hundreds of new towns and villages were established to provide the services necessary for a burgeoning population. Gilbert A. Stelter notes that the *colonial*, or *mercantile*, *period*, during which the mother country in Europe made all major economic decisions, was succeeded in Canada by a new *commercial period*. According to Stelter, this commercial period was characterized by a transfer of economic decision-making power to local commercial interests, by expansion in small-scale production for local and regional markets, and by the introduction of new modes of transport such as steamboats, canals, and railroads.[1] These new systems of transportation, combined with a general diversification of the economy, stimulated the gradual urbanization of Canada and, in particular, the growth of major cities, which now began to supply an increasing variety of products and services to their surrounding regions.[2]

During the first wave of this urbanization, new urban residents habitually removed all existing vegetation, levelled the terrain as much as possible, and redirected and canalized the watercourses. Frequently, as at Granby and Magog in southern Quebec, towns turned their backs on their rivers, after reconfiguring and harnessing them for economic purposes.

Often, these growing towns and cities lacked all visual amenity – their buildings devoid of any architectural quality, crooked, made of raw wooden planks with no hint of paint; their roads dusty and windswept; a complete absence of squares, public parks, and recreation facilities or, alternatively, public places established when the towns were first laid out but left without any embellishment and filled with refuse. Overall, a general and demoralizing ugliness.[3] Even long-established cities – such as Quebec City and Montreal – suffered from a lack of public spaces, since their rapid commercial and demographic expansion had not been accompanied by a corresponding expansion in public space. All of this constituted an "urban frontier," which, just like the rural frontier, needed to be tamed and civilized.[4]

And in fact, just as in the rural milieu, Canada's cities and towns did indeed experience a profound restructuring that made them more liveable, more efficient, and more beautiful. This rebuilding, which began in the middle of the nineteenth century, expressed itself through several urban innovations: the creation of *boulevards* through the urban fabric; the *planting of trees* along main roads (as in the rural milieu); the construction of *esplanades* along the shores of lakes and rivers; the creation and decoration of new *squares* and the embellishment of those that already existed; the construction of *splendid public buildings*, carefully situated on well-landscaped sites; and the realization of *floral gardens and public parks*.

Boulevard and Esplanade

Urban Boulevards

As early as 1860, Quebec City proposed to enlarge Grande Allée, a major avenue leading westward from the built-up area of Upper Town, and to plant trees along both sides. The project was finally realized in 1886,[5] transforming Grande Allée into one of the most beautiful and prestigious streets in Canada, which it remains today. In Lower Town, following a terrible fire that destroyed a large area of the working-class districts of Saint-Roch and Saint-Sauveur in 1866, the city created a fire-break passage between the two sectors by widening an existing street. The street was reconfigured in 1885 to its present form – two traffic lanes, separated by a broad central island that accommodates a pedestrian way, including benches and site furniture – and renamed Boulevard Langelier in 1890. The composition was designed by Charles Baillairgé, an architect and engineer employed by the city of Quebec since 1866.[6] This gifted professional was to exert a remarkable influence on the countenance of his city throughout the second half of the century. A real urban jewel, his boulevard fulfils the role of both a spatial and a symbolic axis, owing to its strategic location between the base of the cliff that separates Upper from Lower Town and the historic Hôpital général de Québec to the north.

Some years earlier, the young city of Toronto laid out an equally important and strategic boulevard, in conjunction with the founding in 1829 of Ontario's first institution of higher learning, King's College, the first component of what would eventually become the University of Toronto. To provide for the new college, its governors bought an extensive site outside the built-up area of the city. To link the college to the town in a stately and impressive fashion, they built a magnificent north-south boulevard right up to the college entrance. Designed by John Wedd, the superintendent of the college grounds, the boulevard – today University Avenue – had an impressive width of 36.5 metres (120 ft). Its central trafficway was flanked on each side by two double rows of pink-flowered chestnut trees that framed pedestrian ways, and its northern termination was marked by a grand multi-level fountain. The boulevard and the site of the college, which today houses the Ontario parliament at Queen's Park as well as the University of Toronto, had already become favourite locations for public promenades and social *rendez-vous* by the middle of the nineteenth century. The present College Street, perpendicular to the boulevard, benefited from a similar aesthetic treatment.[7]

8.2 Broadway, Winnipeg: view west along central mall.

154 CHALLENGES OF AN URBAN AND INDUSTRIAL LANDSCAPE

In the same city, Dr. W.W. Baldwin, father of the celebrated political leader Robert Baldwin ("grandfather of Confederation" along with Louis-Hippolyte Lafontaine), created in 1830 another boulevard, Spadina Avenue, running northward from the lakefront to his residence beyond the city limits. Baldwin subdivided his large property, hoping to exploit the booming real estate market of Toronto, and gave this splendid boulevard to the city. With a large circular island, Spadina Crescent, as its central focus, the boulevard still plays a similar role to that of University Avenue, acting as a major structural axis in contrast to the dense urban grid of downtown Toronto, earning itself the honorary nickname "Broadway."[8]

"Broadway" was the real name of another great nineteenth-century boulevard, this one created in western Canada by the Hudson's Bay Company. The agreement of 1869, by which it ceded to the government of Canada its immense territory of Rupert's Land, still permitted the company to retain extensive landholdings, strategically located throughout the West. One of these properties adjoined its old fur trade post Upper Fort Garry, near the centre of the newly founded city of Winnipeg. In 1874, the company planned a new development on this 500-hectare site, a model city of some sixty blocks, organized in regular fashion on either side of a grand central avenue, Broadway. The boulevard is still a marvel of urban planning and serves as the foyer of many important institutions, including the legislative assembly of the province of Manitoba, constructed in 1910, and Union Station, built in 1911, whose domed concourse majestically terminates the axial space of the boulevard at its eastern extremity. Four rows of American elms, first planted before the debut of the twentieth century, border the sidewalks and the central island, along which a tramway formerly ran.[9]

Windows on the Water: Esplanades on Lakeshore and Riverbank

Almost all of the towns of those times were located close to lakes and watercourses that furnished important connections with the rest of the country and with the outside world. Every town had its port, usually located in the downtown area, a centre of movement and excitement as well as of commerce. Despite the technical requirements of the harbour, a number of municipal authorities created promenades and esplanades along the water, using these sites to advantage as places for recreation and for the appreciation of the aesthetic charms of their lakes and rivers.

In 1861, the mayor of Trois-Rivières, Quebec, J.-E. Turcotte, who lived on the Chemin des Remparts directly above the banks of the St. Lawrence River, ceded the street to the municipality in order to create a park. Thus was born Terrasse Turcotte, a linear esplanade parallel to the river. Partially surfaced in wooden planks, it was embellished with pavilions and decorative lamp standards and enclosed by a wrought-iron fence with columns of cut stone, all under the shade of great elm trees. This terrace long served as the preferred promenade of the residents of Trois-Rivières. For more than a century, it survived the gradual expansion of the harbour installations, but finally these grew to obstruct the views of the water. A general redesign was in order, and this was carried out in the 1980s.[10]

8.3 (left)   Charles Baillairgé and Lord Dufferin

8.4 (facing page, above)   Porte Saint-Louis, Quebec City: one of the nineteenth-century city gates created through the efforts of Charles Baillairgé and Lord Dufferin

8.5 (facing page, below)   Dufferin Terrace, Quebec City

The most famous and spectacular of the nineteenth-century esplanades was undoubtedly Dufferin Terrace at Quebec City. One of a series of improvements to the city that were undertaken in the latter half of the century, this project was the fruit of a collaboration between two remarkable people who were, at first, diametrically opposed on the question of Quebec City's redesign. When the British garrison left in 1871, the city engineer, Charles Baillairgé, started to demolish the old city gates that separated the city centre from its growing suburbs in order to improve circulation. He also proposed to lower the height of the walls that enclosed the historic precinct. The business community supported him in these endeavours. But everything changed when a new governor general, the Irish peer Lord Dufferin, arrived at his new posting in 1872. The viceroy admired the historic character of Old Quebec and its integration with the unique topography of its site. He opposed the elimination of the gates and the diminution of the walls. In his view, "Quebec is one of the most picturesque and beautiful cities in the World, not only from its situation, but also from the diadem of wall and towers by which it is encircled."[11]

Lord Dufferin invited his compatriot, architect William H. Lynn, to advise him on preserving the city walls, creating a continuous path along their crests, and integrating new gates of neo-medieval style. These gates, while permitting the increased circulation desired by Baillairgé, added enormously to the historical and romantic cachet of the Old Capital. For his part, the city engineer not only supported and carried out the plans of Lynn and Lord Dufferin, he also convinced His Excellency to support a personal project that was dear to his own heart: the extension of Durham Terrace, a small public platform, begun in 1838 and enlarged in 1854, along the cliff edge between Upper Town and Lower Town.[12] Built in 1878–79, the new project consisted of an immense wooden terrace along the cliff,

156   CHALLENGES OF AN URBAN AND INDUSTRIAL LANDSCAPE

protected by a guard rail. Five pavilions of exotic shape – designed by Baillairgé in cast and wrought iron (materials he employed habitually and skilfully) – punctuated the terrace's perimeter. Named Dufferin Terrace in honour of its patron, it was "the finest promenade in the world," in the words spoken by Princess Louise at the official opening of the terrace.[13]

One long-proposed waterfront esplanade was not to become a permanent reality. Late nineteenth- and early twentieth-century plans for Toronto invariably included an extensive green space next to Lake Ontario, but the pressure of commerce – based on the expanding role of the Queen City as a railroad hub – consistently overcame the claims for recreational amenity.[14]

Square and Place

Nineteenth-Century Squares: The Montreal Legacy

Montreal, Canada's largest city throughout the nineteenth century, led the way in the creation of new public spaces and the embellishment of existing spaces. During the first decade of the century, the growth of the city's suburbs and a constant increase in commercial pressure had already convinced the city commissioners to have Montreal's old fortifications demolished. This decision gave rise to the Rue des Commissaires, built along the southern boundary of the old city walls, and to the creation of two new public spaces: a public market on the site of the present Place Jacques-Cartier and the Champ-de-Mars, a large parade ground at the northern limit of the old city. Rows of trees – poplars, according to drawings from the period – marked the perimeter of this space, which, despite its military vocation, served Montrealers as a favourite place for leisure-time promenades.[15]

Place d'Armes, one of Montreal's most venerable open spaces, was completely transformed following the construction of the new and immense Notre-Dame Church (1824–29). The *place* took its present square form with the demolition of the original church, which had stood right in the centre of Notre-Dame Street at the highest point of Old Montreal. Between 1847 and 1851, it became an "English square," inspired by the residential squares of Soho and Bloomsbury in London and by Place des Vosges in Paris. The newly landscaped square was enclosed by a cast-iron fence with rows of trees planted along it, both inside and outside. Its central focus, a three-level fountain, was encircled by symmetrically organized beds of grass and shrubs.[16] In 1895, the square welcomed a statue of Montreal's founder, Paul Chomedey de Maisonneuve, an elaborate bronze sculpture executed by the Quebec master Louis-Philippe Hébert (1850–1917).[17]

In creating the subsequent generation of public spaces, Montreal's city commissioners showed great originality and discernment. In a city where urban space seemed to be entirely occupied, they recruited all non-built sites – swamps, markets, and cemeteries – and transformed them into *places* and squares.[18] Place Viger, located outside the old city walls, was built on an ancient marshland that had been filled to create a livestock and hay market; during the years 1844–51, the city greatly enlarged the site and turned it into an elegant square.[19] Horticulture played a

158 CHALLENGES OF AN URBAN AND INDUSTRIAL LANDSCAPE

central role in the design of this large public space, and the many activities it accommodated made it a popular gathering spot. Military bands provided music from a central *bandstand*, and fireworks enlivened summer evenings. This square became the "preferred place for promenades and leisure activities" of Montrealers.[20]

The site that would become Victoria Square was also originally a marshland. Situated to the west of the old city's fortifications, it was acquired by the city in 1810 and filled to become a hay market. Finally, in 1860, it was redesigned as an elegant square and renamed in honour of the queen.[21] In 1872, the governor general, Lord Dufferin, unveiled the statue of Victoria that reigns over the square to this day.[22]

The commissioners also created squares on several recycled cemeteries. The only one of these that still remains is Dorchester Square, previously known as Dominion Square, built on the site of Montreal's principal Catholic cemetery, where the victims of the 1832 cholera epidemic were buried.[23] This site had once been part of the northwestern suburbs of the city, surrounded by orchards, but it was gradually encircled by handsome residences of the well-to-do and then the city's centre of gravity migrated to its environs.[24] Made into a public square in 1870, sixteen years after the last burials, its landscape reflected aesthetic preoccupations that were somewhat different from those of the previous generation. Tall trees were disposed within the space as well as around its periphery; diagonal paths delimited raised areas planted in grass, shrubbery, and formal oval flower beds. Neither fence nor gate indicated its perimeter. This square marked the birth of a new urban archetype that was to serve as a model for a whole series of public spaces created in Montreal in the twentieth century.[25] Dorchester/Dominion Square maintained its original appearance for a very long time; the most important change that it accommodated was the integration into its confines of an astonishing number of statues and monuments.[26] As the best-known and most prestigious of Montreal's downtown squares, it provided the perfect setting for the commemoration of important people and events.

Another opportunity was presented to the civic authorities in 1879, when a hilltop site above the downtown area, destined to become a reservoir, proved inadequate to serve the needs of a constantly growing population. The city reclaimed the site to create Saint-Louis Square,[27] destined to become the centre of a flourishing cultural district at the beginning of the twentieth century. In his definitive history *Montreal in Evolution*, Jean-Claude Marsan emphasizes the Victorian identity of the square. He considers it to be "a typical residential square of the romantic days" through a "general unity of style" that complements the "ornamental profusion" of the façades that enclose it. Marsan notes in a lyrical passage, "The place is surrounded by a halo of antiquity ... wonderfully softened by its crown of trees."[28]

These observations clarify the role of the square in the nineteenth century; it was an oasis of greenery, of tranquillity, and of floral beauty in a densely inhabited milieu. It accommodated a great variety of temporary activities – winter carnivals with ice palaces, fanfares, and band concerts – and allowed a great number of people to find a moment of leisure, but it did not try to attract active games or noisy or structured activities. The nineteenth-century square provided a strikingly successful response to the limited demands that were made of it, making, as Marsan states, a great contribution to the landscape heritage of the Victorian period.[29]

Squares Elsewhere in Canada

Although it was "a small settlement in a rural universe,"[30] the city of Trois-Rivières, in Quebec, also needed green spaces in its central area, given its rapid commercial expansion in the nineteenth century. The private garden of the Hart family, prosperous local merchants, satisfied this need. Bought by the city and transformed into a public space in 1869, Parc Champlain became a magnificent green island bordered by the Catholic cathedral and its dependencies, by the city hall, and by a Presbyterian church. The design of the park followed the classic formula of the English square, as in Montreal: a horizontal grass surface, diagonal paths leading to a central *rond-point*, tall trees – willows brought in from l'Assomption – and floral planting beds. The customary wrought-iron fence enclosed the space, and a bandstand for fanfare concerts, erected in 1882, later accommodated a ground-floor restaurant, contributing to the square's great attractiveness to city residents, the Trifluviens.[31]

The absence of a square or other public space in the original plan of Toronto, drawn up in 1793 (see chapter 5),[32] was redeemed in the following decades as the city expanded to the west. Surveyors allocated parts of the newly laid-out areas to sites for the parliament buildings and the governor's residence and integrated new open spaces to the functional but graceless plan they had inherited. For one of the expansion phases in the 1830s, surveyor H.J. Castle drew the plans for "New Town," which included an urban ensemble designed according to a classic "barbell" configuration: two squares linked by a tree-bordered boulevard.[33] Toronto's two squares – Victoria on the west, Clarence on the east – still exist. They became "green oases," simple grass lawns ornamented with large trees, crossed by a few random paths marked out by passersby. At the centre of Victoria Square, a monument recalls the soldiers and regiments that tried to defend the young city of Toronto – then called *York* – against American invaders during the War of 1812–14. Some of these soldiers still repose in a cemetery that occupies a part of the park. Once a fashionable and elegant district, this neighbourhood succumbed to a wave of industrialization in the mid-nineteenth century. But one can nonetheless still appreciate the fine proportions of Wellington Place, the boulevard that links the two squares, and admire the rows of mature maple trees and the robust façades of the industrial buildings that frame it. The original elegance of this composition is still quite visible despite the passage of 175 years.[34]

In the Maritime provinces, the military surveyors who planned the original town layouts had anticipated the need for squares and green spaces and had integrated such spaces in orderly fashion within the towns' urban fabric (see chapter 5), but for many years, these spaces were not attractively developed. All this changed in the middle of the nineteenth century, beginning in the city of Saint John, New Brunswick, at King's Square. Established in 1783 when the city was founded, this square took on its definitive form in 1847, when the city decided to clear the site, construct a network of perpendicular and diagonal paths, and plant trees. The history of Queen Square in Charlottetown is similar. Up to 1860, it was nothing but a disgraceful cow pasture, although it was the most important of the five green spaces set out at the city's foundation (see chapter 5). Its central location in the city grid and the presence within it of the Colonial Building, today the legislative assembly of the province, was little reflected in its meagre landscape treatment. Finally, in 1884, local citizens organized a campaign on the occasion of Arbor Day,

8.6 Gore Park, Hamilton, ON

an 1872 innovation of the American state of Nebraska that had rapidly gained popularity in the intervening decade. The goal of the campaign was to landscape each of the original five squares of the city. Each square was taken in hand by a committee of citizens, and Arthur Newbery, the city's secretary, prepared the planting plan for Queen Square. Newbery also supervised the planting of 135 trees of eleven different varieties when the work was carried out on Charlottetown's first Arbor Day, the 24th of May 1884. This collective effort also inspired the community to install floral planting beds, lawns, and street furniture; an English gardener who worked in Halifax, George Fletcher, designed these improvements. Other new installations followed: fences, paved paths, a grand fountain designed by Newbery along the lines of the fountain that graced Parliament Hill in Ottawa, and, in 1895, the inevitable hexagonal bandstand pavilion, which was to host band concerts for the next fifty years. Up until 1891, the maintenance of the grounds was assured by a citizens' association, the Charlottetown Arbor Society. Such community participation was common practice for many nineteenth-century public spaces.[35]

From 1860 to the present day, the nerve centre of the city of Hamilton, Ontario, founded in 1816 at the head of Lake Ontario, has been Gore Park, a trapezoidal site enclosed by robust Victorian commercial buildings. At one time, the park had been described as "a disreputable dump and mudhole," but beginning in the 1850s, the city landscaped the square,[36] installing a spectacular central fountain, which generated a hemisphere of sparkling water, and "island plantings" of bright-coloured annuals. Like the squares of Montreal, Gore Park served as a "repository of the public memory," the venue for statues of Queen Victoria, Sir John A. Macdonald, first prime minister of Canada, and the city's principal war memorial.

In western Canada, most municipalities had only existed for a few years, but they were still highly motivated to create and embellish public squares in order to civilize and add greenery to their often unprepossessing downtown areas. Designated in 1884 as a public square in the original plan for Regina, Victoria Park remained derelict until its city was recognized as the capital of the new province of Saskatchewan in 1905. Shortly after that event, the city mandated Montreal landscape architect Frederick G. Todd to prepare a plan for the park. Todd's design, drawn up in 1907 and carried out in subsequent years, included a broad central lawn that served as a playing field, rows of trees on both sides of the four enclosing streets, straight and curved paths inside the park, and an irregularly shaped pond. Looking today at the park, the foyer of "several of the oldest and most beautiful specimen trees in Regina," one finds it hard to imagine that there was not a single tree on the site of the city at the time of its founding.[37]

Achieving the status of a city in 1884, Calgary owes its first square to William Pearce, pioneer of landscape architecture in the West and "father of irrigation in Canada" (see chapter 7). In 1885, as a council member of the Dominion Lands Board, which had just been established at Calgary, Pearce arranged for the site of Central Park (today Central Memorial Park) to be transferred to the city as a gift from the federal government. This gesture was part of Pearce's long-term strategy for the greening of Calgary, a city located in the semi-arid climate zone of southern Alberta but well furnished with water by the Bow and Elbow rivers. Pearce

8.7 Central Memorial Park, c. 1914–19, Calgary

also advised the city to undertake mass tree plantings.[38] In 1911–12, the Carnegie Foundation from the United States constructed the first public library in Alberta in the eastern section of the park.[39]

    The park later benefited from many improvements planned and supervised by a member of the Calgary Horticultural Society and subsequently by R. Iverson, the city parks superintendent. In 1912, Iverson proposed an ambitious project that would include an elaborate orchestra shell flanked by pavilions on both sides, fountains, an equestrian memorial to veterans of the South African War, formal planting beds, and latticework summer houses.[40] William R. Reader, Iverson's successor as parks superintendent, oversaw the design of the project, its realization, and the maintenance of the park from 1913 until the end of his remarkably long and productive mandate in 1942. Through Reader's efforts, the park became widely recognized for the excellence of its elaborate planting, which deployed crabapples, blue spruce, and giant cottonwood poplars around a central "show garden," the colourful geometric planting beds of which recalled the late Victorian

THE GREENING OF THE URBAN LANDSCAPE 163

era. As Reader proudly stated, "This park was undoubtedly the focal point of attraction in the city from the horticultural standpoint."[41]

Bandstands and Multi-level Fountains

The reader may be astonished by the universality of bandstands in the parks and squares of the nineteenth century, not only in Canada, but throughout Europe, the United States, Latin America, and the Antipodes as well. According to the eminent landscape historian Hazel Conway, two events launched the popularity of the bandstand: its appearance in France around 1855, at the Exposition industrielle in Paris, and the construction of the first cast-iron bandstands in the gardens of the Royal Horticultural Society in the Kensington district of London, in 1861.[42] These picturesque kiosks became the points of convergence of squares and parks for almost a century, accommodating musical performances of all sorts – military, classical, popular – activities that were greatly appreciated by the enthusiastic crowds that filled urban public spaces throughout this long period.

Usually built of wood or iron (often mass-produced in factories), bandstands were almost always octagonal or hexagonal in plan, while their columns and roofs took many forms, varying from simple and pure geometry to fantastic complexity. The visual extravagances of some of the latter provide a clue to their likely inspiration: the *chatri*, that domed and pillared pavilion that is the central element of many gardens and building complexes in the Islamic world and in India. And the chatri traces its origins, in turn, to the ancient Persian gardens, which were almost always anchored by a small and elegant pavilion at their central point, the crossing of the four canals typical of the traditional garden of the type *chahar bagh* (four gardens). This might also explain the bandstand's central location, at the middle of a symmetrical composition, in so many of our nineteenth-century squares.[43] If we continue still further back in history, we might find that the ancestor of the chatri was a tent or even a suspended rug, providing a distant evocation of the fluid and playful forms that characterize many of our bandstands. Another formal element played almost as important a role as did bandstands in the structuring of these public spaces: *multi-level fountains*, which were also the beneficiaries of a distinguished genealogy. They trace their origins to the magnificent baroque fountains of Italy, including the fountain designed by architect Carlo Maderno for St. Peter's Square in Rome during the reign of Pope Paul V from 1605 to 1621[44] and to earlier fountains in other Italian cities.[45]

The squares and *places* of Canada's nineteenth-century commercial cities were sophisticated and complex places. Always well maintained throughout this period, they inspired great pride among urban populations.[46] They were full of statues, fountains, ponds, and such unique elements as cannons. Some were showpieces for horticulture, while others sought a more modest appearance, essentially green. These spaces played several urban roles: they were places to relax, to welcome high-ranking visitors, and to carry out religious ceremonies. They also served as places of public assembly for seasonal events. It was in two of these spaces, Place d'Armes and Dominion Square, that the Montreal Winter Carnival was held in the 1880s.

8.8 Drawing of the Ice Palace in Dominion Square, Montreal Winter Carnival, 1889, by Alexander C. Hutchison, architect. The newly constructed St. James' Cathedral (now the Cathedral Basilica of Mary, Queen of the World), a scaled-down replica of St. Peter's Basilica in Rome, is shown in the background.

The carnival's temporary features included sculptures, palaces, and labyrinths, entirely constructed of blocks of ice.

Era of the Landscape Gardeners

Civic and institutional buildings of the time were often set in attractive and elaborate landscapes. As landscape historian Pleasance Crawford explains, these landscapes were usually realized after the buildings with which they were associated were built, sometimes considerably later. Their budgets were limited and often made available only sporadically. But almost all these projects, at least after 1830, seem to have benefited from the contributions of professional designers, who usually identified themselves as *landscape gardeners*. The practitioners of this discipline generally carried out, on the ground, the landscape works they had designed, and sometimes even involved themselves in their long-term maintenance.[47] Landscape gardeners designed almost all the high-quality gardens and site

THE GREENING OF THE URBAN LANDSCAPE 165

developments in Canada, from about 1825 until the ascendancy of the profession of landscape architecture during the second half of the nineteenth century.

Like the great majority of architects of the time, most landscape gardeners came to Canada from the "old countries" of Europe, usually Great Britain and Ireland but also the Low Countries and Germany. In all these lands, the profession of horticulturist had been long established and was supported by excellent training and apprenticeship programs. Among the first of these practitioners to emigrate to the New World, André Joseph Ghislain Parmentier (1780–1830), a native of Enghien in Belgium, was certainly the most famous. Scion of a horticultural family already renowned for its innovations in the cultivation of roses and potatoes, Parmentier immigrated to Brooklyn (New York), in 1824, where he rapidly established a reputation as a nurseryman and landscape gardener. In his well-known nursery, Parmentier displayed fruit trees and other plants, often exotic, as well as a demonstration garden laid out in naturalistic style. In his practice, he designed private gardens for the proprietors of large estates in the Hudson River valley, and provided them with plants from his establishment. His outstanding realization was the villa of Hyde Park, now known as the *Vanderbilt Mansion* and recognized as a national historic site. The New York landscape gardener and author Andrew Jackson Downing states, "We consider ... M. Parmentier's labours and example as having effected directly far more for landscape gardening in America than those of any other individual whatever."[48] Pleasance Crawford and Stephen A. Otto found, among Downing's praises for Parmentier, a reference to works that the latter had apparently carried out in Canada: "[T]wo or three places in Upper Canada, especially near Montreal, were, we believe, laid out by his own hands and stocked from his nursery grounds."[49] This brief reference inspired Crawford and Otto to pursue their researches into Parmentier's endeavours in Canada. They discovered that he had a network of some thirty sales agents who represented his nursery, from New Orleans to Halifax. Their studies indicate that Parmentier undertook several projects in eastern Canada and that in 1830, shortly before his death, he spent two weeks in Montreal meeting clients. Unfortunately, the identity of these clients is unknown, although Parmentier's documents mention the names of Louis-Joseph Papineau and other eminent Montrealers.[50]

Parmentier's activities in Toronto, however, are more precisely known. He apparently prepared a landscape plan for the campus of King's College University (see above), a flat site with little vegetation but traversed diagonally by a small stream, Taddle Creek. The landscape work he proposed included plantings of chestnuts, elms, and white-flowering hawthorns, ordered from an American nursery, for the main access road, along with other trees and shrubs. The execution of this work began in 1830 under the direction of Richard Colemen, a botanist trained in Ireland.[51]

Parmentier also worked on residential projects in Toronto, including Moss Park, located in the northeastern part of the city on one of the *park lots* that dated from its founding. The owner, William Allan, a Scottish immigrant who had achieved considerable success in business, purchased the lot in 1819 and built a substantial house at its southern extremity in 1828, near the main artery Queen Street and

8.9 Open space structure, Toronto, 1830–60. Since its founding in 1793, the city has expanded westward into the military and public reserve and eastward to the Don River, and the harbour has been developed. As originally planned, the range of park lots north of Queen Street provided sites for the villas of wealthy officials and business people; institutions and smaller-scale residential areas have begun to take over this sector.

the prolongation of the same Taddle Creek that crossed the site of the university. The overall site layout – probably designed by Parmentier in 1828–29, since it corresponded exactly to his customary picturesque style – included serpentine roadways, ornamental planting, and clusters of coniferous and deciduous trees. Some of the latter came from his own nursery, including the purple beech, which he seems to have introduced to North America.[52]

A landscape gardener of Scottish origin, William Mundie (1811–1858), settled in Hamilton in 1850, where he designed large private gardens on Hamilton Mountain (the local name for the Niagara Escarpment, which long defined the southern limit of the city). Around 1852, the provincial Department of Education engaged him to design and supervise the development of the grounds of the new Normal School and Model School at Toronto. Mundie worked until 1856 on this long-term project, moving to Toronto in 1855. He planned a "botanical garden" around the main buildings, which were to occupy the central part of the 3.2-hectare site.[53] The garden included more than 200 plant species, a fruit garden, a greenhouse, an area devoted to agricultural experimentation, and playing fields for gymnastics. Mundie also directed the landscape work on the site. Toronto residents so

THE GREENING OF THE URBAN LANDSCAPE 167

appreciated his work that they quickly adopted the school grounds as a public space, to be known as St. James Square.[54]

Mundie also prepared plans for the site of King's College University (the University of Toronto), for which an extensive territory of 42 hectares to the north of the city had been reserved. His first proposal for a botanical garden, sketched out and begun on the site in 1851, was abandoned when the Ontario government expropriated a large part of the university land (that known as "University Park") in order to build the new provincial parliament on the property, now renamed Queen's Park. Mundie continued his work elsewhere on the site, preparing a new general plan for the remaining university land, including the layout of terraces adjoining its first building, University College.[55] His plan shows a network of roadways designed to follow graceful curving alignments, broad lawns punctuated with clusters of trees, and the reconfiguration and integration of Taddle Creek into the new contours of the site. Mundie's plan foresaw a great central space that would provide a dramatic setting for the university buildings and, within these

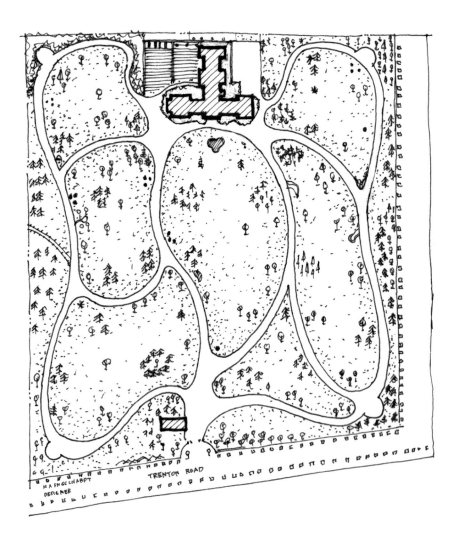

8.10 (above) H.A. Engelhardt

8.11 (left) Site plan for Belleville Institute for the Deaf and Dumb. After H.A. Engelhardt, landscape gardener.

168 CHALLENGES OF AN URBAN AND INDUSTRIAL LANDSCAPE

buildings, interior courtyards to furnish private, intimate, and comfortable spaces for students – the first expression of two spatial themes that would long characterize the campus of the University of Toronto. Following Mundie's untimely death in 1858, the English landscape gardener Edwin Taylor (a former assistant of Sir Joseph Paxton, the great creator of public parks in England) carried out the works conceived by his predecessor.[56]

Another gifted designer, Henry Adolph Engelhardt (1832–1897), gained distinction for his work in civic and institutional milieus. Born at Mülhausen in Prussia, Engelhardt undertook university studies in Berlin and completed his military service before emigrating in 1851 to the United States, where he began his career as a landscape gardener. He worked on the layout of Central Park in New York and on several cemeteries in Virginia and the American Midwest, later moving to Ontario in 1870. On his arrival, he worked on the design of the grounds for two specialized schools: the Ontario Institution for the Education of the Blind at Brantford and the Institute for the Deaf and Dumb at Belleville. In 1871–72, Engelhardt designed, hired the workers for, and directed the landscaping of the grounds of these two establishments, laying out curving access roads and pedestrian promenades, planting conifers and various deciduous trees, and creating attractive settings for the main buildings, which were, as was usual at the time, located at the high points of their sites.[57]

Engelhardt was a major figure among Canadian landscape designers of the nineteenth century. He contributed to the design of other institutions – the Ontario Agricultural College at Guelph, for example – and played an important role in the design and realization of cemeteries and parks (see chapter 10). According to Pleasance Crawford, this unusual character was "well educated in history, agricultural sciences, and the classics, ... was sensitive to natural processes, [and] firmly believed that beauty could elevate the human spirit." Crawford describes Engelhardt's confident, enthusiastic, and sometimes hilarious way of communicating with his clients, as well as his far from orthodox approach to spelling; this last, however, did not prevent him from writing the first English-language Canadian book on landscape design, *The Beauties of Nature Combined with Art*, published in 1872.[58] This book, an advisory manual on the principles of design and the employment of plant material, was oriented to the designers of large private gardens and the grounds of such public facilities as schools, cemeteries, and courthouses.

It is perhaps surprising that the young society of Ontario, barely advanced from its rustic pioneer beginnings, should be concerned with such institutions as normal schools, educational facilities for the handicapped, universities, and colleges. These physical realizations were in fact the symbols of a social transformation. Influenced by reform movements in political affairs and social concerns raised by rapidly expanding Protestant religious denominations, Ontario passed through a profound revolution between about 1830 and 1880, fleeing a past dominated by the aristocracy of the Family Compact in order to redirect itself towards a new social model, more democratic and egalitarian.[59] This social transformation found its physical expression in the creation of great institutions, composed of solid and dignified buildings, set in well planned and gracious landscapes.[60]

9

Public and Private Gardens of the Nineteenth Century

The Victorian Garden

9.1   Halifax Public Gardens

In the nineteenth century, England was the centre of gravity for new ideals and principles in garden design. As an outpost of British culture, Canada was inevitably pulled into the orbit of these ideas, which reflected the preoccupations of a new generation of Britons who had gained their wealth in commerce and industry. This new class had replaced the landed gentry of a previous generation as the dominant group in British society.[1] The "natural" and romantic landscapes of the great landowners were no longer the aesthetic ideal. Members of the new dominant class – energetic, ambitious, and *arriviste* – were, like their predecessors, passionately interested in gardens, but they were particularly fascinated by plants, especially those with vivid flowers.

Everything reinforced and stimulated this interest: the founding of horticultural societies; worldwide expeditions in search of new and exotic plants, often sponsored by these same societies; and the establishment and expansion of botanical gardens, including the Royal Botanic Gardens at Kew, established as a royal

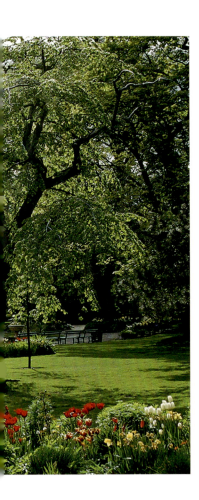

garden in the early eighteenth century and transformed into a national enterprise in 1840. Horticultural magazines lovingly described all of these developments.[2]

This enthusiasm for plants led to a redefinition of the garden. The objective of the garden was no longer to realize painterly compositions in real landform and planting, subordinating each element to a single aesthetic vision of the whole, but rather to dispose its various elements – especially its plants – to best display their unique qualities of colour, form, and texture.[3] This new tendency led to an eclectic approach to design, through which the garden became a complex of specialized and nearly autonomous *mini-gardens*. Each sector of the garden was independently composed and refined: the kitchen garden, the floral garden, the herb garden, the rose garden, the aquatic garden, and so on, like a restaurant that features a Louis XV room, a Polynesian room, etcetera. Technical progress reinforced this new spirit: new tools and new methods of cultivation, larger and more efficient greenhouses, powerful pumps that supplied copious amounts of water for spectacular fountains. All seemed possible to those who had access to this great technical virtuosity.[4]

Based on these general principles, the Victorian garden (so named in honour of the British queen who reigned from 1837 to 1901)[5] was subject to a constant stylistic evolution, repeatedly reinventing itself in response to wide swings in taste. Each decade seems to have brought a new vision of what gardens should be, a vision that would be relegated, in its turn, to the dustbin, as outdated, boring, and ridiculous, in favour of a succeeding wave of design ideas.[6]

Among these numerous waves, a revival of the gardens of the past became a major theme. The Italian Renaissance, walled gardens of the Tudor era, Dutch topiaries, the *parterres* of the French Renaissance, and the herbaceous borders of the English tradition all had their moments of glory.[7] For a time, the rock garden, either naturalistic or fantastic, dominated.[8] During other periods, a particular category of plant – giant conifers, brilliantly coloured tropical flowers, foliage plants in several shades of green, alpine wildflowers, rhododendrons from the remote Himalayan mountains, trees with coloured leaves or unusual forms (pyramidal, fastigiate, weeping) – became the flavour of the week.[9] Geometry and composition were also in play: at times, obsessive symmetry or its opposite dominated; preferences varied from straight lines to fluid serpentine curves; planting beds might flourish in the form of perfectly circular islands or, alternatively, of shapeless amoebas, commas, or vaguely plant-like forms.[10] The Victorians embraced all of this aesthetic diversity, buoyed by the indomitable confidence, exuberance, and enthusiasm that were so much a part of their civilization.

Elements of the Canadian Garden: Creating a Vocabulary

To recreate the garden prototypes that came from overseas, Canadian gardeners needed – as did Canadian agriculture, as described in chapter 7 – knowledge, tools and methods, and plants well adapted to the milieu. The latter could be procured in three different ways: first, by the identification of appropriate native plants and their introduction to the garden; second, by the importation and integration of

9.2　Central Experimental Farm, horticulture section, Ottawa

foreign plants; and finally, by the development of new cultivated varieties, or *cultivars*, capable of thriving under Canadian conditions.[11]

French colonists and botanists had already taken up the first two challenges from the earliest days of New France (see chapter 4). Nineteenth-century pioneers continued to explore these two strategies in all regions of the country. The work of Ontario's two literary sisters Susanna Moodie and Catharine Parr Traill is particularly noteworthy; their books recount the identification and adoption of such native plants as honeysuckle, spirea, red flowering raspberry, and wild gooseberry, and the introduction of marigolds, sweet peas, poppies, and pinks from the "old country."[12] The *botanist-priests* of Quebec also made remarkable contributions. The most famous of these, Abbot Léon Provancher (1820–1892), was the author of *Traité élémentaire de botanique* (1858) and the magnum opus *Flore canadienne* (1862), which addressed the systematic identification of the flora of eastern Canada. Both books were the first of their type to be published in Canada.[13]

Beyond their contributions to agriculture, the central and regional experimental farms (see chapter 7) developed a broad range of hardy and attractive ornamental plants. Immediately upon the establishment of the farms in 1886, Director William Saunders began a research program focusing on garden plants. In 1898, he chose William T. Macoun, son of a botany professor, as horticulturist to the Central Experimental Farm.[14] Macoun's most outstanding employee was Isabella Preston, a horticulture specialist born in England who arrived at the Central Experimental Farm in 1920. Preston undertook a series of experiments from which

172　CHALLENGES OF AN URBAN AND INDUSTRIAL LANDSCAPE

emerged many useful plants, including colourful and hardy lilies, the well-known late-blooming *Preston lilacs*, which remain industry standards, and the charming and disease-resistant *Rosybloom crabapples*.[15] Other agricultural research stations adapted the Rosybloom strain, creating crabapple varieties well adapted to the harsh climatic conditions of the Prairies.[16] During this period and later, in the 1960s, the experimental farms also invested a great deal of effort in the development, through hybridization, of hardy roses with large and attractive flowers. This work resulted in the development (based on the familiar wild rose, *Rosa rugosa)* of the famous *Explorer* series, remarkably tough plants with abundant flowers of diverse colour, floral type, and growth habit.[17] Other experimental farms produced rhododendron and chrysanthemum hybrids, among others, well adapted to various Canadian climates.[18]

Several private nurseries also made major contributions to the development of an ornamental plant vocabulary for Canadian gardens. These included the nursery of Auguste Dupuis in the village of St-Roch-des-Aulnaies, on the south shore of the St. Lawrence River in Quebec,[19] and various Ontario nurseries situated near St. Catharines on the Niagara Peninsula, where soils and climate were favourable. Among these nurseries were those of Linus Woolverton and A.M. Smith at Grimsby, and that of the E.D. Smith Company at Winona. Innovative nurseries were soon established beyond Niagara, throughout the southern part of the province.[20] Several ambitious nurseries were opened on the Prairies towards the end of the nineteenth and beginning of the twentieth century. Through careful selection and grafting, these nurseries developed ornamentals adapted to the region. H.B. Patmore, of Brandon, Manitoba, and Saskatoon, produced the *Patmore ash*; Frank L. Skinner (1882–1967), at his nursery at Dropmore in Manitoba, developed a number of cultivars including the *Dropmore honeysuckle* vine and the *Pocahontas lilac*.[21] At Rosthern, Saskatchewan, Seager Wheeler carried out experiments with flowering plants and fruit trees, while at St. Albert in central Alberta, Georges Bugnet created many hybrid roses, of which the highly resistant shrub variety *Thérèse Bugnet* has become a garden classic.[22]

Sharing Expertise: Horticultural Societies

In parallel to these plant innovations, newly formed horticultural societies were anxious to spread knowledge of garden planting and maintenance. Modelled on the prestigious Royal Horticultural Society in England, associations of this type were quick to establish themselves across Canada, in Toronto in 1834,[23] Halifax in 1836, and Montreal in 1846.[24] Other cities and regions in eastern Canada soon followed.[25] Horticultural associations began to take root in Manitoba in the 1880s and 1890s, and developed all over the West at the beginning of the twentieth century. These associations offered many services to their members: exchanges of seeds, plants, and information; exhibitions and competitions; courses and technical demonstrations; visits to public and private gardens. They also offered their members the opportunity to participate directly in civic projects to make their cities more beautiful.[26]

Magazines and Books

Horticultural societies and producers' organizations initiated a multitude of publications in order to communicate knowledge and product information to those interested in gardens. The first Canadian entry in this field was the *Canadian Horticulturist*, supported by the Fruit Growers' Association of Ontario, published from 1857 to 1934. In 1884, Linus Woolverton of Grimsby, Ontario, succeeded its first editor, Delos W. Beadle, owner of a nursery in St. Catharines. In December 1868, Abbot Léon Provancher began the publication of a monthly periodical, *Le Naturaliste Canadien*, at Quebec City. His objective was to "popularise knowledge of natural history ... for the benefit of the arts, industry and the needs of everyday life."[27] Several books were also published in Canada, among them *The Canadian Fruit-Culturalist* by James Dougall of Windsor, Ontario (Montreal, 1867); numerous volumes on orchards, fruit growing, vegetables, and flowers by the tireless Abbot Provancher from 1862 to 1885; *The Canadian Fruit, Flower, and Kitchen Gardener* by Delos W. Beadle in 1872; and, finally, the first Canadian manual on landscape design, *The Beauties of Nature Combined With Art*, published by landscape gardener H.A. Engelhardt at Montreal in 1872.[28]

Demonstration Gardens

Finally, a number of organizations carried out concrete projects to show how ornamental plants could prosper in diverse climates and soils across the country, and how they could be grouped and arranged to create attractive compositions. The Central Experimental Farm laid out such a garden, designed by an "eminent landscape architect" whose name Director Saunders unfortunately did not specify,[29] on its "campus" in the southwest sector of Ottawa. In its arboretum, adjacent to a model farm and experimental fields, 36 hectares planted with trees, hedges, and ornamental gardens were composed according to the precepts of the romantic movement. The site still has the aspect of a park; since the beginning, the general public has been invited to explore the site, appreciate its beauty, and learn how to grow plants and arrange them in the garden.[30] The Sutherland Forest Nursery Station in Saskatoon also played the role of a *demonstration garden*, attempting to prove to residents of the Prairies that one could create a very attractive garden in that region in spite of its difficult climate. In preparing the plans for the Sutherland station, essentially a vast tree nursery, Herbert Ross, the provincial minister of the interior, designed the southwestern sector as a verdant park, featuring shrub borders and decorative trees in the area adjacent to the superintendent's house.[31]

The Canadian Pacific Railway (CPR) established the most extensive network of demonstration gardens in the country. For seventy years beginning in 1890, this powerful company acted as the "chief gardener for Canada." It supplied station agents across the country with seeds for trees, shrubs, annuals, bulbs, and perennials, from a series of central nurseries and greenhouses. These "station gardens" provided instructions on planting and suggestions for the domestic garden. They contributed to the CPR's subtle campaign to convince the pioneers that they could

9.3   CPR station railroad garden at Medicine Hat, AB, 1887

live well in the West, and helped to show the fertility of the prairie soils. The gardens were designed in the whole gamut of Victorian styles, from circular planting beds bordered in white alyssum, to whitewashed stones, all the way to very elaborate geometric compositions. Lilacs often played a predominant role.[32]

Victorian Gardens in Canada: On the Farm

All these tendencies exerted a powerful influence on the design of farm properties in eastern Canada. The gradually expanding prosperity that had come to rural life in the mid-nineteenth century (see chapter 7) permitted the addition of an aesthetic dimension and a layer of refinement to the farm environment, which until then had emphasized production pure and simple. In *county almanacs*, so popular throughout this period, one can see an unmistakable tendency towards a more elaborate and elegant agricultural setting. Ann Leighton, chronicler of American gardens, perceives "a passion for gardening in however small a compass" on the farms north of the border.

Leighton notes specific elements that expressed this new refinement: circular planting beds filled with annuals, flowering vines climbing up the gallery posts, rose gardens, croquet lawns, and tree plantings along farm roads and streets. These features were often complemented with a *garden house* or small pavilion, a semi-circular carriage entrance, wooden trellises, and fences in various styles.[33]

Classic flowering shrubs – honeysuckle, viburnum, spirea, mock orange – played an important role in the domestic garden. Lilacs, in full individual splendour beside the front door or massed in "wild hedges," seem to have constantly remained among the most favoured shrubs. Deciduous shade trees – maple, silver-leaved poplar, or aspen – and a vegetable garden, beside or behind the house, completed the picture.[34]

Public Gardens

The new-found enthusiasm for gardening inspired several nineteenth-century Canadian cities to create public gardens for the enjoyment of their citizens. Like public squares (see chapter 8), these gardens benefited from the philanthropy and civic actions of public-spirited civic groups. The best-known of these Victorian-era gardens was without doubt the Halifax Public Gardens, in the capital of Nova Scotia. This jewel of the city owes its existence to the Horticultural Society of Nova Scotia, a group formed in 1836 by influential male and female citizens who dedicated themselves to the beautification of their city and to the amelioration of its social conditions. The project sought to create both a scientific garden with the goal of "advancing the art of Horticulture and the science of Botany" and a public garden "to extend a cheerful influence upon private happiness and to exalt and

9.4 Nineteenth-century farmstead landscape at "Easydale," the residence of William Justin, Mississauga, ON, 1877. All the elements of a working farm are present – cropland, woodlot, kitchen garden, barn, and outbuildings – but the main house has been spruced up with arches, quoins, and Victorian wood detailing, while its front yard has become a circular entrance garden with symmetrical decorative planting within an enclosed space defined by rows of coniferous trees. A formal entrance avenue to the farm is also provided.

refine the tone of public morals." On a 2.2-hectare site within the city's original common, transferred to it in 1841 by the province's legislative assembly, the society planted a vegetable garden and flower beds that were soon visited by the public in great numbers.[35] In 1866, a new municipal garden was developed to the north of the society's site, and in 1874 the city of Halifax consolidated the two sites by purchasing the garden of the society. This resulted in a square block of land of some 6.4 hectares in area, well located close to the built-up areas of the city. The following year, the gardens began to take on their definitive form, following the design and under the direction of a remarkable landscape gardener of Irish origin, Richard Power (1841–1934). Trained on the estate of the Duke of Devonshire and formerly employed by Sir Joseph Paxton, Power had later worked at Central Park in New York. In 1872, he became superintendent of the Halifax Public Gardens, a post he occupied continuously until 1915.[36]

Power reorganized the diverse elements on the site to create a new overall composition. He based his plan on a simple spatial structure that included a main network of parallel and perpendicular paths, as well as a series of more intimate curved paths in each quadrant of the gardens. Water played the role of counterpoint: Power modified the shape of an existing large, square pond to create an irregular lake with a central island. Close to the main entrance to the gardens, he reworked an existing watercourse into a chain of small lakes linked by a stream. He gradually elaborated each sector of the site according to a different theme so as to present a variety of contrasting ambiances, closely juxtaposed; this was typical of the Victorian garden.[37] The choice of plants comprised a broad selection of large trees, mostly exotics – copper beech, Japanese larch, Katsura tree – each set out in isolated splendour, often at path intersections, so that every specimen could reach its broadest extent and give its best visual impression to garden visitors.[38] In the northwest sector, dedicated to the memory of the soldiers who had served in the South African War of 1899–1902, the use of many trees of "weeping" habit – willows, birches, elm, cherry – evoked a solemn atmosphere. Elsewhere in these eclectic gardens, colour and vivacity prevailed. To celebrate the fiftieth anniversary of the reign of Queen Victoria in 1887, a magnificent bandstand was constructed in the open area at the centre of the gardens, according to the drawings of Henry Busch, an architect of German origin. Around this highly coloured and decorated wooden structure, some thirty planting beds were laid out, displaying thousands of annual plants from city greenhouses. Other planting beds presented a diverse spectrum of Victorian styles, including clumps of tropical plants, crescents of perennials, carpet bedding (or *mosaïculture*), and several small rock gardens.[39] Flowering shrubs – roses and immense rhododendrons – enriched the spectacle. Elsewhere on the site, other iconographic elements – always essential in a Victorian garden – were integrated with the composition: a new commemorative fountain, allegorical statues of Roman goddesses,[40] a composition of linear flower beds in serpentine form with added flourishes, filled with perennials that provided a constant succession of floral colour.

The gardens were entirely enclosed by a fence, by mounds, and by vegetation. This was intentional. As soon as visitors entered the grounds through their elegant wrought-iron gates, their field of view was entirely occupied by natural objects and they forgot the surrounding city. They had the impression that the gardens extended to the horizon. A garden of this tradition aimed to create an imaginary ideal world, in harmony with the idealism that was so much a part of Victorian literary and socio-political expression.[41] Still perfectly maintained, these gardens are a *tour de force* that express with precision the ideas and forms of the Victorian era. Their remarkable longevity and their fidelity to their roots, which have resisted every stylistic revolution since the Victorian period, are largely due to the continued dedication of a single family, the Powers, and their successors, who have so consistently managed the site. Following his retirement after forty-two years as superintendent, Richard Power continued to contribute to the gardens' development until about 1930. He was succeeded by his son Richard until the latter's career was cut short by his death in an accident. Another son continued to work at the Halifax Public Gardens after the patriarch's death in 1934, and a third was employed at the Boston Public Gardens, another splendid example of the Victorian tradition.[42]

A similar scenario to that of the Halifax Public Gardens was enacted in Toronto through the creation of the gardens and greenhouses now known as Allan Gardens. This civic project was built in the 1850s on the property of George William Allan (1822–1901), mayor of Toronto in 1855 and a member of the Toronto Horticultural Society. Allan inherited the *park lot* on which his father had built his home and garden, Moss Park (see chapter 8), and the younger Allan subdivided the lot and gave some 2 hectares to the Horticultural Society as a site for the creation of a *botanical garden*.[43] Landscape gardener Edwin Taylor, who had previously worked on the site development of the University of Toronto (see chapter 8), drew up the plans for the garden at his own cost. Under his direction, the work was carried out in 1859 and 1860, and the grand opening took place during September of the latter year, on the occasion of the visit of the Prince of Wales, the son of Queen Victoria and future King Edward VII. The garden, oval in form along an east-west principal axis, comprised bands of carpet bedding, hundreds of trees and shrubs, floral beds of varied form, a *rustic pavilion* constructed of great cedar logs, and a three-level floral amphitheatre.[44] The city of Toronto acquired the entire site in 1888 in order to establish a municipal garden, and added a series of exhibition greenhouses, or *conservatories*, inaugurated in 1909. Renamed Allan Gardens in honour of their benefactor, George William Allan, these gardens have retained much of their original colour and liveliness, and still provide a rare oasis of beauty in the eastern sector of downtown Toronto.[45]

The Picturesque Villa, 1830–1860

The most impressive gardens of the period adorned a new wave of villas built, like those of the previous generation, on spectacular natural sites on the outskirts of major cities. As discussed in chapter 5, military officers and high government officials of the colonial period had written that first chapter in the evolution of the villa in Canada, from about 1780 to 1830. The next phase of this evolution was to be directed by a new class of prosperous merchants from the commercial cities. These people, in reaction to the expansion and densification of the nineteenth-century urban milieu, fled the noise, heat, and dust of the towns, seeking to create their own little paradise in calmer environments. Fear reinforced this tendency. Epidemics of cholera, arriving from Europe with the boatloads of immigrants, devastated Canadian cities from the 1830s on, accelerating the flight of those who could escape to the countryside.[46] This movement affected all Canadian cities, large and small. As in the first period of villa creation (see chapter 5), favoured sites offered a sense of isolation, a natural wooded environment, and interesting views. Happily, such sites were to be found close to most urban centres.

Having never been exposed to the classical and Palladian traditions of their forebears, the *nouveaux riches* who created the second generation of villas sought other sources of knowledge. Fortunately, since the end of the eighteenth century and throughout the nineteenth, several well-known garden designers published popular books filled with plans, rules, and instructions, inspired by their knowledge of horticulture and their practices in landscape planning. The first of these authors was Humphrey Repton (1752–1818) of England. Repton had been among the first to identify himself as a *landscape gardener*. The term combined the notions of painting and gardening: "[T]he art [of landscape gardening] can only be advanced and perfected by the united powers of the *landscape painter* and the *practical gardener*."[47] In several volumes published from 1794 to 1818, Repton systematized and popularized the ideas of the great designers and theoreticians of the English garden – natural and picturesque – of the eighteenth century.[48] His books consisted primarily of a series of excerpts from the "red books" that he had prepared for his clients to help them design or redesign their country estates. John Claudius Loudon (1783–1843), eminent British designer of parks and gardens and founding editor of the popular review *The Gardener's Magazine*, republished all the books of Repton in 1840. He used the expression "landscape architecture" to describe the philosophy and works of his predecessor, a very early use of a term that would later be more widely adopted. Loudon later published *An Encyclopaedia of Gardening*, which included a plethora of information on horticultural techniques and the design of public gardens.

The American homologue of these British gardening prophets was Andrew Jackson Downing (c. 1818–1852), born into a family of nurserymen who were well established along the Hudson River, in New York State. Downing borrowed liberally from Repton and Loudon while composing his highly influential encyclopaedia of gardening, *A Treatise on the Theory and Practice of Landscape Gardening Adapted to North America*, later reissued four times between 1841 and 1850.[49] Energetic and enthusiastic, Downing wrote several other books of advice on domestic architecture and horticulture. He edited the popular magazine *The Horticulturist* while designing numerous private and public gardens. Shortly before his tragic death in a boating accident at the young age of thirty-three, he campaigned for the creation of a large public park in New York City, which was undergoing a vertiginous expansion at the time.[50] More sensitive to aesthetics than Loudon (if we may judge by their respective books), Downing considered the design of villas and their gardens according to two distinct styles of design: the *beautiful*, an ideal of calm and harmonious balance, like a gracious and symmetrical elm tree; and the *picturesque*, exemplified by a rugged pine or larch whose irregular and tormented branches bear witness to its combats against storm and tempest.[51]

Downing established a sort of genetic code – a set of rules – for the design of the country house and its grounds: locate the main house on an elevated site so as to benefit from wide views; create an indirect approach road that winds through the forest so as to progressively isolate the visitor from the noise and distractions of the city and the public road; carefully orchestrate the sudden discovery of the house and the view that it enjoys; dispose the more practical and down-to-earth components of the villa – vegetable garden, greenhouses, dairy – simply and functionally, in less visible locations; and locate floral and decorative gardens so as to create a spectacular or elegant *mise en scène* (chosen according to the main aesthetic philosophy – picturesque or beautiful – that has been adopted for the villa and its grounds). In architecture, Downing favoured, in place of the Palladian buildings of another era, Gothic and rustic styles (which relate well to the picturesque approach), along with Greek and Roman neoclassicism and the Italian style (which are appropriate to the aesthetic of the beautiful).[52]

Loudon proposed a third vision of the garden, one he called *gardenesque*. In this approach, "all the trees and shrubs ... are arranged in regard to their kinds and dimensions," and planted at distances that will "best display the natural form and habit of each: while, at the same time, ... unity of expression and of character are aimed at, and attained, as effectually as they were under any other school."[53]

All these philosophies of the garden eventually found their way to Canada. In general, garden design in Canadian villas long remained faithful to the romantic and pastoral inspirations typical of the eighteenth century – the ideal of the beautiful – while gradually absorbing ideas from both the picturesque and the gardenesque approaches as the nineteenth century progressed.

Villas of Quebec City

At Quebec City, the wood industry reached its apogee during the years 1804 to 1850, inciting the *timber barons* and the new bourgeoisie associated with banks and other thriving businesses to demonstrate their wealth and social position by creating a *golden age of villas* (1830–60).[54] For their grand estates, these new magnates chose cliff-top sites west of the city, facing either the St. Lawrence River on the southern margin of the Quebec plateau or the valley of the St. Charles on the north side. By purchasing the lands of old religious orders or of individuals in the community of Sillery and the adjoining suburbs, they appropriated the most spectacular and strategic sites of the Quebec region, according to France Gagnon Pratte, author of the definitive book on the subject.[55] Their villas exemplify the image, promoted by Downing and his colleagues, of a "classic architecture set in a pictorially composed landscape." But this British and American influence was "constrained and modified by the French presence." Since an architectural and artistic tradition had already existed in Quebec for centuries, the villas of the *vieille province* had their own unique signature.[56]

Bois-de-Coulonge

The most spectacular of the Quebec City villas was *Bois-de-Coulonge,* built in a cliff-top setting above the St. Lawrence on a site that had once been owned by Louis d'Ailleboust de Coulonge, a former governor of New France. The project was begun in the 1780s by General Henry Powell of the British Army. Powell built his residence, which he called Powell Place, as a square symmetrical building, with a central pediment over the main entrance.[57] After a subsequent owner renamed the property *Spencer Wood* in 1811, it was purchased in 1835 by wealthy lumber merchant Henry Atkinson, who added colonnades to east and west of the structure, linking the central nucleus to two pavilions at the ends of a linear composition – a classic Palladian ensemble. Atkinson, the president of the Quebec Horticultural Society, aided by his Scottish-born landscape gardener Peter Lowe, also carried out an elaborate landscape plan that fully exploited his 80-hectare site and its splendid views towards the south shore.

9.5   View to the river from the nineteenth-century formal garden at Bois-de-Coulonge, Quebec City. The formal Palladian building that once stood on the platform from which this photograph was taken burned down in the 1960s as its predecessor had done a century before. It has not been replaced, and a simple hedge designates its previous location. In the building's nineteenth-century heyday, the view to the river would have been unobstructed by the trees seen in this photograph.

The design of the area immediately adjacent to the house included flower gardens and specimen trees laid out according to gardenesque ideals. This classic garden included a formal parterre organized around a central circular fountain; a *shade avenue* bordered by trees on both sides; an orchard, stables, and greenhouses to supply tropical plants and exotic fruits. The space between building and cliff edge was occupied by an immense lawn used as pastureland, with irregularly scattered trees, native and ornamental, its limits defined by the native forest of the cliff, composed primarily of sugar maples and red oaks. Behind the house towards Chemin Saint-Louis, a maple forest formed a visual and psychological barrier between villa and city. The access road entered the grounds at the guardian's house or lodge, passed by the fields that provided sustenance to the establishment, and then became a long, formal avenue, carved through the forest to dramatize the transition. Atkinson integrated a number of recreational facilities into the domain: a bowling green, grass-surfaced tennis court, and croquet pitch, along with aviaries for the study of birds. A network of curved paths gave access to the various wooded and open sectors of the site and followed the edge of the cliff, where a "tea room" and *belvedere*, or overlook, provided excellent lateral views up and down the river towards Sillery and the Île d'Orléans.[58]

The garden of Spencer Wood/Bois-de-Coulonge was famous. Even Loudon, in his *Gardener's Magazine* and *Encyclopedia of Gardening*, praised it as a triumph of Canadian gardening. And in 1850, the government of Canada purchased the villa and made it the residence of the governor general.[59] The house burned down in 1860 but was rebuilt and, following Confederation in 1867, served as the residence of Quebec's lieutenant governors until its destruction by a second fire in 1966. It regained its historic name of Bois-de-Coulonge in 1950.

Cataraqui

If the Bois-de-Coulonge is impressive for its grand scale, its formal symmetry, and its splendid spatial composition, the *Maison Cataraqui* located at Sillery, one kilometre to the west on the same plateau, is an elegant and subtle jewel. Perfectly integrated with its site, which slopes downwards to the cliff edge, this villa follows the same compositional structure as its monumental neighbour, but at a greatly reduced scale (the total site area is about 12 hectares) and with a more intimate ambiance. James Bell Forsyth, also a lumber merchant and a participant in several other enterprises of the time, founded Cataraqui around 1831 and spent the next ten years developing its buildings and gardens. Forsyth named the estate in honour of his native city, Kingston (located at the meeting point of rivers and lakes, *Cataracoui* in Iroquois). The second proprietor, Henry Burstall, a relative of Forsyth's and a successful merchant, began building a new country house in 1850, relying on the talents of Edward Stavely, member of a distinguished family of architects who had designed several projects of this type.[60] A simple neoclassical "box" of two stories at the beginning, fronted by an elegant colonnade facing the river, the house and its garden evolved gradually through a series of extensions and elaborations,

182 CHALLENGES OF AN URBAN AND INDUSTRIAL LANDSCAPE

9.6 Maison Cataraqui, Sillery, QC

directed by a series of proprietors and carried out by a succession of highly skilled gardeners. The ensemble thus created is recognized as a masterpiece of its genre.

One of the proprietors, Charles Eleazar Levey, built several extensions in 1866 and added large greenhouses at the rear of the house in 1880. To design the gardens of Cataraqui, he engaged landscape gardener Peter Lowe, who had already worked at Bois-de-Coulonge. Lowe guided the development and maintenance of the Cataraqui gardens for forty years, embellishing the area adjacent to the house with shrubs and flowering vines, and planting large trees on the slope in front of it.[61] In 1905, the villa passed into the hands of the Rhodes family, who occupied it until 1972. Adoptive daughter Catherine, an artist, and her husband, the painter Percyval Tudor-Hart, long assured the maintenance of the buildings and gardens. They entrusted this work to gardeners George Penney and Toussaint-Emmanuel Le Pennec, long-term employees like their predecessor Peter Lowe, and to the Scottish-born landscape architect Mary Stewart, who designed the rock gardens situated along the cliff-edge path, a project carried out in the 1930s.[62]

A visit to the villa indicates that the site has been organized according to the precepts Downing announced for the picturesque garden. A miniature lodge marks the entrance from the Chemin de Cap Rouge. The approach road, straight at

PUBLIC AND PRIVATE GARDENS OF THE NINETEENTH CENTURY 183

first, then meandering, passes through a forested area. One then arrives at a broad clearing and sees an angular view of the house, located on a slightly raised natural terrace. Going around the house, one sees that the façade is oriented to a grassy slope, fairly steep, that descends to the south. The slope, with interspersed large evergreen and deciduous trees, ends at the edge of a wooded cliff face that falls abruptly to the level of the river, 50 metres below. Gardens and buildings evolved continuously; diverse elements appeared and disappeared over the years. Despite these modifications, Cataraqui has retained the essence of its original character to the present day. Among the grand villas created in the environs of Quebec City during this golden age, it is the only one that has been thoroughly conserved.[63]

Villas in Ontario

In the 1830s, on the promontory of Burlington Heights in Hamilton, at the western extremity of Lake Ontario, Sir Allan Napier MacNab (1798–1862), soldier, businessman, and politician,[64] built a grand Italian-style villa, Dundurn Castle. A flamboyant character, MacNab chose a unique site to realize his dream of creating, in the New World, a castle worthy of his Scottish ancestors. He had the benefit of a stunning perspective looking towards Burlington Bay and, beyond, the whole length of Lake Ontario until it merged with the horizon. From the site, he could also view vestiges of First Nations settlements and of fortifications from the War of 1812–14, during which – while still an adolescent – he had played a distinguished

9.7   City façade of Dundurn Castle, Hamilton, ON

9.8 Dundurn Castle façade towards Burlington Bay and Lake Ontario, drawn by Robert Wetherell, architect

role. The irregular landform of his property recalled the Scottish Highlands, the scene of so many of the historical novels that dominated the literature of the period. Several mature oaks and an orchard were deployed about the generally open plateau; the cliff was densely wooded then as it is now.[65]

It would be hard to find a better place for a villa.[66] MacNab and his architect and landscape gardener, Robert Wetherell, were able to exploit the site to maximum advantage. They located the castle, or principal building, at the site most favoured to exploit the views and to permit a gradual approach across the promontory from the main road, to ensure the progressive discovery of the site elements according to the classic scenario. Wetherell chose to locate the entrance to the main house on its "city façade," facing the main road, unlike the villas we have seen at Quebec City. On the opposite face of the building, the dining room and a grand gallery looked out on the garden, the slope to the cliff edge, and the lake. This dichotomy was reinforced by the differing architectural character of the two façades: that facing the city was formal and solemn in contrast to the garden façade, enlivened with playful, irregular towers. Several secondary buildings in various styles were located at various points on the site: stables, pigeon house, and gardener's lodge. William Reid conceived these features,[67] along with a *cockpit* – a small neoclassical pavilion – in precarious equilibrium at the edge of the cliff. The principal tree groupings served to conceal the estate from the main road and to frame a great

PUBLIC AND PRIVATE GARDENS OF THE NINETEENTH CENTURY 185

lawn on the garden side, decorated with floral planting beds in the gardenesque idiom. Further along the plateau was an extensive kitchen garden, organized geometrically around a central fountain and enclosed by a rustic fence reinforced with a hedge of hawthorn and privet. This walled garden was apparently inspired by traditional Scottish landscape practice.[68] Twenty years later, in 1856–57, MacNab decided to modify his landscape by realigning the approach road and adding two new formal terraces. To carry out these modifications, he turned to George Laing (1808–1871), a Scottish-born landscape gardener who had acquired an excellent reputation working on the great estates of the Scottish aristocracy before emigrating to Canada in 1856.[69]

Today, almost all the buildings and structures at Dundurn Castle still exist, along with the major visual effects of the landscape treatment. According to Janet Wright of Parks Canada, "In terms of exterior design, plan, and landscape setting, Dundurn represents the most comprehensive statement of the Picturesque values of Canadian architecture … it surpassed in scale and in lavishness and sophistication of design anything previously known to the young colony."[70]

Southwestern Ontario abounded with propitious sites for villas and experts to create them. In the village of Ancaster, 10 kilometres west of Hamilton, George Laing designed the gardenesque landscape setting for Woodend Villa, a residence constructed in the rural Gothic style for the reeve of Wentworth County, on a site adjoining the escarpment.[71] Further west again, in London, the villa and the gardens of Eldon House (1834), built for the district treasurer, look out grandly on the Thames River from their commanding cliff-top perch.[72] At the cliff's edge, a small hexagonal pavilion exploits views down to the valley; such pavilions, which recall the "follies" in eighteenth-century English gardens, became a common vernacular form in nineteenth-century North America under such names as "gazebo," "garden house," and "summerhouse."[73]

The Cottage Orné

The heyday of these spectacular villas occurred simultaneously with that of a number of smaller houses and gardens of more modest aspirations, located primarily in suburban rather than natural milieus. Inspired by the traditional English rural cottage and representing an idealization of rural life, these houses were known as *cottages ornés*.[74] The buildings were characterized by a low profile, typically a one-and-a-half-storey configuration; a square plan, or an irregular cross, under a roof sloping down in all four directions (and often incorporating dormer windows); long verandas on one or more sides, supported by slender columns, sometimes trellised, with decoratively carved eaves. French doors ensured the integration of interior and exterior. The proximity of ground floor to grade level and their gentle roof slopes "anchored these houses to the ground."[75] This picturesque and refined architecture also recalled certain colonial forms brought from overseas, as we have seen at the Manoir Montmorency on a larger scale (chapter 5).

The western districts of Quebec City offer many excellent examples of the *cottage orné*. At Sillery, the Villa Bagatelle (or Spencer Cottage) is a virtual personification

186 CHALLENGES OF AN URBAN AND INDUSTRIAL LANDSCAPE

9.9 Villa Bagatelle, Sillery, QC. This photo shows the results of a recent restoration of the garden based on the design principles of the original garden.

of the irregular, picturesque cottage. Henry Atkinson lived there from 1850, after renting and later selling his grand villa Bois-de-Coulonge (Spencer Wood) to the government. The neo-Gothic style of the cottage was strongly influenced by the precepts of Andrew Jackson Downing.[76] Its original garden, realized by Peter Lowe, corresponded to the British tradition of the floral *cottage garden*.[77]

Closer to the city centre, on Grande Allée, the main street of Upper Town, the Henry-Stuart House is a classic example of this genre. Sheltered by immense ashes and maples, the house is approximately square in plan and largely symmetrical. Its four roof slopes, interrupted by dormers, curve out to create verandas on the four sides of the building. Built in about 1849 for Maria Curry, the wife of William Henry, the house was occupied from 1918 until 1987 by two sisters, Adele and Mary Stuart, descendants of the celebrated writer Philippe Aubert de Gaspé (see chapter 4) and of members of Quebec City's anglophone bourgeoisie.[78] The house's picturesque garden retains its original cachet. Inside its wooden fence, the front garden consists of a green landscape setting of trees, shrubs, and traditional ground covers. The rear garden is composed of flower beds, footpaths, and a rose garden featuring yellow *floribundas* gaily climbing over a wooden tunnel. Owner Adele Stuart redesigned a part of the garden in the 1930s, in collaboration with the Scottish landscape architect Mary Stewart, and maintained the garden for many decades.[79]

Colborne Lodge, the residence of architect John Howard, built in 1830 west of downtown Toronto, was also an expression of the *cottage orné* stylistic influence. The house, situated within a domain of 66 hectares that Howard named *High Park*, looked out on Lake Ontario from a promontory framed by two ravines. The integration of the building with its site, a typical objective of this type of cottage, was assured by the low-profile format of its two storeys, by French doors, by a minimal change of level between ground surface and gallery, and, finally, by the projection of the living room via a large bay window out into the veranda, which benefited from a splendid view towards the south.[80] Howard conserved the existing forest on most of the site and integrated several symbolic elements into the garden, including an impressive tomb for his wife and himself, encircled by a fence that had once enclosed St. Paul's Cathedral in London.[81] Howard, an accomplished artist and Toronto's most important architect throughout the period 1830–60, left many watercolours of the picturesque and romantic features of his estate and nearby properties, including Grenadier Pond, Lovers' Lane, and the Old Indian Path.[82]

The Last of the Seigneurs

The nineteenth century brought to Canada a unique and surprising fusion of two residential archetypes: the *seigneurial manor* and the *picturesque villa*. The traditional system of land tenure in New France was to experience a last golden age during its final years, before coming to an end in 1854 with the abolition of the seigneuries by the government of the united province of Canada.

The Domaine Joly-De Lotbinière at Pointe-Platon, west of Quebec City on the south shore of the St. Lawrence, is an outstanding example of this cohabitation. It was founded by Julie-Christine, heiress of the Chartier de Lotbinière seigneury, and her French-born husband, Pierre-Gustave Joly, named by his wife as manager of the estate.[83] In 1851, on the heights of the Platon, the couple built a splendid two-storey residence, equipped with galleries at both levels to enjoy the striking views out towards the river. They called their home the Maison de l'Érable (Maple House), a name mirrored by maple-leaf motifs worked into the gallery balustrades.[84] Their son, Sir Henri-Gustave Joly de Lotbinière (1829–1908), continued their project and assumed the title of seigneur. Dedicated to conservation, reforestation, and the wise management of forest resources, Sir Henri served on the executive of many associations devoted to the improvement of agriculture and forestry. In 1883, he initiated the celebration of Arbor Day in Quebec (see chapter

8). Ably assisted by his son Edmond-Gustave, he proceeded with the landscape development of the domain, while simultaneously carrying out on the site a series of experiments in scientific sylviculture. Father and son created an elegant formal parterre, on the river side of the house, and a wooden pavilion, the *Nid des Amoureux* (Lovers' Nest), at the edge of the riverbank. An orchard, extensive kitchen garden, and greenhouse for the cultivation of grapevines were among their other initiatives for the site.[85] Along the entrance road, they planted long rows of deciduous trees, which are now enormous: Lombardy poplars, sugar maples that merged with the native forests, American beeches, and red oaks. They also planted thousands of non-native black walnuts, from various sources. Some of these original trees still exist today, and their descendants are well established. The domain was a lively centre of activities, particularly during the summer, when members of the family, their friends, and their associates arrived by boat from Quebec City.[86]

The Canadian Jefferson

The classic example of the conflation of seigneury and picturesque villa was certainly the Manoir-Papineau, situated on the crest of a low hill overlooking the Ottawa River, halfway between Montreal and Ottawa. Its creator was Louis-Joseph Papineau (1786–1871), the dominant personality of Canadian politics of the era. Papineau called his estate *Monte-Bello*, which means "beautiful mountain" in Italian. This name strangely resembles that which another distinguished politician gave to his domain in a similar setting: *Monticello* (little mountain), the Palladian-inspired villa that was built in the foothills of the Blue Ridge Mountains of western Virginia, between 1768 and 1810, by Thomas Jefferson (1743–1826), third president of the United States.[87]

It was surely no accident that the two residences and their landscape settings bore similar names and followed similar design prototypes. The parallels between their two creators are striking. Both were sons of surveyors who had acquired property and become patricians; in Papineau's case, the old seigneury of the Petite Nation des Algonquins, the largest and most distant of all the lands ceded by the colonial government in the seventeenth century. Both were lawyers, both entered politics at an early age,[88] dedicating themselves to the reform of non-representative colonial systems of government, first through parliamentary means and then through more drastic measures.[89] Both exercised great influence on the critical issues facing their country and saw their desires for change realized, though the manner in which these changes were achieved differed greatly.[90] When their revolutions ended, both spent many years abroad, again in very different capacities.[91] And both spent their final years at their villas in the hills, one in the piedmont of the Appalachians, the other in the Laurentian foothills, occupying themselves with their estates and their gardens. Respected by all, they became the *éminences grises* of their respective societies, and since both were men of letters, each accumulated the largest private collection of books in his country. The parallels extended to their private lives: both created small domestic universes within their buildings and landscapes, carefully integrated with the natural environment.[92]

Shortly after his return from exile in 1845, following a general amnesty, Papineau began the creation of his little universe at Petite-Nation. He located the main house on the *beau mont* of Cap Bonsecours, exploiting a splendid view of the Ottawa River and the fertile agricultural plain to the south. Designed by Papineau himself and realized by architect Louis Aubertin, the house was an eclectic composition of a main Anglo-Norman central block flanked by quasi-Gothic towers. Visitors who approached the villa from the main road entered the site through a stone portal, immediately beside the gardener's lodge, a small neo-Gothic *cottage orné*. They then followed the *allée seigneuriale*, a winding approach road that passed through the Laurentian forest dominated by sugar maples and red oak. The road traversed a carefully orchestrated spatial sequence, crossing a stream, opening up into a clearing around the family's funeral chapel, and passing through dense forest. Finally, on an angular view towards rising ground, visitors made their first discovery of the manor house.

9.10 Manoir-Papineau, Montebello, QC, seen across the Ottawa River. This and the following photograph were taken by Ramsay Traquair, professor of architecture at McGill University, an admirer and student of "the old architecture of Quebec."

Papineau's oldest son, Louis-Joseph Amédée (1819–1903), played a central role in the creation of the villa and its gardens.[93] Father and son's common interest in gardens had a long history: during their exile in the United States following the abortive rebellion of 1837, the whole family visited upstate New York's Hyde Park villa and its gardens, designed by Belgian-American landscape gardener André Parmentier and greatly admired by Andrew Jackson Downing (see chapter 8). Amédée was fascinated by this magic milieu and by the landscape of the Hudson Valley, where a majestic watercourse flowed between steep wooded slopes and broad plateaus. This landscape provided a magnificent setting for the villas of a number of prominent American families and inspired an important artistic movement, the Hudson Valley School of romantic landscape painting.[94] Judging by the numerous resemblances between the two projects, one may suppose that Hyde Park served as an inspiration for the design of the overall site of Montebello.[95] Amédée was a great amateur of landscape architecture, and this predilection had been sharpened by his many visits to gardens and natural sites in the United States and Canada. His extensive knowledge of native trees and interest in botany, combined with his wide reading of romantic literature (a sort of literary equivalent of the picturesque movement)[96] and close familiarity with Downing's writings, made him the ideal person to work on the design of Montebello. His father jokingly chided him for his enthusiastic interest in the American garden writer. Through Amédée, the influence of Downing was visible everywhere within the domain: in the rustic benches distributed here and there; in the many paths that invited the visitor to explore and appreciate the estate; in the picturesque secondary buildings that played a number of symbolic and functional roles.[97] Amédée seems to

9.11　Tea house at Manoir-Papineau, Montebello, QC

PUBLIC AND PRIVATE GARDENS OF THE NINETEENTH CENTURY　191

have been perfectly content with the results of his efforts and those of his father: "It is the most beautiful site and the most handsome country house in Canada."[98]

Birth of the Garden Suburb

It was only a step from the free-standing villa to the *garden suburb*. The first of these was built on a unique site with a unique view – a luxury of the very rich or powerful. The second, a preplanned "district of villas," was laid out on an irregular and often wooded site of irregular topography. Its goal: to provide a villa-like experience for the upper middle class, a much larger segment of the population. In the cities of the second half of the nineteenth century, a time of constant demographic and economic growth, this class of the citizenry was in rapid expansion.

In a sense, Sillery already was a garden suburb, laid out on a grand scale. A broad sector west of downtown Quebec City attracted some forty villas of the anglophone and francophone elites of the *vieille capitale*, distributed along winding lanes through the wooded glades along the clifftops. But these were large traditional villas. The site of the Bois-de-Coulonge measured 80 hectares, that of Cataraqui 12, and these villas were autonomous in many ways so that their distance from the city was not a handicap. As soon as reliable and inexpensive public transportation brought such sites within reach of city centres, a new opportunity presented itself: divide up these attractive natural sites into smaller lots of 0.5 to 1.5 hectares; provide access to them via a new network of roads, curving and elegant like the old country roads already in place (to maintain the bucolic atmosphere); and sell the lots to well-off residents of the central city who wanted to live in a more natural environment and to escape the constant pressure of the rapidly expanding commerce and industry in the city.

Such was the case in Toronto, the largest city of Canada West, which already boasted a population of 30,000 inhabitants at the beginning of the 1850s and was in full expansion mode throughout the decade.[99] To the northeast of the city limits, on a high plateau dissected by two deep wooded ravines and close to the site where Simcoe had built his villa Castle Frank in 1793, several influential city residents had already established themselves on large properties. The family of Sheriff William Jarvis occupied some 44 hectares richly endowed with cedars, maples, oaks, and aspens,[100] along with the wild roses that gave their name to the Jarvis home: Rosedale.[101] Several other estates, similar in size and character, shared the plateau. All were adorned with gardens and fruit trees, and well located to exploit views of the ravines or towards the Don River Valley to the east.[102] In 1854, Jarvis sold most of his land to developers who subdivided it according to a plan prepared by surveyor John Stoughton Dennis, submitted to the city under the name "Rose-Park." The development included sixty-two lots, from 0.3 to 1.6 hectares in area, most of them irregular in shape to conform to the uneven topography. The lots were laid out along curving roads, also carefully integrated into the landscape.[103] Subsequently, other developers divided up the rest of the plateau into parcels of varied dimensions, creating a complex of residential subdivisions known collectively as Rosedale. Almost thirty subdivision plans were filed between 1854 and 1910.[104]

9.12　Map of Rosedale Garden Suburb, Toronto. Beginning at the northern limit of Toronto's Park Lots, Rosedale was located on a plateau dissected by scenic ravines and bordered on the east by the Don River Valley. Following 1850, the large villas and gardens built to take advantage of the views towards these natural features gave way to a network of curving roads serving smaller villas on smaller lots, maintaining the original natural character of the milieu.

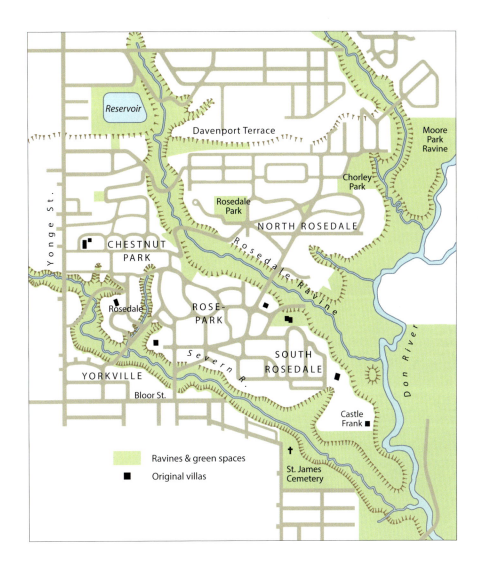

Rosedale thus became one of the first Canadian examples of the garden suburb, a new urban form that resembled a village of little villas, each with its own garden. The fact that Rosedale was laid out by several designers at intervals, over a period of decades, provided the district with a certain variety in road configuration, lot size and form, and dwelling type; yet all these features were integrated to create a coherent ambiance, wooded and tranquil.[105] The neighbourhood also benefited from a diversity of architectural styles – all of the rich panoply of the Victorian period – as well as from a certain demographic diversity.[106] This variety – complemented by its sensitive integration into the natural environment of plateau and ravine – helped to make Rosedale a successful community and a template for the upscale garden suburbs that would be built in other Canadian cities in the late nineteenth and early twentieth centuries.

10.1 Notre-Dame-des-Neiges
       Cemetery, Montreal

10

Taming the Industrial City:
City Parks and Rural Cemeteries

As we have seen in previous chapters, many of the deficiencies of the nineteenth-century commercial cities were corrected by the creation of such traditional urban components as squares and *places*, and of new public gardens. But by the middle of the century, a new challenge awaited those cities. The invention of innovative technologies for the production and transportation of goods, together with the ascendancy of large companies whose giant factories employed thousands of people, began to transform Canadian cities into industrial centres. This industrialization inspired rapid urbanization, to which municipal authorities responded by inventing several new types of public space that had never existed before. The process began with *public* and *private parks* of intermediate scale, followed by *rural cemeteries*, which functioned – surprisingly – as places for public recreation. These facilities, in turn, inspired another type of public space, the *large urban park*, natural and romantic in character. The adoption and evolution of these innovative new spaces occurred at breakneck speed, entirely transforming cities over a period of only a few decades.

The construction of the Lachine Canal in southwestern Montreal, begun in 1829, signalled the start of the industrial revolution in Canada. Capitalizing on the potential of this maritime route to the centre of the continent, Montreal vaulted into the role of Canada's first industrial city, becoming the production centre for a wide range of manufactured products.[1] Other cities followed rapidly, first in the East – Quebec City, Toronto, Halifax, Saint John, Hamilton – and then everywhere in the country. Canada inexorably transformed itself from an essentially rural society to a predominantly urban one. This transformation, however, created new stresses and problems: poverty and social dislocation, destruction of the natural environment, air and water pollution, and the separation of cities from their lakes and rivers by a swath of industrial sites and railroads.

Canada's First Public Parks

The squares, *places*, and public gardens that had served compact commercial cities very well in the first decades of the nineteenth century (1800–40) proved inadequate to satisfy the public-space needs of the rapidly expanding cities of the industrial era. Towards 1850, in response to these new needs, several municipal administrations across Canada established public parks of considerably larger size than their previously existing public spaces, following different aesthetic models and programmatic requirements from those of the small squares of the central city. Located on public lands at the edge of their cities' built-up areas, these new parks measured about 5 to 10 hectares on average. This was a major increase over the city squares of previous years, the largest of which occupied some 1.5 to 2 hectares. Another important difference: the new parks provided facilities for a wide range of recreational activities, whereas the squares and *places* had been essentially passive.

Jack Wright of the University of Ottawa places the birth of this first generation of Canadian parks *before* the main impact of industrialization and urbanization struck the nation's cities. He suggests that these parks were not created as a reaction to urban conditions in Canada, but were instead a transplanting of the new park ideas that were already popular overseas, mainly in Great Britain, ravaged by industrialization and its associated degradation since the last years of the eighteenth century. Since the 1840s, national authorities in Britain had adopted laws encouraging municipalities to create new parks,[2] and the overseas echoes of these events may have inspired the Canadian parks movement, which was almost contemporaneous with that in Great Britain.[3]

Wright identified City Park in Kingston, on Lake Ontario, as the first park of this type to be created in Ontario.[4] During Kingston's brief reign as the capital of Canada, at the beginning of the 1840s, the governor general, Lord Sydenham, assembled land close to the lake on the west side of the city as a site for the future Parliament of Canada. When the government moved the capital to Montreal in 1844, the citizens of Kingston demanded that the 10-hectare property be transformed into a park "for the health and convenience of the inhabitants."[5] The property transfer indeed took place, and work on the park was begun in 1854, following the plans of a landscape gardener from Rochester, New York, on the other side of Lake Ontario. The designer's name has since been lost, but the most likely candidate seems to be Frederick J.M. Cornell, a Rochester native who designed Kingston's rural cemetery of Cataraqui during the same period (see below).[6]

The design of this large municipal park, which has seen little change up until the present day,[7] was the utmost in simplicity. It consisted of a vast lawn, slightly sloping in the direction of the lake and surrounded by large trees. The lawn was divided by an east-west road into a primarily ornamental southern sector, for casual recreation, and a northern sector that accommodated sports facilities, including a cricket field. Carriage roads and paths provided access to the site and encouraged promenades on foot, in vehicles, and on horseback. At the centre of the site, a wooden observatory served as a landmark and point of convergence. In

10.2 City Park with statue of Sir John A. Macdonald, Kingston, ON

later years, a monument in honour of Canada's first prime minister, Sir John A. Macdonald, a Kingston resident early in his career, was erected at the southeast corner of the park. An elegant residential district gradually built up around the park, as happened adjacent to many parks of similar vintage.

Other parks of this type were far more elaborate. Among these was Victoria Park in London, Ontario, which featured an ambitious horticultural display, without, however, rivalling the public gardens – such as the Halifax Public Gardens – where horticulture was the central *raison d'être*. Victoria Park stood on a vestige of London's old military garrison lands, close to the downtown area. In 1874, with the military role of the garrison no longer pertinent, the British government ceded a part of the site to the city for use as a park.[8] In common with almost all the new landscape projects of the time, Victoria Park was designed by a professional, in this case Charles Miller. Miller had begun his career as a nurseryman in Philadelphia, before distinguishing himself as the director of horticulture for the great world exhibition held in the city in 1876, in celebration of the centenary of the founding of the United States. When the exhibition closed, Miller turned his hand to landscape design.[9] In his plan for Victoria Park in London, prepared in 1878, the formalism of the park's general layout – including a central *rond-point* and bandstand – reminds us of the *places* and squares of an earlier generation, but as noted by Nancy Z. Tausky, "These are subordinate to the naturalistic impression created by the curving paths, irregularly shaped gardens, and seeming randomness of the larger plantings."[10] And despite the elaborate and *gardenesque* character of Miller's planting, the park was really a *multi-functional open space*, given the presence of equipment for active recreation and its year-long period of operations. In winter, the city decorated each of the large conifers around the skating rink, creating the ambiance of a whole series of Christmas trees.[11] The park was large enough to permit carriage driveways, a popular way of experiencing the green spaces of the time. Miller also took advantage of the undulating topography of the park to insert a *lily pond* illuminated by electricity.[12]

Other municipalities also welcomed the opportunities offered by abandoned military sites as potential locations for new parks. In 1874, Major's Hill Park became the first public park in Ottawa, benefiting from magnificent views of the Parliament Buildings and the Rideau Canal. It was a lively, colourful, and eclectic park, filled with compositional elements and objects in a variety of styles, including gardenesque flower beds, sculptures, and a picturesque garden pavilion on the edge of the cliff. As in Victoria Park in London, a pond played a major role in defining the personality of the park. The ruins of the old house of Colonel By, the officer who directed the construction of the Rideau Canal, continue to occupy a small corner of this site, which looks out upon his great achievement.[13]

Parks of this size and type sprang up everywhere during the years from 1850 to 1880, in smaller centres as well as in big cities. The Ontario government's 1883 adoption of a law encouraging the creation of parks only accelerated an already-

10.3 Plan of Victoria Park, London, ON. Charles H. Miller, horticulturist and landscape designer, 1878

10.4 Major's Hill Park, Ottawa, c. 1900

established trend.[14] But although this generation of parks added greatly to the viability of towns and cities, their still modest dimensions were insufficient to satisfy the need for open space and greenery of the still growing populations of the cities of the industrial era. And although they were, when established, at the peripheries of their cities' built-up area, continuing urbanization soon surrounded them, limiting their potential for expansion. Inevitably, this enclosure by buildings made the new intermediate parks feel like urban places and not like areas of wild nature in the city. To provide this kind of open-space experience, a whole new range of solutions was needed.

Private Parks: The Age of the Entrepreneur

Private parks offered one response to this unsatisfied demand. Throughout the second half of the nineteenth century and almost up until the present day, imaginative entrepreneurs provided urban populations the chance to enjoy a variety of recreational activities in attractive natural surroundings. Vauxhall Gardens and Battersea Park on the Thames in London, England, served as prototypes for this type of park. Like their models, the Canadian versions were often located on bodies of water, a sure way to enhance their commercial success. In 1882, two private parks on the banks of the Red River, south of Winnipeg's city centre, opened their gates: River Park on the west shore and Elm Park on the east, both located on wooded sites. The promoter was the owner of a tramway line that linked the parks to downtown,[15] an astute strategy that flourished in a number of cities. In Victoria, the British Columbia Electric Company inaugurated, in 1906, an amusement park called Gorge Park (also known as Tramway Park) on a beautiful site along an arm of the sea, at the end of its streetcar line. The ideal spot for picnics and country outings, the park featured many attractions, including a Japanese tea house and garden.[16]

Similar parks served residents of Toronto. Lorne Park, west of the city on Lake Ontario, accessible by boat from downtown, and the Beaches, a series of amusement parks and leisure facilities scattered along the natural lake beaches east of the downtown area, including Kew Gardens, accommodated crowds of visitors for many decades.[17]

In east-end Montreal on the shores of the St. Lawrence River, Sohmer Park delighted city residents from 1889 to 1919 with its unique combination of music in a verdant milieu, a pavilion magically illuminated by electricity, and a carrousel, among other attractions.[18] Later, Dominion Park, further east but still on the river, and Belmont Park, on the northern shore of Montreal Island, facing the Rivière des Prairies at Cartierville, continued the tradition, the latter until 1983.

Private parks certainly offered a partial response to the public's need for open space and facilities for recreation and enjoyment, but they were not a complete solution. They were too small and too expensive, and there was conflict between the activities and facilities that made money for the owners and those that were more likely to satisfy the needs of the population. Moreover, the parks sometimes raised questions of public morality; some cities were reluctant to expose their residents to activities involving alcoholic beverages, for example, or games of chance, considered (by some) to be in defiance of social norms. And finally, many of these parks emphasized activities that, while exciting and frenetic, provided little in the way of peaceful, natural environments for the spiritual sustenance of their citizens. Then, in the 1840s and 1850s, from an unsuspected direction, a new urban phenomenon gained prominence and began to satisfy this need for natural places.

Rural Cemeteries

Surprisingly, the first effective solution to the problem of open space in large cities came from an institution that was little associated with recreation in the natural milieu: the cemetery. A new kind of cemetery was beginning to replace the traditional model, which had usually been located in a churchyard, in a crypt under the church floor, or in an "Old Burying Ground" near the centre of town. In country villages or small, compact pre-industrial towns, such traditional landscapes were often pleasant and bucolic, but in the middle of large cities, rapidly expanding under the impact of industrialization, such cemeteries were subject to serious problems of space and public health. Many urban cemeteries had become

10.5 Mount Royal Cemetery, Montreal. This mid-nineteenth-century landscape demonstrates the classic features of the rural cemetery that were so attractive to the urban populations of the time: undulating topography, clumps of large shade trees, well-kept lawns, colourful planting of lilacs and other decorative shrubs. These "natural" features were complemented by man-made elements including winding paths and sculptured stone monuments.

overburdened common graves, ugly and potentially dangerous. Fearful people imagined that miasmas escaping from these graveyards caused epidemics. It was time to find new ways to dispose of the dead.[19]

At the same time, a profound change in social attitudes concerning death began to call into question the traditional definition of a cemetery. Under the influence of eighteenth-century romanticism, death was more and more being seen not as the end of a life, but as the point of departure for reflection and contemplation on life.[20] Such attitudes first took hold among aristocrats and intellectuals, and then spread among the general population. Their first manifestations were seen in the integration of monuments and memorials into the great gardens of country villas, first in Britain and then in France.[21] A unique Canadian example was the McTavish Monument, a 6-metre stone column erected on the slopes of Mount Royal in 1806 in honour of the fur magnate Simon McTavish.[22] This new attitude towards death, in combination with the many practical reasons to remove cemeteries from densely populated urban areas, created a fusion of the cemetery and the garden that led to the *rural cemetery*,[23] or *garden cemetery*: a burial ground outside the city, located in a healthy and attractive natural milieu on a hill or by a body of water, in which a diversity of monuments to the departed were distributed in picturesque fashion within a pastoral landscape. Given the origins of these new rural cemeteries, it was perhaps inevitable that they would adopt the romantic villa garden (see chapter 9) as their aesthetic model and the source of their design vocabulary, ultimately inspired by the seventeenth-century paintings of Claude Lorrain and Nicolas Poussin and the pastoral landscapes of England.

The first concrete realization of this new tendency occurred at the beginning of the nineteenth century with the building of the Cimetière du Père-Lachaise on a hill to the northeast of Paris, in 1804.[24] The site, Mont-Louis, was already a formal garden, having been laid out as a Jesuit retirement community in the eighteenth century. The designers reinforced the pre-existing axial and symmetrical structure of the garden in the central sector of the site, while creating a network of winding roads and paths on the irregular topography of the hills and plateaus that surrounded it. Originally occupied by native vegetation, the cemetery was rapidly filled with numerous monuments and mausoleums that have given it the ambiance of a miniature city.[25] This new concept of the cemetery evoked a strong response among the British, who began to follow the French example in the 1820s and 1830s.[26] The romantic poet William Wordsworth noted "the softening influence of Nature" to assuage pain and "elevate the emotions."[27] John Claudius Loudon, landscape gardener and writer *extraordinaire* (see chapter 9), reinvented himself as an inspired propagandist for the rural cemetery. He designed several cemeteries in this genre and, in 1843, published an encyclopedic volume that greatly influenced the design of cemeteries throughout Britain.[28]

The new philosophy was also quick to conquer the New World. In 1829–31, the Massachusetts Horticultural Society undertook the first concrete project of this type in North America: Mount Auburn Cemetery in Cambridge, in the suburbs of Boston.[29] Situated on wooded hills, slopes, and valleys, enjoying views towards the Charles River, Mount Auburn was both an experimental garden and a rural cemetery. By integrating curving roads and paths into the irregular landforms of their site, by creating loop roads around the summits of the hills (the highest of which was surmounted by a tower, to better appreciate the view) and lakes in the hollows, the cemetery's designers[30] explicitly followed the example of Père Lachaise.[31] In ensuing years, families and individuals endowed the site with striking monuments in many styles. The philosophy and the landscape of Mount Auburn served as models for the majority of cemeteries everywhere in North America, throughout the Victorian era.[32]

Although the principles of the gardenesque and of eclectic composition were extremely popular at the time, the overall style adopted in the rural cemeteries was instead inspired by an earlier paradigm, the naturalism of the great private gardens of the eighteenth century. The character of particular cemeteries alternated between the *beautiful* and the *picturesque* versions of that tradition, according to the topography of the site in question. It was perfectly normal that rural cemeteries should adopt this prototype: several, including Père Lachaise and the Laurel Hill Cemetery in Philadelphia (1836), had been gardens before their transformation into cemeteries.[33] Thus, in the rural cemetery, the flowing lawns and carefully composed clusters of trees characteristic of the pastoral and romantic parks of

"Capability" Brown, one of the great masters of English landscape gardening in the eighteenth century,[34] trumped the overwrought flower beds and repeated stylistic mutations typical of the Victorian garden (see chapter 9). The commemorative iconography of the eighteenth-century garden, consisting of a few focal elements set in a green landscape, was amplified in the cemetery, spreading over the entire space in a spectacular and romantic *mise en scène*.

Canada's First Rural Cemeteries

The cholera and typhus epidemics that were brought to Canada's port cities from Europe during the 1830s and 1840s rapidly convinced the residents of those cities to abandon traditional methods of burial. The transfer of Montreal's Catholic cemetery from Dominion Square in 1854 (see chapter 8) was a consequence of that crisis. The decade of the 1840s saw the gradual adoption of the new philosophy of cemetery design all across Canada as municipalities and church authorities became aware of projects in the United States. There were some transitional projects. In 1833, for example, faced with the continued expansion of the city and a severe lack of space in the Old Burying Ground (chapter 5), the citizens of Halifax established Camp Hill Cemetery on a part of the old common, beside the Public Gardens. Much like the Old Burying Ground in its arrangement of grave plots in regular rows reinforced by tree alignments, the cemetery nonetheless adopted some of the precepts of the new rural model: it was located on a hill beyond the city limits, in a pastoral environment conducive to promenade and reflection.[35] In Toronto, in 1844, the St. James Anglican Cemetery moved from its downtown churchyard to a new site on the slopes of a ravine in Rosedale, on the edge of the city. The plans were prepared by architect John Howard, a ubiquitous presence in nineteenth-century Toronto.[36]

Mount Hermon Cemetery in Sillery, Quebec, was the first such facility in Canada to model itself entirely on the canons of the rural movement. Approached by the same Chemin Saint-Louis as many of the villas studied in the preceding chapter, this relatively small site (12.8 ha) was effectively designed to exploit its unique location. In fact, the site had already been developed as a villa and summer residence before the Quebec Protestant Cemetery Association purchased it in 1848, with the intent to transfer burials from downtown churchyards to an appropriate location on the outskirts of town. To design the site, the association engaged Major David Bates Douglass, a well-respected military engineer from the United States.[37] Major Douglass, a professor at the American military academy at West Point, had contributed to the design and realization of large engineering projects; he had designed, in 1838–39, the immense Green-Wood Cemetery in Brooklyn, New York, one of the "grand triumvirate of the first and most influential of American rural cemeteries."[38] Similar in topography to Green-Wood, the site of Mount Hermon Cemetery descended sharply from the plateau of Quebec, down to the edge of the cliff that overlooks the St. Lawrence. From the elegant Gothic *cottage orné* at the entrance gate – the residence of the superintendent – a single serpentine road loops its way around the site, providing access to all parts of the cemetery. The

continuous lawn that forms the ground plane is shaded by free-standing trees, often enormous: oaks, white pines, and sugar maples in particular. At the bottom of the slope, on the edge of the cliff, perspectives suddenly open up to offer long and spectacular views of the river, the city of Quebec, and the point of Lévis on the opposite shore.[39]

The charm of this new type of cemetery also inspired the Catholic population – the majority of Quebec City residents – to follow suit. After the adoption in 1855 of a law prohibiting burials within the city limits, the multi-talented architect and engineer Charles Baillairgé planned two new suburban cemeteries to serve Catholics from the francophone community: Cimetière Saint-Charles (1855), on the banks of the river for which it was named; and Belmont (1859), which enjoyed excellent views toward the Laurentians from its location on the plateau at Sainte-Foy northwest of the city.[40] On the southern margin of the plateau, adjacent to Mount Hermon, a third cemetery, St. Patrick (1879), was laid out for anglophone Catholics, principally of Irish origin. All located in natural environments that benefited

10.6 (left)   View from Mount Hermon Cemetery, looking towards the St. Lawrence River and central Quebec City

10.7 (right)   "Broken column" monument at Cataraqui Cemetery, Kingston, ON

204   CHALLENGES OF AN URBAN AND INDUSTRIAL LANDSCAPE

from attractive views, these Catholic cemeteries were nonetheless sited on flatter and more regular sites than their Protestant counterparts, and were laid out according to more formal and traditional geometries, maintaining greater continuity with the historic cemeteries of Quebec.

Whether Catholic or Protestant, all the cemeteries of this epoch were deeply concerned with *iconography*, using sculptural and architectural languages to express messages that were personal, spiritual, social, and even economic. Iconographic elements took on a great variety of forms: the standard vertical gravestones were extremely diverse in form and decoration, while the obelisk and imitation sarcophagus were used to celebrate the famous and prestigious, as were the column and the *stele*, a vertical stone slab. Occasionally, people wanted to commemorate themselves by engaging a well-known sculptor or architect. This was the case with the splendid colonnade and *aedicule* – a shelter or shrine expressed as a small classical building – designed by Baillairgé to surmount the mausoleum of William Venner at the Cimetière Saint-Charles. Mausoleums were, essentially, small buildings inspired by Greek or Egyptian temples, Gothic towers, or Renaissance palaces, constructed above underground vaults in which members of prominent families reposed.[41] Because of its resistance to the ravages of time, granite was the preferred material for sculptural and architectural compositions; limestone and marble were also frequent choices. Luckily, both granite and limestone are available almost everywhere in Canada.

In Protestant cemeteries, messages often appealed to sentiment and symbolism: a broken column to evoke a life cut short, an open book to represent a famous editor. Familiar religious symbols characterized Catholic landscapes: the cross in all its variations, Greek, Celtic, Maltese; angels; allegoric statues, including Desolation and Pain; plant motifs symbolizing the continuation of life.[42] *Calvaires*, ways of the cross, statues of the Virgin Mary and the Saints often figured as landmarks and calls to reflection. In contrast, Jewish cemeteries avoided all sculptural expression except for simple tombstones. No symbols were evident either, with the exception of the six-pointed Star of David, the familiar sign of Judaism.[43] These cemeteries have practised a rather austere tradition of commemoration; memories of the departed are warmly recalled in domestic ceremonies.[44]

Cemeteries on the "Magic Mountain"

Soon after the realization of Mount Hermon, two large cemeteries were installed on Montreal's most visible landmark, Mount Royal. Vestige of an ancient intrusion of igneous magma, this topographic feature evolved to its present form through the erosive impact of water and ice. It consists of a central hollow enclosed by mountain crests that rise to three distinct summits, before descending – abruptly on the east, gradually elsewhere – to the broad plateau that occupies the greater part of the Island of Montreal. Since the time of its first Aboriginal inhabitants, this magic mountain has always exerted an influence and a profound sense of attraction on those who frequent it. We still call it by the name given to it by Jacques Cartier in 1535, when he visited the Native village of Hochelaga, built on its slopes.

Mount Royal Cemetery

The development of the mountain for this new purpose began with the formation, in 1849, of an association that brought together several Protestant and Jewish religious communities of Montreal around the common goal of establishing a cemetery outside the city. In 1851, their group, now formalized under the name the Montreal Cemetery Company, bought a property on the mountain, and the commissioners of the company engaged James C. Sidney (c. 1819–1881) to design the cemetery for them. Experienced in this field, the English-born Sidney had worked since 1849 on the design of Laurel Hill Cemetery in Philadelphia.[45] He was a man of many talents; at different moments in his career, he had worked as an architect, civil engineer, surveyor, and mapmaker, as well as a *rural architect*, an appellation

10.8 Plan of Mount Royal Cemetery, 1852. James P. Sidney, contractor, and James P.W. Neff, architect and engineer. The central stream can be seen on the plan flowing diagonally from upper right to the cemetery entrance at bottom centre, but it is no longer evident on the site except in the latter area. The peripheral loop road is Forest Drive.

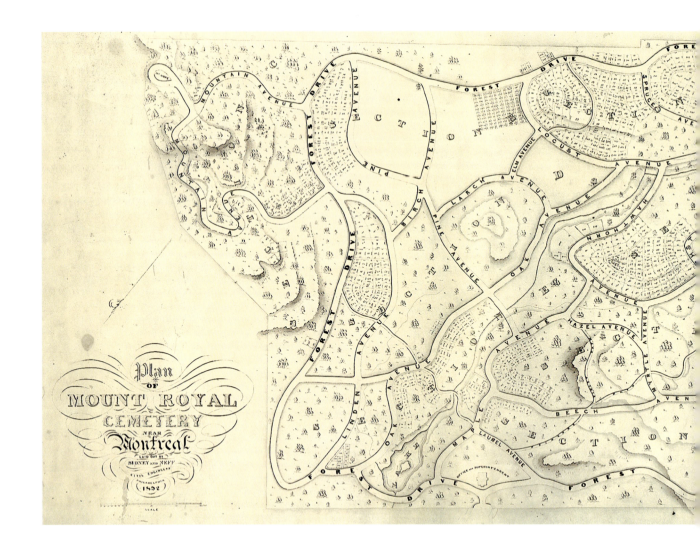

that corresponded to *landscape architect*. He would later be involved in the design of Fairmount Park in Philadelphia and of several other cemeteries.[46] Sidney rapidly drew up the plans for Mount Royal Cemetery in 1852, and then carried them out in the role of contractor, in association with James P.W. Neff, architect and engineer. The official dedication took place in 1854.[47]

The site of the cemetery, which today occupies some 70 hectares, consisted primarily of a wide concave slope in the northeastern sector of the mountain. This slope descended gently down to the plateau, framed by the eastern and northern summits of the mountain, the "Outremont summit" and "Mount Murray." Sidney understood the site and exploited it well, creating one of the best-composed large cemeteries in Canada. As a main structural element, he conserved a stream in the centre of the slope, framing the small watercourse with a road on each side and dyking off its lower extremity to create a small lake. The designer complemented this central natural feature by tracing a long and winding loop road, Forest Road, along the periphery of the site, climbing hills and descending valleys. On each side of this road, a series of smaller loop roads formed an overall lattice pattern that divided the site into some thirty cells. Within each cell, a series of gravesites was laid out in parallel curving rows; across the cells, pedestrian shortcuts provided links to the road network. The essentials of the plan were carried out in the 1850s, and its overall character is still evident.[48] A Gothic gateway and a charming waiting room, built in 1862 according to the plans of Montreal architect John William Hopkins, dramatized the entrance, along with a picturesque headquarters building, later to become the superintendent's residence.[49]

Trees and shrubs played a central role in the cemetery. In the original plan by Sidney and Neff, all the roads were named for different species of trees: linden, maple, pine, hawthorn, and so on. Even today, plant references are associated with almost all the physiographic features of the site: Rose Hill, Lilac Knoll, Oak Ridge, Pine Hill Side. Since the cemetery was created through a process of gradual insertion into an entirely wooded site, sugar maple and red oak, the two native species that most typify the flora of Mount Royal, constitute the majority of all the cemetery's trees and provide a background rhythm on which a large number of horticultural species from diverse origins strike accents and contribute their lively colourful melodies. These include Ivory Silk lilacs, gingko, mass plantings of crabapple and Amur maple, along with white pines and dawn redwood.[50]

The evolution of Mount Royal Cemetery benefited, as did Mount Hermon, from intergenerational continuity in its administration and landscape management. From 1852 to the present century, the members of several generations of the Roy family helped shape the cemetery in the role of superintendent and in other positions. Ormiston Roy succeeded his father in 1898 as the third superintendent and later occupied the post of landscape architect for the cemetery, until his death in 1958. He presided over many major changes, including the transformation from a picturesque Victorian landscape vocabulary to a new image of broad open spaces – the *lawn plan* – accomplished by the placing of memorial plaques level with the ground.[51]

Our Lady of the Snows

Right beside the Mount Royal Cemetery is its Catholic counterpart,[52] Notre-Dame-des-Neiges, officially opened by Montreal's Notre-Dame parish in 1854. The design of this cemetery is a sort of hybrid, representing a fusion of the formal tradition of New France and the romantic new wave; and the physical elements that express these two principal design philosophies are overlaid on a complex landscape consisting of several "landscape units" or physiographic zones. The cemetery's main entrance opens from Côte-des-Neiges Road onto a perfectly axial composition, focused on a familiar iconography (see chapter 4): a central cross flanked by two golden angels in an oval island framed by trees. The axis, perpendicular to the road, continues further across a flat plain, which constitutes the first landscape unit of the cemetery, via an elongated floral bed that terminates in the imposing facade of the cemetery's crypt. The crypt is masterfully integrated into a slope that defines the limits of the plain and constitutes the site's second landscape unit. At the top of this slope is a broad plateau punctuated by low hills that rise gradually to the Outremont and Montreal summits. On the plateau, another sector of the cemetery is laid out in a rectilinear pattern, parallel to the property lines of the site. The regularity of this sector is reinforced by the planting of orderly ranges of trees that follow the lines of the roads, placing this area of the cemetery within the monumental and formal tradition typical of the New World landscape plans carried out by the Sulpicians and other religious orders.[53]

But in the areas that surround and frame these highly structured central zones, we find ourselves in the most romantic of rural cemeteries. Sinuous roads are carefully integrated into the irregular topography, large trees are distributed in quasi-naturalistic fashion within the burial areas, and monuments display a great diversity of forms and dimensions. This bipartite organization recalls that of the Père-Lachaise Cemetery in Paris, where the central formal sector is surrounded by romantic, "natural" landscapes.[54]

Finally, going beyond the plateau, we come across a third landscape approach, borrowed from the rural traditions of New France: a way of the cross that climbs up to a traditional *calvaire*, located close to the Outremont summit, a landscape feature that the cemetery's historians have situated in the long tradition of the "sacred mountain," shared by classical Greece, Judaism, and Hinduism before its appropriation by the Christian religion. They have interpreted the complex overall physical structure of the cemetery as a metaphor for the Christian soul that seeks to come closer to God. The flat, open plain first distances us from the busy world of the living. The shady plateau is a place of purification. Finally, at the summit, luminous horizons proclaim the existence of a transcendent Other World.[55]

Notre-Dame-des-Neiges is certainly large enough to embrace three divergent landscape concepts. It is the largest cemetery in Canada, measuring 138 hectares in area. Almost a million people have been buried there since its original foundation in the 1840s.[56] The founders of the cemetery anticipated its important social role. Faced with the closure of their historic downtown cemeteries, the Sulpician Fathers of Notre-Dame acquired a number of farms on Mount Royal.[57] They confided

10.9 (left) Central axis of Notre-Dame-des-Neiges Cemetery, Montreal

10.10 (right) Family burial chamber in Beechwood Cemetery, Ottawa

the planning of the new cemetery to the eminent Montreal architect and surveyor Henri-Maurice Perrault (1828–1903), the nephew of John Ostell (1813–1892), Montreal's most celebrated architect of the nineteenth century.[58] It was Ostell who designed the cemetery's first buildings in 1854–55, the crypt as well as a combined chapel and superintendent's house, exploiting a picturesque site at the crown of the main slope with a building that employed appropriate Gothic detailing.[59] Perrault later designed several other pavilions, as well as a splendid gateway, erected in 1888–89.[60] Disagreeing with the cemetery's directors concerning the regularity of the layout in the central part of the plateau,[61] he configured the major romantic

CITY PARKS AND RURAL CEMETERIES 209

zones of the cemetery. Sometime around 1850, he participated in the creation of similar landscapes for the Mount Royal Cemetery, designing the serpentine road that provides access to Mount Murray.[62] In his choice of plants, Perrault preferred exotics and horticultural species to native vegetation, of which little was present on the original site. Unlike its neighbour and contemporary, Mount Royal Cemetery, the Notre-Dame Cemetery was established on lands that had already been deforested and cultivated, and was in fact a productive agricultural region well known for its gardens and orchards in the nineteenth century.[63] Today, within its distinguished landscape setting of great mature trees and spectacular and symbolic topography, Notre-Dame-des-Neiges is noted for its unique collection of commemorative architecture and statuary, the richest in Canada.

Rural Cemeteries of Ontario

The explosive expansion of Toronto in the nineteenth century put enormous pressure on all of the city's traditional cemeteries. One of these, the old Potter's Field, had been relocated in 1855 from its original urban site to the new and larger Necropolis, situated north of the city by the Rosedale Ravine. This site quickly proved insufficient, and by 1874, it was apparent that a second expansion, even larger than the first, would be needed. This led to the founding of Mount Pleasant Cemetery, 80 hectares in extent, located well outside the city limits yet easily accessible by its main north-south spine, Yonge Street.[64] Despite its name, Mount Pleasant is neither a mountain nor even a hill. It is a plateau, from which a valley descends gradually towards the southern boundary of the site, eventually merging with the network of ravines that characterizes the city of Toronto.[65] The cemetery's designer was the Ontario landscape gardener Henry A. Engelhardt (see chapter 8), originally from Germany, who had previously designed cemeteries at Port Hope and Belleville, and had published his recommendations concerning the layout and landscaping of cemeteries in his book *The Beauties of Nature Combined with Art*, issued in 1872.[66]

Engelhardt took maximum advantage of his site's irregular topography. Visitors passing through the Gothic *porte cochère* on Yonge Street were quickly directed down into the valley along a chain of lakes and cascades, paralleled by serpentine roads that blended into the irregular landforms. On the plateau, Engelhardt laid out a path system composed of regular circular curves, their intersections embellished with small planted triangles and the occasional larger roundabout at a strategic location.[67] As was often the case with landscape gardeners, Engelhardt not only designed the cemetery, but also directed the construction of the first section of 21 hectares, completed in 1876. He then continued on as superintendent until 1888.[68] The designer and his successors planted thousands of trees of more than 140 different varieties in order to create the natural ambiance that we see today. The plane surfaces of the plateau set the scene for several formal and axial compositions focusing on impressive mausoleums, the resting places of prominent Toronto families – the Eatons, the Masseys – as well as the final dwelling of thousands of more-humble but equally appreciated residents, including the cemetery's creator, Henry Engelhardt.[69]

As soon as rural cemeteries had been established in the larger urban centres, every city and town endeavoured to create one. Thus, between the years 1846 and 1900, there was a remarkable proliferation of new cemeteries, constructed on beautiful natural sites outside towns and villages everywhere in the country. Although all were inspired by a common ideal, each cemetery had its own unique personality. Cataraqui Cemetery in Kingston, which opened in 1853 in response to an epidemic of cholera that devastated the city in 1847, was among the most spectacular and romantic of all the rural cemeteries in Canada, through its masterful exploitation of the natural components of the site. These consisted of a series of small transverse swales or little valleys, oriented east-west, that traversed the long

10.11　Ross Bay Cemetery, Victoria, BC. This historic cemetery contains many family and group plots, including that of the Sisters of St. Ann, originally from Lachine, QC.

CITY PARKS AND RURAL CEMETERIES　211

rectangle of the site at right angles, draining into one main valley, oriented north-south. Several small lakes filled the low points along this valley, and a majestic canopy of conifers reigned over the whole of the site. The cemetery's designer, Frederick James Mott Cornell (1820–1868), was the son of surveyor Silas Cornell, who planned the Mount Hope Cemetery in Rochester, New York, on the opposite shore of Lake Ontario.[70]

Created in 1873, Beechwood Cemetery in Ottawa was built on a hill like most cemeteries of this generation. Precisely at its highest point stood a massive mausoleum and chapel in Gothic style, designed by architect James Mather (1833–1927)[71] and constructed, like all the other buildings of the cemetery, with the bedrock that formed the hill, Ottawa limestone. Visible in exposed outcroppings, this native stone was also used for retaining walls, division walls, stairs, and borders throughout the site. This fortunate decision assured a perfect marriage between man-made interventions and the natural environment. Robert Surtees (1835–1906), a native of England who served as Ottawa's city engineer for two decades, drew the plans for the interlacing curved paths that form the circulation system of the cemetery; these were realized on site by gardener Alpine Grant, who was the first superintendent of Cataraqui Cemetery in Kingston.

Cemeteries in Western Canada

In 1873, the West Coast city of Victoria opened Ross Bay Cemetery on a flat site along the cliff edge, looking out at the Straits of Juan de Fuca. Its planner, Edward Hallandaine (1827–1905), born in Singapore and among the first architects to set up shop in British Columbia, laid out the cemetery on an arrangement of radiating avenues emanating from a central oval.[72] The planting of Ross Bay profited from the generous climate of the southern point of Vancouver Island. Evergreens such as yews, laurels, box, and pines created an effective background for colourful flowering trees, including hawthorn, cherries, and plums.[73] The visitor is astonished to discover that the luxurious hedge that encloses the northern boundary of the site is composed of holly – a reminder of the extensive Christmas holly export business of Vancouver Island, a million-dollar industry that sent holly all over the country until the 1940s.

In Calgary, Union Cemetery was founded in 1890 on a site southeast of the city centre, across the Elbow River. This cemetery was located on a windswept hillside farm, barren of vegetation other than native grasses, overlooking plains that would soon be occupied by the expanding city. The city engineers, Childs and Wilson, planned the site. Union Cemetery began to overcome its barren appearance in 1899 with the debut of a long-term tree-planting program, and a Gothic-style mortuary chapel was erected in 1908 at the topmost point of the site. During his short term of office as parks superintendent (1911–13), Richard Iverson integrated curving paths with the existing regular plan of the cemetery and directed the construction of a stone entrance archway that soon became its symbol. His successor, William R. Reader, superintendent from 1913 to 1942 (see chapter 16), was the champion of Calgary's greening and beautification programs. His interventions

212 CHALLENGES OF AN URBAN AND INDUSTRIAL LANDSCAPE

10.12 Union Cemetery, Calgary

transformed the cemetery into the splendid garden and classic rural cemetery we know today.[74] The rich vegetation and overall ambiance of this cemetery are remarkable, given its location in southwestern Alberta, land of the hot, dry chinook winds – a milieu where the plant vocabulary is severely limited by climate. Everything is done with a small number of carefully chosen plants: Colorado spruce and Scots pine, cottonwood poplar, and the forever tireless caragana, along with lilacs and crabapples to provide seasonal colour.[75]

Character and Configuration of the Rural Cemeteries

The physical arrangements of these cemeteries typically included a continuous fence around their entire grounds, to define the sacred area and ensure security, and a variety of iron railings and stone borders within, to define plots for families and communities. Such communities were often religious – like those hardy missionaries, the Sisters of St. Ann, who occupy one of the oldest sectors at Ross Bay Cemetery, and the Frères des Écoles Chrétiennes at Notre-Dame-des-Neiges – or related to national origin, profession, or affinity groups of various kinds. Besides these special sections of large cemeteries, many entire cemeteries, often of considerable antiquity, are dedicated to particular religious or national groups. This is the case with the cemeteries of two Jewish congregations – Shearith Israel and Shaar Hashomayim – located immediately adjacent to Mount Royal Cemetery,[76] as well as of the Jewish cemetery Beth Israel at Sainte-Foy near Quebec City and the Chinese cemetery at Harling Point in Oak Bay, in the suburbs of Victoria. Both of the latter have been recognized as national historic landmarks.[77]

Malaka Ackaoui, of the firm WAA Inc., served for many years as the landscape architect of the Mount Royal Cemetery and sees in rural cemeteries a metaphor and a reflection of our way of life: the abodes of wealthy families are marked by mausoleums and monuments; dense alignments of repetitive tombstones, in regular rows, remind us of the orderly streets of the middle class; and the straight and uniform ranks of military sections are like dress parades. The location and character of memorials in the Victorian cemetery "reflected the economic and social status of the departed" within a society that was not yet egalitarian.[78]

Emergence of the Landscape Architect

The parks and cemeteries we have just been examining did not emerge from an anonymous, vernacular tradition like the burying grounds or churchyards of previous generations had. Unlike their predecessors, almost all of them were designed by professionals. Among these professionals, *landscape gardeners*, who designed and built projects and often managed and maintained them afterwards – sometimes for decades – began to cede part of their traditional role to *landscape architects*. The expertise of these new professionals was focused on design, preparation of plans, and supervision of work on the site,[79] while the landscape gardener remained responsible for the execution and maintenance of landscape and horticultural work, either as an independent contractor or as an employee of the client or institution involved. The preparation of drawings by one profession and their implementation by another started to become a normal practice during this period.[80] The term *landscape architect*, used to identify the new design-oriented profession, was invented in Scotland in 1828 and had already been used by Loudon in 1840; it gradually became a common expression in professional discourse.[81]

Why this change in the middle of the nineteenth century? Certainly it had something to do with practical considerations, including the increasing number of landscape projects, the complexity and large scale of the work required to realize these projects, and a desire among clients to attain a higher level of quality or originality in design. But the new profession of landscape architecture also brought new perspectives and new values to landscape design: in particular, a moral concern for the pressing social and environmental issues of the day and a belief that landscape could contribute to the successful resolution of those issues.[82]

An additional development: whereas the previous generation of Canadian garden designers had come almost entirely from Europe, most of the landscape gardeners and landscape architects who designed rural cemeteries were Americans. This was not surprising. American designers had already adapted European landscape ideas to the North American context, while the profession of landscape architecture did not yet exist in Canada. And this was a period of enlightenment in the United States, the "American Renaissance," when artists, poets, and writers began to create an American culture distinct from that of Europe.[83] An era of political harmony between Canada and the United States had also begun, reinforcing the traditional commercial relationships between the two neighbours. The eminent landscape architect Horace W.S. Cleveland (1814–1900) of Boston needed to make only a short trip across the Gulf of Maine to participate in the design of Mountain Cemetery at Yarmouth, Nova Scotia, in 1861.[84] Even Canadian-born designers were strongly influenced by American trends; for example, the directors of the Notre-Dame-des-Neiges Cemetery sent architect Henri-Maurice Perrault to visit cemeteries in Boston and New York in preparation for his work on the Montreal project.[85]

Precursors of Public Parks

An unexpected consequence of building these great cemeteries was the powerful attraction they exerted on the general public, including people who had no direct connection with a place of burial. Cemeteries were often the only extensive natural landscapes that were accessible to a majority of urban residents. This phenomenon had already been seen at Père Lachaise Cemetery, which was rapidly seized on by Parisians as a site for promenades, for the enjoyment of architectural features and green spaces, and for biographical lessons in the history of France.[86] Mount Auburn attracted so many visitors that admission was limited to pedestrians and vehicles were refused entry.[87] Notre-Dame-des-Neiges Cemetery became a preferred destination for promenading Montrealers in the nineteenth century, despite the objections of the bishop, Monseigneur Bourget.[88] This popularity of cemeteries suggested to many observers that there was a strong public demand for large, naturalistic outdoor spaces in which people could walk and stroll.[89] In 1849, Andrew Jackson Downing gave voice to this demand as he called for the creation of large city parks and, in particular, for a great natural park in New York City. He based his proposal on the immense popularity of Mount Auburn, an excellent indicator of the need for such facilities.[90] Thus rural cemeteries were in themselves magnificent landscapes that satisfied several functional, aesthetic and recreational needs; but they also served as precursors and as an inspiration for a subsequent innovation that would be even more important in the taming of the industrial city.

11

Taming the Industrial City: The Great Public Parks

11.1 The Seawall in Stanley Park, Vancouver

Efforts to tame the industrial city through the deployment of new kinds of public spaces culminated in the creation of *large, naturalistic urban parks* during the last decades of the nineteenth century and the first years of the twentieth. All the large cities of Canada – and many small and medium-sized towns – equipped themselves with parks of this type. These parks resembled the rural cemeteries that had inspired them. Generous in extent and pastoral in ambiance, from 60 to 800 hectares in area, they were located beyond the city limits, on natural sites well endowed with native vegetation and, if possible, on rough and irregular terrain. The new parks' creators were also attracted to sites by the water – sea, lake, or river – or, in their absence, to landforms that could accommodate an extensive artificial lake.

Mount Royal Park

In 1870, Montreal was the largest city in Canada and the fifth largest in North America. Boasting a population of 115,000,[1] it led the way in commerce, culture, and religion, and was the uncontested centre of finance and industrial production in Canada. Its urbanized area extended from the banks of the St. Lawrence River to the lower slopes of Mount Royal, which provided the city, as always, with a handsome wooded backdrop. Then suddenly, in 1872, the clear-cutting of a large swath of forest on the southern flank of the mountain revealed its vulnerability,[2] inciting the city council to begin purchasing private property on the mountain in order to create a park. The council moved quickly. Between 1872 and 1874, the city acquired some 175 hectares of land.

To design the park, the council chose the most qualified person in North America, Frederick Law Olmsted (1822–1903), the famous landscape architect from New York City. First and foremost a social reformer, Olmsted also possessed great artistic abilities and an innovative technical bent. He was born into a prosperous merchant family in Connecticut and grew up in the northeastern United States during a time of remarkable cultural ferment.[3] In 1858, he collaborated with Calvert Vaux (1824–1895), an architect from Britain who had been the partner of Andrew Jackson Downing, on the design of Central Park in New York, a brilliant work that stimulated the creation of similar parks throughout North America, many designed by Olmsted and his associates.[4]

Olmsted had just terminated his long association with Vaux when he accepted the city of Montreal's mandate in 1874.[5] He had certain reservations concerning the irregularity of the site: "As a general rule rugged and broken ground is the last that should be chosen for a public recreation ground in the immediate vicinity of a large city." But after exploring the mountain, his doubts were calmed: "[I] found myself upon a surface but moderately broken and rugged and essentially an undulating and wooded table-land, from nearly all points of which broad and delightful distant landscapes are commanded."[6] Finally, he concluded that, unlike Central Park, where it had been necessary to construct a large part of the landscape, the key strategy in the design of this park was to fully exploit its natural qualities, its attractive landscapes, and its fine views of the surrounding plain. "You have bought a mountain," he said to the park commissioners, "it would be wasteful to

THE GREAT PUBLIC PARKS   217

try to make anything else than a mountain of it."[7] In seeking the *genius loci*, or "spirit of the place," he divided the site into eight distinct zones, each defined by its physiographic or botanical character. These included, among others, the *Crags*, the rocky countenance that the mountain turns to the city; the *Glades*, a broad zone of open clearings on sloping topography in the northwest of the park; and the *Côte placide*, a gentle slope that descends to the eastern extremity of the park. For each of these landscape units Olmsted established a particular design treatment and a long-term management strategy. His strategy for the Crags, for example, sought to amplify their apparent height as seen from below, while preserving panoramic views from above, by the planting of vines, trees, and compact shrubs, pruned to increase their density and punctuated with the brilliant colours of sumacs in autumn.[8] In adopting this approach, Olmsted was an early precursor of what we would today call "ecological design" or "design with Nature."

Olmsted proposed a network of paths and roads for horse-drawn carriages, carefully integrated into existing topography and vegetation, laid out on gradual slopes so as to permit easy access to the mountain, highlighting a series of strategic vantage points from which to view the surrounding landscapes.[9] He also envisioned the building of several shelters, rustic bridges, and other structures, including a refectory and tower at the mountain's summit.[10] The city required that the plan include a large reservoir; in response, Olmsted designed a great symmetrical pond, surrounded by a formal paved promenade, to be constructed in the Glades sector, where an ancient bog occupied a low-lying portion of the site.[11]

Until 1881, Olmsted continued, by letter, to direct the work shown on his plans.[12] It was a difficult project; he was often disappointed by the decisions of the commissioners and by inconsistent management of the work.[13] But the city finally realized the essential elements of Olmsted's design, and the park became, in the latter years of the nineteenth century, a vital recreation ground for Montrealers,

11.2 Frederick Law Olmsted. This wood engraving, the most well-known image of Olmsted, was based on a photo by James Notman taken in 1893, towards the end of the celebrated landscape architect's career.

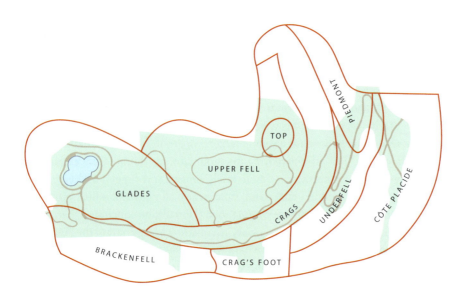

11.3 Plan of Mount Royal Park, Montreal, 1877, showing the ecological zones defined by Olmsted

218   CHALLENGES OF AN URBAN AND INDUSTRIAL LANDSCAPE

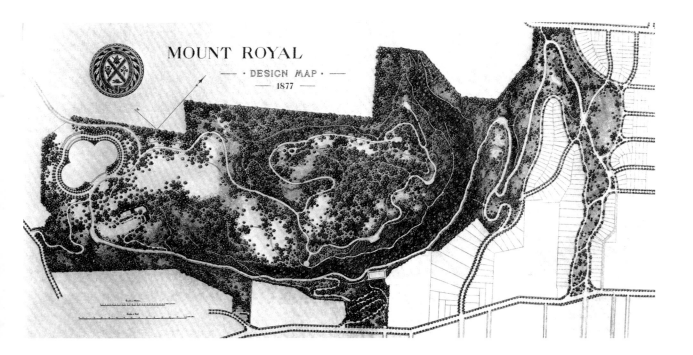

11.4   Mount Royal Park Design Map, 1877. Frederick Law Olmsted, landscape architect. The essentials of Olmsted's plan were realized, particularly in its western and central sectors. The eastern meadows were truncated by the later construction of Park Avenue and new sports facilities at the foot of the mountain. The formal water basin proposed by Olmsted was not carried out when the park was first created, but was eventually constructed in the 1930s in a strikingly different form (see chapters 13 and 18).

who explored it in large numbers on foot, by carriage, and on snowshoes (the most popular sport of the era). Entirely surrounded by the city by the beginning of the twentieth century, Mount Royal Park today accommodates an incredible variety of activities in its diverse pastoral and wild landscapes, landscapes that correspond closely to the four environmental archetypes that Olmsted and Vaux included in Central Park and most of their subsequent large parks: broad pastoral lawns studded with trees, an irregular lake or pond, a formal promenade with elegant structures, and a wild stony "Ramble" with rustic shelters. The fourth of these environments dominates Mount Royal, which many consider the most natural of the Olmsted parks. The park fully satisfies the objectives that Olmsted considered important for his public parks: to create a place of rural beauty that contrasts with the urban environment, a segment of the countryside that permits city dwellers to lose themselves in a different milieu, there to find repose and tranquillity; to provide to the underprivileged members of society the same advantages *within* the city as those provided to the wealthy through their opportunities to visit natural landscapes *outside* it; to promote the integration and fellowship of people of diverse cultures and socio-economic levels and, by doing so, to inculcate the values of democracy.[14]

Large Urban Parks in Eastern Canada, 1870–1900

During the late nineteenth century, almost all the other industrial cities in eastern Canada created similar large urban parks, located beyond (and eventually surrounded by) their built-up areas, each one following the naturalistic and romantic model defined by Mount Royal Park. High Park, on the west side of Toronto, figured among the first of these urban spaces. It was given to the city, in 1873, by John George Howard towards the end of his distinguished career as an artist, surveyor, and architect. His many design contributions to the city include St. James Cemetery and his villa Colborne Lodge (see chapter 9), as well as the latter's adjoining garden. In fact, High Park was his country estate and villa, located on a high plateau that overlooked Lake Ontario, its flat wooded terrain dissected by two deep ravines that drained out to the lake. The western ravine was occupied by the waters of Grenadier Pond, so named for the soldiers who practised their military exercises there in the nineteenth century. The original vegetation regime of the site was that of a black oak savannah, once broadly distributed in southern Ontario but today increasingly rare.

In 1876, the city held a competition for the design of the park, a contest won by the redoubtable landscape gardener H.A. Engelhardt, well known for his contribution to the planning of cemeteries and the site development of public buildings in Ontario. Unfortunately, his design was never realized.[15] The design that was realized, however, has permitted the park to retain its original wooded character up to the present day, and its natural setting and numerous city-sponsored activities have attracted throngs of visitors since the late nineteenth century. One of its most popular activities at that time was tobogganing on the slopes beside the lake.[16]

Point Pleasant Park in Halifax was also a heavily wooded site,[17] situated at the southern extremity of the peninsula that extends out along the shores of Chebucto Bay. It has long served as a strategic bastion to control the sea entrances to the fortress-city that Rudyard Kipling called "the Warden of the North."[18] The park's 75-hectare site has accommodated a multitude of military structures erected over the course of the centuries (including the *Martello* tower constructed by the Duke of Kent; see chapter 5) and called back to duty as recently as the Second World War. The land still belongs to the government of Canada, which rents it to the city for park purposes in exchange for an annual payment of a shilling. This unit of currency bears witness to the great age of the park, which has existed since 1866, well before the great urban parks of Montreal and Toronto. Haligonians had, in fact, used the rocky and wooded site as a park even before it was officially designated as such. They took walks in the forest, held picnics, swam in the ocean, skated on the ponds, and contemplated the sea and the constant movement of ships entering the harbour. And long before the arrival of the European newcomers, the Mi'kmaq people had already occupied this site for use as a summer fishing camp.[19] This site, unlike some other parks, was severely exploited for firewood and for timber for the building of fortifications; later, it was extensively replanted, first with deciduous trees and later with conifers.[20]

Rockwood Park, in the port city of Saint John, New Brunswick, was designed by Downing Vaux (1856–1926), the son of Calvert Vaux, Olmsted's associate on the design of Central Park, and the namesake of his father's first partner, Andrew Jackson Downing.[21] The younger Vaux visited the site in 1896 after the death of his father and submitted his plan and report in 1899.[22] The creation of Rockwood Park was a tribute to the spirit of voluntarism and philanthropy that pervaded the

11.5 Point Pleasant Park, Halifax: view from the eastern shore of the peninsula towards the entrance to Halifax Harbour. Maugher Beach lighthouse is just visible on the horizon.

Victorian period. In 1894, the Saint John Horticultural Association, with the goal of creating a public park, bought a large site in the hills to the north of the city, beginning a process that would eventually create one of the largest parks of this type in Canada, with an area of 880 hectares.[23] Following the Olmstedian model, this unknown treasure was composed of several very different milieus. Above the broad sports fields and active recreational spaces, an entirely unexpected landscape and climatic regime holds sway: a kind of boggy upland heath occupies the park's higher elevations, punctuated by many rocky outcrops, its stunted and contorted vegetation thinly scattered about in highly acidic soils. Clumps of white birch, a multitude of spruce, the mauve-flowered lambkill (sheep laurel), and the Canadian rhododendron flourish. A sequence of artificial lakes provides facilities for swimming and fishing. The impression is one of wild nature, but of course the park is in the midst of a city.

The first great urban park of Quebec City, *Parc Victoria*, also owed its design to a well-known professional, in this case the city architect and engineer, polymath Charles Baillairgé. The park was established at the junction of the densely

THE GREAT PUBLIC PARKS 221

populated industrial districts of St-Roch and St-Sauveur in the Lower Town, not far from the central commercial area of the Victorian era. It was inaugurated in 1897, in time for the celebration of the sixtieth anniversary of Queen Victoria's coronation (thus its name). To create the park, the city purchased a piece of land that was almost completely encircled by a meander of the St. Charles River, a site that was formerly the *Ferme d'îlets* (Island Farm) of the Augustine Sisters, who operated the adjacent General Hospital.[24] Now close to the end of his public career, Baillairgé gave free rein to his penchant for designing everything. He planned the carriage road that wound around the park, the serpentine pedestrian byways, and two iron bridges that provided access for park visitors. He chose the locations where buildings would be sited and personally designed the conservatories for the production of plants destined for the park's garden areas.[25] Sébastien Siné, a gardener working for the city, planted the floral arrangements in 1896–97, and the architects Tanguay & Vallée designed a picturesque-style restaurant pavilion with observation tower.[26]

11.6 Upper lake area of Rockwood Park, Saint John, NB, showing vegetation characteristic of its acid soils and abundant moisture

Major Parks in the Cities of the West

The popularity of these parks in the industrial cities of the East incited cities in the West that had not yet experienced the industrial invasion to create great urban parks as soon as they could. A park of this type was seen as an essential component of any respectable city.

At Fort Victoria (now the city of Victoria) in British Columbia, Governor James Douglas of the Hudson's Bay Company dedicated 71 hectares on a hill beside the sea for the purpose of a public park as early as 1858, only fifteen years after the settlement was founded.[27] The summit of the hill lent itself to the installation of fiery beacons to guide boats crossing the Straits of Juan de Fuca safely into harbour – thus the name of the park, Beacon Hill. The site had already served as the scene for recreational activities, agricultural expositions, and (like Point Pleasant Park) military fortifications[28] before the city sponsored a competition for its design as a park in 1889. The winner of the contest, local landscape architect John Blair (1820–1906), was already an expert in landscape design. Blair was born in Scotland, where he received his training in horticulture before moving to St. Catharines, Ontario, in 1851. His expertise in gardening led him to Chicago in 1865, where he became superintendent of parks. He designed many parks in Chicago and in Colorado Springs, in the American West, before arriving in 1881 on Vancouver Island, where he spent the rest of his life.[29]

Like the romantic literature of his youth, Blair's approach to landscape design was inspired by wild nature.[30] His orchestration of the spatial sequence by which one discovers the park is remarkable.[31] At the entrance to Beacon Hill from the downtown area, the visitor passes across elegant green lawns and between great specimen trees. This transitional zone quickly gives way to a rugged moor-like landscape, its rough landforms colonized with wild grasses, contorted Garry oaks, and broom, which flowers brilliant gold in spring. Reaching the heart of the park, the visitor comes upon an ancient marsh that Blair had transformed into a lake landscape framed by luxurious vegetation, a milieu that resembled an English *paradise garden*.[32] A bridge of rough stone, a witness to Blair's technical virtuosity, is reflected in the waters. Then the visitor undertakes the long and strenuous walk to the top of the hill, passing through wild snowberries (a native plant here), the blue-violet flowers of camas lilies, and the yellow of daffodils, pines silhouetted against the sky; finally arriving on the crest – a sudden majestic view of the straits and the misty mountains of the Olympic Peninsula on the horizon.

The creation of Vancouver's Stanley Park, often considered the jewel in the crown among Canada's urban parks, followed even more swiftly the founding of its city. In fact, the establishment of this park was the first item on the agenda at the first meeting of the city council in May 1886. At the time, the city had only 2,600 residents. In order to create the park, the council resolved to ask the federal government to transfer to the municipality the use of a military reserve that, like Point Pleasant Park on the opposite side of the continent, occupied a wooded peninsula, well located to control the narrow entrance to its port.[33] The government having acceded to its request in 1887, the city proceeded with the development

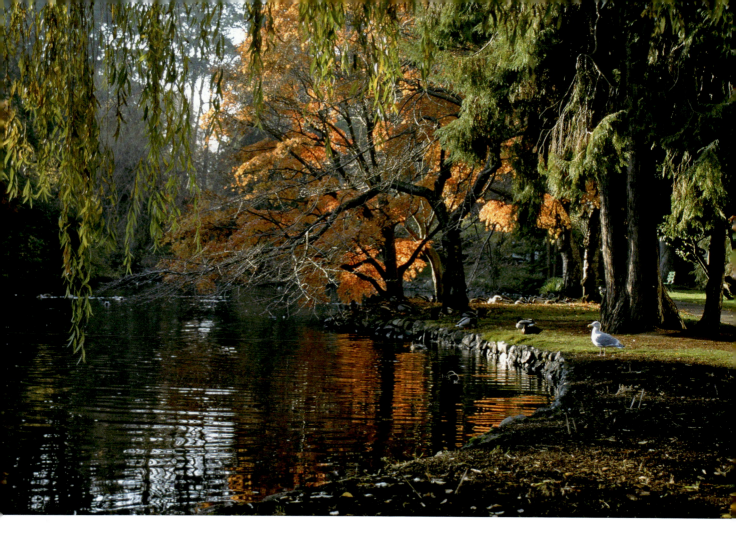

of the park, which was inaugurated in October 1889 by Lord Stanley, governor general of Canada. His vice-regal speech clearly expressed the social objectives of the great urban parks: "To the use and enjoyment of peoples of all colours, creeds, and customs, for all time, I name thee Stanley Park."[34] This was a well-chosen dedication for a city that has been cosmopolitan since its first days but passed through periods of bitter conflict before arriving at its present state of social harmony.

At the beginning, only the sites of Native villages, Salish and Squamish, interrupted the peninsula's dense coastal forest vegetation, dominated by mighty conifers – western hemlock, Douglas fir, and western red cedar – and a vigorous undergrowth of ferns and shrubs. The creation of the park has ensured the survival of most of this forest for some 120 years, the principal vestige of the forest that once covered the site of the entire city of Vancouver.[35]

The design of Stanley Park is the result of a series of successive developments carried out over the years, and not the result of a long-term plan prepared by a landscape architect or other design professional.[36] This process of gradual accretion nonetheless produced a remarkably coherent overall design, consisting

11.7 Goodacre Lake at the heart of Beacon Hill Park, Victoria, BC

essentially of a large number of recreational and athletic facilities carefully inserted within cleared enclaves in the forest, on the park's periphery and adjacent areas. All these facilities were linked by a ring road that encircled the park, and that connected the park to the city via a dyked causeway. This structure cut off the upper part of Coal Harbour, creating a freshwater pond that the Native poet Pauline Johnson christened *Lost Lagoon*.[37] A network of paths promoted the exploration of the shadowy and mysterious forest in the park's interior, just a few minutes' walk from a magnificent esplanade, the *Seawall*, a broad pedestrian and cycle path that traces the entire perimeter of the park, well protected behind a granite wall. The Seawall, one of the great spaces of the country, welcomes thousands of hikers, joggers, and cyclists every day, and offers them unmatched views of the crowded sea lanes on all sides.[38]

The spectacular urban and geographic ensemble of this wooded peninsula, mounted in a setting of sea, downtown towers, and the settled hills and rugged mountains of the north coast, confers a symbolic role on Stanley Park, a role well defined by landscape architect Douglas Paterson: "a classic Canadian park, symbolizing a nation living at the edge of wilderness."[39]

Frederick G. Todd, Canada's Outstanding Landscape Architect

Following the realization of large urban parks in many Canadian cities in the closing decades of the nineteenth century, a second wave of large natural parks would be established in the first fifteen years of the new century. Astonishingly, no less than three of these parks would be designed by a single person: Canada's most important landscape architect of the first half of the twentieth century, Frederick Gage Todd (1876–1948). An American born in Concord, New Hampshire, Todd went to high school in Massachusetts and pursued his education at the state university at Amherst, one of the land-grant colleges discussed in chapter 7. Between 1896 and 1900, he worked in Boston at the Olmsted office, then directed by Charles Eliot (1859–1897) and the two sons of the founder, John Charles Olmsted (1852–1920) and Frederick Law Olmsted Jr. (1870–1957). Todd first came to Montreal during these apprenticeship years as a representative of the Olmsted firm, to supervise ongoing work on the long-term Mount Royal Park project and some residential projects in which the firm was involved.[40] Todd moved to Montreal while working on these assignments and stayed on following their completion. He was the first landscape architect resident in Canada to describe himself with that title.[41] He remained in Canada until his death in 1948, carrying out major projects in all parts of the country throughout a long and illustrious career.[42]

Todd was only twenty-three when he opened his own office in downtown Montreal, on the first day of the new century, 1 January 1900. His connection with the Olmsted office helped greatly in the early years, but he owed his subsequent rapid success to the fact that he "brought to Montreal, and to all of Canada, a level of professional *savoir-faire* that was in great demand."[43] In addition, he developed, early in his career, a distinct philosophy and approach to the design of parks. Todd expressed his design philosophy in terms similar to those used by Olmsted,

11.8   Frederick G. Todd, 1909

THE GREAT PUBLIC PARKS   225

emphasizing the importance of creating a coherent artistic ensemble: "Our first step ... should be to fix firmly in our minds the dominant character of the park ... With the chief character of our park decided upon, everything must be, as far as possible, subordinated to it, and made to accentuate it, making it more impressive and pleasing."[44]

When he was still in his twenties and early thirties, Todd was rapidly entrusted with large and difficult park projects, first in Montreal and then throughout Canada. The first of these, begun in 1904, was Assiniboine Park in Winnipeg. Despite being a frontier town only thirty years before, Winnipeg was already the fourth largest city in Canada in 1904. Its geographic situation at the gate to the Prairies and its key role as a transfer point in the railroad system had allowed it to benefit from a period of vertiginous growth. But the city's growing population was served by only a handful of small parks and squares and a few private parks.[45] Finally, in 1904, the city acquired a site of 117 hectares on the south shore of the Assiniboine River, six kilometres west of its confluence with the Red River. Based on a recommendation from the Olmsted office, the parks committee asked Frederick Todd to prepare a design.[46] Todd imagined a classic park in the Olmsted style: immense lawns for picnics, informal sports, and varied recreational activities; large specimen trees (principally elms, cottonwood poplars, spruce), shrub masses, and intermediate flowering plants (crabapples, honeysuckle, lilacs); winding pathways and grand avenues lined with trees on both sides. At the main entrance in the southeast corner of the park, a stone portal opened onto a vast axial space, a formal courtyard that led diagonally to the centre of the park. The scale of this garden was immense (Todd originally proposed a water basin 200 metres long), the planting simple and robust, in broad masses as required by the generous scale of the planting beds.[47]

Thanks to the great scale of these spaces and the fact that they were almost completely flat, like the surrounding terrain, the park was perfectly integrated into its prairie site. No mounds or hilly topography interrupted this horizontality, with the exception of a gentle wooded slope parallel to the river, the boundary of an old river terrace. Todd used this level change astutely, placing the park's main pavilion at the crest of the terrace, its height and that of the building's central tower reinforcing its role as a landmark, visible from all points in the park. He explained his approach to the design of the park: "In the West, where parks must necessarily be located upon the open prairie, and where at best the open surface is only partly rolling, I have taken as the chief character of the park, the open plain itself ... there is an unbroken view for the distance of about a mile to the far end of the park ... Groups of trees are scattered in the foreground and at intervals over the park, in order to give scale and distance to the view."[48]

The second great park designed by Todd was on the other side of the country, on a historic plateau above the mighty St. Lawrence River: the National Battlefields Park at Quebec City, better known as the Plains of Abraham in honour of the first farmer who cultivated the land.[49] Since the French and British armies had confronted each other a century and a half earlier, the broad open plain on the heights beyond Cape Diamond had been recognized as a powerfully significant

11.9 Aerial view of Assiniboine Park, Winnipeg, looking east. A bridge across the Assiniboine River connects the main southern section of the park to its northern gateway from Portage Avenue. The park pavilion and its tower can be seen at right centre, crowning a gentle terrace parallel to the river.

site, invested with symbolism and meaning, even an aura of sacredness. As the 1908 tercentenary of the founding of Quebec City came closer, influential citizens[50] nominated this legendary site as the ideal place for the commemorations that were envisioned – and what could be nobler than to transform the site into a park!

The site for such a park was still available, but only just. Although the firing lines of the two great battles that had taken place on the Plains – that of September 1759 before the walls of Quebec and that of the following April at Sainte-Foy – extended across their full width,[51] the greater part of this terrain had been developed for urban use. But due to the long-lasting fear of an American attack on the city – there had already been one, in 1775 – the British Army had bought or leased, for purposes of defence, a large strip of land at the top of the cliffs along the river.[52] In 1908, the National Battlefields Commission, through its president Georges Garneau, the mayor of Quebec City (he would preside over the commission until 1939), moved to acquire this undeveloped site in collaboration with other government agencies.[53] Frederick Todd was engaged as the landscape architect of the site in 1908, charged with the task of transforming it into a public park of national significance, a legacy its creators will be "handing down to future generations, with its

THE GREAT PUBLIC PARKS 227

11.10 Frederick Todd's 1913 final design plan of the National Battlefields Park (the Plains of Abraham), Quebec City. The park extends along the escarpment all the way from the vast semi-circular "Parade Ground" in the west to the old city walls at its eastern extremity. At upper left, Avenue des Braves extends north from Grande-Allée to the Monument des Braves at the crest of the slope leading down to the St. Charles River valley.

grandeur and beauty undespoiled, and its historical interest revived and hallowed with the passing of time."[54]

Todd was quite aware of the site's importance – he spoke of it as "a priceless gem" – and of the challenge he faced: "In no other place can we find such grandeur of proportion, such sublime views combined with such a wealth of historical associations."[55] He divided the park into five sections and identified a design strategy for each. He kept as open space the great undulating plateau that descends gradually from the Citadel to the centre of the park, and planted its perimeter in irregular fashion. A second large open area, further west, would become an immense grassy half-circle, the *parade ground*, framed by a row of tall trees and a formal avenue. Todd proposed to retain the wooded escarpment along the river side of the site in its wild state, with the exception of the long, gentle slope at the western extremity of the park, which would be landscaped to recall its military significance. Finally, the *Avenue* and *Parc des Braves* merited a particular landscape treatment so as to properly frame a monument, in commemoration of the soldiers who fell in the Battle of Sainte-Foy, that had been erected some years before at the edge of the escarpment that defines the northern limit of the plateau. Todd accomplished this task by aligning an axial boulevard with the monument, which he framed and dramatized with a formal terrace and naturalistic park. Again, Todd took care to describe his overall intentions with respect to the design of the overall park site: "Nothing can prevent the magnificent views obtainable from these plains from being the great characteristic feature of the park, but the whole park is so bound up in the history of this continent that the opportunity of designing the park in such a way as to perpetuate this history would seem to be much more interesting than to lay it out as an ordinary park, with clumps of trees dotted about, and the whole cut up with walks and drives."[56]

Several years later, in 1911, Todd had a third opportunity to design a great urban park, this time in the old seaport of St. John's, in Newfoundland. Sir Edgar Bowring wanted to celebrate the centenary of the foundation of his family's merchant company, established in St. John's in 1811 and still active in all parts of Canada, by donating a park to the city. He asked Todd to draw the plans for Bowring Park, on a site located some five kilometres west of the city centre, at the confluence of the Waterford River (which continues easterly to the city's harbour) and its tributary South Brook. The plan prepared by Todd's office clearly follows the Olmstedian tradition. At the eastern entry to the park, a dam created a small lake, the *Duck Pond*, at the junction of the two water courses. True to its name, the lake harbours a large population of geese, ducks, and swans. Winding boulevards and pathways, beautifully curved and graded, followed the hills and streams. The latter retain their wild aspect as densely wooded areas in contrast to open, sloping lawns, one of which sets off perfectly the park's main pavilion – the "Bungalow" – located at a dramatic high point, like the pavilion in Assiniboine Park. Planting in the park

11.11 Peter Pan statue in Bowring Park, St. John's, NL

THE GREAT PUBLIC PARKS   229

emphasized native species, including eastern spruce, birch, and mountain ash, complemented by extensive plantings of flowering crabapple and rhododendrons, contributing to the wild effect desired.[57]

Todd visited the site of the park only once, during the design stage in 1912. Following the usual pattern of the time, he delegated the supervision and carrying-out of the work to an assistant who had been working with him since 1911, a landscape architect and civil engineer in his early thirties, Rudolf H.K. Cochius (1880–1944), a native of Holland. Cochius stayed on in St. John's from 1912 to 1917, living with his family in the Lodge building at the entrance to the park.[58] The park was largely realized as planned; however, given the distance between the two collaborators, Cochius benefited from a certain degree of autonomy. He was clearly responsible for designing the reinforced concrete bridge at the east entry; and a particularly appealing aspect of the park, its fanciful fences and furniture made of rough spruce logs and twigs, may have been his pure invention.

Though intimate and modest, Bowring Park is nonetheless one of the most effective and beloved parks in Canada, due to its natural character, its interesting composition that brings together a series of well-defined, sheltered spaces, its charming idiosyncratic elements and artistic placing of diverse sculptures. The latter include a statue of Peter Pan similar to that in Kensington Gardens, London, and two remarkable war memorials (see chapter 15). As Peter Jacobs and Vincent Asselin have noted, these three very different parks demonstrate Frederick Todd's remarkable versatility. While never forsaking the Olmstedian definition of the public park, he avoided the imposition of a stereotyped aesthetic formula on his projects in varied environments, instead seeking to base their designs on historic considerations or *genius loci*, the "spirit of the place," respecting both the particularities of each specific site and the regional landscape setting.[59]

Open-Space Networks

Despite the rapid adoption of the "one great park" idea late in the nineteenth century, city authorities soon realized that their still-expanding metropolitan zones would need other, similar parks to serve new districts. They also understood that a panoply of other green spaces, of diverse scale and type, would soon be needed throughout the city, to complement their flagship park.

In 1889, shortly after its acquisition of Stanley Park, the city of Vancouver obtained a large waterfront property in the eastern sector of the city,[60] a site that had previously belonged to the provincial government; this site was the future Hastings Park. In the 1890s, the city also began to purchase shorefront lands along English Bay, west of Stanley Park.[61] In Winnipeg, a city in full expansion during the 1890s and 1900s, other parks were quickly added to the fledgling network that embraced Assiniboine Park and several small parks and squares in the downtown area. When he was hired by the city in 1907, the new parks superintendent George Champion (1870–1946) – a native of England who had worked at the royal gardens at Kew before immigrating to Ontario in 1897 – was mandated to carry out Todd's plan for Assiniboine Park. At the same time, he was entrusted with the preparation of the designs for a second generation of public parks. This new green wave was to consist primarily of neighbourhood parks in the newly established sectors of the city, as well as a second large suburban park, Kildonan Park. Located on a wooded site that sloped down to the Red River in the northern section of the city, this park was entirely designed by Champion in 1910. Using to advantage his background in ornamental horticulture, the superintendent created a floral garden that is still an impressive component of the park.[62] During his long mandate of twenty-eight years, which finally came to a close in 1935, Champion created several other large public parks, as well as new boulevards, parkways, and sports fields throughout the city.[63]

In short order, Montreal also became a city with several parks. Within a decade of the creation of Mount Royal Park, two more key sites became public open spaces; like Stanley Park and Point Pleasant at the country's antipodes, both of these had previously served as military bases: St. Helen's Island in the St. Lawrence River and the Logan Farm, in the centre of the Plateau Mont-Royal east of the mountain. The latter site became Lafontaine Park, a splendid and heavily used park that accommodated a variety of changing uses over the years, including a zoo and greenhouses, and which has consistently provided an essential verdant milieu in one of the most densely populated districts in Canada.[64]

The Washington of the North?

Besides creating site-specific designs, Frederick Todd also played an important role in the planning of park systems for Canadian cities. In two urban centres of great political importance, he defined the overall pattern for what are perhaps the most coherent and extensive open-space networks in the country: first, the federal capital of Ottawa, in Ontario, and its twin city, Hull (now Gatineau), in Quebec; and subsequently, Edmonton, capital of the province of Alberta. In Ottawa, the story began in 1899 with the creation of the Ottawa Improvement Commission (OIC) by Prime Minister Wilfrid Laurier. The PM instructed the commission to see to the amelioration and beautification of the city and its environs (until that time, the city was an unattractive industrial centre that disfigured both sides of the Ottawa River) so as to create a capital worthy of a great nation. The OIC engaged Todd in 1903, asking him to sketch out a comprehensive general plan for the improvement of the city. Todd carried out his mandate in the short time of only six weeks, submitting in August 1903 his *Preliminary Report to the Ottawa Improvement Commission*, a document of thirty-nine pages, illustrated with photographs, diagrams, and a map of the entire study area.[65]

This was quite a responsibility for a young man of only twenty-seven years, but Todd was equal to the task. First, he redefined Ottawa and its environs to comprise an extensive territory on both sides of the river, including the Gatineau Hills and the Gatineau River to the north of the city of Hull. It would not be an exaggeration to say that he invented the notion of the National Capital Region as we know it today. There is some resemblance between this territory and the federal district around Washington in the United States, which also includes parts of two states

THE GREAT PUBLIC PARKS 231

on opposite banks of a great river. But the parallel ended there: in the first pages of his report, Todd insisted that Ottawa was not to be the "Washington of the North," despite Laurier's announcement to that effect in 1893. The unique site of Ottawa had its own personality, he said, very different from that of the American capital. Its abrupt and spectacular topography, its dynamic rushing river, the Gothic architecture of the governmental buildings – all contrasted strongly with the equivalent characteristics of Washington, DC. To explain these differences, Todd evoked the Reptonian distinction between the *beautiful* and the *picturesque*, insisting that the second philosophy "must obviously form the foundation and keynote of any proposed plans for the future" of Ottawa.[66]

Todd then defined several types of park that the green space network of the region should include, and he selected many specific sites (some of which had already been transformed into parks) in each category. First, he suggested a series of large natural parks (or reserves) outside the city, including a wooded zone along the Gatineau River and the area surrounding Lake Meach (now Meech), in the Gatineau Hills; then he proposed a series of suburban parks, essentially large urban parks, to be distributed in a circle around the city centre. Among these were Rockcliffe Park and its eastward extension, the forest of Lac Leamy in Hull to the north, and the Central Experimental Farm to the south. He also suggested a system of boulevards and parkways that would link these various parks and profit from the splendid views that were available along the watercourses of the region (it should be noted that the OIC had already built the first parkway – a great success – along the Rideau Canal). A parkway in the Gatineau Hills was included in his proposals.[67] Finally, parks for swimming and a number of small parks and squares, located in the various districts of the city, completed the picture.

Despite his efforts, Todd's work was little appreciated by the OIC.[68] The commission did not adopt his proposals and subsequently hired him to design only one other park.[69] So, at first glance, Todd's efforts in Ottawa seem to have been a failure. But a study of the present-day system of parks and parkways in the National Capital Region reveals that almost all the proposals that Todd put forward in 1903 have become a reality during the intervening century.[70] Todd thus succeeded in establishing the pattern for what has since become a magnificent network of open spaces.

Green Ribbons

Todd also sketched out the first draft of an equally splendid network of river parks in Edmonton, which had been selected as the capital of the new province of Alberta in 1905. In the following year, Todd visited the future metropolis at the invitation of the two municipalities (later amalgamated into one) of Edmonton and Strathcona, situated respectively on the northern and southern plateaus that frame the immense valley through which the North Saskatchewan River flows. As at Ottawa, he was requested to examine the city "with a view to reporting on the general scheme for parks and boulevards, which would amply provide for the future needs of the city, as far as these can be foreseen at the present time."[71]

He submitted two separate reports, one to each municipality, in April and May of 1907. In both reports, Todd emphasized the importance of reserving sites for open spaces as swiftly as possible to avoid the enormous costs of acquiring them after urban development had taken place. As at Ottawa, he proposed that the city create several types of parks and boulevards, adapting his recommendations to the particular characteristics of Edmonton. He suggested the creation of several *large urban parks*, which would include a green park on the Hudson Bay Flats (a river-level terrace) and a number of *ravine and hill parks*, embracing a series of wooded ravines that descended to the North Saskatchewan River. He envisioned magnificent continuous *parkways* at plateau level along the escarpments of the great valley. This work had already begun, the city of Strathcona having created Saskatchewan Avenue along the southern rim of the valley. Todd suggested that additional boulevards be laid out as links between the various parks, and proposed a number of small parks and playgrounds, to be established within the various districts of the two cities. He encouraged the planting of trees along the future boulevards, favouring Carolina poplars and Russian poplars for rapid growth.[72]

In 1912, the city followed Todd's recommendation concerning the purchase of the Hudson Bay Flats (this terrain is now Victoria Park, accommodating a municipal golf course), but it made no immediate effort to acquire other properties in the North Saskatchewan River valley[73] – until the day in 1915 when the worst flood in the history of the city destroyed a great number of industries built in the confines of the valley. This event marked a turning point, motivating Edmonton to adopt the conservation of the valley as a guiding principle of the city's official plan. Gradually, the spaces identified by Todd became parks, and the capital of today enjoys a continuous river park that is both a grand visual and recreational resource and an effective means of protection against natural disasters. A plaque in honour of Frederick Todd pays homage to this visionary landscape architect.[74]

Further south in the same province, another visionary brought a similar élan to the creation of a river park system in Calgary. As soon as he moved to the city in 1884, William Pearce (1848–1930), inspector of federal lands, reserved the wooded islands in the Bow River as an ideal site for a park, adding a strip of land along the north side of the river to provide space for a future parkway between the riverbank and a steep slope that follows alongside it. Pearce also reserved land for future park purposes along other sections of the Bow and its tributary, the Elbow River.[75] The overall portrait sketched out by Pearce exerted a long-lasting and positive influence on the evolution of the city's parks. Pearce's long shadow was still in evidence in 1968, when industrial lands located close to the city centre were finally converted into public parkland, creating the green oasis of Prince's Island Park, a true jewel only a few minutes' walk from the downtown skyscrapers (see chapter 20).[76]

Throughout his career, Pearce constantly pressured the city to create parks and playgrounds, and to plant trees, especially conifers. He supported the adoption of Arbor Day, to stimulate the realization of his vision of the city as an urban forest.[77] Pearce's contribution was a determining factor in the creation of Calgary's open-space system, a network that he saw as a coordinated whole, designed in harmony with the climate and environment of the region.[78]

11.12 North Shore Park, Stratford, ON, looking downstream to Victoria Lake

Natural Parks in Smaller Centres

Besides his contributions to major parks and park systems, Frederick Todd designed parks for smaller cities and towns all over the country, including Granby and Valleyfield, Quebec, and the twin cities of Port Arthur and Fort William, Ontario (now Thunder Bay), at the head of Lake Superior.[79] In 1904, the town of Stratford, Ontario, invited him to design a series of parks around a lake newly formed by damming up the river Avon. Shortly after, the Canadian Pacific Railway planned its route across the city through the sites that had been set aside for future parks. Todd forcefully and eloquently recommended the rejection of this proposal, suggesting that the railroad be rerouted elsewhere. By a hair's breadth, Todd's recommendation was upheld by a vote of the citizens and with the gallant support of R. Thomas Orr, president of the city's Parks Commission. Today, this park is the home of the Stratford Shakespearean Festival, initiated in 1953 by the city; yet without the efforts of Frederick Todd, this unique cultural phenomenon and powerful tourist attraction might never have existed.[80]

Other landscape architects were involved in park design in Canada during this period. Charles Ernest Woolverton (1879–1934) was the scion of a family that had been involved in the fruit-growing and horticulture industries in the Niagara Peninsula region since the colonial period. The father, Linus Woolverton, was an orchard manager and editor of the magazine *The Canadian Horticulturist*. The son, Charles, followed the horticulture program at the Ontario Agricultural College at Guelph from 1898 to 1901 and subsequently returned to Grimsby, Ontario, where he established what was probably the first landscape architectural office to be founded by a native-born Canadian, although at the beginning of his career he preferred to identify himself as a *landscape gardener* or *garden designer*.[81] In 1907 and again in 1909, Charles Woolverton worked in the large Boston office of landscape architect Warren H. Manning (1860–1938; with whom his father maintained regular contacts), advancing his knowledge in the design of parks and open-space systems. On his return to Ontario, Woolverton worked primarily in the domain of large private gardens. He approached several Ontario municipalities in search of commissions in park design, and indeed he prepared the plans for Queen's Park in Barrie, Ontario, in 1909, in collaboration with a colleague from the Manning office, George H. Miller. Unfortunately, no documentary evidence has yet been found concerning the realization of the projects he designed at this stage of his career. After a long hiatus from 1914 to 1927, during which he devoted himself to the family enterprise, Charles Woolverton returned to the practice of landscape architecture at the end of his career, in Hamilton and Sarnia, Ontario.[82]

The relationship between landscape architecture and the horticulture industry demonstrated by the Woolverton family was a common pattern throughout the first half of the twentieth century. Many nurseries in southern Ontario, including the E.D. Smith Company of Winona, offered the services of landscape architects as a complement to their sales of plants and garden materials. The Toronto landscape historian Pleasance Crawford has identified several of these professionals by combing through commercial and municipal magazines from 1900 to 1914. Among them were Charles A. Maxson; Max Stolpe, a landscape gardener of German origin who had worked in several European countries; Roderick Cameron, chief gardener at Queen Victoria Park in Niagara Falls up to 1908 and then superintendent of parks in Toronto; and J. McPherson Ross, owner of a nursery in Toronto.[83]

A Remarkable Urban Heritage

The great romantic landscapes of the late nineteenth and early twentieth centuries have provided the background for the lives of all of Canada's urban residents. From their first opening days, these landscapes were immensely popular, occupied by crowds of people engaged in an infinite number of recreational and social activities. We call them simply "The Mountain," or "The Park," and we imagine that they were always as they are now, an inevitable presence. Montreal is unimaginable without Mount Royal Park and the mountain cemeteries; Vancouver inconceivable without Stanley Park. But in fact there was nothing inevitable about these spaces; they were created by city officials and landscape architects as part of a radical restructuring of cities throughout the Western World. These visionaries accomplished almost all the objectives enunciated by Olmsted in the 1860s, and they did much to help our civilization survive the stresses and strains of the urban transformations of the nineteenth and twentieth centuries.

12.1 Lucius O'Brien, *A View of the Rocky Mountains, British Columbia*, 1887

12

Natural Monuments: The Creation of the National and Provincial Parks

Suddenly, in the 1860s, a new kind of green space, the great wilderness park, or *national park*, took form in North America. And in the following century, this new invention was adopted everywhere across the planet. Until this point in our study of parks, squares, green spaces, and recreation places, every design prototype had been imported from Europe, the old civilized continent that offered so much to emulate. Why this inversion of roles? What was this new invention?

The effects of nineteenth-century industrialization on North America were not limited to its urban areas. The raw materials that made possible the accelerated production of every commodity in urban factories had to come from somewhere, and that somewhere was the immense wild hinterland of Canada and the United States, until that time little modified by its Native inhabitants or the scattering of trappers who lived there. Industry made rapid inroads into these territories and changed them profoundly, making entire forests disappear, building dams on most of the rivers, tearing minerals out of remote mountains, and constructing railways everywhere, in order to move resources to their places of transformation.

These devastating changes were often imposed on truly remarkable landscapes. Explorers and visitors to North America had long noted the extraordinary beauty of the country, the variety and the profusion of its visual riches. As we have seen, these landscapes seemed to exist entirely outside the normal experience of Europeans. In 1540, Coronado was astonished by the Grand Canyon, as was the Jesuit father Louis Hennepin by the grandiose scale of Niagara Falls – he was the first recorded European to visit and describe it, in 1678.[1] Captain Cook remarked repeatedly on the great size of the trees seen at Nootka Sound in 1778.[2] By the mid-nineteenth century, the incongruity of large-scale industrial and commercial intrusions within these magnificent landscapes began to arouse strong reactions, favouring the preservation and protection of some of these great natural landscapes against the depredations of mining and forestry. This international movement took a particular turn in North America, the world centre of democracy at the time. The desire to protect nature was combined with the notion that the continent's great landscapes should belong to all the people – everyone should have the right to enjoy them as a component of their national heritage. From the fusion of these two currents of thought was born the idea of the great wilderness park of unspoiled nature.

Beginnings of the Natural Park Movement in the United States

In fact, the national park[3] idea had been prefigured by a number of earlier transformations in ways of thinking and feeling. Literature and philosophy, from Rousseau on, had developed the themes of Nature as good and pure in the face of Man's corruption and of the inherent nobility of those who lived in the wilderness. Romantic poets such as Wordsworth, American transcendentalists like Ralph Waldo Emerson and Henry David Thoreau from New England and poet Walt Whitman from Brooklyn – all idealized wild Nature and promoted its appreciation. Many garden designers tried to create landscapes as powerful as those found in the natural world, and oil paintings by J.M.W. Turner and others expressed the sublimity of natural and imagined landscapes. Painters of the Hudson River School[4] (c. 1840–75; see chapter 9) glorified and popularized the wild country of northern New York and neighbouring states, preparing public opinion to embrace the park idea.

As early as 1832, the majesty of American landscapes inspired artist George Catlin to propose that the US federal government reserve an extensive territory in the West as a "Nation's park, containing man and beast, in all the wildness and freshness of their nature's beauty."[5] This proposition took concrete form in 1864: the federal Congress granted to the State of California, "to prevent occupation and especially to preserve the trees in the valley from destruction," the spectacular Yosemite Valley, sculpted by glaciers through the mountains of the Sierra Nevada, along with its neighbour, the Mariposa Big Tree Grove, home of the venerable giant sequoia trees.[6] To ensure that the park – the nucleus of what would later become "Yosemite National Park"[7] – was properly managed, the state created a commission chaired by landscape architect Frederick Law Olmsted, the celebrated designer of Central Park in New York (see chapter 11) who, by a happy coincidence, had moved to California in 1863. Based on his knowledge of the privatization and destruction of landscapes in the eastern states, Olmsted wrote up a statement of principles defining the *raison d'être* of and the management philosophy appropriate to such magnificent landscapes.[8] He observed that natural scenes exert a positive influence on the psychological well-being of those who are exposed to them over a continuous period. He promulgated his belief that a democratic country must preserve its places of remarkable natural beauty for society at large, and not for a small elite from the privileged classes. Looking at the management of the park, he considered that it should be made accessible to the public through the integration of certain facilities – access roads, firebreaks, pathways to reach scenic viewpoints, some cabins and campgrounds – while nonetheless limiting the physical interventions in the park to the "minimum required to meet the basic needs of visitors." Finally, he recommended that the maintenance, management, and protection of the flora and fauna of the park should follow a regular and structured program, and that measures should be taken to prevent vandalism and exploitation of the park for commercial, forestry, or agricultural purposes.[9]

Thus, at the very beginning of the great natural parks, Olmsted identified the issues that would later preoccupy their designers and administrators, and enunciated visionary policies to deal with them. He deserves to be recognized as the authentic father of the national parks, just as he has been for the large urban parks of North America.[10] Olmsted also foresaw that large-scale tourism would figure importantly and inevitably in the future of the great wilderness parks and would justify their protection. An opportunity to exploit such tourism soon presented itself. This was the era of the transcontinental railways that were being built across Canada and United States at breakneck speed. The natural attractions of the parks offered these enterprises a way to fill their railcars with citizens from back East who wanted to see the magnificent landscapes of the West. Thus, it was not a coincidence that the first "official" national park in the United States – that is, owned and administered by the federal government as the property of all Americans – was

Yellowstone National Park, inaugurated in 1872, located just to the south of the route of the Northern Pacific Railway in what is now Wyoming and Montana.

National Parks Arrive in Canada

The idea of large wilderness parks traversed the frontier between the United States and Canada almost immediately. Nature had been equally generous on both sides of the border, and social customs were relatively similar in both countries; these circumstances created a tourist market in Canada much like that of its neighbour. The natural environment of the Mountain West had already been described in written documents and visual images by early explorers and traders from eastern Canada and the painter-adventurers like Paul Kane who accompanied them (see chapter 6).

As the West became a part of Canada, new visitors brought an increasing awareness of its unique landscapes to easterners. The Canadian Pacific Railway had a lot to do with this, beginning with its dispatching, in 1872, a team of experts under the leadership of engineer Sandford Fleming on a transcontinental journey to identify the most appropriate route for its planned railway, already under construction.[11] Just as it had promoted the agricultural settlement of the West (see chapters 6 and 7), the Canadian Pacific Railway (CPR) recognized the potential value of tourism in the West as an additional means of filling its trains; indeed, American railways had begun to exploit this opportunity a few years earlier. To inform likely customers in the crowded cities of the East of the magnificent attractions of the Rocky Mountains and other spectacular western landscapes, the company engaged or provided free passes for a battalion of photographers and painters, including several employees of the William Notman and Son photographic studio in Montreal.[12] Painters commissioned by the railway included John Fraser, who had begun his career with the Notman studio, Marmaduke Matthews, Frederic Bell-Smith, and Canadian-born (a rarity) Lucius O'Brien. These accomplished artists extolled the beauties of the West in the first decade of the national parks' existence through well-executed works, expressed in a variety of techniques that were strongly influenced by European or Hudson Valley precedents.[13]

Lucius O'Brien provided a further measure of publicity for the wild landscapes of western Canada (and, in fact, for the country as a whole) as the artistic director for *Picturesque Canada*, an elaborate and expensive two-volume compendium of wood-engraved illustrations and accompanying text that described hundreds of urban, rural, and wild natural scenes across Canada, published in instalments from 1882. The text, strongly expressing a new Canadian nationalism, was provided by Rev. George Monro Grant, who had accompanied Sandford Fleming on his 1872 journey and written the report of that expedition.[14]

The challenges Canada faced in creating national and provincial parks were similar to those met by the United States. As in the US, Canadian nature parks had to confront, from the very beginning, an inevitable conflict between the preservation of the parks and their use by the public. The National Parks Law, adopted by the federal government of Canada in 1930, clearly expressed this dichotomy:

"The Parks are hereby dedicated to the people of Canada for their benefit, education and enjoyment, subject to the provisions of this Act and Regulations, and such Parks shall be maintained and made use of so as to leave them unimpaired for the enjoyment of future generations."[15] This passage was inspired by the US National Park Service Organic Act of 1916, copying almost verbatim the original text as written by Frederick Law Olmsted Jr., who followed in his father's footsteps to become a pre-eminent American landscape architect.[16] The paragraph has been retained, essentially without change, in subsequent versions of the Canadian law. The two objectives it identifies seem contradictory; it is obviously impossible to completely satisfy both at the same time. But this conflict was and is central to the definition of our national parks. In fact, we can understand much of the history of these great natural parks as a gradual evolution of our attitudes towards this central paradox.

12.2   Bow River, Banff National Park, AB

The Enjoyment of Resplendent Nature: Great Parks of the West, 1885–1920

The first concrete steps towards Canada's national parks system were taken almost by accident. In 1883, surveyors working for the Canadian Pacific Railway discovered hot springs and cascades in several caverns and basins near the Bow River, along which the railway was proceeding in its long climb through the Rockies. In 1885, the Canadian government reserved a small plot around the springs, to preserve them for the enjoyment of the public.[17] The minuscule terrain was greatly enlarged over the next two years so as to include the magnificent landscapes that surrounded it. In 1887, the whole area became a park, under the name "the Rocky Mountains Park of Canada."[18] A series of laws concerning the natural environment of the park were soon passed, with the objectives of protecting terrestrial and aquatic fauna and controlling private development. But it was clear from the beginning that the federal government and the railway company shared a common goal: the creation of a grand, prestigious tourist resort, aimed at an affluent clientele. The government built the village of Banff[19] on the banks of the Bow River; the CPR built a railway station and a sumptuous hotel – the Banff Springs – on a majestic site near the village. Carriage roads, bridges, and horse trails, to provide easy access to the hotel and the principal attractions of the park, were quick to follow.[20]

Between 1886 and 1895, through the good offices of William Pearce, federal commissioner of mines in Winnipeg and Calgary (known for many other contributions to the Canadian landscape; see previous chapters), the government reserved several other magnificent landscapes as future national parks. All these landscapes had become accessible through the advancement of the rail line into the mountains. Pearce prepared preliminary plans indicating the lands to be included in each park[21] – Glacier and Yoho National parks, which border on the railway's route through the Rockies and the Selkirks in British Columbia; the stunning Waterton Lakes, where the Rockies meet the American frontier; and Lake Louise, a glacier-fed body of water situated higher up in the valley of the Bow, above Banff. Three additional mountain parks were added to the system during the decade

240   CHALLENGES OF AN URBAN AND INDUSTRIAL LANDSCAPE

1910–20, contiguous, as always, to major transportation routes. Mount Revelstoke National Park (1914), adjacent to the CPR line, is an alpine plateau punctuated by vertical summits, glaciers, and spectacular waterfalls. Kootenay National Park (1920) comprises the valley slopes of the Kootenay and Vermilion rivers, where the first wagon road was carved through the Rockies. Further north, the construction of a second transcontinental railway line, the Grand Trunk Railway, set the scene for the creation of the largest mountain park in the West, Jasper National Park, in 1907. A neighbour to Banff Park on the Alberta side of the Great Divide, Jasper included the upper valley of the mighty Athabasca River, at the start of its long journey to the northeast; and the magnificent Columbia Icefield and its pendant, the Athabasca Glacier, last survivors of the age of the glaciers.[22]

With its first interventions in the Rockies and the Selkirk Range, the federal government had set in place the nucleus of what would become a vast system of national parks. It is not surprising that this first generation of national parks was established entirely in the West. Everything in the western landscape – topography, vegetation, distances – seems larger, more striking, more powerful than its eastern counterpart. And since, in the late nineteenth and early twentieth centuries, most of the West had not yet been developed and still remained under the control of the central government, it was much easier to reserve large territories

12.3　Cameron Lake, Waterton Lakes National Park, AB. The mountain face that terminates the lake is in Glacier National Park, Montana.

242　CHALLENGES OF AN URBAN AND INDUSTRIAL LANDSCAPE

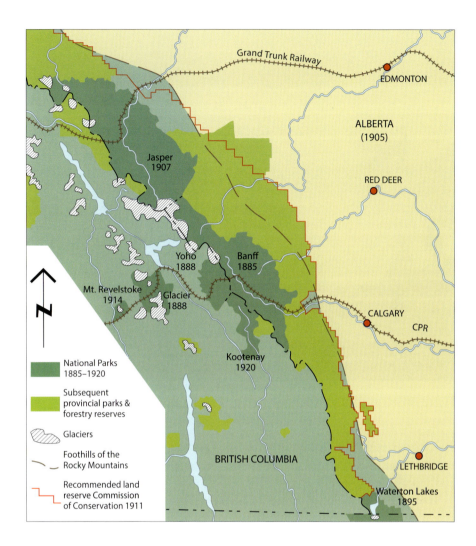

12.4 National parks and reserves in western Canada, 1885–1914. The first wave of national parks, along with a series of subsequent provincial parks and land reserves, formed a continuous protected zone along the crest of the Rockies. The role of the railways in the creation of the parks is evident.

for park purposes there than it was in the largely privatized and more heavily exploited lands of the East.[23] The western parks formed a coherent ensemble linked to the railway network, which was also under federal jurisdiction.

Provincial Wilderness Parks in the East: Protection and Exploitation

During this period of great accomplishment in the West, governments in the East of the continent also established large parks in remarkable natural sites. But it was the Canadian provinces and the American states, instead of the federal governments of the two countries, that initiated this process. Provincial governments had existed, in one form or another, for almost a century in Ontario and Quebec, even longer in the Atlantic region. Alberta and Saskatchewan would not attain provincial status until 1905 and would not control their natural resources or Crown lands – that is, public lands – until 1930.[24] The provincial governments in the

12.5 Niagara Falls, New York and Ontario, seen from the Canadian side. The American Falls are to the left, Horseshoe Falls to the right.

East, however, had long controlled such lands and resources and the federal government had no desire or interest in provoking arguments with these provinces concerning the location of their parks.[25]

The first preoccupation of those who advocated the preservation of natural sites was Niagara Falls, a spectacular natural phenomenon created by the erosion of a deep river gorge some 10 kilometres long into the Niagara Escarpment, a continuous ridge of dolomite that traverses southwestern Ontario in a great arc, from the State of New York to Michigan. A sensational tourist attraction, the falls also attracted a disreputable conglomeration of industries and low-grade commerce, on both sides of the river.[26] The preservation of Niagara Falls for park purposes was largely the result of a long propaganda and publicity campaign waged by the American painter Frederic Church, a member of the Hudson River School, who sketched the falls on many occasions and painted two outstanding panoramic views of them in 1857 and 1867.[27] Church's efforts were ably complemented by those of landscape architect Frederick Law Olmsted (who returned to the East following his sojourn in California) and the governor general of Canada, Lord Dufferin, who gave the first official support to the cause in a speech he delivered in 1878.[28] The energetic Dufferin won the accord of the governments of the State of New York and of Ontario, and finally, by 1885, both governments reserved the land around the falls to create a park.[29] The first reservation in Canadian territory included the gorge and the falls, as well as a wide plateau on the edge of the precipice and a beautiful wooded escarpment that stepped up from the plateau

244 CHALLENGES OF AN URBAN AND INDUSTRIAL LANDSCAPE

to the high plain between Lake Erie and Lake Ontario. The commission remade the plateau as an elegant landscape of lawns and planting beds – Queen Victoria Park – an eclectic juxtaposition of a Victorian flower garden and a magnificent natural spectacle. From this relatively restrained territorial base, the park on the Canadian side expanded gradually but inexorably, eventually comprising a band of green space some 56 kilometres long next to the gorge.[30]

Further innovations occurred in New York and were soon emulated north of the border. In 1885, the state government created a vast public park in the Adirondack Mountains, an extension of the Canadian Shield to the south of the St. Lawrence River. The creation of the Adirondack Forest Reserve envisioned the preservation of the aesthetic and recreational attractions of this wild country of forests and lakes and, in protecting its forests, ensured the provision, in perpetuity, of pure water for the rivers of the state, without which the population and industry of New York could not survive.[31] In Ontario, the Canadian neighbour of New York State, this development was carefully followed. Already placed on its guard by the droughts and floods caused by the deforestation of the early nineteenth century (see chapter 7), Ontarians chose a unique location for a similar park: an elevated plateau in the Canadian Shield, covered with dense forests, and the source of five different river systems that drain the southern part of the province. Originally the homeland of the Algonquin people, these highlands had long been exploited for their forests.[32] In 1885, to eliminate as much as possible the over-exploitation of

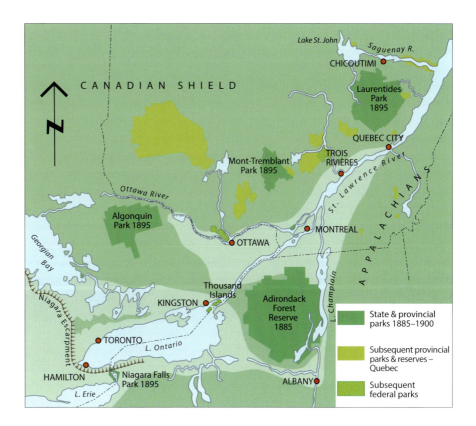

12.6 Natural parks and reserves in eastern Canada and the United States, 1885–1900. Ontario, Quebec, and New York State established the first generation of parks in the East to safeguard long-term water supplies from the Shield and the Adirondacks, and to protect natural wonders like Niagara Falls.

NATURAL MONUMENTS 245

12.7 Mont Tremblant Park, QC, as seen in 1979. This sketch shows the south slope (actually facing southwest) of one of the Laurentians' tallest mountains. Extensive new tourist facilities and ski runs have been added since 1990; the ski slopes shown here were begun in 1938 by American ski enthusiasts.

these resources, Alexander Kirkwood, chief clerk for the agency that administered the sale of Crown lands in Ontario, suggested that the area be preserved as a park. He subsequently chaired the royal commission that convinced the Ontario parliament to create the Algonquin National Park of Ontario in 1893. The government defined the mission of this immense territory as "a public park and forest reservation, fish and game preserve, health resort and pleasure ground for the benefit, advantage and enjoyment of the people of the Province."[33] Algonquin Park, still the largest park in Ontario, espoused several objectives, including the two most fundamental – conservation of the landscape and enjoyment by the public – but also the production of timber, which furnished and still furnishes an important component of its revenues.[34]

In 1895, almost simultaneously with the founding of Algonquin Park, the neighbouring province of Quebec inaugurated its first large natural parks: the Parc de la Montagne Tremblante (today, Parc national du Mont-Tremblant) and Parc national des Laurentides.[35] Like Algonquin Park, both of these parks were immense wooded plateaus in the highlands of the Canadian Shield. Both were located at the frontier between the mixed forest of the Lower Laurentians and the boreal forest of the northern Laurentians. Like Algonquin Park – and, in fact, like the Adirondack Reserve and the Rocky Mountain parks of the West – these two parks were strategically located at the highest points of several watersheds in order to preserve the quality and quantity of water, the critical resource. Later, in 1906, the Quebec government would apply the same principle when establishing the Réserve de la Gaspésie, which protected the sources of all the rivers that drain the Gaspé Peninsula's Chic-Choc Range, a branch of the Appalachians, towards the St. Lawrence and the Baie des Chaleurs.[36] The subsequent creation of wildlife reserves for hunting and fishing pursued the same objective: to protect the forests of mountainous regions and thus assure abundance and perpetual supplies of high-quality water for the whole population.[37]

The First Generation of Natural Parks: Cultural Significance and Exploitation

Wilderness lands, and particularly forests, have played a central role in the formation of the Canadian character. The omnipresent forest has never been far from Canada's *ecumene* – the continuous territory inhabited by human beings – or even from its large cities. Peter Jacobs reminds us that "the forest ... is a critical component of our consciousness, our mind set, and our culture" – it provides an important part of our identity. Jacobs notes that the forest participates in a sort of cultural inversion: when the city becomes dangerous and sinister, the forest is innocent and pastoral.[38]

The forest and the wilderness have powerfully influenced Canadian *images* and *icons*, our perception of who we are, and the writers and artists whose works have interpreted them. In particular, our understanding and appreciation of the great natural parks are inextricably tied to their representation on canvas and in photographs, first in the images created by accomplished nineteenth-century painters such as Frederic Bell-Smith and Lucius O'Brien, mentioned above; then in the powerful oil sketches and majestic large-scale landscape paintings by members of

12.8   Tom Thomson, *Sunset*, 1915. This oil sketch depicts Algonquin Park, ON

12.9   Promotional CPR poster showing recreational development in Banff National Park in the 1930s

NATURAL MONUMENTS   247

the first consciously nationalistic movement in Canadian art, exemplified by the work of Tom Thomson (1877–1917). Thomson, born in Ontario, lived and worked in Algonquin Park from 1913 to 1916. He persuaded his artist friends from Toronto to join him there on painting expeditions. After Thomson's tragic death by drowning in the park in 1917,[39] his friends carried on his mission as the Group of Seven, expressing on canvas a unique and original sense of the Canadian landscape in a vivid and vigorous visual language that went beyond the somewhat conservative, European-influenced work of their predecessors.[40] This new artistic approach was really a pan-Canadian movement. The Group of Seven moved west, north, and east from their Ontario heartland after the First World War. Quebec artist Jean Paul Lemieux produced some outstanding canvasses of natural scenes that were profoundly influenced by Thomson and his colleagues, before developing his own austere and sombre reading of the Canadian landscape. In British Columbia, Emily Carr created a highly personal visual language to describe the giant forests and ancient Native artefacts of the West Coast. Thus the parks movement, which owed its origins in part to the work of Canadian artists, inspired a new generation of Canadian painters.

But those responsible for the parks did not see them as sacrosanct temples of undefiled nature. From the beginning – and even before the beginning – the *ecological integrity* of the national and provincial parks was under threat. Coal mining in Banff and ranching at the Waterton Lakes preceded their reservation as national parks and continued thereafter. The same applied to logging in Algonquin Park and in the first Quebec parks, long after their establishment as places of public recreation. In Quebec, the exploitation of minerals was added to the role of parks as sources of wood and reserves for hunting and fishing.[41] Development of all kinds was encouraged and sponsored by park managers in order to encourage and accommodate tourists.[42] Grand hotels, carriage trails, administration buildings, residences for wardens and supervisors, trail huts, townsites, cottages, fire towers, piers, boathouses, tennis courts, golf courses (often among the first "improvements" to be constructed in a new park), skating rinks – all these facilities were cheerfully welcomed to the early natural parks. These were, in fact, conceived as sophisticated vacation resorts rather than as wild and natural environments; the inaccessibility of the first parks virtually obliged them to seek out an elite clientele who could afford the cost of the long train ride necessary to reach them.[43] But despite all these compromises, the timely acquisition of these great parks ensured their overall protection and established a firm base for the creation of the extended network of parks that we enjoy today.

Conservation Parks, 1910–1930

Even before the full-scale tourist exploitation of the parks ended, a second definition of the national park came to the fore, emphasizing its potential for the *conservation of natural resources*, principally animals and plants.[44] In 1909, greatly concerned with the importance of conserving the resources of the nation, the Canadian prime minister Sir Wilfrid Laurier established the Canadian Commission

12.10 Point Pelee National Park on Lake Erie, ON, a constantly changing sandspit that is a paradise for migratory birds

of Conservation, to be chaired by former minister Clifford Sifton.[45] The newly formed commission was mandated to advise the government on all questions concerning the conservation of resources. The areas of its main concerns were lands and forests, water, hydroelectricity, fisheries, and animals. The commission identified the lands that were to be included in the national parks and forest reserve systems, which they considered vital tools to ensure the conservation of water, flora, and fauna. In 1910, the commission recommended that the government reinforce the seven parks of the "first generation" – all in the Canadian West – by creating a huge Rocky Mountains Forest Reserve, along the entire eastern slope of the Rockies. This was accomplished in 1911. Today, almost all of this territory is included in a chain of provincial parks, wilderness areas, and other protected green spaces that have welcomed a great variety of recreational activities, including the events of the 1988 Olympics at Kananaskis.[46]

In 1915, the commission recommended the creation of a national park on the peninsula of Point Pelee, Ontario, "pointing southerly like a long finger into the western end of Lake Erie."[47] Its goal was to establish a wildlife preserve to protect resident waterfowl and migratory birds. With the government of Quebec, the commission also explored the creation of a bird sanctuary on Percé Rock and the adjacent islands off the Gaspé Peninsula.[48] At the same time, the new Dominion Parks

Branch, established within the Department of the Interior in 1911, emphasized the preservation of large mammals – "charismatic fauna," such as buffalo, elk (wapiti), and moose, along with wolves and black bears – that were in danger of extinction from over-hunting and habitat destruction.[49] The solution: create wildlife reserves where hunting would be controlled or forbidden. The first national park with this specific mission was founded in 1913. This was Elk Island National Park, located in the parklands east of Edmonton. The park protected the last living herd of elk and some 300 plains buffalo, providing the breeding stock for the regeneration of the two species throughout Canada.[50] The creation of the enormous Wood Buffalo National Park in 1922, astride the Alberta–Northwest Territories border, ensured the preservation of the wood buffalo, a related species native to the northern plains.[51]

A Countrywide Park System, 1911–1940

The interventions of the Commission of Conservation reinforced the policies put in place by the first head of the Parks Branch, James B. Harkin (1875–1955), who favoured landscape preservation and promoted the appreciation of wilderness. Harkin wanted "to instill in all Canadians a love of the country and pride in its natural beauty."[52] His other great preoccupation was to extend the park system to all regions of the country and to include within it remarkable landscapes other than the majestic mountain plateaus and peaks that had been favoured up until that time. When he began his mandate in 1911, all the natural parks administered by the federal government were to be found in the two most westerly provinces of the country. But throughout the coming decades, the Parks Branch was to turn its focus towards the eastern and central provinces of Canada.[53] In the East, it would be necessary to choose sites of very different size and character from the extensive regional landscape parks of the West. Most land had been privatized in long-settled eastern Canada, and the public lands belonged to the provinces and not to the federal government. The latter had thus to negotiate with the provinces concerning the choice of sites for new national parks, which would then be ceded to the central government. Then as now, the provinces wanted to maintain control over the economic development within their territories and were thus often reluctant to cede land, even for a desirable purpose.[54]

The Parks Branch's strategy for the first generation of eastern parks focused on establishing a series of small national parks on critical sites that would protect specific physiographic units or representative samples of larger ecosystems. This was the case with the St. Lawrence Islands National Park, situated in the Thousand Islands and founded in 1914 (the site had been placed on reserve in 1904), as well as the Georgian Bay Islands National Park, created in 1929. Just before ceding the rights to natural resources to the three Prairie provinces in 1930, the federal government established two large new parks there: Mount Riding National Park, a long wooded massif that anchors the Manitoba Escarpment some 200 kilometres northwest of Winnipeg, and Prince Albert National Park in Saskatchewan, located in the boreal forest north of the city of that name and close to the confluence of the two branches of the Saskatchewan River.[55] Attracted by the irregular topography

250 CHALLENGES OF AN URBAN AND INDUSTRIAL LANDSCAPE

12.11 Along the Cabot Trail in Cape Breton Highlands National Park, NS

and numerous lakes of these two landscapes, the residents of nearby towns and farms set up vacation communities within them. Both parks established townsites and both accommodated large clusters of cabins, cottages, and semi-permanent tents, which of course did not conform in any way to the stated mission of the national parks.[56]

Finally, in the 1930s, the Parks Branch founded the first national parks in the Atlantic provinces. In 1936, the Cape Breton Highlands National Park, the largest such park in eastern Canada at the time of its founding, was added to the system. Its site included the wild highland plateau of northern Cape Breton Island, part of the Appalachian chain, along with the steep slopes and ribbon of coast where this plateau meets the sea. The highlands, exposed to extreme cold and wind, harbour a stunted subarctic vegetation, unique in the Maritime provinces, and the coast offers truly spectacular views. A single road permits the exploration of the park – the Cabot Trail, built by the government of Nova Scotia between the 1920s and 1950s, featuring vertiginous ascents and descents.[57] In 1937, the Parks Branch inaugurated Prince Edward Island National Park, a long band of terrain on the northern coast of the island, an archetypal landscape that integrates magnificent, peaceful beaches and eroded sea cliffs of red sandstone.

The tourist exploitation of these two parks was based as much on their cultural attributes as on their natural attractions. The fictional story of *Anne of Green*

NATURAL MONUMENTS 251

12.12   Cavendish Beach, Prince Edward Island National Park

Gables profoundly marked the iconography of Prince Edward Island Park.[58] And the interpretive message of the Cape Breton park was strongly based on a Scottish theme, insisting on the Gaelic traditions of the island (while leaving aside its Acadian and English traditions) to deploy a Caledonian nomenclature. The hotel is the "Keltic Lodge"; the golf course, the "Highlands Links."[59] Near a rest stop along the Cabot Trail stands the "Lone Shieling," replica of an old stone shelter that would have been erected by a solitary Scottish shepherd back in the old country.[60]

The parks of that era owed much to Richard W. Cautley (1873–1953), the chief surveyor of the Parks Branch, who researched and recommended potential national park sites at Mount Riding, Manitoba,[61] in New Brunswick, and in the Cape Breton Highlands. Cautley also defined the territorial limits of the latter park and articulated its design philosophy, oriented primarily towards a "discovery experience" by automobile.[62] Although the Parks Branch, during the Harkin era, adopted the preservation of the plant and animal resources of the parks as their central objective, this did not mean that the promotion of tourism and recreational activities had been rejected. Each park of medium or large extent had its own golf course, almost always designed by Stanley F. Thompson (1893–1953), the dean of Canada's golf course architects. Alpine ski slopes, tennis courts, townsites, and vacation communities continued to flourish in the parks, despite the overall philosophy of preservation.[63] In contrast, extractive activities (mining, lumbering, etc.) were banned *de facto* beginning in the 1920s, according to a newly enunciated "principle of inviolability," even though no law explicitly sanctioned this policy. This principle, enunciated by Commissioner Harkin, allowed tourist facilities within the parks while excluding industrial activities.[64]

Parks in the Postwar Years

The other Atlantic provinces had to wait until the end of the Second World War before receiving their first national parks. The aftermath of the war was to have a profound effect on national and provincial parks, principally through rapid growth in Canada's general prosperity and the consequent explosion in car ownership and highway building. Suddenly, a much larger clientele had access to the parks. The number of park visitors would double between 1945 and 1947, and then continue to increase at a spectacular rate in the following years.[65] The new clientele came primarily from the middle class; the days of distant spas frequented by a social elite were long gone. In the face of this increased demand, park planners set in train a major expansion of recreational facilities, campgrounds, and trails, putting less emphasis on conservation.[66]

Green Symbols of Democracy and Their Impact on the Natural Environment

Fundy National Park, founded in 1948 on the southern coast of New Brunswick, facing the Bay of Fundy, was the first new park to confront these revolutionary changes. According to Alan MacEachern, this park expresses a new philosophy, that of *recreational democracy*. An entire panoply of specialized facilities was inserted within the landscape of beaches, cliffs, and forests furnished by Nature. Facilities at Fundy included a golf course (virtually obligatory in any case), a heated swimming pool, a village centre with shops and gas stations, cabins and campgrounds, horse stables for riding, an amphitheatre, and a craft school located in a central clubhouse.[67] To make room for these facilities, park authorities obliterated all original buildings and other signs of habitation on the site – previously occupied for centuries – and proceeded with a major reworking of the landform in the park's central area.[68]

Terra Nova National Park on the east coast of Newfoundland, created in 1957 in the historic dominion that had become a Canadian province in 1949, was the youngest member of this first wave of national parks in the Atlantic provinces. The park did not follow the example of Fundy, seeking instead to present an image of what it really was, a typical coastal landscape of its rugged province.[69] But it was an exception. In general, the uneasy balance between conservation and public use – a permanent characteristic of the national parks system – was in danger of becoming one-sided, leaning too far towards public use. This situation was intensified as time went on, since few new parks would be added to the system during the next fifteen years, while the number of users saw a constant increase.

An overall evaluation of the parks at the beginning of the 1960s would certainly have noted that human activities were strongly affecting the ecological integrity of these milieus, and that their natural qualities had been considerably modified. The building of facilities for tourism, the control of fire,[70] the raising of the water levels of lakes, which flooded shallows and wetlands – all these brought great changes to the living conditions of the wildlife of the parks. Lumbering (in the early years) and deforestation for roads and other purposes indirectly affected many animals.[71] Other interventions were more direct: the killing of wolves and other predators (incredibly, Algonquin's last bounties on wolves were removed only in 1972), the reintroduction of beavers in some parks, the use of pesticides, including DDT.[72] Bears became a tourist attraction, a nuisance, and a danger in the parks.

Rebalancing the Equation

Undoubtedly influenced by the environmental movement of the 1960s (see chapter 21), the Parks Branch moved to restore the balance. In 1964, Ottawa adopted a new national parks policy, expanding on the 1930 National Park Act and establishing a revised philosophy for the parks.[73] The new policy, published in 1969, confirmed that the parks were still there "for the benefit of all Canadians" and that they should remain "unimpaired for the enjoyment of future generations." But this enjoyment would have to be carried out in such a way as to emphasize and show respect for Nature. The law implied that parks should be planned so as to focus the visitor's attention on their important natural features, and that they should not provide facilities that did not contribute to the realization of that goal – that

12.13 Long Beach, Pacific Rim National Park, Vancouver Island, BC. Located on the west coast of Vancouver Island, this park provides a unique view of virtually endless beaches and of temperate rain forest environments that have rarely suffered forest fire. Despite its difficulty of access, overcrowding along the West Coast Trail through the park has become a problem at peak holiday periods.

12.14 Pangnirtung Fjord in Auyuittuq National Park, Baffin Island, Nunavut

is, they should no longer "provide recreational facilities of an urban character." Visitors should be able to enjoy the park without impairing the natural features that attracted them in the first place.[74]

In parallel with the adoption of this new policy, the Parks Branch established a whole new wave of national parks in the 1960s and 1970s, under the direction of the minister of Indian Affairs and Northern Development, Jean Chrétien, later to be prime minister of Canada. Chrétien was personally involved in the extension of the national parks system throughout the country. Some additional western parks were set aside at this time, representing landscape zones previously bypassed: Pacific Rim on the western littoral of Vancouver Island and Grasslands, preserving remnants of the pre-agricultural prairie in southern Saskatchewan. Many parks were established in the Atlantic provinces, and Quebec received its first national parks created by the federal government. Atlantic parks included Kouchibougouac on the Atlantic coast of New Brunswick, Kejimkujik in the forested highlands of Nova Scotia, and Gros Morne in Newfoundland. In Quebec, parks were established at Forillon on the Gaspé Peninsula and La Mauricie in the forested Laurentian Shield. Finally, the first parks were established in the North, so long ignored in the power centres of Canada; these included Kluane in the southern Yukon and Auyuittuq, "the land of eternal snows," located on a high plateau on Baffin Island, accessed by sea via the awesome Pangnirtung Fjord.[75] All these new parks responded to rigorous selection criteria defined by an increasingly professional

NATURAL MONUMENTS 255

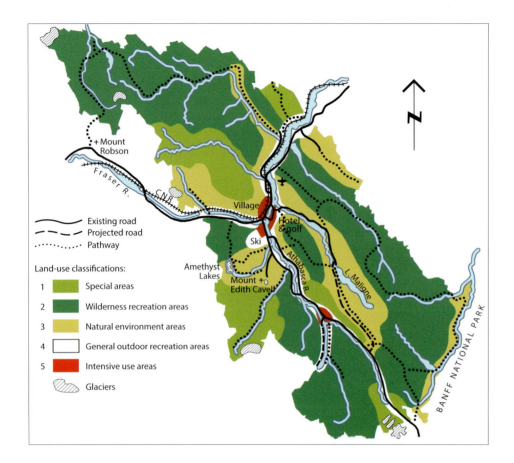

12.15 Land-use zoning plan, 1971, Jasper National Park, AB

parks staff, which included biologists, geographers, geologists, landscape architects, and forestry engineers.

The new parks, as well as most of the existing parks, were subject to an equally rigorous and detailed planning process, carried out in accordance with the rational and scientific approach to design that was characteristic of that period. Following an exhaustive process of site analysis, park areas were zoned by park designers according to five land-use categories.[76] Many of the landscape architecture and environmental design firms of the time were involved in these thorough planning studies. These firms included Donald W. Graham and Associates, from Ottawa; and Project Planning Associates, Richard Strong and Associates, and Hough Stansbury, from Toronto. Inside Parks Canada (even the name of the Parks Branch was changed), Otis Bishopric, Roman Fodchuk, Denis Major, and Reinhart Petersmann figured among the directors and coordinators of these ambitious projects. The projects also benefited from the discipline imposed by public hearings.[77]

Harsh Experiences

The 1964 policy set up far more stringent rules concerning the compatibility of improvements and activities with the principal goals of the parks. This was far different from the free-wheeling response to tourist demand of the 1945–60 period. There would be no new golf courses, swimming pools, or bowling greens in the national parks. Some of these new interpretations of the parks' mission led to controversy, particularly when it came to the removal of long-time residents – and whole villages – from some new parks. Forillon National Park, where the Appalachians meet the sea, is a small mountainous peninsula projecting into the Gulf of St. Lawrence from the larger Gaspé Peninsula. The site of Jacques Cartier's first landfall in 1534, the littoral had been occupied by fishermen for over two centuries. Five villages typical of this traditional maritime culture hugged the coast, their farms and woodlots straggling irregularly up the mountain slopes. The first design studies for the park, in 1970–71, recognized the site as a cultural, as well as a natural, landscape, proposing as the park's theme "a harmony of man, land and sea."[78] But, tragically, this original vision was soon displaced by a narrower concept that focused on the preservation of the natural milieu rather than on the long human history of the peninsula. To create the park, properties were expropriated and several villages were destroyed. Residents of these villages had to leave, rebuilding their lives in a general diaspora after suffering painful personal experiences.[79]

Similar events occurred at Kouchibougouac National Park in New Brunswick. Others went through like experiences with the establishment of new provincial parks during the same period.[80] The policy of eliminating human traces from such parks was part of a high-minded but narrowly focused philosophy prevalent in the 1960s and 1970s, that of *social engineering*, based on the idea that government knew best and would ensure maximum long-term benefits to society, regardless of short-term impacts on individuals and their communities.[81]

Masterpieces of the New Generation

The unhappy events that have just been described do not diminish the excellent quality of the natural and designed landscapes of this generation of parks. And there were some masterpieces among them. In Newfoundland's Gros Morne National Park, the landlocked glacier-cut fjords through the Long Range Mountains and the unique Tablelands, overthrusts of infertile serpentinite from the Earth's mantle, are amazing natural landscapes. And, fortunately, the sacrifices of Forillon and Kouchibougouac residents did affect subsequent park policy, as Gros Morne's boundaries were carefully drawn to exclude a number of little towns like Woody Point, enclaves that are within the overall park territory but remain private lands not subject to stringent park policies.[82] And thanks to the efforts of Susan Buggey and other members of Parks Canada, cultural landscapes are now fully accepted as legitimate components of the national parks, worthy complements to their magnificent natural landscapes.

Another remarkable natural landscape is La Mauricie National Park in Quebec. This park displays the classic landscapes of the Laurentians: mature vegetation characteristic of this kingdom of the maple; hidden beaches and quiet sandbars; cliffs that plunge straight down into long, deep, narrow lakes that fill ancient fissures in the earth's crust, carved out by glaciers.[83] Except for a striking vista straight down the length of Lac Wapizagonke, seen from a masterfully sited viewpoint, the site is seldom as spectacular as the mountain parks of the West or Gros Morne.[84] But the integrity of its natural environment – much of which is owed, paradoxically, to the dozen or so elitist hunting and fishing clubs that controlled it for almost a century[85] – and its carefully balanced development, the result of thorough conceptual studies at both the overall park scale and that of its distinct component areas – provide this unpretentious park with great distinction. A design team directed by town planner Georges Robert, with landscape architect Danièle Routaboule and the participation of the group SEREC, developed the overall master plan for the park, as well as detailed conceptual plans for the various activity areas in each sector. A single parkway, the Route Promenade, provides access to the entire park, including all major recreation and nature-study facilities. This road is a masterpiece of alignment and grading, its trajectory through the park carefully integrated with the natural topography, aligned so as to reveal and frame interesting views, yet located in such a manner as to be invisible from the dozens of lakes within the park.[86]

12.16   The approach to Western Brook Pond, which is enclosed by the cliffs in the background, in Gros Morne National Park, NL. Newfoundlanders call this majestic and powerful fjord a "pond." Coastal deposits have cut off the fjord's access to the sea, so it is a body of fresh, not salt, water.

12.17   Lake Wapizagonke in La Mauricie National Park, QC

Another recent mark of progress in the national parks is a growing collaboration with the First Nations. The original inhabitants of Canada have lived for thousands of years in territories that have become national parks. They have greatly influenced the evolution of the vegetation and animal populations of these territories, without ever destroying their local environments. Today, a major percentage of the total land area of the parks consists of lands donated by the First Nations or owned by them and co-administered with Parks Canada.[87] In general, a strong sense of collaboration inspires this shared management, as can be seen at Gwaii Haanas National Park Reserve, in Haida Gwaii (formerly the Queen Charlotte Islands), off the British Columbia coast. The Haida people have lived in this archipelago for at least 5,000 years. They worked with a coalition of groups from the islands and from outside (including scientist and journalist David Suzuki) to put a halt to the recent devastation of the islands' forests.[88] Today, visitors who enter the park's immense forests of Sitka spruce, western red cedar, and western hemlock are welcomed by Haida Watchmen, who monitor the health of the environment and help their guests to understand both the natural milieu and the totems and houses of the Haida's ancestors, structures that bear eloquent witness to this ancient culture during their gradual reintegration with the Earth.

NATURAL MONUMENTS   259

Representative Landscapes and Ecological Integrity

Since 1972, Parks Canada has redefined its criteria for the selection of new parks, adopting a policy of *representative landscapes*. Each of the country's forty-eight biophysical regions – thirty-nine terrestrial and nine marine – is to be represented by at least one national park. This policy expresses a new goal of preserving landscapes typical of Canada, and not simply the remarkable landscapes that had been protected in the original parks of the nineteenth century. Today, although some regions are not yet represented and others have several parks, an overall equilibrium is being gradually established. The creation of many new parks in the North is a striking accomplishment of this philosophy of representative landscapes. The policy has also been adopted by several provinces, including Quebec, which has decided to create at least one conservation park in each of the forty-four natural regions of the province.[89]

In 1998, a new mode of reflection again redefined the priorities of the national parks. Stimulated by an increasing environmental consciousness among the gen-

12.18 National parks and national park reserves related to the biophysical regions of Canada. Eventually, each region will be represented by at least one national park.

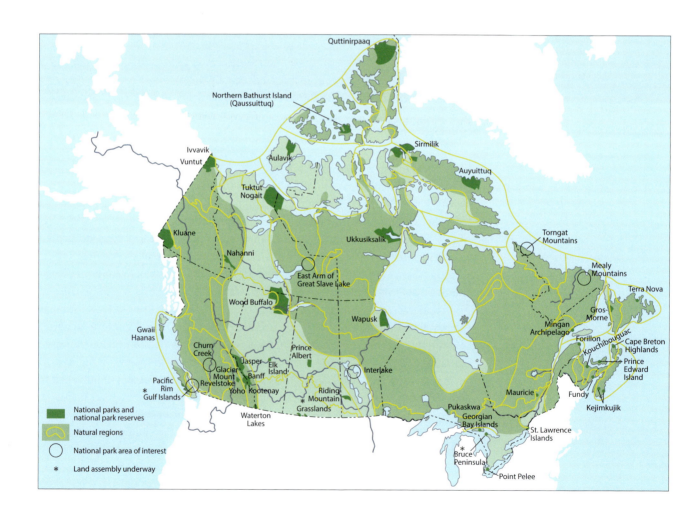

260   CHALLENGES OF AN URBAN AND INDUSTRIAL LANDSCAPE

eral public and confronted by the perception that the parks were suffering from a *loss of ecological integrity*, the minister responsible for the parks asked a group of experts to examine the situation and make recommendations. The committee, which included among its members landscape architect Michael Hough, who had long been involved in conservation issues, stated in its report (published in 2000) that the ecological integrity of the parks was indeed degraded – to various degrees depending on the park, of course – and that the overall situation constituted "a crisis of national importance." Of the thirty-seven parks studied, twenty-two had sustained major or severe impairment; this amounted to 60 per cent of all the parks and included all seven of the original mountain parks of western Canada.[90] In response to this critical situation, the committee enunciated several new principles to guide the management of the parks, including the "precautionary principle," as well as a series of management strategies to put the parks on a path towards recovery.[91] Among their detailed policy proposals, the committee suggested a new regional approach, to prevent the parks from becoming "ecological islands," surrounded by highly modified landscapes. This approach proposed that the national parks be considered as "a key part of the mosaic of conservation lands."[92] The committee also revisited the central paradox of the parks, the apparent conflict between public use and conservation of the environment for future generations, judging that the recent revisions of 1988 and 1999 to the law that defined the national parks gave clear priority to the maintenance and restoration of the parks' ecological integrity, thus relegating park use by visitors and tourists to second place. The committee went further, affirming that, implicitly, even the original law of 1930 did not define a *double mandate*: conservation should always have trumped public use.[93]

An Uneasy but Essential Equilibrium

Looking back at Canada's great natural parks across their 125 years of history, one can see a constant evolution in the perceptions of their *raison d'être*, vacillating between the extremes of conservation and utilization. Regarding the double mandate, it would be comforting, but illusory, to agree with the Committee on Ecological Integrity that the priorities are – and always have been – clear. These unique environments are, no matter what we may feel, parks and not closed ecological reserves, or *chasses gardées*. Their invention was one of the great innovations of North America, an original democratic and social experiment, now exported all over the world.[94] In practice, every time we approach the planning and design of a natural park or a sector or subsystem of such a park, we must strike some balance between the twin objectives of conservation and public use. The riddle of the double mandate remains, but by sensible regulation, by measures for the protection of natural systems, by thoughtful choice and location of appropriate facilities, and by sensitive design of such facilities, each national park should achieve its most appropriate form in relation to its unique landscape. And those who make these choices might still do well to look to the principles enunciated by the Olmsteds, father and son, to provide a template for their decisions.

13.1 Proposed Edmonton Civic Centre, looking south towards the North Saskatchewan River, 1912. Morell & Nichols, landscape architects.

13

New Ideals in Urban Design: Garden City and City Beautiful

Towards the end of the nineteenth century, a powerful reform movement swept through the cities of Canada, transforming urban areas and institutions according to visions of the city that were entirely original. The current of idealism that inspired this movement was a response to unacceptable urban conditions; while the large urban parks and other open spaces created during the nineteenth century had certainly improved the daily life of urban residents, a great number of city dwellers still lived miserably in unhealthy slums. The poverty, chronic diseases, and pollution endemic to urban environments were compounded by traffic jams in too-narrow streets, visual cacophony created by a forest of service poles and wires of all sorts, and an incoherent architectural free-for-all. All contributed to a general ugliness. Between 1890 and 1920, social reformers and design professionals – landscape architects and city planners (there was no distinction between the two practices at the time), architects, a few engineers – envisioned radical changes to Canadian cities.[1] They proposed new models for city planning and design, models in which the *urban landscape* was to play a key role.

Reform Movements

The increasing disparity between rich and poor had created the equivalent of two distinct cities in the large industrial centres,[2] attracting criticism from popular journalists, religious leaders, and even business people and wealthy citizens.[3] In 1897, one of these, Herbert Brown Ames, a Montreal city councillor, published *The City below the Hill*, an analytical report describing the hardships of those who lived down the hill near the factories, in areas lacking parks and proper sanitary facilities. These conditions placed Montreal among the worst cities of Europe or America in terms of mortality rate.[4] Even Canada's great humorist Stephen Leacock bitterly satirized these conditions in his *Arcadian Adventures of the Idle Rich* of 1914, in which he contrasted the difficulties of those "below the hill" with the comfortable lives of those who resided on the slopes of Mount Royal.[5]

Women often played a central role in the reform movements. In Winnipeg, the Mothers' Association and the Manitoba branch of the National Council of Women of Canada (founded by Lady Aberdeen, wife of the governor general) pressured city authorities to create children's playgrounds.[6] Similarly in Montreal, a women's volunteer organization, the Montreal Parks and Playgrounds Association (MPPA), set itself the goal of bringing healthy play environments to the children of the city. Design professionals also became involved: in 1906, the Province of Quebec Association of Architects (PQAA) set up a Civic Improvement Committee (Comité d'embellissements municipaux),[7] and a like committee was formed in Toronto in 1911. The various groups got together: the PQAA and MPPA combined with other militant organizations in 1909 under the banner of the Civic Improvement League (Ligue de progrès civique), creating a broad-based volunteer group that sought progress in green spaces, traffic circulation, housing, sanitary conditions, and civic beauty.[8]

In looking for solutions, the reformers naturally turned to Great Britain, France, and the United States, countries that had already confronted the problems of industrialization and urbanization. In their efforts to change their cities, the native genius of each of these countries combined to give birth to two new philosophies of urban design: the first, British in origin, was the *Garden City*; the second, created in the United States but largely French in inspiration, was *City Beautiful*.

"Alabaster Cities"

The City Beautiful movement was the fruit of a period of great confidence and idealism in the United States. In response to severe problems of health, criminality, and poverty in the dense and dynamic industrial cities of the United States, problems that seemed all but insurmountable, the American business community brought forward a new and ambitious program that expressed the country's sense of national destiny. These problems could be solved; America fed the world, why shouldn't it feed its own citizens? These tawdry cities could be built anew, more grandly, to allow every American citizen to live in as fine surroundings as only princes and aristocrats had done in the past!

The physical inspiration for this urban transformation came primarily from French city planning. Towards the end of the nineteenth century, many young Americans studied at the École des Beaux-Arts in Paris, the most famous school of architecture in the world, to learn how to design the projects that would constitute an American Renaissance.[9] These aspirations first took concrete form on a grand site adjacent to Lake Michigan in Chicago, at the World's Columbian Exposition of 1893, designed by such luminaries as landscape architect Frederick Law Olmsted and architect Daniel Burnham. The image of elegant white buildings formally arranged around an expansive sheet of water[10] inspired cities all over the United States to create new *civic centres*, clusters of magnificent public buildings – city

13.2 Chicago Columbian Exposition Court of Honour, 1893. Looking east towards the Lake Michigan gateway and the enormous central basin at the heart of Olmsted and Burnham's spectacular "White City" composition.

13.3 Rickson A. Outhet, 1918, in a group photograph taken during his time at the US Housing Corporation in Washington. Outhet, who sports a mustache, is at the centre of the photo.

halls, libraries, concert halls – linked to the various sectors of the city by *park-like boulevards*.[11]

Soon christened "City Beautiful," this idea rapidly won over Canadian opinion, primarily through the efforts of designers from outside the country. But a few Canadian-born practitioners sought training abroad and returned with new knowledge and skills to the land of their birth. Among the first of these messengers was a young Montrealer, Rickson A. Outhet (1876–1951), who had gone to Boston in 1899 to study landscape architecture. Besides his academic training at Boston's Bussey Institute, Outhet worked in two offices of landscape architecture, first with Warren H. Manning and then with the Olmsted Brothers, who at that time were engaged in the creation of the Boston parks system. In 1901, the Olmsted office sent Outhet to Washington, DC, to work on the most important urban design project of the time, the McMillan Plan for the rebuilding of the centre of the capital. Inspired by the precepts of the City Beautiful movement, the project was directed by a brilliant team similar to the one that had created the Chicago Exhibition of 1893; its dominant members were architect Daniel Burnham and landscape architect/planner Frederick Law Olmsted Jr., son of the patriarch. Through his participation in this project, Outhet contributed to the creation of the large-scale axial geometry that ties together the various governmental buildings of the city.[12] He subsequently worked for several years as resident landscape architect at the Tuxedo Park estate in rural New York, extending his knowledge of the design and management of villa gardens. Following a systematic visit to the gardens and landscapes of England and the European continent, Outhet returned to Montreal in 1906 and

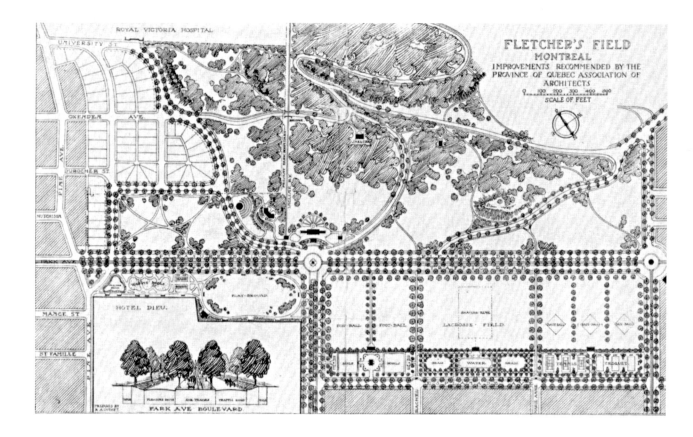

began to practise as a landscape architect. He was likely the first native-born Canadian to identify himself as such. His projects included several private gardens in the more prestigious districts of the city, often carried out in collaboration with prominent Montreal architects Edward and William Maxwell.[13]

Outhet's principal project after his return to Montreal demonstrated the talents in urban design that he had honed in Washington. In 1907 and 1908, he elaborated, for the Civic Improvement Committee of the PQAA, a series of urban design drawings for the central area of Montreal, following the principles that had informed the McMillan Plan for Washington. The six large drawings that Outhet produced for this mandate (one general plan and five sectorial plans) constituted a vast integrated scheme for the reorganization and beautification of central Montreal, a radical reconstruction of the city.[14] Published in 1909, his drawings proposed to solve the city's traffic problems by cutting broad diagonal boulevards through the downtown area, linking Mount Royal and Lafontaine parks with a new avenue – Confederation Boulevard – across the Plateau Mont-Royal, creating new public squares embellished with fountains and sculptures and, next to Mount Royal Park, a recreation park with several sports fields. A second sequence of boulevards and parkways would have connected Mount Royal Park to the banks of the St. Lawrence River, continued along a magnificent riverfront promenade dotted with aquatic parks, and then linked back to the downtown area. A continuous green

266 CHALLENGES OF AN URBAN AND INDUSTRIAL LANDSCAPE

13.4 Rickson Outhet's central Montreal plan, 1909. This is one of the five sectorial plans that Outhet prepared for the Province of Quebec Association of Architects' Civic Improvement Committee. The drawing shows the eastern extremity of Mount Royal Park, as revised by the construction of Park Avenue, the elaborate formal boulevard that crosses the drawing from left to right. The sports field of Parc Jeanne-Mance (formerly Fletcher's Field) is located at bottom right; at bottom centre is the beginning of the unrealized Confederation Boulevard, which Outhet proposed as the central thoroughfare of the Plateau Mont Royal district. The sculptural feature indicated at the intersection of the two axes was built a block north of the location shown: it is the George-Étienne Cartier monument, now the site of Montreal's wildly popular "tam-tam" musical event. At lower left is an enlarged cross-section of Park Avenue showing its four rows of trees.

swath would have encircled the central core of the city. These proposals were clearly reminiscent of the boulevards, plazas, and linear parks that Outhet had worked on and that were currently being realized in Washington.[15]

Other designers, graduates of the École des Beaux-Arts in Paris, proposed new urban configurations expressed in the popular vocabulary of the City Beautiful movement. In 1913, the Montreal architect Jean-Omer Marchand (1873–1936), who had studied at the Beaux-Arts from 1893 to 1902 (and was its first French-Canadian graduate),[16] proposed a new civic centre for Montreal, grouping several imposing public buildings around a splendid central plaza located at the intersection of several major arteries.[17] John McIntosh Lyle (1872–1945) from Hamilton, Ontario, a student at the Beaux-Arts from 1892 to 1896,[18] returned to Canada in 1906 after practising for several years in New York.[19] In 1911, Toronto's Civic Improvement Committee (like that in Montreal, a subsidiary of the provincial association of architects, the Ontario Association of Architects [OAA]) engaged him to prepare an urban design study for the downtown core. Lyle proposed that a grand boulevard, Federal Avenue, connect the new Union Station (of which Lyle would be one of the architects) by the lake, with a great civic plaza to be located to the north between Old City Hall and the law courts, Osgoode Hall.[20] Lyle's plan for this boulevard and plaza was part of a larger scheme for the entire urban area, proposed in 1909 by the Toronto Guild of Civic Art. This organization recommended the creation of diagonal boulevards to resolve Toronto's vexing problem of traffic blockages. It also envisioned an integrated network of parks and green spaces that would benefit from the city's natural features – islands, lake, and ravines.[21]

The wide-open spaces of western Canada furnished a fertile soil for the kind of large-scale projects that were typical of the City Beautiful movement that had become very popular in the American West and Middle West just across the border. In 1912, the City of Edmonton invited the office of Morell and Nicholls from Minneapolis, Minnesota, to prepare an urban-planning study. The two principals of the firm, Anthony Urbanski Morell (1875–1924), a native of France, and Arthur R. Nichols (1880–1970), born in Massachusetts, had worked together in New York before founding their office, in 1909, and embarking on joint careers that would take them throughout the West.[22] The voluminous report submitted by Morell and Nichols was far more ambitious than that written by Frederick Todd five years earlier, touching on circulation and transport, the location of public facilities and urban activities, parks, open spaces, and cemeteries. As in other schemes, they proposed to build diagonal boulevards for the improvement of traffic flow and an imposing civic centre east of the downtown area. This complex would be linked to the existing market square and would accommodate the city hall, a railroad station, a public library, and an art museum. Their two alternative designs for the civic centre, delineated in impressive City Beautiful colour perspectives, were centred on a formal park oriented at right angles to the valley of the North Saskatchewan River, which passes through the city.[23]

This was not the first cross-border foray for the Minneapolis designers. In 1911, they had designed a major residential garden project in Vancouver (see chapter 14), and a predecessor firm, Mufflin and Nichols, had provided the rapidly expanding

NEW IDEALS IN URBAN DESIGN 267

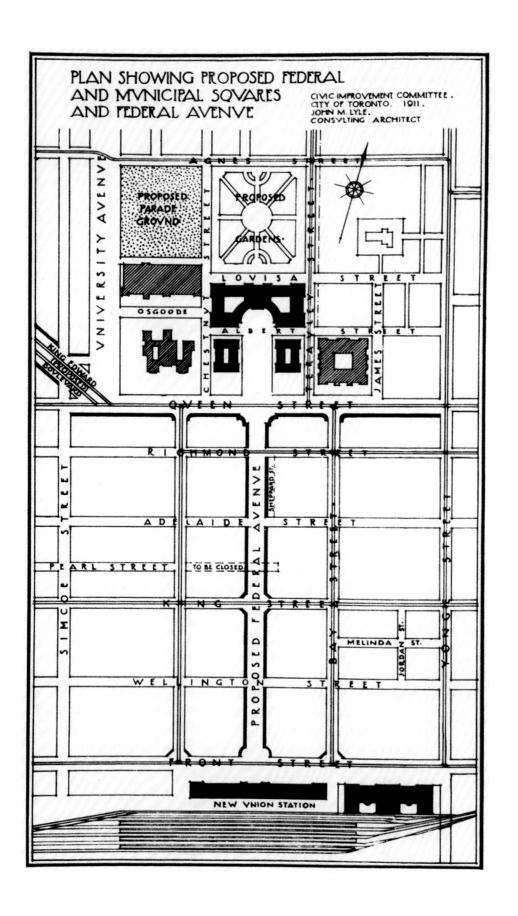

13.5 (facing page) Toronto civic plan, John Lyle, architect, 1911. Although the north-south Federal Avenue that Lyle proposed was not realized, the Union Station was indeed constructed at its southern extremity, as envisaged, and – much later – Toronto's new city hall was built on Queen Street at its northern end, exactly where Lyle drew a complex of civic buildings and a public plaza. The beginning of one of the diagonal boulevards proposed by the Toronto Guild of Civic Art – also not realized – may be seen at middle left.

13.6 (below) Thomas Mawson in his conservatory, Caton Hall, Lancashire, UK

city of Saskatoon with a plan – mostly unrealized owing to financial pressures – that defined a system of parks linked by tree-lined boulevards.[24]

The British Whirlwind: The Projects of Thomas Mawson

Between 1910 and 1915, the principal proponent of the City Beautiful movement in Britain, Thomas Hayton Mawson (1861–1933), visited Canada six times. First invited to deliver a series of lectures on landscape architecture and civic design, Mawson quickly attracted a prodigious number of clients through his expertise and his magnetic personality. He drew plans for the transformation of several cities in the Canadian West, executing a succession of virtuoso urban design performances in his own flamboyant personal style.[25] His energetic approach to urban design was like a tornado ripping through the middle of a city, and like the tornado that devastated the city of Regina in 1912, his impact was spectacular but brief, with a few exceptions.[26]

Born in the industrial north of England, Mawson launched a number of different enterprises, each success leading to a new challenge. A past master of garden design, he was considered by Chadwick to be the "the most successful designer of parks in the first quarter of the century" in Great Britain.[27] During the first ten years of the twentieth century, his compositions tended more and more towards the formal language of City Beautiful. This tendency was at least partly due to the education that his son and associate Edward P. Mawson (1885–1954) received at the École des Beaux-Arts in Paris.[28]

Mawson's career in Canada began tentatively with projects in Ottawa and Niagara Falls that did not result in serious commissions,[29] but he soon found enthusiastic clients further west.[30] The city of Calgary, in full-blown expansion, engaged him in January of 1913 to design an overall development plan for the city. Mawson threw himself into a detailed study of the municipality and, at the beginning of 1914, submitted urban design proposals for the downtown area and a master plan for the extended urban area, all presented on large coloured drawings and in a sumptuous book.[31] His plan proposed a complex network of plazas and boulevards for downtown Calgary,[32] all laid out in relation to a grand boulevard extending from the business district north to the Bow River, where Prince's Island (an industrial site at the time) would be transformed into a public park. The boulevard would then continue across to the northern bank, along which a series of promenades and parkways was to be developed.[33] Transverse to this boulevard between the railroad line and the river, Mawson located a broad rectangular open space, about which the major civic buildings that would constitute Calgary's Civic Centre would be built. Further east, a second north-south boulevard was to be aligned with the existing railroad station and would also link up with a bridge across the Bow. Few elements of this elaborate scheme were realized at the time, but its influence would be felt in future decades.

Following his first visit to Calgary in early 1913, Mawson continued west through the Rockies,[34] to accept a mandate to plan three sectors of Stanley Park in Vancouver, including Coal Harbour, where the road from the city centre entered the park

NEW IDEALS IN URBAN DESIGN   269

13.7   Mawson's plan for central Calgary, 1912–14. His two north-south boulevards run from bottom to top of the drawing, at right angles to the railway line that crosses the city horizontally in the lower half of the drawing. The Civic Centre is a white rectangle that crosses the boulevard to the left, just below the Bow River; Prince's Island Park straddles the boulevard on the south side of the river's main channel. This richly coloured image is reproduced from Mawson's lavishly illustrated presentation book.

across a salt-water lagoon. Mawson prepared four different designs for the site, all reinforcing its role as a "hinge space" between the city and the park. The most ambitious of his proposals would have transformed the lagoon into an immense circular freshwater pond, centred on a symbolic column that would terminate the axis of Georgia Street, the straight boulevard that links the downtown area to the park. Around the pond, Mawson imagined an assembly of impressive civic buildings, contrasting dramatically with a backdrop provided by the noble coniferous forest of the peninsula, the whole ensemble creating a smashing, almost Wagnerian, perspective.[35] But despite his efforts to set up a Canadian office,[36] time and enthusiasm ran out for Mawson's revolutionary projects under the influence of an economic recession in 1913, followed by the outbreak of the First World War in 1914.[37]

The Third Magnet

While downtown City Beautiful proposals focused on the issues of beautification, ease of transportation, and coherent structure of the city, other projects addressed social needs that were of central concern to the reformers, such as improvements in housing quality and in the everyday life of working Canadians. The design of these projects followed the other great model of urban redevelopment of the time, the Garden City, invented by a brilliant British autodidact, Ebenezer Howard (1850–1928), who postulated a new form of human community in his pioneering book *To-Morrow: A Peaceful Path to Real Reform* (1898).[38] Howard envisioned a series of new towns, each having a population of about 30,000 residents and comprising the full range of urban activities, located at sufficient distance from existing major cities to function autonomously. He explained his idea with a diagram that set in competition three magnets: the *city* – dirty and dangerous, but filled with economic potential; the *countryside* – stable and healthy, but impoverished; and the Garden City, combining all the good qualities and none of the defects of the city and the countryside.[39] Other diagrams explored the internal structure of this new form of settlement, organized in concentric bands that corresponded to different urban activities, the whole town encircled by a peripheral *greenbelt* dedicated to agriculture. Howard then linked these concentric bands together with radial boulevards that focused on a central public park. He saw this physical model as a means for achieving a far-reaching economic and social program, uniting all residents in a cooperative enterprise.[40]

In Britain, Howard's ideas attracted the attention of influential members of the governing circle, including the future governor general of Canada, Earl Grey, who had presided at the opening ceremonies of Letchworth New Town in England in 1903.[41] Once installed in Ottawa, Earl Grey brought together, in 1910, several of his British colleagues to discuss housing questions with Canadian reform groups. Besides Thomas Mawson (this was one of the reasons for his first visit to Canada), Raymond Unwin, the architect of Letchworth, and Henry Vivian (1868–1930), member of Parliament and co-founder of a cooperative housing project, were among the participants.[42] Vivian introduced the Canadian reformers to the

NEW IDEALS IN URBAN DESIGN   271

co-partnership system, very successful in Britain, through which private enterprise built demonstration projects in collaboration with workingmen's organizations.[43] This strategy provoked strong interest among the prosperous manufacturers of Toronto; in 1912, several of them founded the Toronto Housing Company to put into practice the principles enunciated by Vivian. They undertook two projects: Spruce Court, west of the Don River, and Riverdale Courts, east of the river in the East York district. These projects, of which the architectural character follows a sort of English cottage style, consisted of dense but intensely liveable row houses and apartments grouped around a series of green courtyards.[44] The architect of both projects was Eden Smith (1858–1949), born in Britain, who had already completed his apprenticeship in the cooperative movement through his design of several houses in the *Arts and Crafts* style for a "mini Garden City" in Toronto – Wychwood Village, where he lived. A somewhat eccentric community, a sort of artists' colony (its founder, a permanent resident, was painter Marmaduke Matthews), the village was subtly integrated into the Davenport terrace and the adjacent slope that connected it to the plain of southern Toronto. This garden suburb remains a charming and unique enclave only ten minutes from the skyscrapers of downtown Toronto.[45]

Aside from socially oriented projects, a considerable number of developer-built housing projects embraced the Garden City model, integrating extensive green spaces, curving roads, and picturesque architecture into their design. The leading Canadian exponent of this approach during the early years of the twentieth century was landscape architect Frederick Gage Todd, who, besides his outstanding contribution to Canada's urban parks (see chapter 11), was very much involved in civic design and in the layout of residential districts. Todd mastered the vocabularies of both the City Beautiful and the Garden City approaches and seemed to be able to fuse their various design motifs into a coherent whole. His first project of this nature was the Bowling Green neighbourhood in Pointe-Claire, a historical agricultural community on the shores of Lake Saint-Louis, west of Montreal, that had become a vacation colony and then a suburb following the construction of a railway line connecting it to the city centre. In 1904–05, Todd and his associates purchased two long-lot farms, perpendicular to the lakeshore and east of the old village, as a site for a residential development. Later adopting the name "Canadian Garden City Homes Limited," the company (with Todd as president) developed the southern part of the site as a residential ensemble in the Garden City spirit and the northern part as a nursery. The latter was gradually transformed into housing lots, following a master plan designed by Todd, until the economic crisis of the 1930s forced a halt to real estate development.[46] In his master plan, Todd designed curving roads and cul-de-sacs to follow the gentle contours of the site; these were lined with large silver maples and other favourite trees, and punctuated with several small parks interspersed within the residential fabric.[47] The first wave of houses (1905–13) established an Arts and Crafts architectural tradition that is still present in the local architectural vocabulary.

The Bowling Green neighbourhood was among the very first Garden City projects to be carried out anywhere in the world. The original publication of *Garden*

272 CHALLENGES OF AN URBAN AND INDUSTRIAL LANDSCAPE

13.8 Bowling Green district, Pointe-Claire, QC, 1905–30, designed by Frederick Todd. Beginning with the housing cluster organized around the small rectangular park near the lake at centre right (the original "Bowling Green"), Todd and his business associates developed this extensive residential community over a period of twenty-five years.

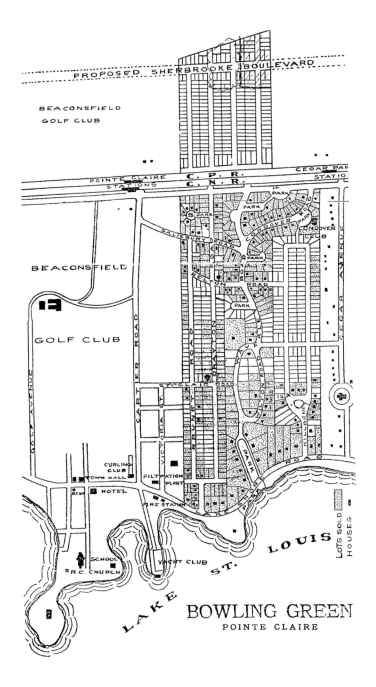

Cities for To-Morrow dated only from 1898, and Letchworth, the first Garden City in its country of origin, had only existed since 1903. The prestigious Hampstead Garden Suburb in London, which would become the most well-known realization in the Garden City genre, was begun a year later than Bowling Green, in 1906.

Frederick Todd was subsequently invited to design new residential neighbourhoods across the country, among them the high-end Point Grey district at the western extremity of the Vancouver metropolitan area (1907), a large multi-functional

NEW IDEALS IN URBAN DESIGN 273

project sponsored by the provincial government. At Point Grey, Todd concentrated civic and commercial facilities around a central *village green* and designated as parks the steep slopes and heavily wooded ravines that were difficult to develop. Around the periphery of the district, skirting the edge of the steep sloping lands that led down to the sea, Todd planned the winding Marine Drive parkway, a magnificent esplanade that took full advantage of available views. In 1913, this road was already described as "the most famous drive on the mainland of the province."[48]

Todd carried out many of these projects for railroad companies, which were major actors in the Canadian real estate industry at that time, controlling large urban properties across the country. On one of these properties, a hilly site located to the east of the town of Point Grey, Todd designed the upscale residential area Shaughnessy Heights, developed by the Canadian Pacific Railway.[49] In this project, realized in 1907–09, Todd again integrated his trademark curving roads into the subtle topography of the site. Main boulevards, incorporating central *terre-pleins*, led gradually up to the crown of the hill; there they converged on a magnificent central park – the Crescent – a great lawn, oval in shape, embellished with a stunning variety of majestic trees and large shrubs.[50]

13.9   The Crescent, the central open space of Shaughnessy Heights, Vancouver

The plans for Todd's residential projects are all informed by his habitual *design signature*: carefully integrated green parks, similar to the village greens by Parker and Unwin at Letchworth; treed boulevards – either formal and impressive or curving and park-like[51] – incorporating linear bands of greenery and little triangles (popularly called "parklets") at road intersections like those seen in the master plans of the Olmsted clan as early as the 1869 plan for Riverside, Illinois; and, frequently, a major open space located at a prominent central location, often at the highest point of the site.

For the Canadian Northern Railway, Todd designed the Town of Mount Royal – first known as "the Model City" – constructed beginning in 1912 in the Montreal suburbs, at the northern exit from the Mount Royal Tunnel, which was built for the project.[52] The design of this new city displayed a striking contrast of formal and curvilinear geometries. At the central point of the city, a small commercial and institutional nucleus and a large central park marked the intersection of two major diagonal boulevards and the north-south commuter rail line. This meta-geometry was superimposed on a traditional rectangular street grid, and in counterpoint to this logical and Cartesian structure, Todd designed a continuous curving parkway loop, halfway between the central node and the periphery of the town, linking together the neighbourhood parks located in each sector of the city. This innovative promenade reflects the spatial concepts of the Garden City, while the formality and symmetry of the great diagonal boulevards clearly take a page from the City Beautiful lexicon.[53] Both of these conceptions of the *parkway* had been classic components of the Olmsted firm's urban design vocabulary, with which Todd was certainly familiar.

Elsewhere in Montreal, another ambitious model city took form during the same period. The city of Maisonneuve, meant to serve both industrial and residential clienteles, had been founded in the 1880s on the eastern edge of the urban area. The goal of its promoters, a group of francophone industrialists led by Alphonse Desjardins, was to create, simultaneously, the "Pittsburgh of Canada" and the "Garden of Montreal." Between 1910 and 1915, the industrialist and developer Oscar Dufresne and his brother Marius Dufresne, the municipality's engineer, transformed the conventional street grid of the city according to the City Beautiful model. Two broad boulevards situated at right angles to each other, Sherbrooke Street and Boulevard Pie-IX (named for the then-current pope), furnished the basic structure of the city and assured its main circulation. A third artery, Morgan Boulevard, provided an elegant axial connection between the civic complex, consisting primarily of a market building and plaza, and a verdant park that terminated its perspective.[54]

The Olmsted Brothers firm in Brookline, Massachusetts, the most prestigious landscape architecture and city planning office in North America for decades, was also very active in Canada during this period. The firm was commissioned by the CPR to plan one of the company's principal properties in Calgary, the Mount Royal district, located southwest of the downtown area on a hill much like that adjacent to its namesake in Montreal. After laying out the northern section of the site in 1907–09, the CPR's assistant land commissioner, Lonsdale Doupe, engaged

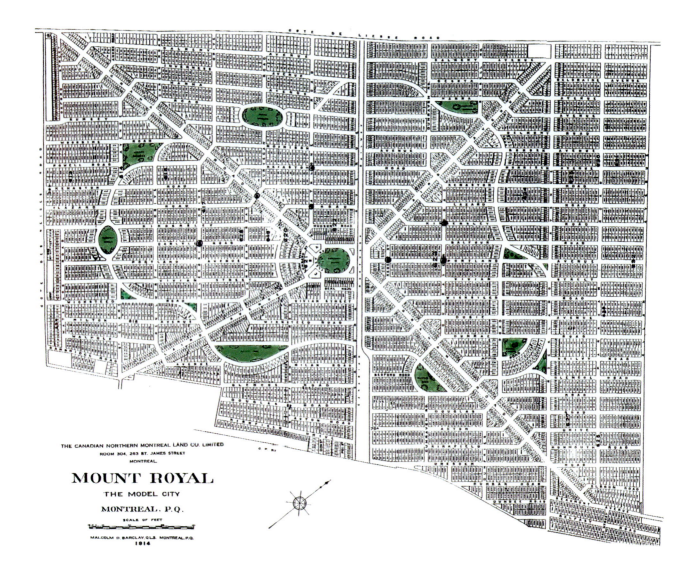

John Charles Olmsted (1852–1920), the older of the two brothers, to take charge of the design for the southern section of the project.[55] Olmsted created a residential neighbourhood with curving roads, well aligned with respect to topography, dotted with clusters of houses encircling small parks that, like Unwin's work in England, recall the traditional village green. The designer conserved for park use a steep escarpment on the eastern side of the sector, as well as the high point of the hill,[56] as Todd often did. Between 1907 and 1913, John C. Olmsted designed another distinguished *residential park*, the Uplands development in the municipality of Oak Bay, adjacent to Victoria, BC.[57] On a 190-hectare site (465 acres) gently descending to the sea, Olmsted again employed his office's customary vocabulary: a network of sinuous roads, sensitively graded, articulated by small triangular or circular parks; a grand central avenue, "Midland Way," following the classic barbell configuration

13.10   Town of Mount Royal, QC, 1914, as planned by Frederick Todd. Drawing by Malcolm D. Barclay, Quebec land surveyor. The railway, lifeline of "The Town," runs through the centre of the plan, from bottom to top. The two diagonal boulevards intersect at a small town centre and park. The meandering "green ring" of parks and parkways is clear on the drawing, but the town, as realized, diverged increasingly from this clear structure as development proceeded by stages.

(see chapters 5 and 22); and impeccably detailed street infrastructure, including underground electrical lines and elegant cast-iron street lamps.[58] Though not anticipated in the original plan, a rocky promontory near the coast in the southeast section of the neighbourhood was acquired by the municipality of Oak Bay and retained as a natural and undeveloped park, preserving the Garry oak savannah typical of the region.[59]

The Olmsted Brothers and their two "graduates," Rickson Outhet and Frederick Todd, were all involved in the design of a garden suburb in Winnipeg, the Tuxedo Park district, adjacent to Assiniboine Park. Outhet had met the developer, Frederick Heubach, during his stay in the United States and had prepared a subdivision plan for his Winnipeg property in 1905, basing his design on a diagonal motif. Heubach also seems to have invited Todd to propose a plan, and the Olmsted office revised the Tuxedo street pattern and prepared a design for a more extensive site in 1910. Finally, John C. Olmsted drew up a competition program based on Garden City principles for the next stage of the project. The proposals of the Olmsted office and, to a lesser degree, those of Outhet, were partly realized; but the death of Heubach in July 1914 called a halt to the development.[60]

The majority of the projects considered above were not really "Garden Cities," properly speaking, but only parts of cities; they were, in fact, "Garden Suburbs" inspired by the Garden City spatial model and philosophy. The number and quality of such projects designed by landscape architects and town planners working in Canada at the time is truly impressive,[61] but it could not be said that their realization satisfied the social objectives of the reform movement that had originally inspired them. The designers' creations were, essentially, handsome and liveable environments for middle- and upper-class residents. Some of these projects found their way to the "top 10" list of desirable Canadian neighbourhoods; all share a sense of community and identity, attracting many long-term residents,[62] and only rarely creating closed enclaves.

Squares and Playgrounds

In one respect the reform movements amply attained their objective: the goal of equipping every district of the city with small urban parks and creating, in each of these parks, a children's playground. The *playground movement* started in Germany in the late nineteenth century as an antidote to the unhealthy conditions of German cities, rapidly expanding at the time. The idea crossed the Atlantic, and during the years 1900 to 1910, pressure groups all over North America urged city councils to create playgrounds and parks in every neighbourhood.[63] The city of Montreal is a good example: gradually, after about 1910, children's playgrounds were increasingly considered as normal city fixtures, in both existing parks and those specially designed for the purpose. These new playgrounds were busy places, well maintained and provided with *monitors* to guide the children's play activities. In Montreal, the neighbourhood parks usually took the form of a square of standard design, with a number of small variations: one or two blocks of the city grid in area, a flat grassy ground surface, many large shade trees (generally

NEW IDEALS IN URBAN DESIGN   277

13.11 Molson Park, Montreal

elms and maples), a geometric arrangement of paths – usually diagonal – and play areas, with equipment for younger and older children in one quadrant of the park. A fountain or bandstand often served as a central feature (the latter date mainly from the 1920s). This simple, almost banal, layout was once described as "more an ambiance than a design," but all of these little green oases have played decisive roles in the districts they serve: they are flexible, offering something for everybody, and they make even the most heavily populated parts of the city, like the Plateau Mont-Royal (long the most densely populated neighbourhood in Canada), eminently liveable.[64] Some of these small parks are real gems, including Molson Park in the Petite Patrie sector and Parc Lahaie in the Mile-End district.

Resource Towns on the Frontier

Outside the metropolitan zones, close to the sources of mineral and energy resources, entirely new cities with a full range of urban functions were taking form at this time. These far-flung *resource communities* were so distant from other settlements that they had no choice but to stand on their own. They were cultural landscapes unique to Canada and a few other countries where primary resources from forests, seas, rivers, and mines formed a central part of the economic base.[65] Towns of this type were often located on challenging sites with irregular topography, offering great aesthetic possibilities to their designers.

The simplest resource community was a *temporary camp*, as seen in the lumber industry. As soon as the trees were cut down and the logs hauled away, the settlement was abandoned and, eventually, disappeared without a trace. *Mushroom towns* of the nineteenth-century mining industry were a next step: simple grid-plan towns, built close to the mine, their population dwindling when the resource ran out, succeeded by a long period of stagnation, as befell the Kootenay ghost towns (see chapter 6). The next wave of resource towns represented another level of community – *company towns* – founded by larger enterprises ready to invest on a large scale so as to integrate their production with the industrial economy that was rapidly taking form.[66] These towns were planned in advance by the companies that created them. From the start, the company provided for infrastructure – electricity, water, sanitary sewers – and often built lodging and commercial facilities, of which they retained long-term ownership.[67]

Towns of this kind had existed for some time. One of the first in Canada was Marysville in New Brunswick, founded in 1883 on a tributary of the Saint John River, a few kilometres north of Fredericton. Marysville's principal products were wood and textiles; the company built the factory, residences for the various classes of personnel, and all community facilities. These diverse constructions were laid out in picturesque fashion, on a sloping site parallel to the river.[68] Some of the first company towns were laid out on the familiar rectangular grid. This was the case with Powell River, a pulp-and-paper town built on the coast of British Columbia in 1911–12 so as to apply the motive power of the river to the apparently endless forests of the BC interior. From the first residential sector, designed as a compact grid overlooking the mill located on the waterfront, the town expanded to the south, over a period of years, in a long crescent parallel to the shore, providing residents with magnificent views of Malaspina Strait and the innumerable islands offshore.[69]

Shawinigan Falls in Quebec was both similar to Powell River and more complex. Some 60 kilometres north of Trois Rivières, the St. Maurice River, one of the largest tributaries of the St. Lawrence, passed through a narrow gorge that descended 58 metres, almost as deep as Niagara.[70] The falls presented a splendid opportunity for the production of electricity and the industries it could power, including chemical and electrochemical enterprises, aluminium producers, and pulp and paper. Shawinigan Falls would become one of the most important industrial centres in Quebec. The principal company, Shawinigan Water and Power, did not retain ownership of all the land but sold property rights to other enterprises and residents; thus Shawinigan was not a company town but an autonomous *multi-industry resource city*.[71] The engineering firm T. Pringle and Son of Montreal laid out the town plan in 1899, locating the commercial centre and workers' residential area on flat lands above the falls and new dam, following the traditional nineteenth-century square grid pattern. The managers' and professionals' residential area was situated on higher ground, on an overlooking plateau, its curving streets following the lines of the natural topography. Other elements of the plan went beyond the traditional stereotype, providing for a large public park at the curve of the St. Maurice River and a linear esplanade along the riverfront.[72] The crest of a steep cliff above the downtown area became the site for an elegant hotel and a great church.[73]

The city of Prince Rupert, on the coast of British Columbia, represents another category of frontier settlement, the *transportation node*, a city located at the exchange point between two modes of transportation. Its northern location (54°

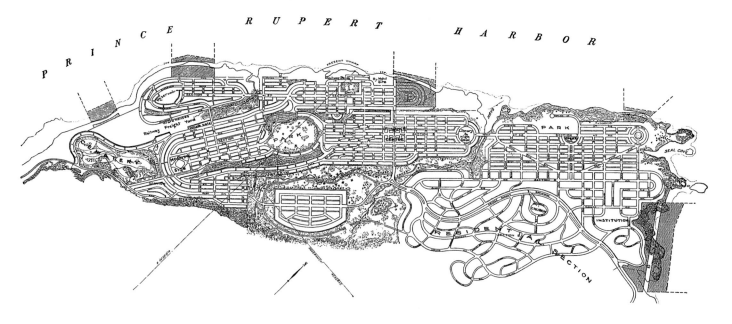

latitude), on a magnificent natural harbour that is free of ice the year round, convinced the owners of a new railway line, the Grand Trunk Pacific (GTP), to choose this site as their western terminus. They hoped to steal a march on their southern rivals by reducing by a full day the sea voyage to Asia. In 1908, the GTP commissioned landscape architects Brett and Hall of Boston to prepare a plan for a city of 100,000 inhabitants. Franklin D. Brett, like so many other landscape architects, had been trained in the Olmsted Brothers office; he had also worked in New York for Charles Platt, a celebrated designer of country villas and gardens, where he met George Duffield Hall (1877–1961). The two opened their own office in 1903.[74] For their imposing site at Prince Rupert, the two Bostonians designed a City Beautiful composition inspired by its complex topography. The downtown area, sited on a terrace that sloped down gradually to the port, consisted of a series of parallel streets terminating on public buildings, enclosed by a second sequence of streets exploiting the site's bowl-like topography in a series of concentric crescent-like streets. As the city's visual focus, BC architect Francis Rattenbury designed a monumental complex of hotel and marine terminal/railway station buildings to be constructed right on the harbour. The landscape architects retained as parks the stream valleys in the urban area, as well as the hilltops and a broad plateau at the edge of the city.[75] This astonishing project, magnificent and daring in the extreme, was only partially realized; the city's population never exceeded 15,000. But today, Prince Rupert is still an extremely stimulating and agreeable city, compact and urbane, its coherent urban structure still totally readable and convincing.

The idea behind all these frontier projects was to establish permanent cities that would extend the Canadian ecumene. The nineteenth-century harnessing of

13.12 "General Plan for the Development of Prince Rupert," BC, 1912. Brett & Hall, town planners and landscape architects. The designers must have examined and understood the site extremely well, for their plan fits its topography of linear hills like a glove. As a result, the sectors that were realized (perhaps two-thirds of the ensemble) follow the original plan very closely. Unfortunately, Rattenbury's striking vision for the railway station and hotel complex facing the harbour (top centre of the plan) did not come to fruition.

these resources was one of the great epics of Canadian history, not only because of the tremendous natural and technical challenges that were overcome, but also in terms of the viable and autonomous cities that were created in harmony with their landscape settings.[76]

Visions of Progress: New Institutions

Most of the City Beautiful projects designed for Canadian downtowns were not realized, but the need for new governmental and educational institutions – a need endemic to a young country in rapid expansion – offered fertile ground for other projects inspired by this model. Among these were the new parliamentary complexes called into being by Canadian Confederation in 1867. This pact restructured political relationships across the continent; the new federal government and each province had to choose a capital city, a site for the governmental institutions, and a design scheme for the disposition of its parliament buildings and public spaces. Governments often located these symbolic projects on pivotal sites that related both to urban structure and to the natural landscape.

The most impressive of these governmental complexes was the federal parliamentary precinct in Ottawa, already chosen as the capital of the united province of Canada by Queen Victoria in 1859. This city owed its location to the meeting of the Ottawa River with a mass of highly resistant limestone bedrock that blocked its passage, creating an abrupt change of level that caused the river to descend in a series of falls and rapids, finally settling into a great peaceful basin enclosed by rocky cliffs. The government chose the highest of these cliffs – the site with the

13.13 "Parliament Square, Ottawa, Ontario," 1873. Calvert Vaux, landscape architect. The overall topography, wrought-iron and stone enclosure, and central pedestrian approach designed by Vaux still exist today. His retaining wall parallel to the Centre Block has been banked and planted, introducing a more verdant character than he envisioned. The diagonal paths have disappeared, but their position may still be detected when seen from the air. Of course, the Centre Block of Parliament changed dramatically when it was rebuilt following the 1916 fire.

most spectacular relation to the river below – as Parliament Hill, to accommodate its legislative buildings. As the highest and most central point of the city, the location was visible from the entire urban region, from both the Quebec and Ontario shores of the historic river. On this sublime site, architects Fuller and Jones erected Gothic-style buildings that were equally impressive.[77] To the south, a formal relationship with the city was established: a dominant central block, secondary wings on each side, the three buildings disposed about Parliament Square, a great symmetrical *cour d'honneur* designed by the New York landscape architect Calvert Vaux,[78] who had only recently ended his long and fruitful association with Frederick Law Olmsted. Vaux's design for the main public space of Parliament, begun in 1873, consisted of a great lawn, sloping down gradually towards Wellington Street to the south and terminated on its northern boundary by a series of stone walls, stairs, and terraces that skilfully resolved some quite difficult grading problems. On the axis of the central tower, at the base of a grand staircase leading to the upper terrace, Vaux placed a fountain at the focus of three axial and diagonal paths.[79] On the north side of the building, a complex panoply of towers, turrets, spires, and variously shaped roofs combined to create a picturesque silhouette like that of a medieval city, establishing a majestic relationship with the Ottawa River, the perfect counterfoil to the classic set-piece public space on the southern façade that links Parliament to the city.[80]

Canada's three Prairie provinces – Saskatchewan, Alberta, and Manitoba – created legislative assemblies in the first two decades of the twentieth century. All adopted similar City Beautiful compositions, placing beaux-arts domed capital buildings in juxtaposition to the great river valleys that were their historic lifelines. On studying the masterful integration of these institutional compositions with their natural and urban environments, it seems that the great plains in the centre of the continent became the authentic heartland and true home of the City Beautiful movement. All three compositions follow a similar format: a formal and symmetrical building complex centred by a colonnade and pediment, surmounted by a hemispherical or octagonal dome.[81] Facing the city, a monumental staircase terminates a strong visual axis and approach. In all three cases, this axis continues through the building and extends beyond, and all axes establish a geographic link with the main watercourse of the city, always a major *ligne de force* in the horizontal landscape of the Prairies.

The first of these legislative assemblies, that of Saskatchewan, is located south of Regina's downtown area and is oriented towards a secondary river, Wascana Creek, which was dammed up to form a magnificent lake. Engaged in 1907 to prepare a preliminary plan for the site, landscape architect Frederick Todd of Montreal sketched out a romantic, pastoral park, following the nineteenth-century natural park tradition, on both banks of the reservoir. On this flowing composition, he superimposed a north-south axis linking the legislative assembly to the lake with a formal and symmetrical flower garden. Todd sited the assembly atop a slight rise at the southern extremity of the axis, which he continued to the north across the lake and along a street beyond the limits of the park.[82] The architects of the building, Edward and William Maxwell of Montreal,[83] elaborated the site

13.14 Civic design plan for Saskatchewan Legislative Assembly and surrounding area, 1912. Plan by Thomas H. Mawson & Sons. North is at the left of the drawing; the legislative assembly is at bottom centre, with its central axis continuing north to and across Wascana Lake. The transverse east-west axis of the legislative assembly building was extended to the east, with a historic fountain acting as a focal point, and the main axis extended to the south (right of drawing) as a great lawn. Although it was not entirely realized, much of Mawson's grand scheme is evident on the site today; his masterful juxtaposition of natural and man-made geometries makes this one of his best works.

282 CHALLENGES OF AN URBAN AND INDUSTRIAL LANDSCAPE

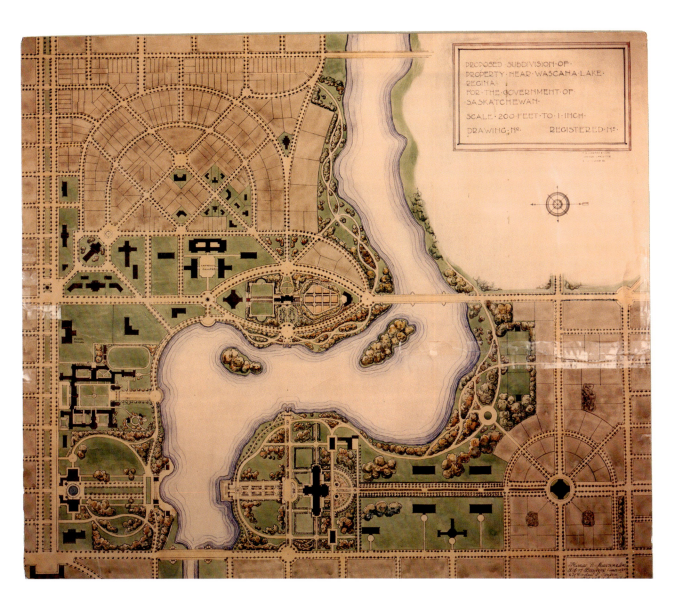

plan in consultation with Todd, but when the moment arrived to proceed with detailed site development, Todd was replaced by the distinguished British designer Thomas Mawson during the latter's visit to the region in 1912.[84] Mawson was given a mandate to prepare a general plan for the city as a whole, including several projected institutions. Working from his Vancouver office, his team drew up an impressive plan that applied the precepts of the City Beautiful movement at a monumental scale. Mawson adopted and amplified Todd's proposals, extending the north-south and east-west axes of the Saskatchewan Legislative Building as main structural lines for the adjoining sectors of the city. His proposals for the immediate environs of the building were carried out, but the 1914–18 war prevented work in other sectors from proceeding.[85]

NEW IDEALS IN URBAN DESIGN   283

The Alberta Legislative Building in Edmonton, constructed in 1908–13, stands on a high plateau on the north bank of the powerful North Saskatchewan River, adjacent to the site occupied by old Fort Edmonton (a site noted by Frederick Todd in his 1907 report; see chapter 11). The building, designed by architect Allan Merrick Jeffers (1875–1926),[86] presented a striking silhouette to observers in the river valley below; this area became a park in 1915, when Fort Edmonton was demolished. In 1912, landscape architects Morell and Nichols of Minneapolis designed a formal entrance court on the north side of the building, on the façade that opened out to the city. Their proposal included avenues embellished with rows of trees, a pool, and fountains, all to be enclosed by other government buildings.[87] The

13.15 Saskatchewan Legislative Assembly and grounds

project was not carried out, but in the 1970s, in preparation for its seventy-fifth anniversary, the province created a great new pedestrian space on the same site, extending the axis of the legislative building to the north and, finally, integrating the composition to the urban grid.[88]

Similarly, after several decades of delay, the Manitoba Legislative Building was finally integrated into the urban environment of the provincial capital at Winnipeg. The parliamentary building was designed by British architect Frank Worthington Simon (1862–1933) and built between 1913 and 1919, its construction period prolonged by the war. Its extensive site, located southwest of the city centre, was strategically positioned between a major boulevard, Broadway (see chapter 8), and the Assiniboine River. The cross-shaped building stood four-square in the centre of a broad green garden. Its entrance façade and the *Golden Boy* that surmounts the dome far above are oriented to the north, source of the province's mineral, energy, and forest resources and symbol of its future.[89] To the south, the building's axis descends to the river. In 1913, the local architect J.D. Atchison proposed to prolong this axis to the north, as far as Portage Avenue, Winnipeg's most important east-west artery. Atchison's design was modelled on the classic Parisian boulevard, framing the roadway with double rows of trees and distinguished buildings – a City Beautiful concept *par excellence*.[90] The project was carried through: many years of gradual progress finally culminated in 1962 with the official opening of today's Memorial Boulevard, its carefully framed perspective terminated by the legislature's dome.[91]

13.16 Victoria Inner Harbour, showing the boat landing and BC Legislative Assembly. The Empress Hotel is located to the left, outside the picture.

NEW IDEALS IN URBAN DESIGN 285

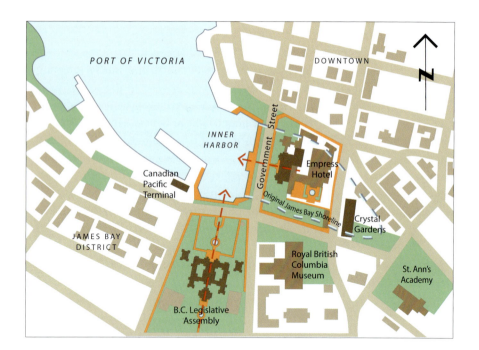

13.17 Urban design of Victoria Inner Harbour, BC. Francis Rattenbury, architect. Sight lines from the legislative assembly (bottom centre) and the Empress Hotel (right centre) converge on the Inner Harbour. Other important and interesting features are nearby – the provincial museum, maritime terminal, parks, and commerce.

It was fortunate that the creation of these legislative buildings coincided so precisely with the ascendancy of the City Beautiful movement, since, as Catherine Macdonald states, "The sense of order and power conveyed by this style ... seemed to embody the vision of progress that was so ardently sought by western Canadian leaders."[92]

Beyond the Prairies, one final Canadian parliament building took form during these years, at Victoria in British Columbia. This building acts as the anchor for a rich and intricate urban design scheme almost entirely designed by one gifted man, architect Francis Mawson Rattenbury (1867–1935). A native of Yorkshire in the north of England, the young architect had only just arrived in Victoria when he won the competition for the British Columbia Parliament Building in 1893. His massive and eclectic structure[93] was once again related to water, facing north across a broad sloping lawn towards James Bay. In 1902, Rattenbury suggested that the shallow and polluted tidal mud flat at the eastern extremity of the bay be filled to create a site worthy of the CPR's projected Empress Hotel, designed by Rattenbury in the château style favoured by the railway companies. The combination of the hotel, the legislative building, and a new and elegant quay created an enclosed Inner Harbour with great theatrical presence, reinforced by the CPR's marine terminal (a sort of giant Ionic temple, also designed by Rattenbury), the Crystal Gardens pool and amusement centre, and the gardens around the hotel and parliamentary complex.[94] Architectural historian Leonard K. Eaton said of Rattenbury's urban composition at Victoria, "His concept for the potential development of the Inner Harbour was brilliant, and to a remarkable extent it has been fulfilled."[95]

Temples of Learning

The first universities in western Canada were also established during the golden age of the City Beautiful movement. The campuses of these institutions generally followed a pavilion arrangement, by which several faculty buildings were organized in relation to a strong central axis, around a great central space.[96] The ideal of a democratic society founded on public education was a powerful inspiration for the provinces of the West, imbued with the spirit of progress that was so typical of the turn of the century.[97] In Saskatoon, the city chosen as the site of the University of Saskatchewan in 1909, Montreal architects Brown and Vallance prepared a master plan that successfully integrated a City Beautiful/beaux-arts plan with collegiate Gothic architecture, built with greystone available on a neighbouring site. The architects defined the structure of the university with two main lines of force: a central axis, perpendicular to the banks of the South Saskatchewan River, and a long curving crescent that defined the access road. The principal buildings were grouped around a great oval pedestrian space, the *Bowl*, aligned with the main axis and terminated, at its eastern extremity, by the main campus building.[98]

In 1912, a young architect and professor at McGill University in Montreal, Percy Erskine Nobbs (1875–1964), was given the responsibility of planning the campus of the University of Alberta at Edmonton. Nobbs worked on the plan in close

13.18 Plan of University of Alberta central quadrangle, 1912, Percy Nobbs, architect. This drawing is part of a much larger panorama showing the entire campus. The early development of the central space and surrounding buildings followed Nobbs's design, but subsequent construction gradually diverged from the model. New construction has begun to reconfirm the original design.

NEW IDEALS IN URBAN DESIGN   287

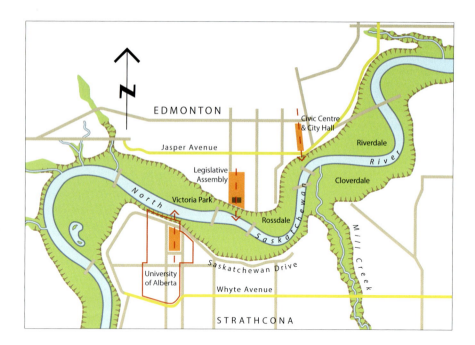

13.19 Urban design of Central Edmonton. Todd's vision of a continuous park sequence all along the valley of the North Saskatchewan, creeping up to the plateau along tributary streams, has been largely realized. The lands around old Fort Edmonton were first laid out on the French long-lot system, perpendicular to the river; this did much to facilitate the establishment of the three axes for public buildings and complexes.

collaboration with the president of the university, Henry Marshall Tory (1864–1947), and architect Frank Darling of Toronto. He organized the campus around a centrally located *grand quadrangle*, its axis perpendicular to the North Saskatchewan River. Residences were positioned on one side of the quadrangle, academic buildings on the other. Nobbs proposed that the place of honour, at the termination of the axis, be occupied by an immense *Convocation Hall*, visible from the other side of the valley. Rows of trees parallel to the enclosing façades completed the composition.[99] With the Civic Centre and the Alberta Legislative Building, the university completed a triumvirate of City Beautiful schemes in Edmonton, all three oriented along axes perpendicular to the river, following the same design strategy as that applied in Paris, where a series of important institutional spaces were conceived as counter-axes in relation to the Seine, backbone of the city.[100]

The University of Manitoba, in existence since 1877 as a federation of anglophone and francophone colleges located on several sites in Winnipeg and St. Boniface, finally consolidated its various components in 1929 on the campus of an agricultural college in the south of the city, within a large meander of the Red River.[101] The campus layout closely resembles a long-term plan prepared in 1914 by the university's first professor of architecture, Arthur A. Stoughton, originally from New York and a former student at the École des Beaux-Arts. Stoughton had proposed a spatial structure that placed the university buildings along both sides of a great central avenue lined with elm trees. He suggested that, at the perimeter of the site, a scenic road be built atop a dyke, or levee, that would protect the campus from the frequent floods caused by the rising waters of the Red River.[102] Finally, new university buildings were located to reinforce the previously existing agriculture campus, rather than at the end of the peninsula as Stoughton had suggested.

13.20 University of British Columbia, view to north along Main Mall, continuing across Burrard Inlet to Bowen Island and Howe Sound. Flag at half-staff in recognition of the recent death of former prime minister Pierre Elliott Trudeau, September 2000.

In 1908, the provincial government endowed the University of British Columbia (UBC) with a magnificent site on the peninsula of Point Grey, at the extreme west of the Vancouver metropolitan area. The original campus occupied only a small part of the *Endowment Lands*, 1,420 hectares that the province gave to the university to assure an ongoing revenue stream as well as to provide for its academic establishment.[103] At the time, the site was largely covered by a dense forest of immense conifers and bordered by steep cliffs that descended to the sea. Following a competition, the province entrusted the design of the campus to local architects George L. Sharp and Charles J. Thompson, seconded by an advisory committee that included landscape architect Thomas Mawson. Together, the committee and the architects chose the site and reworked the master plan (it seems that Mawson prepared a landscape plan) in 1913. The plan for UBC was based on a regular grid of roads and walks, dominated by one key space, the *Main Mall*, a central avenue some 75 metres wide. Later converted to a pedestrian mall, this *allée* traversed the

NEW IDEALS IN URBAN DESIGN   289

entire site of the university. It was framed by a double row of majestic red oaks, planted in 1931, and looked north to a spectacular view of the entrance to the port of Vancouver and to Howe Sound beyond.[104]

Thus, during a single generation of twenty years – including long periods of war and economic difficulty – the four provinces of western Canada all established distinguished university campuses, planned according to the principles of the City Beautiful movement, creating a framework for higher education that would continue to be effective into the far future.[105]

Plan for the National Capital Revisited

One final City Beautiful project, of great significance, was begun just before the First World War precluded city planning concerns. In 1913, the federal government, still seeking to endow Ottawa with the dignity and beauty appropriate for a capital city, set up the Federal Plan Commission, under the direction of Sir Herbert Holt, president of the Royal Bank.[106] The commission engaged Edward H. Bennett (1874–1954), an architect and city planner from Chicago, to propose a long-term plan for the capital.[107] Bennett, a native of England, had studied architecture at the École des Beaux-Arts in Paris before working with Daniel Burnham, the leader of the design team for the 1893 Chicago World's Fair. The two collaborators subsequently prepared urban plans in the City Beautiful tradition for San Francisco

13.21 Ottawa Civic Centre, 1914. Perspective by Bennett and Burnham looking north along Elgin Street and the mostly hidden Rideau Canal. Parliament Hill is at top left, the Ottawa River visible in the background, and the railway station and Chateau Laurier Hotel at right rear.

290 CHALLENGES OF AN URBAN AND INDUSTRIAL LANDSCAPE

and Chicago.[108] Ably seconded by Canadian engineers E.G. Cousins and A.E.K. Bunnell, who addressed the technical aspects of the project, Bennett submitted twenty-seven presentation drawings in late 1914[109] and a report in 1915. His plan absorbed and elaborated many of the suggestions that Frederick Todd had put forward in his 1903 report, proposing the creation of a very large *natural park* in the Gatineau Hills (where Todd had suggested a small forest reserve), a *park network* in the inner city, integrating almost all that Todd had proposed, and the extension of the existing *promenade and parkway system* to include walkways and driveways along canals, rivers, and streams. Although he shared Todd's opinion that Ottawa should not see itself as the "Washington of the North," Bennett proposed several projects that were typical of the City Beautiful approach, including the creation of a civic centre in Hull and a major public plaza (the future Confederation Square) at the intersection of Wellington and Elgin streets with the Rideau Canal, right next to Parliament Hill. Bennett also strongly suggested the establishment of a Federal District Commission to oversee the long-term planning of the capital region.[110] When his plan was submitted, the war was at its full intensity and the government put it on the shelf, but this master plan was nonetheless a key landmark in Canadian town planning.[111] In 1920, a French city planner, Jacques Gréber (1882–1962), sang its praises: "Ottawa is developing a splendid program of beautification along the banks of its river, and is preparing a great plan for its future growth. This document, published by the Federal Plan Commission, provides us with a most interesting lesson in applied city planning."[112]

City Beautiful Abandoned ... and Rediscovered

The sidelining of the new plan for Ottawa reflected the fate of many prewar urban design schemes, and it marked the end of a long succession of optimistic and ambitious urban reconstruction projects. As time passed, the reputation of the City Beautiful approach declined. A later generation judged it to be poorly adapted to the modern city, too grandiose, and irrelevant to the "real issues" of poverty and urban housing.[113] But as professor William Perks of the University of Calgary has stated, the designers of that era responded well to the spirit of the times and to the aspirations of their clients. It is unfair to judge them according to the criteria of another epoch.[114]

And on re-examining the specific projects that we have discussed above from a century's distance, we see that an impressive number of those visionary ideas, despite many vicissitudes, have borne fruit: Toronto's city hall and its grand plaza, Nathan Phillips Square, carried out in the 1960s;[115] Sir Winston Churchill Square in Edmonton, anchored by the city hall and a new public library; in Calgary, the creation of a broad mall that links the downtown centre to the Bow River and the transformation of Prince's Island into a park; in Montreal, busy sports fields in Jeanne-Mance Park and a dramatic monument across the street.[116] All of these were prefigured by City Beautiful designers, on the sites where they were finally carried out. Thus the visionary plans of the City Beautiful movement presaged the great civic spaces of the future.

14

Landscapes of the "Belle Époque"

During the years that preceded the First World War of 1914–18, Canada enjoyed an extended period of peace and prosperity that was reflected in its urban and rural landscapes. The problems of the nineteenth-century city had not disappeared, but much seemed stable and coherent in Canada at the turn of the twentieth century. Medium-sized centres (despite the existence of several large cities, Canada was still largely a country of small towns) and some big-city neighbourhoods could claim to have a high-quality environment: a regularly laid out and spacious street plan; a central square or public park surrounded with dignified public buildings; a city park by the lakefront, river, or waterworks, not far from the mill or factory (which employed a number of residents while adding to the growing quantity of made-in-Canada manufactured goods); and fairgrounds for yearly agricultural and industrial exhibitions. Prosperous family-owned shops were crowded together along the sidewalks of *Main Street*, and from the spacious verandas of their homes, the factory owners, doctors, and other professionals contemplated the shady expanse of *Maple Street*. Well-kept gardens in their backyards featured a variety of familiar plants – lilacs, roses, spirea, hydrangea. And for almost the first time, the average citizen had enough spare time to enjoy the town's public spaces and handsome

14.1 Riverside Park in Stratford, ON (now Cenotaph/Memorial Park), is seen from the south side of the Avon River, towards the western end of the downtown area, in about 1912. Saint James' Anglican Church is visible on the hilltop right of centre.

gardens. Stephen Leacock idealized small-town Ontario of that time: "A land of hope and sunshine where little towns spread their square streets and their trim maples beside placid lakes, within echo of the primeval forest."[1]

This golden age of prosperity was the *Belle Époque*, as described by historian Paul-André Linteau. During the last years of the nineteenth century and the first years of the twentieth, an ambiance of euphoria ruled, at least among the favoured members of society.[2] Leacock recalled the "halcyon days," calm and tranquil, of that era.[3] Reaping the benefits of the opening of the West and the exploitation of mineral and hydroelectric resources,[4] Canada had arrived at a threshold of prosperity. By 1914, all ten of today's provinces had been settled and had elected their own governments who met in their own parliamentary assemblies. Almost all the towns and cities we know today had already been established; with a few exceptions, the Canadian ecumene of today already existed. During the "Laurier Years" – from 1896 to 1911 – Prime Minister Sir Wilfrid Laurier led the country through a remarkable period of rapid population growth, immigration, economic expansion, and increasing affluence, making it possible for him to predict that "[i]t is Canada that shall fill the twentieth century."[5]

Some sense of a Canadian identity was beginning to weld together the very different linguistic, religious, and cultural groups that made up the population, in parallel with the physical integration accomplished by the railways. The first expressions of a culture based more directly on the Canadian experience were to be seen in painting, poetry, and novels.[6] In every region, there existed or were springing up the universities and colleges that would consolidate and nourish this culture, and science had progressed to the point that, for the first time, research carried out at a Canadian university was recognized with a Nobel Prize.[7]

Large Estates and Elegant Gardens

The Canadian countryside experienced a new wave of villas and gardens, built by a new class of business people, wealthier than the local merchants of the nineteenth century. These proprietors were the great industrialists: owners and officers of national banks and railway companies, producers of electricity and coal, of textiles and sugar. They constructed their villas in the suburbs of large cities and in vacation colonies far from urban centres, relying on the railways for access. To design their large houses and elegant gardens, this new class of wealthy patrons hired the best architects and landscape architects of the time, pressing into service the designers of the era's great public projects to create their own private worlds.

Summer Estates in Eastern Canada

Many of these captains of industry lived in Montreal, the nerve centre for their Canada-wide economic empires. From their central headquarters in the *Golden Square Mile* (their residential district on the slopes of Mount Royal),[8] they made plans for summer residences on the outskirts of the city or in natural settings further afield. Locations close to the water were preferred, and thus the small communities of Senneville and Sainte-Anne-de-Bellevue on Lake of Two Mountains, west of the city, saw the construction of a series of rustic castles. Edward Maxwell, his brother William Maxwell, and their associate William Shattuck were the architects of choice, brilliantly interpreting their clients' high aspirations by creating such estates as Bois-Briant for Sir Edward Clouston, general manager of the Bank of Montreal; Pine Bluff for Richard B. Angus, director of the Canadian Pacific Railway (CPR) and president of the Bank of Montreal; and Bois-de-la-Roche, a masterpiece of its genre, for Montreal financier and Senator Louis-Joseph Forget.[9] All these domains were built between 1896 and 1903; each was centred on a great house, the latter two designed in the *château* style (already the classic architectural language for hotels); and all were sited in such a way that their occupants could enjoy panoramic views of the lake. The space between house and lake was typically embellished with loggias and terraces next to the house; a sloping lawn, framed with trees and shrubs, descending to water level; and a beach area on the edge of the lake, equipped with shelters and seats.[10] The buildings were set within extensive sites designed by landscape architects,[11] and each of the three proprietors mentioned above engaged the Olmsted Brothers' office to prepare their landscape plans. The office's young employee Frederick G. Todd, who had worked on the drawings in Brookline, Massachusetts, was sent to Montreal to supervise on-site work. As Todd established himself in Montreal in 1900, his role gradually evolved from that of "the Olmsteds' representative" to that of "professional responsible for the project." But even after this transfer of responsibility, the brothers continued to provide their former employee with professional advice at no charge.[12] Off the island of Montreal, landscape architect Ormiston Roy, long associated with the Mount Royal Cemetery, designed the gardens for the residence of jurist Eugène Lafleur in Hudson Heights, on the other side of Lake of Two Mountains (1912),[13] and the Olmsted Brothers and Frederick Todd were successively engaged, between 1896 and 1903, on the design of the gardens of Fulford Place, the magnificent summer home of George T. Fulford in Brockville, Ontario, located on a plateau above the St. Lawrence River. Much of the original design carried out by John C. Olmsted remains extant, including a striking "Italian garden" composed of annual planting beds arranged symmetrically around a central fountain. Todd's contributions include a "Wild Garden" and "Cascade Garden."[14]

Several hundred kilometres downriver, Sir Rodolphe Forget, nephew of the senator and majority shareholder in the company that provided Montreal with electricity, built a manorial residence, Gil'Mont, on the plateau at St-Irénée-les-Bains, in Charlevoix County.[15] His house, which had electricity and an interior swimming pool, was as impressive as his terraced garden, which offered an unsurpassed view of the river and the mountains. In the village of Pointe-au-Pic at the mouth of the nearby Malbaie River, the Olmsted Brothers designed a somewhat simpler landscape for Mrs. T.D. McCagg, "The Spinney" (1899), contrasting a flower garden, geometric but informal, with the surrounding natural woodland.[16] This region of clifftop villas held a strong attraction for prestigious families from the United States as well as from eastern Canada.[17] Other regions of Quebec and Ontario furnished excellent sites for impressive villas and gardens. Rickson Outhet designed

14.2 Covenhoven, St. Andrews, NB: view to Passamaquoddy Bay

many such projects at Mount Bruno, southeast of Montreal, at Lake Magog in the Eastern Townships, and at Métis in the Gaspé.[18]

At St. Andrews, an eighteenth-century town built on a peninsula in the extreme southwestern part of New Brunswick (see chapter 5), wealthy Montrealers and others established a colony of villas around the venerable Algonquin Hotel, an important railway destination. The architecture of the Maxwell Brothers was well represented, along with garden compositions by the landscape architects with whom the brothers worked on a regular basis. Here as elsewhere along the coasts, sea views were the universal magnet that influenced the villas' siting and design. In 1899, the president of the CPR, Sir William Van Horne (1843–1915), settled on Minister's Island in Passamaquoddy Bay, where he began to design his residence, Covenhoven, by himself, before inviting the Maxwell Brothers to work with him. A substantial house with three gables, a gigantic barn (Van Horne ran a real farm), and a beach pavilion, a miniature circular fortress built right on the coast,[19] were the result of their collaboration. Van Horne's garden descended gradually from the

LANDSCAPES OF THE "BELLE ÉPOQUE" 295

columned gallery of the house, stepping down in terraces towards the rocky beach, each transitional slope planted with flowering shrubs and bright perennials.[20]

Edwardian Gardens in the West

In western Canada, two reconstructed historical gardens demonstrate the landscape approach typical of the Belle Époque. In Kelowna, BC, Lord Aberdeen (governor general of Canada from 1893 to 1896) and Lady Aberdeen built a residence they called "Guisachan," a bungalow recalling Indian colonial traditions, when they established their first ranch in the Okanagan Valley in 1891 (see chapter 6). When they sold the property in 1903, the subsequent owners, Elaine Cameron and her husband, surrounded the house with magnificent perennial gardens that soon became a local landmark. In 1987, the city of Kelowna painstakingly rebuilt these Edwardian[21] gardens to create Guisachan Heritage Park, using Mrs. Cameron's photographs and journal as reference documents. Wooden shelters and garden kiosks act as focal points within an overall composition of planting beds and winding paths.[22] And in Regina, the capital of Saskatchewan, the recent rehabilitation of the gardens of Government House, residence of the lieutenant governor, recall the formal landscape language of the period. Initiated as a celebration of the

14.3 Restoration of the Edwardian garden at Guisachan Heritage Park, Kelowna, BC. Perennials and roses are emphasized, in keeping with the planting of the garden between 1903 and the 1920s.

province's centennial in 2005, the project involved the replanting of traditional tree alignments and floral beds and the restoration of the formal spatial structure of the garden, in the spirit of the original plan of 1894 designed by gardener George Watt.[23]

Great Gardens of the West Coast

Fortunes were made throughout the country during the Belle Époque. In British Columbia, two prominent families invested their industry-generated wealth in outstanding gardens, both on Vancouver Island near the capital, Victoria. The first garden was both physically and financially based on the exploitation of limestone for the cement industry. At the beginning of the twentieth century, Robert Pim Butchart and his wife, Jennie Butchart (1866–1950), established a summer residence beside their limestone quarry at Tod Inlet, at the foot of the Saanich peninsula. In 1904, Jennie Butchart planted a garden around their house, profiting from the mild and relatively humid climate of this favoured environment.[24] Thus began the famous Butchart Gardens, of which she always remained the designer in chief, even though several of the best landscape architects of the time assisted her.

In 1906, Jennie Butchart's project began in earnest with the creation of a Japanese garden north of the house, close to the bay. The opening of Japan to foreign trade and influence in 1868 had opened the door to the discovery of Japanese gardens in the Occident, and Western cultures embraced Japanese gardens, buildings, and crafts – so different from those of European traditions – with fascination.[25] The Japanese concept of the garden, in particular, provoked great interest among the general public, thanks to displays at the world exhibitions in Vienna in 1873, Philadelphia in 1876, and Paris in 1889. An influential book by British architect Josiah Conder, *The Art of Landscaping in Japan*, was published in North America in 1893. The Japanese gardens and pavilions constructed within Olmsted's naturalistic park at the World's Columbian Exposition in Chicago in that same year (see chapter 13) and at the subsequent Louisiana Purchase Exhibition, held in St. Louis in 1904, attracted a great deal of attention and inspired the creation of similar gardens in North America.[26]

To realize her Japanese garden, Jennie Butchart hired Isaburo Kishida, a landscape architect from Yokohama. Kishida had come to Victoria in 1904, at the age of sixty-five, to design the Takata Tea Gardens in the Tramway Park amusement grounds at the Gorge (see chapter 10), in the suburbs of Victoria, in response to a call from his son Yoshitaro (Joe), the gardens' promoter.[27] For the Butcharts, he created a *promenade garden*, inspired by one of the classic garden types of Japan. In a garden of this kind, the visitor meanders through the space on a pre-designed path, ascending and descending slopes, in a milieu that is usually cut off from its surroundings by large trees and where water is almost always present. There is evidence that Kishida ordered garden ornaments and plants for the garden from Japan, including bamboo, Japanese maple, and Japanese black pine.[28]

From 1909 to 1919, Jennie Butchart took advantage of her husband's closing of the quarry to create the *pièce de résistance* of the garden, the spectacular *Sunken*

Garden, in a deep rocky hollow dug out from the native limestone that she would transform into a vale of greenery and flowers. The planting included colourful annuals, shrubs, and small trees such as rhododendrons, cherries, and Japanese maples, framed by western red cedars and Douglas firs, dark conifers that almost entirely obscured the ravaged stone walls of the quarry.[29] Other gardens followed in the 1920s: an *Italian garden* featuring a colourful display of flowers, a *rose garden* laid out on a theme of concentric ovals, a *star-shaped pond*, and a small private garden for Jennie Butchart. She was gradually composing a series of diverse thematic gardens, related to each other in a sequential manner. This eclectic approach had been a standard way of planning the large garden since the mid-nineteenth century, but this garden went beyond tradition. In particular, the Sunken Garden is a unique *tour de force* through its dramatic composition, impeccable maintenance, and stunning colour effects; it is one of the precious jewels of Canadian horticulture.

Jennie Butchart had help; she orchestrated the talents of several widely known designers, including Samuel Maclure (1860–1929), the humble yet brilliant architect of many residences in Victoria and Vancouver, which he realized in a broad

14.4 (facing page, above)
Isaburo Kishida

14.5 (facing page, below)
The Sunken Garden at Butchart Gardens, Victoria, BC, created 1909–19. A sweeping overall impression of this colourful quarry garden is first seen from above, before one descends into the former quarry to explore it in detail. Tall fountains animate the garden, to which dramatic lighting effects are added at night.

range of styles between 1888 and 1930.[30] Maclure assisted Butchart in redesigning her home and several areas of the gardens between 1911 and 1925. Butler S. Sturtevant (1899–1971), an American landscape architect who practised primarily in Seattle and San Francisco, contributed to the design of the rose garden. Several expert gardeners also helped to bring the project to fruition: William H. Westby, originally from England, worked on the Sunken Garden, and a young assistant gardener and future landscape architect, Raoul Robillard (1897–1980), worked on the gardens with his father from 1911 to 1914.[31]

With this project, Raoul Robillard began a long and illustrious career. A native of Normandy in France, he had immigrated with his family to Alberta in 1905, then moved to Vancouver in 1908. His father, Arthur Robillard, had worked as a gardener at the Hycroft Estate, the home of General McRae in the Shaughnessy district, where the grounds had been designed by Minneapolis landscape architects Morell and Nichols. Later moving to Victoria, Arthur Robillard helped create several of the capital's grand gardens, while his son acted as his assistant and translator. It was in these privileged milieus that the Robillards met architect Samuel Maclure, who, appreciating their gardening abilities, recommended their engagement at the Butchart Gardens. Maclure also recognized the young Robillard's talent for design and welcomed him into his office for seven years as an apprentice; while there "he learned the art of landscape design."[32] As a teenager, Robillard made a special contribution to the construction of the University of British Columbia. He accompanied his father and the provincial premier, among others, on a reconnaissance visit to the site of the UBC campus (see chapter 13) before the forest had been cleared. To make sure that the future central mall of the university really lined up with the view towards Howe Sound, he was asked to climb up a tall cedar tree and verify that this was indeed the case – which he did, contributing to the pleasure of all future students and professors of that institution.[33]

It was not limestone but coal that built another outstanding garden near Victoria. Family patriarch Robert Dunsmuir had found and exploited rich deposits of this essential product near Nanaimo, allowing the next generation, James and Laura Dunsmuir, to lead lives akin to royalty. In fact, James Dunsmuir occupied the vice-regal post of lieutenant governor from 1906 to 1909, after serving as prime minister of the province from 1900 to 1902. The residence that the couple began to construct in 1908 bore the title "Castle," and looked like one. Their estate of 270 hectares, Hatley Park, was located some eight kilometres west of Victoria, immediately to the west of Esquimalt Harbour, the principal maritime base of the British navy, and then of the Canadian forces, on the Pacific. The terrain sloped gently down to Esquimalt Lagoon, which adjoined the entrance to the naval base. A Douglas fir forest occupied the northern part of the site, acting as a protective barrier for the landscape of the southern sector, which overlooked the sheltered anchorage and harbour approach called "Royal Roads," in the Strait of Juan de Fuca.

Like the Butcharts, the Dunsmuirs chose as their architect the well-known Samuel Maclure, who had integrated several architectural traditions to create a Tudor/Arts and Crafts style that had become a sort of West Coast vernacular (which persists up to the present day).[34] His design for their residence, which he sited close

LANDSCAPES OF THE "BELLE ÉPOQUE" 299

to the northern limit of the open coastal landscape, organized its many rooms along two principal axes focused on a grand central hall. A square tower over the crossing of the two axes, neo-medieval in form and detail, provided a dramatic focus and justified the building's nickname, Hatley Castle. Maclure often designed gardens to accompany his houses in a naturalistic style that avoided formality and employed mostly native plants. For Hatley Park, he drew up the first site-layout plan and designed a grand open terrace along the south façade.[35]

Just as Jennie Butchart had done, Laura Dunsmuir[36] engaged Isaburo Kishida to create a Japanese garden for her estate, in 1909.[37] Kishida used the water from a little stream west of the house to supply an irregularly shaped lake that would serve as the central element of his garden. A main path followed the edge of the lake and provided access, via a bridge of curving profile, to an island where Kishida constructed a small, elegant pavilion. A rustic shelter occupied a high point of the site, offering a perspective of the entire garden. Azaleas, cherries, and Japanese maples (including, apparently, some plants Kishida had once again imported from Japan) added colour to the garden. Tall conifers and deciduous trees gradually grew up to close views towards the house, focusing attention on the garden and eliminating distraction.[38] The Dunsmuirs hired Brett and Hall, the Boston landscape architectural

14.6 Main building and grounds of Hatley Park, Colwood, BC, 1916, looking north. The castle is at the top of a long grassy slope going down to Esquimalt Lagoon, with dense Douglas fir forest in the background. Terraces and thematic gardens, including an "Italian Garden," are clustered around this main house. The Japanese garden is visible in left foreground.

14.7 Japanese garden at Hatley Park, a contemporary view. The growth of vegetation has divided the open landscape of the early days into distinct spaces, each with its own garden character.

firm that had planned the city of Prince Rupert in the northern part of the province (see chapter 13), to complete the overall site design and plan its detailed landscape development. The overall plan that they designed (and largely realized between 1913 and 1916) resembled in its major features the classic villa gardens of the nineteenth century, such as those at the Bois-de-Coulonge at Quebec City: a winding approach road through the forest, a sudden arrival at a clearing where the house was revealed in a dramatic setting at the crest of a great sloping lawn that descended to the water. Elegant gardens flanked the residence: an *Italian garden* of regular formal geometry, defined by box hedges and a wisteria-covered pergola; and a staircase on the north side of the building, continuing the axis of the main entry up the hill to the *Neptune terrace*, animated by a fountain and statue. To the west of the house and its immediate gardens, Brett and Hall integrated the already-existing Japanese garden with their overall design, mirroring its lake with three small bodies of water as the stream continued its way through a wooded valley down to Esquimalt Lagoon. The functional side of the establishment is located still further west: greenhouses and kitchen gardens, sports fields and a complete farm.[39] In the temperate climate of southern Vancouver Island, the original plants have grown to impressive proportions. Many trees, both exotic and native, are remarkable specimens, including a number of purple beeches, Lawson cypresses, a Chilean araucaria, and a magnificent arbutus.[40]

Before returning to his native country in 1912, Kishida designed another Japanese garden in Victoria, at Clovelly Place, the residence of Sir Frank Barnard, future lieutenant governor of the province.[41] Kishida's gardens were only the first expressions of Asian influence on the gardens of Canada's Pacific coast. They prefigured a vigorous fusion of Western and Eastern ideas that would be a central theme of British Columbia's gardens up to the present day.

New Faces in the East

In eastern Canada, other landscape architects embarked on prolific careers in the 1910s. Of particular note were Howard and Lorrie Dunington-Grubb, two landscape architects from England who arrived in Toronto in 1911 as representatives of Thomas Mawson. On his first foray outside his homeland in 1904, Howard Burlingham Grubb (1881–1965) had enrolled in the agriculture school at Cornell University, in New York State. When he returned to England in 1908 on completion of his studies, Grubb convinced Thomas Mawson to hire him as a junior landscape architect. One year later, he became the director of Mawson's London office,[42] and it was Mawson who introduced him, in 1910, to landscape architect Lorrie Alfreda Dunington (1877–1945), who had already established her own professional office in London. Dunington had been educated at Swanley Horticultural College, the world's first horticultural college for women, founded in 1889 in Kent, England, and dedicated to women in 1891–92.[43] Howard and Lorrie were married in 1911 and, taking the joint name Dunington-Grubb, emigrated to Toronto in the same year. First acting on behalf of Mawson, they soon opened their own office, which quickly acquired an excellent reputation.[44] They participated in residential development projects such as Lawrence Park Estates (1911–12), planned by the English engineer Walter S. Brooke, and the Humber Valley Surveys (1912–15), both garden suburb projects. The design of the gardens for the Old Mill Restaurant in the latter development provided an excellent showcase for Lorrie Dunington-Grubb's expertise in planting design.[45]

Following this promising début, the Dunington-Grubbs went on to have long and productive careers, principally in the region of southern Ontario, carrying out an astonishing number of high-quality landscape projects in a variety of traditional styles. Unable to find suitable plant material for their complex landscape projects, the Dunington-Grubbs founded the still-flourishing Sheridan Nurseries

14.8 Lorrie and Howard Dunington-Grubb, c. 1912

in the rich agricultural region west of Toronto. To manage the enterprise, they engaged the experienced horticulturist Sven Herman Stensson (1877–1938), a native of Sweden who had worked in Denmark and England, inviting him to immigrate to Canada in 1913 with his young family. Together, the Dunington-Grubb and Stensson families established a continuing landscape dynasty in southern Ontario, capitalizing on the natural symbiotic relationships among landscape architecture, the supply and maintenance of plants, and the making of gardens.[46]

A Global Culture

The international mobility of landscape professionals and the inclusion of Japanese gardens in Canadian projects at the beginning of the twentieth century attest to the existence of efficient means of travel and communication among different countries and different cultures. Well before our present era of globalization, economic and cultural internationalism had already flourished in the later years of the nineteenth century and the early years of the twentieth, greatly contributing to Canadian stability and prosperity.

This period was to see a remarkable growth in cross-border commercial exchanges. Peace reigned supreme – no general war had been fought between 1815 and 1914, despite periodic tensions – and a constant technical progress raised living standards yearly. Increasing worldwide prosperity brought a growing demand for Canadian products. People, goods, and money moved freely throughout the world. Undersea cables, excellent train service, and mail delivery twice a day permitted rapid intercity movement of business people and rapid exchange of information and ideas.[47] In the field of environmental design, the latest European ideas on garden cities and town planning quickly appeared in American magazines, available in Canada. A series of international conferences on town planning brought delegates from all the industrialized countries together to share their knowledge.[48]

Landscape Archetypes of Imperialism

Some historians see the period before the First World War as the dénouement of a "long nineteenth century" that lasted from 1789 to 1914. This 125-year period corresponded to the time it took for the consequences of the French Revolution and the Industrial Revolution (which originated in Britain) to spread throughout the world. In Canada, the nineteenth century "lingered like ice on the shaded side of a hill in spring. The real end of the age came in the hot summer of 1914."[49] In memory, this became a legendary "last golden summer of peace."[50] The lost world of that era was dominated by a small number of international empires, each one consisting of a European, American, or Asian *métropole* and its continental or overseas colonies and dependencies. Many principles of that system are unimaginable today, but at the beginning of the twentieth century, imperialism was so universal and powerful that it was difficult to imagine another system.[51]

Great efforts were made by these far-flung empires to tie their heterogeneous and multicultural possessions together into coherent wholes.[52] Some of these efforts were, of course, political and military; others involved common legal and administrative structures; but more subtle efforts were made to create a sense of cultural belonging through art and literature, through shared symbols and legends, including, as an important component, *landscapes*. Despite the great variety of climates, landforms, flora, and fauna represented in their worldwide territories, the empires' use of certain *landscape archetypes* allowed them to establish a sort of spatial continuity, just as the Romans had done by constructing all the towns and cities throughout their empire according to the same plan, that of the *castrum*. Through these landscape archetypes, empires attempted to provide a coherent physical image, a commonality of experience, and a sense of belonging to a great international community.[53]

At different moments in its history, Canada was a member of two of these international communities, first the French Empire and then the British, the most extensive of all. Built through the gradual accretion of territories large and small over several centuries, the British Empire reached its apogee in the second half of the nineteenth century. Its component territories, located in most of the major climatic and vegetation zones of the world, eventually occupied some one-quarter of the Earth's surface and inspired the prideful boast that the sun would "never set" on the empire. Of course, it did, as Rudyard Kipling foresaw in his strangely prophetic poem "Recessional" of 1897.[54]

From the start of the European colonization of Canada, French and British newcomers implanted their familiar landscape archetypes in the New World, beginning with French Renaissance gardens – oriented primarily to food production – at Port-Royal and the *Abitation* of Quebec City. Subsequent centuries saw the official gardens and convent gardens of New France (chapters 3, 4), followed by Georgian town layouts based on a standard grid pattern in the British settlements of the Maritime provinces (chapter 5). Examples of these twin traditions can be seen all over the world: Philadelphia (1683) and Savannah (1733) in the United States were classic early examples of regular city plans, integrating open spaces in an orderly pattern, as were later cities such as Adelaide in Australia (1837) and Christchurch in New Zealand (1850).

Public squares, laid out everywhere within the British colonial world, were symbols of order and permanence as well as much-needed oases of verdure in the burgeoning commercial cities of the nineteenth century. The rise of the romantic movement in the eighteenth and nineteenth centuries profoundly influenced landscape design throughout the empire, both in the villa gardens of the powerful and in visions of the little parish church in the glade, seen on a misty morning across a green meadow – one of many vivid images that figured in collective memories, even among those who had never seen the original.[55] The designers of the great urban parks often incorporated archetypal scenes from this romantic tradition into their creations.[56] Botanical gardens were among the most revered of the landscape archetypes of the Victorian period, as educational as well as aesthetic resources (the Victorians, like us, were passionate about "edu-tainment"). Legacies of the voyages of scientific discovery that had begun with Captain Cook in the eighteenth century (and thus integrally linked to the expansion of the empire), gardens

304   CHALLENGES OF AN URBAN AND INDUSTRIAL LANDSCAPE

of this genre became the treasures of Singapore, Sydney, London, and many other centres. Surprisingly, this tradition did not take root seriously in Canada before the 1930s. The closest approximation – the Halifax Public Gardens, founded in 1836 – was certainly a place for the admiration and study of plants, while also serving as a place of repose for the harried industrial workers of the city's maritime industries.[57]

The British model of the college and university campus also spread to all parts of the world, although the American pavilion model was a close rival (see chapter 13). Like Oxford and Cambridge, the University of Toronto was a federation of autonomous colleges that mirrored, in its first phases of development, their physical pattern of continuous buildings organized around interior courtyards and cloisters (identical to the French institutional tradition, which descended from the same medieval prototypes). A striking feature of the British campus tradition was the role of the sports field as a symbol of physical and moral health, the struggle against obstacles, and equality and team spirit – key values of the nineteenth century – often reaching iconic status. The Battle of Waterloo was said to have been won on the playing fields of Eton,[58] and impeccably maintained lawns for football, cricket, and field hockey were (and are) inescapable components of rural towns, schools, and universities in former empire territories, distant descendants of the common pastures and village greens inherited from the first Anglo-Saxon settlers of England.[59] Even today, it is not seen as incongruous for open spaces surrounded by the most prestigious collegiate Gothic halls of higher learning to be regularly churned into mud by pick-up matches of soccer or North American football. In Victorian mythology, the role of the sports field as a training ground for life was

14.9 McGill University lower campus, Montreal. Hockey matches such as that shown in this nineteenth-century photo by Alexander Henderson are repeated today in the main open space of the McGill campus.

LANDSCAPES OF THE "BELLE ÉPOQUE" 305

14.10 The little church in the vale, a familiar landscape archetype in many regions of Canada: Westmount Park United Church, Westmount, QC

idealized, probably too strongly. During the relatively peaceful years at the end of the nineteenth century, war was seen as a kind of game. The conflation of these two activities, so profoundly different, could be seen in the poems that continued to be studied in English Canadian schools until recently.[60] Such literary expressions might almost be seen as training films for the approaching war.

The use of landscape archetypes as a way of creating a sense of international community was practised by all the empires and quasi-empires of the time – British, French, Russian, Japanese, as well as in the overseas dependencies acquired by the United States in 1898. New landscape forms were routinely imposed on indigenous populations, who too often saw their own cultural landscapes obliterated. During the Belle Époque, the landscapes of British imperialism, like the empire itself, arrived at their apogee in scale and dimension; the magnificent new capital of India at New Delhi (built 1913–31) was its most grandiose expression. But at the other extreme, the rustic villages and country gardens of England long inspired emotional and sentimental attachments in distant corners of the empire.[61]

Legacy of Imperialism

This sentimental nostalgia lingered in Canada at least until the 1950s, primarily among Canadians of British background, who still commonly referred to Britain as "the Old Country." Although Canadians felt varying degrees of enthusiasm for the British Empire,[62] this association clearly resulted in a number of contributions to the country, including several in the domain of landscape. In particular, the governor generals and their spouses helped greatly in the preservation of the Quebec City fortifications, the creation of the Niagara Falls parks, the promotion of municipal reform, the introduction of Garden City ideas and co-partnership housing, and the encouragement of amateur sport.[63] In 1910, the invitations that Earl Grey extended to British designers led to the many projects and realizations of Thomas Mawson across Canada, and brought the most advanced knowledge and theories of the time to the country. In the nineteenth century, Canadian gardens and public spaces benefited from the expertise of the many landscape gardeners, landscape architects, and architects of British and Irish origin who immigrated to Canada. And finally, the landscape archetypes that owe their origins to the British Isles have inspired the creation and influenced the design of a large number of parks and squares across the country.

Victoria Park

Many of these fine landscape features bear a common name in honour of the monarch who presided over the period of Britain's international hegemony for almost two-thirds of a century. Victoria Park, Victoria Square – virtually every city and town under British administration created an open space that bore this name, sometimes a vast green wilderness, sometimes a little postage-stamp square

14.11 Victoria Park, Cambridge, ON. A pick-up hockey game in one of many parks designed by Frederick Todd in Galt, ON, now part of the larger municipality of Cambridge.

LANDSCAPES OF THE "BELLE ÉPOQUE" 307

downtown. There was a first wave of these parks in the early years of Victoria's reign, from 1837 to about 1845, but most date from the Belle Époque – the last years of her reign and the years immediately following her death in 1901. We have already met many of these parks and squares, including the first large urban park of Quebec City, established in 1893, and the downtown squares in Montreal, Regina, and Brantford, Ontario, among others. Victoria Parks of intermediate size grace St. John's in Newfoundland; Moncton, New Brunswick; Cambridge, Ontario; North Vancouver, British Columbia, and include the first completed section of Edmonton's extensive riverside park as well as a gracious cliff-top promenade along the edge of the valley above.

In other open spaces, statues of Queen Victoria are central features. An imposing statue of Victoria is a dominant element in Gore Park, at the heart of Hamilton, Ontario. Elsewhere in the former British Empire, the city of Christchurch, New Zealand, boasts both a Victoria Square downtown, right beside the city hall, and an extensive Victoria Park in its southwestern district; and in Australia, the square that occupies the central position in Adelaide's orderly constellation of public spaces also bears her name. Similar urban features are found in scores of other cities throughout the globe, identifying them with a world order that seemed permanent but which, except for the names of parks and squares, no longer exists.

Stormy Horizon

Several problems shadowed the general brightness of the age. In Quebec, colonization had reached the limits of highly productive agricultural land, but nonetheless continued into areas that were much more difficult to cultivate. A massive emigration began, partially towards western Canada, but mainly towards the United States.[64] "Empire patriotism" often provided an easy excuse for denial of the full benefits of citizenship to various linguistic and cultural communities, First Nations, and immigrants. In large cities, urban problems persisted despite the idealism of municipal reformers and the City Beautiful and Garden City visions of designers.[65]

Internationally, the extended period of peace was drawing to a close. The long nineteenth century was to end with increasing rivalries between empires, a last desperate struggle for colonies, and rampant instability. It would give way to the "short twentieth century," from 1914 to 1991, that would be characterized by ideological confrontations – hot and cold – between powerful nations.[66] The world of the Belle Époque was a good place to live and seemed to be filled with the promise of a long and prosperous future, especially if one lived in Canada. And then the war blew everything away.

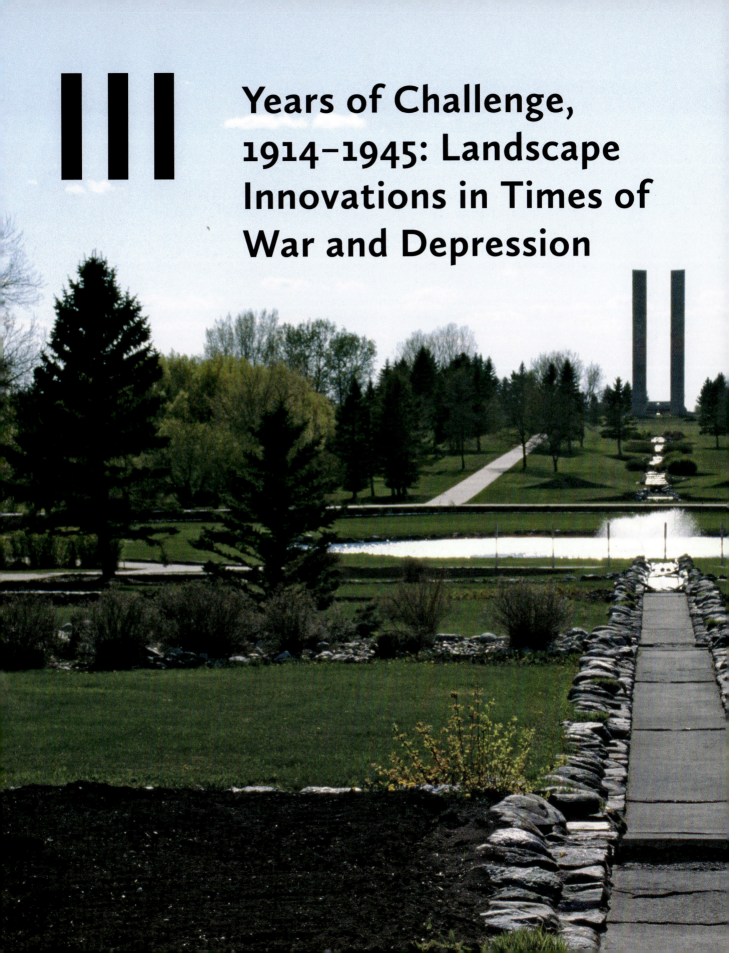

III

Years of Challenge, 1914–1945: Landscape Innovations in Times of War and Depression

15.1 Alex Colville, *Main Street*, 1979

15

Landscapes of Memory: Memorials of the First World War

In almost every town and city across Canada, the most important and strategic site – the centre of the public square, the central axis of the main street, a key location in the park along the river – is devoted to the same thing: a memorial to the Canadian soldiers who served in the First World War, from 1914 to 1918.[1] Our urban centres have been permanently marked by this war – not by bombs, none of which fell on Canadian soil – with the exception of the 1917 explosion in the port of Halifax – but by thousands of such memorials, built mostly in the 1920s and still commanding pride of place in prominent and symbolic locations. No other monuments have replaced or upstaged these in the ninety or more years since their creation.

Whether grand or humble, these memorials are part of the permanent backdrop of our lives. They continue to play an important role in the public landscape of our cities and towns, and their message is still clear, even though some aspects of their symbolism and design may have been obscured with time. They are so universal and familiar that we often do not pay attention to them, like the people who are busily going about their shopping in front of the soldier who stands on the monument behind them in Wolfville, Nova Scotia, in Alex Colville's 1979 painting *Main Street*.[2] The shoppers are occupied with their weekly routine; they are not watching him, but he is watching them.

The Impact of the War on Canada

The First World War had a powerful formative influence on the creation of modern Canada. We have seen in the preceding chapter how the physical progress and prosperity of the country contributed to the beginnings of a distinct Canadian identity, expressed by the first indications of an autonomous and unique culture. The First World War changed all this and set the country on an entirely different path. The war plunged the country into a turmoil that was both to accelerate its growth into nationhood[3] and to nearly tear it apart along its traditional linguistic fault line, over the issue of conscription. Canada was involved in the war from the first day to the last, and its sacrifice was out of all proportion to its size. Of a total population of some 8 million, over 460,000 served overseas in all areas of the Western Front, playing a major role in the Allied victories. Casualties were terrible: some 55,000 killed (1 in 8), more than Canada's losses would be in the Second World War when it had a much larger population, and roughly comparable to the number of American combat deaths in the First World War.[4]

This dreadful sacrifice touched every community and every social class. Among those who perished were the son of Lady Julia Drummond, who had played an important role in Montreal's urban reform movements; the grandson of Amédée Papineau (and great-grandson of Louis-Joseph); the young assistant of architect Samuel Maclure; the son of the mayor of Shawinigan Falls; and Thomas Mawson's youngest son, who would never complete his studies at the École des Beaux-Arts. Those who did not participate directly in the war were also caught in the whirlwind. The private sector of the economy slowed down drastically, and design offices lost their ability to function as many of their younger professionals went to the front. Rickson Outhet and the two principals of Brett and Hall had no work in Canada; they left for Washington to work for the US Housing Corporation, which was responsible for emergency housing during the wartime period.[5] This marked the end of the prolific partnership of Brett and Hall. The School of Engineering at the University of Saskatchewan closed its doors in 1916–17, all the professors and students having enrolled in the military services.[6]

In his poem "Recessional" (1897), Rudyard Kipling had predicted that the world of the Belle Époque would fall away. But no-one could have predicted how quickly the debacle would occur. War had never seemed inevitable, and it could conceivably have been called off at any time up to the mobilization of troops in August 1914.[7] At an international meeting of city planners in Toronto only three months before the outbreak of hostilities, the achievements of German city planning were favourably mentioned,[8] and in spring 1914, Thomas Mawson went to Greece to advise Kaiser Wilhelm on the garden of his summer residence.[9] Then, seemingly overnight, the Great War became an all-encompassing conflagration that overshadowed all other tasks and goals, a titanic struggle that absorbed all energies and had to be won at any cost.

Canada never really recovered from the wounds sustained in this war, one that happened at a time when the country was still an adolescent, at the threshold of maturity, like the young people who fought for it.

Homes for Heroes

In his autobiography, Thomas Mawson recalls the final letter that he received from his son before his death near Ypres in Belgium. The young man described the sacrifices of his fellow soldiers and asked his parents to "do something for our wounded." His request "became a command" for Mawson, inspiring him with a mission to create new towns for veterans. After the war, this mission occupied all his efforts for three years[10] and led to an important public campaign in Great Britain, in support of returning servicemen, that promoted the building of "Homes Fit for Heroes." In response, the British government passed a law in 1919 requiring local councils to build housing for veterans, and provided subsidies to carry out this work.

Mawson himself designed a village of this type in England and, during his last visit to North America in the autumn of 1915, tried to convince Canadian authorities of the importance of building villages for veterans.[11] After the war, in 1919, the Canadian government also instituted a national housing program, furnishing mortgage funds to the provinces to help reintegrate veterans into postwar Canadian society. The complete absence of residential construction during the war, as well as the formation of a large number of new households by veterans returning home, had created a major housing crisis that demanded an urgent response. Although most of the houses constructed under this program were scattered in small clusters throughout metropolitan areas,[12] some new planned communities were built, expressing more coherently the ideals of the time. The town of Lens, Saskatchewan, designed according to the principles of the City Beautiful movement,

is a notable example. Édouard Gaston Deville (1849–1924), Canada's surveyor general, drew up the plans on behalf of the Soldier Settlement Board.[13]

In Europe, the reconstruction of the towns and districts that had been devastated by war was an immediate priority. In Canada, the only site affected directly by the war, the Richmond district in the northern section of Halifax, was similarly targeted for rebuilding. In December 1917, the collision of two ships in the port, one of which was filled with munitions, had caused the largest explosion the planet was to see before the thermonuclear era, bringing complete destruction to a residential quarter of some 130 hectares. Even before the end of the war, the government had set up a relief committee to direct reconstruction work. The mandate to design the new section of the city was given to Thomas Adams, the town-planning adviser to the Canadian Commission of Conservation. Though a defender of the principles of the *City Efficient*, based on the criteria of efficiency and public health (see chapter 17) in opposition to the largely aesthetic values of *City Beautiful*, Adams nonetheless designed a neighbourhood that combined attractive green spaces and a logical and simple spatial configuration to create an impressive model of social housing.[14] The use by architects Ross and Macdonald

15.2 Hydrostone District, Halifax. This photograph shows one of eight block-long green malls around which Adams organized the Hydrostone residential areas. View is towards the southwest, looking away from Halifax Harbour. It is taken from Fort Needham Memorial Park, which, despite being on a substantial hill, did not protect the area behind it from the explosion.

314 YEARS OF CHALLENGE

of a unique system of precast concrete elements to construct the modest houses of the project provided it with an original name, the Hydrostone District.[15] Adams's design provided the development with a short commercial street that bears a striking resemblance to the corresponding sector in the town of Bournville in England, a model for the British Garden City movement.[16]

Commemoration

This willingness to do something concrete for the veterans was accompanied by a desire, widely shared, to recognize their sacrifice in some symbolic way. Extensive landscapes played a major role, beginning with *military cemeteries*, the great majority integrated into already-existing municipal cemeteries. A military section was added to almost all the rural cemeteries that we examined in chapter 10. All follow a standard design that recalls the orderly array of the parade ground: straight rows of simple gravestones, identical except for their inscriptions, without distinction between officers and common soldiers.[17] In Montreal, the military sections of the two great cemeteries, Notre-Dame-des-Neiges and Mount Royal (still Catholic and Protestant, respectively, at the time), are neighbours, separated only by a wrought-iron fence. Other cemeteries were specifically dedicated to veterans. The Field of Honour in Pointe-Claire, Quebec, follows a regular geometry structured by axial sightlines and circles.[18] The recently designated National Military Cemetery is located at the summit of the hill in Beechwood Cemetery, Ottawa.[19]

15.3 Walking north along the Meewasin Trail adjacent to the South Saskatchewan River, Saskatoon. At left is the Vimy Memorial, terminating 20th St. East.

LANDSCAPES OF MEMORY   315

15.4 Memorial chapel, Darlingford, MB

More generally, parks, squares, and other public spaces, which have always served as repositories of the community's public memory, became preferred locations for the commemoration of the service and sacrifice of veterans. Sometimes an entire park has played this role. Veterans Park at Lac-Mégantic, Quebec, is one such example, located at the end of the lake and enjoying a view along its entire length. Five rows of majestic trees march across its broad lawn, perhaps a reminder of soldiers in marching order. Other veterans' parks are found across the country, from Port Coquitlam and Langford in British Columbia to Belleville and Orillia in Ontario. In some places, buildings located within parks have served as memorials. In homage to the Canadian victory at Vimy Ridge in April 1917, architect Frank J. Martin designed the Vimy memorial in Saskatoon, Saskatchewan, an open octagonal pavilion similar to the bandstands that animated Victorian parks. The location of this structure within the urban setting is most striking: it is a feature of Kiwanis Memorial Park, part of the Meewasin Valley Greenway along the South Saskatchewan River, as well as the terminating element of an axis perpendicular to the river, along one of the main downtown circulation arteries. At Darlingford, a little village in Manitoba, the memorial consists of a modest chapel set back from the main street and facing a grand natural perspective complemented by grain elevators. Dr W.R. Leslie, from the Morden agricultural research station, created the small and intimate park that provides a setting for the building, which was designed by architect Arthur Stoughton, first director of the School of Architecture at the University of Manitoba. Adjacent to the altar inside the chapel, a panel recalls the names of all the local participants in the two world wars.[20]

316 YEARS OF CHALLENGE

In some cases, a building or other structure within the peaceful environment of a university campus took on the role of a memorial. Classic examples include Soldiers' Tower at Hart House, the social centre of the University of Toronto, built to the designs of architects Sproatt and Rolph in 1923–24, and the Memorial Gates at the University of Saskatchewan in Saskatoon (1924–27), designed by the architect of the original university buildings, David R. Brown. The latter project grouped pedestrian and vehicular entrances to the campus around a central stone panel commemorating "they who went forth from this University to the Great War of 1914–1918" and did not return.[21]

Roads of Remembrance

In emulation of a British campaign to create *roads of remembrance*, several Canadian cities created living memorial landscapes by planting avenues of trees, often associating each tree with a specific soldier. These avenues made reference to the long, straight roads of northern France, enclosed on each side by rows of elms, so familiar to the soldiers during their many years of service in that landscape. Jonathan Vance has characterized such avenues and groves of trees as "images of natural regeneration" that represented "the promise of everlasting life."[22] Many of

15.5   Next-of-Kin Memorial Avenue, Saskatoon, looking south towards the stone entrance portals. Woodlawn Cemetery is at left. The bronze plaques are supported on separate stands and not attached to the elm trees.

these avenues still exist but have lost their identification as memorials; an example is Sherbrooke Street in the Notre-Dame-de-Grâce district of Montreal, where in 1922 and the following years the Montreal Women's Club organized a program of planting trees and installing identification plaques. Most of the trees on this boulevard have been replaced and the plaques no longer exist. Since 1939, however, the west access road to Mount Royal Park bears the name Remembrance Road.[23] Other similar avenues, from Victoria, British Columbia, to Thunder Bay, Ontario, had virtually lost their identity as remembrance roads by the 1990s.

Memorial Drive in Calgary was constructed in 1922–31 under the direction of William R. Reader, superintendent of parks, on the north bank of the Bow River near the downtown area. It was a magnificent boulevard and linear park framed by 3,000 Russian poplars, each carrying a plaque that honoured a veteran, while a median strip in the middle of the boulevard was dotted with lilacs.[24] In later years, the boulevard lost some of its character as it was transformed into a wide, busy thoroughfare. In Winnipeg, vestiges remain of the avenue of elms that once marked the University of Manitoba's axial entrance road. But one of these historic roads still exists in its original form and in excellent condition: Next-of-Kin Memorial Avenue, begun in 1923 beside Woodlawn Cemetery in Saskatoon. As in Montreal, a women's group, the Imperial Order Daughters of the Empire (IODE), sponsored the project. Close relatives of veterans made contributions towards the purchase of the trees (American elms, the classic street tree of the Prairies) and the fabrication of the plaques, all of which remain in place today as the best example of a "living memorial" in Canada.[25]

Sculptures and Monuments

The great majority of memorials were, however, free-standing monuments and sculptures, strategically located in dramatic settings within the urban landscape so as to maximize their visibility to the general public. In the Atlantic provinces, these important sites are likely to be by the water. This is the case with the simple cross facing the small harbour of Woody Point, a little village on Bonne Bay in Gros Morne National Park, Newfoundland. It is also true of the Newfoundland National War Memorial, the powerful monument on Water Street in the capital, St. John's, with its many figures (sculpted by British captain Basil Gotto, 1866–1954) representing the various civilian occupations and military services of the province,[26] surmounted by an allegorical personification of the spirit of Newfoundland. The landscape setting of this memorial was designed by landscape architect Rudolph Cochius, who had returned to Newfoundland after working on Bowring Park with Frederick Todd. Its swirling staircase rises from the historic waterfront where Britain's first colony was founded some three and a half centuries before, and the monument stands almost directly opposite the legendary port entrance of the Narrows.[27]

St. John's Bowring Park includes two remarkable memorial sculptures, both carefully sited for maximum visual impact: *The Fighting Newfoundlander* (1922) and *The Caribou* (1928). A native of Newfoundland, where the often sterile soils

318 YEARS OF CHALLENGE

15.6 Caribou memorial for the Royal Newfoundland Regiment at Beaumont-Hamel in northern France

support abundant lichens (its main nourishment), the caribou has long been a symbol of the province and, in particular, of the Royal Newfoundland Regiment. Once again, Basil Gotto created the bronze images and Rudolph Cochius designed their landscape settings. The latter placed the caribou, sculpted in a heroic and defiant posture by Gotto, at the summit of a stylized granite escarpment.[28] This composition is identical to that of the five Newfoundland memorials that Cochius designed for the battlefields of Europe, collectively referred to as the *Trail of the Caribou*. The keystone of these sites was the memorial at Beaumont-Hamel, completed in 1924.[29] Here, the caribou, again positioned atop a dynamic and angular rocky crag, was surrounded by the topography of conflict. Trenches and bomb craters were conserved to remain as permanent reminders of the horrors of war, in contrast to the landscapes of the surrounding countryside, which have regained the bucolic aspect that is characteristic of rural France. The other memorial parks, considerably smaller, follow a similar format: the caribou is always situated at the top of a fragment of Newfoundland landscape transplanted to Europe and is always oriented to face the line of trenches that the Newfoundlanders were to attack.[30]

LANDSCAPES OF MEMORY   319

Sculpture and the sea also played important roles in Nova Scotia. The kilted soldier who stands by the shore in Chester, on the south coast, brings to mind the Scottish origins of the early settlers. Its sculptor and donor, Massey Rhind, was also responsible for the allegorical figure representing the city of Halifax on the principal memorial in the provincial capital. This monument is located at the most prestigious and strategic point in the city, on the longitudinal axis of Grand Parade, the eighteenth-century square at the centre of the old colonial downtown grid, halfway between the harbour and the Citadel (see chapter 5). Elsewhere in Halifax, a cross in Point Pleasant Park facing the sea honours the members of the Royal Canadian Navy, for whom Halifax is the principal base on the Atlantic.

In the Maritimes as elsewhere, many of the sculptural figures are remarkable works of art, created by the best artists of the time. One of the most moving is located in Victoria Park in Moncton, New Brunswick: a devastated soldier stands with hanging head and uncomprehending eyes, his face grown old with war. Surprisingly, the sculptor's name is not to be found on the monument; he was Emanuel Hahn (1881–1957), a Canadian of German origin who had lost previous commissions by letting his background be known.[31] Artist Elizabeth Wyn Wood (1903–1966) from Orillia, Ontario, who studied with Hahn before they were married, carried out sculptural works for several memorials, including the moving Welland-Crowland Memorial at Welland, Ontario; but on other projects, she suffered the same fate as her husband, through association: rejection despite winning the commission.[32]

15.7 War memorial at Grand Parade, Halifax, looking north. The city hall is seen at the end of the square's central axis; the clock on one face of its tower is permanently set to the time of the Halifax Explosion.

15.8 Memorial sculpture by Emanuel Hahn, sculptor, at Victoria Park, Moncton, NB

320 YEARS OF CHALLENGE

15.9 Memorial at Vimy Ridge, northern France, seen from the east. Walter Allward, sculptor and designer. The limestone sculpture's two pylons, representing Canada and France, can be seen for many kilometres across the Douai Plain to the northeast. The central statue of the Spirit of Canada, or *Canada Bereft*, is the focal point of the composition.

Those responsible for the building of the memorials often located them at troop-embarkation points. In Sussex, New Brunswick, as in most of Canada, this was the railway station. The station remains, although the trains no longer go there, as in many spots in Canada; in front of it, there is a little railway square, still perfectly kept up, with a small stone obelisk in the centre. On a wall inside the station is an old photo of the troops, assembled in front of the trains mustered to take them to waiting ships bound for Europe. Similarly, in Peterborough, Ontario, a photo in the city hall shows the troops gathered in September 1914 in front of the adjacent drill hall. In a small park midway between the two public buildings stands a remarkable allegorical sculpture in black marble. This dramatic work by Toronto artist Walter Allward (1876–1955) represents Valour turning back Barbarism.

Allward also received the mandate to design Canada's most prominent war memorial, the monument at Vimy Ridge in France, the scene of Canada's greatest triumph – at great human cost – of the First World War. On a broad stone base at the top of the ridge, the sculptor erected two immense columns of white limestone, setting in relief a score of allegorical figures, as in Peterborough, representing Peace and Justice, Truth and Knowledge, the Spirit of Sacrifice and the Spirit of Canada, mourning her dead. Like the memorial park at Beaumont-Hamel, the

LANDSCAPES OF MEMORY 321

Canadian National Vimy Memorial is still surrounded by the ruined landscape of war, unhealed by time.[33] The victory at Vimy, to which the whole Canadian Army contributed, was of tremendous symbolic importance to Canada, as attested by the great number of references, all across the country, to the battle. There is a Vimy Park in Kaslo, British Columbia; in Winnipeg, Manitoba; at Port Colborne, Ontario; and in Outremont, Quebec, and elsewhere; and a Vimy Peak in Waterton Lakes National Park in the Rockies.[34]

Some memorials have a stunning relationship to the urban landscape and to natural topography. A striking example is the powerful sculpture by George Hill (1862–1934) in Sherbrooke, Quebec, that commands the steeply sloping major artery, King Street, and dominates the whole vista down to the St. Francis River and beyond.[35] An equally skilful urban integration, albeit less spectacular, can be observed at Shawinigan, Quebec. The Monument aux Braves is situated within the St. Maurice Promenade, a linear park along the bank of the river that gave life to the city, at the termination of the sightline along the main downtown commercial street. This composition and that of the Vimy memorial in Saskatoon apply identical techniques of urban design. In the provincial capital of Quebec City, the principal war memorial has a place of honour on Grande-Allée, just opposite the parliamentary precinct and adjacent to the entrance to the Plains of Abraham, site of another long-ago conflict and now a wonderful park. The memorial is similar in form to the Sailors' Memorial in Halifax's Point Pleasant Park: a bronze sword

15.10 Cross of Sacrifice facing Grande-Allée and the Colline Parlementaire, Quebec City. The old fortifications and Porte Saint-Louis are at left; the entrance to the Plains of Abraham at right.

322   YEARS OF CHALLENGE

15.11 Cenotaph, Central Memorial Park, Calgary, located at the western entrance to the park

superimposed on a simple, almost abstract, limestone cross. In fact, it is a standard design, the *Cross of Sacrifice*, first designed by a famous British architect, Sir Reginald Blomfield (1856–1942), for the Imperial War Graves Commission. This cross, which symbolizes the integration of ideas typical of the times – patriotism, religion, and sacrifice – is the central element of every Commonwealth cemetery in Europe and an important feature in the military sections of many Canadian cemeteries.[36]

The other classic type of memorial erected everywhere in Canada is the *Cenotaph*, its name derived from Greek words meaning "an empty tomb," in the sense that no-one is buried at the memorial. It was another celebrated British architect, Sir Edwin Lutyens (1869–1944),[37] who designed the modern form of the cenotaph. His first design, sketched up in a single day, was realized as a temporary memorial in Whitehall, London, for the first Remembrance Day in November 1919. Lutyens's design consisted of a rectangular block divided into three sections – base or plinth, main body, cap or crown – bearing standardized inscriptions and symbols. The cenotaph actually represents a tomb supported on a pylon-like shaft, but its abstract character is most keenly read. The only decorations are two laurel wreaths on the sides, flags flown on front and back, and an inscription, originally "Our Glorious Dead." The first temporary cenotaph was subsequently rebuilt with great

LANDSCAPES OF MEMORY 323

refinement in stone; it quickly became the model for such structures everywhere.[38] At the entrance to Victoria Park in London, Ontario, is a classic exemplar. Located right downtown and surrounded by important civic, commercial, and religious buildings, it faithfully follows Lutyens's model in detail: three flags, stone wreaths on each side, inscriptions, and dates, as at Whitehall. A similar cenotaph occupies a place of honour in Gore Park, Hamilton, a square also located in the most central and historic part of town. Other monuments that follow closely the original prototype are found in Montreal's historic square Place du Canada, previously known as Dominion Square, long the centre of gravity of the business and institutional district of the city; and in Calgary, at historic Central Memorial Park.[39]

The proportions of the standard cenotaph were often modified to create a narrower and more elongated rectangle, a column or a *stele*. An example of the latter is seen in the median band of Memorial Boulevard, located on the axis of the Manitoba Legislative Assembly in Winnipeg. A similar columnar cenotaph is located at the central point of Victoria Park in North Vancouver, British Columbia. The park, a long green rectangle, is organized around the grey granite monument,[40] which bears a typical inscription: "In memory of the citizens of North Vancouver city and district who served in the allied forces in the wars 1899–1902, 1914–1918, 1939–1945 and the Korean War. Their name liveth for evermore." Inscriptions for subsequent wars were frequently added to the original memorials erected following the First World War. The great battles in which local residents participated are also indicated – Cambrai, the Somme, Ypres, Vimy. Many of these cenotaphs – though not this one – also bear the inscription "Lest we forget," the refrain of Rudyard Kipling's poem "Recessional," mentioned above and in chapter 14. There have been several French translations of Kipling's words, but a simple variant of the Quebec motto "Je me souviens" seems to be the most widely used.[41]

The popularity of these standard designs was equalled by the enthusiasm for monuments featuring sculptures of people, and these are often the most moving of all. The figures involved were generally soldiers, singly or in groups. Sometimes an angel stands over them as a messenger from God; in other monuments, a woman or an angel comforts a fallen soldier. Such sculptures occasionally seem to be organized in "families," following regional trends. In his study of memories and meanings of the First World War, author Jonathan Vance has identified, in the actions and attitudes of these memorial soldiers, several themes that express the general public's understanding and interpretation of the war. These include the jubilant celebration of victory in the defence of civilization, symbolized by uplifted helmet or rifle; and an alternate vision – not pacifist, but filled with chagrin – that emphasizes the sacrifice and loss of war through downcast eyes or angels carrying those who had perished to Heaven.[42] The triumphant posture of the soldier who stands on the podium at the Manitoba Legislative Building is virtually identical to that of his counterpart on the other side of the Red River, in the cemetery of Saint Boniface Cathedral. The soldiers in the memorials at Victoria Park in Regina, sculpted by R.G. Heughan, and at the city hall in Lethbridge, Alberta, both adopt the stance of *reversed arms* customary for a military funeral service. At Yarmouth in Nova Scotia, Henri Hébert (1884–1950), son of Louis-Philippe,

15.12 (left)   War memorial on the grounds of the Manitoba Legislative Building, Winnipeg, facing Broadway (dedicated 1923). The sculpture, which represents a Canadian soldier celebrating the end of the war, was executed by local artist Marguerite Taylor, while the monument as a whole was designed by Winnipeg architect Colonel J.N. Semmens. Erected by the Winnipeg Soldiers' Relatives' Memorial Association, it is known as the "Next of Kin" monument. Just visible at lower left is the Golden Boy atop the legislative building, in a somewhat similar pose.

15.13 (right)   Memorial at Victoria Park, Regina, SK

created a memorable representation of an exhausted soldier who had just left the trenches.[43] At the National War Memorial in Ottawa, erected on a central site in Confederation Square on the axis of Elgin Street, the British artist Vernon March and his family sculpted some twenty figures in bronze, including ground troops, an aviator, a nurse, and a sailor, who advance towards the conflict through an immense granite arch. King George VI and Queen Elizabeth dedicated this memorial in the spring of 1939, on the eve of another conflagration.[44]

The government of Canada erected the memorial in Ottawa, but this was exceptional. Almost all of these memorials were erected by public subscription and organized by volunteer citizens' groups. Only a handful were carried out by

LANDSCAPES OF MEMORY 325

governments or paid for by wealthy individuals or corporations.[45] This certainly has something to do with the respect that they still elicit and with the considerable variety and originality they display. Memorial Park, the main square in Oshawa, Ontario, is another exception, having benefited from a major contribution from the prominent McLaughlin family. The design of the Oshawa memorial was very elaborate: a central sculpture mounted on a pedestal was flanked by a curving wall built with stones from the battlefields of the war and from each of the Allied nations. The dedication in 1924, itself an elaborate affair, was held before a large crowd that had gathered to hear the speeches and the bands playing.[46] In the nearby town of Whitby, Ontario, both the monument and the dedication ceremony were simpler. Situated in a much smaller park a couple of blocks from Whitby's main "four corners" intersection, the monument was inaugurated in 1922 by guest of honour Lord Byng, governor general of Canada and the former commander of the Canadian Corps during the war. He was greeted by schoolchildren singing a song written for the occasion, "Lord Byng, Canada Welcomes You."[47] The continuing relevance of the Whitby memorial was demonstrated in the days following the tragic events of September 2001 in New York. A hand-made placard with a few flowers was added to the monument as an impromptu message of shared sorrow. It was still there a month later.

Symbols and Themes

Landscape elements were often used in the Canadian memorials to convey ideas and explore themes concerning war, peace, and conciliation, as we have seen at Beaumont-Hamel and Vimy. The most universally recognized landscape element in Canada is without doubt the *poppy*, thanks to the poem "In Flanders Fields," written by Major John McCrae, a Canadian army surgeon. In April 1915, following the second battle of Ypres in Belgium, McCrae was filled with sorrow at the death of a young soldier whom he could not save. His poem described exactly what he saw around him, wind-blown scarlet poppies, pioneer plants that thrive in disturbed soil (like wheat fields, battlefields, and cemeteries). His poem was not a message of peace; it was a call to arms. McCrae implored his colleagues – and the nation – to continue the fight.[48] His symbolism refers back to that romantic but disturbing conflation of war and sports defined in Sir Henry Newbolt's poem "Vitae Lampada" (see chapter 14): he demands that the torch be held high (as in the relay races of classical Greece) and not allowed to fall. This torch has retained its flame for many years, a symbol of defiance and a message affirming the resolution to remain undefeated. It made its appearance in the monument at Vimy, and the line of the poem that refers to it is emblazoned in the dressing room of the Canadiens, Montreal's renowned hockey team. Thus the image that used sports as a metaphor finally came full circle to its athletic origins.

But the poppy, as a symbol, evolved in the opposite direction. Adopted in Canada and elsewhere, it springs profusely into bloom each year during the weeks that precede November 11th, solemnly observed as Remembrance Day. Poppies are not incitements to victory but reminders of sacrifice and loss. The monuments rediscovered at this time of the year are not calls to war but recollections of its cost and futility. In this sense, they should be considered as peace memorials rather than as war memorials, as Shipley eloquently states.[49] Every one of them bears an invisible motto, "Never again."

For several decades, the physical condition of many memorials deteriorated. They still existed, however, occupying the most significant locations in almost every Canadian town. Every year on November 11th, old soldiers solemnly come back to them, along with Boy Scouts, Girl Guides, mayors, and city councillors, but no-one seemed to be really interested in the memorials or in looking after them. However, this unhappy interlude seems to have ended. The last few years have seen increasing numbers of participants at the major ceremonies and sensed greater appreciation of the monuments and the soldiers they represent. In recent times, several memorials have been extensively restored, including Beaumont-Hamel in 2000–05, under the direction of John E. Zvonar, landscape architect with the federal Department of Public Works; and Memorial Drive in Calgary, where, since 2000, the City of Calgary Parks, with the assistance of consulting landscape architects, has established a program of gradual plant replacement through the use of cuttings from the original memorial trees as they approach the end of their life cycle, a process that symbolizes the triumph of life over death.[50] In Ottawa, Phillips Farevaag Smallenberg, Vancouver-based landscape architects and planners, undertook a major reconstruction of the National Memorial in 2006, integrating into it the tomb of the Unknown Soldier; and Canadian architect Julian Smith collaborated with Jacqueline Hucker, architecture and landscape historian, and with architect Daniel Lefèvre of Paris on the restoration of the Vimy Memorial in 2003–07.[51] Several cities, including Winnipeg, Côte-Saint-Luc in Quebec, and Memramcook in New Brunswick, have recently inaugurated new Veterans Parks. The section of Ontario Highway 401 – the Macdonald-Cartier Freeway – that links Trenton and Toronto has been officially named the "Highway of Heroes," and the Quebec government has recently designated a section of Route 20, west of Montreal, as *l'Autoroute du Souvenir*, "Remembrance Highway."

16

Private Gardens of the Twenties and Thirties

16.1 Garden of Uplands Estate, Toronto, designed by L.A. & H.B. Dunington-Grubb and Stensson, landscape architects, 1930

Except for a brief interlude in the 1920s, Canadians were preoccupied with issues of war and depression for the three decades from 1914 to 1945. But remarkably, a number of fine landscape and civic design projects were realized during these troubled years. In particular, the decade following the First World War was a period of energy and effervescence in the art of the garden, especially the private garden, to which many landscape architects dedicated their talents.

After the war, there had been no "return to normal." Instead of resuming the life of the Belle Époque where they had left off, people found themselves in an era of transition. New forces led every aspect of Canadian life, particularly economic life, in new directions. Even before the war, in 1913, the end of the long boom in economic and real estate development was evident and a housing crisis had begun.[1] To these changes were added, after 1918, additional stresses: demobilized servicemen established new families in great numbers (thus aggravating the housing crisis), few jobs for veterans materialized, and the transition from a wartime to a peacetime economy proved more difficult than had been thought.[2] In 1919, the Winnipeg General Strike starkly demonstrated workers' dissatisfaction with their salaries and living conditions,[3] and subsequently, a serious deflation between 1920 and 1923 caused considerable social disruption. For the rest of the decade, an apparent prosperity, based largely on stock market speculation, allowed some to reach higher levels of wealth and status, while providing little benefit to middle-level salaried workers.[4]

These new forces had many consequences for landscape architecture in Canada. While most of those who had practised the profession before the war resumed their careers and the principal offices reopened their doors, their ranks were reinforced by several new professionals from abroad, mostly from Great Britain and the United States. But a new phenomenon was increasingly evident: the enrichment of the profession of landscape architecture by a growing number of native-born Canadians who had been trained in the United States, either in established offices or in university programs of landscape architecture and horticulture – and several of these new recruits were women. The projects that the postwar practitioners undertook did revisit some prewar trends, such as the planning of residential neighbourhoods and resource towns, urban design, and the long-term development of college campuses and the grounds of parliamentary complexes established before the war. The latter was particularly true of western Canada, where the City Beautiful model of the original plans continued to inspire subsequent work. But the age of great public parks and rural cemeteries – the most important accomplishments of Canadian landscape architects from 1870 to 1914 – had definitely ended. Governments and other clients were no longer interested in this type of investment, while rapidly expanding demand in the private sector was focused elsewhere.

The "Country Place Era"

A new generation of influential property owners, descendants of the nineteenth-century captains of industry and of the wealthy industrialists who had come to the fore in new industries (such as automobile manufacturing), created a new generation of villas and country gardens. The economic climate of the time and the skyrocketing stock exchange added to their already substantial fortunes while permitting a significant number of professionals and middle-class business people to achieve a new status of prosperity and prestige.[5] The desire of these groups to display their prosperity in concrete fashion led to the proliferation of large country estates among the more wealthy and, in garden suburbs, to the establishment of *mini-villas* of 1.5 to 2 hectares for the new members of the upper middle class. The owners of these domains, large and small, sought the help of the best architects, landscape architects, and artisans in order to realize their architectural and landscape ambitions.

This was a general trend all over North America. Norman Newton, historian of landscape architecture at Harvard University, has given a name to these years during which private landscape projects took precedence over public projects: the *country place era*.[6] The landscape architects of the period devoted much of their time and effort to projects of this type, as such work enabled them to continue to practise their profession despite a marked decline in the number of large public projects. There was another advantage: millionaires are very demanding clients, generally ready to invest the money required to ensure that a high standard of work is carried out. Thus the landscape architects who designed their gardens were able to hone and perfect their design abilities and work with the finest materials,

PRIVATE GARDENS OF THE TWENTIES AND THIRTIES   329

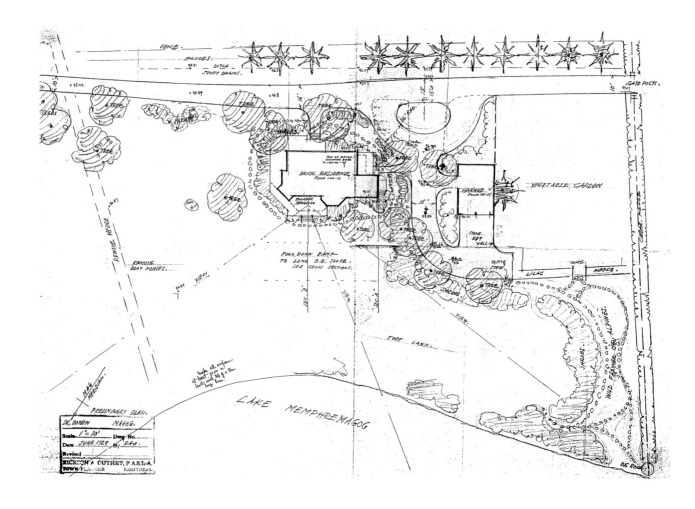

whether mineral – limestone, granite – or vegetal – plant materials. They had the time and the resources to work out the details and refine their compositions.[7]

To build and maintain such ambitious gardens, the magnates of the 1920s and 1930s relied on an army of competent gardeners, many of whom had received excellent training in Europe and were available at modest salaries. To guide the owners in their decisions, a specialized magazine was there to help them: *Canadian Homes and Gardens*, published in Toronto from October 1925 in its definitive format. Well illustrated with large photos, the magazine featured articles densely filled with horticultural tips and instructions in garden building. It was a high-end publication: advertisements for powerful automobiles and motorboats shared the publicity pages with ads for greenhouses, plants, and furniture. A summary stylistic analysis of the gardens that were featured suggests that many owed their inspiration to the works of Gertrude Jekyll (1843–1932) and Edwin Lutyens (1869–1944), as well as their contemporaries in England. The approach of these two brilliant designers was clear and simple: first, the area of the garden was divided by walls or dense hedges into several distinct *outdoor rooms*, each with its

16.2 Sketch plan for garden of country residence, Magog, QC, June 1929. Rickson Outhet, landscape architect. Lake Memphremagog in Quebec's Eastern Townships has long been a favourite location for the country houses and summer cottages of wealthy and middle-class Montrealers. Here, in his typical quick and skilful manner, Outhet has roughed out a preliminary landscape design for a country residence of moderate extent. The house is located at the top of a northwest-facing slope that goes directly down to the lake. Outhet has identified a few key levels and defined (and kept open) the main view, while providing an extensive veranda and pedestrian and car access adjacent to the house. He has laid out major trees and shrub masses in a sketchy manner, without identifying particular species at this early stage. Nonetheless, all major garden areas and vegetation components are shown: decorative planting related to the house, visual barrier between vehicle/service area and main lawn, vegetable garden, shrub masses to frame the lawn, and a wild garden near the site boundary, adjacent to a large rock by the water.

own form and personality; then each space was embellished with complex plant compositions, carefully planned to set up contrasts of plant form and foliage and enriched by the successive flowering of various plants so as to provide a sequence and contrast of colours. Another likely source of inspiration was the work of American architect and landscape architect Charles Adams Platt (1861–1933), whose book *Italian Gardens* (1894) and whose many designs for villas and gardens reflected a sophisticated fusion of the formality and symmetry of the Italian Renaissance with the naturalism of the English picturesque garden.[8] Thomas Mawson, who had mastered this vocabulary in his work in Great Britain, had an influence on Canadian projects, including those of his former employees Howard and Lorrie Dunington-Grubb.

Each month, *Canadian Homes and Gardens* presented professionally designed residential gardens, often featuring a landscape architect who spoke of his or her own work. In the April 1929 issue, for example, Frederick G. Todd described the garden he had designed for the residence of Lady Meredith on the slopes of Mount Saint Bruno, east of Montreal.[9] In January 1929, the magazine's editor, J. Herbert Hodgins, recounted – in a particularly floral literary style – his visit to the gardens of Shadowbrook Estate, a residence situated on a tributary stream of the Don River in Willowdale, Ontario. Designed by landscape architects H.B. and L.A. Dunington-Grubb and built by the landscape company they had created, Sheridan Nurseries (see chapter 14), the gardens followed an almost classic eclectic formula. The house opened onto a wide stone terrace, inspired by the Italian Renaissance, which gave onto a broad lawn sloping down to the wooded stream at the edge of the property. Other functional spaces and thematic gardens, linked together in an orderly geometric array, complemented the main spaces: an intimate rose garden, a kitchen garden, a tennis court, and even a Japanese garden, complete with tea house.[10] Several projects by landscape architect Edwin Kay, another native of England who had worked in the Dunington-Grubb office before setting up on his own account, also figured in the magazine. The articles on his work bear witness to Kay's expertise in the execution of traditional garden components, including rock gardens, shady wooded ponds, and perennial borders, expertise he had apparently gained while managing the "estate of a European nobleman."[11]

In the pages of *Canadian Homes and Gardens*, garden designers also addressed more general questions of design and technique. Edwin Kay provided instructions on pruning deciduous shrubs in March 1926,[12] and Lorrie A. Dunington-Grubb wrote a series of eight articles between 1925 and 1928 exploring such subjects as the use of water in the garden, rock garden composition, and the selection of plants to provide autumn colour. These lively and instructive texts demonstrate the encyclopedic knowledge of plants she had developed and had called into action in her landscape designs.[13] Gordon Joseph Culham, like Rickson Outhet a Canadian graduate of the Olmsted Brothers office in Brookline, Massachusetts, contributed two series of articles to the magazine, beginning with monthly features on the great garden styles of the world (Italian, French, Spanish, English). These were followed by a more general collection of articles concerning the methods and principles of garden design (integration of the garden with the site, planning and

PRIVATE GARDENS OF THE TWENTIES AND THIRTIES 331

zoning, planting design, etc.). All his contributions were liberally illustrated with photos of gardens in Canada and abroad.[14]

The relationship between Culham and *Canadian Homes and Gardens* went beyond journalism. The publisher of the magazine, John Bayne Maclean (1862–1950), was Culham's personal patron.[15] As soon as he became a millionaire, Maclean sponsored a beautification program for his native village of Crieff in Ontario. He was at first assisted in this endeavour by the Olmsted Brothers of Massachusetts. When Maclean needed someone to provide resident supervision of the work at the village, he recruited Culham from the Olmsted office.[16] Culham had already served an interesting apprenticeship. Before he began his professional career, he had served in the Canadian Army during the First World War and had then studied at the Ontario Agricultural College (OAC) at Guelph. While continuing his studies in landscape architecture at Harvard, he helped in the preparation of the New York Regional Plan, an ambitious enterprise directed by Thomas Adams, who had previously played a central role in the Canadian Commission of Conservation (see chapters 15 and 17). In 1926, Culham was recruited by the Olmsted office, where he worked until 1930. When the economic crisis of 1929 led to a sharp decline in professional work, Maclean's offer convinced Culham to leave Boston for Toronto, where he opened an office as a town planner and landscape architect and took on the responsibility for all of Maclean's projects.[17]

Gardens and Designers on the West Coast

The primary focus of *Canadian Homes and Gardens* lay in eastern Canada, particularly the southern areas of Ontario and Quebec, but each issue featured at least one project from British Columbia, often one of the great gardens located along the seacoasts of Victoria or Vancouver or in upscale districts like Shaughnessy Heights or Oak Bay (see chapter 14). During the 1920s and 1930s, many of these projects were designed by *landscape gardeners*, who were not professionally trained in landscape architecture but had a profound knowledge of plant materials and remarkable abilities in design. Raoul Robillard, as an adolescent in the prewar years, had helped his father at the Butchart Gardens (see chapter 14); after the war he became a consummate creator of gardens. He designed and constructed some 1,500 residential and commercial gardens in Vancouver, including several in the large estates on Marine Drive, first laid out by Todd twenty years before. Robillard also designed and executed gardens in Victoria and in West Vancouver.[18]

On the West Coast as in central Canada, many American professionals were involved in landscape work. These included the Morell and Nichols firm from Minneapolis, who designed the Hycroft garden in the Shaughnessy Heights district of Vancouver (see chapter 14).[19] Fred Cole, an eminent garden designer from Seattle, planned the landscapes for many estates in Vancouver, where he maintained an office. His work at "The Gables," the residence of W.G. Murrin on Marine Drive, is a well-known example.[20] Landscape architects of British origin also established themselves in British Columbia. English-born Frank Ebenezer Buck (1875–1971)

16.3   Gordon Culham and Edwin Kay in the 1940s

studied in New York State at Cornell, one of the first universities to offer a degree in landscape architecture, before moving to Montreal in 1911, where he obtained a degree in horticulture at Macdonald College. Buck subsequently worked at the Central Experimental Farm in Ottawa (see chapter 7), assisting the chief of the Horticulture Division, William T. Macoun. His assignments at the farm included writing instruction manuals on gardening, which provided an excellent training for his future role as a professor of ornamental horticulture at the University of British Columbia (UBC), from 1920 to 1949.[21] The versatile Buck also served as the university's landscape architect for many years, directing the landscape work that would gradually transform the site into one of the most beautiful university campuses in Canada. Intensely interested in town planning, Buck participated in the town planning commissions of Point Grey (a city later amalgamated with Vancouver) and other municipalities, and served as president of the Town Planning Institute of Canada during the 1920s. The tree-planting programs along the boulevards and residential streets of Point Grey are a part of his rich legacy. Buck also found the time to design private gardens, including that of Eagles Estate on Deer Lake in Burnaby, a suburb of Vancouver, and to contribute to the planning of the University Endowment Lands at UBC.[22]

Bill Livingstone (1911–1990) personified the strong traditional connection between the landscape industry and landscape architecture. A member of a Scottish family that had founded a nursery in Vancouver in 1912, he already had an excellent grounding in horticulture when he began to work for Fred Cole in the United States in the 1920s. When his apprenticeship was completed, he returned to Vancouver in the 1930s, establishing himself as a landscape designer and contractor. Like other designers, he planned the gardens for many estates in Shaughnessy Heights and on Marine Drive; this led to his 1938 engagement as director of landscape construction for the city of Vancouver. It was there, in the years following the Second World War, that he would create his most significant works (see chapter 19).[23]

Canadian Women in Landscape Architecture

For many years, Lorrie Alfreda Dunington-Grubb was the only Canadian woman who practised landscape architecture as a full professional.[24] Yet many women had been involved in garden design since the nineteenth century, as both amateurs and professionals, without calling themselves "landscape architects." Gardening and landscape architecture were, in fact, among the first disciplines to open their doors to women, who hastened to take advantage of the opportunity. In 1911, an article in the magazine *The Canadian Horticulturist* exhorted women to pursue studies in horticulture and garden design to earn their living.[25] In the 1920s and 1930s, two women who worked as landscape gardeners designed high-end residential gardens in the Quebec City area: Sarahluff Bond created the gardens at the *Groisardières* estate, the residence of Mrs. C.E.L. Porteous on Île d'Orléans;[26] and Mary Stewart refined and augmented the design of the gardens at the Henry-Stuart House and at the villa of Cataraqui (see chapter 9).

The early twentieth century witnessed the founding of three American institutions that offered specialized training to women in these fields: the Cambridge School of Architecture and Landscape Architecture, in Massachusetts (founded 1915); the Pennsylvania School of Horticulture for Women, in Philadelphia (1910); and the Lowthorpe School of Landscape Architecture, Gardening and Horticulture for Women, established in 1901 at Groton, Massachusetts, by Judith Eleanor Low, a graduate of the Swanley Horticultural College in England, where Lorrie Dunington-Grubb had carried out her professional studies (see chapter 14).[27] These three schools, created to combat the obstacles imposed on women by the prestigious Ivy League universities, allowed women to occupy an important position within the landscape architectural profession in the United States during the 1920s and 1930s.[28] Their influence extended to Canada; at least three Canadian women crossed the border to study at the Lowthorpe School, returning to the Toronto region after graduation to make their mark in landscape architecture. They were Helen M. Kippax (born 1890), Frances Steinhoff (1892–1965), and Frances McLeod (1914–1992). Kippax and Steinhoff specialized in the design of residential gardens; one of their colleagues remarked that Kippax excelled in the design of small-scale landscapes and that Steinhoff possessed a masterful knowledge of the world of plants.[29] Like their male colleagues, both wrote many articles for *Canadian Homes and Gardens*; Steinhoff also contributed to the magazine as garden editor from 1939 until 1948, the year she moved to Vancouver with her husband.[30] The Royal Botanical Gardens in Hamilton, Ontario, recently recognized Helen Kippax's contribution to garden design in the province by creating a garden in her honour. The Helen M. Kippax Garden displays some 135 species of native plants and native plant cultivars.[31] Its objective is to inspire and educate the public concerning the benefits of sustainable gardening.[32]

Frances McLeod, generally known by her married name, Frances Blue, was born in Toronto. She worked with Lorrie Dunington-Grubb in 1933, which inspired her to pursue professional studies in landscape architecture at the Lowthorpe School. On completion of her studies and two periods of work in the United States, she returned to Ontario, where she became the unofficial historian of the profession and a vigorous participant in the activities of professional associations, all while directing a commercial farm that she redesigned to create an authentic *ferme ornée*.[33] The efforts and accomplishments of these pioneers and of their predecessor, Lorrie Dunington-Grubb, ensured the long-term acceptance of women into the landscape architectural profession, a profession that continues to benefit from a strong feminine presence.

Some Canadian women remained in the United States after completing their education in landscape architecture. Iris Ashwell, a native of Chilliwack, British Columbia, who had previously worked for Thomas Mawson, graduated in geology from UBC in 1919 before studying landscape architecture at Iowa State College in the late 1920s. She subsequently worked in New York for Annette Hoyt Flanders before moving to Chicago, where she spent most of her career with the Federal Public Housing Authority.[34]

16.4   Helen Kippax, c. 1955, and Frances Steinhoff, 1940s

The Great Gardens

The Parkwood Estate in Oshawa, Ontario, the home of R. Samuel McLaughlin (1871–1972), magnate of the Canadian automobile industry, is among the best examples of the art of landscape architecture as it was practised during this period.[35] This great house, its dependencies, and its gardens have not only been well preserved and maintained as in the time of "Colonel Sam," but they also bear witness to the talent of a succession of eminent landscape designers who worked on different areas of the gardens over several decades, beginning in 1915. On a 5.6-hectare site in downtown Oshawa, already blessed by the presence of large mature trees (the property had been previously occupied by an earlier villa, then recycled as a private amusement park), landscape architects Harries and Hall carried out the first stage of the gardens' construction in 1915–19, in parallel with the building of

16.5 Parkwood Estate, Oshawa, ON, plan

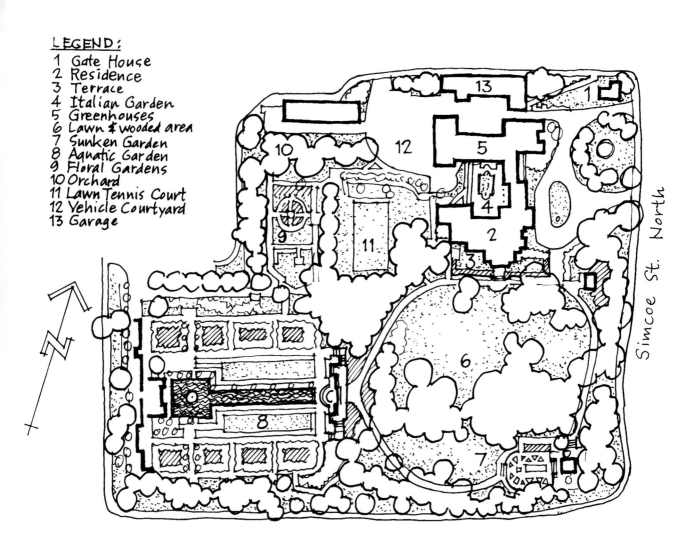

PRIVATE GARDENS OF THE TWENTIES AND THIRTIES   335

16.6 A detail of the Art Deco aquatic garden at the Parkwood Estate, Oshawa, ON, 1935–36, designed by architect John Lyle

the house, designed by Toronto architects Darling and Pearson. Their principal intervention was the creation of a terrace on the south side of the residence and a wide lawn that extended towards the southern limit of the property, a formal composition that gradually melted into an enclosing semi-natural woodland area. Between 1925 and 1928, H.B. and L.A. Dunington-Grubb readdressed the south terrace, in conjunction with the addition of a new gallery to the house, to provide a more direct and fluid access to the lawn area. They also created an intimate sunken garden adjacent to the lawn, a tennis court in a bucolic setting, and an Italian garden enclosed by the house and climaxed by a large pool of water. Finally, in 1935–36, architect John Lyle (see chapter 13) transformed the southwestern corner of the site into a formal aquatic garden featuring a long water basin and fountains disposed along the main axis, designed to be viewed from a raised podium at the east end and from a "tea house" at the west.[36] This garden was a masterpiece of the Art Deco style, which Lyle had mastered. With its curved forms, stylized decoration that recalls natural elements, and symmetrical disposition of sculptures and clipped conifers, it is almost unique among Canadian gardens.[37]

The Parkwood gardens seem to be expressed in the two distinct design languages mentioned above. The structural approach of Jekyll and Lutyens is seen in the use of hedges and cedars to create a series of distinct intimate spaces of varying form and personality, protected from exterior views. The approach of Charles Platt comes through in the planning and details of several of these outdoor rooms, following Italian Renaissance models. In addition, the gardens showcase many interesting experiments with plants, including an early use of Japanese yews, and displays of orchids and palms in extensive greenhouses. Toronto landscape architect George Tanaka was responsible for designing much of the greenhouse planting in the postwar years.

Like the Butchart Gardens on the West Coast, many great gardens of this time were not created by professionals, but instead by dedicated and gifted amateurs. Such was the case with the *Jardins de Métis* or Reford Gardens, located on the Gaspé Peninsula of Quebec at the point where the Mitis River joins the St. Lawrence. The construction of the Intercolonial Railway soon after Confederation had opened up the majestic landscapes of the Lower St. Lawrence coast and the Gaspé Peninsula to tourism, and numerous Montrealers had chosen to establish their cottages and summer homes in the region. In 1918, the creator of the gardens, Mrs. Elsie Reford (1872–1967), had received the gift of a handsome seaside terrain in the area, part of an old seigneury, from her uncle Lord Mount Stephen, one of the founders of the Canadian Pacific Railway. Like Gertrude Jekyll, Mrs. Reford discovered her vocation as a gardener rather late in life. Following a bout of appendicitis in 1926, when she was fifty-four, her doctor advised her to discontinue her favourite pastime, salmon fishing. As a replacement, she threw herself into the creation of a garden on her property, despite her lack of any formal training in the field, and it rapidly became her passion.[38] Over a period of decades, she developed a rich and complex garden on a rugged wooded site, taking advantage of an unusual marine microclimate.

PRIVATE GARDENS OF THE TWENTIES AND THIRTIES 337

16.7 Elsie Reford at High Bank in her garden at Métis, QC, c. 1940

The proximity of the river assured ample humidity and softened extremes of temperature, while abundant snowfalls protected vulnerable plants from the winds and cold of winter. Elsie Reford learned everything and did everything, with the help of local people: planting and transplanting, fabricating soil from its various components, building walls and rockeries. Over the years, she created a series of gardens, linked together by a network of winding paths and integrated into the differing milieus already existing on the site. Many gardens were planted within the shady and intimate environment of a wooded stream valley that passed through the site, gurgling down to the Mitis River – a *stream garden* featuring a multitude of perennials; an *allée* of azaleas; and a *garden of blue poppies* native to Tibet, a special attraction.[39] Lilies and gentians were among other plants of particular interest to Mrs. Reford. The path of discovery that led through these gardens traversed several rustic wooden bridges, built by Mrs. Reford. In a higher and sunnier section of the gardens, lilacs and crabapples displayed their flowers, and up on the plateau that overlooks the entire site and the river, adjacent to Estevan Lodge (the estate's residence, built by Mrs. Reford's uncle), was the *pièce de résistance* of the gardens, the *Long Walk* or *Allée royale*, a 100-metre-long pedestrian avenue enclosed on both sides by colourful mixed borders. The visual impact of this feature was amplified through its contrast with a background of dark spruce trees. In an open and sunny environment beyond the house, paths converged around and across a wildflower meadow towards a cliff-top lookout, which presented a magnificent panorama of the Mitis River and the St. Lawrence, so wide at this point that it is known as "*la mer*" – the sea.[40]

Elsie Reford continued to cultivate her gardens until 1958. She developed a profound knowledge of plants and horticultural techniques and wrote meticulous notes recounting all her decisions, reflections, and experiences. Her journal still helps the present director to develop the gardens according to the ideas of its creator.[41]

At about the same time during the 1920s and 1930s, in Charlevoix County on the opposite side of the river, the first lines were being drawn for another splendid garden, one that would reach its apogee five or six decades in the future (see chapter 22). This garden was that of the domain *Les Quatre-Vents* at Cap-à-l'Aigle, Quebec, also situated along the river on an elevated site that had belonged to one of the historic seigneuries of the North Shore. The 200-hectare site enjoyed the same favourable climatic conditions as the Jardins de Métis, and benefited from striking views towards the little village of Pointe-au-Pic and the confluence of the Malbaie River with the St. Lawrence.

A vacation destination since the 1830s, La Malbaie (also known as Murray Bay) attracted many visitors and summer residents from the United States, urban Quebec, and Ontario. In 1902, the site of Quatre-Vents became the property of Mrs. Maud Bonner Cabot and her husband, Francis Cabot. Their son Higginson, in 1928, built a house in the form of a *pavillon français* on Sunset Hill, at the highest point of the site.[42] Higginson relied on his two brothers-in-law, architect Eddie Mathews (1903–1980) and artist/landscape architect Patrick Morgan (1904–1982), to design the first gardens for his residence. Their composition exploited two perpendicular axes. The first, oriented towards the town of la Malbaie, followed an informal grassy slope down to a swimming pool situated atop a rocky ledge. The second took advantage of a view across intervening pasturelands to the Laurentians beyond. Mathews extended the spaces of the house into the landscape along this axis, creating a sequence of terraces and stairs that descended to grade level. From this point, a *tapis vert* – a linear and axial strip of lawn – descended in successive levels towards a stream-cut ravine that traversed the property. Later, in the 1930s, Morgan constructed a dam to block the stream and create a lake – *Lac Libellule* (Dragon-fly Lake) – and laid out several garden areas perpendicular to the axis of the tapis vert. The resulting spatial structure was later to serve as the starting point for the elaboration of one of the great gardens of Canada.[43]

One of the most original of the owner-designed gardens is located in the Gatineau Hills of western Quebec, where the tenth prime minister of Canada, William Lyon Mackenzie King (1874–1950), created his domain of Kingsmere.[44] It was a decades-long project, like King's political career, that was remarkable for its longevity. King presided over the government of Canada for twenty-two of the years between 1921 and 1950, including half of the Depression era and all of the Second World War. He guided the country through a critical stage of its constitutional transformation from a dependency of Great Britain to the status of an independent country, and carefully managed the delicate equilibrium among its regions and linguistic communities. Yet his public personality was an enigma. It almost seemed that his goal was never to say anything memorable or controversial.[45] His real personality can, however, be seen in the journal that he kept from 1900 until his death, as well as in his gardens.

King's residences and gardens in the Gatineau showed a marked evolution over the years. It all began with a little cabin, *Kingswood*, in an entirely natural forest

16.8 (left)   Allée Royale (The Long Walk), Reford Gardens, Métis, QC

16.9 (right)   Quatre-Vents garden, Cap-à-l'Aigle, QC, looking along the *tapis vert* towards the Cabot residence, rebuilt following a fire in 1956

milieu beside Lake Kingsmere, on a property he purchased in 1903. His next residence was *Moorside*, a larger "country house" that had been constructed on open land at the top of a nearby hill and that he surrounded with gardens. He moved into the house in 1928, and his gardens date primarily from 1930 to 1937. Finally, he reconstructed *The Farm*, an old agricultural establishment that he attempted to exploit commercially, but without much success. This was his home from 1943 on. According to the biographer of his gardens, Edwinna von Baeyer (whose interpretations are based on an exhaustive study of King's journal), these environments allowed King to imagine himself in a succession of idealized roles: the *child of nature* who lives simply in the forest (an ideal that has very deep roots in the Canadian tradition); the patrician *seigneur* who accepts an important public role; the *gentleman farmer*. It was pure romanticism and King was profoundly romantic. His solitary life, the heroic death of his best friend at Lake Kingsmere, and the loss of most of his family within a very short period in 1916–17 undoubtedly influenced his reflections and thoughts.[46] He "saw life as a profound drama" and was constantly in search of the hidden messages that surrounded him.[47]

This romanticism was clearly evident in his gardens, although they resembled in some aspects the *thematic floral gardens* that we have examined (see chapter 9). At Moorside, he created a balustrade-enclosed stone terrace that recalled terraces of Italian inspiration, looking out towards French and English gardens that projected axially from the house into the landscape. These two small gardens were composed, respectively, of annual and perennial flowering plants.[48] But the

16.10 (facing page, above) The French and English gardens of Moorside, at the Kingsmere Estate in the Gatineau Hills, QC

16.11 (facing page, below) The dramatic Abbey Ruins at Kingsmere Estate, strategically located on a hilltop site at the end of a carefully modulated approach sequence

greater part of the landscape received its inspiration from a different model, that of the *picturesque* and *romantic* gardens of the eighteenth century, expressed in rolling lawns, great sugar maples and white pines carefully planted or preserved, and paths of discovery in the forest, leading to secret places, a hidden waterfall and a grotto. And finally, there were the "ruins," assembled on site from the fragments of abandoned or destroyed buildings.[49] King built these ruins at strategic locations in the landscape, in relation to natural and man-made site elements. A curved colonnade on the central axis of his formal garden became a window on the forest, and from the edge of a plateau, the *Abbey Ruins* surveyed the Laurentian forest beyond.[50] The philosophy behind this garden, and indeed behind the entire domain, recalls another garden located in the same range of hills, some seventy kilometres to the east – that of Montebello, the estate of Louis-Joseph Papineau (see chapter 9). Unlike Mackenzie King, Papineau really was a seigneur, and his property was a real seigneury and a real farm. But like his predecessor, King always regarded the past with reverence and tried to connect it to the present through his gardens. It is not surprising that the two men should have been inspired by the same landscape archetype.[51]

King did not create his gardens alone; he relied heavily on friends and experts, often commandeered from government service. Isabella Preston and William Macoun from the Central Experimental Farm helped him in the choice of shrubs and the establishment of his lawns; an architect was involved in the design of his ruins; and landscape architect Ormiston Roy (from the Mount Royal Cemetery) participated in the overall design. But the gardens are nonetheless a perfect reflection of the unique personality of Mackenzie King.[52]

The End of the Country Place Era

These great gardens mark the end of a long tradition. It was still possible, during the 1920s and 1930s, for affluent families to engage the teams of well-trained gardeners who were needed to maintain such gardens at the desired level of quality. During the following decades, this would no longer be the case. The elegance and complexity of these magnificent historic gardens became more and more difficult to preserve, and a new approach to garden design would be needed.[53] But the country place era left an important legacy to the general public. In the absence of private owners sufficiently wealthy or motivated to preserve them, a considerable number of excellent gardens became public resources, recycled as much-appreciated public gardens, living museums, and cultural centres. And their designers had developed the skills and expertise needed to meet the requirements of these ambitious projects, so that when large public projects once again came on stream, they were ready.

17

"The City Efficient": Changing Currents of Urban Development

17.1 Urban design development in downtown Montreal, proposed by the Canadian National Railways. Drawn by the office of Montreal architect Hugh Griffith Jones, c. 1930

Faced with the new economic and social circumstances of the years between the wars, those involved in the movements for urban reform revised their goals. The aesthetically oriented City Beautiful movement and the unlimited optimism that had underwritten it, so widespread before 1914, had to yield to more down-to-earth concerns: the provision of housing at a reasonable cost, the rational and intelligent expansion of cities, and the establishment of high standards of public health. A new paradigm, the *City Efficient*, took its place on the urban agenda.[1]

New methods and new people came forward to realize these new goals. The now discredited master plan, painstakingly drawn up by a visionary planner, gave way to a complex and comprehensive web of standards and bylaws, set in place by teams of technically trained experts. The improvement of the urban environment, which had formerly entailed a heroic effort involving social reformers and artistic designers and lasting two or three years, became a more structured task. Important decisions were placed in the hands of impartial, well-trained civil servants, free

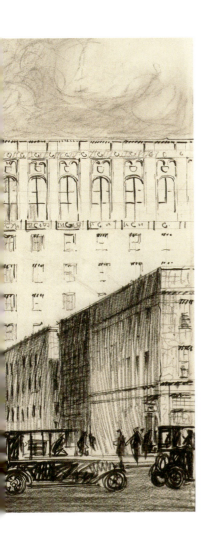

from the arbitrary and corrupt world of politics. Reformers and artists had given way to experts who focused on such current issues as the need for new housing and the "financial plight" of municipalities, the value of orderly and efficient urban layout, and the preservation of property values.[2] Costly, non-utilitarian planning was discredited, giving way to such tools as zoning, minimum standards for lots and buildings, and standard placement of buildings on lots.

Those who were concerned with these emerging issues organized themselves into the new profession of *town planning*. Many of the practitioners of this new discipline were landscape architects and architects who had prepared urban design plans before 1914. They were joined by engineers and surveyors, down-to-earth professionals with few aesthetic pretensions. The latter reclaimed their former position in the planning of cities, emphasizing their systematic training and technical expertise. The acceptance of this new approach was heralded by the adoption of town-planning laws in several provinces between 1912 and 1924 and by the founding, in 1919, of the Town Planning Institute of Canada, which included a number of landscape architects among its charter members.[3]

In Canada, the principal evangelist for the new message was Thomas Adams (1871–1940), the town-planning adviser to the Canadian Commission of Conservation (see chapter 15). Born in Scotland, Adams had served as the first secretary of the Garden City Association in England in 1901, then as secretary and manager of Letchworth, the first Garden City (built 1903–06). Impressed by his reputation in Britain and his active participation in several international town-planning conferences, Canada's federal government invited him to join the Commission of Conservation, seeking to benefit from his expertise in the planning of towns and cities.[4] On his arrival in 1914, Adams proved to be as dynamic in the New World as he had been in the Old. He promoted the adoption of town-planning laws by the provinces and wrote or revised several of them. He prepared a considerable number of plans for new towns and new city neighbourhoods. He helped found the country-wide Civic Improvement League for Canada[5] and the Town Planning Institute of Canada (TPIC), of which he was the first president. Finally, he authored several key reports on town planning and rural development in Canada, as well as a multitude of articles for the conservation commission's magazine.[6]

Adams saw town planning as a system of detailed regulations and controls that could ensure the residents of newly constructed districts a satisfactory degree of amenity, convenience, and cleanliness. In Adams's view, when companies, public agencies, and individuals conformed to such rules, cities would be wholesome and rational; aesthetic quality would be the consequence, and not the goal, of the system.[7] But despite his predilection for the City Efficient, Adams seems to have always fallen back on his Garden City roots when he got the chance to design a real town or a new sector of a big city. This return to his origins may be seen in his design for the Hydrostone District in Halifax (see chapter 15) and for Lindenlea, a miniature enclave east of downtown Ottawa, built in 1918 as a demonstration project to provide a model of low-cost housing for the real estate industry. Here in Lindenlea, Adams created a cluster of comfortable and intimately scaled single-family cottages around a series of small green spaces, the geometry of its road

"THE CITY EFFICIENT" 345

system gently curving to relate to the rolling topography of the site.[8] He also designed, in 1919, the village of Borden Landing on Prince Edward Island, at the terminal of the new ferry route between New Brunswick and the garden island, once again arranging residences and other buildings around modestly scaled public spaces: *station square*, oriented to visitors, and *village square*, oriented to residents. The two open spaces were connected by the town's main commercial street.[9]

Despite the remarkable contribution of Adams and his colleagues at the Commission of Conservation, the government closed down the commission in 1921, after twelve years of existence. Adams went on to a career as a town-planning consultant, remaining as prolific as he had been while a public servant. In 1923, he moved to the United States, where he directed the Regional Plan for New York and Environs, a vast urban and regional planning study, published in 1930 and long considered to be a landmark project.[10]

Return to the Shield: The Continuation of Model-City Ideals

The ideas of the Garden City and City Beautiful movements also maintained their influence in the design of a series of *resource settlements* built during the war or in the 1920s. Great domestic and foreign enterprises, sometimes in collaboration with provincial or federal governments, returned to the mountainous and forested regions of the country, newly accessible owing to the construction of railways to facilitate the exploitation of a new wave of resources. In building towns for the workers in these industries, city planners, landscape architects, and architects generally adhered to the precepts of the Garden City for the design of residential districts, and to those of the City Beautiful for downtowns and commercial areas. The industrial zones usually followed the inexorable logic of the extraction and production processes involved, which often led to impressive architecture and landscapes through the grandeur of their scale and the sculptural simplicity of their forms.

Several of these towns were built in the *Clay Belt*, a swath of land within the Canadian Shield that overlaps northern Quebec and Ontario, where deposits from ancient glacial-era Lake Barlow-Ojibway supported dense forests of balsam fir and white spruce, ideal for the production of pulp and paper. The Temiscaming and North Ontario Railroad initiated the process in 1911, engaging Ontario architect John M. Lyle (see chapter 13) to prepare a plan for the town of Iroquois Falls, located at a major railway junction in Ontario. Lyle conceived a formal and symmetrical plan, similar to the concept that he proposed for the urban design of downtown Toronto in the same year. He laid out radial boulevards centred on the railway station, *rond-points* (traffic circles) and playgrounds, and extensive parks integrated into the geometric structure of the town.[11] Like his Toronto project, this plan was not carried out. The final configuration of the town instead followed a scheme designed in Chicago and elaborated by two Ontario engineer-surveyors, H.S. Crabtree and G.F. Summers, in 1915. They fitted their plan into the natural topography through the use of curving roads and large lots, which permitted the building of single-family dwellings with generous gardens. The Garden City character reflected by these arrangements was reinforced by a program of park and

17.2 Thomas Adams, town-planning adviser to the Canadian Commission of Conservation

17.3 Resource settlements in northern Ontario and Quebec, 1910s–30s. Railways played an essential role in the locations of all of these towns. Some were located with respect to forest resources – pulp and paper towns – while others were established to take advantage of mineral deposits or the hydroelectric power potential of great rivers.

landscape development carried out between 1915 and 1919 under the direction of Montreal landscape architect Leonard Schlemm, who designed several other resource towns, including Baie-Comeau (1937) on the north shore of the St. Lawrence and the garden suburb of Hampstead in Montreal (1914–20).[12]

The tireless Thomas Adams also contributed to the planning of resource settlements, including the towns of Corner Brook, in southwestern Newfoundland, and Kipawa (later renamed Témiscaming), constructed on the Quebec side of the Ottawa River at the southern point of Lake Témiscaming in 1917. Since the best sites of the latter town were already occupied by industrial installations, Adams successfully installed the commercial and residential sectors of the town on steeply sloping terrain by laying out the streets across contours to diminish their longitudinal gradients.[13] He sited the institutional centre and a "village green" on the only available level land, and retained the steepest slopes as forested open-space

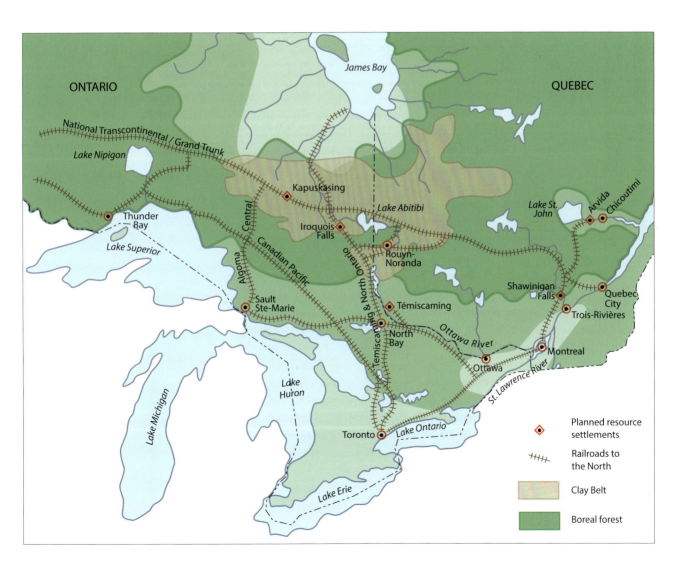

"THE CITY EFFICIENT" 347

reserves.[14] Two other professionals in design subsequently adjusted and refined Adams's plans, the engineer and town planner Allan K. Grimmer, mayor and principal administrator of the city for many years, and Arthur A. Shurtleff (1870–1957), a landscape architect and city planner from Boston, who drafted the definitive plan for the town in 1920.[15] Thanks to the efforts of these three designers, the town became a real Garden City, filled with greenery, to such an extent that it was featured in the prestigious magazine *Canadian Homes and Gardens* in October 1930.[16]

In 1921, the government of Ontario initiated the construction of the "model industrial city" of Kapuskasing, located about 400 kilometres northwest of Témiscaming and similarly destined for the production of paper products.[17] The designers, landscape architects, and engineers of the firm Harries, Hall and Kruse of Toronto and Buffalo, New York, laid out the various components of the town so as to harmonize their plan with the topography and natural assets of the site. They decided to locate the town on a high plateau at a bend in the river, structuring the business zones and central parks according to a formal layout, while basing their plan for the surrounding residential zone on a sequence of curving roads. They kept the banks of the Kapuskasing River and its tributaries as open spaces, establishing a greenbelt in the Garden City tradition.[18]

The partners in the consulting office that designed this project, William Edward Harries (1886–1972), Alfred V. Hall, and Arthur M. Kruse (1889–1980), had long practised in Ontario, individually and in various combinations. Harries and Kruse, born in Buffalo and New York City respectively, had studied landscape architecture at Cornell University from 1906 to 1910, as had Howard Dunington-Grubb (at that time simply Grubb). Subsequently, Harries worked for Thomas Mawson in England, as did Grubb. On his return to North America, he worked with H.B. and L.A. Dunington-Grubb in 1912 and 1913. Hall, Canadian by birth, had worked in the office of Warren Manning (see chapter 13) in Cambridge from 1906 to 1912, together with C. Ernest Woolverton from Grimsby, Ontario. Harries and Hall became partners in 1914 and began a productive practice, based in Toronto and Buffalo, that lasted for several decades. Kruse worked for the United States Housing Corporation in Washington towards the end of the First World War, along with his acquaintance Rickson Outhet and other landscape architects. In 1919, he moved to Toronto and began his collaboration with Harries and Hall, becoming their partner in 1925.[19]

The abundant hydroelectric resources of the Shield that supplied the motive power for the pulp and paper factories also attracted other energy-hungry industries, including the aluminum industry. In 1925, the Aluminum Company of America – "Alcoa" – chose a strategically located site on the Saguenay River in Quebec for a massive aluminum production facility. The company aimed to harness the waters of the *Grande Décharge*, which drains Lake St. John, to produce the electricity that would transform raw materials, imported by train and by water via the Saguenay fjord, into aluminum. To house their workers and professionals, Alcoa built a new city, Arvida,[20] planned by Harry Beardslee Brainerd (1887–1977), an architect and city planner from New York. Brainerd's plan – a masterpiece of

17.4 Plan of Arvida, QC, 1925, Harry Beardslee Brainerd, town planner. North is at the bottom of the drawing; industrial areas are coloured yellow, residential areas light brown, and commercial areas orange. Note the contrasting geometries of axial "City Beautiful" sectors and curvilinear "Garden City" residential areas, similar in layout to postwar suburbs. Green areas are integrated both within and between the residential sectors. This drawing has been attributed to Brainerd's associate, Hjalmar Ejnar Skougor.

graphic presentation – oriented the commercial sector of the city along a north-south axis, perpendicular to the east-west direction of the factories and railway that paralleled the great river. He organized the town's residential districts in hexagonal patterns adjacent to the downtown area, loosening them up into curved forms as they moved further out so as to adapt them to the contours of the terrain. He very effectively exploited the topography of the site, taking advantage of hilltops to provide appropriate settings for parks and important buildings, while establishing linear parks along the stream valleys that passed through residential areas.

The expansion of the city of Shawinigan Falls (see chapter 13) during the 1920s put similar ideas into practice. Following a report submitted by the Olmsted Brothers in 1916, a number of the proposals in the original city plan of 1899 were finally realized. The city planted hundreds of street trees and moved forward with the landscape work for Saint-Maurice Park, located on the river from which it took its name, and for various sites around the installations of the Shawinigan Water and Power Company. This work was carried out according to the drawings of landscape architect Rickson Outhet and of city employees.[21] Outhet also designed, in 1924–25, the landscape treatment of the picturesque Cascade Inn hotel, built on a

"THE CITY EFFICIENT"   349

17.5 A neighbourhood of single-family dwellings in Arvida, QC, 1995. Gabor Szilasi, photographer.

promontory overlooking the town and enjoying splendid views of the St. Maurice River. The city created and reforested other parks during this decade and set up programs to encourage the public to plant trees and shrubs to improve the urban environment.[22]

New Public Projects

The emphasis on private gardens that characterized the 1920s (see chapter 16) was by no means universal. Municipal and provincial governments created a number of significant parks, public gardens, and institutional landscapes during the decade. In 1918, the city of Hamilton, Ontario, purchased 40 hectares of land on the east side of the urban area, in a location that benefited from the magnificent green backdrop of the Niagara Escarpment (locally known as Hamilton Mountain). The city engaged the office of Howard and Lorrie Dunington-Grubb to prepare plans for the site, Gage Park, in the 1920s. This multi-functional park embraced many facilities, including sports fields, a rose garden, an orchestra shell, and a bowling green, articulated by swaths of native vegetation. As an indication of the interprofessional collaboration typical of the period, the versatile architect John Lyle (who had been raised in Hamilton; see chapter 13) laid out a formal plaza and decorative fountain in the park in 1926–27, integrating sculptural elements executed by the Toronto artist Florence Wylie. This same team was to work together on many other projects during the 1930s.[23]

In its realization of Sunnyside Beach Park on the shores of Lake Ontario, the city of Toronto created one of the most popular open-space projects of the 1920s. The site, a natural beach located some seven kilometres west of the downtown area, facing High Park, had been used as a bathing beach since the 1880s. But in 1912, when the Toronto Harbour Commission prepared a long-term plan for the city's lakefront in preparation for a major port-enlargement project, it proposed to integrate the beach and neighbouring lands into a broad network of parks. In

17.6 John Lyle's fountain and plaza at Gage Park, Hamilton, ON. The fountain vista continues across the park to Hamilton Mountain.

"THE CITY EFFICIENT"   351

17.7 View to the breakwater and Lake Ontario from an upper-level archway of Sunnyside Bathing Pavilion, Toronto

constructing a breakwater opposite the beach and using excavated material to expand the port, the commission enlarged the site to create an extensive beach park, flanked by an area parallel to the lake that was shaded by tall deciduous trees. The central focus of the project was a splendid bathing pavilion, designed in 1923 by Toronto architect Alfred H. Chapman, featuring an open-air pool that could substitute when necessary for the somewhat cold waters of the lake.[24] The office of the Olmsted Brothers seems to have had a hand in the design of Sunnyside and the overall park network that was envisaged. While he was drawing up the general plan of 1912, Edward L. Cousins, chief engineer for the Harbour Commission, spent a week at Brookline, Massachusetts, "developing the design" under the direction of Frederick Law Olmsted, Jr. Cousins also studied the landscape configurations and buildings of a number of public beaches in Massachusetts that had been planned by the Olmsted firm.[25] Unfortunately, the commission never realized the largest of the open spaces it proposed, a linear park and lagoon, five kilometres long and 300 metres deep, in the eastern sector of the port.[26]

A remarkable public garden entered its key phase of development in the 1920s – the Reader Rock Garden in Calgary. The city provided a residence for William R. Reader, its superintendent of parks and open space from 1913 to 1942 (see chapters 8 and 15), at the top of a steep hill adjacent to Union Cemetery in the southeastern sector of the city, near the Elbow River. A born gardener, Reader dedicated himself to the transformation of the barren hillside atop which he resided. Starting in 1922, he constructed a series of terraces, stairs, retaining walls, and pathways

17.8 Reconstruction of the Reader Rock Garden in Calgary, 2004–05

made of local stone – including the grey sandstone traditionally used for Calgary buildings – and planted the slopes and interstices with a broad selection of perennials, trees, and shrubs. He levelled the terrain and sowed the area around his house with grass. At the limit of his terrace, where the downward slope began, he built a little shelter from which to enjoy views of the plain and of the sequence of pools and cascades, created by him, that descended towards it. In this garden, Reader planted some 4,000 perennial varieties in diverse growing conditions and carefully documented his many experiments. The site was essentially a collection of test plots to help with the selection of plant materials for Calgary's parks and a tool for instructional and demonstration purposes to show what was possible in this difficult climate.[27] Reader's idiosyncratic and highly personal creation attracted many visitors during the 1950s and 1960s,[28] but it then fell into several decades of decline – even the house was demolished – before its eventual restoration in the twenty-first century (see Epilogue).

Therapeutic Landscapes

The nineteenth century had seen Canada become a country of institutions: people expected their various governments to provide them with a wide array of services previously furnished by their families or by the private sector.[29] These institutions often demonstrated great expertise in the practice of horticulture, using landscape and gardens as a mode of therapy in sanatoria and in hospitals, particularly hospitals that served those suffering from mental illness. Such institutions evolved with the times. Influenced by the new ideals of optimism and generosity of the nineteenth century (see chapter 13), many adopted a new design philosophy, replacing the former practice of sequestration with therapeutic complexes similar to residential colleges in rural surroundings. The belief behind these open and attractive institutions was that beautiful surroundings can change one's life and heal one's ills, and that residents would benefit from fresh air and the absence of urban stress. It was also felt that participation in gardening and farming activities could have therapeutic effects, and these activities became part of the program; residents were encouraged to help produce their own food and to maintain decorative plantings.

Initiated in the United State in the years 1850–80 by the medical directors of mental asylums, this new philosophy was expressed in physical terms through peaceful, green environments featuring extensive lawns, large ornamental trees, and serpentine driveways. Both the ideas and their design manifestations quickly crossed the border into Canada; their impact was soon apparent at the Mimico Hospital near Toronto, founded in the 1880s (today the Lakeshore Psychiatric Hospital), and at the Ontario Hospital at Hamilton, established in 1876. These two institutions were both situated in pleasant and reposeful natural landscapes: the first beside Lake Ontario, the second at the crest of the wooded escarpment of Hamilton Mountain.[30] Although the phalanx of buildings at the top of the slope was somewhat intimidating, the landscape of this institution, which accommodated up to 915 patients, corresponded closely to the new currents of thought. Large

17.9 Grounds of the Ontario Hospital at Whitby, 2001. The landscape character of the hospital complex – curving roads, specimen trees, and shrub masses – was still apparent after the site was abandoned in 1995. Most of the buildings were torn down in 2005–06.

specimen trees of diverse horticultural varieties, massed shrubs, and fluid, curving roads designed to create interesting sequences of movement and perspective were important features of the landscape.

The same philosophy inspired the extensive Essondale (later Riverside) Hospital complex in Port Coquitlam, British Columbia, in the early 1900s. As the principal residence and treatment centre for the mentally ill of the province, the institution expanded to become a community of some 7,000 patients and staff at its apogee in the 1950s. The therapeutic program included clearing the forests in preparation for construction, operating the 200-hectare Colony Farm and a neighbouring stock farm, and tending a dairy herd and a tree nursery to provide plants for government projects throughout British Columbia. In 1912, landscape architect G.K. MacLean and botanist John Davidson (1878–1970) from Aberdeen, Scotland, planned the "first botanic garden in Western Canada" on the Essondale grounds, with the goal of assembling all plants native to the province on this site. Davidson was to move most of the plants of the botanical garden to the University of British Columbia in 1916, but Essondale/Riverview Hospital has maintained its remarkable collection of trees to the present day.[31]

The Ontario Hospital at Whitby (later renamed Whitby Psychiatric Hospital), constructed between 1913 and 1925, was set in a pastoral landscape similar to that of the great nineteenth-century parks. Its overall layout plan followed the City Beautiful approach; it was essentially a *residential village* composed of pavilion-style cottages distributed along a roughly symmetrical network of curving streets, axially related to a central hospital and administrative complex. As in Mimico, the site looked out onto Lake Ontario to the south; Whitby Bay was its neighbour

"THE CITY EFFICIENT" 355

on the east. The landscape treatment, designed by Toronto landscape architects Harries and Hall (apparently their regular partner Kruse did not act as a principal on this project), integrated tall *specimen trees* – elms, oaks, sycamores, purple beeches – into the natural undulations of the site, along with large shrub masses and decorative small trees. Flowering shrubs lined the foundations of the vaguely Tudor-style buildings. Lawn areas, "always perfectly mowed," extended throughout the central area of the autonomous community, punctuated here and there with such recreational facilities as tennis courts and a skating rink. Planting was meticulously maintained by professional gardeners and hospital residents, the latter also playing an important role in the operations of the farm, situated just to the north of the village complex. This farm provided almost all the food for the institution.[32]

Return of Large-Scale Urban Projects

In 1928 and 1929, on the eve of the Great Depression, a period of temporary economic prosperity briefly revived interest in the City Beautiful movement and the idealistic notions of comprehensive design that had been so popular in the prewar world.[33] The projects of these years included ambitious urban design proposals for the central areas of large cities, as well as broad-scale programs that aimed to improve the urban environment over the long term.

City Beautiful Revisited

In Montreal in 1929–30, the Canadian National Railways' proposal to build a new downtown railway station inspired architect Hugh Griffith Jones to imagine an urban-design composition of new buildings flanking McGill College Avenue and culminating in a skyscraper on Dorchester (now René-Lévesque) Boulevard. This tall building would have provided the southern termination for a sightline extending north as far as McGill University. This project bore a striking resemblance to the future Rockefeller Center in New York,[34] and it was a precursor to later developments on McGill College (see chapters 20 and 22). In 1930, the Canadian Pacific Railway quickly unveiled a rival project, designed by New York City architects Fellheimer and Wagner. Their project envisioned the replacement of Windsor Station on Dominion Square with a skyscraper of similar architectural character to the buildings Jones had designed.[35]

In 1929, Toronto's Advisory City Planning Commission put forward an ambitious plan to redevelop the downtown area, envisaging the creation of several grand avenues whose points of intersection were elaborated as public plazas. One might consider their proposal as a neo-baroque vision of the North American city. The new arteries comprised the southern prolongation of University Avenue (the gateway to Ontario's legislative buildings), the reprise of the north-south boulevard between Union Station and the Civic Centre designed by John Lyle in 1911 (see chapter 13), and diagonal boulevards to ease circulation.[36] In the opinion of architect and city planner Ken Greenberg, this project demonstrated an excessive

356 YEARS OF CHALLENGE

preoccupation with the automobile and no concern for the impact of parking lots as well as a frankly cavalier attitude towards the destruction of the existing urban fabric,[37] precursors of tendencies that were to become commonplace after the Second World War. But for the present, both the Montreal and the Toronto projects were overtaken by economic events and not immediately realized.

Urban redevelopment was also an important concern in Ottawa, where the torch lit by Todd and the Holt commission was passed into the hands of city planner Noulan Cauchon (1872–1935). Born in Winnipeg, Cauchon (the son of Manitoba's first lieutenant governor) was among the members of the city planning profession who had come in via the engineering route. He was the director of the Ottawa Town Planning Commission from 1921 to 1935 and a founding member, in 1919, of the Town Planning Institute of Canada, which he served as president in 1924–25. Cauchon was remarkably prolific; he produced numerous plans and texts that focused on the urban design of the capital, including a proposal in 1922 for the entire central area of Ottawa, envisioning a city that would "conform to the dignity, order and beauty which every country demands from its capital city."[38] A complex and brilliant personality, known as an "eccentric dreamer" yet practising a scientific and rational approach, Cauchon sketched out proposals for several specific development projects. These included Vimy Way, a ceremonial route along the cliffs adjacent to the Parliament Buildings; a redesign of Major's Hill Park opposite Parliament, integrating a large public plaza and a national gallery; and the enlargement of Elgin Street, with the creation, at its intersection with Wellington Street, of a great triangular public space that would provide a setting for the capital's war memorial. This last idea of Cauchon's inspired the present Confederation Square, begun in 1928 by the government.[39] Another of his proposals came to fruition in 1927 when Prime Minister Mackenzie King established the Federal District Commission, preparing the ground for a comprehensive approach to urban and landscape issues on both sides of the Ottawa River.

The City Efficient in Western Canada

Even before the First World War, the rapidly expanding cities of western Canada had begun to focus on the efficient organization of urban activities and circulation. In 1913, for example, Saskatoon's city commissioner C.J. Yorath drew up an original and far-seeing plan for a network of major traffic arteries to be superimposed on the city's existing grid of streets. This network included inner and outer "encircling boulevards" and bridges; had it been realized, it might have provided an interesting alternative to the later urban freeway system that was imposed on Saskatoon, as on almost all Canadian cities, in the years following the Second World War.[40]

The Vancouver Town Planning Commission, newly created in 1925, decided to put in place a long-term master plan for the city of 220,000, anticipating its expansion to a population of one million over the next thirty to forty years. To carry out this task, they engaged the American firm of Harland Bartholomew and Associates, based in St. Louis, Missouri, an office that had created plans for some

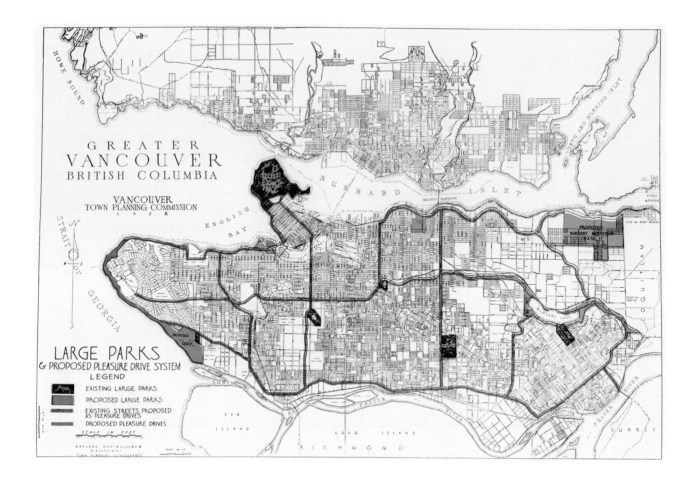

500 cities in North America and elsewhere in the world. The founder, Harland Bartholomew (1889–1989), an engineer and city planner who came originally from Massachusetts, had developed and perfected systematic techniques for the analysis, programming, and design of cities. His firm took some three years to carry out its study and to prepare a plan for Vancouver (1926–28); the Canadian engineer and town planner Horace L. Seymour (1882–1940), who had previously worked with Thomas Adams, acted as the resident director of the work, in close collaboration with Bartholomew's team.[41]

Both Bartholomew and Seymour favoured the City Efficient approach over that of the City Beautiful.[42] Their report was a model of its genre. It began with an excellent historical analysis and contextual study, written in language that was professional but nonetheless highly accessible. It then proceeded to detailed studies of six aspects of the city, including the circulation network, public recreation, and art. Concerning recreation, the report proposed a hierarchical system of parks and other open spaces. The system envisioned a number of *neighbourhood parks* of 8 to 12 hectares; several *large parks* (including the existing Stanley Park on the west of the downtown area and Hastings Park on the east side of the city); and several *new*

17.10 Vancouver city plan, 1928: a plan of the network of large parks and pleasure drives proposed by the office of Harland Bartholomew, city planner. Stanley Park can be seen at upper left centre, with Queen Elizabeth Park below it in the centre of the city, and Hastings Park along the northern edge of the city near the then-existing Second Narrows Bridge. Marine Drive and other thoroughfares loop around the edge of the main peninsula on which Vancouver is built; a spine road (King Edward Avenue) bisects the urban area along its east-west axis, with several north-south arteries also identified as pleasure drives. Burnaby Mountain (where Simon Fraser University was later constructed) and Burnaby Lake are at the right side of the drawing.

parks on Native reserves or unoccupied natural sites, such as the "little mountain" in the centre of the urban area, which would later become Queen Elizabeth Park. A network of *pleasure drives* would ensure the parks' interconnection, and many *public beaches* were to be established, including the entire shore of English Bay between Stanley Park and the University of British Columbia. The plan also proposed the creation of several *mountain parks* outside the city limits – one on the north shore, facing the city across Burrard Inlet (where today's Grouse Mountain ski centre is located), another further afield at Mount Garibaldi (now a provincial park, and a major venue for the 2010 Winter Olympics). The report also suggested the construction of a new bridge and a civic centre at the entrance to the downtown area, and it offered much detailed technical advice.[43]

The long-term impact of the Bartholomew plan was enormous, in particular its section on the open-space network. City administrators followed almost all the suggestions made by Bartholomew and his team, including the creation of a continuous band of parks along the water's edge, the cleaning-up of polluted bodies of water, the conversion to park use of undeveloped terrains, and the extension of the parkway system. The Vancouver of today, which many consider a highly successful city, could not have existed without Bartholomew's visionary plan.[44]

The Garden Suburb on the North Shore

Another major project requiring years of work began in Vancouver towards the end of the 1920s, this time as a private rather than a public endeavour. This was the immense residential development British Pacific Properties, built on the mountain slopes to the north of Burrard Inlet, in the municipality of West Vancouver. The project's initiator, Alfred J.T. "Fred" Taylor (1887–1945), born in Victoria, was a self-taught engineer, a manufacturer and developer of humble origin, who had become wealthy and influential. His involvement with industrial projects took him to England, where he lived for several years and where he persuaded British investors, including the Guinness family (owners of Irish breweries and other enterprises), of the merits of an enormous real-estate development project that he had been putting together since 1928. To realize Taylor's vision, it would be necessary to build a bridge across the inlet at its narrowest point, which implied the construction of an access road across Stanley Park, the city's jewel. Taylor and his associates overcame all obstacles, both physical and administrative. The project was gradually realized between 1931 and about 1947. The design of its first phase, Capilano Estates in the eastern sector of the site, was entrusted to the Olmsted Brothers of Brookline, Massachusetts, still the most prestigious and competent landscape architects and city planners in North America. A huge project, covering about 1,700 hectares in total area – over 4,000 acres – British Properties was, for its time, the largest real-estate development in Canada, and during the difficult years of the Depression, a project of such magnitude was a source of hope for many.[45]

The project director was one of the principal associates of the Olmsted Brothers, James Frederick Dawson (1874–1941),[46] who had assisted and then succeeded John C. Olmsted (see chapter 13) as the principal responsible for the firm's work on

"THE CITY EFFICIENT" 359

the West Coast.[47] The master plan for Capilano Estates that was prepared under his direction was well adapted to the steep slopes of the site. The entrance to the new district was via a straight and formal boulevard (named "Taylor Way" in honour of the developer) that rose steeply across contours of land,[48] leading to a main loop road that provided access to all areas of the project. From this main road, a series of smaller loops and cul-de-sacs served each residential lot. By this arrangement, the site plan eliminated any abrupt changes of level along its thoroughfares. Grading design was uniformly superb, as one would expect from a project bearing the Olmsted signature. At strategic intersections along the main loop road, Dawson inserted small triangles of greenery, transitional elements that had been part of the Olmstedian vocabulary for generations.

17.11 Kitsilano Beach, Vancouver. Now one of Vancouver's most popular beaches, this site was occupied for homestead purposes in the late nineteenth century, then taken over by the CPR. Private citizens and the Vancouver Parks Department repurchased the property to create today's splendid park, which enjoys striking views of downtown Vancouver, Stanley Park, and the entrance to Vancouver Harbour.

As constructed, however, the community did not entirely follow the planning conventions of the Olmsteds' garden suburb model. Although the original design of Capilano Estates included a *village centre* at the head of Taylor Way, as in other urban sectors designed by the Olmsted Brothers,[49] none was ever built; nor, apparently, were the Estates' public parks fully landscaped and equipped in the early years. The green spaces were splendid – natural forest reserves and a beautiful golf course at the centre of the development – but despite its qualities, the course was a private club.[50] The reduction of lot dimensions in the 1940s, in response to market trends, made it more difficult to integrate houses with the demanding topography of the western part of the site and limited the amount of effective open space available for each house. These aspects of the district prefigure typical characteristics of post–Second World War suburbs, many of which were related to the increasing importance of the automobile. But despite these reservations, this was a stunning project, remarkably well fitted in overall terms to its difficult site. Almost every residence turned its face towards outstanding views of the harbour and the city of Vancouver, and beyond as far as Vancouver Island and Mount Baker in the United States. These qualities continue to ensure the ongoing success of the project.[51]

17.12   Postwar development in British Properties, West Vancouver

"THE CITY EFFICIENT"   361

18

Embers in the Shadows: Remarkable Landscape Projects of the 1930s

18.1 Contemporary view (looking downstream) of Promenade du St.-Maurice, Shawinigan, QC

The world depression of the 1930s caused devastation throughout Canada, and it did not spare the practitioners of landscape architecture and its related disciplines. But, paradoxically, the troubled decade from 1929 to 1939 provided us with many of our best gardens and public spaces.

It was not surprising that North America faced an economic downturn in 1929, since, according to Canadian economist John Kenneth Galbraith, "the economy was fundamentally unsound." The apparent prosperity of the 1920s had concentrated wealth towards the top of the social pyramid. Speculation, inflated values, stock market manipulations – all demanded an important readjustment. According to Galbraith, it was never obvious why this readjustment was so severe and so prolonged.[1] And once the crisis had begun in the United States, it was inevitable that Canada would be implicated, given the extensive trade and high degree of integration that already existed between the two economies. The principal effect of the Great Depression was to reduce overall demand and purchasing power for the entire society, leading to falling prices and declines in production of all goods and services. Thus, the average annual production of wheat in Saskatchewan slid from 220 million bushels in 1920–28 to 138 million in 1928–38, and the international price of wheat fell by 60 per cent between 1929 and 1932. The per capita revenue across all of Canada decreased by about 50 per cent from 1929 to 1933; that of Alberta by 60 per cent; and that of Saskatchewan by 72 per cent. In Quebec, 26.4 per cent of unionized workers were unemployed in 1932, and farmers, finding no market for their products, fell back on subsistence agriculture. Cities were filled with unemployed and discouraged people.[2]

The Impact of the Economic Crisis on Landscape Architecture

Members of the "design professions" – architecture, landscape architecture, city planning, engineering, interior design – were among the first to feel these economic changes. Before projects are built, they must be designed and drawn up. Professionals who do this are among the first to sense a period of growth or an economic boom, before the overall society begins to reap the benefits, but they are also among the first to lose their jobs in times of recession or economic crisis. Humphrey Carver (1902–1995), a young British architect newly arrived in Toronto in April 1930, provides a striking description of this process. While seeking work in the city's architectural offices, he and his former classmate visited a succession of offices that had signs on their doors saying the owners had gone out for lunch. In fact, the majority were to be "out to lunch" for seven years. Carver was lucky to find a job in a city planning/landscape architecture firm, Wilson, Bunnell and Borgstrom, an interdisciplinary office that was still benefiting from a backlog of work inherited from the real-estate developments of the prosperous 1920s. But as the year 1930 advanced, the office's activities gradually declined. Employees departed one after the other, often to take their chances in other fields. Finally, in the summer of 1931, the three partners had to close down the firm and move on in different directions. Only one project remained to be completed, and the partner in charge of it, Carl Borgstrom, asked Carver to act as his associate in carrying it out.[3]

The crisis completely derailed the life of Rickson Outhet, one of the pioneers of landscape architecture in Canada. Doubly stricken by the loss of his wife at the beginning of 1929 and by the economic decline that began later in the same year, he left the comfortable family home in Montreal West to live in the wilderness, in a cabin he built himself. Reachable only by boat, his cabin was located 125 kilometres north of the city on the northern shore of Lake Tremblant in the Laurentians. An experienced woodsman, Outhet was able to survive with minimal financial resources, returning to Montreal occasionally to continue his professional practice at a reduced scale, designing only a few small- and medium-sized projects each year.[4] He was not a hermit; he belonged to a group of artists and naturalists who appreciated living in the natural environment. He was indeed an accomplished artist himself, working primarily in watercolours, in a style related to that of the Group of Seven. In the words of Nancy Pollock-Ellwand, Outhet was "an independent-minded man who lived his life in two distinct acts."[5]

Life also changed for the many landscape architects who had specialized in the design of private gardens and country estates during the 1920s. The Depression brought ruin to some of their clients, and a majority of the others were no longer able to spend large sums of money on non-essential projects. The luxury market did not entirely disappear, but it was clear that the era of the country place, as a central support of landscape architectural practices, was finished.[6] Landscape designers and their offices had to turn their talents, which they had finely honed by designing large-scale residential gardens for demanding clients, to other projects. Against all odds, there were such projects.

Great Public Gardens

During the winter of 1929–30, the gravity of the Depression became increasingly evident and governments reacted quickly, primarily through direct action: providing money, food, and other goods to families whose breadwinners were unemployed. Governments at all levels also responded to the crisis by creating public work projects to fight unemployment, and private philanthropy sponsored additional projects. Among the most important of these initiatives, created in this decade thanks to the vision of remarkable civic leaders, were several of the country's great botanical gardens.

"Give her flowers for her corsage!"

This was the plea that Frère Marie-Victorin (1885–1944),[7] a member of the Frères des écoles chrétiennes and professor of botany at the University of Montreal, addressed to Camilien Houde, the mayor of Montreal, in 1935. The prominent educator was comparing Montreal – "Ville Marie" – to a woman, and he exhorted the mayor to offer her a gift other than a "main sewer or a police station" for her three hundredth birthday in 1942. Born Conrad Kirouac to a middle-class family in the Eastern Townships of Quebec and subsequently brought up in Quebec City,

18.2 Frère Marie-Victorin and Henry Teuscher, Montreal Botanical Garden

Marie-Victorin responded to a calling from the church as a young man. He embarked on a teaching career and developed a growing interest in botany. Invited to teach this subject at the Faculty of Sciences of the University of Montreal in 1920, he pursued an active career in research and authored many publications. As early as 1925, he began to promote the creation of a botanical garden in Montreal as a means of initiating the Quebec population into the field of science, which he considered to be the essential foundation for social and economic progress.[8]

In the winter of 1929–30, the economic crisis provided him with the opportunity to realize his dream. Montreal was hard hit: 20 per cent of male workers and 10 per cent of female workers were unemployed at the beginning of June 1931. All three levels of government contributed funds for public works projects, and Marie-Victorin succeeded in convincing Mayor Houde to allocate a large site on the east side of the city – including a garbage dump – for the construction of the Montreal Botanical Garden, and to provide money to build the necessary greenhouses. In 1932, in the United States, Marie-Victorin found his ideal designer for the overall plan, a landscape architect and horticulturist of German origin, Henry Teuscher (1891–1984), dendrologist at the New York Botanic Gardens. Teuscher had received excellent training in Berlin, and he was passionately interested in the idea of building a botanic garden *de novo* and enthusiastic at the possibility of designing it. He immediately began to develop concepts and drawings for the Montreal Botanical Garden and corresponded constantly with Marie-Victorin, all without a contract or a salary, since the financial situation of the garden did not then permit his engagement. The situation changed in 1934 with the return to the mayoralty of Camilien Houde, who revived the city's public works programs after a two-year hiatus. There was little choice, given that 25 per cent of the city's population was currently receiving public assistance. The election of a new provincial

18.3 Planting in the entrance mall area of the Montreal Botanical Garden

government in 1936 provided another important impetus to the project. The new minister of labour, William Tremblay, identified the botanical garden as a key project to be supported by the province's investment program for job creation.[9]

Teuscher was finally able to come to Montreal. His "ideal plan," already well advanced since 1932, was completed in 1937 and published in 1940. Work on the site moved ahead concurrently, largely executed by workers who had no experience in construction. Operations were carried out with hand tools and horses, to maximize the number of people employed. Between 1937 and 1940, up to 3,000 people worked on the site. This first wave of construction included the principal entrance to the garden (embellished with fountains and planting beds of bulbs and annuals), the main building (a fine example of Art Deco architecture), service greenhouses, and a nursery, as well as several specialized gardens. All was carried out according to the master plan prepared by Teuscher, who continued to guide the development of the garden until his retirement in 1962, long after the premature death of Marie-Victorin in 1944. Despite the constant evolution of the garden that has placed it among the very best botanical gardens of the world, it is still easy to recognize its clear structure and overall design coherence – the fruit of the collaboration of its two remarkable creators.[10]

366 YEARS OF CHALLENGE

The Greening of Steel City

In Hamilton, Ontario, the heart of Canada's steel industry, the Great Depression saw the realization of another great botanical garden, one that also owed its existence to the efforts of a highly dedicated innovator, Thomas Baker McQuesten (1882–1948). Scion of a prominent family that had fallen on hard times, McQuesten grew up in Hamilton to become a lawyer, a city councillor, and a member of Hamilton's Board of Parks Management. In 1928, before the economic storm broke, he had already set in motion a long-term plan for the rehabilitation and development of the city's northwest entrance, located on a dramatic site where the waters of a vast marshland – Cootes Paradise – sweep through Burlington Heights, a narrow crest

18.4   Rock garden in the Royal Botanical Gardens, Hamilton, ON

of glacial origin, on their way to Burlington Bay, the western extremity of Lake Ontario.[11]

McQuesten and his colleagues sponsored a design competition for the entire entrance sector and invited Eric Arthur, a professor of architecture at the University of Toronto, to organize it. The plan of Wilson, Bunnell, and landscape architect Carl Borgstrom won the competition, followed by the propositions of Harold and Lorrie Dunington-Grubb and of architect John Lyle.[12] Confronted with financial problems, the Parks Board decided to diminish the scope of the project and to combine the ideas of the three winning contestants. Job-creation funds made available at the beginning of the Depression enabled them to proceed, in 1930–31, with the first stage of the work – the Rock Garden – situated in an old quarry below the crest. Construction of this garden followed the designs of Borgstrom, who carried through the project with his new associate Humphrey Carver. A native of Sweden, Borgstrom had worked in the great gardens of Europe before immigrating to Canada after the First World War.[13] Carver admired the veteran landscape architect's deep understanding of plants and trees and his capacity to comprehend nature and integrate his projects into the natural environment. In later years, according to Carver, we would call his mentor "an ecologist and an environmentalist."[14]

Borgstrom's naturalistic design set a sequence of pools and streams among massive blocks of dolomite at the bottom of the former quarry. He contrasted the vivid colours of bulbs, perennials, and annuals with a solid green backdrop of large conifers, planted on the slopes. This stunning garden constituted the first step in the creation of the Royal Botanical Gardens, one of the great gardens of Canada, which today includes a multitude of component gardens and natural sanctuaries on an extensive site of 1,093 hectares.[15]

Return to Turtle Island

Another magnificent public garden was inaugurated in the 1930s in western Canada, on the frontier between Manitoba and North Dakota: the International Peace Garden, initiated by Dr Henry J. Moore, a horticulturist from Ontario. In 1928, Moore had the idea of creating a garden at the frontier between Canada and the United States, as a symbol of the peace and collaboration that had existed between the two countries since they had last confronted each other on the battlefield in 1814. A bilateral committee of eminent citizens sponsored a public fundraising campaign for the project and chose a site on Turtle Mountain in southwestern Manitoba, a wooded massif with rolling terrain at its summit, overlooking vast plains to the north and south. The plateau had served, for centuries, as a peaceful meeting place for diverse Native peoples – Dakota, Cree, and Anishinabe – who lived in the adjoining territories. It is a unique site, located at the top of a mountain that had always stood above the glaciers, only fifty kilometres from the geographical centre of the continent. Its physical forms are thus more ancient than those of any of the lands that surround it. Despite the considerable distances that

18.5 Central vista of the International Peace Garden on Turtle Mountain, Manitoba/North Dakota. This photograph looks west along the international boundary; the United States is on the left, Canada on the right.

separate the site from larger centres, the groundbreaking ceremony, held in the middle of the Depression in July 1932, attracted 50,000 visitors.[16]

Moore, a professor at the Ontario Agricultural College at Guelph who had also taught at Cornell, prepared the first plan for the garden: a formal and symmetrical composition, almost Victorian in its details, covering the central zone of the immense site of 930 hectares that had been given by Manitoba and North Dakota.[17] His garden served as the point of departure for the design of the overall site, conceived at a much larger scale by landscape architect Hugh Vincent Feehan (1899–1952) of Minneapolis. The final version of the central garden space, carried out according to the drawings of landscape architect Walter F. Clarke of the US National Parks Service in 1966, is the "Versailles of the Middle West": a great axial space 1.6 kilometres in length, oriented east-west along the line of the frontier, embellished by a series of floral terraces and crossed by a sequence of pools and

EMBERS IN THE SHADOWS 369

cascades that terminate in a naturalistic lake on the American side. The central sightline is focused on four abstract towers at the western extremity of the space. The general impression of the garden is one of great unity, and although the whole garden is organized around the line of the frontier, its design is such that the frontier itself is invisible.[18]

Since their creation in the 1930s, these three floral gardens occupy unique positions in the sentiments and the culture of the communities that brought them into being. In all three cases, their creators envisioned them not only as gardens or as ways to combat unemployment, but also as means for the transformation of society. In 1991, Canada Post included depictions of all three among a series of five postage stamps honouring public gardens.[19]

Parks and Civic Projects: Weapons against Unemployment

"Put people to work!" was the motto of the 1930s, and because they could employ large numbers of people who lacked specialized training, public landscape projects provided a crucial means of responding to the challenge. Canadian landscape architects had concentrated on the design of private domains in the 1920s (see chapter 16), but they were quick to turn their hands to public projects in the 1930s. Gordon Culham worked throughout this period on the campus of the University of Western Ontario, located on both sides of the Thames River in London.[20] His designs for the campus landscape followed the tradition of the English pastoral garden, a tradition that married well with the greystone buildings in "collegiate Gothic" style that he located in picturesque fashion on elevated sites, providing views towards the wooded corridor of the river. Besides placing the buildings at Western, Culham oversaw the management of trees on the site and directed reforestation, erosion control, and the opening of perspectives. Culham played a pivotal role in the creation of the beautiful "natural" site of the contemporary university, and in 1966, he was awarded an honorary degree in recognition of his outstanding services to the university. His fellow landscape architect Edwin Kay designed the Alexander Muir Memorial Gardens in Toronto in 1934, on the occasion of that city's centennial celebrations; the gardens, entirely paid for by donations from the general public, presented a symmetrical composition of stone terraces that framed planting beds of colourful perennials and annuals. Removed from their original location in 1951–52 and rebuilt on a new site further north, the gardens' formal terraces step down from Yonge Street (Toronto's principal north-south artery), leading to one of the many ravines that dissect the broad plateau of the Toronto urban area. The gardens create an elegant transition between the geometric forms of the city and the irregular topography and shaded privacy of the ravine landscape.[21]

In Ottawa, the Central Experimental Farm, founded in 1886 (see chapter 7), continued to serve as the centre of Canada's agricultural research establishment and as a vital influence on horticulture and gardening through its research on new plant varieties and its demonstration gardens. By the 1930s, these gardens had

18.6 Alexander Muir Memorial Gardens in Toronto, looking westward from the ravine towards the stepped terraces leading up to Yonge Street

long been favourite cultural and recreational sites for local citizens and visitors to the capital.[22] William T. Macoun, Dominion horticulturist, turned much of the "Farm" (as it was affectionately called) into an attractive garden graced by the latest creations of Isabella Preston and her fellow scientists. On Macoun's untimely death in 1933, the government decided to create a memorial garden in his honour. The assignment was given to a young Guelph-trained landscape architect, R. Warren Oliver, who had returned to Canada after losing his job as a golf-course designer in Florida. The Macoun Memorial Garden was constructed on the site of Macoun's long-time residence within the grounds, which had been demolished after his death.[23] Within the original foundations of the house, Oliver created a splendid sunken garden, organized as a series of flower-lined walkways and grass terraces arrayed around a central pool. He was able to integrate into his design most of the trees that had previously embellished the property, as well as an elaborate perennial border on which Macoun himself had worked for many years.[24]

Projects in the Regions: La Mauricie

The realization of such projects was not limited to larger centres. In Quebec, the industrial cities of the St. Maurice valley, severely affected by the Depression,

EMBERS IN THE SHADOWS 371

18.7 Boulevard Saint-Maurice in Shawinigan Falls, QC, looking upstream shortly after completion of work in the 1930s. In this photograph, the roadway, walkway, and balustrade arrive at the town centre after following the river from Saint-Maurice Park. The elevated overlook is located at top centre; the St. Maurice River is filled with logs, a normal occurrence until the 1980s. The boulevard was recently renamed "Promenade du St.-Maurice" when a bicycle path replaced part of the roadway.

organized a number of back-to-work projects, financed by the Quebec Ministry of Labour. These included work on the Trois-Rivières Exhibition Grounds, which benefited from a splendid new Art Deco baseball stadium; and the development of Parc Saint-Marc in Shawinigan Falls, which included an innovative swimming pool in the same style. The city of Shawinigan also undertook the last stages of the work on Parc Saint-Maurice, designed by Rickson Outhet, in collaboration with municipal engineer E. Alide Delisle, at the beginning of the 1930s. The park included a classic octagonal bandstand, underpinned by an ice cream restaurant as in Trois-Rivières, municipal baths, and a fanciful *vespasienne* (public washrooms and changing rooms for an outdoor pool).[25] This park served as an anchor for one of the most handsome public amenities of the period, the Boulevard Saint-Maurice, built in 1931–32 with the help of the provincial government. The promenade, including a gracious pedestrian walkway (recently supplemented by a bicycle and skate path), followed the edge of the St. Maurice River along the park's waterfront and continued to the west for almost a kilometre, linking the park to the downtown area. At the end of the avenue, an elevated overlook provided a striking panorama of the river, the economic lifeline of the region. Already projected in 1899 in the first plan for the city, the promenade was executed *à la pelle et à cheval* – with shovels and horses – to maximize the manual work required,[26] as had been done at the Montreal Botanical Garden. A continuous precast concrete balustrade and decorative light standards added a touch of elegance. The city's engineering staff prepared the plans and cross-sections for the project,[27] which constituted "without doubt the mark of distinction of Shawinigan," according to the city's popular historian, Fabien LaRochelle.[28]

Thomas McQuesten Expands His Mission

Besides playing a key role in creating Hamilton's Royal Botanical Gardens, Thomas B. McQuesten contributed to many other institutions of his city, particularly McMaster University. In 1928, he succeeded in attracting the university from Toronto, its original location, by offering the institution a large site at the edge of the slope that descends to Cootes Paradise, an enormous wetland that was to be a future component of the Botanical Gardens. The construction of the new campus proceeded throughout the 1930s according to a master plan prepared by landscape architects Dunington-Grubb and Stensson; their plan grouped the university buildings around a great central space and merged the campus smoothly into the natural landscape of the Botanical Gardens. A highlight of the campus was the Sunken Garden, located at the southeast corner of the site: a formal garden laid out around a long rectangular pool, signalling the entrance to the university.[29] The new name of the venerable firm signalled the presence of a new partner, Vilhelm "Bill" Stensson, son of the chief horticulturist at Sheridan Nurseries. Stensson, who had studied landscape architecture at Harvard, was like a son to the Dunington-Grubbs. He became a partner in the firm on his return to Canada, on completion of his studies.[30]

Following his many contributions to the urban design of Hamilton, McQuesten extended his ambitions to the provincial arena. He became minister of transport for Ontario in 1934 and immediately undertook a series of road-building projects that included the Queen Elizabeth Way, a divided, limited-access highway linking Toronto, Hamilton, and the Niagara Peninsula, as well as a series of international bridges to the United States. Job creation was obviously a main goal of these projects,[31] but McQuesten also aspired to create permanent civic works of high quality. As in Hamilton, he assembled his regular team of consultants, a sort of repertory company that included landscape architects Borgstrom and Carver, Dunington-Grubb and Stensson, architect William Somerville, a protégé of John Lyle, and the sculptor Elizabeth Wyn Wood, among others. Named to the Niagara Parks Commission, McQuesten sponsored other projects, including the restoration of historic forts from the War of 1812–14 and the rebuilding of the old river road as a scenic route for automobiles next to the gorge. In 1935, he engaged landscape architect Matt Broman, who had been educated at Kew Gardens in England, as an employee of the commission. Broman subsequently participated in many of McQuesten's initiatives, including the planting along the Niagara Parkway, the creation of an arboretum, and the founding of the Niagara Horticultural School, created to train expert horticulturists and thereby ensure the expert maintenance of the commission's extensive park and garden system.[32]

Directly opposite Niagara Falls and oriented so as to take maximum advantage of spectacular views of the cataracts, the Oakes Garden Theatre (1936) was certainly the *pièce de résistance* of the network of gardens, plazas, and other landscapes that marked McQuesten's contributions to the Niagara area. Built on a site given to the Parks Commission by wealthy industrialist Sir Harry Oakes, the theatre was first sketched out by Borgstrom and Carver, but the fluid and natural

EMBERS IN THE SHADOWS 373

18.8   Oakes Garden Theatre, Niagara Falls, ON

layout that might have been expected from these consultants was very far from the design finally carried out by Dunington-Grubb and Stensson. Their design was theatrical in every sense of the word: its central element was a grand sloping lawn, focused on the falls and framed by numerous pavilions, colonnades, pedestals, urns, staircases, and other familiar site elements, all carried out magnificently in a style inspired by the Italian Renaissance. This architectonic *tour de force* was perfectly complemented by an equally brilliant and detailed exposition of horticulture and topiary.[33]

The Renaissance of Frederick Todd

The dean of Canadian landscape architects, Frederick Todd, had enjoyed a first "golden age" as a young man, between 1900 and 1914 (see chapters 11 and 13). He reached a second professional apogee during the last fifteen years of his life.

When the Depression, against all the odds, opened up new opportunities for landscape architects, Todd had lost none of his talent; indeed, the influence of his work during this period continued until the 1960s and even the 1990s.

Some of the projects Todd had drawn up in the 1900s were still under construction, including the landscape work at the Plains of Abraham (National Battlefields Park) in Quebec City, on which much was done in the 1930s.[34] In 1937, Todd proposed to William Tremblay, the provincial labour minister, that a lake be created in Mount Royal Park in Montreal, at the spot where the original 1877 plan, prepared by his first employer, Frederick Law Olmsted, had indicated a formal basin. Todd prepared the design for the irregularly shaped Beaver Lake with the assistance of his old friend Rudolf Cochius, who had returned from Newfoundland to re-establish their collaboration.[35] The 1937–38 excavations to create the lake revealed that generations of beavers had lived there some centuries before – thus the name of the lake. Todd used the fertile soils dug out from the pond to cover the exposed roots of trees on the mountain, and he had much of the material transported to the Montreal Botanical Garden, under construction at the time, to enrich its planting beds.[36]

Todd also replanned Saint Helen's Island, situated in the St. Lawrence River facing downtown Montreal, in another back-to-work project. His plan included the restoration of the island's historic military installations, the construction of a *Martello tower* (in actual fact, a water tower) to serve as an observation point, the creation of a lake and stream for drainage purposes as well as for aesthetics, playing fields, and a path network to link these facilities. He also integrated into the romantic environment of the island a visionary proposition: the reworking of several smaller islets, shoals, and sandbars near the main island to create a beach peninsula enclosing a swimming lagoon.[37] This imaginative project, partially realized in the 1930s, prefigured both Expo 67 and the Île Notre-Dame Beach Park, opened in 1990.

18.9   Louis Perron, c. 1970

Todd had lost none of his abilities as an urban designer, as proven by his 1939 design for Morgan Boulevard in the Maisonneuve district of Montreal. Other Montreal projects that he designed in the 1930s remained on paper, but they nonetheless served as the first drafts of major works that would be realized in the future: an Olympic Park on the exact site that, forty years later, would be adopted for the 1976 games; and a geological park displaying the attractions of an abandoned quarry in the Plateau Mont Royal, similar in concept to the Complexe environnemental Saint-Michel that would be established in Montreal's Miron quarry in the 1990s.[38]

Louis Perron, Master of Floral Composition

Among the many remarkable landscape projects of the 1930s, the Jardin Jeanne-d'Arc on the Plains of Abraham in Quebec City stands out. Its designer was Louis Perron (1907–1990), "the first landscape architect of French expression in Canada," as he characterized himself. Born the seventeenth of eighteen children to a farming family in rural Quebec, Perron was involved from his earliest youth in market

18.10 Jardin Jeanne-d'Arc, Plains of Abraham, Quebec City. The statue of the Maid of Orleans is the centrepiece of a broad sunken garden, enclosed by tall trees and flowering slopes on all sides.

gardening, ornamental horticulture, and greenhouse operation through the nursery business of his older brother Wilfrid, whose company W.H. Perron et Cie. Ltée was a major force in the Quebec landscape industry. Louis's brother encouraged him to enrol in landscape architecture at Cornell University in upstate New York,[39] and in 1937, shortly after receiving his degree, Louis was invited to design a garden dedicated to Joan of Arc on the Plains of Abraham, sponsored by two American donors.[40]

His long-time association with plants and planting had a profound influence on Louis Perron. Plants were a central presence in his projects, and he composed with a broad palette. The plant lists on his working drawings could easily extend to a hundred varieties or more. It was thus perfectly natural that he should create a floral garden in response to his first professional challenge. His design expression was eclectic; Perron had mastered a number of design vocabularies and did not feel obliged to work within an officially prescribed idiom. The Jardin Jeanne-d'Arc is a wonderful example of his fusion of traditions. Perron's design integrated a symmetrical composition inspired by the French formal tradition, centred on a statue of the Maid of Orleans, enclosed by an English flower garden à la Gertrude Jekyll, featuring mixed borders of annuals, perennials, and conifers, organized according to a carefully orchestrated flowering sequence. This garden is a masterpiece of spatial and floral composition that perfectly expresses its theme of conciliation between two founding peoples of Canada, as Perron intended: "an English floral garden within a French composition."[41]

The Garden as Lifeline

A few owners of large private gardens who were less affected personally by the Depression continued with, and even accelerated, the realization of their gardens so as to help maintain employment for residents of their regions. This was true of Sam McLaughlin at Parkwood in Oshawa and of Elsie Reford at her Jardins de Métis on the Gaspé Peninsula.[42] Another kind of garden came to the aid of urban residents in economic difficulty: the community garden, located on municipal land and offered to citizens as a place to grow vegetables and thus furnish themselves with food, regardless of a lack of jobs. Volunteer associations were called upon to organize these programs. In Montreal, the Ligue des jardins populaires and the Community Garden League managed almost 4,000 communal vegetable gardens.[43] In the Mauricie region, the cities of Cap-de-la-Madeleine, Grand-Mère, and Shawinigan Falls provided lots for their residents to cultivate fruits and vegetables. Their city councils also helped to preserve the products harvested, and the provincial government provided seed and fertilizer. There were more than 1,000 such gardens in the city of Shawinigan Falls alone.[44]

New Buildings and Landscapes in the National and Provincial Parks

The managers of the large natural parks outside the cities profited from government back-to-work funds made available during the 1930s, using them to create a variety of new facilities. The "critical mass" of public works of that era provided the parks with an aesthetic signature that endures to the present day. In 1932, the federal government set up unemployment relief camps, where young men without work were provided with food and dormitory lodging, along with other benefits, in return for working on public projects. Situated far from the cities, these camps, which were similar to those of the Civilian Conservation Corps (CCC) established by President Franklin D. Roosevelt in the United States, accommodated a total of 170,000 men during the life of the program.[45]

Volunteers who signed up for the camps carried out a variety of tasks, including brush removal, reforestation, and the construction of roads and buildings. At Banff National Park, they created a remarkable garden, the Cascades of Time (1934–37), which consisted of a sequence of basins and waterfalls descending the slope, retained and directed by rocks from many different geological formations, arranged

EMBERS IN THE SHADOWS 377

18.11 East entrance gates, Riding Mountain National Park, MB

to provide instruction on the stages of the Earth's geological evolution. The stone and water composition was framed and enclosed by blue spruce trees and mass plantings of annuals and perennials. Architect Harold C. Beckett, a native of Riverside, Ontario, designed both the gardens and the park's administrative building that they surround.[46] On the Prairies, the two national parks (Riding Mountain in Manitoba and Prince Albert in Saskatchewan), along with Whiteshell Provincial Park in Manitoba, provided sites for the relief camps and benefited from the work of their residents. One of their realizations, Wasagaming Village in Riding Mountain National Park, consisted of residential and commercial zones grouped around a central administrative and recreation-oriented nucleus beside Clear Lake. Between the village centre and the lake, a waterside park was planted with American elms, now very large, set in a broad grass lawn. The neighbouring park buildings included a museum (now transformed into an interpretation centre), the park administration building, and a tennis pavilion. A small polygonal bandstand flanked with pergolas stood in the centre of the park, close to the lake shore. Gardener George Lean conceived and planted a miniature English garden behind the museum. The architectural expression of all these buildings followed a common rustic style, using local stone, timber logs, and massive squared timber sections to create a rough and natural visual effect and to allow for the lack of precision expected from artisans who did not necessarily have training in the construction trades.[47] This architectural signature characterizes the great majority of buildings and site works erected in the national parks throughout this prolific period, in

378 YEARS OF CHALLENGE

both Canada and the United States. It has become an integral component of the parks' identity, and some examples – such as the park gate and the complex of residential and administrative structures at the east entry to Riding Mountain National Park – achieve a significant level of architectural distinction.

An Organized Profession

The Depression furnished the conditions and the motivation for Canadian landscape architects to join together in creating a professional association, a crucial landmark in the development of the profession in Canada. By the middle of the 1930s, there was a significant number of landscape architects in the Toronto-Hamilton region; they knew each other and enjoyed getting together; and some shared common ideas concerning the social and political evolution of the country.[48] Several of these professional colleagues met regularly in the garden of a restaurant on Bloor Street in Toronto, the Diet Kitchen.[49] Their informal meetings led to the founding of the Canadian Society of Landscape Architects and Town Planners (now the CSLA), officially constituted at a meeting held in Toronto's Royal York Hotel in March 1934. Nine founding members participated in the creation of the CSLA: Howard and Lorrie Dunington-Grubb, the prestigious leaders of the group, and their partner, Bill Stensson; Carl Borgstrom and his associate, Humphrey Carver; Gordon Culham and Edwin Kay, mentioned above; and two graduates of the Lowthorpe School (see chapter 16), Helen M. Kippax and Frances Steinhoff,[50] known after her marriage as Frances Steinhoff Sanders. It was a diverse group in terms of age, nationality of origin – several members were born in Great Britain, two were of Swedish heritage – and educational background.

18.12 Members of the CSLA and their spouses in the 1940s. Left to right: Humphrey Carver, Douglas McDonald, Norman Dryden, Gordon Culham, Mary Carver, Frances Steinhoff, Edwin Kay. At rear: Howard Dunington-Grubb, J. Vilhelm Stensson.

The association expanded rapidly into Quebec and other parts of Ontario. Montrealers Frederick Todd, his associate N. Boudreau, Leonard Schlemm, and a young Louis Perron joined prior to 1939, accompanied by Norm Dryden from Guelph and Douglas MacDonald, who would later pursue a very successful career in Ottawa.[51] The CSLA eventually expanded to include members from all regions of the country. In 2009, its seventy-fifth anniversary year as the national association of landscape architects, it counted some 1,500 members across the country, in a federation of ten provincial, territorial, and regional associations. The inclusion of town planners in the association's first years indicates the close relationship that had long linked the two professions. It also indicates the devastating impact of the Depression on city planners, who experienced such widespread unemployment that the Town Planning Institute of Canada (TPIC) simply ceased to exist in 1932.[52]

New Landscape Expressions

Bridges as Civic Monuments

Since Canada's earliest settlements, bridges have been built as essential public works, permitting easier communication and circulation. Without conscious design intent, some of these bridges had a striking aesthetic impact, from the spare elegance of the mile-long high-level railway bridge across the Oldman River valley at Lethbridge to the majestic and robust solidity of the bridge at Quebec City that, combined with its remarkable natural setting, produced a powerful visual effect. But for one brief moment in the 1920s and 1930s, Canadian bridges went beyond their usual functional and practical role to become monuments of civic design. Among the best examples of this trend was the High-Level Bridge at the dramatic northwest entrance to the city of Hamilton, another component of Thomas B. McQuesten's far-reaching plan for the transformation of Hamilton. Built in 1931–32 according to the drawings of engineer E.M. Proctor and architect John Lyle, this dramatic bridge had originally been part of the overall entrance plan proposed by Carl Borgstrom in the 1927 competition.[53]

In Regina, 700 men were employed on the enlargement of the Albert Street Bridge, along the grand tree-shaded boulevard that neighbours the legislative assembly and Wascana Lake. These two bridges, integrating sculptures and iconic symbols, are fine examples of the popular Art Deco style.[54] The city of Saskatoon invested its back-to-work funds in the building of Broadway Bridge across the South Saskatchewan River, begun in 1932.[55] The bridge's designer, Dr C.J. Mackenzie, dean of engineering at the University of Saskatchewan, was aided by a team of students. The bridge, now an important city landmark, consists of a series of elegant reinforced concrete arches that are gracefully reflected by the river to create one of the iconic views of Saskatoon, often featuring the Bessborough Hotel in the background.

The Lions Gate Bridge, built in Vancouver in 1937–38, was undoubtedly the most spectacular bridge of the Depression era, thanks to its elegant form and its

18.13 Details of the Hamilton High Level Bridge, ON. Civic projects of this period often displayed a marked contrast between the simplicity of large-scale structures and the fine detail and decorative character of smaller-scale elements at eye level.

strategic position between Stanley Park and the suburbs and mountains on the north shore of Burrard Inlet. All the maritime traffic destined for the port of Vancouver passes beneath the 475-metre main span of this bridge, suspended from its twin towers 111 metres in height. The engineer responsible for the design, Philip Louis Pratley (1884–1958), a native of England who had arrived in Canada in 1906, was already an experienced designer of suspension bridges when he started work on the project. His office, Monsarrat and Pratley, had designed the central span of the Île d'Orléans Bridge, of similar form, in 1935. At Lions Gate, Pratley refined the dimensions of the structural members to achieve more slender sections and elongated proportions without sacrificing stability, and to ensure visual continuity of the road line from one shore to the other.[56] These innovations make a strong contribution to the bridge's aesthetic impact. Local sculptor Charles Marega complemented the steel structure with two dramatic concrete lions, fronting impressive entrance pylons that incorporate abstract motifs in Art Deco style. The pylons were designed by Montreal architect John Wilson Wood of the office of Hugh Griffith Jones.[57]

Another iconic Canadian bridge designed by Pratley, the Jacques-Cartier Bridge (1925–29), links downtown Montreal to the southern bank of the St. Lawrence

EMBERS IN THE SHADOWS 381

18.14 Entrance to the Lions Gate Bridge, Vancouver, drawn by the office of Montreal architect Hugh Griffith Jones, c. 1930

with an intermediate stop at St. Helen's Island – carefully integrated with the new configuration of the park as planned by Frederick Todd – permitting vehicles to reach the island for the first time.[58] Due to its central location in the Port of Montreal, this cantilever bridge has become an essential element in the visual definition of the city.

Golf Courses: Discovering the Landscape through Sport

The Depression years and the decade that preceded them saw the golden age of Canadian golf course design. This was a specialized discipline, practised by a small number of experts who had been trained in landscape architecture or came from the world of golf, and often both. The depth of Canada's Scottish heritage undoubtedly stimulated and sustained the development of golf courses; the Royal Montreal course, founded in 1873 on Fletcher's Field (see chapter 13) on Mount Royal, was the first such facility anywhere in North America.[59]

The dean of Canadian golf course architects, Stanley F. Thompson (1893–1953), was born in Toronto into a family that included five golfing brothers, of whom several (including Stanley) were championship-level players. His studies at the Ontario Agricultural College at Guelph were interrupted by his service in the Canadian artillery during the First World War. Following his return to Canada, Thompson rapidly made his mark as a talented golf course designer in the early 1920s. His golf course in Jasper National Park, constructed in 1926 adjacent to the Jasper Park Lodge hotel, made him an instant celebrity. This led to his engagement for the design of a whole series of courses in other national parks[60] – in 1928, the golf

382 YEARS OF CHALLENGE

course at Clear Lake in Riding Mountain National Park, Manitoba; in 1929, that of the Banff Springs Hotel; and in 1938–39, courses in the Maritime provinces at Green Gables, in Prince Edward Island, and in the Cape Breton Highlands.[61]

Several of Stanley Thompson's courses have become legendary, and some regard his work with feelings that border on reverence.[62] One of Thompson's signature approaches may explain such reactions: he seemed to integrate the forms and details of his courses into those of the larger surrounding landscape with consummate skill. Moving through the rolling landforms of the Highlands Links course at Ingonish in Cape Breton Highlands National Park, for example, one seems to enter into the rhythm of the mountains that shape the horizon. At the scale of the individual hole, Thompson brilliantly exploited the natural elements of the site, whether he was dealing with the lake at Jasper or the natural amphitheatre of the "devil's cauldron" at Banff.[63] Thompson's private courses are equally celebrated; they include the Capilano Golf and Country Club course (opened in 1938) in the British Pacific Properties residential development in West Vancouver (see chapter 17). This course is sensitively integrated into the original topography, following the

18.15 Highlands Links Golf Course, Cape Breton Highlands National Park, NS, looking west from Middle Head Peninsula towards the Highlands

EMBERS IN THE SHADOWS 383

contours on steeper slopes, gradually unfurling the landscape to the golfer, then opening up spectacular perspectives through majestic conifers towards the central city of Vancouver.[64]

During his brief stay with the office of Wilson, Bunnell and Borgstrom in 1930, Humphrey Carver became acquainted with Thompson, who was associated with the firm. To Carver, the legendary creator of golf courses displayed "an extraordinary understanding and artistic sense for the form of a landscape." His ability to create sophisticated landscapes from the rough material of the Canadian wilderness required, in Carver's view, the artistic gifts of a Capability Brown or a Nicolas Poussin, persons whose names were surely unknown to the robust and extroverted Stanley Thompson.[65]

Modernism: The Beginnings of a New Philosophy

The 1930s saw the tentative beginnings of a new aesthetic movement in landscape architecture, that of modernism. Begun in Europe, this revolutionary philosophy of design was linked to the promises of modern technology and internationalism; it rejected traditional styles of design, whether the formalities of the Italian and French Renaissance or the picturesque landscapes of the English garden. Modernism brought simplicity and abstraction of form, along with an emphasis on *function* and on the small private garden. It abhorred elaborate horticulture, which it regarded as being out of touch with modern civilization, emphasizing instead the *social importance* of designers' decisions: one should serve all of society, not just an elite, and one should employ the new technologies, which had already transformed other industries, to realize new social goals. Finally, its expressive vocabulary was to be that of abstract painting and sculpture.[66]

Landscape architecture, in comparison with other fields of environmental design, was slow to convert to the modern movement. In contrast, the modernist paradigm had been a promising new trend in the European architectural world in the years following the first war.[67] There had been a gradual progression towards modern landscape design in France and Belgium in the 1920s and 1930s, including several brilliant creations for the Exposition internationale des arts décoratifs held in Paris in 1925.[68] The torch was then passed to the Americans, through the appointment to the Harvard Graduate School of Design of professor Walter Gropius, founder of the Bauhaus, who had immigrated to the United States in 1938. Gropius inspired a generation of landscape architecture students at Harvard, including Garrett Eckbo, Dan Kiley, and James Rose. Returning from Harvard to California in the late 1930s, Eckbo brought his own vision of modernism to a milieu that was already the meeting place of several great garden traditions and where much experimentation with modern garden design was being carried out by the well-established landscape architect Thomas D. Church. This critical mass would win California the central role in the development of modern landscape architecture for the ensuing decades.

In Canada at this time, the most prominent landscape architectural projects were expressed in derivative formal languages from past traditions; such projects

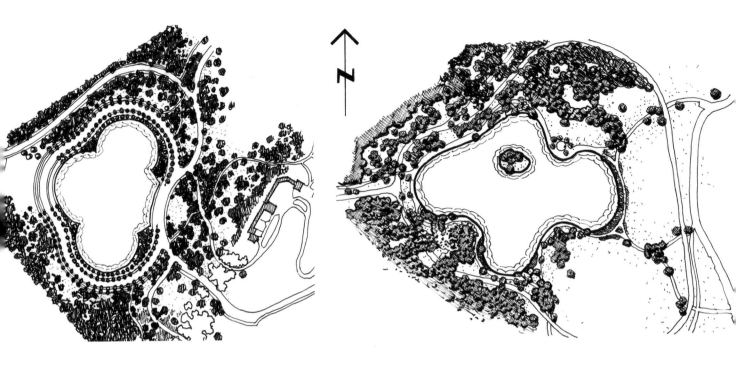

18.16 Comparative plans for Beaver Lake, Mount Royal Park, Montreal. Frederick Law Olmsted's original symmetrical design, 1877, and the free-form "amoeba" of Frederick Todd, 1937.

were often splendid, but not innovative. The Art Deco sculptures and bridges of the 1930s seem to have been the only works in the landscape that embraced the new ideas of modernism. A possible exception might be seen in the irregular amoeba shape (perfectly integrated with the local topography) that Frederick Todd gave to Beaver Lake in Mount Royal Park. The form of this pond was quite different from the symmetrical, neoclassic configuration indicated on the original plan by the park's creator, Frederick Law Olmsted. Do we see the influence of abstract art in Todd's design?[69]

Christopher Tunnard

Paradoxically, the first – and, for many years, the only – book that discussed modernism in landscape architecture was written by a Canadian, Christopher Tunnard (1910–1979): *Gardens in the Modern Landscape*, published in England in 1938. Tunnard was born in Victoria and completed his college studies there before enrolling at the University of British Columbia. In 1929–30, he undertook further study with the Royal Horticultural Society at Wisley in England; staying on in London after completing his courses, he joined a group of British and continental artists and architects who were exploring modernist ideals. Tunnard developed a successful practice in landscape architecture,[70] and two of his projects became early icons of modern landscape design. These were Bentley Wood at Halland, Sussex, and St. Ann's Hill at Chertsey in Surrey, residential gardens for modern homes, located on extensive sites in southern England's "home counties" near London.[71] In these projects, Tunnard embraced modernist themes: continuity between house

EMBERS IN THE SHADOWS 385

18.17 Bentley Wood Garden, Halland, Sussex, UK. Tunnard superimposed the lines and forms of modernism on a mature, naturalistic English garden.

and garden, the use of a vocabulary of form inspired by modern art – integrated, however, with the naturalism of the English garden – and the integration of art to the garden, exemplified by his careful placement of a modern sculpture by Henry Moore as the central focus of his composition at Bentley Wood.[72]

In his book, which is a compilation of several articles he had written for the *Architectural Review* in 1937 and 1938, Tunnard explores the meaning of modernism in the context of landscape.[73] His case studies and illustrations include iconic works of modern painting, sculpture, and architecture as well as contemporary gardens designed by Jean Canneel-Claes in Belgium and his own projects. Shortly after the publication of the book, Tunnard returned to North America at the request of Gropius, to help the latter establish a modernist landscape program at Harvard.[74] His book was well received in Canada. In a review published in the *Journal of the Royal Architectural Institute of Canada* in July 1939, Humphrey Carver (who, while a student in England, had been converted to the modern gospel through his readings of Le Corbusier) stated that Tunnard's book was essential reading for anyone who wished to understand what modernism was about.[75]

A Challenge Well Met

In examining the Canadian experience of the Depression, we see that the profession of landscape architecture, like society in general, reacted rapidly and quite effectively to a critical situation that had never been confronted before that time. In spite of all the difficulties, there seems to have been a spirit of collaboration and mutual support, and against all odds, this period brought forth many stimulating ideas and some of our most impressive works of landscape architecture, in both aesthetic and social terms.

IV Birth of the Modern Landscape, from 1945 to the Present Day

19.1 B.C. Binning residence and garden terrace, West Vancouver, c. 1951

19

Brave New Landscapes: The Postwar Era

In the Canada of 1945, everything had changed. The postwar social landscape would be fundamentally different from what had preceded it, and in response to this new social landscape, new physical landscapes would have to be created.

The most obvious change was the economic boom. Canada was coming out of fifteen years of Depression and war, during which the civilian economy had virtually disappeared, creating a huge pent-up demand on the part of consumers. The immense productive capacity of the country, previously devoted to war goods, was now ready to furnish products for peacetime. In the cities and towns of Canada, everything needed to be done. No private development had been realized since 1930, although the public sector had distinguished itself during the Depression through the construction of socially relevant projects of remarkably high environmental and aesthetic quality (see chapter 18). The commercial downtown areas had seriously deteriorated. The return of the war veterans signalled the debut of the "baby boom" as new families and households formed, making even more acute the housing crisis resulting from the low rate of construction. This crisis was exacerbated by a change in family structure that saw the gradual expansion of the *nuclear family*, in which two, rather than three, generations lived under the same roof.[1] An additional phenomenon was to have a great social impact: unlike what had happened after the First World War, governments were successfully managing the transition from a war economy to an economy of peace. A new wave of social democracy inspired new programs and social benefits that favoured a more egalitarian distribution of the fruits of the newfound prosperity.

New Urban Forms

This combination of circumstances led to a vast expansion of commerce, industry, and real-estate development from 1950 to 1970, a period that Jean-Claude Marsan has defined as the "years of recovery."[2] But rather than continuing to build in the familiar forms of the industrial city, new development followed its own rules. After a century of evolution, the prewar industrial city was dense and compact, organized according to a regular grid of streets and dependably served by tramways that ensured rapid and efficient circulation. This "streetcar city"[3] was composed of many small, semi-autonomous *urban villages*, each with its own local culture, its churches and schools, its commercial street, its movie theatre.

The new postwar city did not resemble this model in any way. Its revolutionary form reflected, more than anything else, the greater and greater prevalence of the automobile.[4] Governments also played a major role in the creation of new urban forms. In his book *The Developers* (1978), James Lorimer emphasized the influence of the Central Mortgage and Housing Corporation (CMHC), founded immediately after the war by Canada's federal government, on the creation of a large-scale real-estate development industry.[5] This governmental initiative aimed to put in place stable and broad-based organizations that would be able to take on the housing crisis and the daunting challenges of reconstructing Canada's central cities. In Lorimer's view, CMHC's policies, combined with the immense social and technological changes already underway and the prosperous state of the economy,

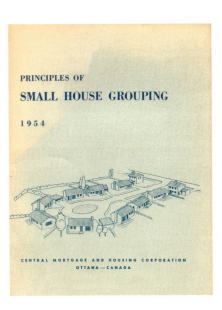

19.2 Cover of a CMHC publication on residential planning, 1954, typical of the easily understood "how-to" documents produced for professionals and the public during Humphrey Carver's tenure as director of research

gave rise to an entirely new development model. This model was based on five new urban elements: the *suburban bedroom community*, served by the automobile; *high-rise apartment buildings*, the principal alternative to living in a bungalow in the suburbs; the *industrial park*, which accommodated, on extensive and well-landscaped suburban sites, industries that no longer needed to be in the city or near a railway; *downtown office towers*; and *decentralized shopping centres*, an inevitable consequence of the move to the suburbs.[6]

A sixth innovation should be added to Lorimer's list: the *freeway*, strongly influenced by the Interstate Highway network that was being established in the United States during the 1950s.[7] The construction of provincial limited-access highways, such as the Autoroute des Laurentides in Quebec in the 1960s and the Macdonald-Cartier Freeway in Ontario, primarily in the 1950s, was paralleled by the creation of a Canada-wide highway system that combined the expertise of federal and provincial authorities across the country. Extremely popular from the very beginning, these freeways soon attracted the majority of intercity traffic, to the detriment of the railways. Some of the first freeways displayed remarkable aesthetic qualities; at their best, they offered a whole new way of perceiving and appreciating the rural and natural landscapes of Canada and provided a new level of individual freedom to the average citizen. Noting the successful contribution of the new freeways to intercity circulation, the leaders of urban communities quickly moved to extend their benefits to the cities, hoping to facilitate easy access to downtown areas. This initiative was to have major unforeseen consequences.

The landscape architect Humphrey Carver played a central role in the creation of these new urban forms.[8] During the war, this founding member of the Canadian Society of Landscape Architects (CSLA; see chapter 18) served in the Canadian Army, where his experiences as an adviser, along with a subsequent period teaching in the Department of Social Work at the University of Toronto – during which he spent much time reflecting on housing problems – led him to a postwar career as a "mandarin" in Ottawa. Emerging as the *éminence grise* of the housing sector in government circles after 1948, he established and directed the research programs of CMHC and promoted the modernization of the house-building industry.[9] Under Carver's direction, CMHC published numerous books showcasing modest architect-designed prototype houses in an effort to encourage and guide residential construction.[10] Interested families and contractors could purchase working drawings for these houses at minimum cost. Suppliers of construction materials and household equipment were quick to focus their advertising on images of "gracious suburban living."

The Shape of the Suburban Milieu

The street configuration of the postwar suburbs was profoundly different from that of the streetcar city. The traditional grid gave way to a pattern based on flowing curves, often including loops and cul-de-sacs to discourage through-circulation. A hierarchical road system favoured T-intersections to promote safety. Low population density and people's desire to live in country-like surroundings militated

BRAVE NEW LANDSCAPES 391

against the construction of sidewalks. In plan, the general impression resembled the curving road layout of residential districts designed by the Olmsted firm and other landscape architects, such as British Properties in West Vancouver or Riverside, Illinois. But the flowing geometry of the new suburbs was seldom the result of subtle adjustments to the contours of a sloping site or to the form of an existing watercourse, as in the Olmstedian developments. It was more likely to be a purely arbitrary arrangement, laid out on flat ground.

The Car Culture

The classic configuration of the new suburb obviously responded to the demands of the automobile, a central influence on North American life in the postwar years. In fact, the automobile era had long signalled its coming ascendancy. The expansion of the Canadian Tire Company, the country's leading supplier of automobile and recreation equipment, had not slowed down since its founding in Toronto in 1922, even during the Depression. This expansion accelerated dramatically after 1950, and by 1959, the company boasted some 190 retail outlets in eastern Canada.[11] The large-scale production of cars became possible as the end of the war freed up the necessary factories, materials, and workers. At that time, North America was self-sufficient in oil, which was easily available at low prices. The discovery of large reserves of "black gold" in Alberta in 1947 and in Saskatchewan a few years later gave further impetus to the growth of a culture on wheels.[12]

Beginning in the 1950s, the first question that a landscape architect or other designer asked when starting a project was "What shall we do with the car?" The first response was to provide surface parking, even in downtown areas. Automobile access and parking areas almost always occupied a major part of the site. For many years, parked cars took up more than half the surface area of some central cities, even invading parks and historic squares. Later, the adoption of multi-storey and underground parking garages lessened the visual impact of parked cars in downtown locations, but the car still reigned supreme in the suburbs. Some auto-oriented suburban phenomena reached their apogee in the 1950s, including the drive-in movie and restaurant, favourite destinations for young people during this era.

The Ascendancy of the Modern Movement

Postwar projects differed from their forebears not only in the new urban forms they represented, but also in their style and character. An aesthetic revolution shook the whole design world in the late 1940s and 1950s. From a marginal movement in the 1930s, supported by a small number of artists and creators, modernism had become the main artistic current in Canada, in landscape architecture and architecture as well as in painting and sculpture. What can explain this abrupt transformation? One explanation lay in the fifteen lost years of the Depression and the war, a period that inspired a profound rejection of the past and an idealistic desire to create a new and better world. Modernism had begun as a radical movement, emerging from the ruins of Europe after the First World War. Canada was finally ready to accept it in 1945. In an autobiography, Carver referred to this readiness: "[T]his was a time of new beginnings, the long-awaited moment in history when great ideals could happily be brought out into the open, and examined, with real prospects of public interest and realization. It was a time for the highest optimism."[13] The moribund forms of the past could not help build this new and optimistic world. In the new circumstances that prevailed, it was the right moment to reinvent everything. Many of the revolutionary or eccentric ideas of 1939 seemed normal – even inevitable – after 1945, in the Brave New World that was coming into being.

Philosophies of the Modern Landscape

The various themes and aspects of the modernist thesis in Canadian landscape architecture, and its differences from traditional approaches, were most clearly outlined in a 1950 issue of the *Journal of the Royal Architectural Institute of Canada*, published at the precise moment of the modernist victory.[14] All the authors featured in this issue focus their attention on the domestic garden, the first object of modernist design. Beginning with the opening article by Tommy Church, the designer of legendary gardens in California,[15] modern landscape architecture is principally defined through its emphasis on *functionalism*. Church puts it clearly: "The landscape architect no longer has a choice between a functional or esthetic approach. Like it or not, the functions of the house have spilled out into the garden and must be provided for." In his 1956 book *The Art of Home Landscaping*, Garrett Eckbo describes a way of organizing the modern garden based on the disposition of functional areas. But instead of dividing "house" from "garden," he imagines a series of zones – living, recreation, service, and contemplation – each of which has both an interior and an exterior component. Thus house and garden overlap and complement each other, each space acting as a continuation of the other.[16]

Even planting had to satisfy functional criteria. Master plantswoman Helen M. Kippax explains how easier access to home ownership by young families in the postwar years means that there will be many more gardens than ever before, and that ease of maintenance will be essential to their non-wealthy, non-expert owners who have little spare time. The era of prewar villas maintained by teams of expert gardeners, to which Kippax and her colleagues had so brilliantly contributed (see chapter 16), was a distant memory.[17] Democratization of the garden had placed a new emphasis on easy, dependable plants.[18] Vilhelm Stensson suggests simple mass plantings to replace the "intricate flower borders, fussy foundation plantings, the clipped trees and hedges" of a bygone era. He goes so far as to encourage the elimination of most plants in favour of permanent architectural elements, much easier to maintain.[19]

The integration of interior and exterior space is explored by J. Austin Floyd, who had completed the master's program in landscape architecture at Harvard following his studies at the University of Manitoba.[20] Like the American landscape pioneers, Floyd advocates "extending … the architectural materials into the garden and allowing the garden to extend into the house in the form of planting beds."[21] This theme was to become one of Floyd's personal trademarks, as evidenced by his subsequent projects (see chapter 20). Similarly, the veteran Howard Dunington-Grubb concludes that "the house of 1950 is so much part of the ground that house and garden must soon become one unit of design. The barrier between indoor and outdoor living is beginning to disappear."[22]

The aesthetic aspect of the modern garden is the preoccupation of other contributors. Jack Nazar, another young landscape architecture graduate from Harvard and the Ontario Agricultural College at Guelph, roundly criticizes the formal layouts and horticultural clichés of traditional parks, which he sees as expensive to maintain and of little use to residents.[23] Garrett Eckbo focuses elsewhere – on the complexity and richness of modern landscape architecture and on the importance of avoiding a doctrinaire approach to design. But he confirms one of the axioms of modernism – that there is a link between landscape architecture and the other arts – in acknowledging the important influence of modern artists and architects on his own rich vocabulary of form.[24]

For his part, Howard Dunington-Grubb is in no way embarrassed to represent the traditional approach to design that is being dragged through the mud by his co-authors. He challenges the view that the modern garden must follow the lead of the modern house. While the new orthodoxy demands "the provision of the greatest amount of use value at the smallest cost," he considers that, as always, the objective of garden design is essentially aesthetic, the creation of "a decorative setting for the house ... most of its horticultural furniture is introduced for decorative reasons only."[25] He also notes that the rapid technological advances of the postwar world were changing society's perception of the landscape and that these advances would render irrelevant many cherished garden traditions.[26]

The Modernist House and Garden in British Columbia

Although modernism in Canada was essentially a postwar phenomenon, several modern residential gardens had already been built in the suburbs of Vancouver in the early 1940s.[27] Canada's West Coast benefited from its proximity to California, where landscape architects Thomas Church and Garrett Eckbo, later followed by Lawrence Halprin, exerted great influence. These designers collaborated with *Sunset Magazine*, a monthly periodical focusing on American homes and gardens of the West Coast. Professional relationships, commonly established on a north-south basis, also played an important role in introducing modernism to Canada.[28] Besides the pervasive California influence, other currents of thought came from Japan – including the "mass planting" approach and the ubiquitous wood deck of modern gardens – and Brazil, a centre of experimentation in plant form and colour, as practised by Roberto Burle-Marx.[29] And the mild climate of the coastal region contributed to the creation of a new way of life and a new approach to house and garden.

But the Vancouver projects found their dominant source of inspiration in the character of their sites, particularly the scenic wooded sites that were increasingly

19.3   Plans of the residence and garden of architect J.H. Porter in West Vancouver, 1950. In the plans, the rectilinear forms of the house are modulated to the irregularity of the landscape through the use of a complex vocabulary of curves and diagonals, reminiscent of forms used in modern painting and sculpture. The upper plan shows garage court at top left and bedroom wing at right; the lower plan shows intermediate-level "adult wing" at left and lower-level living-dining area at right, leading out to the free-form terrace.

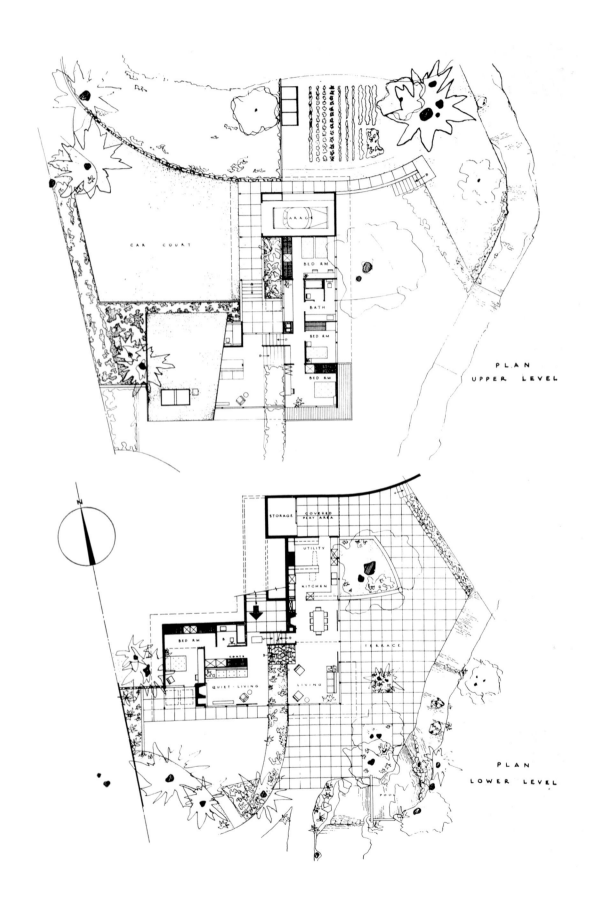

available on the shores of Burrard Inlet. There seem to have been two seminal relationships between house and site: some houses were hidden at the edge of the coniferous forest, expressing a sort of mystical connection between the two, reminiscent of a Haida village emerging from damp, primeval, impenetrable darkness, while others were perched precariously on cliff edges and escarpments, looking out at the infinite space of the western ocean. But the appreciation and exploitation of the *genius loci* of the site in no way diminished the importance of programmatic considerations in the design of the outdoor spaces of these houses. Indeed, outdoor spaces featured careful functional zoning: a car entrance court, a broad paved terrace acting as an extension to the main living-dining space of the house, service and storage area adjacent to the kitchen and utility space, vegetable garden, and sheltered area for children's play. The location and layout of each of these zones were consciously related to each site's unique conditions.

A landmark among the Vancouver projects was the B.C. Binning house and garden (1941), principally designed by the owner, a professor and artist.[30] Inspired by the principles of modernism, Binning sought to create a totally integrated work of art, comprising house, interior furnishings, mural paintings (by himself), and garden, the plan of which married the abstract vocabulary of modern art to the precepts of functionalism. Designed by Binning in collaboration with architects C.E. ("Ned") Pratt and Robert A.D. Berwick, this project inspired and influenced other houses and gardens of the region.[31] The home of architect J.H. Porter in West Vancouver (1950) is a highly successful example of modern design, integrating building and landscape into a continuous composition perfectly fitted to an irregular site. The split-level dwelling steps down a southeast-facing slope to the main living area – located at the lowest level – which opens to a wide concrete terrace, its outer edge defined by natural features. A semi-private "adult suite" is inserted at the half level, and car access is from above. An automobile court and garage adjacent to bedrooms share the upper level, where a vegetable garden occupies a sunny location. The lines of the garden – and even its plants – extend into the house, fusing the fluid geometry of the garden with the regular geometry of the residence.[32]

The redefinition of the house that took place in Vancouver was mirrored by a redefinition of the garden, thanks to several noted landscape architects of the West Coast. The modernist reinvention of residence and garden, far from being the esoteric preoccupation of an elite, swiftly became the new regional vernacular. The widespread adoption of these ideas owed much to the magazine *Western Homes and Living*, later *Western Living*, founded in Vancouver circa 1950, which played a role similar to that of *Sunset Magazine* in California.[33]

The Friedman garden near UBC (1953), designed by landscape architect Cornelia Hahn Oberlander, demonstrates a dramatic, broad-brush approach to planting design, characteristic of the new idiom. Oberlander responded to the challenge of a triangular site, squeezed between two busy streets, and a grove of red alders that was already present on the property. Existing grades dictated a sunken garden, descending to the bedrock where a broad, free-form surface of raked gravel became the central element of the composition. The slopes enclosing the central

19.4 Friedman garden, Vancouver. Mass plantings of junipers and heather cover sloping banks that descend to a sculpture in centre foreground.

space were planted with burning-bush and heather, with fruit trees at the top. Adjacent to the gravel area, bands of rhododendron and mountain laurel were planted in beds of flowing form, which reinforce the main visual theme. The garden's vocabulary of form established an interesting counterpoint with that of the house, designed with rectangular Cartesian discipline in the new regional style of the Pacific Northwest by Fred Lasserre, director of the School of Architecture at UBC.[34]

This garden was among the first Canadian projects of a landscape architect soon to become a leader in the profession. Born in Germany, Cornelia Hahn had always lived with plants. She had her own garden at her childhood home, which she was forced to leave in 1938 in response to the gathering storm clouds that presaged the Second World War and presented an imminent danger to the Jewish community. Her family settled in New Hampshire, where they lived and worked on a market garden farm during the war. Hahn obtained her Bachelor of Arts at Smith College in 1944, then enrolled in the Graduate School of Design at Harvard University, obtaining her degree in landscape architecture in 1947.[35] Her Harvard professors, Christopher Tunnard (see chapter 18) and Lester Collins, "opened her eyes to modernism" and its functional and collaborative principles of design.[36] She began to practise her profession in Philadelphia with architects Oscar Stonorov and Louis

Kahn, both beacons of the modern movement, on public housing projects such as Mill Creek and Schuylkill Falls, in collaboration with American landscape architect Dan Kiley. In 1953 she married H. Peter Oberlander, architect and city planner, whom she had met while at Harvard. The couple moved to Vancouver, where Peter Oberlander had been engaged as the first professor of town planning at UBC, with the mandate of establishing the School of Community and Regional Planning.[37]

Another landscape architect who had recently moved to Vancouver, Desmond Muirhead, also employed the modernist vocabulary with flair and assurance. Born in England in 1923 and a veteran of the Second World War, the flamboyant and talented Muirhead immigrated to Canada, where he studied botany and town planning before beginning to practise. In 1953, he established a partnership with a graduate of the University of California at Berkeley, Clive Justice, who was born in 1926 on Saltspring Island in British Columbia. Muirhead's stay on the West Coast was relatively brief; he soon moved to Florida where he became an expert in the design of golf courses, but he created several memorable landscapes before his

19.5 (below)   Landscape layout and planting plan of the Friedman garden by C.H. Oberlander, 1956. Linear hedges and paths adjacent to the perfectly rectangular house designed by Fred Lasserre give way to flowing curves within the sunken garden. The plan itself can be read as an abstract composition.

19.6 (above, right)   Cornelia Hahn Oberlander in her Vancouver garden, 1989. Photograph by Kiku Hawkes.

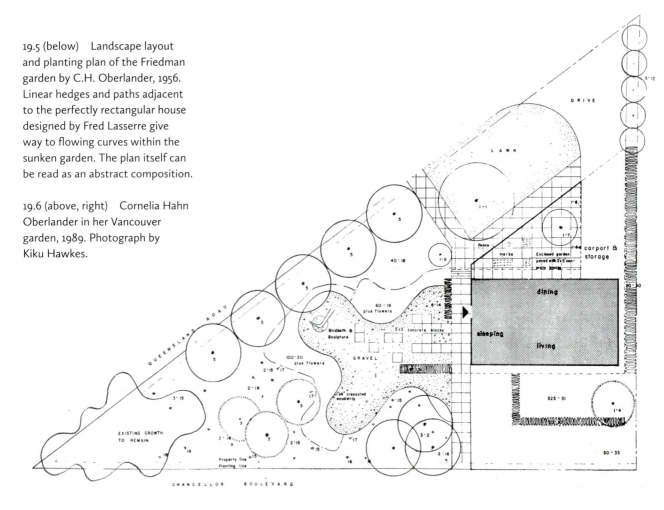

398   BIRTH OF THE MODERN LANDSCAPE

departure.[38] His site design for the Philip Graham House near UBC, for example, demonstrates clearly the fusion of functionalist ideas and the new esthetics characteristic of the period. Each room of this multi-level house, carefully integrated to its sloping site by architect C.B.K. Van Norman, relates to an exterior space, in line with Eckbo's ideas concerning residential zoning. On the street side, the house encloses a rectangular courtyard; on the garden side, a series of small and intimate spaces form extensions to each interior space. Further down the slope, a great open lawn provides a common space enjoying striking views of mountain and sea.[39]

Gardens and Parks across the Country

The new concepts for house and garden that were developed on the West Coast served as examples of efficiency and aesthetic composition for similar work across the country, reinforced no doubt by European texts and examples. The design by J. Austin Floyd for a residential garden in Toronto's Forest Hill Village, published in 1950, is clearly based on the abstract and dynamic forms of modern painting. With considerable skill, Floyd juxtaposed several distinct geometries, his rhythmic and angular forms deliberately at odds with the rectilinearity of the lot lines.[40] In an Ottawa garden designed by Jack Nazar, also published in 1950, modernist principles and forms are clearly in evidence. Nazar has entirely eliminated the traditional "back lawn" in favour of an extensive brick-paved terrace screened from view by a dense cedar hedge;[41] a service courtyard connects strategically to kitchen and garage; and all is expressed in the now-familiar angular and curvilinear vocabularies established by Church, Eckbo, and their California colleagues.

19.7 Beaver Lake Pavilion, Mount Royal Park, Montreal

BRAVE NEW LANDSCAPES 399

19.8 Peguis Pavilion, Kildonan Park, Winnipeg

Other principles and themes were soon grafted onto the basic notions of the modern house and garden that were developed during this key period. These included the relation between the house and the large-scale landscape with respect to views and orientation, and the possibility of freeing the house from its conventional location on the lot and relating it to the path of the sun and to the direction of the prevailing winds.[42] The gardens of this era laid down a basic template that is still central to the Canadian domestic garden today, but the factors that the pioneers of modern design did *not* consider are also significant. These innovators were not concerned about the larger environment, ecological issues, or "sustainable development," an idea that had yet to be invented. In the immediate postwar period, the supply of resources seemed infinite and the burgeoning problems of environmental pollution were far from the minds of people who saw in economic progress an opportunity to improve their daily lives, after many years of hardship.

In the mid-1950s, the continuing expansion of cities motivated municipal governments to create a number of new urban parks, including Angrignon Park in Montreal and Queen Elizabeth Park in Vancouver. The latter was constructed on the "Little Mountain," an igneous intrusion at the geographic centre of the city,

400 BIRTH OF THE MODERN LANDSCAPE

according to the design of Bill Livingstone, the city's director of parks (see chapter 16). Livingstone followed the same strategy as that for the Butchart Gardens and the quarry garden of the Royal Botanical Gardens in Hamilton (see chapters 14 and 18) in that he recycled an abandoned industrial site as an immense space filled with spectacular plants, viewed from an elevated vantage point. In creating this theatrical park, Livingstone exploited the autumn colours of many varieties of Japanese maples and perennials, contrasting them with emerald lawns and dark conifers. With the exception of the acrylic-domed Bloedel Conservatory and an open plaza of exposed-aggregate concrete at the summit of the hill, it cannot be said that this park followed the specific tenets of the modern movement. But gradually, after 1950, the new aesthetic extended its influence from the residential milieu to all types of gardens and parks. Elsewhere in the country, new structures conceived in the modernist vocabulary were integrated into existing parks. The stunning Beaver Lake Pavilion in Mount Royal Park, designed by architects Guy Desbarats and Hazen Sise, is an excellent example. Equally striking is the Peguis Pavilion at Kildonan Park in Winnipeg, erected in the mid-1960s to the design of architects Blankstein, Coop, Gilmore and Hanna, adjacent to a skating pond designed by the city's chief landscape architect, Gunter Schoch.[43] Throughout the following decades, hundreds of large-scale projects were carried out in Canada within the modern idiom. The design of all these environments owed much to the pioneering residential projects of the 1940s and 1950s, an ideal laboratory for the exploration of contemporary design ideas: small-scale, private, and entirely open to freedom of expression.

Innovative Urban Neighbourhoods of the Postwar Era

The residential districts of the new suburbs, their houses constructed all at the same time according to a limited number of standard layouts, often suffered from a banal sameness, a lack of the interesting particularities that are habitually found in older neighbourhoods. And they generally lacked the kind of *landscape signature* that could distinguish one suburb from another. But there were exceptions, even in relatively conventional districts. The southern sector of Sainte-Foy, Quebec, for example, was particularly well integrated into its uniformly sloping site, and virtually every house had its own individual cachet, while maintaining a family resemblance with neighbouring houses.

Aspiring to create something beyond well-designed conventional suburbs, a certain number of inspired developers and designers, in all parts of the country, created alternative neighbourhood layouts (and even whole towns!) that had larger ambitions. The unusual configurations of these districts sought a compromise between two objectives: satisfying the average family's longing for a house of their own, while achieving a sense of community and a sense of place and escaping the total tyranny of the car. Each of these visionary projects included a circulation system designed exclusively for pedestrians, and all were based, to some extent, on Garden City prototypes (see chapter 13).

Cité-jardin du Tricentenaire, Montreal

The first of these developments, located in the Rosemount district of east-end Montreal, was actually begun during the war years and was explicitly motivated by the social ideas of Ebenezer Howard. The project began with the creation of a non-profit association, the Union économique d'habitation (UEH), with the goal of constructing "workers' garden cities" throughout Quebec. The driving force behind the project consisted of two remarkable men: lawyer Joseph-Auguste Gosselin, who had studied workers' housing projects in Europe, and Jesuit priest Jean-d'Auteuil Richard, a native of western Canada who had also benefited from a long period of residence in Europe and who was highly involved in social action. The association's goal was to help its members acquire property, seen as the keystone of social stability and, implicitly, as a means of liberating the francophone working-class community of Quebec from a situation of economic dependency. The religious establishment strongly supported the UEH's housing initiative, which aimed to provide homes for 400 working-class families in Montreal.[44] Christened the Cité-jardin du Tricentenaire in honour of the three-hundredth anniversary of Montreal's founding in 1642, the development was to occupy an extensive territory east of Maisonneuve Park (which was a municipal golf course at the time) and the Montreal Botanical Garden. The original master plan, designed by architects A. Donat Gascon and Louis Parant, would pass through several successive revisions, first at the hands of architect Jean Gagné in 1942 and, finally, by Montreal architect/city planner Samuel Gitterman of the National Housing Administration, an agency of the federal government.[45] Arranged in an organic and fluid configuration, the project consisted of modest single-family houses grouped around a dozen cul-de-sacs shaded by large native trees. Each street was named for the species planted along its roadways – tamaracks on *"rue des Mélèzes,"* with chestnuts, oaks, and cedars on adjoining streets. A linear park – a network of pedestrian paths and common spaces – meandered behind the houses, connecting the cul-de-sacs and leading to a central park and community centre, which originally accommodated the offices of the UEH, a church, and several other community services.[46]

This system of spatial organization was based on that of a new town that had been planned and partially realized in 1928 at Radburn, in the state of New Jersey, by city planner/architect Clarence Stein and landscape architect/planner Henry Wright, along with landscape architect Marjorie Sewell-Cautley.[47] Stein and Wright's town plan was an attempt to adapt Howard's Garden City concept of 1898 to the new reality of the automobile through the creation of a network of protected green spaces that would be reserved for pedestrians and would provide access to all residences, schools, and commercial areas. The Cité-jardin project, an atypical enclave of single-family dwellings in a district of multi-family walk-up residences, is today a very urban suburb, benefiting from the country-like ambiance created by its now-mature giant trees (of all those species!). Despite numerous modifications and adjustments to its buildings, the neighbourhood retains its visual coherence to a remarkable extent and radiates a strong sense of community – a highly successful model of urban habitation.[48]

19.9 Comparative plans of new residential developments and "new towns" of the 1940s and 1950s. The layout of each community demonstrates some elements of the "Radburn Plan" and the Garden City philosophy: cul-de-sacs, loop roads, neighbourhood units, and pedestrian greenways. Main thoroughfares are identified in yellow; commercial and assembly spaces in orange. Public or semi-public parks, pathway routes, and open spaces are in shades of green. Community centres, schools, and commercial buildings are heavily outlined in black.

Cité-jardin du Tricentenaire, Montreal, 1940s

Wildwood Park, Winnipeg, late 1940s

Don Mills, Toronto, 1950s

Kitimat, BC, 1950s

Wildwood Park, Winnipeg

A second Canadian project was, according to legend, even more directly influenced by Radburn. Developer Hubert Bird of Winnipeg is reputed to have seen the New Jersey development from the air while returning by airplane from a visit to New York City. Some years later, after researching Clarence Stein's projects, Bird realized Wildwood Park, a 200-hectare development based on the Radburn layout, in a meander of the Red River in the Fort Garry district of southern Winnipeg.[49] Like both Radburn and Montreal's Cité-jardin, the 1948 Wildwood Park layout,

BRAVE NEW LANDSCAPES 403

designed by architects Green, Blankstein and Russell of Winnipeg, finally consisted of a single highly structured neighbourhood. Within an extensive "superblock," single-family houses were clustered along short automobile access roads, opening on their opposite façades onto a "greenway" system of wooded linear parks that provided pedestrians with a continuous pathway network leading to playground and common areas, without crossing automobile thoroughfares. In contrast to both Radburn and Cité-jardin, which provided access to the houses via a system of cul-de-sacs, the designers of Wildwood adopted a loop system (considered to be more efficient for purposes of snow clearing), following discussions with architect Samuel Gitterman in Ottawa.[50]

Don Mills, Toronto

In the years that followed the war, E.P. Taylor, a Toronto developer and captain of industry, gradually assembled 825 hectares of land northwest of the city, located on plateaus and sloping land between two branches of the Don River. In 1952, with the goal of creating a very extensive new suburb that would include commerce and institutions as well as residences, Taylor engaged a young landscape architect, Macklin Hancock (1925–2010), who was still a student at Harvard at the beginning of the project. Hancock prepared the master plan for what would become the community of Don Mills, destined to receive a total population of 35,000 residents when fully developed. Hancock located a central civic and shopping centre at the crossroads of two major arteries, to serve as the focus for a series of four self-contained neighbourhood units, each comprising single-family residences, a primary school, and local churches. Between the civic centre and the neighbourhood units, Hancock designed a main access road, the Donway, in the form of a closed loop. A *greenway* system exploiting the complex web of existing ravines and river valleys – unbuildable areas traditionally neglected and ignored in Toronto – provided a continuous pedestrian network connecting homes, schools, and community facilities.[51] Finally, industrial sectors were laid out around the periphery of the settlement. This revolutionary project was based on many of the original ideas of Ebenezer Howard (see chapter 13) and of the Radburn design, in particular the *neighbourhood unit* concept that had been first enunciated by planner Clarence Perry during the preparation of the New York Regional Plan in 1929.[52]

Like many other pioneers of landscape architecture, Macklin Hancock came from a family that was involved in horticulture. Born in China, where his grandfather worked as a physician, he arrived in Canada in 1928 at a very young age. His father, Marcus Leslie Hancock (1892–1977), was a professor of horticulture, first in China and subsequently at his *alma mater*, the Ontario Agricultural College (OAC) at Guelph, before establishing Woodland Nursery in the suburbs of Toronto. A great enthusiast for rhododendrons, the senior Hancock gave his collection of these plants to the Montreal Botanical Garden in 1976, where it forms the basis of the Rhododendron Garden, which he laid out and which is named for him. He also founded the Botanic Garden of the University of Guelph, recently redesigned by landscape architecture professor Jim Taylor, where the rhododen-

19.10   Macklin Hancock, c. 1965

dron and azalea garden again bears his name.⁵³ Marcus's son Macklin Hancock also graduated in horticulture at OAC before pursuing his studies in landscape architecture at Harvard.

Kitimat, British Columbia

In a remote area of British Columbia, at the very end of his career, Clarence Stein (1882–1975), the designer of Radburn and dean of American town planning, finally got the chance to plan a whole new city. In 1951, the Aluminum Company of Canada (Alcan) brought him out of retirement to advise on the design of the Garden City of Kitimat, on Douglas Channel in the northwest of the province. Alcan aimed to build an autonomous city harbouring diverse industries – not a company town – with an eventual population of 35,000 – an extremely ambitious proposal. Like Arvida in Quebec (see chapter 17), Kitimat brought in raw materials by boat and train, to be transformed into aluminum by immense quantities of electricity. This energy was to be created by water that had passed through a 16-kilometre-long tunnel under the Cascades, and then transmitted on 82 kilometres of wire through trackless mountains. Stein and his colleagues, architects Albert Mayer and Julian Whittlesey (New Yorkers like himself), planned a city that followed the Radburn principles to the letter. It was composed of five neighbourhood units, each with local stores, a primary school, and churches, arranged on an elevated plateau and on a lower plain around the civic nucleus, where the city hall, a shopping centre, a sports complex, and a hospital were located.⁵⁴ Most of these public activities were lodged in a single building that constituted a sort of combined commercial and community centre.

19.11 A pedestrian pathway connection between neighbourhoods in Kitimat, BC

BRAVE NEW LANDSCAPES   405

The automobile circulation system was strongly hierarchical, breaking down into main arteries, local loop roads, and cul-de-sacs. The green-space network, laid out by the celebrated American landscape architect Dan Kiley in collaboration with Stein,[55] was a crucial component of the overall design. As at Wildwood, the façade of each house was oriented towards a linear park linked to other greenways, creating continuous circulation routes for pedestrians and cyclists throughout the entire city and avoiding conflict with vehicles. Large natural parks, located on hilly sites and along the Kitimat River (which drains the site to Douglas Channel) complement the greenway system. Although the success of some elements of the plan (such as local commerce) has fallen short of expectations, the greenway network has been a tremendous success, constantly used by everyone and kept open throughout the winter to provide continued school access. Despite the vicissitudes of the industrial job market, Kitimat is a stable and permanent settlement, peopled by long-term residents to whom it offers a rich and engaging way of life.[56]

During the 1940s and 1950s, Garden City planning themes were explored at small and medium scale in many other lesser-known projects across the country. In Quebec alone, examples include the St-Jean-Baptiste-de-la-Salle sector of Trois-Rivières by Benoît Bégin, in collaboration with Georges Robert and Georges Daudelin; the Foyer cooperatif in Chicoutimi; and the Plateau du Moulin and Val-de-Grâce projects, also in Chicoutimi, designed respectively by Édouard Fiset and Jean-Claude La Haye.

Shopping Centres and Office Buildings in the Suburbs

The birth of open-mall commercial centres created a new world of shopping for suburban residents: light and airy buildings, organized on a single level around a series of external courtyards embellished with planting boxes, street furniture, fountains, and sculptures. This represented a complete transformation of the commercial environment and was a novel experience for the consumer. Easily accessible by car, comfortable, and provided with large lots for free parking, these shopping centres became symbols of prosperity and well-being. Figuring among the best examples of this genre are the Park Royal Centre in West Vancouver,[57] its open areas designed by landscape architect Philip Tattersfield; Rockland Centre in the Town of Mount Royal (Ian Martin and Victor Prus, architects); and the Don Mills Shopping Centre, designed by John B. Parkin Associates, architects, with Project Planning Associates (PPA), landscape architects. The level of sophistication, comfort, and accessibility offered by these commercial centres created a new rivalry with downtown shopping areas, presenting a challenge that was unheard of before the 1950s and 1960s and that would soon force inner cities to develop major catching-up programs.[58]

A new spirit infused working environments in the suburbs. In the 1950s and 1960s, new office buildings and factories (often combined, the office wing turning an attractive face to the street while storage and production activities were out of sight in the back) were able to spread out over large terrains, since suburban land costs were low. On an extensive property, designers could site their buildings in

19.12 (above)   Interior pedestrian courtyard of a shopping centre in Don Mills, ON, 1959

19.13 (below)   Ortho Pharmaceutical's building in industrial park, Don Mills, ON, set in a pastoral landscape, 1958

harmony with the natural features of the landscape and subtly conceal parking areas with mounds and vegetation while preserving mature trees, vestiges of a previous agricultural vocation, to create a distinctive environment. The building and site of Ortho Pharmaceuticals in Don Mills (John B. Parkin Associates, architects) were an excellent example of this compositional approach. The insertion of crisp and simple modern forms into a mature open landscape provided the same dramatic contrast as that seen in Tunnard's design for Bentley Wood (see Fig. 18.17). The CIBA complex, located near Montreal's new international airport at Dorval, was also an iconic suburban office complex. The CIBA Company left its crowded downtown location to build a new facility on the former site of the Royal Montreal Golf Club, which the club had occupied from 1896 to 1950 before moving to Laval. In this pastoral milieu, graced by a little stream that gurgled past tall elm trees, architect Percy Booth created a precise and elegant composition. The central focus of his design was a circular "satellite" pavilion housing the cafeteria, deftly set in a reflecting pool, square in form. This central feature contrasted with the pure rectilinear geometries of the office block (the exterior cladding of which employed the newly developed technology of the glass curtain wall) and production building. The surroundings, designed by landscape architects McFadzean and Everley of Chicago,[59] continued the lines of the building out into the site, integrating a parking area, paved terraces, and circulation ways into a coherent artistic composition. An abstract sculpture in aluminum (1959–60) by Montreal architect/industrial designer Norman Slater, using triangular forms in bright hues, complemented the natural elements of the landscape.

At their best, suburban office buildings of this generation created an environment that was at once bucolic and technological, a vision of a new world that "erased the boundary between workspace and parkland." As architect Gary Conrath has said of the realizations of this era, "never has the quality of this working environment been surpassed."[60]

Landscape Architects of 1945–1960

Some landscape architects who had begun their practices before the war attained "cruising speed" during the early postwar years; others, though approaching retirement age, continued to distinguish themselves. English-born Robert Savery (b. 1902) had been trained in biology and in botanical and zoological illustration before his immigration to Canada in 1924; he worked in Toronto for the Dunington-Grubb/Stensson and Borgstrom/Carver firms, then became a landscape architect with the E.D. Smith and Sons nursery in Winona, Ontario. After moving to British Columbia in 1935, Savery taught school and opened an illustration studio before returning to landscape architecture with the BC Department of Public Works in 1944, rising to become director of the department's Landscape Division in 1958.[61] Savery's government position involved him in a great number of challenging projects in varying capacities, but his outstanding achievement was undoubtedly the redesign and reconstruction of the gardens at the lieutenant governor's residence in Victoria, Government House, following a disastrous fire in 1957. Savery's design replaced the ruined vestiges of the original 1911 garden, designed by Vancouver landscape architect G.K. MacLean, with a complex and eclectic series of garden spaces carefully integrated together, in the traditional manner of the nineteenth century and the Belle Époque (see chapters 9 and 14). Savery's design took full advantage of the irregularities of the site and the rich horticultural possibilities provided by the Victoria microclimate. The gardens of Government House have continued to evolve through the hands-on involvement of a succession of lieutenant governors, and they have been increasingly opened to the public, both visitors and enthusiastic volunteers.

19.14 View to the summit of the Way of the Cross at St. Joseph's Oratory, Montreal, by Frederick Todd, landscape architect, 1947. The pilgrimage route follows a classic sequence: the garden is entered at a low elevation from which the visitor follows a smoothly curving path that rises gradually up the slope, leading to the progressive discovery of fourteen alcoves defined by vegetation, each with a sculpture executed in Indiana limestone; these are the "stations of the cross." The last phase of the ascent is the steep staircase shown here, with a majestic statue of Christ at the top.

Frederick Todd continued to make significant contributions to the profession and to society until his death in 1948. He was a member of the Montreal City Council between 1946 and 1948 and served as president of the Canadian Society of Landscape Architects in 1946. During this period he completed his last project, the Way of the Cross at St. Joseph's Oratory, an important pilgrimage route in Montreal, where he reprised the traditional themes we have seen in chapter 4.[62] After the death of his wife, Lorrie, in 1945, Howard Dunington-Grubb continued to direct their prestigious office, in collaboration with their former protégé Vilhelm Stensson, now a senior member of the profession, and the latter's wife, Janina Stensson, a landscape architect of Polish origin who joined the firm in 1958 and soon took on a central role. Howard Dunington-Grubb finally made peace with modernism,

BRAVE NEW LANDSCAPES 409

adding modern design to all the other styles he had mastered during his prolific career.[63] In the 1950s and 1960s, the office carried out the landscape design for the grounds of the new Ford Motor Plant in Oakville, Ontario, and the formal and precise gardens in the median of University Avenue in Toronto. Following a brief association with the Dunington-Grubb office, J. Austin Floyd established his own firm in 1956, reaching the top of his form in the 1950s and 1960s with a number of masterful landscape projects, including the site development for the Inn on the Park hotel in Don Mills.

Louis Perron was well engaged in a long and productive career that often called into play his prodigious knowledge of plant materials. Benefiting from his education at Cornell, where he had learned the art of classic "country place" design, he planned the gardens of many large country and city estates for members of Montreal's business elite. But these estate projects were only a small part of Perron's professional *oeuvre*. He also designed many far more modest residential gardens, as well as an astonishing number of parks and playgrounds in dozens of municipalities, everywhere in Quebec.[64] His larger projects included the Parc des Voltigeurs, a provincial park on the St. Francis River in Drummondville, Quebec; three projects at Expo 67; and many golf courses – he was a keen golfer. And like both Dunington-Grubbs, Vilhelm Stensson, Frederick Todd, and Austin Floyd, Perron served as president of the CSLA.[65]

Large Public Projects

Plan for the National Capital

The end of the war finally cleared the way for the realization of several major projects that had been envisioned for years. The long-planned improvement of the National Capital at Ottawa and Hull (now Gatineau) had at last arrived at its decisive moment. Despite the efforts of a succession of consultants and commissions dating back to 1899, the two cities on the Ottawa still resembled factory towns for the wood industry up until the late 1940s.[66] The prime minister, Mackenzie King, had dedicated himself to the transformation of the neighbouring cities into a capital worthy of a great nation. In 1936, while on a visit to the site of the Exposition universelle in Paris, King met the person who was to help him realize his ambition: the exhibition's chief architect and urbanist, Jacques Gréber (1882–1962). A 1909 graduate of the École des Beaux-Arts (along with classmate Ernest Cormier, architect of the University of Montreal), Gréber was already familiar with North America. He had lived there in the late 1910s when he designed Benjamin Franklin Parkway in Philadelphia, one of the last manifestations of the City Beautiful movement in the United States. At King's request, Gréber came to Ottawa in 1937 to help the prime minister achieve one of his long-term goals, the construction of Confederation Square, site of the National War Memorial inaugurated in 1939.[67] Gréber already knew the urban landscape of Ottawa; he had praised the Holt Plan for the capital in his 1920 book *L'architecture aux États-Unis*, which included illustrations from Edward Bennett's report (see chapter 13).

19.15   Jacques Gréber, 1950. Photograph © Estate of Yousuf Karsh

19.16 Master plan for the metropolitan area of Ottawa, ON, and Hull, QC, from Jacques Gréber's *Plan for the National Capital*, 1950. The impressive report prepared by Gréber and his team included many plans at different scales, illustrating his development proposals for various aspects of the capital and its region.

After staying in France throughout the war, Gréber received another appeal from Ottawa at the end of hostilities, in August of 1945. King named him leader of a team of designers whose mission was to prepare a comprehensive plan for the design of the capital, including the surrounding rural and natural territories in both Quebec and Ontario. Gréber worked unceasingly on the plan from 1946 to 1950. He was ably seconded by Canadian architects/city planners John M. Kitchen (a former assistant of Noulan Cauchon, who worked for the city of Ottawa), Édouard Fiset (1910–1994), who, like Gréber, was a graduate of the École des Beaux-Arts in Paris, and landscape architect Douglas McDonald, who had finished his studies at Cornell University in 1937. The master plan they created was based on a detailed study of all the physical and human aspects of the site, in keeping

BRAVE NEW LANDSCAPES 411

with the scientific City Efficient approach then generally accepted. The ideas that had been previously presented by Todd and Bennett were fused with the functional and social preoccupations that underpinned the new study. The master plan was finally published in 1950, just a few days after the passing of its indefatigable champion, Mackenzie King.[68]

The plan proposed a metropolitan transportation scheme, including major arteries and boulevards and a network of parks and parkways along the rivers and canals, to be integrated with similar features that already existed. It envisioned the removal of the wood-pulp factories from downtown Hull, the elimination of railway lines from the centre of Ottawa, and the creation of Gatineau Park, a "green wedge" that would link the city with the Gatineau Hills to the north (a proposal that King had already put forward in the 1930s)[69] and provide for a variety of recreational activities, including camping, canoeing, and skiing. It also proposed the decentralization of government offices to the suburbs, the integration of the Rideau Canal – a military waterway that had lost its strategic significance – into

19.17 "La Mer Bleue" peat bog conservation reserve, one of the outstanding natural areas within the Ottawa Greenbelt defined by Gréber's plan for the National Capital

412 BIRTH OF THE MODERN LANDSCAPE

the city's open-space system, and the creation of an extensive *greenbelt*, with an average width of four kilometres, around the whole Ontario sector of the urban area. This band of open space would embrace both agricultural lands and natural sites, including the splendid peat bog *La mer bleue*, and would serve a variety of educational and recreational purposes.

Unlike the plans of Todd and Bennett, almost all the elements of Gréber's 1950 plan were brought to fruition, and quite rapidly. By 1970, most of the work was done. The realization of the capital plan was the principal task of the Federal District Commission (FDC), which was to transform itself, in 1958, into the National Capital Commission (NCC), a public agency that became a country-wide model.[70] In 1934, the FDC engaged gifted designer and administrator Edward I. ("Ned") Wood (d. 1984), fresh out of Harvard, as their first landscape architect; Wood later became chief landscape architect for the National Capital Commission. At the NCC, while carrying out much design work himself, he also assembled a highly competent team of landscape architects, administrators, and maintenance personnel to manage the diverse green spaces of the commission. Wood oversaw his team's preparation of the detailed plans for the many parks, open spaces, and parkways envisioned in the master plan and brought Gréber's vision to reality. While at Harvard, Wood had experienced first-hand the reconstruction of historic Williamsburg, Virginia, and early in his career, he had studied parkway design at Cornell.[71] These two experiences stood him in good stead in his duties at the FDC and NCC, where the restoration of historic environments and the development of a region-wide parkway system (bringing to fruition an ambitious long-term plan begun early in the century – see chapter 13) were central tasks. Wood envisioned and organized the capital's open spaces – from manicured tulip beds in urban public gardens to natural escarpments and forests in the Gatineau – as a comprehensive, integrated system. He also established a rigorous review and approval process for new projects that were to be constructed within the federal lands. Wood retired in 1966, leaving an impressive legacy in the outstanding environmental character of the National Capital Region.[72]

One of the young landscape architects Wood brought on board was Donald W. Graham, a native of Montreal who had, like himself, studied at Harvard's Graduate School of Design. Soon after his graduation in 1958, Graham was involved in a broad variety of landscape architectural projects, first with the NCC and then as a private practitioner, through his long-lived Ottawa-based office Donald W. Graham and Associates.[73] A key member of the pioneer generation of Canadian-born landscape architects who brought modern design to Canada in the postwar years, Graham carried out a large number of important projects, particularly in the areas of education, parks and national parks, and urban design (see chapters 12 and 20).

Besides his professional activities, Don Graham was instrumental in founding a national magazine for the profession, *The Canadian Landscape Architect*, which he served as editor throughout its existence from 1960 until 1966. A review of the magazine today provides a window into the activities and concerns of Canadian landscape architects during a time of great expansion and enthusiasm. The magazine featured articles by design professionals about their projects and

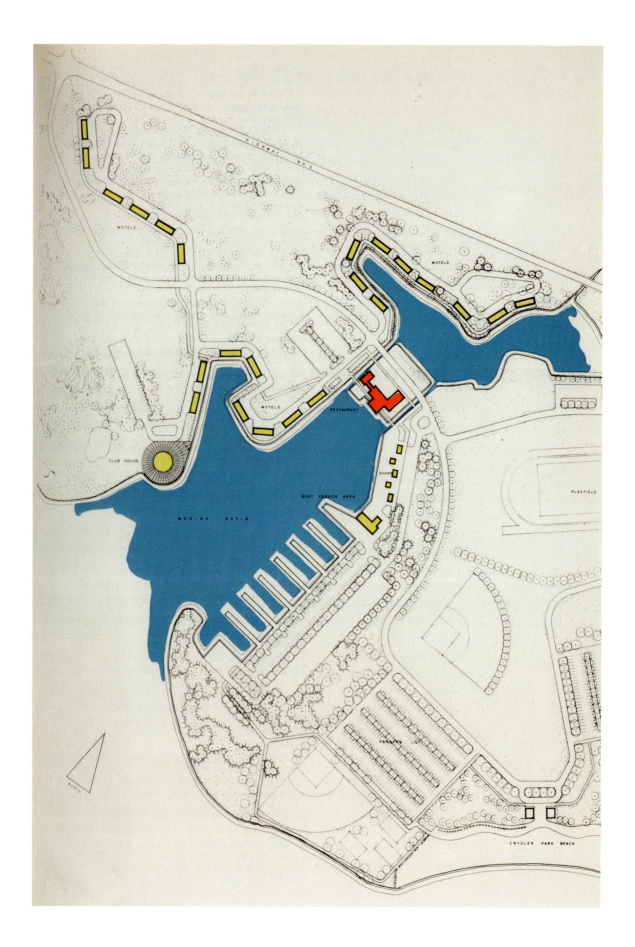

19.18 Plan of the Crysler Park recreation area, ON, one of the new parks integrated into the enormous engineering works of the St. Lawrence Seaway; designed by Project Planning Associates, planners and landscape architects, 1959

philosophies, reports on the progress and growth of the profession (including the founding of professional schools), governmental developments, profiles of significant personalities, and preparations for Expo 67. The magazine was the official publication of the Canadian Society of Landscape Architects and Town Planners, reorganized during this period as a federation of provincial and regional associations and increasingly identified with landscape architecture alone; the reference to Town Planners was gradually dropped from the name of the CSLA, disappearing altogether by the mid-1960s.[74]

Landscapes of the St. Lawrence Seaway

Another government mega-project of the time, the St. Lawrence Seaway, had also passed through a long period of gestation before its realization. This network of canals and navigable waterways represented the fulfilment of a dream that had begun in 1783, the dream of a continuous maritime passage allowing boats to navigate, without barriers, from the Gulf of St. Lawrence all the way to the head of Lake Superior in the centre of the continent, a distance of some 3,800 kilometres. Landscape architects such as Frederick Todd urged the governments involved to treat the landscape as an immense canvas that, designed as an ensemble, could satisfy much broader objectives than those of water transportation alone.[75] The Canadian Society of Landscape Architects proposed that new parks be integrated into the gigantic program of landscape realignment that the project entailed, that some elements of the historic villages that were to be eliminated be preserved, and that native wildlife be protected.[76] Finally, the Ontario–St. Lawrence Development Commission, an agency of the Ontario government, engaged Project Planning Associates to prepare a master plan for all the parks and other sites that would be affected by the giant construction project. PPA was a Toronto firm that had been founded in 1956 by seven associates from different disciplines, including landscape architects Macklin Hancock and Don Pettit, a graduate of Harvard like Hancock. The development of this immense territory included the creation of hydroelectric power stations for Ontario Hydro, idyllic rural environments for passive relaxation, and more elaborate parks for active recreation. In the Montreal region, Louis Perron planned Seaway Park along the south shore of the St. Lawrence River. Other new facilities along the waterway system included public beaches, campgrounds, a bird sanctuary, and the historically themed Upper Canada Village, composed of buildings saved from flooding and newly reassembled to create an educational heritage park.[77]

These great public projects, combined with the expansion of the suburbs, created a completely new family of Canadian landscapes, most of which were situated outside the city centres. But from 1960 on, a landscape revolution also began to express itself within the heart of Canada's downtown areas. This new development will be examined in the following chapter.

BRAVE NEW LANDSCAPES 415

20

Urban Renaissance

20.1 Expo 67, Montreal: the lightweight Minirail "people-mover" zips across this view of the French Pavilion on Île Notre-Dame. Innovative light-reflecting fixtures are seen at left.

The Years of Recovery: The Best of Times, the Worst of Times

When did Canadian landscape architecture achieve its finest hour? Most would choose the 1960s, a decade of remarkable innovations during which landscape architecture established itself as a profession of consequence. Unfortunately, the 1950s and 1960s were also the worst years for landscape architecture: this was the time when we most rapidly destroyed our historic urban landscapes, without really thinking much about it.[1]

These years saw the conflation of a number of tendencies that contributed to this destruction, including the *displacement of urban facilities to the suburbs*, which heralded the debut of a long process of decline in the city centres. In Quebec City, there was good reason for Laval University and several large downtown stores to move seven kilometres west to Sainte-Foy, in the suburbs. There was simply not enough room on Cape Diamond beside the Grand Séminaire for the university to accommodate the major expansion that it needed to make; moreover, the commercial enterprises wanted to be close to the new sectors of the city that were expanding most rapidly. But these displacements greatly diminished the importance of the old downtown area.

The construction of *urban freeways* also encouraged people to leave the central districts of the city for the suburbs. These new freeways disrupted the urban fabric, slashed wide swaths through dense residential neighbourhoods, divided up historic districts, and degraded them with noise, pollution, and general ugliness. Just about every city in Canada welcomed this invasion. The Gardiner Expressway cut off Toronto's downtown from Lake Ontario. Boulevard Saint-Cyrille and the Autoroute Dufferin-Montmorency in Quebec City all but eliminated the pedestrian environment at the very gates of Parliament Hill. A mini-freeway even encroached upon the centre of the small city of Fredericton. Yet somehow a number of cities successfully resisted this general trend, thanks to the intervention of groups of dedicated citizens who opposed the destruction of their city's fabric. In Vancouver, Peter Oberlander, a key figure in this effort, resigned as chairman of Vancouver's Town Planning Commission in 1967 when the city approved a proposal to drive a cross-town freeway through traditional Eastside residential areas. His resignation touched off a political firestorm that ended with the project's cancellation.[2] Vancouver has since survived very well without such disturbing traffic arteries, thanks partially to the creation, decades before, of a boulevard system around the periphery of the city (see chapter 13). In Halifax, a waterfront freeway that would have separated the downtown area from the city's historic port was also sidelined,[3] and a similar freeway proposal that would have slashed through historic Old Montreal was overcome through the efforts of city planners Sandy van Ginkel and Blanche Lemco Van Ginkel.[4] In 1971, the wholesale construction of urban freeways was stopped for good in Toronto when writer and activist Jane Jacobs, recently transplanted from New York City, galvanized the movement to stop the Spadina Expressway, which would have destroyed one of the city's most significant and historic boulevards and its surroundings (see chapter 8).[5]

The *cult of the automobile* also affected parks and squares. In Montreal, parking lots had long since taken over Champ de Mars and part of Victoria Square. In the 1950s, the construction of the Chemin Camillien-Houde on Mount Royal, designed by the prestigious New York landscape architects Clarke and Rapuano, provided a swift and convenient shortcut and a panoramic way of appreciating the mountain's charms, but brought a huge parking lot with it.[6] Other interventions in urban areas across the country eliminated rows of street trees and chopped up green spaces by changing boulevards into urban highways.

Urban renewal, the stated objective of which was to improve the quality of city life and to combat the degradation of "blighted" districts, often meant the demolition of neighbourhoods that could have been salvaged and upgraded, substituting either apartment towers inappropriate for families or office buildings with vast parking areas, like the Radio-Canada Headquarters in Montreal. Sometimes parks were the victims of urban renewal projects. Victoria Park in Quebec City, established in 1895–97 in a meander of the Saint-Charles River, was subjected to a major revision during the 1950s, losing much green space to new public buildings. The city shortened the river so as to eliminate the meander, part of which was subsequently paved over for automobile circulation. The park thus lost its most important natural element.[7]

A *decline in the quality of parks* was seen throughout the country in the 1950s and 1960s. After the Depression and the war – years that had severely constrained activities, personnel, and maintenance budgets[8] – all the equipment and natural features of public parks were in a sorry state. It was in this era that the bandstands, the sculptures, the ponds and basins, and the rustic wooden fences and bridges disappeared from such open spaces as Major's Hill Park in Ottawa, Champlain Park in Trois-Rivières, and Westmount Park, among many others. At the same time, in response to the baby boom, young families needed public spaces to provide recreational facilities for their children. New suburban parks were quickly constructed to meet this burgeoning demand, their design inspired by a different model than that of the traditional urban park. These parks suffered from an oversimplification of their urban landscape program, a limited definition of their *raison-d'être*. Pragmatic and functional considerations, reflected in purely quantitative standards and norms, eclipsed community-oriented aspirations.[9] All this led to new parks (or redesigned old parks) that were, essentially, aggregations of sports facilities – three baseball diamonds, two soccer fields, a *chalet* or service building, and a swimming pool, each identical to all the other service buildings and swimming pools in the city – without topographic variation and lacking any sense of aesthetics or general composition. Each element was isolated from its neighbours by a practical and efficient chain-link fence. The result: parks that were literally and figuratively flat, conveying an overall impression that was banal and boring.

Modernism (see chapter 19) frequently contributed to this loss of quality. At its best, this philosophy stimulated experimentation with abstract forms, colour, and motion, giving rise to original and exciting projects. But when interpreted too literally or unimaginatively, it led to the impoverishment of the design vocabulary, which was cut back to the lowest common denominator of squares and rectangles.

Modernism was a jealous god, serious and intolerant. In the face of its requirements for simple, pure forms, everything fanciful, idiosyncratic, light-hearted, or capricious – even plants – had to give way. Further, because of the difficulty of finding experienced horticulturists in a period of full employment, it was virtually impossible for parks to retain the formal planting beds, floral clocks, and perennial borders of a recent but inaccessible past. The plant vocabulary of parks was gradually reduced to grass, hedges, a few sporadic trees, and an occasional mass planting of annuals.

Parks of such stereotypical design became places for children, not adults. The park lost its traditional role as the guardian of the public memory and was no longer the setting for public assemblies or activities. Worse: the limited number of activities and the habitual underuse of such spaces created a vacuum that was quickly filled with antisocial activities – crime, drugs, vandalism. In the 1960s, some parks were even considered to be dangerous places, off-limits when not actively occupied.[10]

Finally, the new design paradigm ignored or forgot long-established landscape archetypes. New urban thoroughfares were not expected to be integrated and rhythmic compositions of buildings, vegetation, and street furniture, as had been the case with traditional boulevards; they were essentially practical, often austere, and seldom loved. The vigorous expansion of university campuses in western Canada did not project into the future their original City Beautiful plans: at the University of Manitoba in Winnipeg, the main central axis framed by elm trees – once the symbol of the university – was downplayed in a long-overdue restructuring of pedestrian space and circulation;[11] and at the University of Alberta in Edmonton, a new building was constructed within the great central space of the campus.

"People Places"

Despite all the negative tendencies that have just been described, this same period saw some of the most remarkable central-city projects the country has known – an "Urban Renaissance"[12] that expressed, in physical form, the flowering of a new civic culture in Canada. The downtowns of Canadian cities, like their parks, had passed through a long period of deterioration since the beginning of the Depression in 1929. Then, suddenly, both public and private sectors seemed to rediscover the downtown areas and then proceeded to reinvent them. They created lively "people places," exciting and well-appointed outdoor spaces that welcomed city residents. These projects heralded a more open, creative, and joyous spirit in Canadian civic life. During the 1960s, Canada moved into the vanguard of world architecture and design for the first time, breaking a tradition of adapting ideas from abroad that had lasted for generations. The new projects had style, flair, and originality; it was as if a whole country full of dull, hard-working people who had dutifully shouldered the burdens of the Great Depression and the war decided to have a little fun and express themselves, for a change.

Nowhere was this more true than in Toronto, where the building of a strikingly modern new city hall and plaza (1961–65), the result of an international

20.2 The skating rink at Nathan Phillips Square, Toronto City Hall, framed by three abstract arches. Toronto's Old City Hall is seen in this view from the centre of the plaza, looking towards the southeast.

competition won by Finnish architect Viljo Revell (in collaboration with Toronto architects John B. Parkin and Associates), marked the city's evolution from a staid, reserved past to an open-minded and multicultural future. The public plaza in front of City Hall, Nathan Phillips Square, is resolutely modern in composition: a great open space, almost without detail, enclosed by a raised passageway that connects it to neighbouring buildings. At its central focus – a skating rink and reflecting pool of perfectly rectangular form – stand three abstract arches.[13] The square provides the ideal ambiance for large public assemblies and serves as the anchor and point of departure for several other open spaces, public and quasi-public, that work together to create a rich spatial and experiential sequence extending south towards Lake Ontario. This linear sequence is the modern equivalent of the beaux-arts axis that John Lyle imagined sixty years before (see chapter 13). It includes such outdoor spaces as the Toronto-Dominion Centre (1962–73) and Commerce Court (1968–72), the nerve centres of two of the country's giant banks, both designed by famous modern architects, Mies van der Rohe and I.M. Pei and Associates of New York, respectively.[14] Two interior spaces also form part of the sequence: Eaton Centre (designed in 1973 by architects Zeidler and Roberts), a great multi-storey commercial gallery, roofed in glass and animated by basins, fountains, sculptures, and 100,000 visitors per day;[15] and landscape architect J. Austin Floyd's open-air garden within the Sheraton Centre Hotel (built in 1972 across the street from City Hall), a tract of wild forest mysteriously relocated to an upscale urban environment.[16]

In Quebec, the Quiet Revolution (1960–70 approximately) dramatically redirected the province's church-dominated traditional culture towards a new kind of society that was to be secular, progressive, and technologically oriented. Its

20.3 (above) Plan of downtown Toronto showing its evolving urban design structure in the 1960s and 1970s. Historic landmark buildings are shown in brown; new buildings of the 1960s and 1970s in grey; interior pedestrian connections in yellow; new plazas and public squares in orange; and planted areas in green. Note the similarity between the route of John Lyle's apocryphal north-south "Federal Avenue" of 1911 and the main interior pedestrian route developed during the 1960s and 1970s.

20.4 (below) The interior garden of the Sheraton Centre Hotel, Toronto. All floors of the hotel open onto this central space, which features large trees in raised concrete planting boxes and a thundering waterfall. Although it is entirely enclosed by the hotel, it is in fact an exterior space separated from the building's interior by full-height glass walls, permitting the use of locally grown plants.

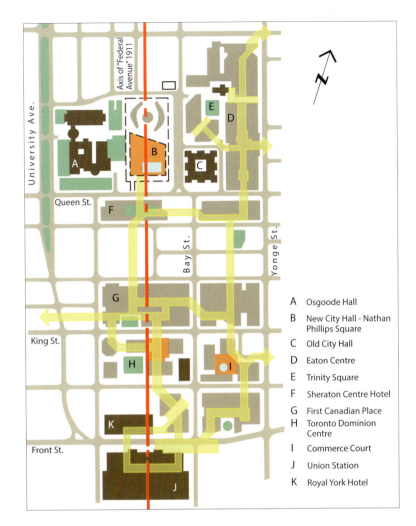

A Osgoode Hall
B New City Hall - Nathan Phillips Square
C Old City Hall
D Eaton Centre
E Trinity Square
F Sheraton Centre Hotel
G First Canadian Place
H Toronto Dominion Centre
I Commerce Court
J Union Station
K Royal York Hotel

20.5 (facing page, above) The central plaza of Place Ville Marie, Montreal, c. 1962, looking north through the complex to McGill College Avenue, McGill University, and the eastern flank of Mount Royal. PVM's trademark cruciform tower is on the right.

20.6 (facing page, below) Stream and pool sequence of the hotel garden atop Place Bonaventure, Montreal

20.7 (below) Rideau Canal and National Arts Centre, Ottawa, looking southward from the Plaza Bridge, which connects Rideau and Wellington Streets

architectural and landscape symbol was Place Ville-Marie (1959–64), a stunning downtown office and shopping complex. The project's New York developer, William Zeckendorf of the Webb and Knapp company, and its designers, I.M. Pei and Associates (project director, Henry N. Cobb) with local architectural consultants Affleck, Desbarats, Dimakopoulos, Lebensold, Michaud, Sise (known informally as Arcop),[17] created a whole new central focus for the city, opening up a broad paved plaza on the axis of an avenue connecting the city's business centre to McGill University and Mount Royal Park.[18] Its plaza, conceived as a great outdoor room, resembled an elegant Italian piazza, entirely devoted to pedestrians, paved with colourful exposed-aggregate concrete and illuminated at night by stylish clusters of white globes. Simultaneously, its underground shopping concourse ushered in Montreal's "underground city," which linked businesses together and to the stations of the newly constructed Metro system, soon to expand in all directions. The cross-shaped tower and central location of "PVM" made it an instant landmark; it became a favourite meeting place and scene of outdoor assembly for Montrealers, literally creating a new kind of public milieu that had not previously existed[19] and giving Montreal a vibrant image of urban sophistication.

Other equally revolutionary projects followed, notably Place Bonaventure, an immense convention centre and merchandise mart crowned by the magnificent roof garden of the Hotel Bonaventure. The garden was designed by landscape

20.8 Garden of the Provinces, Ottawa

architects Sasaki, Dawson, Demay from Boston, assisted by local consultant John Schreiber. The building, again designed by the Arcop group (principal designers Ray Affleck and Eva Vecsei), furnished an appropriate microclimate for the garden and incorporated a series of technical innovations that resolved the many problems of structure, drainage, insulation, and irrigation involved. Masao Kinoshita, the lead designer of the garden, created a remarkable fusion of Japanese spatial composition and aquatic garden design, with Nordic vegetation and local granite and limestone.[20] The garden forms a green ring between the hotel's central public facilities and its individual rooms, which are situated around the building's perimeter, providing a high degree of privacy. Connecting corridors and bridges between the central area and the rooms divide the garden into four quadrants; these are tied together by a continuous stream and pool sequence that recalls the "promenade garden" of the Japanese tradition.

A few streets to the east, between 1967 and 1972, the city planning and architecture firm La Haye-Ouellet developed the conceptual design for Complexe

424 BIRTH OF THE MODERN LANDSCAPE

Desjardins, an enormous interior public plaza enclosed by significant public- and private-sector buildings designed by several of Quebec's top architectural firms, the whole complex occupying an entire city block.

In Ottawa, the architects and landscape architects of the National Capital Commission (NCC) continued to realize the Gréber plan (see chapter 19) under the direction of landscape architect Ned Wood and, after his retirement in 1965, that of Don Pettit, a founding member of the Project Planning office in Toronto. Pettit, the chief landscape architect of the NCC from 1966 to 1985, was backed up by a team of landscape architects and other professionals that included Roman Fodchuk and Ed Holubowitch. Adjacent to Parliament Hill in Ottawa, the NCC finalized the construction of Confederation Square and the transformation of the Rideau Canal into a prominent landscape feature favoured by pedestrians and skaters (the canal has been billed as the "longest skating rink in the world"). Beside the canal and again designed by the architects of the Arcop group, Canada's National Arts Centre was erected in the late 1960s. Like Place Bonaventure, the roof of the centre was treated as a garden, designed this time by landscape architects Hough, Stansbury of Toronto.

To the west of the Parliament Buildings is the Garden of the Provinces, a jewel of modernism designed by Donald W. Graham (and first envisioned in the Gréber plan). The garden, opened in 1962, demonstrates a spare elegance in its careful detailing of natural stone paving and stairs, its integration of sculpture, and its exploitation of the aesthetic possibilities of water, featuring basins, fountains, and sculptures created by Norman Slater and Emil Vandermeulen.[21] A recent refur-

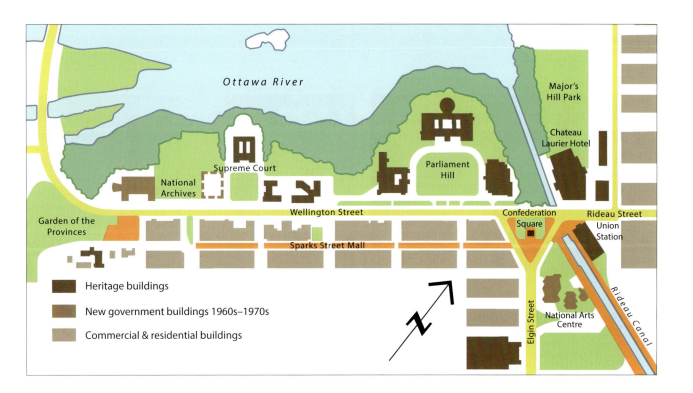

20.9 Downtown Ottawa, 1960–70. Main boulevards and thoroughfares are shown in yellow; new plazas and pedestrian spaces in orange; parks and planted areas in light green; and forested slopes in dark green.

URBAN RENAISSANCE   425

bishment by the federal government has returned the garden to its original character. These exciting projects, along with the realization of the Sparks Street Mall that converted the main shopping street of downtown Ottawa into a pedestrian space (Watson Balharrie, architect, among others),[22] constituted a critical mass of attractive and interesting landscapes, well integrated with the natural features of Ottawa. Together, these landscapes reinforced the city's role as the national capital and as an important destination for Canadians and foreign visitors.

In Winnipeg, the Urban Renaissance was expressed through a number of projects of intermediate scale. Denis R. Wilkinson, a landscape architect of British origin who had carried out his studies at the University of Pennsylvania and worked in Philadelphia and San Francisco, arrived in the city in 1963 to teach at the University of Manitoba and to act as campus landscape architect. During his short five-year stay in Winnipeg, Wilkinson designed a considerable number of projects that gained him a reputation as one of the best modern landscape architects in the West.[23] His design for the Maitland Steinkopf Gardens in the downtown area (1967), a multi-level space framed by two municipal buildings, including the Centennial Concert Hall, is a good example. Wilkinson's simple palette consisted essentially of poured-in-place concrete and trees (birches and conifers), which he arranged in regular right-angle geometries. Through his able exploitation of this minimalist vocabulary, Wilkinson succeeded in creating an elegant space – stimulating to pass through – by the modulation of steps and landings, the arrangement of successive spaces in echelon, and the positioning of a water basin and fountain jets as focal elements.[24] Elsewhere in the downtown area, the local office Lombard North employed a similar vocabulary of forms and materials in their design for Centennial Library Park (built 1974–77). The firm's landscape architects Scott Burbidge and Doug Paterson created a sheltered space, again animated by water basins and fountains, that offered a quiet setting for impromptu performances.[25]

20.10　Entrance area and detail view, Maitland Steinkopf Gardens, Winnipeg

426　BIRTH OF THE MODERN LANDSCAPE

20.11 (above)   Stephen (Eighth) Avenue Mall, Calgary. Beyond the simple exclusion of automobile traffic and the preservation of existing buildings, the careful integration of street trees, sidewalks with textured paving, and attractive site furniture established a design vocabulary for the transformation of a former mixed-circulation shopping street into a successful pedestrian mall.

20.12 (below)   View to downtown Calgary from Prince's Island Park in the Bow River, the result of a long-term beautification plan begun by landscape architects Man, Taylor and Muret in 1968

Like Ottawa, many cities closed one of their major thoroughfares to cars in order to create a *pedestrian mall*. In Calgary, the Stephen Avenue Mall, which transformed the former Eighth Avenue into a pedestrian space, was a remarkable success from the outset, thanks to its careful integration into the overall urban design plan for the downtown area. This lively public space provides the visitor with an opportunity to appreciate the robust and well-proportioned sandstone buildings that enclose it, some of which date from the late nineteenth century.[26] The street and its stores maintain their human scale through the limitation of the number of storeys that face onto the mall, while, behind these facades, high-rise buildings are discreetly inserted to maintain economic viability. Street furniture, special paving materials and patterns, itinerant merchants, and musicians all contribute to the creation of a highly stimulating urban environment. Downtown Calgary experienced many other important changes during this period, including the transformation of the former industrial site of Prince's Island in the Bow River into a public park and the creation of a direct pedestrian connection from downtown to the park.

URBAN RENAISSANCE   427

The masterpiece of the West Coast was undoubtedly the Robson Square complex in Vancouver. From 1973 to 1980, architect Arthur Erickson and landscape architect Cornelia Hahn Oberlander redesigned a large swath of the central city to create a three-block-long composition of building, plazas and gardens – "a skyscraper turned on its side" – integrating the provincial law courts and a number of other office and commercial activities into a fascinating multipurpose urban milieu. Intimate paths, sunny sidewalk cafés, dense tree planting in rows and clumps, and pedestrian passageways above and below street level created a new focus of popular activity[27] – a welcoming and inviting milieu diametrically opposed to the stolid and intimidating personality typical of law court buildings. This project was an early example of the *green roof* approach, featuring plants suitable for city conditions, planted in a lightweight growing medium to create a linear park and urban oasis on top of the building. Robson Square also broke new ground through the use of *stramps* (pedestrian ramps integrated with staircases) and the installation of pools and waterfalls over office areas with transparent roofs.

Open-space innovations such as those described above were to be found in urban centres of all types, as witnessed by the many new plazas and refurbished

20.13 Lower-level courtyard at Robson Square, Vancouver, 1981. Looking northeast, with waterfall in foreground, sidewalk cafés and performance area at lower level. In the rear left is architect Francis Rattenbury's old courthouse, now the Vancouver Art Gallery; the matching shelters on both sides of Robson Street were designed as reflections of the gallery's dome.

city squares that enlivened the downtown areas of medium-sized and small municipalities as well as those of major cities. Successful examples from the late 1960s and early 1970s included the Place de l'hôtel de ville, a roof-terrace plaza and informal theatre designed by landscape architect Jan Hoedeman adjacent to the city hall in Quebec City; and the elegant Parc de la Francophonie within the parliamentary precinct of the *vieille capitale*, then undergoing rapid and far-reaching expansion. Designed by John Schreiber, the latter project is a sunken amphitheatre-like space that serves as a popular venue for Quebec City's many festivals; it is fondly referred to as "Le Pigeonnier," in honour of the sculptural pigeon-house at its centre, created to attract the pigeons that had long been comfortably ensconced on the surrounding government buildings. The reconstruction of Champlain Park in Trois-Rivières, Quebec, by landscape architect Georges Daudelin gave a new life to that historic square through the integration of large water basins and fountains of contemporary allure.

Centennial Plaza in Victoria, British Columbia, brought new life to a key site in the old business district. Created in 1962 in honour of the city's centennial by landscape architects Justice and Webb (a new partnership that brought together Clive Justice and Harry James Webb after the departure of Desmond Muirhead),[28] this plaza is a fine example of the artistic originality of its creators. Their three-

20.14 "Stramps" connecting upper and lower plaza levels at Robson Square, Vancouver

20.15 (above) Parc de la Francophonie, Quebec City. Looking northwest across the park towards "Complexe G," one of the large government buildings constructed during the Quiet Revolution. The pigeon-house is the small structure at right.

20.16 (below) Central sculpture and pool at Centennial Plaza, Victoria, BC

20.17 (facing page) Sunken courtyard at the Confederation Centre of the Arts, Charlottetown, PEI, leading down to the main pedestrian concourse within. The austere and abstract landscape composition is modulated by the use of subtly hued Wallace sandstone as exterior cladding on the buildings. This stone was used in the original construction of the adjacent PEI Province House.

dimensional design encompassed the entire site in a radio-concentric geometry that spun out from a central sculpture and pool, bringing unity to a space that was enclosed by an exceptionally heterogeneous collection of buildings, including the old Victorian city hall.[29]

Charlottetown, Prince Edward Island, also benefited from the creation of an outstanding new plaza, the Confederation Centre of the Arts (1964), designed by the Arcop group and architect/planner Norbert Schoenauer of Montreal following a nation-wide competition.[30] Constructed right beside the province's legislative assembly at Queen Square, the central open space in the original colonial town plan, the complex was built in commemoration of Charlottetown's role in bringing about the confederation of Canada's provinces a century before. The design succeeded where it would have been very easy to fail. Through the division of the new building into several distinct components, each one smaller and lower than the assembly building, Schoenauer ensured that the enormous new complex would not dominate the historic jewel at the centre of the square. The landscape and overall site treatment created a sort of modern Greek sanctuary, using sculptural modulation to create an appropriate base for monumental buildings.[31]

New Landscapes in Governmental Precincts

Surprisingly, several of these lively and vivacious places were related to the monumental and imperious legislative buildings of the various provinces. In Regina, the availability of public lands on both shores of Wascana Creek, adjacent to the site of Saskatchewan's legislative assembly, inspired provincial, municipal, and university authorities to collaborate on the planning of Wascana Centre, an immense urban area. The directors of the project, which was begun in 1961, commissioned architect/city planner Minoru Yamasaki of Detroit and landscape architect Thomas D. Church (1902–1978) of San Francisco to prepare a master plan for the overall site, comprising a total area of 800 hectares. The consultants' plans, submitted in 1962 and 1967 and developed gradually over two decades,[32] involved the refurbishing of the parliamentary environs and the creation of new parks and recreation areas along the water, as well as an administrative centre, exhibition galleries, and the campus of the University of Regina.[33] Landscape architect Ken Dockham, director of operations for the Wascana Centre Authority, coordinated the preparation of detailed plans and the realization of the various components of this ambitious project.

The forecourt of the Alberta Legislative Assembly in Edmonton is an outstanding example of a humane, relaxed, and democratic public space, following its redesign and expansion between 1978 and 1982. Most of the year, the pools and fountains of the forecourt (which extends the axis of the building to the north, as proposed in the 1912 City Beautiful proposal drawn by landscape architects Morell and Nichols) provide a solemn and dignified setting for this significant building. But on sunny summer days, in particular Canada Day on the 1st of July, they are transformed into an immense aquatic garden, where tens of thousands of people enjoy themselves by rollicking in the water, listening to music, and eating hotdogs – the apotheosis of the "people places" of the 1960s and 1970s.

Why These Innovations?

The flowering of creativity and originality that provided Canada with these outdoor spaces can be partially explained by simple need. Downtowns had been neglected for decades and no longer corresponded to the requirements of the society that had evolved; the central cities had to be revived. But there were also several other relevant factors. Opportunity undoubtedly played a role: almost every Canadian city had large areas of vacant or underused land in its central area, often belonging to railroad companies. The financial and physical resources were present: a general prosperity reigned and the high productivity of former war industries had been transferred to those of peace. There was also, very importantly, a public will for change: people were ready for a major cultural transformation. The social changes of the 1960s were most clearly visible in Quebec, with its Quiet Revolution, but it seemed that each region of Canada was searching for a new social paradigm, one that was more tolerant, more open, more sophisticated, and less constrained by the dogmas of the past. This new awakening applied both to serious concerns,

20.18 Forecourt of the Alberta Legislative Assembly on Canada Day, 1 July 2008. The forecourt design was the result of a 1975 competition won by architects McIntosh, Workun and Chernenko of Edmonton. Yasuo Matsumara was a principal designer.

such as the elimination of discrimination, and to questions of lesser gravity, such as whether one might enjoy lunch in a sidewalk café, previously almost unthinkable in Canada.[34] Although much less dramatic and thoroughgoing than the profound transformation experienced by Quebec during this period, it is not an exaggeration to say that each province had, in a sense, its own quiet revolution.

Studies of people's behaviour in urban settings also contributed to this transformation. Until the 1960s, designers seldom carried out serious research on the activities of people in city environments. Thanks to the studies and publications of Jane Jacobs (1916–2006), a brilliant journalist from New York who moved to

URBAN RENAISSANCE   433

Toronto in 1969, all this was to change. In her first book, *The Death and Life of Great American Cities* (1961), Jacobs stated that "people do not use city open space just because it is there and because city planners or designers wish they would."[35] She also signalled the importance of diversified neighbourhoods in attracting people and encouraging a variety of activities throughout the day. She sought complexity and diversity in the urban milieu, in opposition to the excessively functionalist and simplistic approach of the time. Jacobs's ideas had a powerful influence on urban design; her discoveries opened the door to a series of further studies, including those by Clare Cooper Marcus at the University of California at Berkeley, that provided professional designers with a theoretical base upon which to design outdoor spaces in a more socially enlightened manner than had previously been possible.[36] These ideas spread rapidly into Canada; Cooper Marcus, for example, served as a guest professor at the University of Manitoba in the 1970s.[37]

Dramatis Personae

The simultaneous alignment of all these factors in the early 1960s could not have assured the creation of excellent public spaces without the presence of one final ingredient: the human resource, the *talent*. Where did the designers of these spaces come from? After all, there were only a handful of landscape architects in Canada in 1948, many of whom, like Frederick Todd, were nearing the end of their careers. There were no schools of landscape architecture in Canada – these were still twenty years in the future – and the schools of architecture offered no systematic training in the field of landscape, although, as always, a certain number of architects had an instinctive feel for the landscape, without having any specific training. Arthur Erickson and Ron Thom, for example, perhaps because of the powerful West Coast landscapes that surrounded them, demonstrated a brilliant capacity to integrate their buildings into the landscape. The profession of town planning was getting back on track after a long hiatus, thanks largely to the influence of Humphrey Carver, chair of the CMHC (Central Mortgage and Housing Corporation) Research Committee; its secretary, Peter Oberlander; and Harold Spence-Sales, founder of the city planning program at McGill University. But planning had now become a distinct profession, having little overlap with landscape architecture – one could no longer depend on city planners to be landscape architects as well. Nonetheless, landscape architects did come forward in response to the postwar challenge, and they came from three different worlds.

Canadian Pioneers: The "Greatest Generation"

A considerable number of young Canadians studied landscape architecture abroad, almost entirely at learning institutions in the United States (where degrees had been offered in this discipline since 1900), both in land-grant colleges (see chapter 7), traditionally related to agriculture and horticulture, and in prestigious universities that brought landscape together with architecture and fine arts.[38] These studies were greatly facilitated by CMHC's establishment, under the direction of Carver and Oberlander, of a scholarship program to permit Canadian graduates in architecture and other disciplines to pursue advanced studies in landscape and planning outside Canada, before these subjects were offered in Canada. The careers of many future professionals were made possible by these scholarships.[39] Following the example of Louis Perron, Quebecers who undertook studies in landscape went mostly to the land-grant school at Cornell University in Ithaca, New York, which had an excellent reputation in botany and natural sciences. Benoît Bégin spent five years there, gaining diplomas in both landscape architecture and city planning. André Chartrand, André Lafontaine, Ulric Couture – the nucleus of the future landscape design team of Montreal's Parks Department, destined to be, for many years, the largest landscape architectural office in Canada – were all Cornell graduates, while André Sauvé, who was to practise in the private sector, carried out his studies at the University of Massachusetts at Amherst, also a land-grant college. Their contemporary Georges Daudelin studied at the École nationale supérieure de paysage de Versailles, the oldest school of landscape architecture in France, before embarking on a career in both the private and the public sectors.

Future professors Hugh Knowles and John Neill, natives of Ontario, finished their bachelor's degrees at the Ontario Agricultural College (OAC) at Guelph before beginning their advanced studies at Michigan State and Oregon State universities, respectively. Many other pioneers from eastern Canada were trained at OAC, including Estyl Mooney, from the Maritime provinces, and George Tanaka, originally from the West Coast. Others obtained a first degree from OAC or Macdonald College (part of McGill University in Montreal) before going in the 1950s to Harvard, the great "multiversity" of New England, home of the first university program in landscape architecture in the United States. This group included Macklin Hancock, Don Pettit, and Donald W. Graham of Montreal. They benefited from the teaching of the legendary Hideo Sasaki, director of the landscape school at Harvard throughout this period, who was also an outstanding practitioner whose firms were involved in a number of major Canadian projects.. Many young candidates from western Canada chose the University of California at Berkeley. Clive Justice arrived at Berkeley from British Columbia in 1953, to be followed in 1957 by Edwin "Jack" Walker, Victor Chanasyk, Roman Fodchuk, and Ed Holubowich, all from the Prairies, "headed to California for sun, fun and adventure."[40] Others succeeded them at Berkeley in the 1960s, including Cameron Man and Garry Hilderman from Manitoba. The pilgrimage to the prominent universities of the East also continued in the 1960s: Brad Johnson of Toronto and Peter Jacobs from Montreal went to Harvard, while Alex Rattray studied at the University of Pennsylvania.

A key point: many members of this generation of designers began their studies on their return from service in the Second World War. Hancock had been a fighter pilot, Neill had driven a tank "all across Europe,"[41] Clive Justice had served in the Canadian Army in England, Harry Webb (Justice's associate) in the Merchant Marine, and George Tanaka in Intelligence.[42] Benoît Bégin was in training with the navy when the end of the war intervened, while architect Jean Ouellet, who was to work closely with landscape architects throughout his career, was a member of the RCAF's famous Alouette Squadron of medium and heavy bombers operating from Britain and North Africa.[43] The discipline and humility that carried them through those difficult times affected their entire lives and professional careers, as they did for all those described in the moving books by writer Barry Broadfoot and journalist Tom Brokaw.[44]

The "Brilliant Europeans": Culture and Experience

Canada also benefited from the contributions of landscape architects, architects, and urbanists from Europe who, leaving that war-shattered continent, found a fertile ground for their talents on our shores. Most had already been educated in landscape architecture in the excellent horticultural academies of Europe or in architecture or urbanism in its historic universities. The broad culture and technical knowledge of these people enriched the world of design in all parts of Canada.[45] Several of these landscape architects came from Germany, including Gunter Schoch, who arrived in 1954 and eventually became the chief landscape architect of the city of Winnipeg, where he designed and managed many important urban projects over several decades.[46] Klaus Bartholl and Eckhard Schirde-wahn worked together for many years as partners in their firm Parkway Planning Associates, with offices in Ottawa and Montreal. Reinhart Petersmann worked at Parks Canada before establishing his own design office in Halifax, and Friedrich Oehmichen, a master of design with plants, pursued a long and rewarding career as a professor at the University of Montreal, along with his colleague of French background Danièle Routaboule, born in Algeria. Other French citizens who became part of the Canadian design community included Tunisian-born Georges Robert, who combined the skills of landscape architecture and city planning during his long practice as a design consultant based in Trois-Rivières, and Georges Hou-plain, who left his native France to undertake a fruitful career with the municipal government of Quebec City.

John Schreiber, born in Poland, arrived in Montreal in 1951 after graduating in architecture from the University of Glasgow, to begin a productive career as a designer and builder of highly original projects and as a professor at McGill University. Janina Nalesc-Korckuc Stensson was also of Polish origin; already a well-known landscape architect in the land of her birth before her marriage to Vilhelm "Bill" Stensson, she moved to Ontario in 1958, becoming a partner in the historic office of Dunington-Grubb and Stensson. From northern Europe, Latvians Val Lapins and Edwin Skapsts both came to Montreal, where Skapsts would become the head of the city's landscape architecture team. Their compatriot Alexander Budrevics settled in Toronto, where he opened his office in 1950 – an office that continues to operate today under the direction of Arnis Budrevics, his son. Sigurd Hoff from Norway played an essential role in the design of parks, roads, and urban planting for the government of Saskatchewan.[47] Hans Hageraats, originally from the Netherlands, also practised his profession in the governmental milieu, as the head of landscape architecture at the federal Ministry of Public Works in Ottawa. Jan Hoedeman, also of Dutch birth, long practised in both private and academic sectors at Quebec City and Montreal, while Belgian native Alfred de Vynck worked primarily in the public sector and was a mainstay of the Quebec professional association.

Despite the brief periods that British-born Denis Wilkinson and Desmond Muirhead spent in Canada, both had an important impact on the early modern landscapes of their respective cities of Winnipeg and Vancouver. Other landscape architects of British origin, Phil Tattersfield and Michael Hough, settled permanently in Canada, enjoying long and illustrious careers in their adopted cities of Vancouver and Toronto as designers of innovative projects and leaders of the profession.

American Transplants: Quiet Competence

A third wave of landscape architects, this time from the United States, joined the other two groups during the 1960s and early 1970s. They came in response to an extraordinary expansion of demand for landscape architects in Canada, while the United States was undergoing a period of instability. Largely recruited from the Midwest heartland of the country, many had mixed academic backgrounds combining baccalaureates from the land-grant colleges with master's degrees from Harvard, Berkeley, or the University of Pennsylvania, three of the best-known university centres for this discipline. Such training provided them with a practical and detailed knowledge of the profession, along with a larger overall perspective. This was an excellent preparation for roles in teaching and in directing design teams, principally in the private sector. Like the Europeans, they settled in all parts of the country: Peter Klynstra from Illinois became an influential presence in the Maritimes; John Lantzius from Harvard Graduate School of Design and Don Vaughan from the University of Oregon brought innovative design contributions to British Columbia; and Charlie Thomsen from Illinois came to teach in Winnipeg, where James Taylor from Iowa had already begun a career that would subsequently take him to Calgary and eventually to an academic post at Guelph. Warner Goshorn directed the landscape architecture office at the City of Montreal; Walter Kehm and Richard Strong, graduates from Harvard, and Jim Stansbury were much involved in professional and university circles at Toronto and Guelph; and Cecelia Paine, from Illinois, worked in both the public and the private sector in Ottawa before undertaking a teaching career at the University of Guelph. In the public sector, the National Capital Commission in Ottawa benefited greatly from the expertise of transplanted American landscape architects, including that of King Harvey, Bob Hosler, Jim Clark, and many others.

New Multidisciplinary Offices

Inevitably, this influx of Americans and the reintegration of Canadians who had been educated in the United States led to an increasingly American definition of landscape architecture in Canada. The broad influence of the US model touched as much on design methodologies and the visual signature of designed landscapes as on questions of office organization and management. One aspect of this Americanization was the establishment of large multidisciplinary firms that, while often led by landscape architects, included professionals from other disciplines (engineering, architecture, urbanism, natural sciences, etc.), creating organizations with the skills and competence needed to handle large-scale, complex projects.

The trend began in Toronto with the formation of Project Planning Associates in the 1950s (see chapter 19); it continued in the 1960s, which saw the creation of Sasaki Strong, founded by Richard Strong in association with the director of his alma mater, the Harvard landscape school, Hideo Sasaki (1919–2000, founder of one of the most influential offices in the United States) and Hough Stansbury, formed by Michael Hough and Jim Stansbury.[48] The pattern repeated itself in western Canada: the Man Taylor Muret office was founded in Winnipeg in 1966, bringing together Cameron Man and James Taylor, former classmates at Berkeley, and engineer Claude Muret. The striking success of this firm led to its rapid expansion to Calgary and Vancouver, where it combined with the office of John Lantzius. Now a multi-city operation, it brought in experts in biology, geography, and economics so that it could respond to new opportunities offered by environmental projects in northern Canada, reconstituting itself as the Lombard North Group Ltd.[49] The office of Hilderman Crosby Feir Witty was also established in Winnipeg, following a similar model.[50]

Subsequently, a second generation of large multidisciplinary offices was born, often through permutations and combinations of the personnel of the first generation, as experienced associates set out to try their wings in new partnerships. These new offices included Johnson Sustronk Weinstein in Toronto; Landplan Collaborative Ltd. in Guelph and its associated firm Pacific Landplan Collaborative in Vancouver; and EDA Collaborative in Toronto. In Ottawa, the offices of Parkway Planning, Donald W. Graham and Associates, and Corush Laroque Sunderland took on large master planning projects that were coming on stream, as did the Halifax-based firm CBCL Ltd, which absorbed a Montreal-based city planning office that employed Peter Klynstra in 1972. In Montreal, planner Jean-Claude La Haye and architect Jean Ouellet created a highly competent multidisciplinary firm that was to serve as a training ground for many future landscape architects and other professionals. All the above firms were well placed and well structured, ready for the new challenges of the times.

Expo 67 and Its Impacts

The greatest of these challenges – and the climax of the Urban Renaissance – was Expo 67 in Montreal, built on a natural and artificial archipelago in the middle of the St. Lawrence River in celebration of the centennial of Canadian Confederation in 1967. For the site of the "world exposition," Mayor Jean Drapeau and his advisers decided to consolidate the many large and small islands, rocks, shoals, and sandbars of the river in order to create a single large urban park, making a reality of Frederick Todd's dream of thirty years before (see chapter 18),[51] and of proposals from other designers in previous decades, dating as far back as 1895.[52] The

20.19   Bird's-eye view of Expo 67, Montreal, July 1967. View from the southwest, showing the parks of Île Notre-Dame in the foreground, Île Saint-Hélène beyond, and the Island of Montreal in the background. The pavilions of Canada, Ontario, Quebec, France, and Great Britain line the large lagoon in the middle of the photo; the Americans' geodesic dome and the Soviet Union's massive pavilion confront each other, in full Cold War symbolism, across the narrow channel between the islands.

construction of this site proved to be an epic struggle. It required virtually all the excavation materials from the building of Montreal's Metro and several downtown projects, collected over a period of years, to furnish the necessary fill.[53] With this material, supplemented by enormous amounts of rock from the river, the Expo Corporation enlarged St. Helen's Island, both upstream and downstream, and created a new island beside it, Île Notre-Dame; the two islands were separated by a narrow channel; and one of the quays of Montreal's port, renamed Cité du Havre, completed the site.[54]

Under the director of installations, Colonel Edward S. Churchill, and the chief architect, Édouard S. Fiset,[55] the enormous park gradually took form according to a master plan. The first draft of this brilliant document was put together rapidly

URBAN RENAISSANCE 439

20.20 Walkway to the inverted pyramid Katimavik – "meeting place" – in the Canada Pavilion at Expo 67

in a hectic "charrette" – an intensive collaborative design session – by a small group of designers in 1963. The team was first led by Claude Robillard, Montreal's director of planning and a close confidant of Drapeau's, but following Robillard's premature death, responsibility was passed to local planners Sandy van Ginkel and Blanche Lemco van Ginkel, Montreal architect André Blouin, landscape architect Macklin Hancock of Project Planning, and architects Ray Affleck and Fred Lebensold of Arcop, among others.[56] The preliminary plan that emerged from this intense collaboration among very different personalities was then developed in detail over the next two years by design teams responsible for each sector of the site. Architects and planners Moshe Safdie, Adèle Naudé, Jerry Miller, and Steven Staples, who had previously played important roles during the master-planning

440 BIRTH OF THE MODERN LANDSCAPE

stage, were among those who directed these teams.[57] The plan envisioned a continuous web of canals, lakes, grand plazas, pedestrian ways, and parklands as a magnificent setting for national, provincial, commercial, and thematic pavilions. The "World's Fair" explored many aspects of its principal theme, "Man and His World," inspired by French author Antoine de Saint-Exupéry's book *Terre des hommes*.[58] Its goal was to celebrate the role of the individual in the progress of civilization – a profoundly optimistic and positive philosophy, typical of the 1960s when all things seemed possible. More than a mere commercial exposition, Expo 67 sought to achieve lofty goals in terms of cultural communication and urban innovation. And physically, the coherent and structured organization of the site somehow tied together the heterogeneous collection of pavilions that was typical of such expositions, avoiding any sense of visual discontinuity.

Landscape architects, city planners, and architects played a determining role in the design and realization of Expo 67. The complexity and scale of the project, and the centrality of landscape to the concept of the exposition, required the services of virtually every landscape architect practising in Canada and of many who came temporarily from abroad; some fifty to sixty landscape architects were involved in the overall project, including the pavilions and public spaces.[59] The office of Sasaki, Strong, and James E. Secord planned the amusement centre La Ronde; a consortium comprising Project Planning Associates (with Macklin Hancock acting as porte-parole), Dunington-Grubb and Stensson (represented by Janina Stensson), and Austin Floyd planned the exhibition sector of Île Notre-Dame; while Donald W. Graham and Associates, in collaboration with Georges Daudelin and Otis Bishopric, laid out the extensive park in the southwestern sector of the island, a network of lakes and ponds in a seemingly natural environment of wooded glades and hills.[60] Don Graham played an essential role in ensuring landscape coherence throughout the entire site, based on an expression of the Canadian landscape from the Atlantic provinces to British Columbia. Robert Calvert, of Project Planning, was the central "organization man" who coordinated the timing and logistics of the many landscape architectural contracts involved in the project.[61] Pierre Bourque, a young horticultural engineer recently returned from his studies at Vilvoorde in Belgium,[62] directed on-site planting work throughout this enormous park.

The individual pavilions and other installations also featured elaborate and original landscape treatments, integrated with the general concept. Children's World, designed by John Schreiber, created a fantasy world centred on an antique merry-go-round. At the Canada Pavilion, Cornelia Hahn Oberlander created the "Creative Centre for Play" for children aged five to twelve, complete with mounds, a tunnel, a grand canal with a Nova Scotia dory – everything to stimulate children's creativity, a concept that she would develop in the ensuing years through her work with the Children's Task Force on Play at CMHC and her designs for some fifty imaginative playgrounds.[63] Douglas Harper, a landscape architect from Montreal,[64] and John Lantzius designed the landscape for Habitat 67, the revolutionary housing complex conceived by young Montreal architect Moshe Safdie.[65] Landscape architects who worked for the City of Montreal, coordinated by department head Warner S. Goshorn, laid out the gardens for the Alcan Aquarium at La Ronde and planned

URBAN RENAISSANCE 441

20.21 "Creative Centre for Play" at the Canada Pavilion, Expo 67. The Nova Scotia dory was a popular attraction throughout the summer of 1967.

several other sites. Louis Perron was responsible for the landscape design of three sites, including the Rose Garden situated on St. Helen's Island. The principal public plaza on the site, the imposing Place des Nations, was the work of architect André Blouin.

Expo 67 was a miniature city, experimental and revolutionary, a magical place widely viewed as a prototype for a new urban vision and a model for the real cities of the twentieth century. It offered, for instance, a redefinition of urban transportation: several innovative movement systems linked Expo 67 together, including a sleek elevated monorail, the cozy "Minirail" people-mover, pedestrian walkways, bicycle chariots, even canal boats... everything but the car! It brought together the most imaginative architecture and industrial design of the time. Original benches, light standards, and other site furniture, designed by Luis F. Villa and Frank Macioge Associates, contributed greatly to the overall ambiance of Expo;[66] Montreal industrial designer Norman Slater also contributed to site lighting and signage. Many buildings were memorable, and two among them became iconic symbols of the era: Habitat 67, the much-admired residential milieu and technical tour-de-force; and the American Pavilion, an elegant manifestation of the geodesic dome invented by R. Buckminster Fuller.

Expo 67 was a great success for Canada. Some 50 million visitors came to the exposition, easily satisfying the initial goal of improving communication throughout the world. The technical triumphs and social collaboration it engendered were remarkable. At the annual meeting of the International Federation of Landscape Architects (IFLA) held in Montreal in 1968, the president of the federation called

442   BIRTH OF THE MODERN LANDSCAPE

Expo 67 "the most important landscape architectural project of the twentieth century"![67]

Projects influenced by Expo 67

The most successful World's Fair in modern times, Expo 67 set the agenda for all such expositions that have taken place since 1967, each of which has been called "Expo" and has emulated the Montreal model of cultural communication and exploration of new urban visions. Expo 67 also influenced many similar projects involving the close integration of natural and man-made landscape. Among these was Toronto's Ontario Place, a great exploitation of that city's Lake Ontario waterfront, which had been neglected for decades. Realized in 1970 according to the designs of landscape architects Hough, Stansbury, Michalski Ltd., this multi-purpose amusement and education park on a three-island site in Toronto's harbour integrated an open-air amphitheatre, a huge children's play centre, and a number of up-to-date technical exhibits, housed in several spectacular pavilions designed by architect Eberhard Zeidler.

Founding of the Provincial Associations and Professional Schools

A less obvious but equally important effect of Expo 67 was the greater visibility given two young professions, landscape architecture and industrial design, which

20.22 Innovative and extensive water-park playground at Ontario Place, Toronto, integrating many different forms of play and types of play equipment. This was one of the earliest and most successful such installations.

URBAN RENAISSANCE 443

undoubtedly stimulated the founding of programs in the two disciplines at the University of Montreal in 1968. The influx of landscape architects to Quebec before Expo 67 had already encouraged the establishment of the Association des architectes paysagistes du Québec (AAPQ) in 1965. These two events were of crucial importance to the growth and recognition of the profession in Quebec, and they were paralleled by similar developments across Canada.

Since, in Canada, the provincial governments are in charge of regulating the professions, the setting up of provincial associations is an essential step for every profession that is seeking recognition. The landscape architects of British Columbia were the first in the country to organize at the provincial level, in 1961, when they formed an association that in 1964 would be named the "British Columbia Society of Landscape Architects" (BCSLA). They succeeded in their quest for professional recognition in 1968, thanks to the dedicated work of Phil Tattersfield and John Neill, among others, when the BC government reserved the use of the title "landscape architect" to members of the BCSLA.[68] The Quebec association, following its formation in 1965 under first president Warner S. Goshorn, also sought official recognition of the profession of landscape architecture, but in 1974, despite the efforts of Danièle Routaboule and other members, the government of Quebec refused their request. However, use of the professional title is nonetheless protected by a long-term understanding with the Ordre des architectes du Québec, the professional association of the province's architects. The campaign for official recognition proceeded more smoothly in Ontario, where the efforts of a province-wide professional association, created in 1968 from the "central chapter" of the CSLA, were rewarded in 1983 by a provincial law reserving their title. Gradually, landscape architects from the other provinces, regions, and territories became sufficiently numerous to form associations in all jurisdictions across the country. These associations now sponsor a great variety of educational activities for their members, administer procedures for admission to practice, and organize many programs for the promotion of the profession.

Professional education was the other *sine qua non* to ensure the continuity of the profession of landscape architecture in Canada, the only certain means of providing a dependable supply of new recruits. Already in the early 1950s, Howard Dunington-Grubb had raised this point with the government of Ontario.[69] These discussions would finally bear fruit in 1964 with the creation of the first landscape architecture program in a Canadian university, at the University of Guelph – newly created on the foundations of the old Ontario Agricultural College – under the direction of Victor Chanasyk. In 1965, a second landscape architecture program opened its doors at the University of Toronto, with Michael Hough and Richard Strong as founding directors.[70] In Quebec, Louis Perron had taught courses on a variety of landscape architectural subjects for many years, both at Montreal's École des Beaux-Arts and at Macdonald College of McGill University. In the 1960s, he addressed a brief to the Parent Commission, which had been formed to modernize Quebec's education system, urging the creation of a school of landscape architecture at university level. His efforts were crowned with success in 1968 with the fusion of two pre-existing institutions, the Institut d'urbanisme and the

École d'architecture, to create a new Faculty of Environmental Design (Faculté de l'aménagement) at the University of Montreal. The faculty offered a new four-year program in landscape architecture, the only French-language program in North America, under the direction of Douglas Harper, a veteran of Expo 67.[71] Shortly thereafter, the University of Manitoba inaugurated a course of study in landscape architecture, offering a professional training program at the master's level in 1972, with Alexander Rattray as director. On the West Coast, University of British Columbia horticulture professor and campus landscape architect John Neill had long taught courses in landscape and horticulture. Finally in 1970, he became the founder and first director of a bachelor's program in landscape architecture at UBC, located in the Department of Botanic Science.[72]

The emergence of provincial associations, the founding of five university degree programs, a three-year diploma program at Ryerson Polytechnical Institute (today Ryerson University) in Toronto, and college-level courses in several provinces produced a growing stream of young Canadian professionals who rapidly took their places in the fast-growing profession. These new landscape architects – "made in Canada" – found work in public, parapublic, and private sectors, and many founded their own firms, in outlying regions as well as in big cities. The scale and quantity of professional work continued to expand, and already, at the end of the 1970s, a changing of the guard was evident. The founding generation slowly began to step back, while the graduates of the new Canadian schools moved forward into increasingly important roles.

The Democratization of Learning: New and Expanded University Campuses

The accession of the discipline of landscape architecture to university status was characteristic of a general cross-Canada trend of the 1960s and 1970s: the expansion and democratization of higher education. Under the double impulsion of the baby boom and a revolutionary commitment to make a university education available to all qualified students, new programs, new faculties, and entirely new universities were created across the country to respond to the needs of the postwar society for specialized expertise. From this time forward, each province saw education as the keystone of its continued prosperity and the birthright of its citizens.

During the late 1960s, almost all existing universities saw great expansion. Increases in student registrations from 5,000 to 25,000 were not unusual. Most campuses had to be replanned to permit the construction of new buildings and to accommodate the now universal presence of the automobile. The response to the latter often involved the entire reorganization of the vehicular circulation network within the campus, locating parking areas and access roads on the periphery, served by a loop road, thus reserving the heart of the university precinct for pedestrians. Typical of such reorganization was that carried out at the University of Manitoba in Winnipeg between 1958 and 1965, following renovation plans prepared successively by professors of architecture Arthur Mudry and James Stovel, the office of Sasaki, Walker and Associates in Boston, Denis Wilkinson, and Bob Allsopp.[73]

Wilkinson also prepared detailed plans for several landscape areas within the campus, including extensive green areas and intimate paved courtyards.[74]

Newly constructed universities and colleges were often configured in accordance with the same strategy. At the University of Victoria, founded in 1963, a circular service road enclosed a continuous pedestrian precinct in which the main university buildings were organized around a central university quadrangle. The campus plan was designed by architects Wurster, Bernardi and Emmons and landscape architect Lawrence Halprin of San Francisco, along with local landscape offices Justice and Webb, John Lantzius, and Don Vaughan and Associates. The Canadian Coast Guard College, built in the 1970s by the federal government near Sydney, Nova Scotia, followed the same spatial archetype. The landscape design of this campus, laid out by Reinhart Petersmann, attempted to achieve a harmonious integration of the developed zones of the campus with the surrounding forested environment.

Elsewhere in the Maritimes, the Université de Moncton in New Brunswick was created in 1963 as the flagship francophone university in the region. The university's site plan was laid out by planner Georges Robert, landscape architect Danièle Routaboule, and Jean Issalys as a series of academic and residential clusters disposed around cloister-like pedestrian spaces, designed to provide shelter from winds and linked together to form a car-free central mall. Parking and service areas were located, as usual, at the periphery of the campus.[75]

Georges Robert's office also worked closely with architect Jean-Marie Roy (1925–2011) on a remarkable project in the western sector of the Quebec City urban area. The *Campus intercommunautaires de Saint-Augustin* at Cap Rouge brought together several institutions of higher education, representing religious communities that had previously worked in isolation. The institutions were housed in distinct, jewel-like white pavilions arranged in a complex, asymmetrical configuration dictated by topography, held together by an elegant modernist site and planting plan by landscape architects Georges Daudelin and Danièle Routaboule.[76] In contrast, the layout of the new campus of Laval University at Sainte-Foy in the suburbs of Quebec City, designed by architect and planner Édouard Fiset, remained markedly traditional. The adoption of the ring road and peripheral parking schema (described above) permitted Laval's central academic area to be planned around a great pedestrian green space, consisting of a broad north-south mall intersected by a transverse east-west axis, one branch of which terminated on the university's symmetrical and traditional chapel-seminary building.[77] Seen from the air, the classical axis and cross-axis plan of the central pedestrian space forms a giant cross, about which the university buildings are laid out in an orderly fashion. But aside from details of the chapel and the occasional Quebec or university flag, this is the only cross to be seen. Founded in 1852 as a religious institution, Laval was now the principal secular university in the capital region, and its move to the suburbs was the outward and visible signal of this dramatic secularization. Thus, an interesting paradox: the traditional institution at Cap Rouge was expressed in a strikingly modernist landscape vocabulary, while that at Sainte-Foy, which represented a revolutionary educational philosophy and opened higher education to a

20.23 Layout and landscape plan of the Campus intercommunautaires, Cap-Rouge, QC, 1965–68. George Robert, city planner, and Jean-Marie Roy, architect. Drawn by Danièle Routaboule.

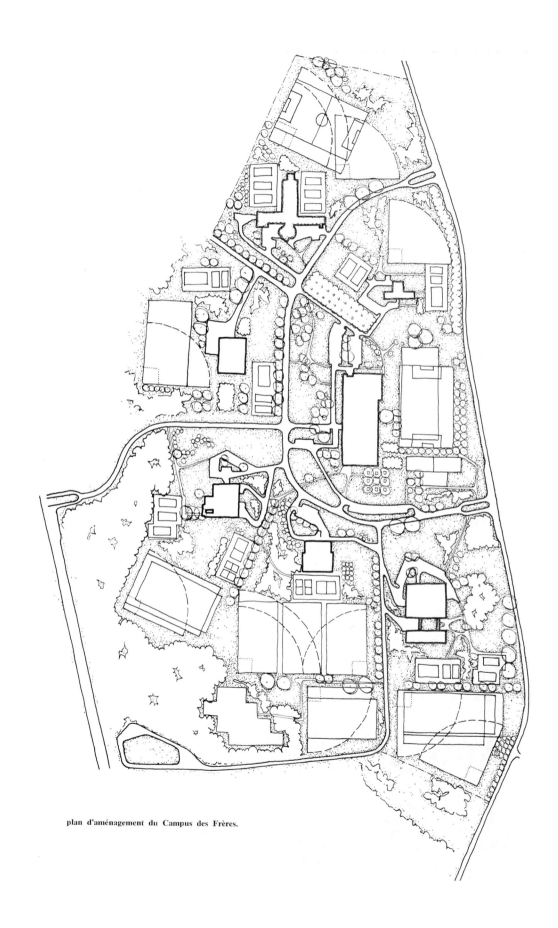

plan d'aménagement du Campus des Frères.

20.24 Entrance to the pedestrian passage providing access to the hilltop campus of the Université de Montréal, Montreal

greatly expanded student body, was laid out on traditional design principles seen in western Canada sixty years before, with ancestry dating back to the University of Virginia in the early 1800s. This paradox helps illuminate the complex and nuanced course of the Quiet Revolution in Quebec, where the Catholic Church was a key agent – in its sponsorship of modern ideas in architecture and landscape, as in some other fields – of the societal changes that were rapidly to diminish its own power and influence.

The Université de Montréal, once a colony of Laval and now Quebec's largest university, also undertook an ambitious expansion program in the 1960s, expanding into the undeveloped sectors of its existing site on the north side of Mount Royal. Besides locating many new buildings around newly created public spaces, the multidisciplinary design firm La Haye-Ouellet-Reeves resolved the access problems bequeathed by Ernest Cormier's brilliant and monumental 1920s campus plan. Their design brought pedestrians and vehicles from the flat plain below to the main campus on the plateau above: pedestrians via an ingenious underground moving ramp (later linked to the Metro), vehicles by a sweeping and elegant new parkway.

Ontario's college and university system also experienced tremendous growth in the 1960s and 1970s. The provincial government established or authorized a number of entirely new universities in areas of the province hitherto unserved. The expansion of existing institutions was guided by new and comprehensive master plans that tried to create environments conducive to learning, employing redesigned pedestrian and vehicular circulation systems (carefully separated for security and comfort), extensive planting and paving, and pleasant public spaces.

448 BIRTH OF THE MODERN LANDSCAPE

Landscape architecture firms elaborated many of these projects, including those of Donald W. Graham and Associates at the University of Ottawa and Carleton University in Ottawa.

In 1964, Macklin Hancock returned to his alma mater, formerly the Ontario Agricultural College and now the University of Guelph, to prepare a new master plan for the expansion of that venerable institution. He devoted all of the central areas of the university to pedestrians and relocated all access roads and parking areas to the circumference, where he concealed them with planted mounds. Hancock created a main pedestrian street, paved with brick, that traversed the entire campus from south to north, linking together the principal campus spaces and historic buildings and serving as a main circulation spine. Around a central public node, situated at the crossing of this pathway and the principal east-west artery of

20.25 Great central assembly space and monumental staircase leading to the Academic Quadrangle at Simon Fraser University, Burnaby, BC

20.26   Westward view from the coulee towards the principal building of the University of Lethbridge, AB

the campus, were grouped the principal public buildings of the university, including the Student Centre and Library.

Many of the new universities that were founded during this period brought forward exciting innovations in landscape and architecture, particularly in the dramatic and well-integrated siting of what were called "megaprojects." In the suburbs of Toronto, architect John Andrews and landscape architect Michael Hough worked together to integrate Scarborough College with its site on the edge of a long lacustrine terrace, so convincingly that the building itself seems to have become a geological feature. Vancouver's Simon Fraser University (1963–67), located at the summit of suburban Burnaby Mountain, was conceived by its architects Erickson and Massey as an "acropolis of learning."[78] The university buildings enclosed a series of majestic outdoor spaces, including the *stepscape* of its great central gallery[79] and the green university quadrangle, treated in powerful geometric fashion by landscape architect John Lantzius, with the assistance of project landscape architect Don Vaughan. Architect Arthur Erickson was also the designer of another icon of Canadian architecture and landscape, the University of Lethbridge (1967) in southern Alberta. In the wide-open, virtually treeless golden landscape of the Oldman River valley, Erickson's great, simple, and implacably horizontal building

20.27 Champlain College of Trent University, located along the Otonabee River in Peterborough, ON. At the rear of this photo, a glacial-era drumlin, typical of this part of Ontario, provides spatial definition to the campus. This view from the bridge, looking northwest, shows the complete consistency of materials sought by architect Ron Thom to create a harmonious overall environment for the campus.

parallels the river far below, bridging right across a tributary coulee and recalling the form of the historic mile-long High Level Bridge to the east.

Trent University (1964–68), beautifully integrated into the rolling landscape of glacial-era drumlins along the Otonabee River in Peterborough, Ontario, is another great academic environment. Its architect, Ron Thom, had gained fame as one of the pioneers of the modernist residence in Vancouver (see chapter 19). Thom, who seemed to have an innate comprehension of the landscape, based his design for the overall site on the traditional layout of medieval residential colleges.[80] As chief designer for the Thompson, Berwick and Pratt office in Vancouver, Thom also orchestrated the reprise of a traditional monastic institution at Massey College, University of Toronto, surely one of the finest academic spaces in the country (1963).[81]

The landscape, architectural, and planning achievements of the 1960s and 1970s are among the most innovative and most appreciated projects ever undertaken in Canada. In some cases, their originality and their consummate execution have placed them among the best projects worldwide of the era. For the first time, Canadian designs influenced realizations across the planet, instead of faithfully following international prototypes as had always been the case until those remarkable years.

21

Birth of an Environmental Conscience

21.1   Reconstructed wetland, Don Valley, Toronto, adjacent to the Don Valley Brickworks

The central motive of human intervention in the Canadian landscape has always had to do with its subduing and exploitation for economic purposes, but an important secondary theme has frequently played counterpoint to this principal theme: that of the conservation and protection of the environment and the landscape, the pursuit of what we today call *sustainable development*. This dual motivation has animated both society as a whole and the design professions, including landscape architects, who consider themselves to be "stewards of the environment."[1] Over the last forty years, the balance between the two themes seems to have undergone a major shift, expressed in a growing environmental consciousness in professional circles and, thankfully, among the general population of Canada. At the planetary scale, landscape architects have often marched in the vanguard of the environmental movement, and Canadians, whether landscape professionals or not, have made strong contributions to this movement throughout the years.

Sustainable Design: A Historic Legacy

A desire to conserve the environment seems to have been present since the very beginnings of human settlement in Canada. Without idealizing the relations between the First Nations and the environment, it is clear that the Native peoples of Canada managed, exploited, and manipulated the landscape to their advantage for millennia, during which the scale and the impact of their interventions never seriously threatened the landscape resources on which they depended (see chapter 2). Later, in the colonies established by European newcomers, the choice of sites and the disposition of new cities were related to the natural environment in an intelligent and sustainable way. As we have seen (chapters 4 and 5), the settlements of New France and the grid-plan cities of the Maritimes such as Charlottetown, Halifax, and Saint John were often brilliantly integrated into the original topography. Built on sloping sites and plateaus to ensure good drainage and security, these dense, compact towns were always located on excellent sheltered harbours protected from rough water by projecting headlands. They all preserved common green spaces for a variety of purposes: the park along the St. John River in Fredericton, for example, has almost always protected the city from flooding. The founders of other cities often retained outstanding natural features for open-space use, simultaneously protecting their cities from natural disasters and providing them with magnificent parks, such as Montreal's islands and mountain; Toronto's ravines and escarpment, along with the necklace of islands that protects its port; and the Niagara Escarpment at Hamilton, preserved as a forested slope to protect the city below from landslides and erosion. Almost all the cities of the Prairies were built on the plateau, leaving the valleys of the rivers that traverse them in open space, thus avoiding flood damage and providing such cities as Saskatoon, Edmonton, and Lethbridge with splendid linear park systems. On the West Coast, the artistic integration with the natural landscape of Marine Drive, the boulevard that parallels the edge of the sea all around Vancouver's western peninsula, helped enable that city to avoid the urban-freeway invasion of the 1960s and 1970s. The retention of forested slopes along the margin of the peninsula also prevented erosion of the glacial deposits that form the substrate of most of Vancouver, a sensible protection measure. Many of these far-seeing acts of preservation and design have resulted in landscapes that are central elements of their respective cities, creating an environmental legacy from which we have much to learn.

But this environmental wisdom was far from universal. As we have seen, the exploitation of Canada's vast territories for furs, wood, and other riches of the land and sea did much to devastate rural and wilderness landscapes. Similarly, the impacts of nineteenth-century industrialization and urbanization made the cities of that era all but unliveable, polluted with smoke and dust and ravaged by disease and social conflict. These episodes of devastation subsequently inspired programs of reform and mitigation that at least partially redressed the situation.

Governments were much involved in these programs of environmental protection. At the beginning of the twentieth century, the federal government, with its creation of the Commission of Conservation, set in place an energetic watchdog organization charged with monitoring the supply of all the country's resources, in collaboration with the appropriate agencies, and assuring their long-term sustainability (see chapters 12 and 17). The disbanding of this commission in 1921 constituted a major defeat for the conservation of Canada's resources.[2] In the 1930s, the Prairie Farm Rehabilitation Act promoted a number of effective strategies to combat the terrible droughts of that period,[3] while research carried out at the experimental farms and stations across the country produced new knowledge, new plant varieties, and new soil conservation techniques to help overcome the agricultural crisis.[4]

Pioneers of Conservation in Canada

Across the country, through their research and publications, many individuals advanced the cause of environmental conservation. Born into an Ontario farming family in 1902, George Angus Hills began a farming career on the Prairies in 1919, later pursuing studies at the Ontario Agricultural College (OAC) at Guelph, starting in 1934. Through his work on the Ontario soil survey, Hills became an expert pedologist and subsequently elaborated a soil classification system that linked the characteristics of soil profiles to local environmental conditions. His system of analysing soils helped to explain their influence on agricultural production and their capacity to resist deterioration.[5] Hills then went to work for the Ontario Department of Lands and Forests in 1944, where he focused his research on the soils in the northern reaches of the province (including the rich lands of the Clay Belt) so as to identify the most promising locations for agricultural development. He later directed the province's research work in forest productivity, from 1954 to 1967.[6] These diverse experiences helped Hills to develop a comprehensive system of land classification for agricultural, forestry, recreational, and other purposes. His 1961 publication, *The Ecological Basis of Land Use Planning*, became a classic work in the field of land analysis and planning. Some of the concepts and tools developed by Hills are universally employed today in landscape planning at the regional scale: the division of natural continuums into graduated classes for

21.2 Angus Hills, c. 1972, and Pierre Dansereau, 1984

purposes of analysis and comparison; the concepts of *capability*, *suitability*, and *feasibility* for their potential applications to sites and landscapes; the division of large territories into *landscape units*; and the use of alternative hypothetical scenarios to explore the likely impacts of different interventions in the landscape.[7]

Pierre Dansereau (1911–2011) was another leader in this domain, a pioneer who has always been in the avant-garde of the environmental movement. Born in Outremont, Quebec, Dansereau obtained his baccalaureate in arts at the University of Montreal and in science at the Institut agricole d'Oka (an early indication of his intellectual versatility) before undertaking doctoral studies in plant taxonomy at the University of Geneva. A disciple and collaborator of Frère Marie-Victorin (see chapter 18), he was one of the first to teach ecology at the University of Montreal, from 1940 to 1950. Dansereau then continued his academic career in the United States, as a professor at the University of Michigan and at Columbia, and served as assistant director of the New York Botanical Garden before returning to the Montreal university milieu, where he taught at both the University of Montreal and the newly founded Université du Québec à Montréal (UQAM). His international research, carried out in such diverse locations as Brazil and New Zealand, helped him to develop a broad overview that was evident in his classic volume *Biogeography: An Ecological Perspective*, published in 1957. This book painted a comprehensive portrait of the field of ecology and touched on questions of conservation and urban ecosystems. The importance of his insights may be seen in the fact that, for decades, references to his book continued to appear in ecology texts by other authorities.[8] He later elaborated a detailed model of the interactions among the various components of the ecosphere, social as well as biophysical.[9] The fact that the Science Pavilion at UQAM, where he taught for many years, today bears his name is a clear indication of the esteem that his contributions to ecology have merited.

These two Canadian pioneers of ecology and environmental planning provided outstanding early examples of ways to understand the environment and to make decisions that affect it positively. The events of the following decades were to bring their theories and methods of analysis to prominence.

The 1960s: Public Concern for the Environment

In response to accelerating demand for natural resources during the postwar period, governments once again became interested in the study and inventorying of these resources. In 1961, the federal government began the Canada Land Inventory (CLI), a system of ecological information and analysis that could serve as a basis for decision-making on land allocation and use.[10] The land classification system developed by Angus Hills in the 1950s greatly influenced the structure and content of the CLI.

In the early 1960s, in parallel with governmental and university-based initiatives, the North American public evinced a new and growing interest in landscape and the environment. Throughout the continent, the postwar period had seen an unprecedented expansion of mining and industrial operations, along with rapid suburban expansion and, in Canada, the opening of the North. This growing economic activity brought prosperity and increased demand for materials and products of all kinds, leading inevitably to increasing impacts on rural, urban, and wilderness environments. Air and water pollution and the accelerating destruction of natural landscapes did much to arouse a new environmental preoccupation. Touched off by the American scientist Rachel Carson's famous book *The Silent Spring* (1962), an ecological movement – based on a collective environmental epiphany, a *prise de conscience* – was sweeping through university and professional circles everywhere in North America, and landscape architects were at its forefront.

New Tools for Landscape Analysis

Regional planning – the systematic planning of a natural landscape region – became a useful means of organizing long-term use of the environment and the landscape. This was still landscape architecture, but at a very large scale. To manipulate the immense amount of information that one had to have to work at this scale, new tools were needed. Such tools were developed in the late 1960s, primarily at American universities. Professor Ian McHarg at the School of Architecture of the University of Pennsylvania invented a system of map overlays of ecological, social, and economic information that brought rigour and logic to the making of decisions that would have an impact on the environment. McHarg's 1969 book, *Design with Nature*, expresses the writer's Faustian philosophy, profoundly influenced by his childhood memories of both the industrial slums of Glasgow and the green hills of the Scottish countryside.[11] It describes his principal projects as a series of attempts to insert human infrastructures rationally into landscapes that are under pressure of development. McHarg explains in detail his methodology for relating the varying capacities of different sites to the biophysical demands made on them by various human uses so as to create development plans that would integrate ecological and social considerations.[12]

   McHarg's simple but effective methodology led to computerized systems for land analysis and the testing of alternative development scenarios, making use of the "computer-graphics" laboratories of professor Carl Steinitz of Harvard (in which Montreal student Peter Jacobs participated), and finally to the sophisticated GIS (Geographic Information Systems) employed today by a panoply of professions as cartographic tools and occasionally as inputs for decision-making processes. Other new methods included a systematic approach to the study of the *visual impacts* of various types of development within landscapes of differing character. Peter Jacobs and Douglas Way of Harvard University carried out much of the early experimental work in this area towards the end of the 1960s.[13]

Canadian Projects

Several graduates of the programs at Pennsylvania and Harvard – originally from Canada, the United States, or other countries – came or returned to Canada in the late 1960s and early 1970s, bringing with them a new gospel of ecological design. Michael Hough, following his studies with Ian McHarg at Pennsylvania, moved to Toronto and, working with several generations of associates, including James Stansbury and Carolyn Woodland, applied his unique perspective to environmental projects in northern Ontario and many other locations.[14] His office developed, in collaboration with the government of Ontario, the *Lakealert* strategy, a set of guidelines for cottage developments adjacent to lakes, seeking to avoid the twin problems of encirclement and eutrophication that were, until that time, their likely destiny.[15]

In western Canada, other offices undertook similarly ambitious projects of regional analysis and landscape planning. The Lombard North Group, from its offices in Winnipeg, Calgary, and other western cities, worked on environmental impact evaluations for the Mackenzie Valley Highway and the Maple Leaf Line, a pipeline in the North. Their large-scale project in suburban Calgary, Fish Creek Park (realized 1973–81), was the first provincial park to be created by the province of Alberta in an urban region. The designers adopted a policy of conservation for the great majority of the 1,300-hectare site, consisting primarily of the valley of Fish Creek, a stream that passes through the southern margins of the city before joining the Elbow River.[16] Strict ecological zoning permitted the cohabitation of bird sanctuaries with trails for hiking, cross-country skiing, and bicycle riding. More intensive activities were concentrated around an artificial lake used for swimming and skating. Another noteworthy project: in 1977, the office of Hilderman Feir Witty and Associates of Winnipeg and Saskatoon completed a landscape analysis of Last Mountain Lake and Flying Creek, located in Saskatchewan's Qu'Appelle

21.3 Phasing and Staging Plan of Fish Creek Provincial Park, Calgary, 1976, by Lombard North Group Ltd. Based on a detailed ecological analysis, this large-scale landscape planning project defined conservation and development zones (large numbers on plan), proposing a design strategy for each, in a manner similar to that used by Olmsted at Mount Royal Park, Montreal, in 1877.

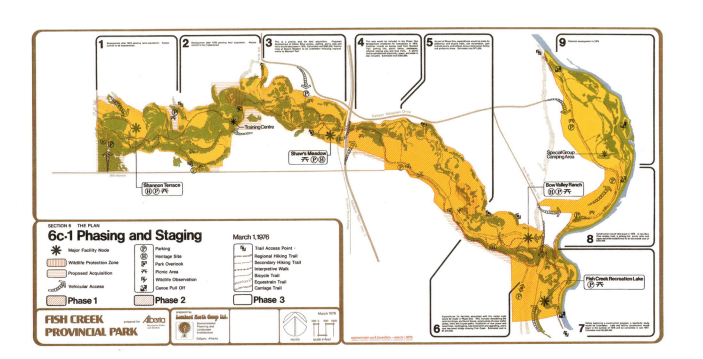

BIRTH OF AN ENVIRONMENTAL CONSCIENCE   457

21.4 Poster for the PEI Ark Project, by Solsearch architects, Charlottetown, 1976. The New Alchemy Institute of Woods Hole, MA, and Souris, PEI, initiated this innovative project with support from the government of Canada. Its central component was a greenhouse-laboratory, powered by solar collectors, direct sun, and a new high-tech windmill that stored heat in rock beds and warm-water fish culture containers. The goal was to create a self-sufficient environment for a family who lived in a dwelling integrated into the main structure. Fanciful lettering and vivid colours, as used in this drawing, were a prominent feature of countercultural graphics.

Valley. Their study of the physical and aesthetic character of this region, a favourite "cottage country" destination for residents of Regina, established the ground rules for subsequent decisions concerning its management and development.[17]

Birth of a "Counter-culture"

Parallel to the technically oriented projects of design professionals, the new environmental consciousness also expressed itself in the pursuit of concrete, direct, on-site experiments. These experiments followed, in general, two opposing scenarios: on the one hand, environments with lower ecological impact were fashioned by using sophisticated new technologies; on the other, idealistic communities were created far from the cities, in landscape settings of great natural beauty, by using simple technologies. Those who embarked on these two forms of experimental discovery were the representatives of a "counter-culture" consisting of small, highly motivated groups of like-minded people all over North America.

A community belonging to the first category, the New Alchemists (John Todd, Nancy Jack Todd, and Bill McLarney) in collaboration with Solsearch Architects (Ole Hammarlund and David Bergmark), created the Ark Project on an isolated site near the coast of Prince Edward Island. They tried to make a closed ecosystem, using only plants, sun, wind, water, and fish. Their highly scientific and systematic project, begun in 1976, sought to avoid dependency on the polluting and dangerous technologies of the times by relying on natural biological processes.[18]

At the other end of the country, at Rose Harbour in Haida Gwaii (formerly the Queen Charlotte Islands) off mainland British Columbia, a different experiment was underway. Several young families and friends attempted to create an autonomous community, far from civilization, based on traditional and even disappearing technologies. Their goal was radical: to live well and self-sufficiently, in harmony with the environment, producing all their food and energy themselves. The site they chose was an old whaling station, the long-abandoned vestige of an over-exploited and ravaged resource. They built their little village by hand with

21.5 Rose Harbour community, Haida Gwaii, BC. Second-growth hemlock, Sitka spruce, and western red cedars shelter the hand-crafted houses of this small "low-tech" village where art and music flourish. Vegetable gardens and abundant fish resources permit a large degree of self-sufficiency. The rusty spherical object at centre right is a vestige of the long-departed whaling industry.

BIRTH OF AN ENVIRONMENTAL CONSCIENCE   459

great creativity, occupying a clearing on a peaceful harbour, sheltered by a forest of giant conifers. Unlike most communities of this type, Rose Harbour has survived to the present day.

Legal Protection

Other responses to the environmental crisis relied on legal and institutional structures. From the beginning of the 1970s, legislatures across the country adopted many new measures to identify, mitigate, and control environmental "insults." These included legal requirements for environmental impact statements on government and some private projects, environmental codes and standards, and the establishment of agricultural zoning in British Columbia (1972)[19] and Quebec (1978), to preserve precious high-quality farmland from rampant urbanization. The territories of both these provinces are immense, but only 2 per cent of the area of Quebec consists of arable land and, in British Columbia, the best agricultural lands among the 5 per cent of its territory that can be farmed are found in the province's most highly urbanized region, the Lower Mainland near Vancouver.

The North: Frontier and Homeland

In 1972, the federal government was confronted with a major environmental challenge when several large companies proposed to build a natural gas pipeline along the valley of the Mackenzie River. This proposal, which coincided with the oil crisis of the early 1970s, envisaged the transport of natural gas from the Mackenzie Delta and the Beaufort Sea (in the Arctic Ocean) to markets in southern Canada and the United States. Parliament appointed a commission of inquiry to evaluate the project in all its ramifications and to ascertain its advantages and disadvantages. The resulting study constituted a critical landmark for all subsequent reflections on the Canadian environment. Chosen in 1974 to direct the inquiry, British Columbia judge Thomas R. Berger organized a series of meetings in every village in the Yukon and Northwest Territories, in order to study the effects of the project on their residents, and commissioned a number of detailed ecological studies. His report, *Northern Frontier, Northern Homeland* (1977), recommended against the construction of a pipeline across the Yukon and proposed a delay of ten years in the construction of a pipeline in the Mackenzie Valley, to allow the time necessary for the settlement of Native land claims and the development of appropriate programs and institutions. Berger also recommended the creation of several parks and wildlife reserves to protect the caribou, belugas, and migratory birds of the Western Arctic. He underlined the indissoluble relationship between cultural and social issues and environmental issues, of particular importance to the Native people of the territories. And finally, Berger proposed a set of guidelines and mitigation measures that would be necessary for the construction of any such infrastructure in the future. His recommendations established a model for projects of this kind. The breadth and depth of the "Berger Report" were exemplary, establishing a high standard for all later work in this field.[20]

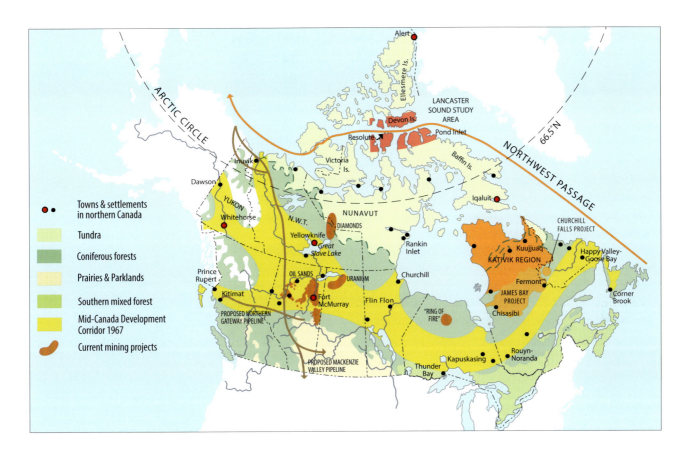

21.6 Development sites and study areas in northern Canada. These are shown in yellow, orange, and red against a background of summary vegetation zones with which they are often associated. Formerly a mere fiction or a vain hope, the Northwest Passage (orange line) is quickly becoming a reality.

Development of the North

The protection of the Canadian North is a dominant environmental concern. It would be easy to consider this immense territory, rich in resources and sparsely populated, as simply an inexhaustible legacy of resources just waiting to be "opened up" to an implacable exploitation for the benefit of southern Canada.[21] This will to exploit was expressed, in subliminal fashion, in the Mid-Canada Development Corridor study, carried out in 1967 by lawyer Richard Rohmer and Acres Research and Planning Limited as a step towards the development of resources in the Canadian North. The Mid-Canada report suggested the construction of new railroads, roads, and industries across a wide band of territory within the boreal forest. This detailed and comprehensive study – a model of its kind – was, however, oriented strongly towards resource development and did not include the human and ecological impacts of northern development within its major areas of concern.[22] But it did present a coherent and integrated long-term approach to northern development, in contrast to the uncoordinated single-resource strategies that were then (and are now) far too common.

The Lancaster Sound Regional Study, published in several volumes in 1982, addressed a much broader field of issues. The federal government commissioned the

BIRTH OF AN ENVIRONMENTAL CONSCIENCE   461

study in response to a proposal to transport oil from the Western Arctic through the Northwest Passage, via Lancaster Sound, to European and southern markets. Placing emphasis on the unique cultures and landscapes of the North, the chair of the public hearings, Peter Jacobs, a professor of landscape architecture at the University of Montreal who had studied regional design at Harvard, insisted on the adoption of a consensual method of decision-making. The imposition of southern technologies was to be avoided, and the application of scientific knowledge to the study was complemented with the insights of *traditional ecological knowledge*,[23] contributed by the Inuit of the High Arctic. The study included an exhaustive cartographic inventory of biophysical and social milieus as well as an evaluation of six alternative development scenarios, varying from *no new development* to the establishment of a *non-renewable resource economy*.[24]

For many years, Jacobs also chaired the regional government agency responsible for evaluating the environmental impacts of projects proposed for northern Quebec. Established after the construction of major hydroelectric projects in the James Bay region, the Kativik Environmental Quality Commission oversaw a great variety of interventions, from gigantic mining projects to infrastructure changes for small municipalities.[25]

Northern Settlements

The construction of mines and dams has profoundly changed the North during the last half-century. To the existing Native villages and camps were added several planned towns, often based on prototypes that came from the South. The village of Chisasibi in Quebec, situated on the southern bank of the Grand River (la Grande Rivière), which flows into James Bay, is a good example. Begun in 1980–81 when the old village of Fort George was scheduled to be abandoned, the construction of Chisasibi (which means "great river" in Cree) was an offshoot of the immense James Bay hydroelectric project undertaken by Hydro-Québec. The planning of the village was aided by a series of scale-model simulations, displayed in group meetings that brought together members of the Cree communities from both coastal and interior areas, Inuit families, non-Natives who were to be future residents of the community, and city planners from the office of Daniel Arbour et associés in Montreal. Architect/city planner Marie Lessard, subsequently a professor at the University of Montreal, acted as director of the design team. The design proposals partially resembled the circular plans of traditional First Nations camps (as described in chapter 2), and the layout of the plan that was finally adopted retained many aspects of these proposals.[26] The overall village plan was similar to that for Radburn, New Jersey (see chapter 19): a series of housing clusters grouped around a large central space, allowing easy pedestrian access to all the larger public buildings in the village centre (school, hospital, shopping/community centre). This plan corresponded to the social structure of the community: very often, extended families would move into the same housing cluster, creating "mini-communities" of relatives.[27] The fragility of the northern environment quickly became evident through the loss of many trees (blown over by the wind as soon as the continuity

21.7 Yellowknife, NWT. From the Bush Pilot's Monument at the top of a rocky park in picturesque Old Town (foreground), the tall buildings of New Town on the plateau are visible on the horizon.

of forest cover was interrupted) and the drying out and subsequent wind erosion of silty surface soils. Despite these setbacks, the creation of artificial soils using sand, native silt, and the rich organic matter provided by a nearby peat bog permitted the re-establishment of vegetation within the village precinct.

The capital of the Northwest Territories, Yellowknife, demonstrates the complexity and richness of urban life in the North.[28] It is a vibrant city, home to a spirit of enterprise and adventure yet still small-scale and familiar, entirely unlike the usual stereotype of a dismal mining town. In fact, seven different towns coexist within its confines. Certainly there is a *mining town*, the municipality's original *raison d'être*, but it is largely invisible today, since the gold mines, now closed in any case, were always outside the main townsite. The unique "*Old Town*," situated on a peninsula in Yellowknife Bay, an arm of the immense Great Slave Lake, was built in random fashion on the rocks of the Shield; everything here is irregular, crooked, and charming.[29] The Native village *N'Dilo*, home of the Dene community, is located at the extremity of an island that is the prolongation of the Old Town peninsula; some of its original brightly painted cabins remain. At a kilometre's distance from the older sections of town, the high-rise buildings of "*New Town*," built primarily in the 1960s, stand atop a plateau, presenting a stunning urban

21.8 Looking south across Frame Lake to the low dome of the NWT Legislative Assembly in Yellowknife

image. This district, which is the downtown area of the city of 12,000 (almost half the population of the Northwest Territories), was laid out in a regular rectangular street grid.[30] In fact, it is almost identical in mission and configuration to the colonial towns of the eighteenth century (see chapter 5), except that the modern buildings lack any cachet and there is no public square. Instead, the steps of the centrally located *post office* stand in as an informal social gathering place.[31] Yet New Town is in many ways a sophisticated and cosmopolitan town centre, boasting many fine urban features.

Beyond the downtown area, *recent suburbs* extend across the plateau; landscape irregularities have here been eliminated in order to create a milieu that resembles the neighbourhoods that surround every city in southern Canada. Another vestige of the rich frontier-town past, a unique and original *house-boat community* – a colourful and eccentric armada of small craft – floats in Yellowknife Bay.

The seventh Yellowknife is most impressive: it is the *symbolic and official precinct* of major institutions, anchored by the Legislative Assembly of the Northwest Territories, built in 1992–94. This building and its landscape setting (the products of a close collaboration among architects Gino Pin, of Pin Matthews, Yellowknife; Matsuzaki/Wright, of Vancouver; and landscape architect Cornelia Hahn Oberlander) constitute a masterpiece of environmental design. The ensemble is

464   BIRTH OF THE MODERN LANDSCAPE

perfectly integrated into its site adjacent to a peat bog and lake, yet only a few minutes' walk from the downtown core. The shallow dome of the Legislative Assembly crowns a circular meeting hall, which represents the process of decision-making by consensus employed by assembly members in their deliberations. The flag of the territories was the first in Canada that did not incorporate a symbol from a European country, just as this building was the first parliament that did not follow a standard spatial model inherited from Europe. In order to unify the assembly and its site, Oberlander preserved the natural vegetation that surrounded the project, and mended construction-damaged areas by carefully transplanting mats of plants and soil to the damaged locations. Since no native plants were available in nurseries in Yellowknife, Oberlander arranged to have seeds gathered from bearberry or kinnikinnick, wild grasses and sedges, saxifrage, and local arctic rose. These seeds were planted and grown in Vancouver, then transplanted to the site two years later, where they survived well as true children of the North.[32] An elegant detail: one approaches the building via a slightly elevated concrete slab, cantilevered out over the adjacent soil, which seems to float over the natural landscape.

Hiatus and Reprise

Towards the end of the 1970s, the ecological movement experienced a distinct loss of momentum. Its victories – laws and regulations, protected landscapes – were assured, but the enthusiasm that had marked its beginnings in the 1960s gradually dissipated. Economic difficulties that continued until the mid-1980s were perhaps among the causes. Landscape architects' concern with the environment somehow diminished in favour of other preoccupations. Even the technical innovations they had pioneered (including GIS) lost much of their interest for practitioners. But a new wave of reflections and realizations was in the works.

21.9   Michael Hough

The City, an Ecosystem

In his book *City Form and Natural Process* (1984), Toronto landscape architect Michael Hough (1928–2013) explored a radical hypothesis: that the city is itself an ecosystem and we must understand it and work with it as such. Hough explores the concept of *urban ecology*, by which the mineral and biological components of the city constitute an ecosystem as authentic as a forest or a desert. He considers this to be a troubled ecosystem, often suffering from a lack of biodiversity, from loss of such resources as rainwater, from an imbalance in chemical nutrients, and from an approach to urban design that favours monoculture and sterility in lieu of biological richness. Hough examines the state of air, water, soil, plants, and animals in the city and exposes our illogical everyday practices, which are – in his view – no way to manage an ecosystem.[33] He provides examples of best practices, sometimes from his own extensive body of work; in 1995 and 2004, in subsequent editions of his book, Hough returns to the projects he had examined in earlier editions, to trace the evolution of key ecosystems over time.

Sustainable Development

Known up until this time as the *ecological movement* or the *conservation movement*, the concern for environmental affairs found a new name in 1987 with the publication of the Brundtland Report, *Our Common Future*, by the United Nations' World Commission on Environment and Development. In the report, the commission's president, Gro Harlem Brundtland of Norway, used the term *sustainable development*. This term was quickly to become the expression of choice to describe the broad but diffuse environmental movement. According to the report, "Sustainable development is development that meets the needs of the present without compromising the ability of future generations to meet their own needs."[34] By its use of the word *development*, the new expression implicitly accepted the necessity of economic progress, which the term *conservation* seemed to oppose.

Since 1987, thanks to the Brundtland Report, the expression "sustainable development" has spread throughout the world, but in fact, the origins of both the term and the concept it expresses had already been invented some years before, and their roots were Canadian. Maurice F. Strong, born in Manitoba in 1929, was secretary general for the first conference organized by the United Nations on the subject of the environment, the Stockholm Conference on the Human Environment, in 1972. A highly competent business person and a champion of conservation, Strong pronounced in his opening address for the conference the basic principles of sustainable development: "There is no fundamental conflict between development and the environment. Environmental factors must be an integral feature of development strategy if the aim of human endeavour is to increase the welfare and not merely to increase the gross national product."[35] Strong asked Barbara Ward and René Dubos to write a preparatory document for the conference; their report, entitled *Only One Earth*, would later become one of the iconic texts of the environmental movement. In his subsequent positions as director of the UN Environment Program in Nairobi, as a member of the Brundtland Commission, and as secretary general of the UN Conference on Environment and Development held in Rio de Janeiro in 1992 (the "Earth Summit"), Strong constantly advocated international cooperation to realize the objectives of sustainable development.[36]

In 1980, the International Union for the Conservation of Nature (IUCN), an agency of the United Nations, adopted the *World Conservation Strategy*. In April of 1984, the president of the IUCN's Environmental Planning Commission, Peter Jacobs, organized an international congress that welcomed the representatives of seventeen countries to Montreal, to discuss the means of achieving sustainable development and to assess the success of realizations to date. The delegates' presentations were, in general, more strongly oriented towards in-depth analyses of problems rather than towards concrete solutions.[37]

The Brundtland Report focused on all of these experiences, and many others, in defining a global policy for the promotion of the ideals of sustainability, bringing environmental concerns before a world audience and incidentally gaining worldwide currency for the now-international expression. The report defined certain fundamental concepts of sustainable development: the primacy of satisfying human needs, in particular of those less favoured economically; the notion of the *carrying capacity* of a landscape, its limited ability to respond to present and future needs, and the corollary that this capacity depends on the degree of technical advancement and the level of social organization; and the necessity to avoid practices that would require elaborate measures of mitigation in the future.

An additional note concerning Canada's relationship to the Brundtland Report: the French translation of the report was carried out by Quebec's Ministry of the Environment. The French version of this vital document, *Notre avenir à tous*, was published in June 1988 and subsequently distributed in francophone milieus worldwide.[38]

Projects Aspiring to Sustainability

Since 1987, there has been a tremendous flowering of projects that sought to put into practice the precepts of sustainable development everywhere in the world. While these projects represented, to some extent, a rebirth of the ecological movement of the 1960s and early 1970s, they went beyond the well-meaning and often unscientific "save the world" approach of that movement by focusing on measurable achievements and realizable – if less heroic – goals. New experts who had benefited from rigorous scientific and ecological education replaced the designers of the "first ecological era," who, despite their dedication to the missions they strove to accomplish, did not always possess the necessary scientific base.[39] The new projects touched on a great variety of different domains, some modest and unassuming, others ambitious, complex, and spectacular.

Green Roofs

A manifestation of the first category is the conversion of inert roofs lacking visual or ecological interest into attractive landscapes, efficient and even productive. During the 1990s, a new generation of "green roof" technology allowed beautiful gardens to be created in unusual locations, while simultaneously reducing the heating costs of buildings and conserving rainwater, thus diminishing the need for artificial drainage and irrigation systems.

Roof gardens have of course existed for some time in Canada, beginning with such innovative projects as Montreal's Hotel Bonaventure Garden, completed in 1966 (see chapter 20). Other gardens and outdoor plazas were constructed on the roofs of underground parking garages in downtown areas all across the country. All of these gardens had the disadvantage of being very heavy, which required massive and expensive reinforced-concrete structures to support them. In the early 1990s, several technical innovations, most of them originating in Europe, made possible a new wave of ultra-light roof gardens. These could be installed on roofs that had never been designed to support gardens, as witnessed by the garden of the Urban Ecology Centre in Montreal.[40] Such gardens could partially answer the open-space needs of disadvantaged neighbourhoods that would derive great benefit from them; such was the case with the roof garden of the Portland

21.10 Reconstituted salmon stream at Mission Creek Greenway, Kelowna, BC

Hotel, a Vancouver residence for homeless people, designed by Cornelia Hahn Oberlander.[41]

Management of Watercourses

The control of surface waters has also made great progress in recent years. The use of retention ponds and check dams, the naturalization of stream and river banks, and direct filtration through the soil were among an ensemble of strategies that sought to prevent floods, diminish the need for investments in underground drainage systems, and provide habitat for fish and waterfowl. In southwestern Alberta, the Pine Coulee Irrigation Project (1996–98), directed by Ron Middleton, landscape architect for the provincial government agency Alberta Infrastructure, integrated mitigation measures into the construction of an irrigation reservoir in order to preserve spawning grounds for pike and to ensure the conservation of balsam poplars along the stream banks.[42] Mission Creek Greenway, at Kelowna in the Okanagan Valley of British Columbia, recreated a stream that had suffered severe impacts at the hands of agriculture, the forest industry, and channelization. The creation of an essentially artificial waterway – although "natural" in both appearance and performance – was the preferred solution to ensure the migration and reproduction of the *kokanee*, the landlocked salmon of British Columbia's interior lakes. At Ruisseau des Hérons on Nuns' Island in Verdun, Quebec, Vincent Asselin of WAA Inc., in collaboration with the engineering firm BGH-Planning, designed a flexible and efficient system to control storm-water flow, thus dramatically reducing the costs of subterranean drainage while creating an attractive watercourse bordered with native plants.

Renaturalization

Planting can make a major contribution to the control of water runoff and of erosion on stream banks and lake margins, as has been demonstrated by its reintroduction in several milieus that had long been denuded of vegetation. *Phytotechnology* has played a central role in the long-term project to regenerate the shores of Lake Ontario, the object of a very detailed study undertaken by a royal commission directed by the former mayor of Toronto, David Crombie, from 1988 to 1992. The thirteen volumes of the study and its final report, *Regeneration: Toronto's Waterfront and the Sustainable City* (1992), proposed an ecosystem-based approach to the design of the diverse zones along the lakeshore and defined a series of objectives and detailed guidelines to regenerate this long-neglected resource.[43] In parallel, the study *Bringing Back the Don* (1991) propounded a plan of action to rehabilitate the Don River on the east side of the city, which had become a polluted and largely canalized watercourse.[44] These studies later took concrete form through a considerable number of specific projects. The multidisciplinary office Hough Woodland Naylor Dance Leinster of Toronto planned and oversaw the renaturalization of the Humber Bay Shores, the severely disturbed delta at the mouth of the Humber River on the west side of the city, integrating a footpath network and intimate, low-impact public gathering places to create an

21.11 Humber Bay Shores rehabilitation project, Toronto, looking east towards the city across rebuilt shorelines and newly planted vegetation

BIRTH OF AN ENVIRONMENTAL CONSCIENCE 469

21.12 (above)   Natural vegetation in Tommy Thompson Park (Leslie Street Spit) on the Toronto waterfront. View to the northwest towards the grain elevator of the Canada Malting Co. in Toronto's industrial sector.

21.13 (below)   Vestiges of the scrap materials used to create Tommy Thompson Park, such as these bricks and blocks eroded by wind and weather, may still be seen among the volunteer growth that is gradually taking over the site.

21.14 (facing page)   Beach Park, Île Notre-Dame (Parc Jean-Drapeau), Montreal. Natural processes played a central role in maintaining the water quality of this urban beach, designed to appear as natural as possible and to recall the lakes and country hotels of the Laurentians. The Bathing Pavilion at left was designed by architects Reeves, Auger, and Boisvert.

environmentally sustainable public waterfront.[45] The designers worked with a firm of coastal engineers to ensure that issues of shoreline dynamics were properly addressed and that a viable land-water interface was achieved. The same office prepared a master plan for the rehabilitation of a part of the Don River Valley: the Don Valley Brickworks, an abandoned industrial site that had once exploited the rich glacial clays and shale bedrock of the locale. The project was carried out in stages during the 1990s: the historic buildings were rehabilitated by architects Oleson Worland, while landscape architects of the Landplan Group and the City of Toronto Division of Parks and Recreation designed recreational landscapes and an artificial wetland with several ponds.[46] Downstream, near the mouth of the Don, a 144-hectare site in Lake Ontario transformed itself into a natural park. Tommy Thompson Park actually began as a gigantic landfill dumped into the lake by the Port of Toronto to provide for a major expansion, but the port extension was found to be unnecessary even before its completion. Spontaneous "volunteer" plant growth subsequently endowed the many-branched linear site with a rich vegetative cover comprising hundreds of native plant species. The park, also known as the Leslie Street Spit, has become a favourite venue for exploration and exercise

21.15 Ecological land-use planning study of North Dartmouth, NS, by EDM Ltd. of Halifax, 2000. Computer analysis of a database of ecological and geographic information led to the development of "suitability maps" that served as a basis for deciding on the most appropriate uses – residential, habitat preservation, business park – for the various zones within the site.

by city residents on foot and bicycle. It offers visitors splendid views of Toronto's downtown towers and has become a sanctuary for thousands of birds, all without ever being the object of any official planning.[47]

Artificial Ecosystems

During the final decades of the twentieth century, the advancement of ecological knowledge permitted the creation of viable artificial ecosystems; the wetland in Toronto's Donlands, mentioned above, is an example. In Montreal, several successive projects trace the evolution of this domain. First, a peat bog garden was reconstructed on Île Notre-Dame (part of the former Expo 67 site) for the Floralies 1980 horticultural exhibition, carried out by a team from the Montreal Botanical Garden under the direction of its head, Pierre Bourque. Then, ten years later on the same island, the Montreal Beach Park opened its doors to 5,000 visitors per day. Designed by landscape architects WAA Inc. for the Montreal Parks Department in collaboration with engineers BGH-Planning and the Montreal Botanical Garden, this swimming park was centred on an artificial beach, and a central component of the experimental project was a series of plant-filled lagoons or "filter lakes" – artificial wetlands – that served as a means of purifying water for the swimming area.[48]

In Nova Scotia, the Halifax-based office Environmental Design & Management Ltd. (EDM) developed considerable expertise in the analysis of the *carrying capacity* of sites through the use of geographic information systems, combined with current computer technology. Principal Margot Young and her associates employed these systems to define detailed suitability maps for residential, industrial, open-space, and other land uses, bringing up to date the methods pioneered by McHarg and developed by Carl Steinitz, with whom Young had studied at Harvard. And in a 1996 project reminiscent of the now-demolished Ark in Prince Edward Island, EDM designed a system that used solar energy for the treatment of waste water in the small village of Bear River in Annapolis County, Nova Scotia. Following the success of this first municipal solar-aquatic sewage treatment system in North America, EDM included tourist-oriented infrastructures in the project to accommodate the numerous visitors interested in studying the design.[49]

Future Prospects

The projects just described were based on scientific knowledge and specialized research. Unlike those of the early ecological movement of the 1960s, they were far from marginal: large corporations and knowledgeable institutions were now involved in place of the small and obscure groups of the 1960s. And currently, a rapidly increasing number of professional and non-governmental organizations are bringing together experts from a great variety of disciplines – and from all corners of the world – to explore and build on the principles of sustainable development.[50]

22.1 *Granite Assemblage*, West Vancouver, looking east from Ambleside Landing to the Lions Gate Bridge between Stanley Park (right) and the North Shore

22

Beyond Modernism: New Currents in Landscape, 1975–2000

All the projects of the 1960s and 1970s mentioned in chapter 20 as high points of Canadian landscape design had been realized within the universal idiom of modernist design. But during the 1970s and early 1980s, a constantly growing force of opinion began to attack the previously impregnable ramparts of the modern movement. This was first signalled by a general dissatisfaction with "faceless buildings" and "windswept plazas" – a dissatisfaction soon followed by a wholesale rejection of the forms of modernism and the cult of progress that underpinned them. Among the reasons for this rejection were a lack of human warmth in buildings and landscapes of all kinds and the obliteration of specific cultural and regional references in favour of the abstract and universal forms of modernism. A general incoherence of urban form resulted from the juxtaposition of modern projects, which no longer seemed to add up to an attractive cityscape as premodern projects had done. Certainly, the best modern projects were always humane, well integrated into their context and capable of making a contribution to the urban milieu. But criticism focused on the general visual quality of the modern environment, which many people found austere and uninspiring. This rejection led to a series of new experiments and projects that did not follow a universal philosophy, as had modernism, but were instead tentative, diverse, and largely unrelated, despite occasional overlapping. With surprising swiftness, landscape architecture – along with other art forms – turned to a new paradigm loosely labelled "postmodernism."[1]

Rediscovery of History

Among these new developments, a renewed interest in history was an important general trend. When modernism occupied the stage, there was no room for historic gardens and buildings, which were considered irrelevant to modern conditions. A new view, born in the 1970s, insisted on the relevance of historic gardens and landscapes, and even proposed the use of references to past landscapes in new projects. In the words of Jean-Claude Marsan, these were the "years of re-appropriation."[2]

Montreal's Champ de Mars, the city's former parade square that had been converted to a parking lot in 1920, was reborn as a contemporary open space following a competition in 1985. The design by Farley/Schreiber/Williams of Montreal tried to tell the story of the diverse periods and transformations through which the site had passed, through the overlapping and superposition of references to the former nineteenth-century parade ground and the remains of the eighteenth-century fortifications.[3] Vestiges of the old city wall from French-regime days were included as an integral part of the design. The revival of traditional civic design forms that had

22.2 The cloister garden in Trinity Square, Toronto

been long out of fashion was another expression of this tendency, as seen in Trinity Square, Toronto, designed by Moorhead Fleming Corban McCarthy, landscape architects (successors to the Sasaki Strong office), in 1985. The designers created a complex and eclectic reinterpretation of a traditional monastic garden, adjacent to the Eaton Centre and Trinity Anglican Church. A serene and peaceful cloister garden, enclosed on four sides by rows of carefully matched little-leaf linden trees, is an outstanding component of this project.[4] With no communication between their authors, similar cloister-garden designs were created in the 1980s in two other Canadian cities: Cathedral Place in Vancouver (Paul Merrick Architects, with Phillips Farevaag Smallenberg and Cornelia Hahn Oberlander, landscape architects) and Place de la Cathédrale in Montreal (WZMH Architects and WAA [Williams, Asselin, Ackaoui et associés], landscape architects).

The long-forgotten urban boulevard also experienced a rebirth at this time, in several locales.[5] In the 1980s, Montrealers finally saw the reconstruction of McGill College Avenue, connecting McGill University and Place Ville Marie, as designed by the landscape architects of the City of Montreal Parks Service with Montreal architect Peter Rose. This theatrical space has since become a favourite location for summer art exhibitions, jazz concerts, and other civic activities.[6] At the southern end of the avenue, landscape architect Sandra Donaldson, with the help of consultant John MacLeod, carried out a major redesign of the plaza of Place Ville Marie, defining pedestrian circulation paths with raised boxes within which a wide variety of trees and shrubs now flourish.

The cities of Ottawa and Gatineau benefited from the creation of a new avenue reminiscent of the City Beautiful era – Confederation Boulevard, a ceremonial route constructed over a period of years to define and delimit the federal government precinct in Ottawa and Gatineau. The boulevard's designers were a multi-disciplinary office formed in Toronto in 1979 by Roger du Toit, Robert Allsopp, and John Hillier, experienced practitioners in architecture, landscape architecture, and city planning. In 1983, the office, then called du Toit Associates Ltd., worked in close collaboration with the National Capital Commission (NCC) to develop a preliminary overall concept for the boulevard; its subsequent realization required some twenty years. The boulevard route took the form of an irregular loop that crossed the Ottawa River twice so as to link and integrate the various federal buildings in the two cities (including those that were then under construction, the National Gallery of Canada and the Museum of Civilization). It included Wellington Street directly in front of the Parliament Buildings, tying in with Elgin Street at Confederation Square (site of the National War Memorial; see chapters 15 and 18) and with the road to Rideau Hall, residence of the governor general, at a new square that would later become the site of the Peacekeeping Monument. Composed of a divided vehicular right-of-way with broad esplanades for pedestrians and cyclists on each side, the boulevard featured an array of traditional elements: single and double rows of maples; elaborate lamp standards, equipped to support banners; paving built with durable and attractive materials.[7] By encircling the federal precinct, the boulevard reinforces the identity of Parliament and other governmental sites and buildings, establishing a contrast with the workaday commercial

22.3 (previous page) Drawing of the view from the refurbished plaza of Place Ville Marie, Montreal, looking north along the newly rebuilt McGill College Avenue towards McGill University, with Mount Royal in the background. The rebuilding of this tree-lined boulevard inspired the construction of several new office and commercial buildings in an area of the city that had seen little recent development. Drawing: Sandra Donaldson, landscape architect, 1988.

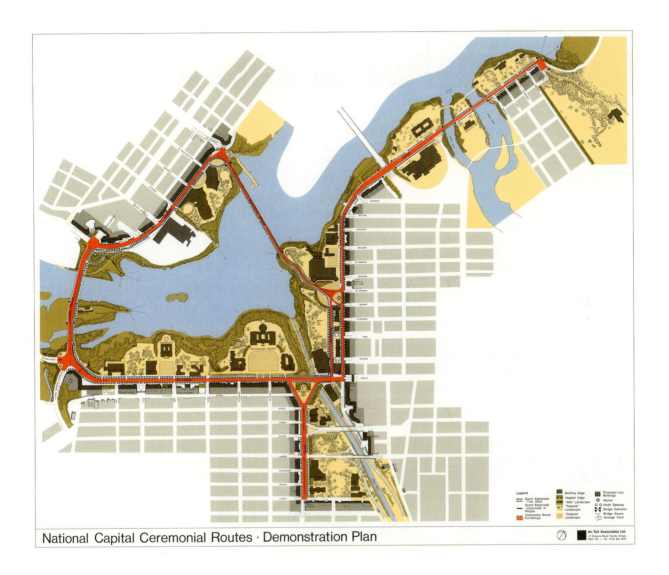

National Capital Ceremonial Routes · Demonstration Plan

22.4 Plan of Confederation Blvd., Ottawa-Hull, by du Toit Associates Ltd., 1983. The office soon became du Toit Allsopp Hillier.

world that surrounds it; the design report summarizes this duality in the expression "town and crown." This urban concept is also based on two key insights, one physical and one social. The first is the drama of the site, a vast three-dimensional space principally defined by the relation of the Parliament buildings to the river, reinforced by cliffs and promontories, museums and the north shore landscape – the great central public space of the capital. The second reality is historic, concerned with the long-standing social, linguistic, and economic division between Ottawa and Hull. The boulevard may be seen as a symbolic contribution to the long-term efforts, ongoing since 1903, to equalize and unify the capital's entire metropolitan area and, implicitly, the country it represents.[8]

A block south of Wellington Avenue, a more recent thoroughfare of downtown Ottawa was transformed in the 1980s. The Sparks Street Mall, an innovative

BEYOND MODERNISM 479

22.5 Entrance to the newly transformed Sparks Street Mall, Ottawa, 1988, looking northwest. The East Block of the Parliament Buildings is seen in the background.

pedestrian street from the 1960s, suffered from physical decline at the same time as it faced increased competition from new downtown commercial centres. In response to this challenge, Cecelia Paine and Associates, landscape architects, prepared a revitalization plan in collaboration with the American landscape firm SWA Group (originally Sasaki Walker Associates). The new design for the mall employed a minimalist vocabulary featuring elegant lighting, movable planters, granite paving, and lightweight structures that provided support for climbing vines, maintaining a maximum of open space to permit sidewalk cafés, musical presentations, and other public activities. Timed fountains provided drama and focus.[9]

In parallel with the rediscovery of historic precedent and detail in new projects, a powerful current of the time focused on the conservation, protection, and refurbishment of historic landscapes, often going as far as complete reconstruction. Designers, educators, and other urban residents reacted strongly to the demolition or threat of demolition of historic buildings. Although such structures no longer seemed to serve their original purpose or meet the financial goals of their owners, they were still valued by many people. These enthusiasts formed pressure groups and associations with like-minded colleagues, rapidly achieving influence and some success in delaying or preventing the destruction of heritage buildings. Almost every city and town in Canada soon boasted preservation organizations, and these organizations lost no time in linking together to form regional, provincial, or national associations such as the Conseil des monuments et sites du Québec, founded in 1975 by France Gagnon Pratte, and the Heritage Canada Foundation, founded in 1973. These and other groups brought conservation issues to public attention through a wide variety of publications, from impromptu photocopied newsletters to professionally edited magazines.

The area of concern of such organizations expanded in the 1980s to embrace historic landscapes – both vernacular and designed – as well as buildings. Heritage Canada, for example, established an ambitious program dedicated to the preservation of Main Streets in towns across Canada in 1980, under its executive director, architect and historian Jacques Dalibard (1935–2007), who had previously played a leading role in the reconstruction of the Fortress of Louisbourg on Cape Breton Island. Serious efforts to document historic landscapes to ensure authenticity in their protection and restoration began with a few pioneers, including historian Susan Buggey, head of the Cultural Landscapes section of Parks Canada in Ottawa-Hull, and architect John Stewart (who had also been involved in the Main Street program), co-founder in 1984 of Commonwealth Historic Resource Management Ltd. in Perth, Ontario, with architectural historian Harold Kalman. Canadian and American experts with a broad range of interests in the field founded the Association for Preservation Technology (APT) in 1968 to share knowledge and coordinate efforts, and a decade later, in 1978, several members of APT who were particularly concerned with the protection of landscapes formed the Alliance for Historic Landscape Preservation (AHLP).[10] Many landscape architects in both private firms and the public sector developed and applied specialized expertise in the restoration field. Private consultant Cecelia Paine and Associates of Ottawa planned and coordinated an ambitious program of restoration and development for a significant site of the country place era, the Mackenzie King Estate in Gatineau Park, Quebec (see chapter 16), completed in 1986.[11] And many historic landscapes were rehabilitated through the efforts of Parks Canada employees; Linda Dicaire, for example, worked on the gardens of Rideau Hall, the Ottawa residence of Canada's governor general, and the village and battlefield at Batoche in Saskatchewan (see chapter 6), among other projects, in collaboration with a group of professionals in related fields.

Other notable preservation and restoration projects of this period included the central area of Dawson City in Yukon Territory, recalling its halcyon era during the gold rush of 1898 (see chapter 6); the sheds and docks of the Historic Properties along the old commercial waterfront of Halifax;[12] the Parc de l'Artillerie in Quebec City; and a network of canals throughout Ontario – the Rideau and the Trent-Severn system – that had played such an important strategic and commercial role in the nineteenth century. In parallel with this movement to preserve cultural landscapes, a similar effort to protect Canada's natural landscapes was under way. Such organizations as the Nature Conservancy of Canada (1962) led this endeavour.

Rebirth of the Floral Garden

This interest in history was related to another phenomenon that began in the mid-1970s: a tremendous revival of interest in horticulture and flower gardens. Such gardens had been rejected out of hand by modernism as hopeless relics of a past civilization, with the exception of abstract mass plantings of bright-coloured annuals. Then suddenly, the garden as a floral exhibition came back to life, and every part of the country saw the development of new and impressive flower gardens.

The Annapolis Royal Historic Gardens in Nova Scotia, begun in the 1970s according to the designs of architect–landscape architect Peter Klynstra (1944–2010) from the office of CBCL Ltd. in Halifax, and then maintained and elaborated by head gardener Peter Pelham, took full advantage of the mild climate of the Annapolis Valley.[13] They consist of a series of traditional thematic gardens – a rose garden, a knot garden (inspired by the Tudor era), Victorian planting beds – combined with several original and striking elements, including a tunnel arbour covered with golden chains of laburnum, a garden of decorative grasses that merges imperceptibly with a neighbouring wetland, and an Acadian house and garden displaying plants used in the traditional culture of Acadia. The last includes an orchard of seventeenth-century cultivars and a potager (kitchen garden) featuring root crops, herbs, and vegetables identified in diaries from the period, enclosed by a traditional willow hedge. Like the Annapolis gardens, the Kingsbrae Horticultural Garden at St. Andrews in New Brunswick, located in the heart of the early twentieth-century vacation colony, is composed of several floral gardens of diverse inspiration and ambiance. Begun in 1998, Kingsbrae has become an impressive tourist destination. Further north, the New Brunswick Botanical Garden, founded at Edmundston in 1993, has also followed the classic botanical garden pattern, combining several thematic gardens in a unified composition. The Devonian Botanic Gardens in the suburbs of Edmonton, established in 1959 by the University of Alberta, has evolved into its present form since about 1975. The original site consisted of derelict landscapes and abandoned industrial properties, but through the restoration of natural ecosystems and the planting of horticultural varieties, the garden's planners have created a varied complex of diverse gardens, including the magnificent Kurimoto Japanese Garden, designed by Tadashi Kubo

22.6 Annapolis Royal Historic Gardens, Annapolis Valley, NS

of Osaka.[14] In Vancouver, the closing of the Shaughnessy Heights golf course heralded the creation of the Van Dusen Botanical Garden, opened to the public in 1975. Veteran landscape architect Bill Livingstone directed the landscape work in the garden until 1976, at which point head gardener Roy Forster took over.[15] After a third of a century, the original plants of the Van Dusen Garden have achieved a level of maturity in Vancouver's mild climate, and such unique features as the garden's Rhododendron Walk are truly impressive. These projects are but five examples from a considerable number of excellent gardens of this type, founded or extensively redeveloped across the country during the last three decades of the twentieth century.

Some gardens originated because of special events. This was true of Floralies 80, an international garden festival held under the auspices of the Montreal Botanical Garden, directed by Pierre Bourque. Open throughout the summer of 1980 on the Expo 67 islands, the Floralies included such innovative projects as the Aquatic Garden of the City of Laval (designed by Friedrich Oehmichen, landscape architect) and the Peat-Bog Garden – a real peat bog, saved from a soon-to-be-flooded sector of the James Bay project and brought to the island site by trucks that had delivered equipment to the hydroelectric construction site in the North.[16] These highly original gardens were neighbours to classic French and English flower gardens, designed by experts from those two countries in the styles that we associate with their great garden traditions,[17] and to dozens of other floral gardens representing countries, cities, and provinces.

This period also witnessed the revival, refurbishing, and further elaboration of several noted private gardens, including the Jardins de Métis in Quebec's Gaspé region. At the suggestion of Henry Teuscher, landscape architect and conservator of the Montreal Botanical Gardens, the government of Quebec had purchased the gardens in 1961 in order to open them to the public.[18] But by 1995, unable to continue its administration of the property, the government sold the site to a non-profit association, Les amis des Jardins de Métis (Friends of the Métis Gardens). Under the presidency of Alexander Reford, great-grandson of the gardens' creator, Mrs. Elsie Reford, the Friends undertook an ambitious program of revitalization and animation of this historic site, bringing it to new levels of achievement (see chapters 16 and 24).[19] At the Quatre-Vents garden in Cap-à-l'Aigle, Quebec, Francis Cabot (1925–2011), who had inherited the domain in 1965, also built on the work of his family predecessors to create one of the outstanding gardens of North America. Beginning in the 1970s, Cabot expanded the geometrical garden components that had been designed by architects Eddie Mathews and Pat Morgan (see chapter 16), adding onto them a series of new outdoor rooms that were related to the existing spatial structure by a system of axes and cross-axes. The new spaces included Goose Allée, a narrow rectilinear avenue lined with perennials, located parallel to the tapis vert, which proved a popular place for the garden's geese to promenade; and a sequence of square and linear gardens defined by native cedars, animated by pools of water and cascades, and punctuated by sculptural elements.[20] From this intricate complex of intimate spaces, views opened out to the larger landscape of the Laurentians to the north. Cabot continued his landscape initiatives beyond the immediate zone of his residence, strategically locating architectural features

22.7 Pigeon-house and its garden at Quatre-Vents, Cap-à-l'Aigle, QC

within the natural landscape and creating new gardens of diverse inspiration, including a stream garden, a music pavilion, a moon-shaped bridge,[21] a pigeon-house garden (with the participation of Benoît Bégin), and a ravine garden featuring a Japanese pavilion and tea house by Hiroshi Sakaguchi of California.[22] All these features are based on particular gardening traditions, but each is also a totally original creation, thanks to its unique interpretation by Francis Cabot. The garden as a whole is distinctive both for the authenticity and impeccable execution of each of its components and for the integration of each of these into the overall composition, always in sympathy with the surrounding natural landscape.

At a completely different scale, the private garden of architect Arthur Erickson – which he designed and personally created in the 1960s in a residential district of

22.8 Arthur Erickson's garden in Vancouver, looking north towards the house (a converted garage) from the enclosing mound. The central reflecting pond and wooden deck are seen in the foreground.

Vancouver – anticipated the broad interest in gardening that was to characterize the closing decades of the twentieth century. Inside a high cedar palisade, Erickson devoted almost every square foot of his standard corner lot to the garden; his house, a tiny converted garage, sits immediately next to the lane at one extremity of the property. A single gesture establishes the basic spatial structure of the garden: the creation of a great central pond, which opens up the view, and the deposition of the excavated material in a mound behind the pond, which closes it. The interposition of elements perpendicular to the main line of sight – shrubs, rock arrangements, and a hovering wooden deck – conceals the boundaries of the lake and induces a feeling of infinite space in this little intimate universe.[23]

The new wave of interest in horticulture stimulated the rediscovery of a number of garden archetypes and plant types that had been put aside for years: the aquatic garden, perennial borders, decorative grasses.[24] Even *mosaiculture* (carpet bedding), an art that was thought to have entirely disappeared,[25] flourished once more. The summer exhibition Mosaiculture Montréal 2000, organized by the city of Montreal under the direction of landscape architect Lise Cormier, attracted huge crowds to the site of Montreal's Old Port, which led to its continued presentation during the two following summers. The explosion of interest in public gardens was accompanied by a great enthusiasm for residential gardening among the general public, coupled with a rapid expansion of the horticultural, garden lighting, and irrigation industries and an astonishing proliferation of garden books and magazines, in both English and French.

Recycling of Industrial Sites and Greening of the Waterfronts

In the postwar period, North America changed from an industrial society to a "post-industrial" society, in which the majority of citizens made their living in the service sector rather than in manufacturing. This transformation made obsolete a great number of traditional industries and led to the abandonment of much of the enormous urban and rural territory they had occupied. This dramatic change inspired a movement to recycle some of these disaffected industrial terrains as public spaces. Beginning in the 1970s, the government of Canada was faced with the challenge of the old ports of Quebec City, Trois-Rivières, Montreal, Vancouver, and Toronto (among others), as well as of the Lachine Canal in Montreal, all of which had lost much of their traditional vocation, the latter due to the building of the St. Lawrence Seaway in the 1950s.[26] In the space of a few years, the government (in partnership with other organizations) reconstructed many sites that had long been dedicated to industrial uses and railroad installations, opening them to the public and to a variety of recreational activities.

The pioneering Granville Island project (1977) in Vancouver created an exciting water-oriented recreational milieu from an abandoned and obsolete industrial site. The commission responsible for the project, directed by Peter Oberlander, chose to retain almost all the old buildings and rehabilitate them to accommodate tourist facilities as well as commercial and recreational activities. Even automobile

22.9 (above)   A view of Granville Island, Vancouver, showing the robust character of the street furniture elements, designed to provide continuity in the transformation of the existing industrial environment into a cultural, entertainment, and commercial waterfront milieu.

22.10 (below)   The Music Garden, Toronto Harbourfront. New waterfront condominium developments are seen in the background.

circulation was maintained on the site, without adding sidewalks; the result was a stimulating collage, charming and eclectic. The designers, architects Norman Hotson and Joost Bakker with landscape architects Don Vaughan and Associates, developed a robust and unpretentious vocabulary of street furniture, awnings, and new structures, inspired by the island's existing industrial character.[27] In Toronto, new commercial and residential developments, combined with a continuous boulevard, Queen's Quay, finally provided access to the shore of Lake Ontario, long isolated by industry. Among a series of new lakefront landscapes, the elegant and well-detailed Music Garden of 1999 stands out. It was designed by artist and landscape designer Julie Moir Messervy from Vermont, in collaboration with cellist Yo-Yo Ma and the City of Toronto's landscape architects and other professionals. The garden is a sequence of six thematic spaces, each of which translates a movement of Bach's First Suite for Unaccompanied Cello into landscape terms.[28]

The country's largest industrial-recycling project was almost certainly the Forks in Winnipeg, situated on the former railway lands that long prevented access from the city's downtown to the Red and Assiniboine rivers, an important symbolic site that had long been a common meeting place for First Nations tribes, before European settlement. As a result of a collaborative effort by federal, provincial, and municipal authorities that began in earnest in 1987,[29] the enormous site was host to a series of projects, carried out in several stages to eventually constitute an immense multi-purpose public park. The design of the park was also a collaborative effort, involving offices Hilderman, Witty, Crosby, Hanna and Associates; architects Étienne Gaboury and Cohlmeyer Hanson as overall site planners; and Cynthia Cohlmeyer Landscape Architect. Later project designers included Van der Zalm and Associates and Scatliff, Miller and Murray Inc.[30] The park landscapes they created included a public market, an amphitheatre, and a marina that together function as a metropolitan-scale place of public assembly. Natural areas that had survived the industrial epoch were preserved and reinforced with extensive planting of native riparian species, and a number of quiet sitting areas and active locales for specialized recreation, including a spectacular skate park, were integrated into the overall design.[31] The immense success of this project, which redeemed the site at the confluence of two great rivers by restoring its historic role as a gathering place for many peoples, subsequently stimulated the realization of additional major projects on adjacent underdeveloped sites.[32]

Linear Recreation

In the early 1970s, traditional forms of organized recreation began to give way to informal and nature-related leisure activities, often linear in physical configuration. For half a century, recreation in public parks had focused on team sports – baseball, football, hockey – carried out in formalized environments. These classic mass-participation activities evolved into more informal recreational activities, primarily practised by small groups or individuals in natural milieus. The new phenomenon of *linear recreation* constituted a major transformation in the use, and then in the form, of public spaces. City and rural park departments began to

BEYOND MODERNISM   489

22.11 Amphitheatre and marina at The Forks, Winnipeg. The park includes continuous promenades along the banks of the historic Red and Assiniboine rivers.

create new pathways for bicycling, jogging, and cross-country skiing, which eventually linked up to form complex networks of urban and rural trails, often well integrated with natural features such as hills, escarpments, and waterways.

In St. John's, Newfoundland, the Grand Concourse Authority developed a highly coherent and comprehensive path system throughout the urban region, under the direction of Neil Dawe, landscape architect.[33] The Calgary pathway and bikeway system, some 550 kilometres in length, links all parts of the city, taking particular advantage of river and creek corridors.[34] Montreal's Lachine Canal bikeway has become amazingly popular, and the National Capital Commission's extensive path network in Ottawa-Gatineau provides access for pedestrians and cyclists to parks and open areas within the city, in Gatineau Park and along the Rideau Canal in Ottawa, the latter functioning in winter as the "world's longest skating rink."[35] In both rural and urban areas, the "rails to trails" movement has converted hundreds of kilometres of old railway rights-of-way to skiing and bicycle paths. Examples include a municipal trail network in Fredericton, New Brunswick, as well as the former route of the P'tit train du Nord between St. Jérôme and Mont Tremblant in Quebec, as popular with cross-country skiers in winter as it is with cyclists in summer. In Toronto, the closing of the Belt Line urban railroad added an important internal link to an already widespread network of paths and trails that took full advantage of the many interconnecting ravines threading their way through the city.

Rehabilitation of Historic Parks

Many long-established parks that had deteriorated over the years were finally "made over" in the 1990s. The city of Montreal entirely rehabilitated Mount Royal Park, the flagship of Canada's great urban parks, through a step-by-step program of repair and reconstruction that will require twenty years to be fully realized.[36] The second large park of Vancouver, Hastings Park near the city's eastern boundary (which has always lived in the shadow of its more celebrated confrere Stanley Park), was also the object of a major rebuilding effort. Following a long-term plan prepared by landscape architects Phillips Farevaag Smallenberg, the city removed obsolete facilities and equipment that had been installed over the last century and no longer served their original purpose. A stream that had long been confined to an underground pipe was "daylighted" – excavated and replanted – to create a natural sanctuary in a part of the city that is very densely inhabited; several new thematic gardens were also added.[37] At Veterans Park in the town of Lac-Mégantic, Quebec, municipal authorities undertook an ambitious program of replanting, in accordance with the designs of Claude Lachance, landscape architect, to restore the five majestic rows of trees, aligned parallel to the lakeshore, that had originally been the outstanding feature of the park. The western extremity of the refurbished park was destroyed in the railroad accident that devastated Lac-Mégantic in July 2013, but the majority of this magnificent park has survived.

Thematic Environments and Special Events

The expansion of commercial and educational horizons, allied with striking innovations in construction techniques, gave rise to a series of fantasy-based and representational projects that allowed people to experience exotic (or purely imaginary) environments. First emerging in "fun" environments in closed-mall shopping centres, such as Fantasyland in the West Edmonton Mall,[38] and in theme parks, such as Canada's Wonderland in Toronto (1981),[39] this approach was soon adopted by serious educational institutions like the Toronto Zoo (1980), a large-scale exterior site planned by Johnson Sustronk Weinstein (Brad Johnson, project director) that shelters animals in landscape environments that reflect their original habitats. A similar goal inspired the Montreal Biodôme (1992), a sequence of interior spaces that encompass four realistic ecosystems of the Americas, inhabited by animals from their respective zones.[40] The designers and builders of these projects have become remarkably skilful in manipulating advanced materials – glass-fibre reinforced plastics, pneumatic concrete, specialized concrete additives – to simulate natural environments or to create totally imaginary milieus. In these imaginative and sometimes fanciful projects, the traditional boundaries that divide landscape, interior design, set design, and theatre have disappeared. Similar trends were seen in major recreation centres such as Whistler Village in British

BEYOND MODERNISM   491

Columbia (Don Vaughan & Associates, landscape architects) and Mont Tremblant in Quebec. Both of these ski resorts and their associated residential villages used theatrical composition and carefully chosen materials to create unified and highly successful visual themes; the latter was transformed into a virtual simulacrum of an alpine village.

The largest project of this nature was the Expo 86 world exposition in Vancouver, a linear city of fantasy built on a derelict industrial and railway site on the north shore of False Creek, just south of downtown. An additional component, the stunning Canada Pavilion, reminiscent of a fleet of tall-masted clipper ships, was located on the opposite side of the downtown area, on Burrard Inlet. A multidisciplinary in-house design team, with Cynthia Girling as senior landscape architect and Eriks V. Eglite as senior site planner, prepared the master plan for the exhibition. Richard Strong served as director of site development for the early stages of the project, and many BC landscape firms were involved in the design of specific elements and systems within the site. Chief Architect Bruno Freschi directed the design of the major exhibition buildings, which he based on a modular concept in order to provide some architectural coherence to the necessarily heterogeneous exposition. Landscape pulled the diverse areas of the site together through a well-structured circulation system of major and minor plazas and corridors, creating a network of paths that "verged on an abstraction of a medieval town."[41] The theme of Expo 86 was transportation, and many of its most memorable features built on this idea in an imaginative way, including the fantasy hit of the fair, "UFO-H2O." This was a children's playground organized around a "silvery spaceship in a watery Martian landscape" that provided an infinite number of creative ways for children and adults to get wet. Principal designers were North Vancouver artist John Gilbert and WET Enterprises of Burbank, California.[42]

The 1988 Calgary Winter Olympics brought forth a panoply of excellent design work both in natural mountain environments and in Calgary's downtown and suburban areas. Nakiska Ski Area on Mount Allan in Kananaskis Provincial Park, west of the city in the foothills of the Rockies, was chosen as the centre for alpine/downhill events. Designers Ecosign Mountain Recreation Planners Ltd., Landplan Associates Ltd. (Garth Balls, principal), and Mountain Planning and Management carefully inserted a complex network of ski slopes into the steep and densely forested mountain environment, with the help of a multidisciplinary planning team that included environmental scientists and engineers. This large team worked closely together on a tight schedule to minimize environmental impacts and integrate mitigative measures where necessary.[43] The popularity of the Olympic events necessitated the construction of visitor centres, lodges, and support facilities of all kinds to accommodate great numbers of spectators in the least disruptive manner. Many buildings constructed for these purposes were designed in abstracted vertical form and clad with natural materials to mirror the rhythms of the forests surrounding the site.[44]

Cross-country and related events were accommodated at the Canmore Nordic Centre, realized according to a master plan designed by landscape architects Carson-McCulloch Associates Ltd. of Calgary with the help of a similar multidisci-

492 BIRTH OF THE MODERN LANDSCAPE

22.12 Kananaskis Village, AB

plinary team of consultants and advisers. Built from scratch on a previously unexploited mountainside site, the visitor facilities and ski trails benefited from an iterative series of design decisions. The design team gradually "homed in" on the final trail alignment scheme through several successive approximations on site, fitting the trails to the natural landscape while respecting the strict competition regulations of the Olympics.[45]

Postmodern Plazas

A wave of new public and private plazas made their appearance in Canadian downtowns in the 1980s. Their design responded to a series of new considerations that had not applied to the simple and often spectacular spaces of the previous generation. Where Place Ville Marie sought a pure visual expression and did not aspire to communicate any message other than that of the landscape itself, the new plazas were seeking richer and more complex forms of expression and communication. There was a growing emphasis on the designed landscape as a work of art and not simply as an environment in which to live one's life. Designers tried to add new levels of comprehension, to enrich the landscapes they were creating by associating them with ideas, just as the romantic gardens of the eighteenth century had tried to communicate ideas of the picturesque or sublime. This approach was seen as early as 1988–89 in landscape architect-artist Don Vaughan's iconic sculpture/landscape *Granite Assemblage* at Ambleside Village in West Vancouver, a former ferry landing and now a local town centre.[46] Vaughan's sculpture is composed of immense granite cubes that march out into the sea west of the Lions Gate Bridge, juxtaposing a variety of surface textures, smooth and rough. Installed in a man-made tide pool, the sculpture provides a dramatic focus for Ambleside Landing Park, designed by landscape architects Durante and Partners, and is a significant North Shore landmark. Since its creation, a new generation of designers across the country have experimented with new idioms of landscape architectural expression: using metaphor, irony, and humour; telling stories through landscapes; creating projects with multiple levels of meaning; and superpositioning different

22.13 Two of the Ontario landscapes "collected" by the designers at the Village of Yorkville Park, Toronto: waterfall and granite outcrop. The thematic landscapes are lined up in series, corresponding to the alignment of Victorian houses across the street.

494 BIRTH OF THE MODERN LANDSCAPE

22.14 Allegorical column sculptures by Melvin Charney in the Garden of the Canadian Centre for Architecture, Montreal, 1990, illustrating aspects of the city's architectural history. Photo: Robert Burley

interpretations in a kind of palimpsest. Landscape architects had begun to explore new aesthetic realms.

Among installations that exemplify this approach, the Village of Yorkville Park in Toronto stands out. The city organized an international competition in 1991 to select a design for this park close to the downtown area, located on a former parking lot beside a short commercial street. The winning scheme, submitted by American landscape architects Martha Schwartz/Ken Smith/David Meyer and local architects Oleson Worland, confront the visitor with a somewhat tongue-in-cheek collage of a dozen familiar Ontario landscapes, both natural and cultural, including marshland, pine grove, apple orchard, herbaceous border, and decorative tires. These culminate in a clearing dominated by a huge granite dome, a piece of the Canadian Shield transplanted to the city.[47] If most public gardens consist of spaces that tell no story, or of spaces organized in sequence like a classic novel, Yorkville

BEYOND MODERNISM 495

Park is instead a series of distinct short stories, with a surprise ending. First met with puzzlement and even hostility, the garden is now a cherished landmark for Yorkville residents and for the city as a whole.

Several projects built in Montreal in the 1980s and 1990s explore similar approaches to landscape design. The Garden of the Canadian Centre for Architecture (1987–89), designed by artist-architect Melvin Charney (1935–2012) and landscape architects Gerrard and Mackars of Toronto as part of the museum complex established by CCA founding director Phyllis Lambert, recalls the history of the site through the introduction of low walls that symbolize the old cadastral lines, of open fields, and of apple orchards on each side of the garden. It also "reflects on" the main building of the CCA, on the opposite side of the boulevard, by constructing a partial mirror image of that historic building's façade. Sculptures along the southern edge of the park – allegorical columns created by Charney – also make reference to the history of the district and of Montreal.[48]

Pure spatial design with few overtones or levels of interpretation still survived, however. An example may be seen in the mid-1990s courtyard of the Faculté de l'aménagement at the University of Montreal, designed by Parent Latreille Associates on the basis of an original landscape plan by Christian Deshaies, Sandra Barone, Maxine Raymond, and Hélène Blondin.[49] The designers integrated a dramatic stepscape to exposed sections of the existing rock ledge that marks the continuation of the lower slope of Mount Royal beneath the university.

22.15 Courtyard at the Faculté de l'aménagement, Université de Montréal, looking south towards the university's main campus on Mount Royal, marked by architect Ernest Cormier's signature central tower

22.16 Place de la FAO in Quebec City's Lower Town

Vancouver was host to several new and interesting downtown plazas, including Park Place, built adjacent to Christ Church Cathedral in 1985. The plaza is a shady brick-paved refuge bordered by tall, thundering waterfalls. Designers were local firm Don Vaughan & Associates and New York landscape architect Paul Friedberg, known for the revolutionary approach to the urban landscape that he had initiated in the gritty "projects" of his home town. In 1995–97, at a strategic intersection in Quebec City's Lower Town, the city's landscape architect André Plante designed a modest classic: Place de la FAO, a public square that commemorates the foundation of the United Nations' Food and Agricultural Organization at Quebec City in 1953. Within a complex and intimate space, Plante created a landscape of waves, interpreted in paving blocks of contrasting colours, from which projects a sculpture that resembles a ship's prow – *La Vivrière*, realized by artists Richard Purdy, François Hébert, and Carmelo Arnoldin. The space as a whole makes reference to the city's maritime past and to the agricultural richness and fecundity of the planet.[50]

Explicitly Canadian Landscapes

Japanese and Chinese gardens are essentially figurative forms that represent and interpret natural landscapes specific to Asia. The *alpine gardens* that figure prominently in many botanical gardens are also dramatizations, in urban settings, of the wild landscapes of the mountainous sectors of Switzerland and neighbouring countries. Some favourite garden types have been based on cultural rather than natural archetypes; an example is the *cottage garden*, which expresses the English ideal of a small domestic garden, comfortable and filled with familiar flowers.

BEYOND MODERNISM 497

We have gardens of all these types in Canada, which means that we have been inspired by the natural and cultural landscapes of Japan, England, France, Switzerland, and so on, but seldom by those of Canada or any of its regions. However, since about 1980, for the first time we are beginning to be inspired by archetypal Canadian landscapes. Devonian Square in Toronto, constructed in 1978 according to the drawings of landscape architects Richard Strong Steven Moorhead Ltd. (including Margaret Kwan, designer), was a component of Ryerson Community Park, the overall site-development program that aimed to unify the heterogeneous campus of Ryerson Polytechnical Institute (now Ryerson University) through the creation of a continuous and coherent landscape setting.[51] The plan of the park is simple – a great pond, almost circular, framed by a horizontal brick-paved surface, gently shaded by honey-locust trees distributed almost at random – and its visual character is defined by the presence of a dozen immense glacial rocks. The scale of the rocks, standing in the water or overlapping land and water, immediately recalls the landscapes of the Canadian Shield to the north.[52] The rocks are sufficiently large that they define spaces within the pond, through which skaters swiftly glide when the basin becomes a skating rink in winter.

22.17 (below)   Glacial rocks at Devonian Square, Toronto

22.18 (facing page)   The Taïga Garden at the National Gallery in Ottawa, featuring exposed rock ledge and Nordic vegetation. View looking northwest from the Peacekeeping Monument towards the gallery's central tower – sometimes interpreted as a *rappel* of the Peace Tower – which shelters a dramatic interior space.

498   BIRTH OF THE MODERN LANDSCAPE

22.19 Bouctouche dune stabilization and recreation site, New Brunswick, looking westward along the barrier dune at the mouth of the Bouctouche River. The elevated wooden walkway prevents damage to the vulnerable beach grasses and other vegetation that help maintain its stability. In the years since this photograph was taken, vegetation has recolonized the old road visible between the beach and the walkway.

In two projects on neighbouring sites in Ottawa, Cornelia Hahn Oberlander pursued similar themes. At the National Gallery of Canada (1983–88) designed by architect Moshe Safdie, she modelled the principal garden on the landscapes of the Canadian Shield as immortalized in the paintings of the Group of Seven, which occupy a place of honour in the gallery. Her Taiga Garden, specifically inspired by

A.Y. Jackson's painting *Terre Sauvage,* was installed on the exposed bedrock of the site, subtly complemented by glacial rocks placed by the designer. The garden's vegetation is primarily composed of plants native to the climatic zone located some 100 kilometres to the north (jack pine, tamarack, white birch, arctic willow, and bearberry, among others), reinforced by a few exotics. The plants were shaped like *bonsai* into stunted and irregular forms – against every rule of conventional horticulture – to support the theme.[53] Immediately opposite the gallery, the Peacekeeping Monument, an NCC project built in 1988–92, occupies a strategic location at a major intersection of Confederation Boulevard. The design, a collaboration among Oberlander, Richard Henriquez Architects, and sculptor Jack K. Harman, was inspired by a European landscape that was all too significant to Canadians – the ruins of war, colonized by colourful wildflowers.

Other projects were based on the vernacular landscape traditions of Canada, rather than on its natural landscape elements. Such was the case with a series of related interventions constructed in the mid-1990s around Bouctouche Bay in northeastern New Brunswick, a historic centre of Acadian settlement. The Bouctouche Bay Ecotourism Project sought to increase employment opportunities in the area

22.20 The Oodena Celebration Circle at night, The Forks, Winnipeg, 1993–2005

BEYOND MODERNISM 501

while improving the natural environment and reinforcing the region's rich cultural traditions. Landscape architects BDA Ltd. (James Sackville, principal), with Architects Four as consultants, planned the Dune de Bouctouche Irving Eco-Centre, integrating a two-kilometre raised wood walkway along a vulnerable barrier dune that had been subjected to heavy use. BDA also participated in the design of the nearby Pays de la Sagouine tourist complex, which includes a restaurant, theatre, and interpretive centre designed by Élide Albert, architect. The famous novel and play *La Sagouine*, by local resident Antonine Maillet, was the inspiration for the latter complex, which recalls the imaginary fishing village where the events of her literary work took place. The design of buildings and landscape elements in all sectors of the project was inspired by the vernacular construction methods typical of the region. A trail network links together the various tourist attractions and the town of Bouctouche.[54]

A family of explicitly Canadian projects display or dramatize the artefacts and symbols of the First Nations. This current seems to have begun in 1976, with the construction of the Museum of Anthropology of the University of British Columbia, a simple and powerful building conceived by Arthur Erickson, located on the edge of the plateau where the university stands. Its landscape, designed by Cornelia Hahn Oberlander, integrated native plants (which were very difficult to obtain at that time; they had to be sought out on Haida Gwaii, the Queen Charlotte Islands), a pond, and an irregularly shaped gravel beach, a subtle foreground for magnificent Haida "big houses" and totems of the Native peoples of the Northwest.[55] The Wanuskewin Heritage Park in Saskatoon, in the Meewasin Valley of the South Saskatchewan River, interprets the cultures of the First Nations of the Prairies, explaining such landscape features as medicine wheels and tipi rings.[56] In Winnipeg, landscape architects Hilderman Thomas Frank Cram, inspired by the role played by large rocks and circular forms in Amerindian cultures, created a stunning outdoor space within the Forks complex, the Oodena Celebration Circle. This ceremonial assembly space, on the site of a historic First Nations meeting place, is named for a Cree word that denotes the "centre of the city." A circle of massive masonry elements defines the area, with supporting steel "celestial guideposts" disposed around a sacred space, its centre marked by the symbol of the sun.[57] Other symbols within the amphitheatre, 60 metres in diameter, relate to many Aboriginal cultures.

23.1 The Gate of Harmonious Interest at the entrance to Chinatown, Victoria, BC, built in 1981

23

Landscapes for a Multicultural Society

When it adopted the Multiculturalism Act of 1988, the government of Canada stated that "multiculturalism is a fundamental characteristic of the Canadian heritage and identity, and that it provides an invaluable resource in the shaping of Canada's future."[1] The law affirms the principle that Canada is a nation of immigrants with diverse cultural backgrounds and that these traditions enrich us all.

The dimensions of this cultural diversity, which has existed since the beginning of the country, are impressive: 4.8 million immigrants – 224,000 per year, on average, from extremely varied countries of origin and with highly diverse religious convictions – entered Canada in the fifteen years preceding 2006.[2] The integration of these recent newcomers into Canadian society, as well as that of their immediate predecessors, has generally proceeded well. And although most have identified themselves with Canada's already established cultures, they have done this within the typically Canadian model of a *multicultural mosaic*, in contrast to the official American ideal of a unified culture or *melting pot*.

This process has not been without intolerance and difficulties,[3] and clearly, not everything has been resolved. But systematic discrimination in Canada started to fade in the 1960s – yet another quiet revolution of that time – and subsequently, barriers and prejudices have disappeared at an impressive rate. This required a process of reconciliation between governments, community groups, and citizens, and as a result, despite faults and shortcomings, the multicultural society has become an effective reality, celebrated as an achievement and an indication of our evolution as a society.

Impacts of Multiculturalism on the Landscape

How is this phenomenon expressed in the landscape? As Dolores Hayden has explained in her 1995 book *The Power of Place*, urban and rural landscapes are important to the people who inhabit them; they carry *meanings* and *messages* that vary according to the culture of the community and of the individual.[4] Thus each community within Canada, in parallel to its participation in the general culture, also has its own *sacred places*, tied to its own unique history. These places might be gardens or landscapes designed specifically for this purpose or locations associated in some other way with the difficult and rewarding trajectory of a particular immigrant group. Taken together, these places may tell the story of a community. But this story is not universally legible. Often, a place of great significance to one group has little meaning for those who do not share the culture in question. Such places may be entirely unknown – like the Polish cemetery in Saint-Jérôme, Quebec, for example – or, if they are known, may be neither recognized nor appreciated.

If landscapes exert a profound influence on people, the inverse is equally true: inevitably, people influence and modify the landscapes in which they live, and these influences tend to be particularly rich and complex in a society of multiple cultures.

Multiculturalism affects the landscape in several ways. First, it does so through the spontaneous creation of places and environments that express the collective personality and traditions of particular groups. Such places are often superimposed on the regular street grid of an urban milieu, as Mordecai Richler describes St. Urbain Street in Montreal. In the rural milieu, this would correspond to the Mennonite *strattendorf* "street villages" and the Ukrainian four-corner settlements that exist within the regular quarter section geometry of the West (see chapter 6).

Second, in the last forty years, city officials and private groups have made great efforts to celebrate the new multicultural society through the creation or modification of public spaces. This intention has been expressed in plazas, gardens, and civic monuments that recognize the contributions of particular communities and communicate their values and cultures to the general society. Quite rapidly, the traditional use of public space, which was to impose the ideology of a dominant culture, gave way to a new use, one that reflected openness to diversity, cooperation, and integration without assimilation, as well as accommodation and reconciliation towards minority groups. For the designer, this is not easy to achieve; there is always a risk of unknowingly stumbling into condescension or caricature.

Finally, more subtle cultural influences are evident in the incorporation of themes, motifs, and design features of particular cultures into landscape projects of the general society. Such influence has been widely seen in Canada. The presence, for example, of Chinese and Japanese garden features – including stone arrangements, plant species, and spatial configurations – have enriched the landscape vocabulary of such projects as Devonian Park at Ryerson University in Toronto and Place Bonaventure in Montreal.

A Multicultural Urban Milieu: St. Lawrence Boulevard, Montreal

Among the most famous multicultural milieus in Canadian cities, St. Lawrence Boulevard in Montreal, also known as "the Main" (it was briefly called "Main Street" in the nineteenth century), stands out.[5] A legendary street like Broadway in New York, Portage and Main in Winnipeg, Wilshire or Sunset boulevards in Los Angeles, St. Lawrence was the first street to be extended outside Montreal's old city walls. It grew into a thriving suburb, Faubourg Saint-Laurent, which became the favoured destination for immigrants arriving at the port of Montreal, thanks to its location perpendicular to the port's central hub. Successive generations of immigrants established themselves in mixed residential-commercial areas along the boulevard. The Main also came to be a sort of neutral territory between what were for many years primarily English-speaking districts to the west and predominantly French-speaking neighbourhoods to the east.[6]

The architectural and landscape character of this vibrant street is a perfect mirror of its social character: lively, complicated, heterogeneous. A journey along its length, from south to north, reveals a series of neighbourhoods, each of which provides a home and celebrates the presence of a different cultural community. Immediately to the north of the narrow streets and public buildings of Old Montreal, Chinatown – the *Quartier chinois* – announces itself with an enormous arch that integrates Chinese forms and symbols, including sculptures of lions. The City of Montreal built the arch in the 1980s as part of a program to celebrate the cultural

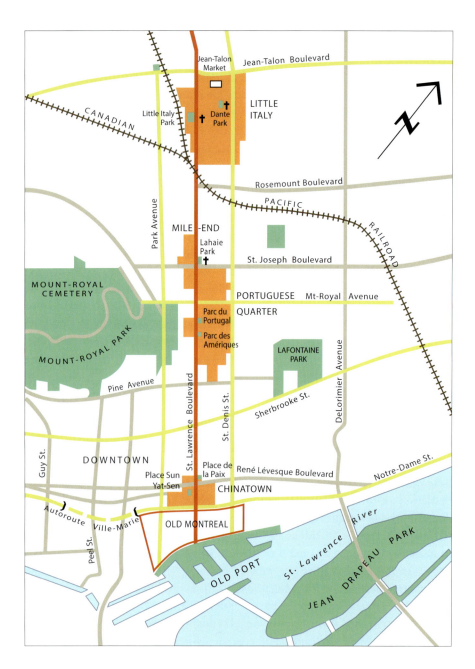

23.2 Map of St. Lawrence Boulevard in central Montreal (indicated in red), showing its relation to the port and original settlement of the city, and to a series of public urban spaces that play important social roles in the neighbourhoods along the boulevard.

diversity of the city's neighbourhoods. Beyond the arch, the visitor is captivated by the messy and lovable environment that is typical of Boulevard St-Laurent at this latitude – signs in Chinese and Vietnamese, windows filled with exotic merchandise, sidewalks crowded with pedestrians and boxes of vegetables, the boulevard filled with vehicles, all contributing to a vibrant and popular urban scene.

Over de la Gauchetière Street, the main east-west axis of the Quartier chinois, the city again has built arches – somewhat smaller – to identify the limits of the

506 BIRTH OF THE MODERN LANDSCAPE

district. And here, once more, the arches follow Chinese models in form, colour, and detail. Just off de la Gauchetière, one block west of St. Lawrence is Sun Yat-Sen Park, a small open space ideal for sitting and talking, animated by a Chinese-style pavilion. The park was named for the revered statesman who helped found the Chinese republic in 1912 and who was its first president.

In the early 1950s, the first of a wave of Portuguese immigrants arrived in Montreal and established themselves on the plateau above Sherbrooke Street, along both sides of the Main.[7] The visual signature of this community is the polychromatic painting of house façades, a gesture of identification by the individual and the community. These bright colours have been called "the poetry of the street."[8] In 1975, Montreal mayor Jean Drapeau changed the name of a small green space in the heart of the Portuguese quarter to Parc du Portugal "in honour of the pioneers of that community who have been here for 20 years."[9] Some twelve years later, following a request from the Portuguese community to redesign the park to better represent the Portuguese culture, the city proceeded with a complete rebuilding of the traditional green square. The new design consisted primarily of a paved plaza featuring elements and structures inspired by villages in Portugal: tiled entrance pillars, a marble column recounting Portuguese history (which had previously been displayed in the Portuguese pavilion at Expo 67), and a fanciful bandstand with Iberian detailing.[10]

This park was very popular with the senior generation of the Portuguese community, but also attracted members of many other groups (not necessarily of Portuguese origin or descent), who "sorted themselves out" by appropriating different areas of the park – punks, seniors, children, among others.[11] The space, as redesigned by the landscape architects of the City of Montreal, was undeniably Portuguese in character, but there was some criticism. The association Sauvons Montréal, a local group that has done much to promote quality design in architecture, city planning, and landscape, gave it a *prix citron*, indicating a negative evaluation of the project, which the judges perhaps considered to be kitsch (or *quétaine* in local parlance).[12]

The Portuguese immigration occupied a territory that was once the heart of the Jewish district of Montreal, as members of that group moved to the suburbs from the 1950s on. But vestiges of the previous occupation can still be seen in the continuing presence of many specialized restaurants and businesses, such as Schwartz's Delicatessen, which still offers the best smoked meat in the world. Nearby, a workshop produces gravestones inscribed in Hebrew, its courtyard opening out onto the boulevard and providing a glimpse of a trade and an enterprise that refuse to die.[13]

Just as the Luso-Canadians began, in their turn, a gradual exodus to the suburbs, a new population of Latin-American origin began to arrive in the district. The city made a gesture of recognition to this community by creating a second plaza, this one called "Parc des Amériques" and located a block south of the Parc du Portugal. Designed by city landscape architect Carlos Martinez, a native of Guatemala who graduated in landscape architecture at the University of Montreal, this park is a largely paved plaza organized about a central stone arch, reminiscent

of the architectural traditions of the Mediterranean and Latin America. The built elements of the square are complemented by colourful plantings, tropical in appearance, which somehow survive in Montreal's challenging climate.

At the corner of the Main and St. Joseph Boulevard, a major east-west artery, the visitor comes upon Parc Lahaie. This is a very difficult kind of open space: a traditional green square with tall trees and simple, continuous grass surfaces, a classic Montreal vernacular form (see chapters 9 and 13). There are perhaps twenty of these squares in central Montreal; they play a vital role as amenities within the most densely populated neighbourhoods in the city. Like many of its confreres, this square is related to a major public building – in this case an enormous church with the picturesque name of Saint-Enfant-Jésus-du-Mile-End.[14] The park is heavily occupied and used, even on the coldest days of the year. One could consider this square to represent Montreal's traditional Franco-British mainstream culture, cohabiting with a number of neighbouring spaces inspired by other cultures.

Further north, beyond the railway underpass (an important territorial marker), is the large district known as "Petite Italie." Once again, the city has contributed to the neighbourhood's identification by erecting an arch, supported on granite pillars (and more chic and modern than those further south), to mark its boundaries.

23.3 (left)   The entrance to Parc du Portugal on St. Lawrence Boulevard, Montreal. The marble column from Expo 67 is at centre right, on the axis of the tiled entrance pillars; the bandstand is at far left.

23.4 (right)   The façade of Schwartz's Delicatessen on St. Lawrence Boulevard in Montreal

508   BIRTH OF THE MODERN LANDSCAPE

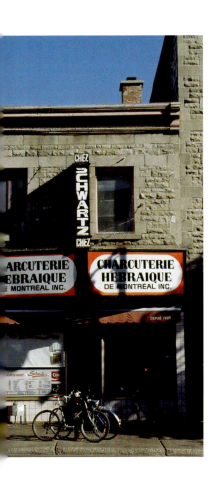

Boulevard Saint-Laurent is full of life here – specialized boutiques, sidewalk cafés, lots of Italian flags, especially during World Cup matches (traffic jams last for hours after an Italian victory). It is a modest district, but the streets here have a lot of character, thanks to the high degree of attention given to the details of the buildings and the public landscape. Even the backyards are embellished with brio and enthusiasm. And right in the neighbourhood is the Jean-Talon Market, where buying high-quality food is a form of recreation and socialization.

As one would expect, the largest church in Little Italy was built on St. Lawrence Boulevard, once again facing a classic green square centred on a traditional *kiosque à musique* or bandstand. The city renamed this square "Parc de la Petite Italie," but unlike Parc du Portugal, the design didn't change in any way to reflect the new name (although, of course, an Italian flag flies from the park's flagpole). The church has fallen on hard times and, like many others in Quebec, has recently been converted to condominiums. Paradoxically, another nearby church is far from closing: Notre-Dame-de-la-Défense, the principal church of the Italian community. This church is located next to Dante Park, a formal and symmetrical open space with gravel surfacing (all of which suggests, without being explicit, Italian landscape traditions); the recently redesigned park focuses on a bust of the famous Italian writer. Like the parks dedicated to other communities that we have seen, this space makes a deliberate gesture to Montreal's Italian community.

These parks and squares constructed in honour of different cultural groups and communities are *landscapes of inclusion* that recognize the multiple sources of the city's vitality. But the city became less enthusiastic about this approach to public parks in about 1990 and stopped systematically creating such spaces.[15] Officials did not explain the reasons behind their decision, but one might postulate several possibilities: the members of different cultural communities move from one district to another; a gesture for one community may be seen as shortchanging another, whether or not it is viewed as a rival; with so many communities in the city, there will never be enough parks to cover every group; and finally, in a democracy, "parks should be for everyone" and should not be identified with just one segment of the overall community. Whatever its reasons, the city reoriented its policy to what some observers have termed the "pasteurizing" of the parks.[16]

Gardens as Witnesses to Multiculturalism

On other fronts, the practice of making special landscapes to recognize special groups continued. In recent decades, many associations and institutions created new gardens to demonstrate the landscape traditions of other nations and cultures. The elegant Dr. Sun Yat-Sen Classical Chinese Garden,[17] located in Vancouver's old Chinese quarter, is a particularly striking example, through its authenticity and painstaking attention to detail. This garden (realized in 1985–86) took its inspiration from one of the classic gardens of the Ming Dynasty (1368–1644), representing a scholar's garden in Suzhou, the city considered to have attained the highest level of garden art in China.[18] The principal landscape architect of the garden, Wang Zu-Xin, worked together with Don Vaughan and Associates, landscape architects

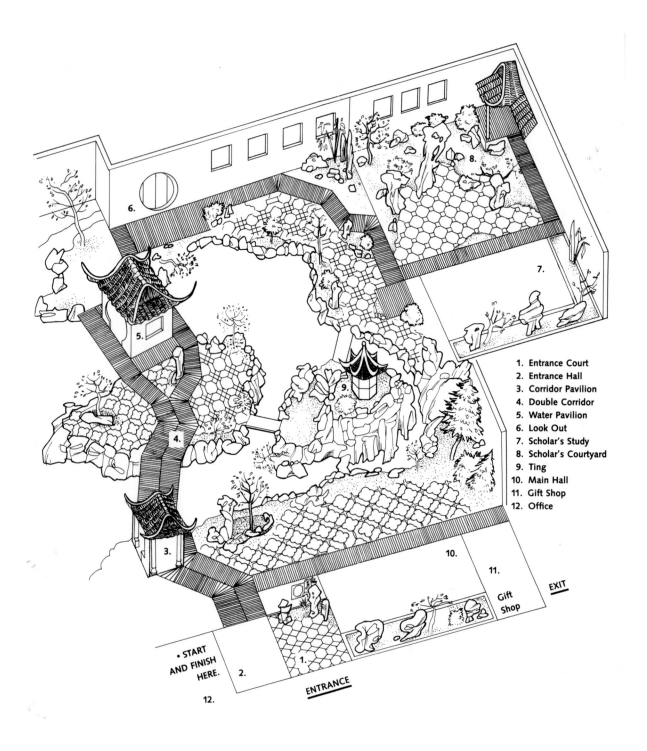

1. Entrance Court
2. Entrance Hall
3. Corridor Pavilion
4. Double Corridor
5. Water Pavilion
6. Look Out
7. Scholar's Study
8. Scholar's Courtyard
9. Ting
10. Main Hall
11. Gift Shop
12. Office

23.5 Isometric view of Dr. Sun Yat-Sen Classical Chinese Garden, Vancouver. The garden is explored along an irregular looped path, carefully designed to provide contrasting views and spatial configurations. From the entrance at bottom left, the visitor proceeds in a counter-clockwise direction around the far side of a miniature lake, finally arriving at a quiet and secluded Scholar's Courtyard at the far corner of the site. The return journey passes across a rocky island punctuated by an elevated "Ting" pavilion, and thence to the main exhibition hall at the end.

23.6 The Italian Gardens, part of the Hastings Park redevelopment project in Vancouver. Designed by Phillips Farevaag Smallenberg, landscape architects. The gardens include Italian-inspired sculptures and fountains along with children's play areas and facilities for court games, including tennis, basketball, and bocce.

from Vancouver, and Joe Y. Wai, architect. A group of Chinese artisans provided by the Suzhou Garden Administration Team fabricated and assembled many garden components.[19] A considerable number of the plants employed in the Vancouver garden were of similar varieties to those found in the gardens of Suzhou, since the climates of the two cities are quite similar.[20] The Sun Yat-Sen Garden's rocks are from Lake Tai, the source of the highly eroded limestone formations that are so much a part of the original Suzhou gardens.[21] Elsewhere in Vancouver, the redevelopment of Hastings Park on the Eastside (see chapter 22) included a striking and dramatic new Italian garden in honour of the large Italian community that has long resided in the neighbouring Hastings Sunrise district.

Between 1987 and 2001, the Montreal Botanical Garden created three new gardens honouring different communities and bringing to the general population a

LANDSCAPES FOR A MULTICULTURAL SOCIETY 511

knowledge of the gardening and landscape traditions of those communities. The Japanese Garden (opened in 1988), designed by Japanese landscape architect Ken Nakajima (1914–2000), director of the Consolidated Garden Research office in Tokyo, was conceived as "a garden for Canada inspired by Japanese gardens" and not as a traditional Japanese garden.[22] Nakajima (who, as the designer of the garden of the Japanese pavilion at Expo 67, was already familiar with Montreal) wanted to integrate the garden into its milieu. It should be far more open and expansive than most traditional gardens in Japan, he stated, "since Canada is so large [*hiroi*]." Nakajima's intentions came through in the great openness of the final design and in the rocks he selected, peridotite blocks from the heartland of asbestos production in southeastern Quebec. But much of the garden is traditional: like most Japanese gardens in the New World, its spatial organization follows the classic scenario of a *promenade* or *stroll garden*, and it features many of the archetypal and much-admired compositional elements of the Japanese garden – a large pond of curvilinear outline, a quiet stream, a strategically located viewing pavilion, a zigzag *yatsuhashi* bridge – that respond to the expectations of those visitors who are looking for an "authentic Japanese garden experience."[23]

A few years later, in 1991, a new project was unveiled: the Montreal Chinese Garden, built by a team of designers and artisans from Shanghai as part of a program of international cooperation organized by Pierre Bourque, who, as director of the Botanical Garden, initiated and orchestrated all of its new features. Le Wei Zhong, architect and landscape architect, director of the Shanghai Landscape Architecture Design Institute (SLADI), was the chief designer of the garden, while Wendy Graham, of the city's Parks Department, was the landscape architect responsible for coordinating the project in Montreal. The clear objective of this garden was to recreate, in Montreal, the character, ambiance, and details of a traditional Chinese garden; in fact, like the Dr. Sun Yat-Sen Garden in Vancouver, it was modelled on the gardens of the Ming Dynasty (1368–1644). In this type of classic garden, characteristic of the cities of Suzhou and Hangzhou in the southern region of the country, the aesthetic impact was based on contrast and harmony among four key elements: planting, water (an expansive lake was usually the common unifying element of these gardens), rocks, and architecture.[24] As in Montreal's Japanese garden, a propitious and unexpected choice of stone – in this case the rugged *breccia* of St. Helen's Island – played an important role, contributing to the spectacular topography of a "mountain" and surrounding hills, their form and colour in sharp contrast to the stone from Lake Tai in China that was used for the buildings.[25]

A third such project was the First Nations Garden, opened in 2001. The goals of this garden went beyond those of its predecessors: it was a gesture of recognition and reconciliation towards Quebec's eleven First Nations, dedicated on the anniversary of a great treaty signed three centuries before – the Great Peace of Montreal. The designers, landscape architects Williams, Asselin, Ackaoui and Associates (WAA), included several Native peoples' elements in their composition, including an Inuit *inukshuk* and a tipi representing forest-dwelling nations. The garden also made frequent reference to traditional symbols that carry special meaning for the First Nations, including widely recognized circle and turtle

23.7 First Nations Garden, Montreal Botanical Garden. This section of the garden, highlighting forest-dwelling First Nations, juxtaposes a traditional tipi against a setting of coniferous trees. The colourful flowering plant is fireweed, a northern native plant that can be used for food in a variety of ways.

motifs. A principal purpose of the garden was to explain the relationship between First Nations peoples and the natural environment, in particular the large number of plants used by Natives. It also aimed to demonstrate to all citizens the contributions of the first inhabitants of Quebec and to provide a meeting ground and a place for cultural exchange.[26] This was not a new idea: in the 1930s, the original landscape architect of the Botanical Garden, Henry Teuscher, had included such a garden in his master plan (see chapter 18).[27]

All these gardens had something in common: their creation and their success were only made possible through constant discussion and close collaboration of the design teams (including consultants and the Botanical Garden's scientific and professional personnel) with members of the different cultures involved, whether from distant countries or from the First Nations of Quebec.

A Case Study: Landscapes of Significance to the Japanese-Canadian Community

It is impossible within the scope of this book to identify and study the landscapes that carry special meaning for all of Canada's many cultural groups. But a preliminary exploration of such significant landscapes can be carried out for a particular group. Canadians of Japanese origin or descent are – as we have seen – the legatees of a great garden-making tradition; they also identify with certain symbolic landscapes and "sacred places" within the overall Canadian landscape. The vicissitudes of history have linked these landscapes to a series of common experiences shared by many members of the Japanese community, and a common theme relates these landscapes to one another.

The first immigrant from Japan arrived in Canada in 1877. Like most of those who would follow, he lived and worked in the maritime environments of British Columbia, that broad band of land and sea where fish and other natural riches were abundant.[28] Many of the new arrivals gravitated towards the little fishing village of Steveston on the Fraser River delta south of Vancouver, now part of the city of Richmond. It was the centre of the West Coast salmon fishery, where Japanese immigrants and their descendants worked in the fishing-boat flotillas and in the canneries.[29] Japanese immigrants were also involved in the lumber industry and in a variety of agricultural activities, including dairying, planting orchards, growing strawberries in the Okanagan Valley, and harvesting sugar beets in the irrigated lands of southern Alberta.[30]

We have seen how the Japanese, very soon after their arrival in Canada, started making gardens. The achievements of Isaburo Kishida at the Butchart Gardens and at Hatley Park (see chapter 14) are well known, but certainly many people less

23.8 Asahi baseball game at the Powell Street Grounds (Oppenheimer Park) in Vancouver, 1939

23.9 New Denver in the Slocan Valley, Kootenay region, BC, the location of one of the major internment camps during the Second World War. Looking east along the main street (6th Avenue) towards the Selkirk Mountains.

celebrated than Kishida planted simple vegetable plots and decorative gardens beside their houses or bunkhouses.

The Japanese community also congregated in urban areas, particularly in the area of Powell Street and Main Street, east of downtown Vancouver. It was not a fancy neighbourhood, but it soon became a real community, convivial and intimate – Japanese Town.[31] One of the features of community life was baseball, which was played in the Powell Street Grounds, a well-equipped baseball field that served as the district's central park. As in the United States, this typically North American sport permitted young Canadians of Japanese ancestry to distinguish themselves. They played as well as, and often better than, their Caucasian rivals. The local *Asahi* (morning sun) team almost always won, becoming a real West Coast legend in the 1920s and 1930s. Thus, despite the many forms of discrimination to which Japanese Canadians were subject in that era, they found a level playing field on the diamond.[32]

All this came to an abrupt end after the bombing of Pearl Harbor in Hawaii in December 1941. A few weeks later, the Canadian government confiscated and sold off the whole Japanese fishing fleet. Twenty thousand people of Japanese origin or ancestry were removed from their homes and sent to remote "camps" in the ghost towns of the Kootenay mountains in the BC interior (see chapter 6) or to work camps further east.[33] Surfacing once again was the tragic theme of exclusion that

LANDSCAPES FOR A MULTICULTURAL SOCIETY 515

23.10 Bay Farm Internment Camp, Slocan Valley, BC, c. 1942, seen from cedar forest above

has run through Canadian history, suffered for centuries by the First Nations in the residential schools and through the loss of their lands, and by the Acadians during the *grand dérangement* of the 1750s. It was a hard time for the Japanese Canadians: families divided, prohibited from returning to the West Coast before 1949 (well after the end of the war), denied the right to serve in the Canadian forces before 1945, pressured to "return" to Japan after the war. But despite everything, there were some positive elements. The camps in the interior were not prisons with barbed wire; they were clusters of simple cabins adjacent to old, semi-abandoned towns. The mountains and lakes in these deep valleys were magnificent, and many of the exiles appreciated the natural environment despite all their hardships, as attested by the autobiographies of David Suzuki and other evacuees.[34] And even in the camps, baseball survived as both a recreational activity and a means of contact with non-Japanese.[35]

Gardens of Reconciliation

In 1981 Joy Kogawa, who had lived through the relocation camps as a child, published a moving account of the wartime experience of Japanese Canadians in her novel *Obasan*, providing many of her fellow Canadians with some understanding of those terrible times. Kogawa's widely read book shed light on what had been a long-hidden chapter of Canadian history, since, in general, members of the Japanese-Canadian community had been reluctant to discuss their wartime experiences. Both before and after the publication of Kogawa's book, gestures of commemoration and reconciliation have been made towards these events, and – perhaps because of the Japanese culture – most of these commemorative gestures were gardens.[36]

One of these gardens of reconciliation was the Momiji Garden, built in 1993 in Hastings Park on Vancouver's East Side. *Momiji* means "maple" – surely the perfect name for a Japanese garden in Canada. In fact, the great variety of *Acer palmatum* (Japanese maple) cultivars available in British Columbia permitted the creators of the garden, the Vancouver Japanese Gardeners Association, to base its design on just one plant, which is very unusual. The garden also features beautifully executed stone paving and walls, the curving forms and construction techniques of which recall those of medieval Japanese castles. On one of the walls, a plaque lists the names of the park's creators and benefactors, accompanied by a dedication to multiculturalism. The inscription states that the garden is "a celebration of the many people who make up Canada's unique cultural mosaic, and the remarkable history and contribution not only of our Japanese Canadians but of all Canadian citizens. Rocks and Japanese maple trees, flowers and waterfalls, all in perfect

23.11 Nitobe Garden on the campus of the University of British Columbia, Vancouver: view of the lake and smaller-scale vegetation in light filtering through giant conifers above

harmony. A magnificent reflection of cultures coming together and signifying what it means to be Canadian." What the plaque doesn't say is why the Momiji Garden is here at Hastings Park. In fact, Japanese Canadians had been here before, lodged in the stables of the old racecourse. This was the assembly point for 8,000 Japanese Canadians before they were shipped off to the interior.[37] This must have been very hard for people who use the same word – *kiree* – to mean both "clean" and "beautiful."

On the campus of the University of British Columbia in Vancouver, the first postwar garden of reconciliation was realized in 1959–60. The Nitobe Garden honours Inazo Nitobe (1862–1933), a most remarkable man. Born in Japan, Nitobe studied in the United States and married an American. He tried to become a "bridge across the Pacific" (his expression), explaining Japanese ideas to the West and vice versa. A career diplomat, he served as undersecretary of the League of Nations, and before his death in Victoria, BC, in 1933, he tried, in vain, to change the flow of events that were leading inexorably towards the Second World War.[38] His portrait on the Japanese 5,000-yen note provides an indication of the high esteem in which he was held by his fellow citizens. By invoking the memory of this unusual person, the Nitobe Garden, created in the often bitter postwar years, can be seen as an attempt to reconcile Japan and the West after the disastrous events that began at Pearl Harbor and ended at Hiroshima and Nagasaki.

The general configuration of the garden corresponds, once again, to the classic model of a stroll garden, offering several ways to explore a hilly landscape by walking around and across a central linear pond. Gigantic native conifers shelter the garden and create a magnificent ambiance, allowing the filtered light to illuminate 200 plant species of both native and Japanese origin. Within the garden, there is a rustic and colourful tea house and small tea garden. All was designed and the construction directed on the site by Professor Kannosuke Mori (1894–1960) from Chiba University in Japan, with the constant support of John Neill (1916–1999), founding director of the Landscape Architecture Program at the University of British Columbia, who acted as local coordinator and facilitator. Roy Sumi assisted in the construction of the Memorial Garden and became its first gardener.[39] Recently, in 1993, a general restoration of the garden was carried out, including the rebuilding of the pond and rockwork and the construction of a traditional protective wall around the site, along with a new approach path and entrance gate. The rehabilitation work was designed and supervised by Shunmyo Masuno, director of Japan Landscape Consultants and a Zen Buddhist priest. Don Vaughan of Vancouver acted as local consultant.[40]

As their local project to celebrate Canada's centennial in 1967, the citizens of Lethbridge in Alberta decided to create an authentic Japanese garden, in honour of the many Nikkei – people of Japanese ancestry – in the region, the majority of whom had left the West Coast during the war, moving inland to harvest sugar beets, and their descendants. Despite hard work and harsh conditions, many of the wartime evacuees who worked on these farms – in order to keep their families together – stayed on in the Lethbridge area after the war.[41] The city invited Dr. Tadashi Kubo of Osaka Prefecture University,[42] with his associate Mas Sugimoto, to

23.12 The lake and pavilion of the Nikka Yuko Japanese Garden, in Henderson Lake Park, Lethbridge, AB. The building houses meeting and activity rooms as well as a traditional Japanese tea room.

design the Nikka Yuko Garden (which means "Japan-Canada Friendship Garden"), on a municipally owned site in the extensive grounds of Henderson Lake Park.[43] If the Lower Mainland around Vancouver is an ideal climate for a Japanese garden, the opposite is true of semi-arid southern Alberta. Yet the character of this garden is totally Japanese, despite the minimal plant vocabulary permitted by hot summers, hard winters, and chinook winds. This *tour de force* has been accomplished through judicious plant choice from a very limited palette,[44] combined with expert maintenance. An irregular lake of curving outline once more serves as the central organizing feature of the park; all the wooden pieces for the garden's diverse structures and its large tea pavilion were prefabricated in Japan and assembled on the site. Within the pavilion is a tea room with a view to the garden, and in a walled area beside it, there is another type of Japanese garden, called *kare-sansui* (dry river), a garden of contemplation typical of Zen Buddhist design, composed of raked white gravel and meticulously placed rocks.

Japanese gardens were also created in the Kootenay mountains near Slocan Lake, where several of the relocation camps were built. This area had undergone a huge mineral boom in the late nineteenth century. While it lasted, fortunes were made in lead, zinc, and silver, but eventually the mines ran out and the people abandoned such once-lively settlements as New Denver and Silverton, which became virtual ghost towns. The few residents who remained were only too happy to receive an influx of thousands of exiled Japanese Canadians in 1942. Relatively cordial human relationships seem to have been established between the exiles from the coast and the region's long-term residents.[45] This era has been commemorated by the Nikkei Internment Memorial Centre at New Denver, situated in the section of the "Orchard" that used to be occupied by the little wooden cabins, each housing two families, that the Nikkei themselves had to build (in contravention of every international agreement on the treatment of prisoners).

The commemorative site, sponsored by the Kyowakai Society, is centred on a garden designed by gardener Roy Tomomichi Sumi of Vancouver (who had worked on the Nitobe Garden) and built by volunteers in 1993–94. As a child, Sumi had passed the war years in another camp a few kilometres north of New Denver. He tried to keep things simple, using the *kare-sansui* technique to minimize the need for extensive maintenance, and he integrated the design of the garden with the magnificent natural landscape over the fence, in the Japanese tradition of "borrowed space" or *shakkei*. The central element in the garden is a dry river that symbolizes past, present, and future. The past is shown by a tortuous, rocky, and irregular stream. This gives way to a strong river, representing the present ... and then, finally, to the future, seen as a broad, calm, and peaceful lagoon.[46] A surprising symbolic element is found in the garden: the stumps of trees, rare in Japanese gardens. Perhaps the meaning of these features is the same as that of the broken columns found in nineteenth-century rural cemeteries: the tragedy of lost youth, of lives cut short.

In the same town, looking out directly on Slocan Lake, there is a second public garden, the Kohan Reflection Garden. Begun in 1988 by gardener Ray Nikkel and maintained by the Slocan Lake Garden Society (a non-profit volunteer association

23.13 Garden of the Nikkei Internment Memorial Centre, New Denver, BC. A Japanese maple, azaleas, ferns, and junipers frame the dry stream and rock composition of this evocative garden, punctuated by a stone lantern.

23.14   The use of traditional components of the Japanese garden – enclosing wall, stone, and colourful fine-leafed maple – provides a distinct Japanese character to the Kohan Reflection Garden in New Denver, BC.

known as the "SLUGS"), the Kohan garden is a Japanese-inspired garden. Its dramatically composed design incorporates a great many garden concepts from the Japanese tradition (including its "borrowing" of the space of the lake, which is virtually an extension of the garden).

A final irony at New Denver: the Japanese Canadians constructed their wooden cabins so well (their community included many carpenters and builders) that they are much in demand today, almost seventy years later. In fact, many of these sturdy cabins have been moved to private lots and have become comfortable modern residences.

Landscapes as Places of Meeting and Conciliation

All of these gardens show that landscapes can be significant contributors to the healing of social wounds, and many exemplify the role of landscape architecture as an impetus towards reconciliation. The history of the Japanese-Canadian community is also commemorated through other former scenes of Nikkei collective life, communicating important messages to their community and sometimes to the larger society as well. In the village of Steveston, now surrounded by condominiums like those springing up everywhere in Vancouver, a monument recalls the Japanese-Canadian fishermen and cannery workers who once lived there. Parks Canada has rebuilt several buildings and other installations of the old fishing station, including the house and garden of one of the families. A grove of cherry trees or *sakura*, of great symbolic importance in the Japanese culture, has recently been planted.[47] Further east, a distinctly Canadian adaptation of Japanese design themes can be seen in the work of landscape architect George Tanaka, who had been evacuated to northern Ontario in 1942 and who subsequently spent many years as the national executive secretary of the Japanese Canadian Citizens' Association before beginning his professional career at age forty-one.[48]

In Vancouver, the Powell Street Grounds still survive under the new name of Oppenheimer Park, in honour of the city's second mayor. Some Japanese Canadians came back to the neighbourhood after the war, but much of the eastern section of downtown Vancouver has fallen into a nightmare of drugs and degradation. Despite this, the volunteer association Tonari Gumi planted eight commemorative cherry trees in the park in 1977, and every summer the Japanese community – and others – gather there to celebrate the Powell Street Festival. Over thirty-five years old, the festival presents such activities as *taiko* drumming, *odori* dancing, flower and bonsai exhibits, a tea ceremony, "hip-hop fusion," and, inevitably, a baseball game.[49] The legendary Asahi team has not been forgotten: Canada's National Film Board made a film about the Asahi baseball team, which has recently been enshrined in the Canadian Baseball Hall of Fame in St. Mary's, near Stratford, Ontario.[50]

However, Oppenheimer Park could not escape controversy. Discussions concerning the recent rehabilitation of the park at first envisaged the elimination of most of the heritage cherry trees. This suggestion elicited sharp reactions, particularly from members of the Japanese community, who insisted on the preservation

23.15 Public "charrette" meeting held in Oppenheimer Park, Vancouver, in 2008, to discuss goals and ideas for the park's redesign. Participants were encouraged to write down and sketch out their proposals.

of what they saw as symbols of a revered past and a heroic struggle, and who quickly set up the Coalition to Save the Legacy Sakura to advance their views. Yet the park, as one of the most heavily used public spaces in the city, has to respond to the needs of a great variety of different users. And many of these other users, including First Nations residents, homeless people, representatives of a convent and a Buddhist temple, and soccer players, were going through their own difficult struggles at the time of the discussions. No design solution that focused narrowly on the needs and traditions of one particular user group would have been appropriate, in terms of either function or meaning. What constitutes a clearly understood symbolic language for one group may be completely incomprehensible to others.[51] Finally, compromise was reached through a series of community meetings involving city officials, representatives of community groups, and space2place, the Vancouver landscape architects who were chosen by the city to facilitate the compromise process. The firm's principal, Jeff Cutler, led the discussions and integrated the many suggestions that ensued into a final design that provided for a wide range of activities, users, and facilities. Most stakeholders were very satisfied with the results. The majority of the heritage cherry trees were saved, and even reinforced by a row of new cherries, so the park remains a sacred place for the Nikkei community while providing a green and peaceful haven for many others.[52]

Most of the landscapes described above bear special significance for the Japanese-Canadian community, and some may be considered sacred spaces. Even today, every issue of *Nikkei Voice*, the monthly newspaper that maintains contact among the members of this community across the country, makes reference to Powell Street or Oppenheimer Park, the relocation camps in the BC interior, or the various friendship/peace gardens created since 1945. And every other community in Canada – whether based on national origin, religion, or other shared social

23.16 Plan of the new design for Oppenheimer Park, 2008–10, based on discussions at the public meetings. The heritage cherry trees are in a cluster adjacent to the children's play area (pink colour). A new row of cherry trees was planted along the diagonal path starting from bottom left. A baseball field was maintained in the top-left quadrant of the park, and a new multi-purpose field house was built at top right, shown in yellow.

background – has similar attachments to places and landscapes that have marked their own unique history in this country.

The survival of another place of significance to Japanese Canadians has also been assured. Efforts had been underway for a number of years to preserve the house in Vancouver's Marpole district where author Joy Kogawa had passed her childhood years before the *dérangement* of 1942. The goal of this campaign was to create "a centre for Canadian and international writers ... enabling new writing about our human rights and our evolving multicultural and intercultural society that make Canada unique in the world."[53] The expropriation of the house was never envisioned – once is enough – but finally, in May of 2006, the Land Conservancy of British Columbia purchased the property, transforming Joy Kogawa's dream into reality. On her return home, she noticed that the old cherry tree in the backyard, where she had played as a child, was still flowering.[54]

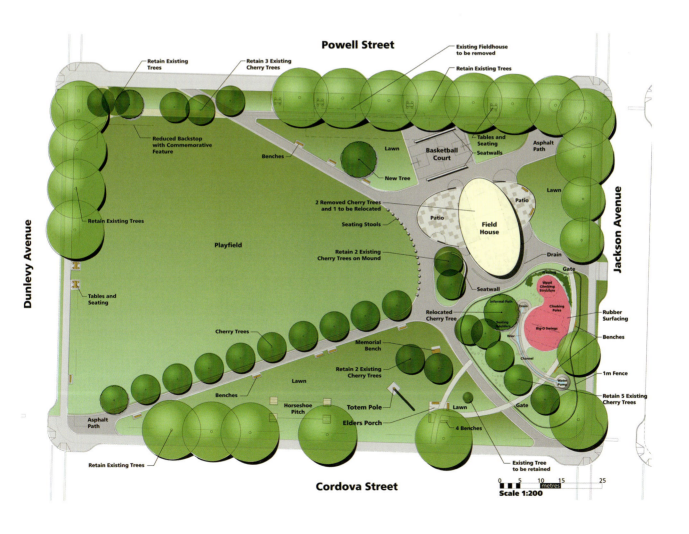

LANDSCAPES FOR A MULTICULTURAL SOCIETY 525

24.1 View from rehabilitated land towards oil sands operations area, near Fort McMurray, AB

24

The Twenty-first Century: Canadian Landscapes in a Time of Rapid Change

The first decade of the twenty-first century was a period of rapid change that affected all aspects of Canadian society and destabilized the natural and cultural landscapes. Given this complex and dynamic situation, it is difficult to predict the directions in which landscape architecture will evolve. It is even difficult to tell which recent developments are significant and which are less pertinent, or merely ephemeral. But a few facts can be noted, concerning both the general social context and the development of landscapes, that may permit us to make some preliminary sketches of a scene that is not yet clear, and perhaps to strike a draft agenda of what landscape architects will need to focus on in the coming decades.

The chief characteristic of today's world is *globalization*, the elimination of international barriers to the free exchange of goods and services. The many consequences of this powerful trend include the weakening of national and regional particularities in favour of international values and images; the primacy of the private sector over the public; the consolidation of vast enterprises at the scale of the planet; and a continuing tendency towards secularization in the majority of developed countries. A "rush for resources" engendered by the economic expansion of China and India, combined with increasing global demand for oil, has put great pressure on the natural resources of Canada. And the dynamism of the newly integrated world economy, in the absence of effective controls, created extreme financial situations similar to those of the 1920s.

The Evolution of a Profession

If we shift our focus from the global situation to the status of landscape architecture in today's Canada, one thing is certainly clear: the profession has greatly matured in the nearly fifty years since the founding of Canada's first professional schools in 1965. Graduates of the Canadian schools are now established everywhere in the country; they have made (and are continuing to make) a huge contribution to the creation of parks, gardens, and public spaces, and are actively participating in educational institutions, local government, private firms, and public agencies. This is the generation that Cecelia Paine has called "the Third Wave," the landscape architects who followed and built on the achievements of the profession's founders and its postwar pioneers.[1]

The great majority of current landscape work across the country is being designed by this generation of landscape architects, and the number and variety of landscape projects are infinitely greater than could have been imagined half a century ago. At that time, it was normal for professionals from abroad to design such projects in Canada; today, this is rare. At the same time, Canadian landscape architecture has gone international. Increasingly, private and even public offices have carried out large-scale, high-profile projects outside Canada, in such diverse countries as the United States, France, Germany, Chile, and China.[2] Certainly, the profession remains less visible than several other disciplines within the field of environmental design; it has only been accorded full professional certification by three of the ten provinces. But the National Battlefield Commission's installation of a bust of Frederick G. Todd on the Plains of Abraham in June 2008 as part of the celebrations of the 400th anniversary of Quebec City's founding, the 2009 advancement of Cornelia Hahn Oberlander as Officer of the Order of Canada, and the induction of Garry Hilderman as a member of the order in 2010 bear witness to broad recognition and appreciation of the profession by the public at large. Other marks of recognition include the investiture of Claude Cormier and Vincent Asselin as Chevaliers de l'Ordre du Québec in 2009 and 2012 respectively, the induction of several landscape architects as members of the Royal Canadian Academy of Arts,[3] and the dedication of a historic plaque in Edmonton honouring Todd for his pioneering work on the design of the city's open-space network in 1907.

Redefining the Garden

Among the graduates of the Canadian professional schools, a new generation of young designers has taken advantage of the opportunities offered by garden festivals and summer exhibits to take public landscapes into new aesthetic territory. In chapter 22, we saw an opening of landscape design to the expression of new ideas through the use of humour, irony, and the superposition of several levels of meaning. Landscape architects have since continued to explore new themes and to try them out in ephemeral and experimental gardens. A key point of departure for the most recent wave of explorations has been the International Garden Festival, an annual event held at the Jardins de Métis in the Gaspé region of Quebec since the summer of 2000. Already, in the 1990s, Alexander Reford and the foundation over which he presided had revitalized the historic gardens founded by his great-grandmother (see chapter 16). At the beginning of the new century, with the support of associates Philippe Poullaouec-Gonidec of the University of Montreal's

School of Landscape Architecture and Chair of Landscape and Environment, and Denis Lemieux, on leave from Quebec's Ministère de la Culture, where he had promoted architectural competitions for public buildings, Reford founded the International Garden Festival, an annual event that would expand the definition of the garden – "push the envelope" – by inviting international designers to design and build experimental gardens.

The master plan for the festival's site, adjacent to that of the original gardens, was designed by Montreal landscape architects VLAN Paysages (Micheline Clouard and Julie Saint-Arnault) in collaboration with the architectural office Atelier in situ. In approaching the festival grounds, the visitor follows a winding path through a forest, a pathway that provides a sort of spiritual transition from the historic gardens to the assembly and arrival space of the new festival. From there, one enters a series of small, intimate spaces along the top of the slopes that extend down to the St. Lawrence; it is in these spaces that the invited designers have created their experimental gardens.

Each year, the designers work within a general theme, but there are no restrictions as to choice of materials or artistic and intellectual approach.[4] In the first summer of the festival in 2000, the landscape architectural group Espace DRAR (Patricia Lussier and Anna Radice) used vernacular and discarded materials such as recycled bottles and rolls of chicken wire to create a whimsical, engaging, and child-friendly garden entitled *Not in My Back Yard*. Susan Herrington, a professor of landscape architecture at the University of British Columbia (UBC), contributed a movable garden, *Surf and Turf*, that included vertical grass panels that rotated to offer changing views of the river. The garden recalled, metaphorically, the creation of the original Jardins de Métis by Elsie Reford.[5] Finally, the star of the festival's first year was, by unanimous agreement, Montreal landscape architect Claude Cormier's *Blue Stick Garden (Jardin de batons bleus)*, a creation that used no plants whatsoever, but rather a collection of vertical sticks, its composition inspired by the *Allée royale*, a classic horticultural *tour de force* of the original gardens by Mrs. Reford, consisting of an axial composition of two mixed borders (see chapter 16). Cormier's sticks were painted with four tones of blue to create a subtle, shimmering colour effect, making a gesture towards the famous Himalayan blue poppies cultivated by Mrs. Reford.[6] A final, surprising dénouement awaited unsuspecting visitors as they turned to leave the space: the reverse side of every stick was painted a brilliant, complementary orange-red.

A native of rural Quebec, Cormier studied agronomy at the University of Guelph and landscape architecture at the University of Toronto. During his early career in late 1980s Montreal, he contributed original design ideas to several large projects and created a number of exciting ephemeral "stage-set" designs for local night clubs, presaging the direction of his future work.[7] In 1993–94, Cormier enrolled in Harvard University's Graduate School of Design, studying the history and theory of design while benefiting from the teaching of such iconoclastic landscape architects as Martha Schwartz. On his return to Montreal, he designed a series of highly personal and stimulating landscape projects in Canada and abroad, both ephemeral and permanent, filled with colourful allusions to popular culture.[8] With these

CANADIAN LANDSCAPES IN A TIME OF RAPID CHANGE 529

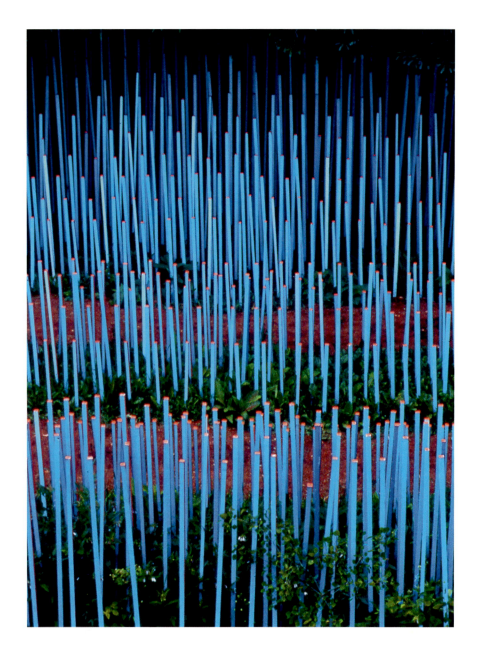

24.2 The Blue Stick Garden at the first Métis Garden Festival at Métis, QC, 2000

24.3 (facing page) "Entre ciel et terre," an ephemeral garden at the Flora International Exhibition at Montreal's Old Port, in 2006. Materials in this non-organic garden, designed by Catalyse Urbaine, included varicoloured translucent plastic and recycled glass aggregate, which create fascinating visual effects.

projects, including the exterior esplanade and interior *Lipstick Forest* at Montreal's convention centre, *Blue Tree* (composed of thousands of Christmas balls) at the Sonoma Garden Festival in California, and his *Solange* installation that wrapped coniferous trees in bright silk flowers at Lyon in France,[9] Cormier gradually extended his reach and reputation from the local to the international, putting landscape architecture on the front page and becoming something of a celebrity, an unusual role for a member of a profession that has too often sought comfortable obscurity and shunned the limelight.

Following the overwhelming popular success of the Festival international des Jardins at Métis, other avant-garde garden exhibitions took form, including the International Flora Montreal exhibit in the city's Old Port in summer 2006. Organized by a number of public and private organizations and coordinated by landscape architect Raquel Penalosa, artistic director, this exhibition provided landscape designers, both established and upcoming, with an occasion to explore new perspectives in garden design. The abstract compositions created by Montreal ensembles NIP Paysage (which includes partners Mathieu Casavant, France Cormier, Josée Labelle, Michel Langevin, and Mélanie Mignault) and Catalyse Urbaine (Juliette Patterson and Michel Langlois) injected colour and humour into the garden festival.[10] Claude Cormier reconstructed his *Blue Stick Garden* from Métis (one of several repeat performances at various exhibitions around the world), and as always, it proved to be a crowd favourite. The Flora garden festival was repeated in 2007, inspiring many original approaches to garden design, whether technically or environmentally advanced, whimsical, ironic, or humorous.

Restoring Urban Equilibrium

In the 1990s and in the first decade of the twenty-first century, Canadian downtowns finally began to reclaim their dominant position they had lost to the suburbs in the 1950s and 1960s. Using a variety of strategies, including direct investments, strategic partnerships, and long-term rehabilitation plans, central cities were able to revitalize their old urban cores and attract, once more, residents and businesses.

No Canadian urban centre was hit harder by the exodus of the 1950s than Quebec City. The "old capital" lost its downtown university and its main business district, previously located in the St-Roch sector, and even the downtown that remained – including the city's Chinatown and the approaches to Parliament Hill – was cut up by urban freeways or eventually demolished to make way for urban renewal projects that never materialized. At last, under the reform administration of Mayor Jean-Paul l'Allier, elected in 1989 and backed up by a highly professional team in the municipal government,[11] Quebec City regained lost ground, rebuilding its historic "flagship" downtown areas and endowing them with a new and stimulating urban character. In collaboration with the Commission de la Capitale nationale du Québec (CCNQ)[12] and other partners, the city embarked upon a series of innovative projects aimed at reinventing the downtown area and correcting the errors of the 1960s. The mayor and his associates sought a broad spectrum of public and professional opinion in defining their strategies and, following the counsel of Ken Greenberg, the former director of urban design for the city of Toronto, initiated their rebuilding program by creating a green space that was envisioned as a *catalyst for development*.[13] This was the St-Roch Garden, completed in 1993 to the plans of a consortium that included landscape architects WAA Inc. of Montreal, the environmental design group Option Aménagement, and GGLC Architects of Quebec City. The garden was an integral part of a larger urban composition planned by Montreal architects/city planners Cardinal Hardy et associés, who deftly welded the new street pattern to the city's original layout, instead of creating a closed

24.4 View of Quebec City's St-Roch Garden, seen from the Upper Town. The garden's creation acted as a catalyst for the redevelopment of a declining neighbourhood. Some of the new buildings that were built after the garden's realization are seen in the background.

enclave. As hoped, the garden project stimulated the reconstruction of the entire St-Roch district, which has now become one of the most successful urban quarters in North America.[14]

Concurrently and in the following years, the city and the CCNQ realized other projects, notably the reconstruction of an intimidating urban freeway, Boulevard Saint-Cyrille, which was reborn as a tree-lined avenue and promenade, Boulevard René-Lévesque.[15] They moved on to the redesign of Parliament Hill and its environs in 1996–98, upgrading the landscape setting for Quebec's historic Hôtel du Parlement and creating new symbolic gardens and a Promenade des Premiers Ministres, on a raised terrace parallel to René-Lévesque Boulevard.[16] Later, in 2000–02, at the northwest entrance to the city centre, the transformation of a freeway deserted by pedestrians into a convivial and active urban boulevard, Avenue Honoré-Mercier, provided a dignified and appropriate approach to the parliament buildings, while creating an attractive, pleasant, and stimulating environment for pedestrians and revitalizing business.

The two-decade-long urban transformation of the Old Capital eventually extended out beyond the city centre, culminating in the creation of the Promenade Samuel-de-Champlain, opened in 2008 as one of the keynote projects marking the 400th anniversary of the city's founding. The promenade is a 2.5-kilometre waterfront green space in a theatrical setting on the St. Lawrence River. The plan integrates pedestrian and bicycle paths and a discreet vehicle route into a splendid greenway punctuated with waterside focal areas featuring fountains, a viewing tower, seating and water-play areas, and sculptural elements.[17]

Besides contributing to the correction of the excesses of the 1950s and 1960s, the ambitious Quebec City projects attracted many new economic and cultural activities to the city centre. Several private offices and public agencies worked in various combinations on the design and realization of the various projects; participants included landscape architect André Plante and several other professionals from the Quebec City municipal government; urbanist Serge Filion and the planning staff of the CCNQ; architects and urban designers Groupe Daoust-Lestage; landscape architects and planners WAA Inc.; environmental designers Pluram-DAA; and Option Aménagement of Quebec City, among others.

Similar projects sprang up across the country. At the University of Alberta, the latest phase of reconstruction has begun to remove inappropriate intrusions into the great central space designed by Percy Nobbs (see chapters 13 and 20), re-establishing the spatial structure of his original beaux-arts plan. We are also seeing the reinsertion of some of the charming, fanciful, and playful elements that had been eliminated from parks and green spaces during their period of decline in the 1950s. Thus the Grand Concourse Authority, in its recent rehabilitation of Bowring Park in St. John's, Newfoundland, reconstructed the delightful fences of rough spruce logs and twigs that had once graced the park.

Completing the Work of the Twentieth Century

Some landscape projects have taken decades, or even a century, to be completed. This has been the case with the park systems of several Canadian cities; the classic example is that of the open-space network of Ottawa and Gatineau, from its original definition in the first report of a young Frederick Todd in 1903, to its virtually complete realization in the years following the Second World War. The propositions of Harland Bartholomew for Vancouver also required some four decades to be more or less fully carried out.

This pattern has recently been repeated in the city of Edmonton, where Frederick Todd set out in 1907 his vision for a great network of greenways based on the majestic North Saskatchewan River and its many tributary streams and ravines. The city authorities proceeded slowly and deliberately to transform the former industrial sites and abandoned lands of the broad valley – 60 metres deep and up to 1.6 kilometres wide – into a park. Direct purchase by the city, donations from service clubs like the Kinsmen, conversions into golf courses, and a major investment by the provincial government at the end of the 1970s – all contributed to the gradual realization of a continuous green ribbon some 90 kilometres long, all across the metropolitan region.[18] Work on the Louise McKinney Riverfront Park, among the recent components of the park in Edmonton's central sector, was finished in 2007, exactly a century after Todd had tabled his first proposals.

24.5 A section of the continuous North Saskatchewan River Park adjacent to downtown Edmonton, looking west. This view includes Louise McKinney Riverfront Park in the middle distance and, further along the river, several other parks and public areas.

This park, designed by Doug Carlyle of the Carlyle + Associates office in Edmonton, had been proposed in earlier concept plans by EIDOS Consultants.[19] The park steps up from the river in a series of slopes and terraces towards Millennium Plaza, an assembly area for summer concerts on an intermediate terrace, focusing on the elegant steel and glass Shumka Stage. In the 1990s, Carlyle also authored the design of Victoria Promenade, a linear park that looks out over the oldest component of the network, Victoria Park.[20] All of these municipal parks contribute, in turn, to a still larger plan developed by the Alberta government, the Capital Region River Valley Park, of which the master plan was designed by EIDOS Consultants Inc., under the direction of Robert Gibbs, landscape architect. The valley park is an immense green space that traverses the whole of the region, measuring some 7,400 hectares in total area and offering a vast range of recreational and educational possibilities that include hiking, cross-country skiing, canoeing, sports fields, and a science centre.[21] In turn, this very extensive scheme has been integrated into an even larger-scale regional plan, which envisions an ecological network for the entire urban region.[22]

One of the most extensive urban rebuilding projects in the country's history is the ongoing reconstruction of the Toronto waterfront. Occupied for more than a century by impassable port facilities, railways, and industry, and separated from the downtown area by the intimidating Gardiner Expressway of the 1950s and 1960s, enormous areas fronting on the harbour had lost their *raison d'être* and became available for redevelopment in the closing decades of the twentieth century. A few isolated waterfront projects, including the highly successful Music Garden, were realized from the 1970s to the 1990s (see chapter 22). Further afield, the rehabilitation of the Don Valley Brickworks site and the mouth of the Humber River began a long-term rehabilitation process for the two river valleys that circumscribe central Toronto (see chapter 21). But Toronto, wisely, did not stop after this first wave of improvements. In the waterfront area opposite downtown Toronto, public open space and design character were still discontinuous and uncoordinated; and pedestrian movement was pinched between the water and a busy boulevard that provided no space for bicycle traffic.[23] The city moved to improve this situation, undertaking a second series of step-by-step rebuilding projects

24.6 Victoria Promenade, a narrow linear park at the top of the escarpment above Edmonton's river park. A simple and low-key construction consisting primarily of well-detailed paving, guard-rails, benches, and shade trees, provides a high degree of urban amenity in a strategic location.

536 BIRTH OF THE MODERN LANDSCAPE

based on the studies directed by former mayor David Crombie from 1988 to 1992 (see chapter 21). Crombie's studies had proposed an ecosystem approach to the regeneration of the entire length of the metropolitan waterfront.

A new public body, the Toronto Waterfront Revitalization Corporation, created in 2001 by the federal, provincial, and municipal governments, provided overall guidance for this complex and far-reaching process, coordinating the activities of an ensemble cast of public and private participants. The corporation divided the entire development area into a number of sectors, from the Billy Bishop island airport to the mouth of the Don River. Within these sectors, specific projects are now taking form or are already completed, providing accommodation for thousands of new residents, a number of new retail and office sub-centres, and a wide variety of public open spaces – to finally realize Toronto's early dream of a great public esplanade along the lake.[24]

These open spaces run the gamut of size, materials, character, and style. At the micro-scale, a series of "wavedecks" were constructed in 2008–09 in the Central Waterfront sector opposite downtown, providing elegant terminations of several north-south streets, including historic Spadina Avenue. These undulating and challenging natural-wood structures, designed (as was the master plan for this

24.7 Toronto waterfront developments and proposals, 1980s–2012. A series of new developments have already transformed Toronto's long-neglected relationship to the harbour and the lake; recent proposals, if realized, promise to further extend this new vision. A comparison between the currently proposed shoreline and that of Toronto's site in 1793 shows a complete reconfiguration of the original natural environment.

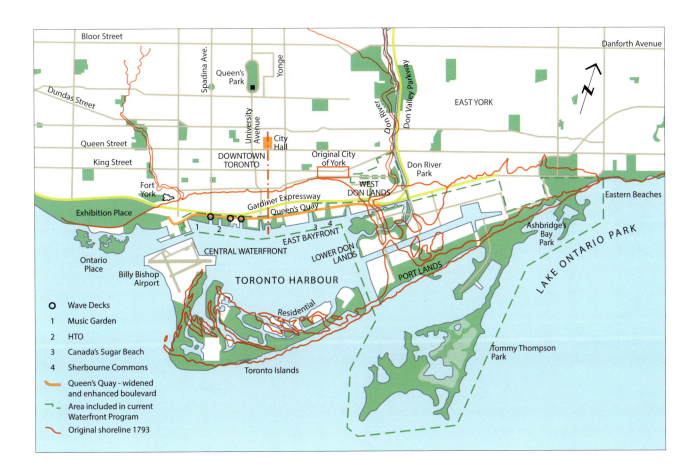

sector)[25] by Amsterdam firm West 8 in collaboration with DTAH (du Toit Allsopp Hillier), provide seating areas and stimulating access routes for pedestrians and cyclists along the lakefront.[26]

In this and the adjoining waterfront sector are two attractive and whimsical urban beaches. The first, HtO, carried out in 2007, features an array of artfully located parabolic grass mounds, punctuated by spreading willow trees, and a sandy platform next to the water, equipped with comfortable "Muskoka" wooden chairs[27] sheltered by cheery yellow parasols. The designers were Toronto landscape architect Janet Rosenberg + Associates, Montreal-based Claude Cormier Architectes Paysagistes Inc., and Toronto architects Hariri Pontarini.[28] Claude Cormier continued to explore the urban beach theme in his subsequent Canada's Sugar Beach project, completed in 2010, in the neighbouring East Bayfront Precinct.[29] Further east in this sector, landscape architects Phillips Farevaag Smallenberg designed Sherbourne Commons, a 1.6-hectare swath of green space between Lakeshore Boulevard and the waterfront, with a central pool and water feature that are transformed into a skating rink in winter.

24.8 A sandy urban beach enlivened by colourful parasols and vernacular Muskoka chairs link Canada's Sugar Beach on the Toronto waterfront to cottage country traditions. The name relates to the Redpath Sugar factory on the neighbouring site. The Toronto Islands are seen in the background.

538   BIRTH OF THE MODERN LANDSCAPE

The West Don Lands to the northeast and the Lower Don Lands on the man-made platforms that long housed the industrial port of Toronto will complete the long-term rehabilitation of the entire southern reach of the long-suffering Don River. Within the latter sector, planned by a team led by Michael van Valkenburgh Associates of New York, with Greenberg Consultants providing urban design expertise, the river's hitherto canalized mouth will be rebuilt in a more naturalistic configuration as the centrepiece of a major park surrounded by new neighbourhoods.[30] Finally, the peninsulas and islands that project out into Lake Ontario, many of which (including Tommy Thompson Park – see chapter 21) have never been developed, will be combined with the extensive beaches east of the Don River to create a huge new green space, 375 hectares in extent, called Lake Ontario Park,[31] based on an overall conceptual plan by New York's James Corner Field Operations and landscape architects and ecological restoration consultants Schollen and Company Inc. of Richmond Hill, Ontario.

Creating the Sustainable City of the Twenty-first Century

The transformation of downtown Quebec City, the Edmonton river-park system, and the Toronto waterfront are all motivated by a new image of the city, compact and green, that responds to the objectives of sustainable development (see chapter 21), unlike the postwar model that consisted of suburbs deployed over a huge urban zone, accessible primarily by car. In Quebec City, the migration of thousands of new residents into a district that is close to the employment opportunities, services, and cultural attractions of the central city diminished the need for cars, freeways, and gasoline while increasing conviviality. In Edmonton, a very large proportion of the population now has access to high-quality green space close to their own residence.

The city and region of Vancouver, among all the major urban agglomerations of Canada, have gone furthest in this direction. At the metropolitan scale, the phenomenon of "Vancouverism" has inspired much praise and many imitations around the world.[32] It is a philosophy of urbanism, put forward by the city's planning staff under the direction of former director of city planning Larry Beasley, that aims to attract a great number of residents into the urban core, to be accommodated in high-rise apartment buildings in integrated neighbourhoods, with commercial and institutional services nearby. To complement this primary urban focus, the regional government is expanding the metropolitan transport system along new rapid-transit lines to link the existing suburbs to the centre city. The "densification" of the urban fabric around the stations of these new transport systems and the exploitation of every occasion to create new green spaces within the new, denser developments should also help to ensure the long-term success of the model through the creation of a higher quality of life. Vancouver's family of strategies is indeed beginning to create a more compact and green metropolis than one sees in other North American cities of comparable population.[33] Certainly, the natural and legal constraints on Vancouver – the limited space available in the

Lower Mainland and the 1972 decision to conserve the region's agricultural lands, the most productive in the province – required a significant augmentation in the average density of the city, long known as a city of small single-family dwellings. Vancouver's urban constraints are as severe as those that apply to the island city-state of Singapore, so it is not surprising that the central area of Vancouver has started to resemble its Asian counterpart.

Transforming these grand intentions into concrete form will depend entirely on the city's capacity to generate *sustainable residential neighbourhoods*. In this domain, Vancouver is once again in the avant-garde of theory and practice. The carrying-out of research in the field of sustainable development has long been a preoccupation of the landscape architecture program of the University of British Columbia. The projects and publications of professors Patrick Mooney, Patrick

24.9   A prototype design for sustainable development, Vancouver, 2006, by the Design Centre for Sustainability at the University of British Columbia. Issues of sustainability that are explored in this study include the interface between city and agricultural land, greenways designed for a variety of traffic modes, and compact neighbourhoods.

Condon, and former chairperson Cynthia Girling have been largely oriented to the design of local communities according to the principles of ecological viability. Girling, in her book *Skinny Streets and Green Neighborhoods*, written in collaboration with Ronald Kellett, explores the ecological potential of the various components of the North American city. They identify these components as *green infrastructure* – the small-scale network of open spaces that do the "ecological work" of the neighbourhood; *green fabric* – the large parks and the "urban forest" that create a milder microclimate; and *green streets* – the parts of the environment that receive and filter urban storm waters and return them to earth.[34]

During the past twenty years, Condon and UBC's Design Centre for Sustainability, of which he was the long-time director and is now a senior researcher, have organized a series of *design charrettes* (intense work sessions that bring together many participants, both citizens and experts, in accordance with a pre-established working procedure) to explore the design possibilities of specific sites. Their Surrey Design Charrette of 1995 applied principles of sustainable development to sites within the Vancouver suburb of Surrey.[35] A recent and even more ambitious charrette, held in several areas of the Vancouver region in 2006, explored the urban and landscape implications of the creation of a sustainable city for a regional population of 4 million inhabitants within fifty years.

Sustainability: Research and Practice

Landscape departments in universities all across the country are currently carrying out research in the realm of sustainable development. For the past two decades, for example, Professor Robert D. Brown, former director of the School of Environmental Design and Rural Development at the University of Guelph, has worked with graduate students and recent graduates on design with climate and microclimate, exploring issues of wind, solar radiation, and air quality, particularly in urban areas. Brown has focused on the development of new design tools and the dissemination of new knowledge through publication in widely used student and professional manuals as well as normal academic media, and through his recently published book, *Design with Microclimate*.[36]

Research findings in sustainable development are mirrored in professional practice, as a new and nation-wide wave of landscape architecture and planning offices moves into this rapidly expanding field of endeavour, assisted by new scientific knowledge and informational technologies. In Vancouver, Catherine Berris Associates Inc., founded in 1985, has developed expertise in the use of GIS (geographic information systems) as a tool for mapping and analysis, and for three-dimensional modelling and animation. This strong technical base supports the firm's work on broad-scale open-space plans for municipalities and on watershed management plans. Calgary landscape architectural office O2 Planning and Design, directed by Douglas Olson, specializes in large-scale landscape and ecological planning. The firm's projects include many regional and metropolitan development plans, based on detailed ecological and spatial analysis and collaboration with public and private stakeholders.

As the principal of Schollen & Company Inc., based in Toronto and Shanghai, Mark Schollen has carried out many regional resource-management projects. His firm's work includes master plans for Toronto's three main river systems (Don, Humber, and Rouge) and involves stormwater management, erosion control, habitat enhancement, and rehabilitation of damaged watercourse environments. Montreal landscape architect and city planner Michel Fontaine and his firm, Medialand Inc., also focus on land reclamation and site enhancements, promoting environmentally positive development and biodiversity. They have developed particular expertise in quarry reclamation and the restoration of ecosystems damaged by large-scale industrial operations, using two- and three-dimensional visual simulation techniques as tools for design and communication.

These and other similar firms are in the vanguard of what will likely become a central preoccupation of all the design professions. The full achievement of the objectives of sustainable development will present new challenges to our whole society and, in particular, to landscape architects, who will have to apply their knowledge at every level, from detailed microdesign to large-scale planning. In the urban sphere, these professionals will have to be able to design attractive and stimulating urban spaces that will accommodate large numbers of people, employing extremely durable materials with great attention to detail. They will have to help design neighbourhoods that will facilitate social integration and satisfy the needs of very different people in relatively small and concentrated spaces. A mastery of the full range of plant materials, native and horticultural, will be required to ensure the perpetuity and lasting beauty of these spaces. Landscape architects will need to carry out detailed studies on how existing neighbourhoods work in order to integrate new, smaller-scale movement systems. And finally, they will have to preserve and enhance the natural systems within park networks, maximizing their capacity to collect and filter rainwater, and return it to the water table to prevent erosion and flooding and reduce dependence on underground drainage and irrigation systems.[37]

A Crisis in Resources

Canada's economic prosperity – since the beginning of human habitation by the First Nations and up until the present day – has been largely based on the exploitation of its natural resources, which have seemed to be miraculously abundant. Fish, furs, wood, agriculture, mining, and petroleum have succeeded and overlapped each other as the central focuses of this exploitation. Even today, despite the strong environmental ethos that inspires many Canadians, the country's post-industrial economy is profoundly dependent on its natural resources. They are what the world wants from Canada.

Exploration for and extraction of these resources have accelerated in recent years, against the background of an expanding world economy,[38] inspiring concerned observers to present eloquent exposés of irresponsible practices in books, magazines, films, and television. Dr David Suzuki's long-running CBC television series, *The Nature of Things*, and his crusades against the destruction of old-growth forests, along with Richard Desjardins's film *L'Erreur boréale/Forest Alert*, concerning the forest industry in Quebec, are vivid examples.[39] The images by Canadian photographer Edward Burtynsky featured in the 2007 film *Manufactured Landscapes* provide a powerful indictment of the wrecked landscapes left behind by large-scale industrial activities throughout the world.[40]

Tar Ponds and Tar Sands

What are the issues in this debate? Have we learned anything from previous experience? To answer this, it may be instructive to compare today's practices to those of the past. An interesting comparison can be made between one of the oldest industrial extraction processes in Canada – the mining of coal on Cape Breton Island – and one of the most recent – the exploitation of the oil sands of northern Alberta. In many respects, the two industries resemble each other. First, both owe their existence to the transformation of the plant residues of ancient forests by powerful tectonic forces in the remote past. Millions of years later, the very first Europeans to arrive in these New World territories stumbled on both of the resources in question. In the 1500s and 1600s Spanish and French sailors noticed the coal seams embedded in the cliffs on the east coast of Cape Breton Island,[41] and the journals of North West Company trader Peter Pond document the "sticky black sand and pools of bitumen" he encountered when he first entered the watershed of the Athabasca River in 1778.[42] Subsequent stages of development of the two industries were also similar. At the beginning, small-scale producers had to overcome major technical difficulties – in the case of the oil sands, this was a titanic struggle – eventually establishing important local industries.

Later, investments from outside the area were necessary for expansion, and this led to dilution or loss of local control, in favour of Montreal investors in the case of Cape Breton[43] and multinational enterprises in Alberta.[44] Then, gradually, both industries became the backbone of their respective regional economies and the lifeblood of a growing population that worked harder and harder to get at a resource that did not give itself up easily. At Glace Bay, New Waterford, and other towns founded by the coal companies, miners dug tunnels that extended out as far as 5.5 kilometres under the sea. The oil in Alberta's three oil sand deposit regions lies hidden at least 60 metres under the boreal forest and muskeg, a difficult landscape to traverse, and it takes the form of a thin film of hydrocarbon that is bound up with a minute amount of water and sand particles. Companies have to excavate enormous holes to get at the oil or must drive it from its underground lair with the help of boiling-hot steam.[45]

The environmental impacts – *negative externalities*, as the economists put it – are also similar. The Cape Breton mines were always a dangerous place, and decent salaries and working conditions were only won through implacable struggle. The owners of the mines and of the steel company that grew up alongside them did little to reduce the environmental effects of the smoke, mine tailings, and chemical outfalls into the surface waters that they produced.[46] When the resource ran out, the people and the environmental impacts remained. No-one had prepared

24.10   View through security fence of the heavily polluted Sydney Tar Ponds, not far from a residential sector of Sydney, NS, 2003. In 2013, the first step in reclaiming this site took form in the creation of a 68-hectare green space.

a transition plan to help the Cape Bretoners adjust to the decline of the industry. This decline was not used as a building block for a new Cape Breton economy; the community inherited only unemployment, chagrin, and resentment. The unique culture of the people of Cape Breton and some creative innovations[47] diminished the human damage to some extent, but since the departure of the coal and steel industries, the region has faced much difficulty.

The physical legacy was almost as discouraging as the economic legacy. The "Sydney Tar Ponds," actually an arm of the sea horribly polluted by PCBs, heavy metals, aromatic hydrocarbons, and other substances emitted by the steel factory over the years, remain a stubborn challenge, despite the investment of hundreds of millions of government dollars to clean them up. The problem is made worse by the location of the ponds within the most densely urbanized area on the island.[48]

The "Athabasca Tar Sands" (as originally named; now known as the "Oil Sands" and found to occur in two additional locations besides the Athabasca region of Alberta) are both similar to and different from the coal mines of Cape Breton. First, a lot more money is involved in the Alberta projects exploited by Syncrude, Suncor, and the other companies that followed them; at the height of the boom, salaries were generous to the point that the wage scale of the entire province was distorted.[49] And the environmental impacts are also infinitely greater. Surface deposits from the Maritime coal mines are minuscule in comparison with the immense excavations and spoil deposits created by the process used to extract oil from the tar sands, which consists essentially of excavating all the overburden, retrieving and grinding up the oil-bearing sands, and then adding a mixture of hot water and caustic to them to separate the petroleum from other components. The materials that remain after this process are deposited in huge sedimentation ponds, toxic and dangerous for the birds that are naturally attracted to them. Another method of extracting the resource, known as "in situ" extraction, has much less impact on the surface of the ground, but both hot water and in situ extraction processes require enormous quantities of water from the nearby natural systems, principally the Athabasca River. This industrial use calls into question both the quantity and the quality[50] of the water that eventually reaches the Peace-Athabasca Delta at the western extremity of Lake Athabasca, some 200 kilometres to the north. One of the largest freshwater deltas in the world, this immense region of lakes, streams, and marshes had already been affected by the 1968 construction of the W.A.C. Bennett Dam on the Peace River, 700 kilometres to the southwest in British Columbia.[51] For the moment, the "oil mines" are situated close to the Athabasca River, but their impacts extend much further. Flying over northeastern Alberta, one has the impression that every square mile of territory has a hole dug in it or a survey line cut through the spruce woods and the muskeg.[52] And considering potential positive impacts, the secondary benefit offered by many mining enterprises in the past – the creation of new communities that would be viable over the long term, the extension of the ecumene – does not seem to have applied here.[53] The only real city or town in the region is Fort McMurray, founded in 1870 and already inhabited by 100,000 people. Those who work in mines located further north live in temporary camps.[54]

CANADIAN LANDSCAPES IN A TIME OF RAPID CHANGE 545

24.11 (facing page)   Aerial view of a small part of the immense Peace-Athabasca Delta in northern Alberta, about 160 kilometres downstream (north) from the oil sands developments near Fort McMurray, AB. A vast and complex wetland where two great river systems meet before their waters flow north to the Mackenzie and the Arctic Ocean, this delta and the plant and animal life it supports are greatly affected by changes in water quantity and quality.

24.12 (above)   View of tailing pond and extraction operations at the Suncor oil sands project, about 20 kilometres north of Fort McMurray

24.13 Reforested land, part of the rehabilitation efforts undertaken by the Suncor Corporation on land that had been disturbed by oil sands operations

Is the Athabasca region destined to recapitulate the harsh destiny of Cape Breton, where industry demanded a high human and ecological cost that we are still paying, hundreds of years after the first exploitation? The oil sands investments are so huge and the demand for oil so broad that it would be unrealistic to imagine that Alberta will stop exploiting this resource (slowing the expansion and fine-tuning production over the long term is, however, quite plausible).[55] The immense amounts of money that will be generated by the sale of hydrocarbons over the life of the resource should make it possible to carry out a serious and well-planned program of landscape repair and renaturalization. This indeed corresponds to the political will of the province and to the stated intentions of the producing companies.[56] But do we have the necessary knowledge to do this? Will it even be possible to reconstitute these devastated landscapes and return them to something like their previous states? It seems obvious that, confronted by the great scale of such present-day *dérangements* of the landscape, we can no longer blithely follow our classic approach to landscape exploitation (see chapters 6, 7, and 8), which consisted of a first phase of thoughtless destruction, followed by an energetic program of rehabilitation after the fact. It would be much more sensible to build mitigation and renaturalization into the extraction process, to see the whole operation as a carefully planned-out continuum. By 2007, the Suncor Corporation had rehabilitated 4,600 hectares of disturbed land (on which some 300 woodland buffaloes now live) and planted 4.5 million trees and shrubs.[57] The grasslands and newly established woodlands within the rehabilitation zone seem stable and in good health, but they are not the same as the original landscapes – primarily spruce forest and muskeg – that they replaced. And the total area of the lands that are slated for eventual oil development is considerably greater than this already huge site. The challenge is enormous and of tremendous importance for the future of Canada, a country that will long depend on natural resources to ensure its economic survival. If there was ever an opportunity to proceed with measured and careful exploitation, to create viable human communities, and to carry out the research necessary to identify appropriate measures of protection, mitigation, and rehabilitation – and to invent whole new technologies, if necessary – it is here. The oil sands represent a unique challenge for Canada to make a major contribution to sustainable development worldwide.

The Continuing Wilderness

Although the theme of this chapter is change, it must recognize one aspect of the Canadian landscape that persistently refuses to disappear: the northern wilderness. Although the frontier is being constantly pushed back by urban expansion, ice roads, and diamond mines in the lands "north of sixty,"[58] this vast area is still largely untouched and, according to John Ralston Saul, will always be; Southern Canadian models cannot be applied in the North.[59] Five kilometres beyond the limits of Yellowknife or Pangnirtung, the Canadian Shield reasserts its presence and "civilization" disappears. Saul speaks of a "permanent frontier" that defines Canada as a cultural entity distinct from the United States or the European countries, from which we import most of our cultural models,[60] and defines our thinking on many levels. This may explain the continuing popularity of a sublime and pristine vision of the Canadian wilderness as expressed in painting almost a century ago by Tom Thomson and the Group of Seven. Over the last twenty years, exhibitions at several major Canadian galleries have presented this important native school, in almost adulatory tone, to a new generation of Canadians, who received it with great enthusiasm, to the consternation of some art critics who question the contemporary relevance of this long-exploited subject matter.[61] The cultural imprinting that coloured much of Canadian poetry with the concept of the sublime in the eighteenth century, as postulated by poet Susan Glickman, remains an important part of the Canadian identity.[62]

Challenges of the New North

Beyond questions of symbolism and identity, real and complex challenges face landscape architects as they confront new needs at the edge of the frontier. As Iqaluit, capital of the recently constituted territory of Nunavut (1999), goes through a stunningly rapid expansion in population and construction, new parks and open spaces are under development to provide for the needs of newcomers and long-time residents. Such development programs have been carried out in many previous municipalities, but in Iqaluit's location on Baffin Island, situated hundreds of kilometres beyond the treeline, the designers of these facilities must work with a drastically reduced vocabulary of materials compared to their counterparts in southern Canada. Plants are limited to extremely hardy, low-growing shrubs and ground covers, which have their own, sometimes spectacular, palette of colours; timber is a precious commodity, imported to the region, its use carefully limited to essential purposes; and stone and rock in every form and variety become the essential physical components of landscape architecture. Iqaluit Square, the community's centrally located public plaza, is a striking case in point. Realized in 2004 under the guidance of consultant Office for Urbanism and landscape architect John Laird, the assembly space of the square is defined by an ellipse of large rocks – the Elders' Circle – that recalls traditional winter house forms, symbolically oriented to the North and focusing on a central circular podium. Stonework was carried out by Mary Crnkovich of Touchstone Masonry.[63]

There is, on the other hand, no shortage of attractive – even remarkable – undeveloped sites that can, with minor interventions, become great natural parks, easily accessible from urban areas and villages. Such is the case of Sylvia Grinnell Territorial Park, designed by local firm Aarluk Consulting, located on high ground above a fast-moving braided river just ten minutes from central Iqaluit, a favourite gathering place with stunning views towards Frobisher Bay.[64] But these views are now changing from year to year, pointing up another challenge for landscape designers, as for everyone else in the North. The rapid acceleration of climate change in these high latitudes is rapidly changing the abundance and distribution of sea ice and the melting of permafrost.[65] The long-term impacts of these changes are as yet only dimly seen, but they will certainly be enormous.[66]

Another striking change in the North is seen in attitudes towards large-scale development projects. Where, in the 1970s, Aboriginal communities were among the strongest opponents of the proposed natural gas pipeline along the Mackenzie Valley (see chapter 21), the current version of this very project has recently been approved, without fanfare, by Canada's National Energy Board – with the support and, indeed, the participation of three of the four Native peoples who had originally stood against it. This new collaboration between First Nations and giant resource companies is the result of several new factors: a much more equal division of profits and jobs among the protagonists; the resolution of many Native land claims, involving the transfer of title to extensive land parcels; and – less positive though seemingly inevitable – the decreasing involvement of Aboriginal people in a traditional land-based economy. While not all the development projects are objects of enthusiastic collaboration and while many tensions remain, the rhythm of northern development will certainly accelerate. A new balance between Native values, economic growth, and ecological fragility must be sought, requiring ever more sensitive analysis and design at the regional scale.[67]

A Time of Rapid Change

In this as in virtually every other sphere, change is the rule. New social and economic structures, international as well as local, are bringing sudden and striking transformations to the Canadian landscape. Everything that is familiar to us is subject to transformation. The impact of the automobile, for example, is increasing rather than decreasing, the consequence of sixty years of urban and suburban evolution. Every landscape architect who has practised for a number of years has been urgently called back to enlarge parking lots designed thirty years ago that were then perfectly adequate. The ideal of the "family car" of the 1950s seems hopelessly insufficient today. A similar fate has come to long-established golf courses, even the classics designed by Stanley Thompson; most are going through major rebuilding programs to adapt them to changes in both equipment and attitudes towards the sport.

Transformation of the Agricultural Landscape

The effects of rapid change are particularly evident in Canada's agricultural landscapes. Research carried out by Gérald Domon and Julie Ruiz at the Chair on Landscape and Environment of the University of Montreal's Faculty of Environmental Design has identified new tendencies across the country. All these trends seem to be moving towards larger and larger farms that are fewer and fewer in number. This evolution accentuates the differences between regions: on the highest-quality agricultural lands, such as those of the St. Lawrence Lowlands, there is at once a loss of farmland to urbanization, an expansion of the total area under cultivation, and an intensification of exploitation (more corn and soybeans, less traditional pastureland and oats). To enlarge their fields, farmers are cutting down hedgerows that formerly divided the landscape, along with isolated trees, those evocative sentinels that contribute so much to the landscape heritage of the Lanaudière region and other rural areas of Quebec.[68] In less-productive territories such as the Eastern Townships and the Mauricie, much farmland has been simply abandoned since 1951; undergrowth and forest have invaded them, creating landscapes that are more and more enclosed and blocking once-classic views. Over fifty years, 80 per cent of Quebec's pastureland area has disappeared, the consequence of changes in the dairy industry. Many archetypal landscapes are becoming more and more rare.[69]

The same winds of change are buffeting the plains of western Canada. The consolidation of smaller farms to create larger corporate farms with larger fields has led to the uprooting of more and more shelterbelts, eliminating what had been a classic element of the regional landscape for more than a century.[70] This physical change parallels the decline of the traditional small-scale family farm, an institution that has long played a central role in the cultural, economic, and democratic evolution of Canada, but which is proving less and less viable in competition with larger enterprises.[71]

Fading Icons

The focal elements of Canada's vernacular landscapes are also disappearing or, if they continue to exist, are little by little losing their meaning. On the Prairies, the traditional wooden *grain elevators* are being eliminated as rapidly as the railway lines that used to serve them, in favour of a small number of much larger *terminal elevators* located in major centres like Medicine Hat. The towns and cities of the West are thus losing their principal landmarks and a large part of their identity. In Quebec and elsewhere in French Canada, the *silver spire of the parish church* is no longer the symbol of a universal religious community. Many urban churches have been transformed into libraries, condominiums, or residences for senior citizens, and those in rural areas often attract only 10 per cent of the number of parishioners served in previous generations.[72] In the Maritime provinces and on other seacoasts and lakeshores, technological progress – radio beacons and satellites – has increasingly diminished the role of the *lighthouses*, which once proudly stood on guard for our shipping. Some will remain as museums or restaurants, but in general, these icons of the Canadian landscape have lost their function and meaning. It is as if the images on all those postage stamps and dollar bills were just fading away.

If key elements of Canada's traditional symbolic landscapes are in decline, what is the symbolism of the landscapes that we are creating today? Is there even a place for symbolic landscapes that communicate meaningful messages? A cynic would nominate the typical landscape of the *urban fringe*, the commercial hodge-podge

24.14 A tall reinforced-concrete terminal elevator on the flat prairie outside Medicine Hat, AB. This structure provides a marked contrast to the comparatively smaller wooden country elevators seen in the distance at lower right. These are the same elevators shown in illustration 7.4.

24.15 A typical landscape of the urban fringe. Looking north towards the city, this photograph shows the road towards downtown Hamilton, ON. A similar picture could have been taken on the outskirts of almost any other Canadian city during the first decade of the twenty-first century.

of the suburban shopping strip, displaying its familiar international iconography, identical throughout North America and making inroads in other parts of world.[73] The same logos, the same generic buildings, almost no native landscape character comparable to that conveyed by the great elms or cottonwoods on the main streets of East and West a few decades ago.

The Centrality of Landscape

Yet despite today's pressures and challenges, there has never been greater interest in Canada's cultural, natural, and historic landscapes. Canadians use the landscape more and in new ways, take pride in local landscape character, and spend a lot of time outside in all sorts of environments that were once derelict or entirely unexploited.[74] And they increasingly see themselves as stewards of the land, seeking ways to escape the improvident destructiveness of the past. Hundreds of private associations have dedicated themselves to the protection and conservation of landscapes. The Conseil du paysage québécois, founded in 1994, brings together professional associations and regional groups that share a common desire to protect the landscapes of Quebec and to bring them to public awareness. Another example is the River Valley Alliance in Edmonton, which promotes the creation and preservation of a metropolitan park network through its sponsorship of the Capital Region River Valley Plan.[75]

Canadian landscape architects, artists, and designers continue to create memorable and meaningful landscapes, as these pages have shown. And research interest at the university level has never been so intense: *landscape studies*, marginal only thirty years ago, now constitute an important field of research for planners, ecologists, anthropologists, geographers, and urban and environmental historians, as well as landscape architects. Identification with the landscape remains a central component of the national identity, as landscapes still figure centrally on recent Canadian postage stamps and banknotes. Their messages are different from those of the past: the rural, wild, or productive landscapes shown on former generations of our money gave way in 2001–04 to a new series of images that expressed the theme *Canadian Journey*, displaying images that often made reference to cultural and symbolic landscapes.[76] Among them, sculptures by Haida artist Bill Reid and other expressions of First Nations cultures; poppies and memorials of war and of peacekeeping; children playing hockey on a frozen pond or slough. In this last nostalgic image, for which Canadian folklore has long reserved a special place, the cultural landscape merges with the personal landscape that everyone carries within – the place where he or she learned to skate as a child; "the cottage," the site of the warmest family memories for many Canadians; or the street where one grew up – to become a sort of *landscape of reference* carried throughout life. Despite threats and transformations, landscapes are important, as always; they will continue to play a central role in our culture.

24.16   Hockey on the pond: an archetypal Canadian landscape image, illustrated on the five-dollar bill from the Canadian Journey series, begun in 2001. The quotation on the banknote is from *The Hockey Sweater* by Roch Carrier (1979); the young woman wears number 9, as did legendary right wingers Maurice Richard and Gordie Howe.

EPILOGUE: THE CONSERVATION OF HISTORIC AND SIGNIFICANT LANDSCAPES

It is normal that we should wish to preserve our inherited landscapes; many of them are beautiful, functional, sustainable, and of great significance to us. Yet the predominantly economic focus of today's world requires all landscapes, whether historic or contemporary, to constantly justify their existence according to new criteria of financial determinism and social relevance. Faced with this pressure, can we indeed find reasons to protect and preserve historic landscapes? And if so, how do we do it?

In fact, the conservation of landscapes can be justified for many reasons. First, *aesthetic quality*: landscapes that demonstrate excellence in their design and execution, that appeal directly to the senses and the spirit, should be conserved, just as other works of art are. And certain landscapes that are not exceptional, but are *perfect examples* of a specific period or style of landscape design, such as Art Deco or the gardenesque, should also be preserved. Other landscapes are worthy of conservation through their role as *authentic witnesses*, not to a "high style" of design, but rather to a vernacular tradition that is typical of Canada as a whole, or of a particular culture, as are the Ukrainian cemeteries of the West.

Another set of reasons that motivate landscape preservation has to do with the *natural world*, including representative examples of specific ecosystems and geological formations, water systems, or unique plant communities. A major *raison d'être* of the national and provincial parks is to protect landscapes of this category. And as for landscapes that have been shaped by human intervention, an outstanding *horticultural achievement* could merit preservation. Finally, a landscape's *influence or association with important events or people* can motivate a decision to conserve it: an original project that established a new trend, a milieu that served as the setting for historic events or framed the life of an important historical personage, or a landscape designed or executed by a noted designer or gardener.

The preceding list is more than a preliminary survey; it corresponds closely to the criteria proposed in 1994 by the Historic Sites and Monuments Board of

Canada in their guide to the recognition of parks and gardens of national import-ance.[1] But once a decision has been taken concerning the conservation of a natural, cultural, or designed landscape, what strategy should be adopted? There are in fact many alternatives. Agricultural zoning and the creation of greenbelts and parks have conserved extensive natural, rural, and wild landscapes. Concerning cultural and designed landscapes, the best protection is often provided by a long-term pro-prietor who carries out continuous maintenance operations and consistent land use over a long period; the Ursuline Monastery in Quebec City and the Halifax Public Gardens provide excellent examples of this. The sensitive conversion of landscapes that have lost their traditional function to permit compatible new uses is often a valuable strategy, as shown by the many "old ports" and other obsolete industrial landscapes that have been transformed into areas of public recreation across Canada.

It is obvious that the limited availability of money, personnel, and resources will prevent us from "museifying" a large number of landscapes, but treating some landscapes as living museums is entirely appropriate and has long been prac-tised by government agencies and non-profit associations everywhere across the country.[2] Parks Canada is the outstanding practitioner of this approach through its programs of preservation, rehabilitation, and restoration when appropriate, and interpretation of historic buildings and landscapes, including their "human-ization" with people in period costume to make history seem real. Many of the sites examined in this book owe their survival or their renaissance to this agency: the Fortress of Louisbourg in Nova Scotia (the classic example), the Motherwell Homestead and Batoche in Saskatchewan, the fur trade posts of Fort Langley and Lower Fort Garry, among others. The provinces also play a vital role, as seen to great effect at Covenhoven in New Brunswick and Writing-on-Stone in Alberta.

Preservation Methods and Techniques

In carrying out their projects of landscape rehabilitation and restoration, these agencies have a number of useful and ingenious techniques at their disposal. While these techniques were called into play in the conservation and restoration of many different kinds of landscape, the restoration of a series of residential land-scapes, of varying scale, over the last forty years demonstrates the application of a considerable variety of approaches. In the 1970s, the buildings and gardens of Bellevue, an Italian-style villa constructed in 1843 in Kingston, Ontario,[3] were re-built by Parks Canada.[4] This villa, built on a site that slopes down towards Lake Ontario, had been rented by Canada's future prime minister John A. Macdonald in 1848. The agency reconstructed the house true to its original flamboyant com-position, which featured a central tower and a variety of picturesque roof forms, and painted it with the vivid colour scheme typical of the mid-nineteenth century.[5] To recreate the landscape setting, the professionals involved undertook archival research and carried out a detailed analysis of the site. In the absence of precise information concerning the site layout in the time of Sir John A., this research enabled them to create a garden in close accord with the styles and plant materials that were current in Kingston in the years from 1850 to 1860. The final site development includes an orchard (which displays a selection of apples of traditional varieties), an ornamental garden centred on a fountain, a pavilion or summer house, and a kitchen garden planned out in squares. Plants for the gardens were chosen from nursery catalogues of the time.

Parks Canada adopted a similar approach in its reconstruction of Ardgowan House, situated in the suburbs of Charlottetown in Prince Edward Island. In their effort to recreate the garden adjacent to the house (which, like Bellevue, had been the home of one of Canada's Fathers of Confederation),[6] the design team, including Thomas Gribbin and Judith Tulloch, and project manager Brian Gallant of Parks Canada, undertook two kinds of research. On the one hand, they undertook

25.1 The formal front garden of Ardgowan House, Charlottetown, PEI, organized around a circular planting bed. The utilitarian components of the garden, including a kitchen garden, are on the opposite side of the house in this restoration by Parks Canada.

THE CONSERVATION OF HISTORIC AND SIGNIFICANT LANDSCAPES 557

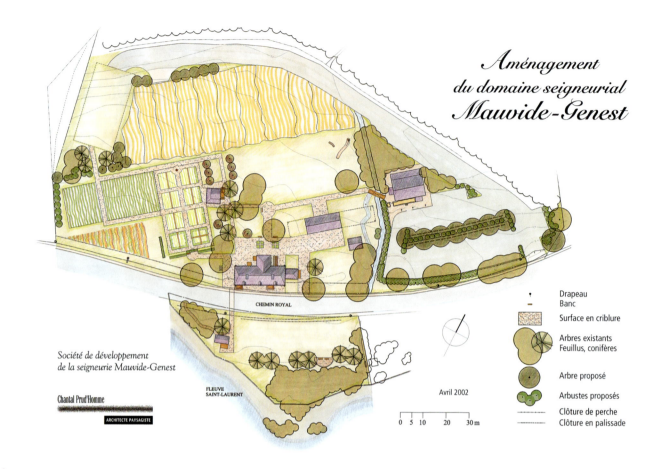

studies specific to the site (soil and seed analyses, archaeological excavations, documentary research) and on the other, studies of the general horticultural and cultural context (illustrations of contemporary houses and gardens, lists of the plants employed in other gardens on the island, books and tools that were available at the appropriate period).[7] The fusion of these two categories of knowledge allowed the team to design a site layout that was typical of the gardenesque ideas of the Victorian period, including a circular planting bed with an immense *Rosa rubrifolia* as its central focus, playful components such as rustic wooden furniture (painted white), and several plants little known elsewhere, notably the goat's-beard with its spectacular flowers and the delicate *rose d'Acadie*, a white single-flowered rose reputed to have accompanied the first European colonists to these shores.[8] Landscape elements were chosen to relate to typical activities of the time: archery, croquet, lawn tennis, and garden parties. A similar documentary approach was used to prepare authentic plans for a garden typical of New France, at the Mauvide-Genest Seigneury on Île d'Orléans, presently in the process of realization according to the drawings of landscape architect Chantal Prud'homme, a consultant to Parks Canada.

25.2 Landscape restoration plan of the grounds of the Mauvide-Genest Seigneury in Saint-Jean, Île d'Orléans, QC, by Chantal Prud'homme, landscape architect, for Parks Canada. At the centre of the drawing, the old *manoir*, built in 1734, stands next to Chemin Royal, the road that follows the periphery of the historic island. Vegetable garden and orchard are located above and to the left of the *manoir*. Beige circles and clumps indicate existing vegetation.

Sometimes restorers are fortunate in having access to the original documents. In Calgary, the celebrated Reader Rock Garden (see chapter 17), which had fallen into ruin after many decades as a major public attraction, was completely restored according to Superintendent Reader's original design, based on the drawings and notes of its creator. Even Reader's house, which had been demolished, was reconstructed. Landscape architect Michelle Reid of the City of Calgary directed the restoration project, with Anne Charlton as overall coordinator. The garden was reopened to the public in 2006 as a historic public park and as evidence of the devotion of its creator to his adopted city. Once again it serves as a site for experimentation, demonstration, and education, to "explore the scope of horticultural possibilities in Calgary."[9]

Progress in Landscape Conservation

Today, the initiatives taken in the 1970s and 1980s (noted in chapter 22) have matured into a widespread movement of landscape conservation and rehabilitation, increasingly based on scholarship and research. Government agencies at all levels pursue landscape conservation objectives. At the federal level, Parks Canada plays a major role through its administration of some 167 of the country's 950 National Historic Sites, many of which involve important cultural and natural landscapes. Other levels of government, along with foundations and private groups, are responsible for the remaining sites. Parks Canada personnel and experts from Public Works and Government Services Canada carry out detailed studies of potential sites and solicit input from knowledgeable citizens, academics, and professionals across the country. Their studies are provided to members of the Historic Sites and Monuments Board of Canada (HSMBC), an advisory group that prepares recommendations to the Minister of Canadian Heritage concerning sites to be recognized and protected. Senior landscape architect John Zvonar of Public Works, who advises the HSMBC on landscape conservation concerning a cross-section of federal departments and sites, served as the 2012 president of the Alliance for Historic Landscape Preservation (see chapter 22), which continues its efforts to expand knowledge about and protection of heritage landscapes at the scale of North America. The Association for Preservation Technology (also described in chapter 22) is now active in thirty countries around the world, and the Society for the Study of Architecture in Canada (SSAC), a learned society founded in 1974, increasingly provides a forum for the discussion of Canada's historic landscapes as well as its historic buildings, both through presentations at its annual meetings, held in diverse regions of the country, and through its quarterly journal *Architecture in/au Canada*. An additional resource for the study of Canadian historical landscapes is provided by a number of architecture-based university programs and government-supported Canada Research chairs at several universities across the country.

Besides the growing knowledge of historic landscapes, important progress continues to be made on their preservation. The Main Street program of the Heritage Canada Foundation has benefited more than a hundred cities and towns; every year, the foundation awards the prestigious Prince of Wales Prize to a community that has demonstrated exceptional care for its historic environment, and the Gabrielle Léger Medal for achievement in heritage conservation by an individual. In Quebec, the Conseil des monuments et sites du Québec, directed for many years by France Gagnon Pratte, has published the quarterly magazine *Continuité*, dedicated to historic buildings and landscapes, since 1982.

Large numbers of seminal reports, studies, and articles now define methods and strategies that are useful in landscape preservation; among the most comprehensive is Parks Canada's *Standards and Guidelines for the Conservation of Historic Places in Canada*, first published in 2003, to which all of Canada's provincial and territorial governments contributed.[10] Many of these governments have established their own policies concerning recognition and protection of natural and cultural landscapes,[11] and increasingly, these landscapes are central to their economic strategies and a source of pride and identification for their citizens.[12] Well-known personalities in a number of fields have provided strong support for landscape protection and have not hesitated to become involved in controversial issues and projects; they include Phyllis Lambert, founding director of the Canadian Centre for Architecture in Montreal, David Suzuki (whose foundation carries out outstanding environmental research), and the Academy Award–winning film animator Frédéric Back, among many others.

Yet despite all these organizations, programs, and support, all is not won. Landscape preservation is still an unpredictable and hazardous affair, and setbacks occur regularly. During the years it has taken to write this book, a number of the landscapes or landscape elements described have been seriously compromised, and some have disappeared altogether. In some cases, great damage has been done by powerful forces of nature; such was the case in the devastation of two of Canada's outstanding large urban parks in the first decade of the new century. Vancouver's Stanley Park and Halifax's Point Pleasant Park – already closely linked in terms of their geographic settings and the circumstances of their acquisition as parks (see chapter 11) – were both struck by powerful storms, Point Pleasant by Hurricane Juan in the fall of 2003 and Stanley Park by the storm of December 2006. In both cases, human efforts and the resurgent forces of nature itself are creating new park landscapes that will be different from those of the past, yet fascinating and inspiring. And in both cases, the devastation of the parks led to controversy concerning their man-made vulnerability and the right way to rebuild them.[13] But most of the damage to significant Canadian landscapes has been the consequence of human action or inaction – through neglect or a misapplication of the real-estate doctrine of "the highest and best use of land," which too often leaves out fundamental social, aesthetic, and symbolic concerns. Damage and destruction of this kind will not be so easily remedied.

ACKNOWLEDGMENTS

My first thanks are to my wife, Sachi Williams, who supported me enthusiastically throughout this ambitious project and actively contributed to it at every stage. She helped establish the first definition of the book, accompanied me on most of my project visits during the research phases of the work, often to distant corners of the country, and participated in discussions with designers and resource people. She also contributed to the transcription of rough notes and early manuscripts, reviewed and provided comments on draft and final texts, acted as a sounding board for ideas and approaches, and carried out the onerous task of preparing the bibliography.

I have received great help from an "inner circle" of close collaborators and advisors, who share an interest in Canada's landscape architectural history. These include my long-time colleague Peter Jacobs, *professeur titulaire* at the École d'architecture de paysage, University of Montreal; Susan Buggey, former *professeure associée* at the same school and previously head of the Historic Services division of Parks Canada in Gatineau, Quebec; landscape architect Cornelia Hahn Oberlander, OC, Vancouver, well known for her many outstanding landscape projects; and Vincent Asselin, CQ, landscape architect, who was my partner for many years at WAA (Williams, Asselin, Ackaoui and Associates) in Montreal. All of these friends and colleagues, along with many others, opened up their personal libraries and document collections to me unstintingly, shared their research findings, drawings, photographs, books, and personal files, and I am most grateful to them. The voluminous and orderly files of Peter Jacobs, including his extensive collection of documents concerning Frederick Todd, provided much essential information, as did the imposing box of documents loaned to me by Cornelia Oberlander, who also helped to develop the thematic approach used in the book in an October 2000 discussion in Vancouver with Sachi Williams and me. In that same year, at the very beginning of the project, Susan Buggey assembled a distinguished group of experts in landscape history to provide me with a half-day briefing in the Gatineau offices of Parks Canada. Peter Jacobs and Vincent Asselin organized professional conferences and collaborated with me on extensive magazine articles, exploring themes and ideas that contributed to the book.

Many other designers, historians, and professors across the country provided similar generous support. Pleasance Crawford gave me full access to her unique library of documents concerning historical landscapes in Ontario. Cecelia Paine, professor at the University of Guelph and long-time president of the Landscape Architecture Canada Foundation, provided untiring support in the effort to ensure the publication of the book and helped considerably with the illustrations. John Zvonar of Public Works Canada has been a dedicated collaborator and has supported many aspects of the project. In 2005, he invited me to present a review of cultural landscapes in Canada to a government team concerned with landscape history; this meeting was held in the same room as my briefing of five years before and in the company of many of the original participants – a most gratifying experience that provided an ideal opportunity to structure and clarify the content of the book. Many friends and colleagues suggested sites and projects to visit (and often visited them with us), including landscape architects Doug Carlyle of Edmonton and Wendy Graham of Montreal, city planner Isabel Corral of Victoria and Montreal, professors Charlie Thomsen, Ted McLachlan, and Jean Trottier of the University of Manitoba, and University of Guelph professors Cecelia Paine, Jim Taylor, Walter Kehm, and Nancy Pollock-Elwand (now at the University of Calgary). Bev Sandalack from the University of Calgary suggested key projects to visit in that city, while architect Gino Pin provided insight and guidance to Yellowknife. Acting director Don Luymes and professors Susan Herrington, Patrick Mooney, and Patrick Condon of the University of British Columbia all contributed much-appreciated knowledge and advice, as did my University of Montreal colleagues Danièle Routaboule and John Macleod. Béatrice Sokoloff and Rachel Lévy offered early encouragement and advice on modes of expression and translation. Wendy Shearer of Guelph, Ontario, and Claude Arsenault and David Byers of Pointe-Claire, Quebec, provided insights on particular cultural landscapes.

This book was also very much a family affair. My son, Dan Williams, prepared and composed the digital maps and plans and compiled the plant glossary. My sister, Dr. Laura Molnar; my brothers, John and David Williams; and my cousins Lorna Cassels and Alan Carmichael cheerfully acted as guides to many urban and rural landscapes; my daughter-in-law, Josée Lavoie, transcribed research notes and preliminary texts. The far-flung Wakamatsu and Ando clans enabled my wife and me to visit many US sites that are closely related to Canadian projects, as did the Howse family in England and France. The precise recollections of my late mother, Hazel Ieleen Williams, gave me background information and salient detail concerning the landscape evolution of southern Ontario from the 1910s through the 1950s. Many friends throughout the country also served as local guides and accommodated us in their homes. Kitty Forrestal furnished expert guidance to the Maritime provinces and, along with Bob Russell, opened doors to many important sites in Nova Scotia and Prince Edward Island. Koichi Kobayashi furnished excellent guidance to the landscape heritage of the Pacific Northwest of the United States, which provided important insights to that of British Columbia.

My publishers and their editorial teams have been extremely helpful, patient, and supportive. At McGill-Queens University Press, I extend my profound thanks to editor Jonathan Crago for his continuing guidance and sage advice, to Jessica Howarth for her dedicated work in putting the book together, to managing editor Ryan Van Huijstee for his invaluable contribution, and to Judith Turnbull for her thorough and careful copy-editing. At the Presses de l'Université de Montréal, I express my appreciation to Director Antoine Del Busso and to editors Nadine Tremblay, Florence Noyer (who provided me with much early help and encouragement), and Yzabelle Martineau. I also express my sincere thanks to Olga Duhamel, who carried out the *révision linguistique* of the French-language text and did much to assure the coherence and fluidity of the book; to Bénédicte Prouvost, who carried out with precision the task of editing the French text; and to Garet Markvoort for her expert design of the book.

I have received extremely generous financial support from the Landscape Architecture Canada Foundation over a period of many years, and I extend my thanks to its board members and donors for their patience and confidence in this project. I hope this book justifies their steadfast support. I am also most grateful to the Canada Council and to the Canadian Federation for the Humanities and Social Sciences for their generous support, and to the Canadian Society of Landscape Architects (CSLA/AAPC), its members, and its component associations – in particular the Association des architectes paysagistes du Québec – for their unwavering help and advice. The generous help, provided at critical moments of the project, of several colleagues and companies with whom I have worked for many years, is also much appreciated. In particular, I would like to extend my thanks to Murray Goodz. The Faculté de l'aménagement of the University of Montreal, my home base throughout the project, supported this work in many diverse ways, including the provision of financial assistance at a critical juncture and the grant of a sabbatical year in 2000–01. I undertook much of the initial research and early writing of the book during that period, both at U de M's École d'architecture de paysage and during a stay of several months as a visiting scholar in the Landscape Architecture program at the University of British Columbia. During this stay, UBC's St. John's College provided me with a congenial *pied-à-terre*, surrounded by enthusiastic students from many lands, for my study of the rich landscape heritage of the Pacific region. My thanks to the college staff and students, who were gracious hosts.

I also owe my thanks to the marvellous staffs at many libraries and archives throughout Canada. First and foremost, to the personnel of the University of Montreal libraries, particularly that of the Faculté de l'aménagement (including Ginette Melançon-Bolduc, Alphonse Hébert, chief librarian Lyne Bélanger, and all their colleagues), the Bibliothèque des lettres et sciences humaines, and the library of rare books and special collections and its former director Sarah de Bogui. I also owe a great debt to the McGill University libraries, especially the John Bland Canadian Architecture Collection and its conservator Ann Marie Holland and her assistants, and to the Blackader Library and its former director Marilyn Berger.

The unique collection of landscape architecture drawings and documents in the McLaughlin Library at the University of Guelph is a rich source of information on the work of the country's leading landscape professionals, and I owe gratitude to several UBC libraries, including those of the Faculty of Agriculture and the departments of Architecture and City Planning. The Historic Sites division of Parks Canada provided invaluable documentation on Canada's historic sites – particular thanks are due to Nathalie Clerk and Don Bienvenu – and Ottawa architect Rickson Outhet kindly made available to me the extensive archive of his grandfather, landscape architect Rickson Outhet. I also owe thanks to the Bibliothèque et Archives nationales du Québec, the City of Edmonton Archives, the J.J. Talman Regional Collection at the University of Western Ontario Archives, the City of Toronto Reference Library, Library and Archives Canada, and the Association des architectes paysagistes du Québec (AAPQ), which opened their archives to me. Finally, the outstanding Pointe Claire Public Library in my own municipality provided access to a broad range of general books and periodicals.

The owners, designers, and stewards of many significant Canadian landscapes received my wife and me graciously and helped me understand their sites. These included, in Quebec, Francis Cabot at Quatre-Vents, Alex Reford and Denis Lemieux at the Jardins de Métis, and Soeur Gabrielle Noel at the Monastère des Ursulines in Quebec City; in Ontario, David Leinster, the Humber Bay project and Don Valley Brickworks, and John Gilchrist, Wychwood Park, Toronto; in Newfoundland, Jim Ronan at Bowring Park in St. John's; in British Columbia, the Watchmen of Haida Gwaii, Elizabeth Whitelaw, and Cheryl Cooper, executive director and conservator of the Arthur Erickson House & Garden Foundation; and in Alberta, Doug Carlyle for many of his Edmonton projects.

I would like to thank all those who consented to be interviewed for the book, including landscape architects Macklin Hancock, Cornelia Hahn Oberlander, Clive Justice, Don Vaughan, Phil Tattersfield, Adrienne Brown, Alfred de Vynck, and Dan Matsushita; Chris Phillips of Phillips Farevaag Smallenberg and Jeff Cutler of space2place, Vancouver; Carolyn Woodland of Hough Woodland Naylor Dance Leinster, Toronto; Ann Milovsoroff of the Royal Botanical Gardens in Hamilton; and Robert Gibbs and Stefan Johansson of EIDOS Consultants, Edmonton. Others include city planners Peter Oberlander of Vancouver, Andrew Hoffman of Montreal, and Gwen Sewell and R.M. Thompson of Kitimat and Prince Rupert, BC; André Delisle and Isabelle Cadieux of the Château Ramezay Museum in Montreal; Natalie Humenuk-Bourke of Parks Canada, Wood Buffalo National Park; Janet Bingham of Vancouver; Bill Dale, Victoria; and Director Rob Wright and professor Pierre Bélanger of the University of Toronto.

Many friends, relatives, and associates lent or gave me books and other documents. Among these were Marie-José Fortier, Julie Jackson, Sylvie Lavoie, Daniel Chartier, Danièle Routaboule, Patrick Mooney, Dr. Laura Molnar, Catherine Macdonald, Eila Milne, Chantal Prud'homme, and Nancy Tausky. Others provided illustrative material; most of these are credited in the illustrations list. Richard Russell provided computer know-how, while Josée Lavoie and Michael Guetta transcribed research notes and early drafts of the manuscripts. Others reviewed portions of the text, among them Don Graham and Wendy Graham, Peter Jacobs, Susan Buggey, Cornelia Oberlander, Alex Reford, Claude Cormier, Larry McMann of Victoria, Diana Moser of the Oil Sands Discovery Centre, and David Williams, who provided both general comments and corrections on the entire text and specific input on geological matters. I also extend my gratitude to the anonymous evaluators who read the book in its manuscript form and reviewed the illustrations, and provided extremely detailed and valuable comments and suggestions. I am most grateful for their suggestions and have incorporated almost all of them into the book. Finally, I must apologize to those who have helped with this and other aspects of the project, but whose names I have inadvertently omitted.

In writing this book, I have been very conscious of my debt to those with whom I was fortunate to study. I owe a great personal debt to my professors in the history of architecture at McGill University, the brilliant and urbane Peter Collins (author of *Changing Ideals in Modern Architecture*, 1965) and John Bland, a pioneer in the study of Canadian architectural history and founder of the John Bland Canadian Architecture Collection at the McGill University Library. At the University of California at Berkeley, I studied landscape history with Margaretta Darnall and John Brinckerhoff (J.B.) Jackson of New Mexico; the latter, more than any other landscape writer, has traced the connections between everyday North American life and the great issues of the rural and urban landscape. I am also indebted to Clare Cooper Marcus at the University of California, who provided insight on the social meaning of the landscape; to my mentors John Schreiber and Norbert Schoenauer of McGill University; and to Winthrop Judkins, my professor of art history at McGill.

Finally, I have been helped in developing the themes and ideas in the book through invitations to address professional and scholarly gatherings and organizations, and to write a number of articles for periodicals in Canada and abroad, including for *Landscapes/Paysages*, *Trames*, *Architecture in/au Canada*, *Continuité*, *Ground*, *Landscape Architecture* (US), and the Chinese magazine *Landscape Architecture*. And, through their participation in my University of Montreal course focusing on Canadian landscape history, my students have greatly helped me to refine and clarify the ideas I have explored in this book.

LANDSCAPE ARCHITECTURE CANADA FOUNDATION

The Landscape Architecture Canada Foundation (LACF) has been a supporter of this book since its inception. The following individuals, firms, and component associations of the Canadian Society of Landscape Architects made special contributions through LACF to ensure publication of this seminal work.

Benefactors
Williams, Asselin, Ackaoui & Associates
British Columbia Society of Landscape Architects
David Reid

Patrons
Atlantic Provinces Association of Landscape Architects
Baker Turner
Catherine Berris Associates
Cecelia Paine
Claude Cormier and Associates
Corban and Goode
Corush Sunderland Wright
Dillon Consulting
Don and Wendy Graham
Doug Carlyle
du Toit Allsopp Hillier
Durante Kreuk
EIDOS Consultants
Employees of the Direction des grands parcs,
    City of Montreal

Faye Langmaid
Harrington McAvan
IBI Group (DAA)
Interbase Consultants
ISL Engineering and Land Services
James Taylor
John MacLeod
L.A. West Associates
Manitoba Association of Landscape Architects
NIP Paysage
O2 Planning & Design
Option Aménagement
Peter Jacobs
PMA Landscape Architects
PWL Partnership Landscape Architects
Quinn Design Associates
R. Kim Perry & Associates
Richard Mark Schollen
Salmona Tregunno
Saskatchewan Association of Landscape Architects
Stantec Consulting
Strybos Barron King
The MBTW Group
Victor Ford & Associates

Advocates
BDA Landscape Architects
Sara Gruetzner

Chantal Prud'Homme, architecte paysagiste
Crosby Hanna & Associates
Daniel Chartier
Don Naylor & Associates
Douglas Paterson
Ekistics Planning and Design
Friedrich Oehmichen

Glenn Group
Jane Durante
Jean Landry
Objectif paysage
Phillips Farevaag Smallenberg
Pierre Bouchard
Scott Torrance, Landscape Architect

CORPORATE SUPPORTERS

Canderel Management Inc.
Pointe-Claire Plaza
Reliance Construction Group
Southwest One Complex, a division of Dorchester Oaks Corporation
Tolchinsky and Goodz, Architects

ILLUSTRATIONS

Photographs and black and white drawings by Ron Williams unless otherwise noted.
Coloured maps by Dan Williams unless otherwise noted.

1.1 Sketch – aerial view of the Canadian Shield   13
1.2 Map of the major physiographic regions of Canada   15
1.3 Map of the glaciers and their aftermath   16
1.4 Map of the climatic regions of Canada   18
1.5 Map of the vegetation regions of Canada   19

2.1 Head-Smashed-In Buffalo Jump, Porcupine Hills, AB   22
2.2 Map of First Nations homelands and cultural sites in Canada   24
2.3 Plan of Iroquoian village, Ontario. Sketch after J.V. Wright, "The Nodwell Site: A Mid-14th Century Iroquois Village." *Canadian Archeological Association Bulletin*, no. 3 (1971)   27
2.4 Longhouse at the Sainte-Marie among the Hurons reconstruction, Midland, ON   27
2.5 Aerial view of medicine wheel at the Ellis Site in southern Alberta. Photo by John Brumley, Habre, Montana, with permission. Courtesy of Jack Brink and Karen Giering, Royal Alberta Museum   29
2.6 Inuksuk, Kuujjuaq, Nunavik, QC. Photograph by Stéphane Cossette, provided courtesy of Mr. Cossette   31
2.7 Totems at Ninstints, Gwaii Haanas National Park, BC   32

2.8 Serpent Mounds, Rice Lake, ON   34
2.9 Horse petroglyph, Writing-on-Stone Provincial Park, AB   35

3.1 Thaddeus Holownia, *St. John's, NL*, image 3 in series *St. John's, NL, 1981–2006*. Courtesy of Thaddeus Holownia   37
3.2 Map of fisheries and early settlements of the Atlantic region   39
3.3 Street scene, St. John's, NL   40
3.4 Reconstruction of the *habitation* at Port-Royal National Historic Site, NS   41
3.5 Dike and *aboiteaux* system used to drain salt marshes in early Acadia   42
3.6 Map of Acadian settlement areas before and after the *Grand dérangement* of 1755   43
3.7 Evangeline Memorial Park, Grand Pré, NS. Bird's-eye view looking north, by Nobbs & Hyde, architects, Montreal. John Bland Canadian Architecture Collection, McGill University Libraries, accession no. 151   45
3.8 St. Thomas Church, Memramcook, NB, seen from approach road across valley   46
3.9 Tantramar Marshes, NB   47

4.1 Sketch of Saint-Siméon, QC   49
4.2 Map of seigneuries and settlements of New France, 1663–1760   50
4.3 *"Abitation"* at Quebec City, 1613. Wood engraving 17 × 23 cm, based on a drawing by Samuel de

Champlain, 1608. Library and Archives Canada/ MIKAN no. 3919911   52

4.4   Vegetable garden at the Sainte-Marie among the Hurons reconstruction, ON   53

4.5   "Plan de la ville de Montréal." Plan of Montreal in 1725 by Gaspard-Joseph Chaussegros de Léry. Ink and watercolour on paper, 52 × 74 cm. Archives nationales (France), Centre des Archives d'outre-mer, Aix-en-Provence   56

4.6   Reconstruction of the King's Bastion barracks, Fortress of Louisbourg National Historic Site, NS   57

4.7   Sketch of Place Royale, Quebec City   59

4.8   Plan of Place d'Armes showing Sulpician "Vieux Séminaire" and garden, Montreal   60

4.9   Garden of the Ursuline Monastery, Quebec City   64

4.10   Domaine des Maizerets, Quebec City   65

4.11   Sketch of linear settlement pattern in rural Quebec   68

4.12   Cemetery, Grandes-Piles, QC   71

4.13   Town of Grandes-Piles, QC, seen across the Saint-Maurice River   72

4.14   Wayside cross, Saint-Mathieu-du-Parc, QC   73

4.15   *Calvaire*, Saint-Élie-de-Caxton, QC   74

4.16   View from the *calvaire* overlooking Saint-Élie-de-Caxton, QC   75

5.1   *Castle Frank – A House erected by Gov. Simcoe near York, Upper Canada*, watercolour, 18.2 × 19.1 cm, June 1796, Elizabeth Simcoe – Sketches, Simcoe family fonds, F 47-11-1-0-231, Archives of Ontario   77

5.2   Map of British colonization in Maritime Canada, 1749–1820   78

5.3   Plan of eighteenth- and nineteenth-century Halifax   79

5.4   Comparison of British colonial town layouts in the United States and Canada   81

5.5   King's Square, Saint John, NB   83

5.6   The Old Burying Ground (St. Paul's Church Cemetery), Halifax   84

5.7   The "three sisters," Mahone Bay, NS   86

5.8   Lighthouse, Louisbourg, NS   87

5.9   Twelve-sided barn at Mystic, QC   90

5.10   Map showing areas of British settlement in Upper Canada, 1760–1840   91

5.11   Map of Toronto (York), Upper Canada: original site and early settlement, 1793   95

5.12   Victoria Park, Brantford, ON   96

5.13   "Plan of the Town of Goderich, Upper Canada, founded by the Canada Company, 1829," printed map, hand-coloured, 22 × 28.5 cm, Joseph Bouchette; engraved by J. & C. Walker, reduced by F. Cattlin. Folder N-6045, accession no. 50666, Archives of Ontario   97

5.14   Macdonnell Street, Guelph, ON. Image provided by the City of Guelph   98

5.15   Manoir Montmorency (Kent House), Montmorency Falls, QC   99

5.16   James Woolford, *Uniacke House, Mount Uniacke*, NS. Oil painting, c. 1830, Nova Scotia Archives and Record Management Photograph Collection, 20080083   100

6.1   "Immigration to Manitoba and the West," c. 1883. CPR poster, 70 × 20 cm. Canadian Pacific Archives (A6418)   103

6.2   Map of the principal physiographic regions and features of western Canada   104

6.3   Map of fur-trading posts and missions in western Canada, seventeenth to nineteenth centuries   106

6.4   Lower Fort Garry, north of Winnipeg   108

6.5   Map of the Red River Settlement, MB, 1820 (after A. Amos, *Report of Trials in the Courts of Canada* [London: John Murray, 1820]), compared with the plan of Winnipeg today   111

6.6   Father Pandosy's Mission, Kelowna, BC   112

6.7   Cemetery and cathedral, Saint-Boniface, MB   113

6.8   Way of the Cross and parish church, Lebret, Qu'Appelle River Valley, SK   115

6.9   Church and presbytery, Batoche, SK   116

6.10   High-level bridge, Lethbridge, AB   117

6.11   Map of a typical township layout in western Canada, late nineteenth century   119

6.12   *Strattendorf* ("street village"), Neubergthal, MB. Courtesy of the municipality of Neubergthal   120

6.13   Shelterbelt, Neubergthal, MB   121

6.14   St. Michael's Ukrainian Orthodox Church and cemetery, Tolstoi, MB   122

6.15   Mormon temple and surrounding park, Cardston, AB   123

6.16   McIntyre Ranch, Magrath, AB   125

6.17   View of islands and mountains in Juan Perez Sound, Haida Gwaii, BC   127

6.18   Map of the original city limits and founding institutions, Calgary, AB   128

6.19   Sandon, abandoned mining town in southeastern British Columbia   129

6.20   Village of Lund, on the "Sunshine Coast" of British Columbia   130

7.1 William Kurelek, *Prairie Farm*, 1976. Painting. Reproduced from W.O. Mitchell, *Who Has Seen the Wind*, Toronto: Macmillan of Canada, 1976, 67. © The Estate of William Kurelek. Courtesy of the Wynick-Tuck Gallery, Toronto   133

7.2 "The Shanty in the Bush," from *The Eastern Townships – Information for Intending Settlers*, 1881. A first-generation farm in the Eastern Townships of Quebec. Library and Archives Canada/C-005755, MIKAN no. 2953446   135

7.3 Strathmore farm, Alberta, c. 1910. CPR demonstration farm. Canadian Pacific Archives (NS1307)   138

7.4 Country grain elevators, Medicine Hat, AB   139

7.5 Barn and house, Motherwell Homestead, Abernethy, SK   141

7.6 View through front gate to fields, Motherwell Homestead, Abernethy, SK   142

7.7 William Pearce, c. 1880s. Glenbow Archives, Calgary, NA-339-1   143

7.8 Vineyard, Okanagan Lake, BC   143

7.9 Main building and central oval at the original campus of Macdonald College, Montreal, 1925. Archives, Faculty of Agricultural and Environmental Sciences, Macdonald Campus, McGill University   146

7.10 View of barns and experimental fields, Central Experimental Farm, Ottawa. Library and Archives Canada/PA-034408, MIKAN no. 3318676   148

7.11 Apple blossoms near Wolfville, NS. Nova Scotia Information Service, photographer unknown, c. 1956. Nova Scotia Archives & Record Management, access no. NSIS 10433   149

7.12 Map showing the distribution and classification of agricultural lands in Canada   151

8.1 Victoria Square, Montreal, c. 1887, photograph by Wm Notman & Son. © McCord Museum, accession no. VIEW-1565.A.2   152

8.2 West-facing view on Broadway, Winnipeg   154

8.3 Charles Baillairgé, photograph by J.E. Livernois, c. 1874. Bibliothèque nationale de France, SGPORTRAIT-307, © Société de géographie, Paris, with permission; "The Earl of Dufferin, K.P.," c. 1881–84. Engraving 16.7 × 24.6 cm, from a photograph by Topley Studio, Ottawa. Library and Archives Canada, accession no. 1952-10, MIKAN no. 2907655   156

8.4 Porte Saint-Louis, Quebec City   157

8.5 Dufferin Terrace, Quebec City   157

8.6 Gore Park, Hamilton, ON   161

8.7 Central Memorial Park, c. 1914–19, Calgary. Glenbow Archives, Calgary, NA-1604-94   163

8.8 Burland Lithographic Co., printer, Alexander Cowper Hutchison, architect. "Ice Palace – Montreal Carnival, 1889," lithograph, DR2004:0004. Collection Centre Canadien d'Architecture/Canadian Centre for Architecture, Montreal; Don de l'hon. Serge Joyal, CP, OC/Gift of the Hon. Serge Joyal, PC, OC   165

8.9 Map of nineteenth-century open space structure, Toronto   167

8.10 H.A. Engelhardt, after a nineteenth-century drawing provided by Pleasance Crawford   168

8.11 Tracing of site plan for Belleville Institute for the Deaf and Dumb, 1871, after a drawing by H.A. Engelhardt, landscape gardener, provided by Pleasance Crawford   168

9.1 Halifax Public Gardens. Photograph by Sachi Williams   170

9.2 Central Experimental Farm, horticulture section, Ottawa   172

9.3 Canadian Pacific Railway station and garden at Medicine Hat, AB, 1887. Glenbow Archives, Calgary, NA-2003-18   175

9.4 Farmstead landscape at "Easydale," residence of William Justin, Toronto Township (now Mississauga), ON. From J.H. Pope, *Illustrated Historical Atlas of the County of Peel, Ont.* (Toronto: Walker & Miles, 1877), 3   176

9.5 View to the St. Lawrence River from the formal garden at Bois-de-Coulonge, Quebec City   181

9.6 Maison Cataraqui, Sillery, QC   183

9.7 City façade of Dundurn Castle, Hamilton, ON   184

9.8 "Dundurn, the Residence of Colonel the Honorable Sir Allan Napier Macnab," drawn by Robert Wetherell, architect; engraving by Bennett. Garden façade of Dundurn Castle   185

9.9 Villa Bagatelle, Sillery, QC   187

9.10 Manoir-Papineau, Montebello, QC, seen across the Ottawa River. Photograph by Ramsay Traquair. John Bland Canadian Architecture Collection, McGill University Libraries, accession no. 101616   190

9.11 Tea house at Manoir-Papineau, Montebello, QC. Photograph by Ramsay Traquair. John Bland Canadian Architecture Collection, McGill University Libraries, accession no. 101629   191

9.12 Map of Rosedale Garden Suburb, Toronto   193

10.1 Notre-Dame-des-Neiges Cemetery, Montreal   194

10.2 City Park with statue of Sir John A. Macdonald, Kingston, ON   197

10.3 Plan of Victoria Park, London, ON. Charles H. Miller, landscape gardener, 1878. Black and white photograph of ink and watercolour drawing on paper. J.J. Talman Regional Collection and Research Collections Centre, The University of Western Ontario Archives, RC60267   198

10.4 Major's Hill Park, Ottawa, c. 1900. Courtesy of National Capital Commission   199

10.5 Mount Royal Cemetery, Montreal   201

10.6 View from Mount Hermon Cemetery, looking towards Quebec City   204

10.7 "Broken column" monument at Cataraqui Cemetery, Kingston, ON   205

10.8 Plan of Mount Royal Cemetery. James P. Sidney, contractor, and James P.W. Neff, architect and engineer, 1852. Courtesy of the Mount Royal Cemetery   206

10.9 Central axis of Notre-Dame-des-Neiges Cemetery, Montreal   209

10.10 Family burial chamber in Beechwood Cemetery, Ottawa   209

10.11 Ross Bay Cemetery, Victoria, BC   211

10.12 Union Cemetery, Calgary   213

11.1 The Seawall in Stanley Park, Vancouver   216

11.2 Frederick Law Olmsted, 1893. Wood engraving by T. Johnson, from a photograph by James Notman. US Library of Congress, call no. AP2.C4 (General Collections), reproduction no. LC-USZ62-36895 (b&w film copy negative)   218

11.3 Plan of Mount Royal Park, Montreal, 1877, showing the ecological zones defined by Olmsted   218

11.4 Mount Royal Park Design Map, 1877, by Frederick Law Olmsted, landscape architect. Frederick Law Olmsted National Historic Site, MA. Courtesy of the late John Schreiber   219

11.5 Point Pleasant Park, Halifax   221

11.6 Upper lake and heath area of Rockwood Park, Saint John, NB   222

11.7 Goodacre Lake in Beacon Hill Park, Victoria, BC   224

11.8 Frederick G. Todd, Montreal, 1909, photograph by Wm Notman & Son. © McCord Museum, accession no. II-175018   225

11.9 Aerial view of Assiniboine Park, Winnipeg   227

11.10 "Quebec Battlefields Park, Quebec, Canada," 1913, coloured drawing by Frederick G. Todd, landscape architect. Plan of National Battlefields Park, Quebec City. Courtesy of the National Battlefields Commission, Archives Department   228

11.11 Peter Pan statue in Bowring Park, St. John's, NL   229

11.12 North Shore Park, Stratford, ON   234

12.1 Lucius O'Brien, *A View of the Rocky Mountains, British Columbia*, 1887. Watercolour, 47.8 × 70.5 cm. Library and Archives Canada/accession no. 1989-514-4, C-097668, MIKAN no. 2897759   236

12.2 Bow River, Banff National Park, AB   241

12.3 Cameron Lake, Waterton Lakes National Park, AB   242

12.4 Map of national parks and reserves in western Canada, 1885–1914   243

12.5 Niagara Falls, New York and Ontario   244

12.6 Map of natural parks and reserves in eastern Canada and the United States, 1885–1900   245

12.7 Sketch of Lac Tremblant and Mont Tremblant Park, QC, 1979   246

12.8 Tom Thomson, *Sunset*, 1915. Oil on wood-pulp board, 21.6 × 26.7 cm. National Gallery of Canada, Ottawa, accession no. 4701   247

12.9 "Banff in the Canadian Rockies," c. 1935. CPR poster. Canadian Pacific Archives (A6519)   247

12.10 Point Pelee National Park on Lake Erie, ON   249

12.11 Along the Cabot Trail in Cape Breton Highlands National Park, NS   251

12.12 Cavendish Beach, Prince Edward Island National Park   252

12.13 Long Beach, Pacific Rim National Park, Vancouver Island, BC   254

12.14 Pangnirtung Fjord in Auyuittuq National Park, Baffin Island, Nunavut   255

12.15 Land-use zoning plan, Jasper National Park, AB. After Government of Canada, *Jasper National Park Provisional Master Plan*, 1971   256

12.16 Western Brook Pond in Gros Morne National Park, NL   258

12.17 Lake Wapizagonke in La Mauricie National Park, QC   259

12.18 Map of national parks and national park reserves related to biophysical regions of Canada   260

13.1 "Proposed Civic Center Looking South, City of Edmonton, Alberta, Canada," by Morell and Nichols, landscape architects, 1912. Ink and watercolour on paper. City of Edmonton Archives no. EA-362-67   262

13.2 C.D. Arnold, photographer. The Court of Honour at the World's Columbian Exposition, view looking east. Chicago, 1893, by D.H. Burnham and Co.,

Architects. Chicago History Museum, black and white photographic print, accession no. ICH1-025626   265

13.3   Rickson A. Outhet, 1918, in a group photograph taken during Outhet's employment with the US Housing Corporation, Washington. Photograph courtesy of Rickson Outhet, architect   265

13.4   "Fletcher's Field, Montreal, Improvements Recommended by the Province of Quebec Association of Architects," ink drawing by Rickson Outhet, landscape architect and town planner, 1909. John Bland Canadian Architecture Collection, McGill University Libraries   266

13.5   "Plan Showing Proposed Federal and Municipal Squares and Federal Avenue," by John Lyle, architect, 1911. Downtown Toronto civic plan, from *Construction*, July 1911, 51   268

13.6   Thomas H. Mawson in his conservatory, Caton Hall, Lancashire, UK. Reproduced from Thomas H. Mawson, *The Life and Work of an English Landscape Architect*, Percy Brothers, 1927, illustration 68   269

13.7   Plan for the central area of Calgary, by Thomas Mawson, landscape architect and town planner, 1912–14. Reproduced from presentation book. Canadian Architectural Archives, Libraries and Cultural Resources, University of Calgary, Image no. MAW C25B, Fig. 09, accession no. 59A/79.15   270

13.8   Bowling Green district, Pointe-Claire, QC, 1905–30, Todd. Courtesy of Jim Laverdière and Janet Wygergangs, Pointe-Claire   273

13.9   The Crescent, Shaughnessy Heights, Vancouver   274

13.10   "Mount Royal, The Model City, Montreal, P.Q.," 1914 plan drawn by Malcolm D. Barclay, Quebec land surveyor, showing town plan by Frederick Todd. Archives de Ville Mont-Royal, QC   276

13.11   Molson Park, Montreal   278

13.12   "General Plan for the Development of Prince Rupert," 1912. Brett & Hall, town planners and landscape architects. Courtesy of the Department of City Planning, City of Prince Rupert, BC   280

13.13   "Parliament Square, Ottawa, Ontario," 1873. Lithograph from *Belden Illustrated Atlas of the Dominion of Canada*, Toronto 1881   281

13.14   "Proposed Subdivision of Property near Wascana Lake, Regina, for the Government of Saskatchewan," by Thomas H. Mawson & Sons, 1913. Plan for the grounds of the Saskatchewan Legislative Assembly and adjacent area, Regina. Wascana Centre Authority, courtesy of Mike Marmona and Ken Dockham   283

13.15   Aerial view of the Saskatchewan Legislative Assembly and grounds at Wascana Lake, Regina. Toronto Reference Library   284

13.16   Legislative Assembly of British Columbia and boat landing at Victoria Inner Harbour, BC   285

13.17   Plan of Victoria Inner Harbour and surrounding area, BC: urban design structure   286

13.18   Perspective view of University of Alberta central quadrangle, by Percy Nobbs, architect, Montreal, 1912. John Bland Canadian Architecture Collection, McGill University Libraries, dossier 89   287

13.19   Plan of Central Edmonton: urban design structure and North Saskatchewan River valley   288

13.20   University of British Columbia, view to north along Main Mall   289

13.21   Ottawa Civic Centre, 1914 perspective by Bennett and Burnham, town planners. Reproduced from Gréber, *L'architecture aux États-Unis, Tôme Second*, 141–3   290

14.1   Riverside Park, c. 1912, Stratford, ON (now Cenotaph/Memorial Park). From Thomas Adams, *Rural Planning and Development in Canada*, 259   292

14.2   Covenhoven, St. Andrews, NB: view to Passamaquoddy Bay   295

14.3   Edwardian garden at Guisachan Heritage Park, Kelowna, BC   296

14.4   Isaburo Kishida, sketch portrait after Takata, *Nikkei Legacy*   298

14.5   Sunken Garden at Butchart Gardens, Victoria, BC   298

14.6   Main building and grounds at Hatley Park, Colwood, BC, 1916; Japanese garden at left in middle ground. Image D-03021, courtesy of the Royal British Columbia Museum, BC Archives, call no. I-52900   300

14.7   Contemporary view of Japanese garden at Hatley Park   301

14.8   Lorrie and Howard Dunington-Grubb, c. 1912. Photograph courtesy of Sheridan Nurseries   302

14.9   "Playing Hockey on the Skating Rink, McGill University, Montreal, Quebec," by Alexander Henderson. Silver-albumen positive photograph on paper, 15.1 × 20.4 cm. Library and Archives Canada, file MSG0814, no. R10846-0-0-E, MIKAN no. 3349908   305

14.10   Westmount Park United Church, Westmount, QC   306

14.11 Victoria Park, Cambridge, ON 307

15.1 Alex Colville, *Main Street*, 1979. Acrylic polymer emulsion on hardboard. © A.C. Fine Art Inc., by permission 311
15.2 Hydrostone District, Halifax 314
15.3 Vimy Memorial from Meewasin Trail, Saskatoon 315
15.4 Memorial chapel, Darlingford, MB 316
15.5 Next-of-Kin Memorial Avenue, Saskatoon 317
15.6 Caribou memorial for the Royal Newfoundland Regiment, Beaumont-Hamel, France 319
15.7 War memorial at Grand Parade, Halifax 320
15.8 Memorial sculpture by Emanuel Hahn, sculptor, at Victoria Park, Moncton, NB 320
15.9 Canadian National War Memorial at Vimy Ridge, northern France, by Walter Allward, sculptor and designer 321
15.10 Cross of Sacrifice at the entrance to the Plains of Abraham, Quebec City 322
15.11 Cenotaph, Central Memorial Park, Calgary 323
15.12 War memorial at Manitoba Legislative Assembly, Winnipeg 325
15.13 Memorial at Victoria Park, Regina, SK 325

16.1 "The sunken pond garden at 'Uplands,' Toronto," by L.A. & H.B. Dunington-Grubb and Stensson, landscape architects. Photograph from *RAICJ* 9, no. 10 (October 1932): 224 328
16.2 Preliminary plan for grounds of the country residence of Dr. Bowen, Magog, QC, by Rickson Outhet, landscape architect, June 1929. Pencil and ink on tracing paper. Courtesy of Rickson Outhet, architect 330
16.3 Gordon Culham and Edwin Kay. Photograph by Frances Blue, 1940s, courtesy of Cecelia Paine 332
16.4 Helen Kippax, photograph by Milne Studio Ltd., Toronto, c. 1955. © David Milne, Toronto; courtesy of David Milne. Library & Archives Canada, accession no. 1994-341 DAP, MIKAN no. 20232. Frances Steinhoff, photograph by Frances Blue, 1940s 334
16.5 Plan of the Parkwood Estate, Oshawa, ON 335
16.6 Detail of aquatic garden, Parkwood Estate, Oshawa, ON 336
16.7 Elsie Reford at High Bank in the Reford Gardens, Métis, QC. Photograph by Robert Wilson Reford, c. 1940, courtesy of Les jardins de Métis and Alexander Reford 338
16.8 Allée Royale (The Long Walk), Reford Gardens. Photograph by Louise Tanguay, 2005, courtesy of Les jardins de Métis and Alexander Reford 340

16.9 Quatre-Vents garden, Cap-à-l'Aigle, QC 341
16.10 French and English gardens at Moorside, Kingsmere Estate, Gatineau Hills, QC 342
16.11 Abbey Ruins, Kingsmere Estate, Gatineau Hills, QC. National Capital Commission. Courtesy of Cecelia Paine 342

17.1 Urban design development in downtown Montreal, Canadian National Railways. Drawing by Hugh Griffith Jones, architect, Montreal, c. 1930. John Bland Canadian Architecture Collection, McGill University Libraries, accession no. 21 344
17.2 Thomas Adams, town-planning adviser to the Canadian Commission of Conservation, photograph c. 1921. Nova Scotia Archives and Records Management, negative no. N-7204, digital accession no. 200200129. © Michael Simpson, by permission 346
17.3 Map of resource settlements in northern Ontario and Quebec, 1910s–30s 347
17.4 Plan of Arvida, QC, 1925, by Harry Beardslee Brainerd, town planner. Courtesy of Alcoa and the Archives Department of the Ville de Saguenay, QC 349
17.5 Gabor Szilasi, photographer. Workers' housing and landscaping on Rue Vaudreuil at the corner of Rue Burma, looking northeast from south Arvida, 1995, 40.6 × 50.8 cm, PH1995:0081. Collection Centre Canadien d'Architecture/Canadian Centre for Architecture, Montreal © Gabor Szilasi 350
17.6 Fountain and view to escarpment at Gage Park, Hamilton, ON 351
17.7 Sunnyside Bathing Pavilion, Toronto 352
17.8 Photograph of Reader Rock Garden residence and surroundings, Calgary, following reconstruction, 2004–05. Photograph by The City of Calgary Parks, courtesy of Michelle Reid 353
17.9 Ontario Hospital, Whitby (abandoned 1995) 355
17.10 "Large parks & proposed pleasure drive system," city plan of Vancouver, 1928, by Harland Bartholomew, city planner. Reproduced from Bartholomew, *A Plan for the City of Vancouver*, 200. http://www.archive.org/stream/vancplnincgen00vanc#page/200/mode/2up 358
17.11 Kitsilano Beach, Vancouver 360
17.12 Postwar development in British Properties, West Vancouver 361

18.1 Promenade du St.-Maurice, Shawinigan, QC, contemporary view 362

18.2 Frère Marie-Victorin in his office at the Institut botanique, Montreal Botanical Garden, 1939. Photograph by Albert Dumas; Henry Teuscher in the Jardin économique at the Montreal Botanical Garden, 1936. Division de la gestion des documents et d'archives de l'Université de Montréal, 1FP,03127 and E01185FP09962   365

18.3 Planting in the entrance mall area of the Montreal Botanical Garden   366

18.4 Rock garden in the Royal Botanical Gardens, Hamilton, ON   367

18.5 International Peace Garden, Turtle Mountain, Manitoba/North Dakota   369

18.6 Alexander Muir Memorial Gardens, Toronto   371

18.7 Boulevard Saint-Maurice, Shawinigan Falls, QC, 1930s. Archives de la Ville de Shawinigan   372

18.8 Oakes Garden Theatre, Niagara Falls, ON   374

18.9 Louis Perron, photograph from office brochure, c. 1970. Reproduced from *The Canadian Landscape Architect*, Spring 1960, 31   375

18.10 Statue and garden, Jardin Jeanne-d'Arc, Plains of Abraham, Quebec City   376

18.11 East entrance gates, Riding Mountain National Park, MB   378

18.12 Members of the CSLA and their spouses in the 1940s. Photograph by Frances Blue. Reproduced from Cecelia Paine, ed., *Fifty Years of Landscape Architecture: The Canadian Society of Landscape Architects 1934–1984, Proceedings of the 50th Jubilee Conference*, 3   379

18.13 Details of Hamilton High-Level Bridge, ON   381

18.14 Sketch of south entrance to the Lions Gate Bridge, Vancouver; Hugh Griffith Jones, architect, Montreal, c. 1930. John Bland Canadian Architecture Collection, McGill University Libraries, accession no. 21   382

18.15 Highlands Links Golf Course, Cape Breton Highlands National Park, NS   383

18.16 Comparative plans for Beaver Lake, Mount Royal Park, Montreal, after F.L. Olmsted, 1877, and F.G. Todd, 1937   385

18.17 Bentley Wood Garden, Halland, Sussex, UK, Christopher Tunnard, landscape architect. Sketch based on Tunnard, *Gardens in the Modern Landscape*, The Architectural Press, London 1948, 68   386

19.1 National Film Board, creator, photograph of B.C. Binning residence and garden terrace, West Vancouver, c. 1951. Gelatin silver print 19.3 × 24.1 cm, ARCH175846. Collection Centre Canadien d'Architecture/Canadian Centre for Architecture, Montreal; Don de Jessie Binning/Gift of Jessie Binning   389

19.2 Cover of CMHC publication on residential planning, 1954   391

19.3 Plans of the J.H. Porter residence and garden, West Vancouver, 1950. From Birmingham, "Residential Work," *RAICJ* 27, no. 9 (1950): 305   395

19.4 Friedman garden, Vancouver   397

19.5 Plan of the Friedman garden, Vancouver, by Cornelia Hahn Oberlander, 1956; courtesy of C.H. Oberlander   398

19.6 Cornelia Hahn Oberlander in her Vancouver garden, 1989. Photograph © Kiku Hawkes, Vancouver; courtesy of Kiku Hawkes   398

19.7 Beaver Lake Pavilion, Mount Royal Park, Montreal   399

19.8 Peguis Pavilion and pool, Kildonan Park, Winnipeg. City of Winnipeg photograph, courtesy of Catherine Macdonald, Winnipeg   400

19.9 Comparative plans of new residential developments and "new towns" of the 1940s and 1950s in Canada   403

19.10 Macklin Hancock, photograph courtesy of Cecelia Paine   404

19.11 Pedestrian pathway system at Kitimat, BC   405

19.12 Shopping centre at Don Mills, ON, 1959. John B. Parkin and Associates and Fisher, Tedman and Fisher, architects. Photograph by Panda Associates, Toronto, project no. PAN 59963, Canadian Architectural Archives, Libraries and Cultural Resources, University of Calgary, image no. 59963-48, accession no. 181A/84.02   407

19.13 Ortho Pharmaceutical Co. building and landscape, Don Mills industrial park, ON, 1958. John B. Parkin and Associates, architects. Photograph by Panda Associates, Toronto, project no. PAN 58689, Canadian Architectural Archives, Libraries and Cultural Resources, University of Calgary, image no. 58689-1, accession no. 146A/83.1   407

19.14 Way of the Cross at St. Joseph's Oratory, Montreal. Photograph by Sachi Williams   409

19.15 Yousuf Karsh, photographic portrait of Jacques Gréber, 1950. Library and Archives Canada, MIKAN no. 3711435. © Estate of Yousuf Karsh, courtesy of Julie Grahame   410

19.16 "Ottawa-Hull and Environs," *Plan for the National Capital*, Plate 9, 1950, by Jacques Gréber, city planner. National Capital Commission, Ottawa. Available at the website of Queen's University, Kingston,

ON: https://qshare.queensu.ca/Users01/gordond/planningcanadascapital/credit.htm. Courtesy of Professor David Gordon   411

19.17 "La Mer Bleue" peat bog conservation reserve in the Ottawa Greenbelt   412

19.18 Plan of Crysler Park recreation area, St. Lawrence Seaway, by Project Planning Associates, planners and landscape architects. *Canadian Architect* 4, no. 8 (August 1959): 46–53   414

20.1 Minirail "people-mover" at French Pavilion, Île Notre-Dame, Expo 67, Montreal. Photograph by Andrew Hoffman   416

20.2 Skating rink at Nathan Phillips Square, Toronto City Hall   420

20.3 Map of downtown Toronto urban design structure, 1960s and 1970s   421

20.4 Sheraton Centre Hotel, Toronto, interior garden   421

20.5 Place Ville Marie, Montreal, mid-1960s. Photograph courtesy of Ivanhoé Cambridge, Montreal   422

20.6 Roof garden of Place Bonaventure, Montreal. Photograph by John Schreiber, c. 1978   422

20.7 Rideau Canal and National Arts Centre, Ottawa   423

20.8 Garden of the Provinces, Ottawa   424

20.9 Map of downtown Ottawa open space structure, 1960–70   425

20.10 Steinkopf Gardens, Winnipeg. Photographs courtesy of Charles H. Thomsen, Winnipeg   426

20.11 Stephen (Eighth) Avenue Mall, Calgary   427

20.12 View to downtown Calgary from Prince's Island Park in the Bow River   427

20.13 View towards lower-level courtyard at Robson Square, Vancouver, 1981   428

20.14 "Stramps" connecting upper and lower plaza levels at Robson Square, Vancouver   429

20.15 Parc de la Francophonie, Quebec City   430

20.16 Centennial Plaza, Victoria   430

20.17 Confederation Centre of the Arts, Charlottetown   431

20.18 Forecourt of the Alberta Legislative Assembly on Canada Day, 1 July 2008   433

20.19 Aerial view of Île Notre-Dame, Expo 67, Montreal, July 1967. Photograph by Andrew Hoffman   439

20.20 View of the walkway leading to the Katimavik of the Canada Pavilion, Expo 67, Montreal, QC, 1967, unknown photographer. Gelatin silver print 24 × 19.3 cm, ARCH255814. Collection Centre Canadien d'Architecture/Canadian Centre for Architecture, Montreal; Don de May Cutler/Gift of May Cutler   440

20.21 Children's playground, "Creative Centre for Play," Canada Pavilion, Expo 67. Courtesy of Cornelia Hahn Oberlander   442

20.22 Water-park playground at Ontario Place, Toronto   443

20.23 Plan of Campus intercommunautaires de Saint-Augustin, Cap-Rouge, Quebec, 1965–68, George Robert, city planner; landscape design by Danièle Routaboule and Georges Daudelin. Drawing by Danièle Routaboule, by permission. Originally published in *Architecture-Bâtiment-Construction*, October 1966, 30   447

20.24 Pedestrian entrance to campus of the Université de Montréal, Montreal   448

20.25 Central assembly space at Simon Fraser University, Burnaby, BC   449

20.26 View from the coulee towards the University of Lethbridge, AB   450

20.27 View of Champlain College, Trent University, Peterborough, ON, from bridge across the Otonabee River   451

21.1 Reconstructed wetland, Don Valley, Toronto   452

21.2 Angus Hills, c. 1972. Photograph by Ted McLachlan. Reproduced from *Landscape Planning* 6, no. 2 (1979): 101; Pierre Dansereau, photograph taken during an interview with the magazine *Dimension Science*, published by the National Research Council of Canada, 1984. Université du Québec à Montréal, Service des archives et de gestion des documents, Fonds d'archives Pierre-Dansereau, document 22P-810: F3/12   454

21.3 Phasing and Staging Plan of Fish Creek Provincial Park, Calgary, AB, 1976, by Lombard North Group Ltd. Courtesy of Jim Taylor and Lombard North Group Ltd.   457

21.4 *The PEI Ark*, 1976. Two-colour lithograph. Courtesy of David Bergmark and Ole Hammarlund, BGHJ Architects collection. Reproduced from Steven Mannell, *Atlantic Modern*, 60   458

21.5 Rose Harbour community, Haida Gwaii, BC   459

21.6 Map of development sites and study areas in northern Canada   461

21.7 View from the Bush Pilot's Monument, Old Town, looking towards New Town, Yellowknife, NWT   463

21.8 Northwest Territories Legislative Assembly, Yellowknife, seen across Frame Lake   464

21.9 Michael Hough, sketch portrait based on a photograph   465

21.10 Mission Creek Greenway, Kelowna, BC   468

21.11 Humber Bay Shores rehabilitation project, Toronto   469

21.12 Tommy Thompson Park (Leslie Street Spit), Toronto waterfront   470

21.13 Eroded bricks and volunteer growth at Tommy Thompson Park   470

21.14 Beach Park, Île Notre-Dame, Montreal. Photograph courtesy of WAA Inc.   471

21.15 Land-use suitability map, North Dartmouth planning study, 1994, by EDM Ltd., Halifax. Courtesy of Margot Young, EDM Ltd.   472

22.1 *Granite Assemblage*, West Vancouver. Photograph by Anthony Redpath, courtesy of Don Vaughan   474

22.2 Trinity Square, Toronto   476

22.3 Perspective drawing of McGill College Avenue, Montreal, from Place Ville Marie, 1988. Courtesy of Sandra Donaldson, landscape architect. Drawing by Andrew Dunbar, Éric Turcotte, and Sandra Donaldson   477

22.4 Plan of Confederation Blvd, Ottawa-Hull, 1983, by du Toit Associates Ltd., Toronto. Courtesy of DTAH   479

22.5 Entrance to redesigned Sparks Street Mall, Ottawa, 1988. Courtesy of Cecelia Paine   480

22.6 Annapolis Royal Historic Gardens, NS   483

22.7 Pigeon-house and garden at the Quatre-Vents garden, Cap-à-l'Aigle, QC   485

22.8 Arthur Erickson's garden, Vancouver   486

22.9 Granville Island, Vancouver   488

22.10 Music Garden, Toronto Harbourfront   488

22.11 The Forks, Winnipeg. Courtesy of Cynthia Cohlmeyer Landscape Architect, Winnipeg   490

22.12 Kananaskis Village, AB. Photograph from CSLA Awards Archive, McLaughlin Library, University of Guelph, ON   493

22.13 Village of Yorkville Park, Toronto   494

22.14 Robert Burley, photographer. View of the Temple-Silo Allegorical Column, with Shaughnessy House in the background, Canadian Centre for Architecture Garden, Montreal, 1990. Chromogenic colour print, 35.5 × 44.7 cm, PH1990:0159. Collection Centre Canadien d'Architecture/Canadian Centre for Architecture, Montreal. © Robert Burley, 1990   495

22.15 Stepped courtyard, Faculté de l'aménagement, Université de Montréal, Montreal   496

22.16 Place de la FAO, Quebec City   497

22.17 Devonian Square, Toronto, c. 1985   498

22.18 Taiga Garden, National Gallery, Ottawa   499

22.19 Bouctouche dune stabilization and recreation site, NB. Photograph by Jay Belyea for J.D. Irving Limited, Saint John, NB. Courtesy of James Sackville, BDA Landscape Architects Ltd., Sussex, NB, and J.K. Irving   500

22.20 Oodena Celebration Circle, The Forks, Winnipeg, MB. Courtesy of Garry Hilderman, Hilderman Thomas Frank Cram, Winnipeg   501

23.1 Entrance gate to Chinatown, Victoria. Photograph by Susan Buggey   503

23.2 Map of St. Lawrence Boulevard, Montreal, showing public urban spaces and neighbourhoods   506

23.3 Parc du Portugal, St. Lawrence Boulevard, Montreal   508

23.4 Schwartz's Delicatessen, St. Lawrence Boulevard, Montreal   509

23.5 Isometric drawing of Dr. Sun Yat-Sen Classical Chinese Garden, Vancouver, from Keswick, Oberlander, and Wai, *In a Chinese Garden*, 24. Courtesy of Dr. Sun Yat-Sen Classical Chinese Garden Society and Suzhou Garden Administration, with Joe Wai Architects and Don Vaughan, landscape architect   510

23.6 The Italian Gardens, Hastings Park, Vancouver   511

23.7 First Nations Garden, Montreal Botanical Garden   513

23.8 Reggie Yasui, "Asahi player at bat," 1939. Baseball game, Powell Street Grounds (Oppenheimer Park), Vancouver. Japanese Canadian (Nikkei) National Museum, 2010.26.25 (Ken and Rose Kutsutake Collection)   514

23.9 Main Street, New Denver, Kootenay region, BC   515

23.10 "Bay Farm Internment Camp, Slocan Valley, BC," c. 1942. Japanese Canadian (Nikkei) National Museum, 1995.139.1.2 a-c   516

23.11 Nitobe Garden, UBC Campus, Vancouver. Photograph by Sachi Williams   517

23.12 Nikka Yuko Japanese Garden, Lethbridge, AB   519

23.13 Garden of the Nikkei Internment Memorial Centre, New Denver, BC   521

23.14 Kohan Reflection Garden, New Denver, BC   522

23.15 Oppenheimer Park: public "charrette" meeting to discuss redesign of the park, 2008. Courtesy of space2place design inc., landscape architects, Vancouver   524

23.16 Plan of new design for Oppenheimer Park, Vancouver, 2008–10. Courtesy of space2place design inc., landscape architects, Vancouver, BC   525

24.1 Oil sands development and rehabilitated land, Fort McMurray, AB 526

24.2 "Blue Stick Garden," Métis International Garden Festival, QC. Photograph by Louise Tanguay, courtesy of Claude Cormier et associés 530

24.3 "Entre ciel et terre," garden at International Flora Montreal exhibition, 2006 531

24.4 St-Roch Garden, Quebec City 533

24.5 North Saskatchewan River Park and downtown Edmonton 535

24.6 Victoria Promenade, Edmonton 536

24.7 Map of Toronto waterfront developments and proposals, 1980s–2012 537

24.8 "Canada's Sugar Beach," Toronto waterfront. Photograph by Waterfront Toronto/Nicola Betts, courtesy of Claude Cormier et associés 538

24.9 Sustainable development prototype design, Vancouver, by the Design Centre for Sustainability, University of British Columbia. Drawing by Bob Worden, Design Centre for Sustainability, courtesy of Patrick Condon and Sara Barron 540

24.10 Sydney Tar Ponds, Sydney, NS 544

24.11 Peace-Athabasca Delta, northern Alberta 546

24.12 Suncor oil sands project, view of tailing pond and extraction operations 547

24.13 Rehabilitated land, Suncor oil sands operation 548

24.14 Terminal elevator, Medicine Hat, AB: the changing scale of Canadian agriculture 552

24.15 Landscape of the urban fringe, Hamilton, ON 553

24.16 Hockey on the pond: landscape image on the Canadian five-dollar bill. Courtesy of the Bank of Canada 554

25.1 Garden and residence of Ardgowan House, Charlottetown, PEI, restored by Parks Canada 557

25.2 "Aménagement du domaine seigneurial Mauvide-Genest," by Chantal Prud'homme, landscape architect, for the Société de développement de la seigneurie Mauvide-Genest, 2002. Landscape restoration plan, Mauvide-Genest Seigneury, Île d'Orléans, QC. Courtesy of Chantal Prud'homme 558

APPENDIX: GLOSSARY OF PLANTS MENTIONED IN THE TEXT

BROADLEAF TREES

English Name	Botanical Name	French Name
Alder	*Alnus*	Aulne
Alder, Red	*Alnus rubra*	Aulne rouge/Aulne de l'Orégon
Apple	*Malus*	Pommier
Apple, Wild	*Malus pumila*	Pommier sauvage
Apples, McIntosh	*Malus domestica* 'McIntosh'	Pommier McIntosh
Arbutus, Pacific Madrone	*Arbutus menziesii*	Madrone du Pacifique, Arbousier de Menzies
Ash	*Fraxinus*	Frêne
Ash, Patmore Red	*Fraxinus pennsylvanica* 'Patmore'	Frêne de Patmore
Ash, Red	*Fraxinus pennsylvanica*	Frêne rouge
Ash, White	*Fraxinus americana*	Frêne blanc, Frêne américain
Aspen, Trembling Aspen, Quaking Aspen	*Populus tremuloïdes*	Faux-tremble, Peuplier faux-tremble, Tremble
Beech, American	*Fagus grandifolia*	Hêtre américain, Hêtre à grandes feuilles
Beech, Copper	*Fagus sylvatica* 'Purpurea,' *F. s.* 'Atropunicea'	Hêtre pourpre
Beech, Purple	*Fagus sylvatica* 'Riversii'	Hêtre pourpre de Rivers
Birch, Grey	*Betula populifolia*	Bouleau gris
Birch, Paper	*Betula papyrifera*	Bouleau à papier
Birch, Yellow	*Betula alleghaniensis, B. lutea*	Merisier, Bouleau jaune
Black Locust, False Acacia, Common Locust, Acacia	*Robinia pseudoacacia*	Acacia, Acacia blanc, Faux-acacia, Robinier faux-acacia
Cherry	*Prunus, P. cerasus*	Cerisier
Cherry, Black	*Prunus serotina*	Cerisier noir
Cherry, Pin; Wild Red Cherry	*Prunus pennsylvanica*	Cerisier de Pennsylvanie, Petit merisier
Cherry, Bird	*Prunus padus*	Cerisier à grappes

Chestnut, Horse-Chestnut	*Aesculus hippocastanum* (not a true chestnut)	Maronnier d'Inde
Chestnut; Red Horse-Chestnut	*Aesculus x carnea*	Maronnier à fleurs rouges
Chokecherry, Red Chokecherry	*Prunus virginiana*	Cerisier de Virginie
Crabapple, Dolgo	*Malus x* 'Dolgo'	Pommetier 'Dolgo'
Crabapples, Rosybloom:		Pommetiers 'Rosybloom':
Almey Crabapple	*Malus x* 'Almey'	Pommetier 'Almey'
Sutherland Crabapple	*Malus x* 'Sutherland'	Pommetier 'Sutherland'
Thunderchild Crabapple	*Malus x* 'Thunderchild'	Pommetier 'Thunderchild'
Crabapple, Siberian	*Malus baccata*	Pommier russe, Pommetier de Sibérie
Dogwood, Pacific; Western Flowering Dogwood	*Cornus nuttallii*	Cornouiller du Pacifique, Cornouiller de Nuttall
Elm	*Ulmus*	Orme
Elm, American	*Ulmus americana*	Orme américain
Elm, Siberian	*Ulmus pumila*	Orme de Sibérie
Elm, Dropmore	*Ulmus pumila* 'Dropmore'	Orme de Sibérie 'Dropmore'
Gingko	*Gingko biloba*	Gingko, Arbre à quatre-écus
Hawthorn	*Crataegus*	Aubépine
Honey Locust	*Gleditsia triacanthos*	Févier
Katsura-Tree	*Cercidiphyllum japonicum*	Arbre de Katsura, Cercidophylle du Japon
Laburnum, Golden-Chain Tree	*Laburnum anagyroides, Laburnum x watereri*	Cytise à grappes, Aubour, Cytise faux-ébénier
Lilac, Common	*Syringa vulgaris*	Lilas commun
Lilac, Ivory Silk	*Syringa reticulata* 'Ivory Silk'	Lilas 'Ivory Silk'
Linden	*Tilia*	Tilleul
Linden, Little-Leaf	*Tilia cordata*	Tilleul à petites feuilles
Maple	*Acer*	Érable
Maple, Amur	*Acer ginnala*	Érable ginnala, Érable de l'Amour
Maple, Bigleaf	*Acer macrophyllum*	Érable à grandes feuilles
Maple, Japanese	*Acer palmatum*	Érable du Japon
Maple, Manitoba; Box-Elder, Ash-Leaved Maple	*Acer negundo*	Érable à giguère, Érable du Manitoba, Érable négundo
Maple, Norway	*Acer platanoïdes*	Érable de Norvège
Maple, Silver	*Acer saccharinum*	Erable argenté
Maple, Sugar	*Acer saccharum*	Érable à sucre
Maple, Vine	*Acer circinatum*	Érable circiné
Mountain Ash	*Sorbus*	Sorbier
Mulberry, Weeping	*Morus alba pendula*	Murier pleureur
Oak	*Quercus*	Chêne
Oak, Garry	*Quercus garryana*	Chêne de Garry
Oak, Red	*Quercus rubra*	Chêne rouge
Palm	*Phoenix, Washingtonia, Chamaerops, Rhapis spp.*, etc.	Palmier
Peach	*Prunus persica*	Pêcher
Pear	*Pyrus calleryana*	Poirier
Plum	*Prunus*	Prunier
Plum, Wild	*Prunus americana*	Prunier rouge américain
Poplar, Balsam	*Populus balsamifera*	Peuplier baumier

Poplar, Carolina	*Populus X canadensis* 'Eugenii'	Peuplier de Caroline
Poplar, Cottonwood	*Populus deltoïdes*	Peuplier deltoïdes, Liard de l'Ouest
Poplar, Lombardy	*Populus nigra* 'Italica'	Peuplier de Lombardie
Poplar, Russian	*Populus deltoïdes x petrowskyana*	Peuplier de Russie
Russian Olive	*Elaeagnus angustifolia, E. hortensis*	Olivier de Bohème
Saskatoon, Western Serviceberry	*Amelanchier alnifolia*	Amélanchier à feuilles d'Aulne, A. de Saskatoon
Serviceberry	*Amelanchier canadensis*	Amélanchier du Canada
Sycamore, Plane-Tree	*Platanus occidentalis*	Platane d'Occident, Sycomore
Walnut; Black Walnut, American Black Walnut	*Juglans nigra*	Noyer, Noyer noir
Willow	*Salix*	Saule
Willow, Arctic	*Salix purpurea* 'Gracilis'	Saule arctique
Willow, Weeping	*Salix babylonica*	Saule pleureur

CONIFEROUS TREES AND SHRUBS

English Name	*Botanical Name*	*French Name*
Araucaria, Chilean; Monkey-Puzzle	*Araucaria araucana*	Araucaria, Désespoir des singes
Cedar, Arborvitae	*Thuya (Thuja)*	Cèdre, Thuya
Cedar, Eastern; Eastern White Cedar	*Thuya occidentalis*	Cèdre blanc, Thuya de l'Est
Cedar, Western Red	*Thuya plicata*	Cèdre rouge de l'Ouest, Thuya géant
Cedar, Yellow; Port Orford Cedar	*Chamaecyparis nootkanensis*	Cèdre jaune, Cyprès jaune, Faux-cyprès jaune
Fir, Balsam	*Abies balsamea*	Sapin baumier, Sapin blanc
Fir, Douglas	*Pseudotsuga menziesii*	Sapin de Douglas
Giant Sequoia, Giant Redwood	*Sequoiadendron giganteum*	Séquoia géant
Hemlock	*Tsuga*	Pruche
Hemlock, Western	*Tsuga heterophylla*	Pruche de l'Ouest
Juniper	*Juniperus*	Genévrier
Larch, American; Tamarack	*Larix laricina*	Mélèze laricin, Tamarac
Larch, Japanese	*Larix leptolepis*	Mélèze du Japon
Lawson Cypress	*Chamaecyparis lawsoniana*	Faux-cyprès de Lawson
Pine	*Pinus*	Pin
Pine, Black; Austrian Pine	*Pinus nigra* 'Austriaca'	Pin noir, Pin d'Autriche, Pin noir d'Autriche
Pine, Eastern White; White Pine	*Pinus strobus*	Pin blanc, Pin blanc de l'Est
Pine, Jack	*Pinus banksiana*	Pin gris
Pine, Japanese black	*Pinus thunbergiana*	Pin noir japonais
Pine, Mugho	*Pinus mugo mughus*	Pin mugho
Pine, Ponderosa	*Pinus ponderosa*	Pin ponderosa, Pin à bois lourd
Pine, Red	*Pinus resinosa*	Pin rouge
Pine, Scots	*Pinus sylvestris*	Pin sylvestre, Pin écossais
Redwood, Dawn	*Metasequoia glyptostroboides*	Métaséquoia de Chine
Spruce	*Picea*	Épinette
Spruce, Black Hills	*Picea glauca densata*	Épinette blanche Densata
Spruce, Colorado	*Picea pungens*	Épinette du Colorado
Spruce, Colorado Blue	*Picea pungens* 'Glauca'	Épinette bleue du Colorado

GLOSSARY OF PLANTS MENTIONED IN THE TEXT 581

English Name	Botanical Name	French Name
Spruce, Engelmann	*Picea engelmannii*	Épinette bleue d'Engelmann
Spruce, Koster Blue	*Picea pungens* 'Koster'	Épinette bleue de Koster
Spruce, Norway	*Picea abies*	Épinette de Norvège
Spruce, Red	*Picea rubens, P. rubra*	Épinette rouge, Prusqueur rouge
Spruce, Sitka	*Picea sitchensis*	Épinette de Sitka
Spruce, White; Eastern Spruce	*Picea glauca*	Épinette blanche
Tamarack, Larch	*Larix laricina*	Tamarac, Mélèze
Yew	*Taxus*	If
Yew, Japanese	*Taxus cuspidata*	If japonais

BROADLEAF SHRUBS

English Name	Botanical Name	French Name
Azalea	*Rhododendron spp.*	Azalée
Burning Bush	*Euonymus alatus*	Fusain
Caragana, Common Caragana, Russian Pea Shrub	*Caragana arborescens*	Caragana, Arbre aux pois, Caraganier, Caraganier de Sibérie
Cranberry, Highbush; Pembina	*Viburnum trilobum, V. edule*	Viorne trilobée, Pimbina
Dogwood, Red Osier	*Cornus stolonifera*	Hart rouge, Osier rouge, Cornouiller
Dogwood, Yellow-Twig	*Cornus flaviramea*	Cornouiller à bois jaune
Gooseberry (commercial)	*Ribes uva-crispa*	Groseiller (commercial)
Gooseberry, Wild; Northern Gooseberry	*Ribes oxyacanthoides, R. setosum*	Groseiller sauvage, Groseiller du Nord
Himalayan Blackberry	*Rubus discolor, Rubus armeniacus*	Ronce discolor
Holly, English; Christmas Holly	*Ilex aquifolium*	Houx commun
Honeysuckle	*Lonicera*	Chèvrefeuille
Honeysuckle, Dropmore Scarlet	*Lonicera x brownii* 'Dropmore Scarlet'	Chèvrefeuille 'Dropmore Scarlet'
Hydrangea	*Hydrangea*	Hydrangée, Hortensia
Kalmia, Mountain Laurel	*Kalmia latifolia*	Kalmia, Laurier
Lambkill, Sheep Laurel	*Kalmia angustifolia*	Kalmia à feuilles étroites
Laurel, English	*Prunus laurocerasus*	Laurier-cerise
Lilac, Pocahontas	*Syringa x hyacinthiflora* 'Pocahontas'	Lilas 'Pocahontas'
Lilac, Preston	*Syringa x prestoniae*	Lilas de Preston
Mahonia, Oregon Grape	*Mahonia aquifolium*	Mahonia à feuilles de houx
Mock-Orange	*Philadelphus*	Séringat
Privet	*Ligustrum vulgare*	Troène
Raspberry, Flowering	*Rubus odoratus*	Ronce odorante
Raspberry, Red Raspberry, Garden Raspberry	*Rubus idaeus, R. idaeus x strigosus, R. strigosus*	Framboisier, Framboisier des jardins
Rhododendron, Canadian	*Rhododendron canadense*	Rhododendron du Canada
Rhododendron, Pacific	*Rhododendron macrophyllum*	Rhododendron à grandes feuilles
Rose Floribunda	*Rosa polyantha x hybrid tea*	Rosier floribunda
Rose, Acadian	*Rosa rugosa alba*	Rose d'Acadie
Rose, Arctic; Prickly Wild Rose	*Rosa acicularis*	Rosier arctique
Rose, Redleaf	*Rosa rubrifolia, R. glauca*	Rosier à feuilles rouges
Rose, Rugosa; Wild Rose	*Rosa rugosa*	Rosier rugueux
Roses, Explorer series: 'Samuel de Champlain'	*Rosa* 'Samuel de Champlain'	Rosiers, série 'Explorateurs': Rosier 'Samuel de Champlain'

'Martin Frobisher'	*Rosa* 'Martin Frobisher'	Rosier 'Martin Frobisher'
Salal	*Gaultheria shallon*	Menziésie ferrugineuse, Salal
Salmonberry	*Rubus spectabilis*	Ronce remarquable, Ronce élégante
Snowberry	*Symphoricarpos albus*	Symphorine
Spiraea, White; Meadowsweet	*Spiraea alba, S. latifolia*	Spirée blanche, Reine des prés
Spirea, Bridal Wreath	*Spiraea x vanhouttei*	Spirée de Vanhoutte

GRASSES AND HERBS/ANNUALS AND PERENNIALS/VINES AND GROUNDCOVERS

English Name	*Botanical Name*	*French Name*
Alfalfa	*Medico sativa*	Luzerne
Bamboo	*Bambusa, Phyllostachys, Sasa spp.*, etc.	Bambou
Barley	*Hordeum vulgare*	Orge
Barley, Foxtail; Wild Barley	*Hordeum jubatum*	Orge sauvage, Queue d'écureuil
Beans	*Phaseolus, Vicia spp.*, etc.	Fèves
Bearberry, Kinnikinnick	*Arctostaphylos uva-ursi*	Raisin d'ours
Bell Flower, Bluebell	*Campanula*	Campanule, Raiponcette
Black-Eyed Susan, Brown-eyed Susan	*Rudbeckia hirta*	Rudbeckie
Blue Grama	*Bouteloua gracilis*	Boutelou gracieux
Bog Rosemary	*Andromeda polifolia*	Andromède
Bulrush, Cat-tail	*Typha*	Massette, Quenouille
Camas Lily, Quamash	*Camassia quamash*	Camassia, Camassie, Quamash
Camas Lily, Blue; Common Camas	*Camassia esculenta*	Camas commun
Carnation	*Dianthus caryophyllus*	Oeillet des bois
Chrysanthemum	*Chrysanthemum*	Chrysanthème
Columbine	*Aquilegia canadensis*	Ancolie du Canada
Coneflower, Narrow-leaved	*Echinacea angustifolia*	Échinacée à feuilles étroites
Coneflower, Purple	*Echinacea purpurea*	Échinacée
Corn, Sweet Corn, Maize	*Zea mays* varieties	Maïs, Blé d'Inde
Dusty Miller	*Artemisia Stelleriana*	Barbette, Armoise de Steller
Fescue, Red	*Festuca rubra*	Fétuque rouge
Fescue, Rough	*Festuca scabrella*	Fétuque scabre
Fiddleheads, Ostrich Fern	*Matteucia struthiopteris*	Fougère à l'autruche, Têtes de violon
Gentians	*Gentiana, Dasystephana spp.*	Gentiane
Goat's-beard	*Aruncus dioicus*	Barbe de bouc, Aronce dioique
Goutweed	*Aegopodium podagraria*	Égopode podagraire, Herbe aux goutteux
Grape, Common Grape	*Vitis vinifera* varieties	Vigne commune
Grape, Wild	*Vitis riparia*	Vigne sauvage, Raisin sauvage
Grass, Western Wheat	*Agropyron smithii*	Blé sauvage de l'Ouest/Agropyre de l'Ouest
Heather	*Calluna vulgaris, Erica spp.*	Bruyère
Indian breadroot, Prairie Turnip	*Psoralea esculenta*	Navet de prairie, Pomme de prairie, Pomme blanche
Iris, Blue; Larger Blue Flag	*Iris versicolor*	Iris versicolore, Clajeux
Lily, Madonna	*Lilium candidum*	Lis blanc
Little Bluestem	*Andropogon scoparius*	Schizachrium à balais
Marigold	*Tagetes*	Souci

GLOSSARY OF PLANTS MENTIONED IN THE TEXT 583

Needle and Thread, Spear Grass	*Stipa comata, Hesperostipa comata*	Stipe chevelue, Stipe comateuse
Northern Calypso, Venus' Slipper, Fairy slipper	*Calypso bulbosa, C. borealis*	Calypso bulbeux
Oats	*Avena sativa*	Avoine
Orchids	*Calypso, Cypripedium, Orchis spp.,* etc.	Orchidées
Pansy	*Viola tricolor*	Violette tricolore, Pensée
Peanut	*Arachis hypogaea*	Arachide
Peony	*Paeonia*	Pivoine
Peony, Chinese; Common Garden Peony	*Paeonia lactiflora*	Pivoine de Chine
Pepper	*Capsicum frutescens*	Poivron
Pink	*Dianthus*	Oeillet
Poppy, Himalayan Blue	*Meconopsis betonicifolia, M. baileyi*	Pavot bleu des Himalyas
Poppy, Red; Scarlet Poppy	*Papaver rhoeas*	Coquelicot, Pavot rouge
Potato	*Solanum tuberosum*	Pomme de terre, Patate
Prairie Crocus, Pasque Flower, Prairie Anemone	*Anemone patens*	Anémone des prairies, Crocus, Pulsatille multifide
Rye	*Secale cereale*	Seigle
Saxifrage	*Saxifraga*	Saxifrage
Sedge	*Carex*	Laîche
Small White Lady's Slipper	*Cypripedium passerinum*	Cypripède oeuf-de-passereau
Soybean	*Glycine max*	Soja, Soja jaune
Squashes	*Cucurbita spp.*	Courges
Sweet Pea	*Lathyrus odoratus*	Pois de senteur
Tulip	*Tulipa*	Tulipe
Vanilla	*Vanilla planifolia*	Vanille
Wheat	*Triticum aestivum, T. vulgare, T. sativum*	Blé
Wheat, Hard; Durum Wheat	*Triticum durum* or *Triticum turgidum*	Blé dur
Wild Rice	*Zizania aquatica, Z. palustris*	Riz sauvage, Zizanie des marais
Wintergreen, Mountain Tea	*Gaultheria procumbens*	Thé des bois, Petit thé

REFERENCES

Brickell, Christopher, and Trevor Cole, eds. *Practical Guide to Gardening in Canada.* Montreal: Reader's Digest Association (Canada), 1993

Cole, Trevor. *Nouveau guide illustré du jardinage au Canada.* Montreal: Sélection du Reader's Digest 2000

Farrar, John Laird. *Les Arbres du Canada.* Canada: Fidès/Service canadien des forêts 1996

– *Trees in Canada.* Markham, ON: Fitzhenry & Whiteside 1995

Government of Canada. *Flore du Canada/Canadian Flora.* Ottawa: Secretary of State, Translation Bureau 1974

Hosie, R.C. *Arbres indigenes du Canada/Native Trees of Canada.* Ottawa: Ministère de l'environnement, Service canadien des forêts 1969

Knowles, Hugh R. *Woody Ornamentals for the Prairies.* Edmonton: University of Alberta 1989

L.H. Bailey Hortorium, Cornell University. *Hortus Third: A Concise Dictionary of Plants Cultivated in the United States and Canada.* New York: John Wiley 1976

Marie-Victorin, Frère. *Flore laurentienne.* Montreal: Presses de l'Université de Montréal 1964

Pellerin, Gervais. *Répertoire des arbres et arbustes ornementaux.* Quebec City: Hydro-Québec 1998

Sunset Books. *Western Garden Book.* 8th edn. Menlo Park, CA: Sunset Publishing Corp. 2007

NOTES

INTRODUCTION

1 Danièle Routaboule, poster of the École d'architecture de paysage, Université de Montréal, 1977; Pleasance Crawford, Edward Fife, and Ina Elias, "Landscape Architecture," *Canadian Encyclopedia* (2012).

2 For example, in the bylaws of the Association des architectes paysagistes du Québec.

3 Personal conversation with Danièle Routaboule.

4 von Baeyer, *Ontario History* 89, no. 2 (1997): 97–102.

5 Unlike the symbols on the same common items of our American neighbour, which are largely abstract or built symbols of their republic.

6 Atwood, *Survival*, 40–9.

7 Canadian programs of higher education in landscape architecture were established quite late, beginning sixty-five years after the first programs in the United States.

8 Primarily France, Great Britain, and the United States.

9 Many of these influences have been described by John Ralston Saul in his 1998 book *Reflections of a Siamese Twin*, his recent book *On Equilibrium*, and his speeches on animism (i.e., CSLA Vancouver 2006). Saul considers the frontier to remain very much a part of the Canadian reality, although it was officially closed a century ago in the United States.

10 The International Council on Monuments and Sites (ICOMOS), the Canadian Society of Landscape Architects (CSLA), and the Association des architectes paysagistes du Québec (AAPQ).

11 J.B. Jackson, *Discovering the Vernacular Landscape*, x–xi.

12 Many historians, including Simon Schama and Alan McEachern, have written fascinating books about landscape, as have geographers, cultural anthropologists, and others.

CHAPTER ONE

1 Leacock, *Canada: The Foundations of Its Future*, 3.

2 Canadian diplomat Hugh L. Keenleyside referred to the Canada-US border as "geographically illogical" and "a typical human creation." See MacLuhan, "Canada: The Borderline Case," 226.

3 Kraulis, *The Canadian Landscape*, 10.

4 As an example, the Oak Ridges Moraine of southern Ontario seems to have become the natural boundary of the Greater Toronto Area.

5 Northrop Frye, "Conclusion," in Klinck et al., eds., *A Literary History of Canada*, 821–49.

6 Vigneault, "Mon pays." Literally, "My country is not a country, it is winter."

7 Rowe, *Forest Regions of Canada*, 6–11 and map; Cannings and Cannings, *British Columbia: A Natural History*, 172–9.

8 Natural Resources Defense Council; see http://www.nrdc.org/land/forests/boreal/intro.asp.

CHAPTER TWO

1 Most authorities place the arrival of North America's first peoples some 15,000 to 25,000 years ago, during the glacial era. As the glaciers receded, Native peoples moved from the south into newly accessible Canadian territories. Athapaskan peoples of northwestern Canada arrived approximately 8,000 years ago and the Inuit in several waves from about 2,000 BCE to 1,000 CE. See Pringle, "The First Americans," for a summary of some recent research.

2 Ray, *I Have Lived Here Since the World Began*, 6–21.

3 Waugh, *Iroquois Foods*, 71–8, 117–29; Brisson, "Au coeur de Montréal," 9–11.

4 Quimby, *Indian Life in the Upper Great Lakes*, 123.

5 Interpretation panel, Fortress of Louisbourg, NS.
6 Kirk, *Wisdom of the Elders*, 192.
7 Waugh, *Iroquois Foods*, 2–6. This system of cultivation had expanded gradually into new territories since its beginnings in Mexico as the "milpa" system some 3,000 years ago.
8 Ibid., 78.
9 Ibid., 72–7, 103–7, 111–14.
10 Ibid., 79–99.
11 Ibid., 4–5.
12 Bird, "Settlement Patterns in Maritime Canada," 385–404; Flynn and Syms, "Manitoba's First Farmers," 4–11; Government of Manitoba, *The Prehistory of the Lockport Site*, 11.
13 Mann, "1491," 41–53; Nelson and England, "Some Comments," 33–43.
14 Buggey, *An Approach to Aboriginal Cultural Landscapes*, 2.
15 These Manitou spirits inspired the names of the province of Manitoba and Manitoulin Island in Ontario.
16 Poet Pauline Johnson recounts one version of this story in *Legends of Vancouver*, 39–42.
17 Shelton, "Places for the Soul," 76–83.
18 According to Alain Beaulieu, *Les Autochtones du Québec*, 24. New villages were established at intervals of ten to thirty years; various other authorities provide differing figures.
19 Mann, "1491," 50, 53; Krech, *The Ecological Indian*, 103–4.
20 Ibid., 50; Krech, *The Ecological Indian*, 42–3. This process was observed over a period of twelve years of American agricultural settlement in Illinois in the mid-nineteenth century, and described in *Scientific American* in April 1863; re-cited in *Scientific American* 308, no. 4 (2013): 91.
21 R. Louis Gentilcore and J. David Wood, "A Military Colony in a Wilderness: The Upper Canada Frontier," in J.D. Wood, ed., *Perspectives on Landscape*, 32–50.
22 Konrad, "Distribution, Site and Morphology of Prehistorical Settlements," 6–31.
23 Beaulieu, *Les Autochtones du Québec*, 22–7.
24 *Canadian Encyclopedia*, article "Iroquois."
25 Upton, *Architecture in the United States*, 111.
26 Brumley, *Medicine Wheels on the Northern Plains*, 2–3.
27 Ibid., 3–6.
28 Ibid., 7–9.
29 Ibid., 37, 50.
30 Hallendy, *Inuksuit*, 44–9.
31 G.F. MacDonald, *Ninstints*, 2.
32 Drucker, *Indians of the Northwest Coast*, 3–9.
33 Smyly and Smyly, *Those Born at Koona*, 16–18.
34 Chittenden, *Official Report*, 64.
35 G.F. MacDonald, *Ninstints*, 7–16.
36 Ibid., 15–39.
37 Smyly and Smyly, *Those Born at Koona*, 24; Barbeau, *Totem Poles*.
38 Stewart, *Looking at Totem Poles*, 31–44.

39 Buggey, *An Approach to Aboriginal Cultural Landscapes*, 4–5.
40 Ibid., 5.
41 Tanner, *The Settling of North America*, 24–7.
42 University of Saskatchewan, "Crooked Lake Provincial Park," http://www.interactive/usask.ca/tourism/ sask_parks/crooked.html.
43 Kenyon, *Mounds of Sacred Earth*.
44 Conrad and Hiller, *Atlantic Canada*, 31.
45 Ontario Parks, *Petroglyphs: The Teaching Rocks*, 2001.
46 Halmrast, *Story on Stone*.
47 For one example of this, see G.F. MacDonald, *Ninstints*, 2, 47.
48 Krech, *The Ecological Indian*, 79–83.
49 These themes are explored by John Ralston Saul in his book *A Fair Country: Telling the Truths about Canada*. See particularly Part 1, "A Métis Civilization," 3–107.

CHAPTER THREE

1 Davis, *Natural History Map of Nova Scotia*; Buczynski and Marceau, *Le Grand Voyage des Continents*.
2 Conrad and Hiller, *Atlantic Canada*, 36–8; McAleese, *Full Circle: First Contact*.
3 Campeau, *The Beginning of Acadia*, 1–40; Easterbrook and Aitken, *Canadian Economic History*, 23–8.
4 Cartier, *Voyages of Jacques Cartier*, 10.
5 Hamelin and Provencher, *Brève histoire du Québec*, 7–8.
6 Cartier, *Voyages of Jacques Cartier*, 51–2, 65.
7 Easterbrook and Aitken, *Canadian Economic History*, 24–8.
8 Ibid., 28–35.
9 In his study of the cultural landscape and vernacular architecture of Tilting, on Fogo Island, Newfoundland, Robert Mellin provides an apt characterization: "rugged land, strong people, fragile architecture." Mellin, *Tilting*, 27–67.
10 Kalman, *A History of Canadian Architecture*, 1:94.
11 The name of the territory, Acadia, was perhaps inspired by the appellation "Arcadia," a poetic reference to the peaceful landscapes of ancient Greece, applied to the Atlantic coast by the explorer Verrazano in 1524. See Campeau, *The Beginning of Acadia 1602–1616*, 30–1. The influence of local First Nations place names (Shubenacadie, Passamaquoddy, etc.) may also have played a role in the naming of Acadia.
12 Campeau, *The Beginning of Acadia*, 29–31, 41–3, 58–60.
13 Davis, *Natural History Map of Nova Scotia*.
14 Trottier and Lacasse, *Port Royal and Its Inhabitants*, 2–5; Parks Canada, *Lieu Historique National de Grand-Pré*, 1999.
15 Conrad and Hiller, *Atlantic Canada*, 51–3; Trottier and Lacasse, *Port Royal and Its Inhabitants*, 5–10; M-J. Fortier, *Les jardins d'agrément*, 66–70.
16 Conrad and Hiller, *Atlantic Canada*, 52.

17 Thurston, *Tidal Life*, 82–3.
18 Cormier, *Les Aboiteaux en Acadie*, 38–55.
19 Ross and Deveau, *The Acadians of Nova Scotia*, 32–3.
20 Thurston, *Tidal Life*, 83; Lockerby, "Colonization of Île St.-Jean," 22–30.
21 Moore, *Fortress of Louisbourg*, 6–8.
22 Ibid., 52.
23 Ross and Deveau, *The Acadians of Nova Scotia*, 60–5.
24 Ibid., 65–7.
25 Boudreau and Chiasson, *Chansons d'Acadie*, Preface; Ross and Deveau, *The Acadians of Nova Scotia*, 65.
26 Longfellow, *Evangeline*, Introduction by C. Bruce Ferguson, 6–8.
27 Parks Canada, *Grand-Pré National Historic Site*, guide, 1999.
28 Parks Canada and Memramcook Valley Historical Society, *Guide*.
29 Published in 1890 as *Canadians of Old* (New York: D. Appleton).
30 Roberts, "Tantramar Revisited."
31 Thurston, *Tidal Life*, 88.
32 Ibid., 82–5.
33 Ibid., 82, 85–91.

CHAPTER FOUR

1 Simard, *L'art religieux des routes du Québec*, 39.
2 Bégin, "Québec et Montréal," 11; Tessier, *An Historical Guide to Québec*, 17.
3 Delaney and Nicholls, *After the Fire*, 1–3, 57–69.
4 Casanova, *Une Amérique française*, 113–36.
5 Marsan, *Montreal in Evolution*, 70–96.
6 Ibid., 93–5.
7 Bégin, "Québec et Montréal," 10.
8 Ibid.
9 Bernier et al., *Québec, ville militaire*, 70–2.
10 Bégin, "Québec et Montréal," 11; Mendel, "Québec: Ville du patrimoine mondial."
11 Lambert, Stewart, and Canadian Centre for Architecture, *Opening the Gates of Eighteenth-Century Montreal*, 24.
12 Bégin, "Québec et Montréal," 11.
13 In his encyclopedic study of North American cities, Reps describes the "charm and interest" of the French colonial towns: "[I]n such cities as Quebec or New Orleans, where the original French character has not been entirely obliterated, the quality of the urban scene or townscape surpasses virtually anything else of its kind in North America." *The Making of Urban America*, 56.
14 Marsan, *Montreal in Evolution*, 70–4; Lambert, Stewart, and Canadian Centre for Architecture, *Opening the Gates of Eighteenth-Century Montreal*, 23.
15 Reps, *Town Planning in Frontier America*, 85–105.
16 Parkman, *Montcalm and Wolfe*, 388.

17 Biagi, *Louisbourg*, 62–7; McLennan, *Louisbourg from Its Foundation to Its Fall*.
18 Bégin, "Québec et Montréal," 15.
19 Bergeron, *Les places et halles de marché au Québec*, 22.
20 Ibid., 8.
21 Bégin, "Québec et Montréal, 11.
22 Bergeron, *Les places et halles de marché au Québec*, 5.
23 Bégin, "Québec et Montréal," 11; Côté, *Place-Royale*, 56–87.
24 Bergeron, *Les places et halles de marché au Québec*, 20–1.
25 Bégin, "Québec et Montréal," 11–12; Côté, *Place-Royale*, 123.
26 Tessier, *An Historical Guide to Québec*, 97–104.
27 Aubert de Gaspé, *Les Anciens Canadiens*, 18; Charbonneau, Desloges, and Lafrance, *Québec, ville fortifiée*, 368.
28 Tessier, *An Historical Guide to Québec*, 97–104.
29 Bergeron, *Les places et halles de marché au Québec*, 9.
30 O'Neill, "The Gardens of 18th Century Louisbourg," 162–3.
31 Ibid., 163–4.
32 Ibid., 163.
33 Bégin, "Québec et Montréal," 14.
34 M-J. Fortier, *Les jardins d'agrément en Nouvelle-France*, 198–215.
35 M-J. Fortier, "Deux exemples de jardins civils à Montréal," 67–74.
36 M-J. Fortier, *L'intégration d'un jardin historique aux activités du musée*, 14.
37 J. Trudel, *Un chef-d'œuvre de l'art ancien du Québec*, 17.
38 Conversation with a member of the Augustinian order during a visit to the grounds, 2004.
39 Conversation with Sœur Gabrielle Noël, responsible for the Centre Marie-de-l'Incarnation, 2004.
40 Cornut, *Canadensum plantarum*, 20–1.
41 Tessier, *An Historical Guide to Québec*, 122–3.
42 Kalm, *Travels into North America*, 2:183–5.
43 Easterbrook and Aitken, *Canadian Economic History*, 38–40.
44 Marcel Trudel, *Initiation à la Nouvelle-France*, 183–91.
45 Bland, *Sainte-Anne-de-Bellevue*, 17.
46 Kalm, *Travels into North America*, 2:242–4.
47 Jacobs and Fortin, *Évolution de l'architecture de paysage au Québec*, 6–7; Lavoie, "Pourquoi notre urbanisme est-il québécois?," 12–14; Marsan, *Montreal in Evolution*, 34–41.
48 R. Lamontagne, *Jean Talon*, 62.
49 Jacobs and Fortin, *Évolution de l'architecture de paysage au Québec*, 8–9.
50 Deffontaines, *Le rang*, 26.
51 Ibid.
52 L'amicale Notre-Dame-du-Vieux-Moulin, *Le moulin de Pointe-Claire*, 3.
53 Aubert de Gaspé, *Canadians of Old*, 101.
54 G. Lamontagne, *Beaumont 1672–1972*, 17–31.
55 Carver, *Cities in the Suburbs*, 6.
56 Deffontaines, *Le rang*, 23.

57 Bland, *Sainte-Anne-de-Bellevue*, 17–19.

58 Michaud, "Analysis of the Architectural Landscape," 43.

59 Simard, *L'art religieux des routes du Québec*, 40; Kalm, *Travels into North America*, 2:248.

60 Ibid., 28.

61 Ibid.

62 Hémon, *Maria Chapdelaine*, 44–56.

63 Hamelin and Provencher, *Brève histoire du Québec*, 30–1.

CHAPTER FIVE

1 Reps, *The Making of Urban America*, 119–38.

2 Bacon, *Design of Cities*, 217–20.

3 Raddall, *Halifax: Warden of the North*, 18–36.

4 Michael Hugo-Brunt, "The Origin of Colonial Settlements," in Gertler, ed., *Planning the Canadian Environment*, 60–3.

5 Cuthbertson, *Lunenburg*, 2, 3; discussion with Brian Cuthbertson, June 2001.

6 Ibid., 3.

7 Cumming, "Charlottetown," 24.

8 J. Jacobs, *Death and Life*, 92–106.

9 Rogers and Tuck, *Charlotte Town*, 14–16; Cumming, "Charlottetown," 24.

10 Conrad and Hiller, *Atlantic Canada*, 100.

11 Rees, *Land of the Loyalists*, 76–7; Forbes and DeGrace, "Two Hundred Years of Planning," 25.

12 Fredericton Heritage Trust, *Walking Tours of Fredericton*.

13 Colonel J.W.F. DesBarres, provincial governor and an experienced cartographer, drew up this original plan in 1786, probably influenced by new residential developments in England. Michael Hugo-Brunt, "The Origin of Colonial Settlements," in Gertler, ed. *Planning the Canadian Environment*, 66–8; Rees, *Land of the Loyalists*, 63–4.

14 Never touched by fire or industrial development, St. Andrews remains one of the best-preserved eighteenth-century towns in Canada, as recognized by its status as a "national historic district." St. Andrews Chamber of Commerce, *St. Andrews-by-the-Sea Historic Guide*, 2001.

15 Rees, *Land of the Loyalists*, 74.

16 A donation from the city's military band.

17 Bormke, *See Saint John*, 10. The Old Burying Ground was refurbished in 1994–95 according to the design of British landscape architect Alex Novell.

18 Raddall, *Halifax: Warden of the North*, 34.

19 Baird and Richards, "Halifax: Ten Buildings to See," 22.

20 Montgomery, *Anne of the Island*, 24–8.

21 Rees, *Land of the Loyalists*, 61–2; Gowans, *Looking at Architecture in Canada*, 66–9.

22 My thanks to Kitty Forrestal of Middleton, NS, for introducing me to this traditional expression.

23 Irwin, *Lighthouses and Lights of Nova Scotia*, viii. Lighthouses are not only found on Canada's ocean coasts, but are also widely distributed along rivers, on the Great Lakes, and on smaller lakes.

24 Irwin, *Lighthouses and Lights of Nova Scotia*, 71–4.

25 Rees, *Land of the Loyalists*, 56–8.

26 Wynn, "The Maritimes," 181.

27 Rees, *Land of the Loyalists*, 14.

28 Conrad and Hiller, *Atlantic Canada*, 91–2, 97.

29 Views of these landscapes are unobscured by billboards along the roads; their absence is presumably influenced by the opinions of Anne of Green Gables on this subject. See Montgomery, *Anne of Avonlea*, 42, 118–24; J. Clark, "Anne of Green Gables Still Rules."

30 Rees, *Land of the Loyalists*, 17–18; Conrad and Hiller, *Atlantic Canada*, 92–3.

31 Rees, *Land of the Loyalists*, 21.

32 Ibid., 12–13; Conrad and Hiller, *Atlantic Canada*, 100.

33 Rees, *Land of the Loyalists*, 40–1.

34 Ibid., 13–15; Conrad and Hiller, *Atlantic Canada*, 102.

35 This was to become a fundamental characteristic of Canadian agriculture in all regions. In Ontario in 1871, for example, 84 per cent of those who farmed and occupied rural land were owners. See Ross and Crowley, *The College on the Hill*, 11.

36 Jacobs and Fortin, *Évolution de l'architecture de paysage au Québec*, 34–6; Marsan, *Montreal in Evolution*, 145.

37 Baldwin, *Métis, Wee Scotland of the Gaspé*, 12–25.

38 Jacobs and Fortin, *Évolution de l'architecture de paysage au Québec*, 30.

39 Hamelin and Provencher, *Brève histoire du Québec*, 52.

40 Jacobs and Fortin, *Évolution de l'architecture de paysage au Québec*, 30.

41 Rajotte-LaBrèque, "Les Cantons de l'Est," 11–14; Hamelin and Provencher, *Brève histoire du Québec*, 53.

42 Baskerville, *Ontario: Image, Identity and Power*, 43–50.

43 R. Louis Gentilcore and David Wood, "A Military Colony in a Wilderness: The Upper Canada Frontier," in J.D. Wood, ed. *Perspectives on Landscape*, 32–42.

44 Scott, "Utilizing History," 179–87.

45 Carver, *Compassionate Landscape*, 167–8.

46 Scott, "Utilizing History," 185.

47 Ibid.

48 Ermatinger, *Life of Colonel Talbot*.

49 Brunger, "Early Settlement," 122–4.

50 James M. Cameron, "The Canada Company and Land Settlement," in J.D. Wood, ed., *Perspectives on Landscape*, 141–58.

51 Conrad and Hiller, *Atlantic Canada*, 111.

52 Tessier, *An Historical Guide to Quebec City*, 51.

53 Easterbrook and Aitken, *Canadian Economic History*, 191–200; C. Grant Head, "An Introduction to Forest Exploitation," in J.D. Wood, ed., *Perspectives on Landscape*, 78–84.

54 Scott, "Utilizing History," 187; Strickland, *Twenty-Seven Years in Canada West*, 1:196.

55 Strickland, *Twenty-Seven Years in Canada West*, 1:53, 74–6, 297–302, 253–5.

56 Ibid., 1:196.

57 County of Huron Economic Development Services, at http://www.investinhuron.ca.

58 Greenberg, "Toronto: The Unknown Grand Tradition," 37–42; Arthur, *Toronto, No Mean City*, 9–14; J.R. Wright, *Urban Parks in Ontario, Part 1*, 58–60.

59 According to an information plaque in the square, this is one of the few parks whose plan was explicitly based on the design of the Union Jack, "in recognition of the connection between Upper Canada and Great Britain."

60 Jackson, "The Nineteenth Century Rural Landscape," 140–4.

61 Strathdee, *Bayfield*, 4–5.

62 J.R. Wright, *Urban Parks in Ontario, Part 1*, 40–1.

63 Rees, *Land of the Loyalists*, 19.

64 J.D. Hunt, *Gardens and the Picturesque*, 24–6; Hunt and Willis, *The Genius of the Place*, 1–30.

65 Gagnon Pratte, *L'architecture et la nature à Québec*.

66 Thus the name "Kent House," often applied to this estate. Gagnon Pratte, *L'architecture et la nature à Québec*, 278–80; SEPAQ, *Le Sault de Montmorency*, 3–7.

67 Raddall, *Halifax: Warden of the North*, 114–20; Baird and Richards, "Halifax: Ten Buildings to See," 24.

68 Raddall, *Halifax: Warden of the North*, 116, 129; Baird and Richards, "Halifax: Ten Buildings to See," 21.

69 Rees, *Land of the Loyalists*, 20–36.

70 Ibid., 37; Nova Scotia Museum, *Uniacke Estate Museum Park*.

71 Arthur, *Toronto, No Mean City*, 15.

72 Their topographic drawings originally sought to describe the lay of the land for military purposes of attack, defence, or occupation, but the artists often turned their skills to landscape sketching for its own sake, as a study or personal reflection. Marylin J. McKay, *Picturing the Land*, 46–63.

73 Named for their son Francis.

74 Glickman, *Picturesque and Sublime*, viii–ix.

75 Raddall, *Halifax: Warden of the North*, 28.

76 Exemplified by the writings of Alexander Pope.

77 Including industry, sense of duty, tenacity, and respect for authority.

CHAPTER SIX

1 Thompson and Nelischer, "Oskuna Ka Asusteki," 129–32.

2 Ibid., 141–3.

3 Cannings and Cannings, *British Columbia: A Natural History*, 11–20.

4 Huck, *Exploring the Fur Trade Routes of North America*, 156.

5 Easterbrook and Aitken, *Canadian Economic History*, 84–7.

6 Thomas, *Cook*, 4–5, 361–5.

7 Glavin, *The Last Great Sea*, 111, 116, 133–7, 140–5.

8 Krech, *The Ecological Indian*, 175–206.

9 Huck, *Exploring the Fur Trade Routes of North America*, 168–77.

10 Easterbrook and Aitken, *Canadian Economic History*, 321–6.

11 For example, the population of the nineteenth-century fur-trading post at Fort Langley, BC, was truly international, including West Coast First Nations, French Canadians, Scottish traders originating mainly in the Orkney Islands, Iroquois, and Hawaiians, among other groups. See McKelvie, *Fort Langley*.

12 Barman, "Family Life at Fort Langley," 16.

13 Parks Canada, Western Region, *Management Plan: Fort Langley*.

14 McKelvie, *Fort Langley*, 60–1.

15 Barman, "Family Life at Fort Langley," 16–23.

16 Easterbrook and Aitken, *Canadian Economic History*, 171; McKelvie, *Fort Langley*, 54–6; Cole, "Archibald McDonald's Fort Langley Letters," 34.

17 Spry, *The Palliser Expedition*.

18 William Francis Butler, "The Great Lone Land," in Gruending, ed., *The Middle of Nowhere*, 36–8.

19 Roy, *Enchantment and Sorrow*, 37; K. Ouellet, *L'importance du paysage*, 15–20.

20 France, Spain, Russia, Britain, and the United States all sent scientific or commercial missions to the North Pacific during this period. These missions also had a geopolitical dimension.

21 Thomas, *Cook*, 8; Glavin, *The Last Great Sea*, 128; Justice, *Mr. Menzies' Garden Legacy*, 49. The role of botanist was often combined with that of ship's surgeon, similar to the *médecins du roi* of New France.

22 Including conifers western red cedar, yellow cedar, Douglas fir, Sitka spruce, and western hemlock; broadleaf arbutus (Pacific madrone); and many shrubs, including mahonia and salal. See Justice, *Mr. Menzies' Garden Legacy*, 22–5, 36–40, 46–50, 64, 88, 101–6, 112.

23 Knapp, *Plant Discoveries*, 225–32.

24 De Galaup de Lapérouse, *Voyage autour du Monde*, cited in Litalien, "Les missions exploratoires du Pacifique nord," 7. A brilliant naval commander, Lapérouse was the uncle of Pierre-Jacques Traffanel de la Jonquiere, governor general of New France 1746–52.

25 De Galaup de Lapérouse, *Journal*, vol. 1.

26 Justice, *Mr. Menzies' Garden Legacy*, 65.

27 M.J. McKay, *Picturing the Land*, 54, 72–5, 147–9; Goldfarb et al., *Expanding Horizons*, 54, 69, 73.

28 Catherine Flynn and Barbara Huck, "A Continental Crossroad," in Huck, ed., *Crossroads of the Continents*, 46–65.

29 This pattern was followed by settlers of various backgrounds and was not limited to those of French culture.

30 Easterbrook and Aitken, *Canadian Economic History*, 180–6.

31 MacEwan, *French in the West*, 125–38. The original riverside farm layout and the old *rang* and cart track to the west have defined the urban pattern of the city of Winnipeg right up to the present day. These principal roads became today's legendary Portage and Main.

32 MacEwan, *French in the West*, 11–18.

33 McKelvie, *Fort Langley*.

34 Juliana Haynes, "Okanagan Wines"; and Robert M. Hayes, "Accommodation in and around Kelowna," in Kelowna Museum, *Kelowna*, 24–8, 33–41.

35 Brémault, *Bienvenue à Saint-Boniface*, 8–9, 12–13.

36 Ibid., 30–1.

37 Ibid., 12–13.

38 G. MacDonald, *A Good Solid Comfortable Establishment*.

39 Easterbrook and Aitken, *Canadian Economic History*, 343–8, 381–3.

40 Krech, *The Ecological Indian*, 123–6; Tolton, *The Buffalo Legacy*, 2–3.

41 Mary Weekes, "The Last Buffalo Hunter," in Gruending, ed., *The Middle of Nowhere*, 31.

42 Tolton, *The Buffalo Legacy*, 10–27; Krech, *The Ecological Indian*, 139–42.

43 Grant, *Ocean to Ocean*, 1–9.

44 Berton, *The National Dream*; Lightfoot, "Canadian Railroad Trilogy."

45 The US government established the Public Land Survey System through the Land Ordinance of 1784 and the Northwest Ordinance of 1787.

46 Corboz, "La dimension utopique," 63–8; J.B. Jackson, "Jefferson, Thoreau & After," in Zube, ed., *Landscapes, Selected Writings of J.B. Jackson*, 4–5; J.B. Jackson, "The Accessible Landscape," in Jackson, *A Sense of Place*, 3–4. Jefferson writes, "Cultivators of the earth are the most valuable citizens. They are the most vigorous, the most independent, the most virtuous, and they are tied to their country and wedded to its liberty and interests by the most lasting bands" (letter to John Jay, 23 August 1785). See also Maumi, *Thomas Jefferson*, 129.

47 Sifton, *The Conservation of Canada's Resources*.

48 John B. Jackson, "A Pair of Ideal Landscapes," in Jackson, *Discovering the Vernacular Landscape*, 16.

49 Stephen Leacock, a farmer and economist before becoming Canada's most famous humorist, discussed the stumbling blocks of the land division system: "[T]he system was suited for only one kind of farming, done in one way, in one kind of country. It shuts out all the old neighbourliness of the river group ... It means dependence on one or two kinds ... of grain crop, and on the export market and foreign trade." Leacock, *Canada*, 207.

50 Leonard O. Gertler, "Some Economic and Social Influences," in Gertler, ed., *Planning the Canadian Environment*, 86–7.

51 Dick, *A History of Prairie Settlement Patterns*.

52 Government of Manitoba, *La colonisation par les Mennonites*.

53 Ukrainian government website, http://www.ukraine-eu.mfa.gov.ua/eu/en/30909.htm.

54 Personal communications from professors Ted McLachlan and Charlie Thomsen, University of Manitoba, June 2002.

55 Site visit to Tolstoi with Alliance for Historic Landscape Preservation, 2002, with Charlie Thomsen and Ted McLachlan as guides; Kalman, *A History of Canadian Architecture*, 2:512–15.

56 Gabrielle Roy, "Hoodoo Valley," in Roy, *Garden in the Wind*, 107–19.

57 Reps, *The Making of Urban America*, 466–72.

58 Like the Mennonites, the Mormon community sought concentration rather than dispersal of its members, for social and religious purposes, and in both cases, the Canadian government allowed exceptions to the normal rules of farm layout. Robert Hirano, presentation at Society for the Study of Architecture in Canada (SSAC) conference, Lethbridge, AB, June 2005.

59 Renovations in 1991 included a "garden of contemplation" by Alberta landscape architect Garth Balls, well integrated with the original composition.

60 Dean, Heidenreich, McIlwraith, and Warkentin, *Concise Historical Atlas of Canada*, plate 16, "The Move to the West."

61 MacEwan, *French in the West*, 195–210.

62 Dean, Heidenreich, McIlwraith and Warkentin, *Concise Historical Atlas of Canada*, plate 16.

63 Doull, *Motherwell Homestead National Historic Park*; Ellwand, "A Homestead Restored," 10–12; Parks Canada, *Lanark Place*, 24–5.

64 Gruending, *The Middle of Nowhere*, 2–3.

65 J.H. Thompson, *Forging the Prairie West*, 63–6; D.M. Wilson, *Cowley, Alberta: History*, http://www.crowsnest-highway.ca.

66 McIntyre, *The McIntyre Ranch*.

67 CELA conference, Lincoln University, Canterbury, NZ, June 2004.

68 Roy and Thompson, *British Columbia: Land of Promises*, 32–44.

69 Glavin, *The Last Great Sea*, 147–53.

70 Mike Steele, *Vancouver's Famous Stanley Park*, 11–14; MacKay, *Empire of Wood*, 6–19.

71 Glavin, *The Last Great Sea*, 153.

72 Ibid., 153–6.

73 P. Oberlander, "The 'Patron Saint' of Town Planning," in Gertler, ed., *Planning the Canadian Environment*, 36–41.

74 Ibid. City planner Peter Oberlander suggests that New Westminster's sophisticated town layout was inspired by that of contemporary districts in England, including new sections of Bath and London suburbs Bloomsbury and Kensington.

75 History Book Committee, *Raymond Remembered*, 8–9.

76 Norris, "Old Silverton, British Columbia 1891–1930," 148; Katherine Gordon, *The Slocan*, 45–89.

77 The same approach was used, for the same reasons, at the village in Waterton Lakes National Park, Alberta.

CHAPTER SEVEN

1 Turner, "The Significance of the Frontier in American History."

2 The St. Lawrence Valley and Acadia in the eighteenth century, the Maritime provinces before 1800, southern Ontario at the beginning of the nineteenth century, followed by the Prairies towards the end of the century as well as the "Last Coast" in British Columbia from mid-century on, where the progression from log cabin to elegant Tudor mansion was encompassed within a single generation.

3 Kenneth Kelly, "The Impact of Nineteenth Century Agricultural Settlement," in J.D. Wood, ed., *Perspectives on Landscape*, 64–77; J.D. Wood, *Making Ontario*.

4 Ibid., 65–6; Scott, "Utilizing History," 189–90.

5 In her book *Roughing It in the Bush*, Susanna Moodie recalls the discouragement she felt shortly after her arrival in the Lakefield district, where her sister had already settled, and the pleasure she experienced in the same place a few months later. In contrast, her sister Catharine's attitude was always implacably positive. Moodie, *Roughing It in the Bush*, 151–5; Gray, *Sisters in the Wilderness*; Traill, *The Backwoods of Canada*, 122–9.

6 C. Grant Head, "An Introduction to Forest Exploitation," in J.D. Wood, ed., *Perspectives on Landscape*, 94–109.

7 Scott, "Utilizing History," 186–7.

8 Kenneth Kelly, "The Impact of Nineteenth Century Agricultural Settlement," in J.D. Wood, ed., *Perspectives on Landscape*, 67–8.

9 Ross and Crowley, *The College on the Hill*, 11–12.

10 Kelly, "The Impact of Nineteenth Century Agricultural Settlement," 67. Rice Lake is only a few kilometres from the original farms of the Strickland family.

11 Ibid., 67–8.

12 Scott, "Utilizing History," 187–95.

13 Ross and Crowley, *The College on the Hill*, 11–12, 42.

14 Scott, "Utilizing History," 192–3.

15 Ibid., 189–93.

16 Ibid., 190–1.

17 Ibid., 190.

18 Huck, *Exploring the Fur Trade Routes*, 186–7, 195.

19 In the absence of trees, houses were built entirely of sod, around a floor of tamped earth.

20 Friends of the Motherwell Homestead, *Waiting for the Train*, 10–14; James M. Minifie, "Homesteader," and Maria Adamowska, "Beginnings in Canada," in Gruending, ed., *The Middle of Nowhere*, 77–82, 71–3; Dick, *Farmers "Making Good,"* 59–65.

21 Friends of the Motherwell Homestead, *Waiting for the Train*, 14–20, 69–74; James M. Minifie, "Homesteader," in Gruending, ed., *The Middle of Nowhere*, 77–82; Dick, *Farmers "Making Good,"* 34–51.

22 "Canadian Pacific's Agricultural Roots Go Back to Helping Early Homesteaders," *CP Rail News* 14, no. 13 (3 October 1984).

23 Grasses included drought-tolerant species such as western wheatgrass and blue grama, as well as little bluestem, which flourishes in moister environments. Indian breadroot figured among edible native tubers.

24 Critical Wildlife Habitat program, *Manitoba's Mixed-Grass Prairie*.

25 Campbell, "Wheat," in *The Canadian Encyclopedia*, 3:1936.

26 Silversides, *Prairie Sentinel*, 5–9.

27 Ibid., 15–23.

28 Ibid., 7–8.

29 Anstey, *One Hundred Harvests*, 215–16; Wilks, *Browsing Science Research*, 157.

30 Ellwand, "A Homestead Restored," 10–12; Parks Canada, *The Motherwell Homestead*.

31 Ellwand, "A Homestead Restored."

32 Ibid.; Parks Canada, *The Motherwell Homestead*.

33 Lee, *William Pearce*, 1–7, 14–4; Donaldson, "For Beauty and Use," 78.

34 Donaldson, "For Beauty and Use," 75–83.

35 History Book Committee, *Raymond Remembered*, 5–43, 44.

36 Takata, *Nikkei Legacy*, 100–1.

37 Probably inspired by policies adopted in Utah and California. See K.W. Wilson, *Irrigating the Okanagan: 1860–1920*, ch. 2.

38 Lord Aberdeen, a future governor general of Canada, and his formidable wife (the founder of the Victorian Order of Nurses, among other organizations) were involved in the development of Coldstream, where irrigation nourished 25,000 fruit trees – apples, pears, and cherries – along with many fruit-bearing shrubs and hops, rapidly maturing plants that provided immediate revenue during the long wait for the first tree fruit. See Wuest, *Coldstream*, 15–21, 51–5.

39 Dendy, "One Huge Orchard," 99; Kenneth Wilson, "The Greening of Kelowna," in Kelowna Museum, *Kelowna: One Hundred Years*, 3–41.

40 Juliana Haynes, "Okanagan Wines"; Kenneth Wilson, "The Greening of Kelowna"; and "Irrigation – Catalyst for Change," in Kelowna Museum, *Kelowna: One Hundred Years,* 24–8, 33–41, 118–19.

41 Mitchell and Gardner, *River Basin Management: Canadian Experiences,* 279–95.

42 Ibid. A 2010 study states that 2 million acres (800,000 ha) of "inherently wet but fertile land" was brought under cultivation in Manitoba between 1895 and 1935. See Venema, Oborne, and Neudorffer, *The Manitoba Challenge,* 42.

43 J.D. Wood, *Making Ontario,* 138.

44 Ross and Crowley, *The College on the Hill,* 77.

45 L.M. Wolfe, *Son of the Wilderness,* 91–7; Badé, *The Life and Letters of John Muir*; Cox, "John Muir and His Canadian Friends." Muir's letter on this subject, addressed to a former professor, became his first publication.

46 http://www.sierraclub.org; Ross and Crowley, *The College on the Hill,* 77; http://www.ksmart.on.ca/hollandmarsh, 16 February 2006; personal recollections of Mrs. Hazel I. Williams, a resident of rural Ontario during this period.

47 Deschênes, *Histoire de l'horticulture au Québec,* 130–4.

48 Several of these new institutions were eventually to be ranked among the most prestigious American universities.

49 Snell, *Macdonald College,* 40–1, 55–9.

50 Ross and Crowley, *The College on the Hill,* 14–17.

51 http://www.historicplaces.ca/en/rep-reg/place-lieu.aspx?id=10655.

52 Ells, *Shaped through Service.* The college has merged with Halifax's Dalhousie University; it now forms that university's Faculty of Agriculture.

53 Bumsted, *The University of Manitoba,* 21–7.

54 Snell, *Macdonald College,* 55–9.

55 Ross and Crowley, *The College on the Hill,* 77–9, 120–2.

56 Ibid., 122.

57 Galbraith, *A Life in Our Times,* 7–8.

58 Anstey, *One Hundred Harvests,* 3–7; Friends of the Motherwell Homestead, *Waiting for the Train,* 20–1.

59 Anstey, *One Hundred Harvests,* 3–9. Carling had previously helped create the OAC at Guelph.

60 Anstey, *One Hundred Harvests,* 11–13, 63. When he became director of the experimental farms, Saunders was already a well-known pharmacist, botanist, and entomologist, a founding member of the Royal Society of Canada, and a professor at the University of Western Ontario, in London. He should not be confused with his American contemporary William Saunders (1822–1900), botanist and landscape architect. The parallels between the lives and careers of these two men with the same name are striking. Born in Scotland, Saunders (the American) studied horticulture before emigration to the United States in 1848, the same year that his homonym came to Canada. He designed large private gardens, cemeteries, and other landscape projects and, in 1862, became superintendent of the Department of Agriculture's experimental gardens

in Washington, the same post that Saunders the Canadian would eventually occupy in Ottawa. See Reuben Rainey, "William Saunders," in Birnbaum and Karson, *Pioneers,* 327–32.

61 Anstey, *One Hundred Harvests,* 370–96.

62 Ibid., 125–44, 151–8; Friends of the Motherwell Homestead, *Waiting for the Train,* 47, 105.

63 Anstey, *One Hundred Harvests,* 211–12; Sarjeant, "Three Million Trees a Year," 34–41; Dick, "The Greening of the West," 12–17.

64 Anstey, *One Hundred Harvests,* 211–12, 216–17.

65 Ibid., 212–13; Friends of the Motherwell Homestead, *Waiting for the Train,* 105–7. Marquis wheat was famous beyond Canada's borders. Widely adopted in the United States, it "helped win the war," according to Ted Steinberg in *Down to Earth: Nature's Role in American History,* 136.

66 Anstey, *One Hundred Harvests,* 247–50.

67 Roos, *The McIntosh Apple,* 19–21.

68 This variety has been crossed with many others by Canadian experimental farms to create such familiar apples as Lobo, Melba, and Spartan. See Roos, *The McIntosh Apple,* 5–9.

69 Dubé, *Charlevoix: Two Centuries at Murray Bay,* 32–109; Villeneuve, *Paysage, mythe et territorialité,* 24–5, 74–96, 201–63.

70 Personal recollection of Mrs. Hazel I. Williams, told to the author in 2003.

71 M.J. McKay, *Picturing the Land,* 63–73.

72 Ibid., 70–3, 92–103.

73 Ibid., 104–15, 137–45.

74 Ibid., 112–15, 137–40.

CHAPTER EIGHT

1 Gilbert A. Stelter, "The City-Building Process in Canada," in Stelter and Artibise, eds., *Shaping the Urban Landscape,* 5, 10–18; Larry McCann and Peter J. Smith, "Canada Becomes Urban," in Bunting and Filion, eds., *Canadian Cities in Transition,* 69–99. Work on the Lachine Canal in Montreal and the Welland Canal in Ontario began in 1821 and 1824 respectively, and Canada's first railroad was built in 1836. By 1860, the rail network in the Maritimes, Quebec, and Ontario (then Canada East and Canada West) extended a total length of 3,200 kilometres. See Desloges and Gelly, *The Lachine Canal,* 20–2; Mika and Mika, *Railways of Canada,* 14–19.

2 Stelter, "The City-Building Process in Canada," 10–14; McCann and Smith, "Canada Becomes Urban," 74–7. The proportion of the population that lived in urban areas increased from 8 per cent in 1821 to 18.3 per cent in 1871.

3 J.R. Wright, *Urban Parks in Ontario, Part 1,* 30; Gentilcore and Wood, "A Military Colony in a Wilderness," in J.D. Wood, ed., *Perspectives on Landscape,* 42–3.

4 Ville de Québec, *Saint-Roch*.
5 Melançon, *Parcs, espaces verts et dynamique urbaine*, 6.
6 Ville de Québec, *Saint-Sauveur*, 18–19; Cameron, *Charles Baillairgé*, 127.
7 W. Dendy, *Lost Toronto*, 134–7; Arthur, *Toronto, No Mean City*, 208.
8 W. Dendy, *Lost Toronto*, 8, 133; Arthur, *Toronto, No Mean City*, 30.
9 Gillies, *Street of Dreams*, 22–9, 34–41, 66–77.
10 Gamelin et al., *Trois-Rivières illustrée*, 65, 105–9, 140.
11 Cameron, *Charles Baillairgé*, 115–16; Drolet, "The Mighty Empire," 18–24.
12 On a site where a terrace had existed since the time of Governor Frontenac.
13 Cameron, *Charles Baillairgé*, 118–19; *Gazette* (Montreal), 20 May 2000, H6; Drolet, "The Mighty Empire," 18–24.
14 Greenberg, "Toronto: The Unknown Grand Tradition," 37–46.
15 De Laplante, *Les parcs de Montréal*, 23.
16 Choko, *Les grandes places publiques*, 34–7; Marsan, *Montreal in Evolution*, 141.
17 Choko, *Les grandes places publiques*, 46, 52–3.
18 Ville de Montréal, *Plan directeur de Montréal: Espaces libres, 1955*, 6.
19 Choko, *Les grandes places publiques*, 111–13.
20 Ibid., 118 (translated by R.F.W.).
21 Ibid., 65–9; De Laplante, *Les parcs de Montréal*, 26, 37–8.
22 Choko, *Les grandes places publiques*, 77–81.
23 Marsan, *Montreal in Evolution*, 295.
24 Ibid., 294–6; Choko, *Les grandes places publiques de Montréal*, 143–53; De Laplante, *Les parcs de Montréal*, 51.
25 These public spaces have survived with little change, and today, their forms and their character seem virtually inevitable. As former Montreal city planner Mark London asked in 1989, "Why would you do anything different with a square?"
26 Choko, *Les grandes places publiques de Montréal*, 161–81.
27 De Laplante, *Les parcs de Montréal*, 51.
28 Marsan, *Montreal in Evolution*, 296.
29 Ibid., 291–6.
30 Gamelin et al., *Trois-Rivières illustrée*, 103.
31 Ibid., 108, 120.
32 Greenberg, "Toronto: The Unknown Grand Tradition," 37–46.
33 R. Brown, *Toronto's Lost Villages*, 19–20.
34 Ibid., 20.
35 Cullen, "The Late Nineteenth Century Development," 1–20; Kalman, *A History of Canadian Architecture*, 1:112, 2:568–9; Hennessey and MacDonald, "Arthur Newbery," 25–9.
36 Newlands, "The History and Operations of Hamilton's Parks"; J.R. Wright, *Urban Parks in Ontario, Part I*, 70–7.
37 Architects in Association and Daly, *Victoria Park Conceptual Master Plan*; *Saskatchewan Herald*, 30 September 1882, cited in J.W. Brennan, *Regina*, 12.
38 Barraclough, *From Prairie to Park*, 4–5; Donaldson, "William Pearce," 233–4.
39 The chief librarian, scandalized by the sorry state of the rest of the park, described it as an "unsightly wilderness of sand and scrub." Barraclough, *From Prairie to Park*, 25.
40 Ibid., 22–5, 30–5; http://www.calgarypubliclibrary.com/calgary/historic_tours.
41 Barraclough, *From Prairie to Park*, 80.
42 Conway, *Public Parks*, 49; Conway, "Royal Horticultural Society Bandstand," 214–16.
43 Conway, *Public Parks*, 49–52; Habibi-Shandiz, *L'idée du paradis et les jardins safavides*, 410, 411; personal communication from Mme Habibi-Shandiz, February 2005.
44 Bacon, *Design of Cities*, 130–5.
45 Tchikine, "The 'Candelabrum' Fountain Reconsidered," 257–69.
46 P. Crawford, "Of Grounds Tastefully Laid Out," 4–7; Conway, *People's Parks*.
47 P. Crawford, "Of Grounds Tastefully Laid Out," 4–7.
48 Downing, *A Treatise*, 40–1; Leighton, *American Gardens of the Nineteenth Century*, 128–32.
49 Downing, *A Treatise*, 40–1.
50 Crawford and Otto, "André Parmentier's 'Two or Three Places in Upper Canada.'"
51 Ibid.
52 This garden no longer exists; the park that presently occupies the site is of recent vintage. Toronto architect John Howard, who designed an addition to the house, prepared two watercolour sketches that show the garden's appearance in 1834. See Bain, "George Allan and the Horticultural Gardens," 231–51.
53 This is today one of the principal open spaces of the Ryerson University campus.
54 Bain, "William Mundie," 298–308; Pleasance Crawford, "Of Grounds Tastefully Laid Out," 4–5.
55 A masterpiece of Victorian exuberance, built in 1856–59 to the drawings of architect Frederick Cumberland. See Gowans, *Looking at Architecture in Canada*, 142–5.
56 Bain, "William Mundie," 300–7.
57 P. Crawford, "H.A. Engelhardt," 30–5; P. Crawford, "Park and Cemetery Landscape Design in Canada," 7–9.
58 P. Crawford, "H.A. Engelhardt," 30–4, 36–8.
59 Baskerville, *Ontario, Image, Identity and Power*, 86–9, 94–6, 147–51.
60 This new wave of social infrastructure was the secular equivalent of the comprehensive network of institutions established by the Catholic Church in Quebec during the same period (1840–60). See Hamelin and Provencher, *Brève histoire du Québec*, 60–3.

CHAPTER NINE

1 Elliott, *Victorian Gardens*, 21.

2 Ibid., 11–12.

3 Ibid., 22–3, 187–97.

4 Ibid., 16–17, 28, 82–3.

5 Victoria had a personal connection to Canada. Her father was the same Duke of Kent who had left his mark as a military commander and creator of buildings, fortifications, and gardens at Quebec City and Halifax (chapter 5).

6 Elliott, *Victorian Gardens*, 40.

7 Ibid., 55–78, 118–21, 133–43, 159–65.

8 Ibid., 40–8, 94–7, 175–80.

9 Ibid., 13–14, 26–33, 49–51, 87–9, 116–18, 152–9, 180–4.

10 Ibid., 42–6, 61–2, 174.

11 In her book *Rhetoric and Roses*, Edwinna von Baeyer describes how the world of horticulture reacted to these challenges. See also Deschênes, *Histoire de l'horticulture au Québec*; C. Martin, *A History of Canadian Gardening*.

12 Traill, *The Backwoods of Canada*, 190–5, 248–9; Gray, *Sisters in the Wilderness*, 174; Moodie, *Roughing It in the Bush*, 175–8. Traill's interest in botany became increasingly scientific, as witnessed by her book *Canadian Wild Flowers* of 1868, admirably illustrated with watercolour engravings by her niece Agnes Fitzgibbon, the daughter of Susanna Moodie, and in her broader and more detailed work *Studies of Plant Life in Canada or Gleanings from Forest, Lake and Plain*, published in 1885.

13 Deschênes, *Histoire de l'horticulture au Québec*, 37–46; Vermette, *L'abbé Léon Provancher*, 1–13.

14 Smith and Bramley, *Ottawa's Farm*, 50–4. Macoun was subsequently named Dominion horticulturist in 1910.

15 Ibid., 56–8, 95–7; Anstey, *One Hundred Harvests*, 255–6; Isabella Preston, "A Few Lilies for Canadian Gardens," 112, 115–16. The name Macoun gave to Preston's crabapples was perhaps inspired by a passage in the famous 1866 poem "Snow-Bound" by John Greenleaf Whittier, still immensely popular in the 1920s.

16 Including the picturesque "Almey," a collaboration between the Morden agricultural station in Manitoba and the Sutherland Forestry Nursery Station near Saskatoon. The latter station also developed the Rosybloom "Sutherland" and the spectacular "Thunderchild" varieties. Anstey, *One Hundred Harvests*, 247–9.

17 Including the varieties "Martin Frobisher," "Samuel de Champlain," etc. This project began in Ottawa under the leadership of Felicitas Svejda and continued at the Assomption Station in Quebec. Anstey, *One Hundred Harvests*, 253–4; Wright, "The New Ottawa Roses," 24, 47, 50.

18 Ibid., 252–6.

19 Dupuis also acted as a sort of "horticultural ambassador," representing Canada at international exhibitions and conferences. His diverse publications included a volume written in collaboration with William Saunders, director of the experimental farm program: *Horticulture au Canada/La culture fruitière au Canada*, published in 1900. Deschênes, *Histoire de l'horticulture au Québec*, 48–59.

20 Von Baeyer, *Rhetoric and Roses*, 130–2; notes from Pleasance Crawford.

21 As well as other successful cultivars, including the "Dropmore" Chinese elm, widely used for shelterbelts, and many hardy roses and lilies. See Lee, *Skinner's Nursery*; von Baeyer, *Rhetoric and Roses*, 132–5, 168–70; Lyle Dick, "The Greening of the West," 12–17.

22 Dick, "The Greening of the West."

23 P. Crawford, "The Roots of the Toronto Horticultural Society," 125–39.

24 Although there had been short-lived organizations in Montreal as early as 1811.

25 Horticultural societies were founded in Charlottetown and Hamilton in 1850 (William Mundie was a founding member of the latter), Quebec City in 1851, London and St. Catharines in the 1860s, and Ottawa in 1893.

26 Notes from Pleasance Crawford; von Baeyer, *Rhetoric and Roses*, 39; Deschênes, *Histoire de l'horticulture au Québec*, 50–7; C. Martin, *A History of Canadian Gardening*, 70–1, 91–9.

27 Provancher wrote most of the articles. Against all the odds, this magazine is still being published today. Its primary objective remains the same and is pursued "in an environmental perspective and with a concern for conservation" (translation by R.F.W.).

28 Von Baeyer, *Rhetoric and Roses*, 142–4, 148–51; Deschênes, *Histoire de l'horticulture au Québec*, 38–40.

29 There are a couple of leading candidates. An Ottawa newspaper reported in 1887 that James Fletcher, the farm's chief of entomology and botany, was to lay out an arboretum and botanical garden on the site in the following year; see Smith and Bramley, *Ottawa's Farm*, 19. And Charles Miller, director of horticulture for the Philadelphia Centennial Exhibition of 1876 and designer of Victoria Park in London, Ontario, in 1878 (see chapter 10), was known to the experimental farms' chief, William Saunders, and John Carling, their governmental champion, both of whom were from London and had supported Miller's design of the park (see Behr, *Victoria Park*). Miller had also prepared plans for the Ontario Agricultural College (OAC) campus at Guelph, another Carling project (see chapter 7). http://www.historicplaces.ca/en/rep-reg/place-lieu.aspx?id=10655.

30 Historical Services Branch, *Central Experimental Farm*, 1275–84; Anstey, *One Hundred Harvests*, 11–13; Susan Buggey, personal communication, August 2002.

31 Sarjeant, "Three Million Trees a Year," 34–41. This garden long functioned as a place of recreation and instruction

for residents of the region, attracting up to 3,000 visitors to weekend picnics in the 1930s.

32 Impressive gardens also underlined the central role of the CPR on the Prairies, and the planting and maintenance of a garden helped to maintain the morale of isolated employees. See von Baeyer, *Rhetoric and Roses*, 14–33; Deschênes, *Histoire de l'horticulture au Québec*, 60–4; C. Martin, *A History of Canadian Gardening* 87–9, 95.

33 Leighton, *American Gardens of the Nineteenth Century*, 269–70.

34 Skinner, "With a Lilac by the Door," 35–8; Montgomery, "A Garden of Old Delights," 274–9.

35 Alex Wilson, "The Public Gardens of Halifax," 179–80.

36 Ibid., 181–3.

37 Ibid., 182–3.

38 Ibid., 183; Hazel Conway describes this approach to planting in *People's Parks*, 164–5.

39 Alex Wilson, "The Public Gardens of Halifax," 183–7.

40 Ibid., 187–90.

41 Ibid., 190; Lindgren, "Public Gardens – A Victorian Ideal," 1, 14–19. Victorians sought such ideal worlds through exoticism – visits to real places in other times and locations – Treasure Island, the Arabian Nights – or in fantastic worlds that had never existed (Neverland, Erewhon, Alice in Wonderland, the science fiction of Jules Verne).

42 Obituary notice for Richard Power, Halifax 1934, provided by Dave Tanner of Nova Scotia at http://www.archiver.rootsweb.com/th/read/BOSTON-STATES/2005-06/1119708973; Alex Wilson, "The Public Gardens of Halifax," 191.

43 P. Crawford, "The Roots of the Toronto Horticultural Society," 125–39.

44 Perhaps inspired by a similar amphitheatre in Regent's Park in London, England, built in the form of concentric circles by the Royal Botanic Society.

45 Bain, "George Allan and the Horticultural Gardens," 231–51; P. Crawford, "The Roots of the Toronto Horticultural Society," 125–39; J.R. Wright, *Urban Parks in Ontario, Part II*, 26–9.

46 Gagnon Pratte, *L'architecture et la nature à Québec*, 49–53.

47 Repton, *Sketches and Hints*, xiii.

48 Ibid., 1794; Repton, *Observations on the Theory and Practice of Landscape Gardening*, 1803; Repton, *Fragments on the Theory and Practice of Landscape Gardening*, 1816.

49 Downing's influence as an "arbiter of taste" made him the Martha Stewart of his time. See Schuyler, *Apostle of Taste*.

50 Downing, "A Talk about Public Parks and Gardens" and "The New York Park."

51 Downing, *A Treatise*, 63–72.

52 Repton, *Observations*, 13–14; Repton, *Sketches and Hints*, 90–2; Downing, *Treatise*, 336–40, 378–80. André Parmentier had also enunciated a series of "rules of composition" for North American villas, with which Downing

was surely familiar. Leighton, *American Gardens of the Nineteenth Century*, 129–32.

53 Loudon, *The Landscape Gardening and Landscape Architecture of the Late Humphrey Repton*, vii–ix.

54 Gagnon Pratte, *L'architecture et la nature*, 49–53.

55 Gagnon Pratte analyses seventy-three examples of this rich burst of creativity.

56 J. Wright, *Architecture of the Picturesque*, 105–16.

57 Gagnon Pratte, *L'architecture et la nature*, 208–10.

58 Fernet-Beauregard, "Le Bois de Coulonge," 11–13; J. Wright, *Architecture of the Picturesque*, 105–7; Déry, Rocray, et associés, *Étude sur l'état de santé*, 8–81; Gagnon Pratte, *L'architecture et la nature*, 52–4, 208–10.

59 The site was rehabilitated in 1984 by the Société immobilière du Québec, following a master plan by landscape architect Anne-Carole Beauregard, and is presently administered by the Commission de la capitale nationale du Québec (CCNQ) as a resource for public recreation and a symbolic site in the heart of the capital. Fernet-Beauregard, "Le Bois de Coulonge"; Sommelier, *Le Bois-de-Coulonge*.

60 F. Smith, *Cataraqui*, 12–21.

61 J. Wright, *Architecture of the Picturesque*, 125.

62 F. Smith, *Cataraqui*, 47–112; P-L. Martin, *Promenades dans les jardins anciens*, 108–11.

63 In the nick of time: after the death of Catherine Rhodes in 1972, the property was scheduled for subdivision and development, but it was instead purchased by the Quebec government in 1975 and restored in the 1990s to its former grandeur. F. Smith, *Cataraqui*, 123–4.

64 Of humble origins, MacNab prospered in real estate and railroad promotions before serving as speaker of the Legislative Assembly of Upper Canada in 1835 and as prime minister of the combined province of Canada in 1854–56. He was a member of the Family Compact, which controlled the government of Upper Canada until 1840. Bain and Leonard, "The Landscape of Dundurn Castle," 208–18; Badone, *Dundurn Castle*, 5–17, 33–7.

65 F. Graham, *The Landscape of Dundurn Castle*, 523, 529; J. Wright, *Architecture of the Picturesque*, 73, 80; Bain and Leonard, "The Landscape of Dundurn Castle," 208–9.

66 Indeed, this auspicious site had already attracted attention. In the 1790s, Elizabeth Simcoe had painted two watercolour sketches that anticipated Dundurn Castle's view down the lake from Burlington Heights.

67 There is some uncertainty as to the respective design contributions of Wetherell and Reid.

68 F. Graham, *The Landscape of Dundurn Castle*, 529–34; J. Wright, *Architecture of the Picturesque*, 78–80; Bain and Leonard, "The Landscape of Dundurn Castle," 209–14.

69 F. Graham, *The Landscape of Dundurn Castle*, 534; Bain and Leonard, "The Landscape of Dundurn Castle," 214–15.

70 J. Wright, *Architecture of the Picturesque*, 78.

71 Grimwood, Scott, and Watson, "George Laing," 52–64. Laing's plan is still on display in the house, which serves as the headquarters of the Hamilton Regional Conservation Authority.
72 The site of this villa had also been previously scouted by the indefatigable Elizabeth Simcoe. She had chosen virtually the same location for the future governor's residence, when London was briefly considered as a possible capital of Upper Canada. See Tausky, *Historical Sketches of London*, 32–3.
73 Leighton, *American Gardens of the Nineteenth Century*, 129–32, 3–5.
74 J. Wright, *Architecture of the Picturesque*, 45, 54–5; Gagnon Pratte, *L'architecture et la nature*, 109–11.
75 J. Wright, *Architecture of the Picturesque*, 127–33; Gagnon Pratte, *L'architecture et la nature*, 109–18.
76 Gagnon Pratte, *L'architecture et la nature*, 106–7, 179–80; Gagnon-Guimond, "Le Jardin de Bagatelle," 36.
77 As does its present-day garden, planted in the 1980s: roses, lilacs, azaleas, and ferns, viewed from a winding pathway that follows and traverses a charming brook. Gagnon-Guimond, "Le Jardin de Bagatelle," 36.
78 Clerk, *Maison Henry-Stuart*, 3–5, 8–11, 14–15; J. Wright, *Architecture of the Picturesque*, 129; Gouvernement du Québec, *Les chemins de la mémoire*, 20; Gagnon Pratte and Ouellet, "La Maison Henry," 57–9.
79 Since the death of Adele Stuart in 1987, the Conseil des monuments et sites du Québec has occupied the house and assured its preservation, along with its gardens and furnishings.
80 Arthur, *Toronto, No Mean City*, 57–63; Hales, *Historic Houses of Canada*, 94–7.
81 City of Toronto, *Virtual Collection – John Howard*, http://www.toronto.ca/culture/howard.
82 Arthur, *Toronto, No Mean City*, 57–9; Hales, *Historic Houses of Canada*, 94–7.
83 Leclerc, *Domaine Joly-De Lotbinière*, 12–15.
84 Ibid., 16–17.
85 Ibid., 20–3.
86 In his spare time, Sir Henri served in both federal and provincial cabinets, including a period as prime minister of Quebec (1878–79); in the final years of his career, he was named lieutenant governor of British Columbia. Leclerc, *Domaine Joly-De Lotbinière*, 18–28; Hamelin, "Joly De Lotbinière."
87 Papineau had studied the events and issues of the American Revolution of 1776–83; his book collection included many volumes written by or about its protagonists. On visiting Philadelphia in July 1838, he sought out the scenes and artefacts of the revolution (L.J.A. Papineau, *Journal d'un Fils de la Liberté*, 202, 207–8). When he died, the book *Vie de Washington* was among those found at his bedside. Rumilly, *Papineau*, 259.
88 Jefferson was elected to the Virginia Assembly in 1769 at the age of twenty-five, Papineau to that of Lower Canada in 1809, at twenty-three, becoming its speaker in 1815. See Padover, *Jefferson*, 25–34; F. Ouellet, "Louis-Joseph Papineau," *Canadian Dictionary of Biography*, 10:621; Rumilly, *Papineau*, 11–23.
89 Both were responsible for the key documents of their respective movements: the American Declaration of Independence, written by Jefferson in 1776, and the "92 Resolutions" (which called into question the governmental system of Lower Canada), conceived by Papineau and presented in the assembly in 1834. Padover, *Jefferson*, 35–44; F. Ouellet, "Louis-Joseph Papineau," 621–3, 627–9; Rumilly, *Papineau*, 89–98; and Leacock, *Baldwin, Lafontaine, Hincks*, 137–40, 281–303.
90 Padover, *Jefferson*, 55–71; F. Ouellet, "Louis-Joseph Papineau," 631; Rumilly, *Papineau*, 200: "This result constituted a victory for Papineau over the long term" (translated by R.F.W.). But Papineau himself never agreed with this conclusion.
91 F. Ouellet, "Louis-Joseph Papineau," 631; Padover, *Jefferson*, 73–92; Rumilly, *Papineau*, 164–214.
92 Padover, *Jefferson*, 187–217; F. Ouellet, "Louis-Joseph Papineau," 632; Rumilly, *Papineau*, 243–66; Parks Canada, *Manoir-Papineau*, brochure-guide.
93 Prud'homme, *Manoir-Papineau, lieu historique national*.
94 Including villas of the patrician Rockefeller and Roosevelt families and such "men of letters" as writer Washington Irving, telegraph inventor Samuel Morse, and painter Frederic Church, a leading member of the Hudson Valley School.
95 L.J.A. Papineau, *Journal d'un Fils de la Liberté*, 189–90. Louis-Joseph Papineau may have met Parmentier when the latter visited Montreal in May 1830, since Parmentier later used his name as a reference. Crawford and Otto, "André Parmentier's 'Two or Three Places.'"
96 Ibid., 137, 187, 201, 228, 369–88, 485, 610, 816–31, 875–6; Collins, *Changing Ideals*, 48–50, 57–8.
97 L.J.A. Papineau, *Journal d'un Fils de la Liberté*, 816–17.
98 Ibid., 830 (translation by R.F.W.).
99 Fischer, "Garden Suburb," 193–6; B.H. Crawford, *Rosedale*, 29.
100 B.H. Crawford, *Rosedale*, 13–14.
101 Fischer, "Garden Suburb," 96. The residence was an old farmhouse to which several additions had been made by the ubiquitous John Howard. B.H. Crawford, *Rosedale*, 14.
102 B.H. Crawford, *Rosedale*, 97, 105.
103 Ibid., 26–9; Fischer, "Garden Suburb," 196–7.
104 B.H. Crawford, *Rosedale*, 32–7.
105 Ibid., 30–1.
106 Ibid., 31; Fischer, "Garden Suburb," 197; Cruickshank and de Visser, *Old Toronto Houses*, 223.

CHAPTER TEN

1 Desloges and Gelly, *The Lachine Canal*, 111–15.
2 J.R. Wright, *Urban Parks in Ontario, Part I*, 62; Chadwick, *The Park and the Town*, 44–52.
3 J.R. Wright, *Urban Parks in Ontario, Part II*, 43–4.
4 J.R. Wright, *Urban Parks in Ontario, Part I*, 64–70.
5 Ibid., 66.
6 Ibid., 67; Jennifer McKendry, "The Rural Cemetery Movement in Ontario: The Role of Cataraqui Cemetery, Kingston," in Beck, Moffet, and Smith, *Conserving Ontario's Landscapes*, 27–32.
7 J.R. Wright, *Urban Parks in Ontario, Part I*, 70.
8 D.R. Poulton and Associates, *Restoration Master Plan for Victoria Park*; Tausky and DiStefano, *Victorian Architecture*, 124–5.
9 Milroy, "A Crowning Feature," 147–58. Miller has also been credited with preparing a landscape plan for the Ontario Agricultural College at Guelph. See http://www.historicplaces.ca/en/rep-reg/ place-lieu.aspx?id=10655.
10 Tausky, *Historical Sketches of London*, 17–18.
11 This practice has continued to the present day.
12 These carriage driveways were opened to cars in the twentieth century, but are now reserved for pedestrians.
13 Torrance and Thakar, *Major's Hill Park and Nepean Point*.
14 J.R. Wright, *Urban Parks in Ontario, Part I*, 84.
15 Ted McLachlan, "Privately Owned Parks and Their Influence on Open Space Development in Winnipeg," in *International Symposium*, 261–6; C. Macdonald, *A City at Leisure*, 3–4.
16 Segger, *Victoria*, 197–9.
17 Lorne Park Estates Historical Committee, *A Village within a City*; Luka, "From Summer Cottage Colony to Metropolitan Suburb," 18–31.
18 Lamonde and Montpetit, *Le Parc Sohmer de Montréal*, 37–73.
19 Etlin, "Père Lachaise and the Garden Cemetery," 211–22; Curl, *A Celebration of Death*, 134–5; Schuyler, "The Evolution of the Anglo-American Rural Cemetery," 291–304.
20 "There is a voice from the tomb sweeter than song, there is a recollection of the dead to which we turn ever from the charms of the living … The grave of those we loved – what a place for meditation. There it is that we call up in long review the whole history of virtue and gentleness, and the thousand endearments lavished upon us almost unheeded in the daily intercourse of intimacy." Washington Irving, quoted in McPherson, *Picturesque Quebec*.
21 These monuments included neo-classical urns, pyramids, and columns; family mausoleums in garden settings; and recreations of the Arcadian landscapes in which the heroes of antiquity were presumed to have been laid to

rest. J.D. Hunt, *Gardens and the Picturesque*, 75–102; Etlin, *The Architecture of Death*, 171–97, 199–209.
22 The column is gone, but a granite memorial was installed on the site in 1942, and other vestiges of the overall composition remain. The City of Montreal is currently studying the remaining elements of the memorial and preparing an interpretation strategy.
23 So called because of its location outside the city's built-up area.
24 Etlin, "Père Lachaise and the Garden Cemetery," 211–22; Curl, *A Celebration of Death*, 154–67.
25 Etlin, "Père Lachaise and the Garden Cemetery," 211–22; Curl, *A Celebration of Death*, 161–7.
26 Although some cemeteries in colonial India apparently prefigured developments in Britain. Curl, "The Design of the Early British Cemeteries," 223–54.
27 Schuyler, "The Evolution of the Anglo-American Rural Cemetery," 294.
28 Loudon, *On the Laying Out, Planting, and Managing of Cemeteries*.
29 Schuyler, "The Evolution of the Anglo-American Rural Cemetery," 291–304.
30 General Henry A.S. Dearborn and the physician/botanist Jacob Bigelow (both members of the Horticultural Society), helped and succeeded by surveyor and engineer Alexander Wadsworth. Curl, "The Design of the Early British Cemeteries," 252; Blanche Linden, "Jacob Bigelow" and "Henry A.S. Dearborn," and Arthur Krim, "Alexander Wadsworth," in Birnbaum and Karson, eds., *Pioneers*, 22–5, 82–5, 420–2; Rotundo, "Mount Auburn," 265–6.
31 Etlin, "Père Lachaise and the Garden Cemetery," 221–2.
32 Rotundo, "Mount Auburn," 255–67; Schuyler, "The Evolution of the Anglo-American Rural Cemetery," 295–7; Schuyler, *The New Urban Landscape*, 44–6.
33 Etlin, "Père Lachaise and the Garden Cemetery."
34 Lancelot "Capability" Brown (1716–1783) designed some 170 gardens, principally for the country estates of wealthy landowners. His nickname was based on his penchant for convincing his clients of the "capabilities" of their properties for landscape improvements. See J.D. Hunt, *Gardens and the Picturesque* and *The Genius of the Place*, for extensive treatment of the man and his career.
35 Awalt, *Camp Hill Cemetery*, 8–12.
36 Arthur, *Toronto, No Mean City*, 134.
37 Treggett, *Le Cimetière Mount-Hermon;* Schuyler, *The New Urban Landscape*, 45–7.
38 Schuyler, "The Evolution of the Anglo-American Rural Cemetery," 291–304. The others were Mount Auburn and Laurel Hill.
39 Since 1865, four generations of the same family, the Treggetts, have succeeded each other as superintendents of the cemetery, undoubtedly helping to ensure the preservation of its original design.

40 Guay, "L'évolution de l'espace de la mort à Québec," 24–7; Clerk, *Le cimetière Mont-Royal*, 159–217.

41 Sanders, *Calgary's Historic Union Cemetery*, vi; Labbé, "L'objet funéraire," 28–32.

42 Labbé, "L'objet funéraire," 28–32.

43 Ibid.

44 Guay, "L'évolution de l'espace de la mort à Québec," 24–7.

45 Young, *Respectable Burial*, 21–9; Clerk, *Le cimetière Mont-Royal*. Receiving no response to their request for advice concerning the choice of a designer from Andrew Jackson Downing, the commissioners followed a recommendation from the superintendent of Laurel Hill.

46 Aaron Wunsch, "James C. Sidney," in Birnbaum and Karson, eds., *Pioneers*, 360–3.

47 Young, *Respectable Burial*, 30–1.

48 Although the central stream has long since disappeared.

49 Ibid., 63–7.

50 Mount Royal Cemetery, *The Trees of Mount Royal Cemetery*.

51 Young, *Respectable Burial*, 106–23.

52 At the time of its founding; today the cemetery is multi-denominational.

53 Bisson, Brodeur, and Drouin, *Cimetière Notre-Dame-des-Neiges*, 43–4, 46, 51.

54 Etlin, "Père Lachaise and the Garden Cemetery," 211–22; Bisson, Brodeur, and Drouin, *Cimetière Notre-Dame-des-Neiges*, 45–6.

55 Bisson, Brodeur, and Drouin, *Cimetière Notre-Dame-des-Neiges*, 36–7, 70.

56 Ibid., 1.

57 Ibid., 2.

58 Marsan, *Montreal in Evolution*, 194–7, 212–14. Perrault had worked with his uncle on the design of Montreal's Old Court House (1851–57) and designed its new city hall in 1874–78 with the assistance of Alexander C. Hutchison.

59 Bisson, Brodeur, and Drouin, *Cimetière Notre-Dame-des-Neiges*, 53–9.

60 Ibid., 69–75. This gateway was later demolished.

61 Ibid., 44.

62 Young, *Respectable Burial*, 67.

63 The previous history of the site may explain why the great majority (90%) of the cemetery's trees consist of only eight varieties, including elm, serviceberry, chestnut, crabapple, and various maples. The regular plan of the cemetery's central plateau section may also reflect the influence of the villa gardens that previously occupied the property. Bisson, Brodeur, and Drouin, *Cimetière Notre-Dame-des-Neiges*, 27, 46.

64 Clerk, *Mount Pleasant Cemetery*, 2, 9–11; Coutts, "Easeful Death in Toronto," 8–10.

65 Filey, *Mount Pleasant Cemetery*, 14–16.

66 Pleasance Crawford, "H.A. Engelhardt (1830–1897)," 30–5; Pleasance Crawford, "Park and Cemetery Landscape Design in Canada," 7–9. Engelhardt also worked on the design of Union Cemetery in Port Hope and Glendale Cemetery in Belleville.

67 This rhythmic configuration continued to the eastern limit of the site in Engelhardt's original plan. Curves were much less pronounced in a later section of the cemetery, built to the east of Mount Pleasant Road, which divided the site in two after its construction in 1919. Clerk, *Mount Pleasant Cemetery*, 14.

68 P. Crawford, "H.A. Engelhardt (1830–1897)," 30–5; P. Crawford, "Park and Cemetery Landscape Design," 7–9.

69 P. Crawford, "Park and Cemetery Landscape Design," 8.

70 Jennifer McKendry, "The Rural Cemetery Movement in Ontario," in Beck, Moffet, and Smith, *Conserving Ontario's Landscapes*, 27–32. At the entrance to the cemetery is a *cottage orné*, a control post, and a superintendent's residence. The first occupant of the residence, landscape gardener Alpine Grant (1811–1874), would later pursue a distinguished garden-making career in Ottawa.

71 Beechwood Cemetery, *Great Canadian Profiles*.

72 J. Adams, *Historic Guide to Ross Bay Cemetery* 6, 3; Segger, *Victoria*, 342.

73 J. Adams, *Historic Guide to Ross Bay Cemetery*, 6.

74 Sanders, *Calgary's Historic Union Cemetery*, 1–4.

75 Many pioneers of the region have found their final home in Union Cemetery, among them William Pearce, whose tombstone bears a replica of the signature that he inscribed on so many documents that preserved or created the landscape icons of the Canadian West. Sanders, *Calgary's Historic Union Cemetery*, 10–11.

76 Young, *Respectable Burial*, 35–7.

77 Hucker, *Beth Israel Cemetery*; Clerk, *Harling Point Cemetery*.

78 Malaka Ackaoui, "De la mémoire à l'art, l'évolution du cimetière Mont-Royal vers le 21ième siècle," in *International Symposium*, 4–7.

79 Along with practitioners of other disciplines, including architects, engineers, and surveyors.

80 The birth of the landscape architectural profession in the mid-nineteenth century was preceded by that of the engineering and architectural professions. See Morgan, "The Emergence of the American Landscape Professional," 269–89; Elliott, *Victorian Gardens*, on the "demise of the head gardener."

81 Its ascendancy was not universally welcomed. Although he used the term in the title of his book, Horace Cleveland considered the expression to be somewhat pretentious and felt it was more applicable to the profession's future aspirations than to its present role. See Cleveland, *Landscape Architecture According to the Wants of the West*, preface.

82 The unique personality and values of Frederick Law Olmsted undoubtedly influenced this new professional motivation; see following chapter.

83 Tunnard and Reed, *American Skyline*, 142–53.

84 Jackson and Brown, "Coming to Light," 5–9.

85 Bisson, Brodeur, and Drouin, *Cimetière Notre-Dame-des-Neiges*, 44.

86 Etlin, *The Architecture of Death*, 335–58.

87 Schuyler, "The Evolution of the Anglo-American Rural Cemetery," 295.

88 Bisson, Brodeur, and Drouin, *Cimetière Notre-Dame-des-Neiges*, 62.

89 Schuyler, "The Evolution of the Anglo-American Rural Cemetery," 302; Schuyler, *The New Urban Landscape*, 54.

90 Rotundo, "Mount Auburn," 266; Downing, "A Talk about Public Parks," and "The New York Park."

CHAPTER ELEVEN

1 Census of Canada 1871.

2 P. Jacobs, "Beyond Parks," 228.

3 Rybczynski, *A Clearing in the Distance*, 23–62; Beveridge and Rocheleau, *Frederick Law Olmsted*, 10–20. Considered to be the founder of landscape architecture in North America, Olmsted made important contributions in many other domains, including the struggle against slavery and the organization of the US Sanitary Commission during the American Civil War. He designed parks and other landscape projects in many American cities, and the firm he established remained in existence until the 1950s.

4 Olmsted met Andrew Jackson Downing in 1851, shortly before the celebrated author's tragic death. Downing introduced Olmsted to Vaux, whom he had recruited as an associate during a visit to Europe. See Kowsky, *Country, Park and City*, 13–22, 52, 96; Rybczynski, *A Clearing in the Distance*, 161.

5 Olmsted had already visited Montreal, on a pleasure trip in 1873. Murray, "Frederick Law Olmsted," 165; Seline, *Frederick Law Olmsted's Mount Royal Park*, 36–7.

6 From Olmsted's preliminary report, *Report of Fred. Law Olmsted on Mount Royal Park*, submitted in 1874.

7 Murray, "Frederick Law Olmsted," 166.

8 Ibid., 168.

9 Ibid., 167.

10 Seline, *Frederick Law Olmsted's Mount Royal Park*, 94–8.

11 Ibid., 78–82. This part of the plan was not carried out until the 1930s; see chapter 18.

12 Ibid., 37; Rybczynski, *A Clearing in the Distance*, 321–5.

13 The client often diverged from Olmsted's plans and did not supply a timely survey drawing. Changes were made to the site boundaries and road patterns without his being informed. This required the replanning of parts of the park and prompted Olmsted, in 1881, to publish his final report to the city as a public letter, copies of which he sent to members of the city's cultural elite and the newspapers. Olmsted, *Mount Royal Park, Montreal*, 1881.

14 Schuyler, *The New Urban Landscape*, 85, 92–5.

15 P. Crawford, "Park and Cemetery Landscape Design," 7–8.

16 There was some controversy about tobogganing on Sundays; this apparently conflicted with Ontario's Lord's Day Act, which banned overly active forms of recreation on the Sabbath. See Homel, "Sliders and Backsliders," 25–34.

17 Kitz and Castle, *Point Pleasant Park*, 13.

18 Rudyard Kipling, "The Song of the Cities," 1896. The poet's sobriquet for Halifax was adopted by Thomas Raddall as the title for his well-known history of the city.

19 Kitz and Castle, *Point Pleasant Park*, 40–3.

20 Ibid., 43–7. Heather and Scots pine played a role, as one might expect in Nova Scotia. This new forest was extremely vulnerable to infestation and high winds, and was devastated by Hurricane Juan in September 2003. Rehabilitation is currently underway.

21 Joy Kestenbaum, "Downing Vaux," in Birnbaum and Karson, *Pioneers,* 409–12.

22 Martin and Segrave, *City Parks of Canada*, 79–82; Kowsky, *Country, Park and City*, 356n111.

23 Martin and Segrave, *City Parks of Canada*, 79–82. Halifax Public Gardens had a similar origin (see chapter 9).

24 Noppen and Morisset, *L'architecture de Saint-Roch*, 29–31; Ville de Québec, *Saint-Roch*, 19–20.

25 Cameron, *Charles Baillairgé*, 127; Ville de Québec, *Saint-Roch*, 20.

26 Noppen and Morisset, *L'architecture de Saint-Roch*, 31; Cameron, *Charles Baillairgé*, 150; M. Bélanger, *Le Parc Victoria*, 3–5, 12–17.

27 Segger, *Victoria*, 197.

28 Ibid., 197–9; Martin and Segrave, *City Parks of Canada*, 109–12.

29 Dale, "John Blair," 27–30; P. Crawford, "Historical Perspectives: Savery and Blair," 20; William A. Dale, presentation at 1994 CSLA Congress, Victoria; and interview, November 2000, Sidney, BC. Bill Dale and Pleasance Crawford of Toronto kindly shared with me their documents concerning this park and John Blair.

30 "This gentleman was born in Scotland, and took his first lessons in landscape gardening from the forest, the mountains and the lakes of that land ... His taste was formed by a familiarity with those wild and picturesque scenes which Scott has so graphically pictured in his 'Lady of the Lake.'" Article by "F.B.N," *Chicago Evening Journal*, c. 1865, provided by Bill Dale.

31 P. Crawford, "Historical Perspectives: Savery and Blair," 20–1.

32 As defined in Hyams, *The English Garden*, 163, 172–4. Historian Martin Segger has characterized the design of Beacon Hill Park as "a charming piece of romantic landscape gardening." Segger, *Victoria*, 155, 196–9.

33 Woodcock, "Savage and Domestic," 169–71; Coutts, *Stanley Park.*

34 Woodcock, "Savage and Domestic," 171–2; Coutts, *Stanley Park*, 301; Steele, *Vancouver's Famous Stanley Park*, 15–16.

35 Although some cutting was carried out within the park at various times. Steele, *Vancouver's Famous Stanley Park*, 9–11; Coutts, *Stanley Park*, 305.

36 Hinds, "Evolution of Urban Public Park Design," 69; Tate, *Great City Parks*, 157–63.

37 Johnson, *Legends of Vancouver*, 95–6.

38 This enormous project was carried out over six decades, 1917–80, first by Superintendent S.W. Rawlings and then, for thirty-two years, by mason Jimmy Cunningham. Martin and Segrave, *City Parks of Canada*, 106–7; Steele, *Vancouver's Famous Stanley Park*, 20–4; Woodcock, "Savage and Domestic," 171.

39 P. Jacobs, "Frederick G. Todd," 27–34; Tate, *Great City Parks*, 163.

40 Asselin, *Frederick G. Todd*, 8; P. Jacobs, "Frederick G. Todd," 27–34.

41 P. Crawford, "Historical Perspectives," 9–10.

42 P. Jacobs, "Frederick G. Todd," 27.

43 Asselin, *Frederick G. Todd*, 10.

44 Todd, "Character in Park Design," translated by Peter Jacobs.

45 C. Macdonald, *A City at Leisure*, 3–8; C. Macdonald, *Making a Place*, 22–3; City of Winnipeg, *Assiniboine Park*, 1–4; Cavett, Selwood, and Lehr, "Social Philosophy," 27, 31–3.

46 C. Macdonald, *A City at Leisure*, 11–12, 16, 27; City of Winnipeg, *Assiniboine Park*, 5–6.

47 C. Macdonald, *A City at Leisure*, 27–8.

48 Todd, "Character in Park Design," translated by Peter Jacobs, 3, 22; City of Winnipeg, *Assiniboine Park*, 9–12; C. Macdonald, *A City at Leisure*, 17–21.

49 Jacques Mathieu and Alain Beaulieu, "The Name and the Location," in Mathieu and Kedl, *The Plains of Abraham*, 25–33; Claude Paulette and Jacques Mathieu. "The Natural Park: A Romantic Garden," in Mathieu and Kedl, eds., *Les Plaines d'Abraham*, 203–37.

50 Including Sir Georges Garneau, mayor of Quebec City; Honoré-Julien Chouinard of the Saint-Jean-Baptiste Society; architect Eugène Taché, and the governor general, Earl Grey. The federal government directed the project and the provincial governments of Quebec and Ontario made important contributions.

51 Lacoursière, *Le champ des batailles*, 16–25.

52 The site of the park had previously accommodated circuses and agricultural fairs, sports (cricket, lacrosse, golf, horse races), military parades, and great assemblies, including the "first national festival of French Canadians" on 24 June 1880. Donald Guay, "Sports, Culture, and Leisure, 1800–1900," in Mathieu and Kedl, *The Plains of Abraham*, 137–71.

53 Paulette and Mathieu, "Creating the Perfect Park," in Mathieu and Kedl, *The Plains of Abraham*, 214–25.

54 Todd, *Quebec Battlefields Park Report*, 1.

55 Ibid.

56 Todd, "Character in Park Design," translated by Peter Jacobs, 3.

57 Martin and Segrave, *City Parks of Canada*, 83–5.

58 As was common practice in those days, Cochius likely returned to Montreal occasionally to work with Todd on the park design, and discussions likely proceeded by regular correspondence throughout the project, as it had between Todd and the Olmsted office in earlier years. See Versteeg, "Rudolph H.K. Cochius."

59 P. Jacobs, "Frederick G. Todd," 28–30; Asselin, *Frederick G. Todd*, 20; Todd, "Character in Park Design," translated by Peter Jacobs.

60 P.E. Roy, *Vancouver: An Illustrated History*, 49.

61 Woodcock, "Savage and Domestic," 173.

62 C. Macdonald, *A City at Leisure*, 16–23; C. Macdonald, *Making a Place*, 2:4–6.

63 C. Macdonald, *A City at Leisure*, 28–31.

64 Société d'histoire et de généalogie du Plateau Mont-Royal, "Cahier souvenir."

65 Todd, *Preliminary Report to the Ottawa Improvement Commission*; D.L.A. Gordon, "A City Beautiful Plan," 275–6; D.L.A. Gordon, "Frederick G. Todd," 29–33.

66 Todd, *Preliminary Report*, 9; D.L.A. Gordon, "A City Beautiful Plan," 275–6; D.L.A. Gordon, "Frederick G. Todd," 29–33.

67 D.L.A. Gordon, "Frederick G. Todd"; Todd, *Preliminary Report*, 32–3.

68 Delays in payment, questioning of bills, replacement of approved designs by in-house concepts designed by civil servants, and so on. See D.L.A. Gordon, "Frederick G. Todd," 29–57.

69 Ibid.

70 Ibid.

71 Todd, "Report and Accompanying Plans Showing Recommendations for Parks and Boulevards," submitted to city of Edmonton in April 1907; parallel document submitted to city of Strathcona in May 1907. These two reports were similar to Todd's Ottawa report in content and approach.

72 Abma and Gibbs, *Frederick G. Todd*, 1–3.

73 Herzog, "A Legacy of Vision."

74 Abma and Gibbs, *Frederick G. Todd*, 3–4.

75 Donaldson, "William Pearce," 234; Sandalack and Nicolai, *The Calgary Project*, 12–13, 25–7.

76 Sandalack and Davis, *Excursions into the Cultural Landscapes of Alberta*, 157–9.

77 Pearce's own house and garden in the eastern part of the city on the Bow River were "a model of landscape planning and horticulture." Sandalack and Nicolai, *The Calgary Project*, 13, 25–7; Donaldson, "William Pearce," 234–7.
78 Donaldson, "William Pearce," 238–9, 242–3.
79 J.R. Wright, *Urban Parks in Ontario, Part III*.
80 Ibid., 162–6; letter from Todd to R. Thomas Orr, Stratford Park Committee, 31 December 1904.
81 P. Crawford, "Charles Ernest Woolverton," 17–19.
82 Ibid., 19–20.
83 P. Crawford, "Historical Perspectives," 9–10.

CHAPTER TWELVE

1 Louis Hennepin, *Description de la Louisiane nouvellement découverte au sud-ouest de la Nouvelle France* (Paris, 1683), 23–49.
2 Cook and King, *A Voyage to the Pacific Ocean*, 2:204, 222, 231–2; Thomas, *Cook*; Justice, *Mr. Menzies*, 79.
3 A note on nomenclature: in North America, large natural and wilderness parks have been created and are administered by federal, provincial/state, and territorial governments. While the term "national parks" has generally been reserved for federally run parks in Canada and the US, it was used for several early provincial parks in eastern Canada and has been applied to Quebec's provincially owned parks since their reorganization in 2001.
4 Including Thomas Cole, Frederic Church, and Albert Bierstadt.
5 H.M. Chittenden, *Yellowstone National Park*, 78.
6 Ranney, *Papers of Frederick Law Olmsted*, 5:512–13.
7 Following several decades of desultory administration by California, the park was expanded and reverted to federal ownership between 1890 and 1905.
8 Ibid., 488–511. Olmsted filed his report in April of 1865; he already knew the site well, having camped out in the Big Tree Grove and in Yosemite Valley on several occasions from 1863 to 1865. See Rybczynski, *A Clearing in the Distance*, 236–8.
9 Beveridge and Rocheleau, *Frederick Law Olmsted*, 207, 466–8; Rybczinski, *A Clearing in the Distance*, 257–9.
10 Mumford, "Frederick Law Olmsted's Contribution," 101–16.
11 Described in Grant, *Ocean to Ocean*.
12 Among these were Benjamin Baltzly, Charles Horetzky, Alexander Henderson, Oliver Buell, and Notman's sons William and George.
13 Marylin J. McKay, *Picturing the Land*, 147–63.
14 Grant, *Picturesque Canada*. Grant and O'Brien's monograph was based on *Picturesque America*, a similar book published in the United States in 1872–74; see Brian Foss, "Word and Image," in Goldfarb, ed., *Expanding Horizons*, 179–81. A similar multi-volume publication, issued in Britain in 1875, presented picturesque sites in Europe.
15 National Parks Act, S.C. 1930, sect. 4; Bourdages, Bouchard, and Trépanier, *Les parcs naturels*, 6.
16 Sontag, *National Park Service: The First 75 Years*, 18–19.
17 Lothian, *A Brief History*, 22.
18 Ibid., 23; Bourdages, Bouchard, and Trépanier, *Les parcs naturels*, 4.
19 Named for the Scottish birthplace of a CPR director. Lothian, *A Brief History*, 33.
20 Ibid., 24–5; Todhunter, "Banff and the Canadian National Park Idea," 33–9.
21 Lothian, *A Brief History*, 27–8.
22 Ibid., 52.
23 Ibid., 82.
24 Ibid.
25 Seibel, *Ontario's Niagara Parks*.
26 Ibid., 10–14.
27 François-Marc Gagnon, "The Forest, Niagara and the Sublime," in Goldfarb, ed., *Expanding Horizons*, 34–6, 38–47.
28 Seibel, *Ontario's Niagara Parks*, 22–4; Michael O'Neill, "Les parcs provinciaux," 34–6.
29 Seibel, *Ontario's Niagara Parks*; Barnsley and Pierce, *The Public Gardens*, 10–11. Frederick Law Olmsted was a member of the commission that established the park on the American side, and he collaborated with his associate Calvert Vaux on the design of a linear park along the river and the gorge. Beveridge and Rocheleau, *Frederick Law Olmsted*, 210–13.
30 Seibel, *Ontario's Niagara Parks*, 27–8; Barnsley and Pierce, *The Public Gardens*, 9–12. This park also included a gigantic hydroelectric power station, Ontario's oldest; its successors still supply some 25 per cent of the province's hydroelectric power. Thus Niagara Falls, now a world heritage site, constituted the first extensive natural park in the province and a main source of Ontario's twentieth-century prosperity.
31 Schneider, *The Adirondacks*.
32 Addison, *Early Days in Algonquin Park*, 2–28.
33 Ibid., 8–9, 40.
34 Ibid., 28.
35 Michael O'Neill, "Les parcs provinciaux," 35; Bourdages, Bouchard, and Trépanier, *Les parcs naturels*, 53–5.
36 This reserve would be recognized as the Parc national de la Gaspésie in 1937. Its initially stringent rules concerning forestry and mining were subsequently relaxed. See Bourdages, Bouchard, and Trépanier, *Les parcs naturels*, 56; Gouvernement du Québec, *Les parcs québécois*, 1:16.
37 This was also an objective of the western parks. As early as 1907, the law that reserved the territory of the future Jasper National Park underscored the role of forests in

conserving water resources. See Lothian, *A Brief History*, 52.
38 P. Jacobs, "Folklore and Forest Fragments," 85–101.
39 A monument and a plaque, installed on a promontory at the head of Canoe Lake, recall his memory.
40 Marylin J. McKay, *Picturing the Land*, 163–5, 169–72; Goldfarb, *Expanding Horizons*, 284–9.
41 Bourdages, Bouchard, and Trépanier, *Les parcs naturels*, 87–8. This continued until a new parks law totally redefined the objectives and practices of Quebec's park system in 1977. See Gouvernement du Québec, *Les parcs québécois*, 1:16–19
42 Todhunter, "Banff and the Canadian National Park Idea," 33–9; J.G. Nelson, *Man's Impact*, 80–1.
43 This began to change as automobiles gained access to the parks around 1910, finally permitting middle-class tourists to benefit from the parks.
44 Developments in the United States reinforced the Canadian concern for conservation. In 1907, President Theodore Roosevelt, an enthusiast for the national parks, met with the governors of the states to discuss the conservation of resources; following the success of this conference, he convoked a second, to which he invited the leaders of other countries, including Canada. See Girard, *L'écologisme retrouvé*, 40–58.
45 Ibid., 49–85; Alan H. Armstrong, "Thomas Adams and the Commission of Conservation," in Gertler, ed., *Planning the Canadian Environment*, 17–21.
46 Girard, *L'écologisme retrouvé*, 172–3; Canadian Commission of Conservation, *Annual Report 1913*, 63–5.
47 Lothian, *A Brief History*, 85. The southern extremity of Pointe Pelee is a favourite staging area for migratory birds on their routes south and north.
48 Girard, *L'écologisme retrouvé*, 23–5, 224–8.
49 Lothian, *A Brief History*, 47–51, 63; Bourdages, Bouchard, and Trépanier, *Les parcs naturels*, 6.
50 Lothian, *A Brief History*, 47–51.
51 Ibid., 63–8.
52 Foster, *Working for Wildlife*, 79; see also Lothian, *A Brief History*, 33; von Baeyer, *Garden of Dreams*, 206; MacEachern, *Natural Selections*, 25–33.
53 Lothian, *A Brief History*, 68–78, 82–107; MacEachern, *Natural Selections*, 37–43.
54 Fortunately, the large provincial parks of the first generation already assured some protection of extensive territories in Ontario and Quebec.
55 These two parks are associated with the legendary spokesman for conservation Grey Owl (Archie Belaney, 1888–1938), a champion of Canada's wilderness environments. His cabin in Prince Albert National Park is still a destination for pilgrimages.
56 Lothian, *A Brief History*, 67–78.
57 Barrett, *Cape Breton Highlands*, 30–5.
58 In fact, those responsible for the park had green paint applied to the gables of the house that had supposedly inspired Lucy Maud Montgomery when she wrote her much-appreciated books. See MacEachern, "The Greening of Green Gables," 27; MacEachern, *Natural Selections*, 73–4.
59 Acadian, First Nations, and other Cape Breton traditions were neglected in favour of the Caledonian heritage; today we would call this "branding" (often an effective means of promotion).
60 This romantic symbol reflects a Scottish exile's nostalgia for the Highlands. It makes reference to an 1829 poem often credited to John Galt, founder of the cities of Guelph and Goderich in Ontario. See chapter 5; Lothian, *A Brief History*, 94–100.
61 Lothian, *A Brief History*, 33, 75, 104.
62 Many of the natural features of the parks bear names given to them by Cautley, including the Amethyst Lakes and the Starlight Mountains in Jasper National Park.
63 Bourdages, Bouchard, and Trépanier, *Les parcs naturels*, 5–6.
64 Commissioner Harkin introduced this principle, with the support of the Alpine Club of Canada, as part of a campaign to prevent excessive development of water resources for hydroelectric purposes in the national parks. See MacEachern, *Natural Selections*, 42, 175–84.
65 Lothian, *A Brief History*, 144; MacEachern, *Natural Selections*, 119–20.
66 MacEachern, *Natural Selections*, 160–3.
67 Ibid., 120–2; Lothian, *A Brief History*, 112–13.
68 Government of Canada, *Fundy National Park Provisional Master Plan*, 7–8, 20; MacEachern, *Natural Selections*, 6–7, 122–3.
69 Lothian, *A Brief History*, 115–22; MacEachern, *Natural Selections*, 6–7, 144–5, 239.
70 Accomplished through firebreaks, observation towers, and reforestation of burnt-out areas.
71 Creating new browse for deer while removing habitat from other species.
72 Mosquitoes have always been a problem in the parks, as attested to by visitors to these territories, from Champlain in 1611 to the tourists of today.
73 Bourdages, Bouchard, and Trépanier, *Les parcs naturels*, 8–9.
74 Government of Canada, *National Parks Policy*, 2–5, 23.
75 Lothian, *A Brief History* 148–50; Miller et al., *The Land That Never Melts*, 17–44, 115–16.
76 "Special areas," including unique or particularly vulnerable natural sites; "wilderness recreation areas," with few improvements other than footpaths; "natural environment areas," providing a natural background and usually accessible by vehicle; "general outdoor recreation areas," for moderately intense activities such as swimming; and

"intensive-use areas" such as townsites. See Government of Canada, *Fundy National Park Provisional Master Plan*, 12–13.

77 Bourdages, Bouchard, and Trépanier, *Les parcs naturels*, 19–22.

78 Beauchemin-Beaton-Lapointe, *Master Plan, Forillon National Park*. The original general plan, which maintained the villages, was coordinated by Charles Beaubien and Pierre Major, assisted by landscape architect Rick Moore and a team of specialized advisers. Roman Fodchuk contributed to the original development concept at the Parks Service in Ottawa. See Le Geyt, *Changing the Face of Canada*, 1:9.

79 The story of this dispossession was explored in 2001 by Lionel Bernier, a native of the region who had participated in the events of the time as a young lawyer, in the form of a novel, *La bataille de Forillon*.

80 There were and are other prototypes for the creation of natural parks in populated zones, such as the *parc habité*, seen in France's Parc national des Cévennes, created in 1970. This park includes some 91,000 hectares of diverse landscapes and remains home to about 42,000 people. See Lise Cormier, *Schéma régional d'aménagement récréo-touristique*, 96–109, 122–34, and annexes 9, 10.

81 This was the time of urban renewal and disruptive downtown freeways (see chapter 20) and of rural displacement through ambitious airport developments.

82 Lothian, *A Brief History*, 128–9.

83 As was the parallel bed of the St. Maurice River, which forms the eastern boundary of the park.

84 The park's territory varies from about 150 to 500 metres in elevation, considerably less topographical variation than that seen in the examples cited.

85 Lafleur, *Documents du Club Shawinigan*; Allard, *Documents du Club WOCOP inc.*

86 Engineers were Tremblay, Héroux and Associates of Trois-Rivières.

87 Parks Canada, *"Unimpaired for Future Generations"?*, 2:7–3, 4.

88 Suzuki, *The David Suzuki Reader*, 280–9.

89 Bourdages, Bouchard, and Trépanier, *Les parcs naturels*, 63–4.

90 Parks Canada, *"Unimpaired for Future Generations"?*, 2:1–9. Even the gigantic Wood Buffalo National Park, almost impossible to reach and offering few tourist facilities, was subject to "considerable" degradation.

91 Ibid., 2:1–17, 18.

92 Ibid., 2:9–1, 2.

93 Ibid., 2:2–2 to 2–5. Virtually all Canadian provinces and territories, like the federal government, are currently upgrading their parks towards higher standards of ecological integrity.

94 H.M. Chittenden, *The Yellowstone National Park*, 84: "Never before was a region of such vast extent as the Yellowstone park set apart for the use of all the people without distinction of rank or wealth." Also see MacEachern's discussion of the double mandate, *Natural Selections*, 227–8, 278–9n3. A recent television series on the US national parks by the celebrated documentary producer Ken Burns was entitled *America's Best Idea*.

CHAPTER THIRTEEN

1 Germain, *Les Mouvements de réforme urbaine à Montréal*, 47–51.

2 Bégin, "Québec et Montréal," 19.

3 Rutherford, "Tomorrow's Metropolis," 435–55. Religious leaders included J.S. Woodsworth, Methodist minister, author of two books preaching social equality, and a pioneer of the social-democratic movement in Canada.

4 Ames, *The City below the Hill*; De Laplante, *Les parcs de Montréal*, 63; Méthot, "Herbert Brown Ames," 18–31.

5 Leacock, *Arcadian Adventures with the Idle Rich*, ch. 1.

6 C. Macdonald, *A City at Leisure*, 35. Through these associations, such women as Montrealer Julia Drummond exercised considerable influence on city authorities in the early 1900s; see Wolfe and Strachan, *Practical Idealism*. In Toronto, the Playgrounds Association and the Guild of Civic Art took up the causes of playgrounds and urban beautification (G. Hunt, *John M. Lyle*, 83–4; *Proceedings of the Sixth National Conference on City Planning*). Regina's horticultural association supported the creation of parks and boulevards, while the Regina City Planning Association promoted garden suburbs, social housing, and the improvement of sanitary conditions. See Brennan, *Regina*, 83–4.

7 Wolfe and Jacobs, "City Planning," 50.

8 Bégin, "Québec et Montréal," 19–20; Wolfe and Jacobs, "City Planning," 51.

9 Tunnard and Reed, *American Skyline*, 150, 138–42; G. Hunt, *John M. Lyle*, 12–22.

10 Tunnard and Reed, *American Skyline*, 142–4. A visit to the Chicago Exposition inspired Wellesley College professor Katharine Lee Bates to include a reference to "alabaster cities" in her 1893 poem "America the Beautiful."

11 Robinson, *Modern Civic Art*, 5–10.

12 Pollock-Ellwand, "Rickson Outhet," 140–50; *Canadian Municipal Journal*, November 1912, 475; Lévesque and Jacques, "Rickson A. Outhet," 27–8, 54–5.

13 Pollock-Ellwand, "Rickson Outhet," 163–5; *Canadian Municipal Journal*, November 1912, 475 (Pleasance Crawford files). In 1911, Outhet also planned a major addition to Westmount Park, integrating the qualities of a large natural park with those of a park for active recreation. See "Sketch Plan for Addition to Westmount Park," *Westmount News*, 5 August 1910.

14 Pollock-Ellwand, "Rickson Outhet," 151–6. Outhet's drawings received input from William Maxwell (who had visited the Chicago Exposition) and other members of the PQAA.

15 Pollock-Ellwand, "Rickson Outhet," 156–61; France Vanlaethem, "Building the Metropolis," in Gournay and Vanlaethem, eds., *Montreal Metropolis*, 137–40; Jeanne M. Wolfe and Peter Jacobs, "City Planning and Urban Beautification," in Montreal Museum of Fine Arts, *The Architecture of Edward & W.S. Maxwell*, 50–5; Bassnett, "Visuality and the Emergence of City Planning," 21–38; Bégin, "Québec et Montréal," 19–20; Lévesque and Jacques, "Rickson A. Outhet," 5–35, 58–60.

16 Marsan, *Montreal in Evolution*, 219. Marchand designed, among other projects, the St. Boniface Cathedral in Manitoba and the rebuilding of the central block of the Canadian Parliament in 1916.

17 Wolfe, "Montréal: Des plans d'embellissement," 24–7.

18 G. Hunt, *John M. Lyle*, 12–17; McArthur, *A Progressive Traditionalist*, 4–15. Lyle and Marchand were fellow students at the École des Beaux-Arts.

19 G. Hunt, *John M. Lyle*, 24–7; McArthur, *A Progressive Traditionalist*, 15–23.

20 G. Hunt, *John M. Lyle*, 83–5; McArthur, *A Progressive Traditionalist*, 57–9; Harold Kalman, *A History of Canadian Architecture*, 2:667–8.

21 Greenberg, "Toronto," 37–46; Bassnett, "Visuality and Emergence of City Planning," 21–38; G. Hunt, *John M. Lyle*, 83–5; McArthur, *A Progressive Traditionalist*, 56–62.

22 Gregory Kopischke, "Anthony Urbanski Morell and Arthur R. Nichols," in Birnbaum and Karson, *Pioneers*, 253–7. Morell and Nichols met as employees in the New York office of Charles Leavitt, landscape engineer, who carried out several projects in Canada, including a town plan for Kitchener-Waterloo.

23 Morell and Nichols, *A Report on City Planning for the City of Edmonton*, 52–6.

24 Delainey and Serjeant. *Saskatoon: The Growth of a City, Part I*, 37.

25 T.H. Mawson, *Life and Work*, 161–231; Beard and Wardman, *Thomas H. Mawson*, 24–33; Vandermeulen, "Roots 1: Mawson," 2, 9–11.

26 Brennan, *Regina*, 83.

27 Chadwick, *The Park and the Town*, 221–3. In addition to the many projects he carried out, Mawson was a prolific writer and a founder of Britain's Institute of Town Planning (1914) and its association of landscape architects (1929). See Vandermeulen, "Roots 1: Mawson," 2, 9–10; Waymark, *Modern Garden Design*, 33.

28 T.H. Mawson, *Life and Work*, 7–9; Beard and Wardman, *Thomas H. Mawson*, 5–21; D. Mawson, "Roots '8': Life and Works," 5–11.

29 D.L.A. Gordon, "From Noblesse Oblige to Nationalism," 3.

30 T.H. Mawson, *Life and Work*, 187–8, 201; *New York Times*, 16 December 1913.

31 T.H. Mawson & Sons, *Calgary: A Preliminary Scheme*. The originals of Mawson's drawings were lost for many years but finally turned up in 1977 in a garage in suburban Calgary, where they had served as wall panelling. See also Morrow, *Calgary: Many Years Hence*, 63.

32 T.H. Mawson, *Life and Work*, 201; Morrow, *Calgary, Many Years Hence*, 14–15.

33 Morrow, *Calgary: Many Years Hence*, 27–57. Some of these proposals echo the ideas of William Pearce (see chapters 6, 7, and 9), who was the president of Calgary's Town Planning Commission when Mawson was working in the city. Pearce served as Mawson's guide during his visit to Calgary and provided him with copies of plans and reports that explained Pearce's ideas concerning the city's future development, which Mawson acknowledged in his report. Donaldson, "For Beauty and Use," 240; Donaldson, "William Pearce," 79.

34 Mawson was awestruck by these mountains (so much that, for once in his life, he had to stop working); "sentinels of eternity" he called them – "Nature at her grandest, aloof, austere, inexplicable, and incomparable." T.H. Mawson, *Life and Work*, 202–3.

35 T.H. Mawson, *Life and Work*, 203–6; Beard and Wardman, *Thomas H. Mawson*, 29, 33; *Vancouver Daily Province*, 26 September 1912, 1; Dalrymple and Dusen, "Coal Harbour Plan"; Thomas H. Mawson, "Vancouver, A City of Optimists," 7–13.

36 Mawson established an office in Vancouver in spring 1913, under the direction of his second son John William Mawson (1886–1966) and his nephew Robert Mattocks (c. 1887–1948), both of whom were recent graduates of the University of Liverpool's Department of Civic Design, which Mawson senior had founded.

37 T.H. Mawson, *Life and Work*, 227; Beard and Wardman, *Thomas H. Mawson*, 33; Mike Steele, *Vancouver's Famous Stanley Park*, 113–18. While Mawson's Calgary proposals seem to have been shelved, his proposal to create a sparkling freshwater pond at Vancouver's Coal Harbour was realized and later immortalized by Métis poet Pauline Johnson as "Lost Lagoon," but with none of the civic embellishments Mawson had imagined.

38 Republished in 1902 as *Garden Cities of To-Morrow*.

39 Howard, *Garden Cities of To-Morrow*, 46.

40 Ibid., 52–3; Choay, *L'urbanisme*, 15–16, 21–2. Howard hastened to note that his diagrams were merely schematic and that the design of a real Garden City would have to be adapted to its site.

41 Donor of the Grey Cup, symbol of Canadian football supremacy. The tea blend of that name is identified with his great-grandfather, British prime minister in the 1830s.

Letchworth was the first new town designed according to Howard's precepts.

42 City Improvement League of Montreal, "For a Better Montreal," 12–13.

43 Members bought shares in the company, and profits were restricted to a limited dividend of 5 per cent.

44 Purdy, "This Is Not a Company," 75–91; T. Adams, "Philanthropic Landmarks," 3–21.

45 Ron Fischer, "The Development of the Garden Suburb," 193–207; Annmarie Adams, "Eden Smith," 104–15. While these two projects corresponded closely to the Garden City ideal in terms of physical design, the cooperative aspect did not succeed; the apartments were rented rather than being held in co-ownership.

46 Matthews, *A History of Pointe Claire*, 124, 135–8, 185.

47 The plan of the Bowling Green sector recalls that of subdivisions designed by the Olmsted firm as far back as Riverside, Illinois, in 1869. As a member of that office, Todd would certainly have been able to familiarize himself with such projects.

48 "Superb Highways and Scenic Beauties Bring Many Visitors to This District," *Pointe Grey Gazette*, 14 June 1913, 13. In the design of this road, Todd employed easy curves and kept slopes to a maximum of 3 per cent, decisions that were to have important repercussions half a century later (see chapter 20).

49 Named for its president Thomas Shaughnessy. Todd was preceded on the job by an engineer of Danish origin, L.A. Davick. According to Professor Larry McCann of the University of Victoria, when Davick's plan did not satisfy CPR officials, Todd was invited to offer a new version (personal communication, based on CPR archival records).

50 Straley, *Trees of Vancouver*, xxi–xxiii.

51 Such as the splendid central boulevard defined by double rows of maples at Leaside, a Toronto district that he planned for the Canadian Northern Railway in 1912.

52 Following a financial *coup de théâtre* that saw all the properties for the new town purchased in a relatively short period of time. A popular but incorrect legend holds that all these purchases were carried out on the same day (L.D. McCann, personal communication).

53 McCann, "Planning and Building the Corporate Suburb," 259–301; P. Jacobs, "Frederick G. Todd and the Creation of Canada's Urban Landscape," 30–1. Although well within Montreal's metropolitan area, the Town of Mount Royal is, of all the projects examined, the closest to an autonomous Garden City. The plan of the town, with its residential, civic, and commercial functions arranged in concentric circles (with industrial areas at its periphery), its radio-concentric geometry, and its internal greenbelt, bears an uncanny resemblance to Ebenezer Howard's original sketch layout for the Garden City idea. Seven years earlier, Todd had prefigured this town plan in a similar layout for Victoria Park in Regina, virtually identical in composition, but at the scale of a single city block.

54 Paul-André Linteau, "The Development and Beautification of an Industrial City: Maisonneuve, 1883–1918," in Stelter and Artibise, eds., *Shaping the Urban Landscape*, 304–20.

55 Corbet and Simpson, *Calgary's Mount Royal*, 8–21.

56 Ibid.

57 Throughout the early years of the twentieth century, John Olmsted was in charge of the firm's projects in the West and the Pacific Northwest, creating a solid body of work in British Columbia, Washington, and Oregon. See Hockaday, *Greenscapes*.

58 McCann, *Oak Bay*, 2–3.

59 Originally used by First Nations peoples to harvest camas bulbs, the site functioned as a farm and market garden area before it became a park in the 1950s (L.D. McCann, personal communication). See also Collier, Morbin, and Jennings, *Invasive Species Management Plan*.

60 Pollock-Ellwand, "Rickson Outhet," 156–60; P. Jacobs, "Frederick G. Todd," 29–30; L.D. McCann, personal communication.

61 In particular, the productivity and impact of Todd and Outhet were remarkable for two designers who were just beginning their careers. Mawson was everywhere, and the impact of the Olmsted firm and other Americans, such as Warren Manning, was also quite significant.

62 Anecdotally, many such communities have attracted several succeeding generations of the same families.

63 De Laplante, *Les parcs de Montréal*, 68–70, 86–7.

64 P. Jacobs, "Beyond Parks," 225–35.

65 Pelletier and Samson, *L'ancienne aluminerie de Shawinigan*, 11–12.

66 Fulton, *Powell River Townsite*, 484–5.

67 Ibid., 492. Fulton characterizes relations between the founding companies and the residents of such communities as combining both progressive and regressive tendencies. On the one hand, owners often demonstrated a somewhat paternalistic concern for the welfare and happiness of the workers (which helped to reinforce the productivity of the industry), while on the other, residential areas were often hierarchically zoned to create a system of official or unofficial segregation according to economic status and ethnic or racial background.

68 As planned by owner Alexander "Boss" Gibson (1819–1913). Company-built facilities included churches, schools, a covered skating rink, and a meeting hall. D. Johnson, *Historic Marysville*.

69 Fulton, *Powell River Townsite*, 486–93. Town extensions were designed by the townsite manager, architect/town planner John McIntyre (1878–1957). Residential areas featured large lots with attractive *craftsman-style* houses, complemented with churches, company stores, a hotel, and many sports facilities. Powell River became the largest

newsprint producer in the world, and the town has preserved its sense of community and its physical heritage to the present day.

70 Lemelin, *Shawinigan, un siècle d'énergie*, 21–5.

71 Filteau, *L'épopée de Sha8nigan* [sic], 77–123; Normand Brouillette, "Shawinigan Falls: Ville de l'électricité, ville de l'industrie," in R. Fortier, ed., *Villes industrielles planifiées*, 51–9.

72 Lanthier and Brouillette, "Shawinigan Falls de 1898 à 1930," 42–7; Brouillette, "Shawinigan Falls: Ville de l'électricité," 64–72.

73 Filteau, *L'épopée de Sha8nigan* [sic], 160. These two installations may be seen as focal institutions of the two principal cultural groups who composed the city – tradition-oriented francophone workers and anglophone professionals from urban centres.

74 M. Kaplan, "Hall, George Duffield (1877–1961)," in Birnbaum and Karson, *Pioneers*, 156–8. Hall was the son-in-law of Charles Hays, president of the GTP. Brett and Hall long maintained an office in Montreal, where they planned subdivisions in Westmount, among other projects.

75 Hall, "The Future Prince Rupert," 97–106. Rattenbury's striking architectural composition was never carried out, but much of Brett and Hall's astonishing and far-seeing town plan was realized.

76 Lambert, "Canada: Urban Architecture and the Social Contract."

77 Use of the Gothic style established a relationship with the Parliament Buildings in London, newly rebuilt in that style in the 1840s following a disastrous fire, and thus confirmed Canada's British connection, of central importance at the time. The eclectic and picturesque composition of the Ottawa buildings expressed the ideals of the High Victorian period. Gowans, *Looking at Architecture in Canada*, 145–50; Bacon, *Design of Cities*, 226–7.

78 Perhaps on the suggestion of Governor General Lord Dufferin; see J.J. Stewart, "Notes on Calvert Vaux's 1873 Design," 1–27.

79 Ibid., 1–27; J.J. Stewart, "Landscape Archaeology," 65–70; Graham, "The Landscape Design of Parliament Hill," 39–44. In this central space, defined by rows of elm trees and a wall of stone and wrought iron along its southern boundary on Wellington Street, Vaux's biographer sees reflections of the planning and detail of Vaux's magnificent terrace in Central Park, New York. Kowsky, *Country, Park and City*, 246–8.

80 Gowans, *Looking at Architecture in Canada*, 145–51. Gowans compares the spatial configuration of the parliamentary complex to that of a baroque palace.

81 This configuration reflects that of many American "state-houses" built during the same period (1880–1910), including those in such border states as Minnesota, Wisconsin, and Montana; all were inspired by the Capitol

in Washington. See Tunnard and Reed, *American Skyline*, 145–7; Kalman, *A History of Canadian Architecture*, 2:555–6.

82 Goodspeed, "Saskatchewan Legislative Buildings," 61–88; Rees, "Wascana Centre," 219–32.

83 The "French connection" still prevailed: William Maxwell, the younger of the two brothers, had studied in a Paris atelier associated with the École des Beaux-Arts.

84 Todd had suggested that the provincial authorities plant thousands of trees for the forestation of the site and the city; many of these trees did not survive. Malcolm Ross, the province's landscape architect, awarded the next stage of the project to Mawson. Goodspeed, "Saskatchewan Legislative Buildings," 75–7; Barnhart, *Building for the Future*, 86–7; Rees, "Wascana Centre," 221–4.

85 Goodspeed, "Saskatchewan Legislative Buildings," 75–7; Barnhart, *Building for the Future*, 87–93; Rees, "Wascana Centre," 224–7.

86 Kalman, *A History of Canadian Architecture*, 2:555–7. Born in Rhode Island, Jeffers was familiar with the state house in Providence, which followed the same pattern as those of Minnesota and Wisconsin.

87 Government of Alberta Archives, Edmonton.

88 Government of Alberta, *Alberta Legislature Grounds*. Imaginative drawings can exert a forceful influence across decades or even centuries.

89 Kalman, *A History of Canadian Architecture*, 2:558–9; C. Macdonald, *Making a Place*, 49–50; D.A. Ross, "Manitoba Legislative Buildings"; Government of Manitoba, *Guide to the Manitoba Legislative Assembly*. In fact, all three of the Prairie provinces' legislative buildings face north.

90 C. Macdonald, *Making a Place*, 43–5. Atchison was the designer of the first pavilion in Assiniboine Park.

91 Ibid., 50.

92 Ibid., 33.

93 Barrett and Windsor-Liscombe, *Francis Rattenbury*, 16–21, 29–34, 51–60. The BC legislative building anticipated the broad façades and central domes of the Prairie parliaments, which were built in the following decades.

94 Barrett and Windsor-Liscombe, *Francis Rattenbury*, 124, 148–60.

95 Segger, *Victoria*, 9.

96 The original prototype for campus layouts of this type was Thomas Jefferson's plan for the University of Virginia, designed and built in Charlottesville from 1812 to 1826.

97 Padover, *Jefferson*. Stephen Leacock remarked on the strange fact that the new provinces of Alberta and Saskatchewan "began where older civilization ends" – with the founding of universities, literary societies, and liberal professions: "The University of Saskatchewan rose, literally, on the empty prairie, on the high ground that overlooks the sweeping slopes of the Saskatchewan Valley." Leacock, *Canada*, 213.

98 Kerr, *Building the University of Saskatchewan*; D.R. Brown, "The University of Saskatchewan," 109–17.

99 Although only the academic buildings were designed by Nobbs, a uniform building height and common vocabulary of brick and stone ensured visual coherence to the campus, up until the 1950s. Bilash and Sitwell, "Words into Buildings," 4–20; Wagg, *Percy Erskine Nobbs*, 1–4, 45–51, 59–61.

100 These include such major public projects as the Jardin des Plantes, the Place de la Concorde, Les Invalides, the Palais de Chaillot, and Parc Citroën.

101 Bumsted, *The University of Manitoba*, 24–5, 64–5; C. Macdonald, *Making a Place*, 46. Various sources indicate that Olmsted Brothers was also involved to some extent in the planning of the university sites.

102 Bumsted, *The University of Manitoba*, 1–8, 23–8; C. Macdonald, *Making a Place*, 45.

103 An approach similar to that seen in the *land-grant colleges* of the United States. Klassen and Teversham, *Exploring the UBC Endowment Lands*, 9–11; Patrick Mooney, unpublished text provided to the author at UBC in 2000.

104 T.H. Mawson, *Life and Work*, 230–1; Vancouver *Sun*, 4 and 11 November 1913; Vancouver *Daily Province*, 4, 6, and 12 November 1913; Victoria *Colonist*, 4, 8, and 11 November 1913; Vancouver *Daily World*, 15 November 1913; Vancouver *News-Advertiser*, 4 and 11 November 1913.

105 The astonishing Thomas Mawson was implicated in the planning of no less than four Canadian universities, including a brief participation in the first efforts to create the University of Calgary and a major contribution to the campus design of Dalhousie University in Halifax, in collaboration with Toronto architect Frank Darling. Other landscape architects from outside the country were also active in designing university campuses across the country; the well-known American practitioner Warren H. Manning, for example, prepared the development plan for St. Francis-Xavier University in Antigonish, Nova Scotia.

106 D.L.A. Gordon, "A City Beautiful Plan," 275–300.

107 Despite the efforts of both Todd and Mawson to win a contract as design consultant for the project.

108 Bennett, who worked for forty years on various aspects of the plan for Chicago, succeeded Burnham as the leading American city planner. Bennett prepared planning studies for many cities in the United States and abroad. D.L.A. Gordon, "A City Beautiful Plan"; Draper, *Edward H. Bennett*, 7–24.

109 Including several striking watercolour perspectives by Jules Guerin, who had done the celebrated illustrations of Burnham's Chicago plan.

110 D.L.A. Gordon, "A City Beautiful plan," 275–300; D.L.A. Gordon, "Frederick G. Todd," 29–57; Gréber, *L'architecture aux États-Unis,* 2:141–3.

111 D.L.A. Gordon, "A City Beautiful Plan."

112 Gréber, *L'architecture aux États-Unis*, 2:147 (translation by R.F.W.).

113 W. Van Nus, "The Fate of City Beautiful Thought in Canada, 1883–1930," in Stelter and Artibise, eds., *The Canadian City*, 162–85.

114 Perks, "Idealism, Orchestration and Science," 1–28.

115 Located at the precise spot where John Lyle had proposed his civic centre and plaza. G. Hunt, *John M. Lyle*, 83–5.

116 Erected in honour of George-Étienne Cartier and an important gathering place for Montrealers. Several components of Rickson Outhet's network of boulevards and riverside parks have now been realized, and the currently projected transformation of the Bonaventure Autoroute into an urban boulevard will continue this process (Montreal City Plan, 2009).

CHAPTER FOURTEEN

1 Leacock, *Sunshine Sketches*, preface.

2 Paul-André Linteau, "The Development and Beautification of an Industrial City: Maisonneuve, 1883–1918," in Stelter and Artibise, eds., *Shaping the Urban Landscape*, 313, 320.

3 Leacock, *Canada*, 203–4.

4 New technologies for the production and application of electrical energy, demonstrated at Shawinigan in Quebec and at Niagara Falls in Ontario and soon to be made available to the population as a whole, promised a new era of prosperity.

5 Prime Minister Sir Wilfrid Laurier, in a speech to the Canadian Club of Ottawa, 18 January 1904; often quoted as "The twentieth century will belong to Canada."

6 Leacock, *Canada*, 214–16.

7 Ernest Rutherford won the Nobel Prize in Chemistry in 1908 for his nuclear research conducted at McGill University.

8 Mackay, *The Square Mile*.

9 Gagnon Pratte, *Country Houses*, 60–89.

10 Ibid., 62–9, 102–4. The great Canadian actor Christopher Plummer, who grew up in these buildings, describes his childhood world as a "tiny atoll of privilege in a late-blooming fin de siècle" and recalls "that other universe of grace and values" that it represented. Plummer, *In Spite of Myself*, 10–31.

11 The site layouts generally included several secondary buildings and landscape features. Bois-Briant, the domain of Prime Minister John Abbott, had extensive gardens, a model farm that included orchards and Guernsey cattle, and spacious conservatories, before its rebuilding in the 1890s. Plummer, *In Spite of Myself*, 16–17.

12 Correspondence between Frederick Todd and Frederick Law Olmsted, Jr., 1911. This was both a professional and

fraternal courtesy and a means of clarifying the legal responsibility for the work.

13 Gagnon Pratte, *Country Houses*, 102–4.

14 Christyna Prokipchuk, "Fulford Place, Brockville, Ontario," in du Prey and Farr, *Ah, Wilderness*, 62–7.

15 Dubé, *Charlevoix*, 102–4.

16 Ibid., 105, 198–202.

17 Ibid., 111–62.

18 Rickson Outhet archive, Ottawa.

19 Van Horne, an accomplished artist, used the upper floor as a studio.

20 Montreal Museum of Fine Arts, *The Architecture of Edward & W.S. Maxwell*, 145–6; Gagnon Pratte, *Country Houses*, 132–8; "My Dream Is of an Island Place," 32–3. Little of the original vegetation remained owing to deer browsing during a long period of neglect, but the government of New Brunswick eventually purchased the property, which it administers as a protected historic site.

21 That is, created during the reign (1901–10) of King Edward VII, son of Victoria. Williams, "Edwardian Gardens," 90–103.

22 Central Okanagan Heritage Society, *Guisachan Heritage Park*; "Guisachan," in Kelowna Museum, *Kelowna, One Hundred Years of History*.

23 "The Residence of Saskatchewan's Lieutenant Governor," 22.

24 Mosquin, *The Butchart Gardens*, 8–9.

25 The first Far Eastern influences on Western gardens had occurred long before. A flurry of interest in Chinese and Japanese gardens that had begun in the late seventeenth century contributed to the evolution of the naturalistic garden in Europe, although the extent of this influence has always been subject to debate. The closing of Japan to foreign contact in 1603 under the Tokugawa Shogunate precluded any significant communication with the West for two and a half centuries. Japan's isolation finally ended with the Meiji Restoration of 1868, which actively sought Western contacts, imported Western ideas, invited Western architects and scholars to Japan, and sent Japanese missions abroad, setting off a half-century of growing enthusiasm for things Japanese in North America and elsewhere.

26 Kuitert, "Japonaiserie in London and The Hague," 221–38; Goto, "The First Japanese Garden," 93–4.

27 Takata, *Nikkei Legacy*, 75–6; Wolf, "Isaburo Kishida," 1–2; Mosquin, *The Butchart Gardens*, 5–6, 9, 21. The Tea Garden met with much commercial success on its opening in 1907 and remained popular until 1942.

28 Takata, *Nikkei Legacy*, 76; Allison, "Finding Kishida."

29 Alexandra Mosquin, of the Historical Services section of Parks Canada, links this recycling of an ugly and disreputable industrial landscape to the many turn-of-the-century reform movements led by women (see chapter 13). Mosquin, *The Butchart Gardens*, 17.

30 Ibid., 22–3; Bingham, *Samuel Maclure*, 67; Segger, *The Buildings of Samuel Maclure*, 61–70, 77–162.

31 Mosquin, *The Butchart Gardens*, 22.

32 Conversation with Janet Bingham, 8 November 2000, and her notes from an interview with Raoul Robillard, 5 November 1977; Bingham, *Samuel Maclure*, 67; McAlpine, "Sculpting with Flowers"; Boyd, "A Man Who Makes Beauty."

33 Conversations with Adrienne Brown and Cornelia Hahn Oberlander, October 2000.

34 Segger, *The Buildings of Samuel* Maclure, 77–162, 217–18; Bingham, *Samuel Maclure*, 2–10, 122.

35 Segger, *The Buildings of Samuel Maclure*, 175–91; Bingham, *Samuel Maclure*, 67, 90–100.

36 Laura Dunsmuir is presumed to have coordinated the architectural and landscape work for Hatley Castle; her husband was not deeply involved (Bingham, *Samuel Maclure*, 91–2; Segger, *The Buildings of Samuel Maclure*, 218). A copy of *The English Flower Garden* by William Robinson (first published in 1883) was found in Laura Dunsmuir's personal library; according to Robillard, Samuel Maclure habitually relied on Robinson's texts for guidance in the design of gardens. See Mills and Clerk, *Hatley Park*, 219–39.

37 Allison, "Finding Kishida"; Martin Segger, "The Architect" and "The Construction Phase," in Castle, ed., *Hatley Park*, 62–93.

38 Martin Segger, "The Construction Phase," in Castle, ed., *Hatley Park*, 89.

39 Ibid., 78–9; Brett, "Developing a British Columbian Estate," 161–6; "'Hatley Park' at Victoria, B.C.," 15–18; Lugrin, "Hatley Park."

40 Castle, *Hatley Park*, 155–9.

41 Coley, "A Bit of Nippon on Our Pacific Coast " 29–31, 56.

42 Milovsoroff, "For the Love of Gardens," 101–33; T.H. Mawson, *Life and Work*, 143–4.

43 Swanley Horticultural College's distinguished graduates include British landscape architect Dame Sylvia Crowe, author Gertrude Webb, and Frances Perry, a well-known horticulturist. The school was destroyed by bombing in 1944, and its successor is now associated with the University of London.

44 Milovsoroff, "For the Love of Gardens," 101–33.

45 Fischer, "The Development of the Garden Suburb," 201–6.

46 Milovsoroff, "For the Love of Gardens," 101–33; Sherk, "The Principals, Sven Herman Stensson."

47 Keynes, *The Economic Consequences of the Peace*, 9–12.

48 *Architectural Record*, 1900–09; *Proceedings of the Sixth National Conference on City Planning*.

49 Shipley, *To Mark Our Place*, 47; Hobsbawm, *The Age of Revolution*, 99; Hobsbawm, *Age of Extremes*, 22–3.

50 Although others remembered this period as one of corruption and decline that could only be excised and purified by a catastrophic conflagration. See Vance, *Death So Noble*, 136–40.

51 Ferguson, *Colossus*, 169–99.

52 Ibid., 105–6.

53 Casid, *Sowing Empire*.

54 Kipling wrote his prescient poem for the sixtieth anniversary of the beginning of Queen Victoria's reign. Britain was at the height of its power at the time, but Kipling doesn't talk about that. Instead, he warns his compatriots against *hubris* – an excess of pride – and asks them to remember the sacrifices of those who have defended their empire, which, like other empires, will not last. His refrain "Lest we forget" was to figure among the inscriptions on war memorials after 1918; see chapter 15.

55 Gowans, *Looking at Architecture*, 121–7; Collins, *Changing Ideals*, 47–58, 67–9, 100–5; Hoskins, *The Making of the English Landscape*, 85–8.

56 A straight line can be drawn between the first parks of this tradition, created in England by Sir Joseph Paxton and others, and the parks realized in the United States and Canada, via the influence of Frederick Law Olmsted, who visited and was inspired by the British parks. Rybczynski, *A Clearing in the Distance*, 85–95, 179–82.

57 Martin and Segrave, *City Parks of Canada*, 25–8.

58 Popularly attributed to the Duke of Wellington.

59 Hoskins and Stamp, *The Common Lands of England & Wales*.

60 Including "Vitae Lampada" ("The Torch of Life," 1897) by Sir Henry Newbolt, where the reader is instantly transported from a cricket match in the familiar confines of the "school close" to a desperate battlefield crisis. Another Victorian poem included in Canadian readers until recent times, "Invictus" (1875, William Ernest Henley), has recently inspired a film with a sports-related but more peaceful theme.

61 Singh, "Sir Edwin Lutyens," 38–43; Hoskins, *The Making of the English Landscape*, 85–8. The village tradition is exemplified in Rupert Brooke's 1912 encomium to his native village, "The Old Vicarage, Grantchester":

> Say, do the elm-clumps greatly stand
> Still guardians of that holy land? …
> Stands the Church clock at ten to three?
> And is there honey still for tea?

62 Many Canadians evinced great enthusiasm for the empire, and some – including Stephen Leacock – supported closer ties with Great Britain through an "imperial federation." Prime Minister Laurier, concerned that this could lead to a loss of identity for communities within Canada, did not encourage such initiatives. See Hutchison, *The Unknown Country*, 107–8.

63 Through the donation of the Stanley Cup (hockey) and the Grey Cup (football), among other contributions. Recent governor general Adrienne Clarkson's donation of a cup to honour the women's hockey champions of Canada is a continuation of this tradition.

64 Hamelin and Provencher, *Brève histoire du Québec*, 75–8.

65 Shirley Spragge, "A Confluence of Interests: Housing Reform in Toronto, 1900–1920," in Artibise and Stelter, eds., *The Usable Urban Past*, 247–67.

66 Leacock, *Social Criticism*, 3–11; Hobsbawm, *Age of Extremes*.

CHAPTER FIFTEEN

1 The author rediscovered these monuments while visiting public squares and main streets across the country during his research for this book. This accidental research led to a more systematic study. Ron Williams, "Memorials of the First World War and Their Continuing Importance in Canadian Cities," in AHLP, *Landscapes of Peace and Commemoration*, 1–5.

2 Colville was a war artist in France and the Netherlands during the Second World War. See Burnett, *Alex Colville*, 202–4, 213.

3 Some writers and historians consider the war to have been a decisive influence in defining the young nation that was just beginning a process of consolidation and development. See Hutchison, *The Unknown Country*, 108–10; MacMillan, "After the Great War"; Morton, "Was the Great War Canada's War of Independence?"; Vance, *Death So Noble*, 226–41.

4 Morton, "World War I," *Canadian Encyclopedia*, 1972–5. The Royal Newfoundland Regiment lost 712 of its 801 soldiers in the first forty-five minutes of the Battle of the Somme on 1 July 1916, at Beaumont-Hamel in northern France. Of the 816 men of the Calgary Highlanders who took part in a counterattack in April 1915 at St-Julien, near Ypres in Belgium, only 174 were at roll call the following day. From its total complement of 5,909 officers, non-commissioned officers (NCOs), and soldiers, the Royal 22nd Regiment from Quebec lost 3,575 dead and wounded, a 60 per cent casualty rate. Of 280 Canadians of Japanese descent from the West Coast who served in France, less than half returned. Memorials at Beaumont-Hamel; St-Julien, Quebec City; and Stanley Park in Vancouver commemorate these particular sacrifices. Christie, *For King and Empire*, 15–19; Boissonnault and Lamontagne, *Histoire du Royal 22e Régiment*.

5 This agency was directed by Frederick Law Olmsted, Jr.

6 http://www.usask.ca/gallery/uofs-buildings/home_memorial gates.

7 Massie, *Dreadnought*, 869–77, 900.

8 *Proceedings of the Sixth National Conference on City Planning*, 92–3, 114–19.

9 T.H. Mawson, *The Life and Work*.

10 Ibid., 245–7, 259–70, 297–302. A 1977 article on Mawson noted "his social awareness (and) concern for people ... made him stand out above the typical designer of that period." Vandermeulen, "Roots 1: Mawson," 9.

11 T.H. Mawson, *The Life and Work*, 249–58.

12 Wade, "The 'Sting' of Vancouver's Better Housing 'Spree,'" 92–8.

13 Wolfe, "Our Common Past," 12–34; Charrett, *Planners and Planning*, 14. The name "Lens" referred to a French town in the Pas-de-Calais, near Vimy Ridge. Deville, who had been appointed surveyor general of the Dominion Lands Survey in March 1885, assured the accurate survey of the twenty-mile-wide CPR railway belt that crossed western Canada.

14 Latremouille, "The Hydrostone District, Halifax," 5–7.

15 Ibid., 5–6; Jébrak and Julien, "Hydrostone's Heritagization," 61–6. This same material had been used to build a whole company town in Minnesota in 1913–15: Morgan Park near Duluth, planned by Morell and Nichols, landscape architects.

16 Sutow and Murphy, *Worse Than War*; Baird and Richards, "Halifax," 16–24; Simpson, "Thomas Adams in Canada," 1–15; Weaver, "Reconstruction of the Richmond District in Halifax," 36–47.

17 Malaka Ackaoui, "De la mémoire à l'art, l'évolution du cimetière Mont-Royal vers le 21ième siècle," in *International Symposium*, 4–7.

18 It is possible that Frederick Todd designed this cemetery, which is similar in layout to his Montreal Memorial Park of 1934. The Field of Honour has recently been designated a National Historic Site.

19 Established in 2001, based on the previously existing military section of Beechwood Cemetery.

20 Information provided by University of Manitoba professors Charlie Thomsen and Ted McLachlan during a site visit, AHLP annual meeting, May 2002.

21 D.R. Brown, "The University of Saskatchewan," 109–17.

22 Vance, *Death So Noble*, 47–8.

23 Fulton and Graham, "Canada's Roads of Remembrance," in *International Symposium*, 164–8.

24 Sandalack and Nicolai, *The Calgary Project*, 63–4.

25 Fulton and Graham, "Canada's Roads of Remembrance," 164–8.

26 Before entering Canada as a province in 1949, Newfoundland was a separate dominion. Some sources credit the bronze sculptures to English sculptors F.V. Blundstone and Gilbert Bayes.

27 Shipley, *To Mark Our Place*, 88.

28 Kavanagh, "Historical Research of Bowring Park," 9–11; Shipley, *To Mark Our Place*, 114.

29 Zvonar, "Where Poppies Grow: Protecting One Memory of the Great War," in AHLP, *Landscapes of Peace and Commemoration*, 1–7; Versteeg, "Rudolph H.K. Cochius and the Creation of Bowring Park," 1–9; Christie, *For King and Empire*, 3, 26–37, 117–29. Other memorials designed by Cochius include Guedecourt, Masnières, and Monchy-le-Preux in France, and Courtrai in Belgium, names familiar to stamp collectors who treasured the famous 1919 Trail of the Caribou series (Newfoundland issued its own stamps prior to joining Confederation).

30 Cochius lived in France throughout the realization of the memorial sites. A generation later, his son Rudolph, born in France during this period, died in the D-Day attacks as a member of the Canadian Army. Christie, *For King and Empire*, 121–9; Versteeg, "Rudolph H.K. Cochius," 1–9.

31 Shipley, *To Mark Our Place*, 93–5, 137; Vance, *Death So Noble*, 140, 206–7.

32 Baker, *Emanuel Hahn and Elizabeth Wyn Wood*.

33 Hucker, "Vimy," 39–48; Vance, *Death So Noble*, 66–70.

34 Names of many other places recall locations, events, and personalities of the war; see Vance, *Death So Noble*, 201–2.

35 A photograph of this monument, in its spectacular urban and natural setting, long figured in public-school geography texts across Canada.

36 Fellows, *Sir Reginald Blomfield*, 103–6.

37 Gradidge, *Edwin Lutyens*, 75–8, 152. Lutyens is better known in landscape architecture for his elegant country houses and gardens, often designed in collaboration with Gertrude Jekyll.

38 Lutyens's design recalls the simple standing stones of ancient Celtic *menhirs* and other archetypal memorials. Shipley, *To Mark Our Place*, 143.

39 The Calgary memorial is aligned, on the axis of the square, with a magnificent equestrian statue, executed in 1914 by sculptor Louis-Philippe Hébert (1850–1917), that commemorates the veterans of the South African War of 1899–1902.

40 Shipley, *To Mark Our Place*, 171.

41 Most commonly, "Nous nous souviendrons" and "Souvenons-nous."

42 Vance, *Death So Noble*, 16–70.

43 Shipley, *To Mark Our Place*, 136–7.

44 Ibid., 53–63, 141–2. A member of this family, Sydney March, realized the war memorial on the grounds of the provincial legislative assembly in Victoria.

45 Ibid., 53–67.

46 Ibid., 84.

47 Both of these dedications were attended by the author's mother, Hazel I. Williams, who recalled that "a big fuss was made of Lord Byng." She kept the Whitby program for

eighty-two years and remembered every word of the song, which she sang to the author shortly before her death in 2004 – an indication of the importance that people have attached to these memorials up to the present day.

48 McCrae, "In Flanders Fields," 1915. In the French-language adaptation, *Au champ d'honneur*, by Colonel Jean Pariseau, chief historian of the Ministry of National Defence, the torch that figures in the original version was changed to the *oriflamme*, sacred banner of the French kings, which communicates a similar symbolic message.

49 Shipley, *To Mark Our Place*, 116.

50 Zvonar, "Where Poppies Grow," in AHLP, *Landscapes of Peace and Commemoration*, 1–7; Douglas Clark, "Memorial Drive," 14–15; consultants at Calgary included Cathy Sears and David Spencer of Stantec Consulting Ltd.

51 Zvonar, "Where Poppies Grow"; D. Clark, "Memorial Drive," 14–15; J. Smith, "Restoring Vimy," 49–56.

CHAPTER SIXTEEN

1 Walter Van Nus, "The Fate of City Beautiful Thought in Canada, 1883–1930," in Stelter and Artibise, eds., *The Canadian City*, 172–3; Walter Van Nus, "Towards the City Efficient: The Theory and Practice of Zoning, 1919–1939," in Artibise and Stelter, eds., *The Usable Urban Past*," 226–46.

2 Galbraith, *The Great Crash*, 182–91.

3 Artibise, *Winnipeg*; Easterbrook and Aitken, *Canadian Economic History*, 564–7. Fifteen per cent of the city's population laid down their tools. The strikers assembled in Victoria Park near the Red River before marching on the downtown area; this perhaps explains the subsequent disappearance of this park, seemingly the only Victoria Park in Canada that no longer exists.

4 Galbraith, *The Great Crash*, 7, 76, 142.

5 Ibid., 6–28.

6 Newton, *Design on the Land*, 427–46.

7 Newton notes this same tendency in American projects of the period. See his *Design on the Land*, 427–8, 446; Gagnon Pratte, *Architecture et nature*, 157–62.

8 Platt's projects were published in 1913 in *Monograph of the Work of Charles A. Platt*. See also Newton, *Design on the Land*, 372–84; Keith Morgan, "Platt, Charles A.," in Birnbaum and Karson, *Pioneers*, 297–300; and Morgan, *Shaping an American Landscape*. Platt designed some projects in Canada, including the Château Dubuc at Chicoutimi, Quebec, in collaboration with Ellen Biddle Shipman, one of the first women to practise landscape architecture in the United States. Morisset, Noppen, and Dieudonné, *Patrimoines modernes*, 77.

9 Todd, "Where Nature Is Abetted," 26–7, 54.

10 Hodgins, "Shadowbrook," 16–20, 50. The advertisements for Sheridan Nurseries that appeared in each issue of the magazine feature a series of projects by the Dunington-Grubb office as well as provide publicity for the nursery company. Taken as a group, they formed a virtual handbook of gardening, as did, for a subsequent generation, the nurseries' annual colour catalogues of plants. See, for example, "Alpines and Perennials for Spring Planting," a Sheridan advertisement published in the April 1928 issue.

11 Gianelli, "Almarie," 37; Humphrey Carver, "The People and the Times: The Founding of the CSLA," in Paine, ed., *Fifty Years of Landscape Architecture in Canada*, 13–31.

12 Kay, "How and When to Plant Deciduous Shrubs," 90, 94, 96.

13 For example, "The Value of Water as a Garden Feature," 26–7, 64, and 66 in the September 1926 issue.

14 For example, "The French Style," 27–9, 58, and 60 in the April 1930 issue; and "We Make a Plan for the Estate," 28–9, 56, and 58 in the May 1930 issue.

15 A "son of the manse" – born into the family of a Presbyterian minister in a small village near Guelph, Ontario – Maclean became a giant in Canada's publication industry, founding *Maclean's Magazine*, the *Financial Post*, and other periodicals and establishing what is, still today, a formidable commercial empire.

16 Chalmers, *A Gentleman of the Press*; Beveridge and Hoffman, *Master List*, 77. In the Olmsted office, Culham played an important role in the design of Fort Tryon Park in New York City, undertaking research on historical landscapes in Spain to help reconstruct the medieval cloisters that are a central feature of this park on the Hudson River.

17 Chalmers, *A Gentleman of the Press*; Carver, "The People and the Times," 24–9; correspondence between Culham and H.V. Hubbard of the Olmsted Brothers office, April 1926–August 1930, provided by Peter Jacobs.

18 Justice, "Vancouver's Tree Heritage," 5–6; McAlpine, "Sculpting with Flowers"; Boyd, "A Man Who Makes Beauty."

19 Coley, "The Terraced Gardens of Hycroft," 31–3.

20 Correspondence between Fred Cole, W.G. Murrin, and Frank E. Buck, 1934–46, provided by Cornelia Hahn Oberlander.

21 Buck, *Planning the Home Lot*, 1915.

22 Justice, "Vancouver's Tree Heritage," 5–6; Justice, "Three Landscape Legacies," 79–104; Haaf and Meredith, *Frank E. Buck*.

23 "Bill Livingstone," obituary notice, *SiteLines*, November 1990.

24 "This Month's Who's Who," 7.

25 Houlton, "Gardening as a Profession," 32–3.

26 Hodgins, "An Italian Garden on Île d'Orléans Cliffs," 22–5, 106, 108; "Sarahluff Bond," 37. In the November 1925 issue of *Canadian Homes and Gardens* (vol. 3, no. 11, p. 15), Hodgins praised Bond's creation: "Without question it is the finest private garden in Eastern Canada."

27 Anderson, *Women, Design, and the Cambridge School*; letter from Frances Blue to Pleasance Crawford, 3 March 1982, provided by Pleasance Crawford.

28 Anderson, *Women, Design, and the Cambridge School*, 1–22, 73–4, 10–35. Among the professors at the Lowthorpe School was Canadian architect and planner John A. Parker. See also Blue, *A Short History of the CSLA*.

29 Carver, "The People and the Times," 26–9.

30 Often known by her married name, Frances Steinhoff Sanders. See Donaldson, "Landscape Architecture in Canada," 17–23; Carver, "The People and the Times," 26–9; Steinhoff Sanders, "Oasis on the Roof," in von Baeyer and Crawford, *Garden Voices*, 56–7.

31 Designed by Martin Wade Landscape Architects of Toronto and sponsored by Kippax's nieces, the Stedman sisters of Brantford, ON.

32 Royal Botanic Gardens, "Helen M. Kippax Garden."

33 P. Crawford, *CSLA Bulletin*, July 1993, 4; see also Blue, *A Short History of the CSLA*.

34 Justice, "Three Landscape Legacies," 101. Clive Justice later gave Ashwell's book collection to UBC.

35 Beatty and Hall, *Parkwood*, 14–19, 50–62.

36 McArthur, *A Progressive Traditionalist*, 182–6.

37 Beatty and Hall, *Parkwood*, 58–62; "A Garden Unique in North America," 30–7.

38 Reford, *Reford Gardens*, 12–28; Reford, *The Reford Gardens: Elsie's Paradise*, 25–56. Elsie Reford was also a principal participant in the founding of the Women's Canadian Club of Montreal (a philanthropic organization); she helped organize the 300th anniversary of Quebec City in 1908; and she served overseas during the First World War. See Reford, *Reford Gardens*, 12–13.

39 The blue poppy, *Meconopsis betonicifolia*, has become the symbol of the Reford Gardens. Coincidentally, this plant is also the floral emblem of the Butchart Gardens on the opposite side of the country, where it is called *Meconopsis baileyi*.

40 Reford, *Reford Gardens*, 34–63; Reford, *The Reford Gardens: Elsie's Paradise*, 57–61.

41 The ongoing stewardship of the gardens is assured by the Amis des Jardins de Métis, under the direction of Alexander Reford, the great-grandson of Elsie Reford; see chapter 22.

42 Cabot, *Greater Perfection*, 53–6; Des Gagniers, *Un jardin extraordinaire*, 19–30; Dubé, *Charlevoix*, 45–61, 92–4, 97–8.

43 Cabot, "Les Quatre Vents," 30–3; Cabot, *Greater Perfection*, 56–63, 94–101; Des Gagniers, *Un jardin extraordinaire*, 61–88; Dubé, *Charlevoix*, 192–5, 236–9.

44 The name "Kingsmere" already existed; the domain was not named for Mackenzie King. Von Baeyer, *Garden of Dreams*, 23.

45 Hutchison, *The Incredible Canadian*, 82–5.

46 King played an important role in the raising of a sculpture of Sir Galahad, in honour of his lost friend, in front of the Parliament Buildings in Ottawa.

47 Von Baeyer, *Garden of Dreams*, 12–13, 145–8, 192–218.

48 Messier, *Mackenzie King Estate*, 56–63; von Baeyer, *Garden of Dreams*, 117–27.

49 King sought architectural stones from many sources for this work, including stones from the British Houses of Parliament, sent to him after their bombardment. Von Baeyer, *Garden of Dreams*, 172.

50 Messier, *Mackenzie King Estate*, 65–81; von Baeyer, *Garden of Dreams*, 156–74.

51 Von Baeyer, *Garden of Dreams*, 25–7, 70–1, 202. King's grandfather, William Lyon Mackenzie, had been the ally and Upper Canada counterpart of Papineau in the 1837 rebellion. And like Papineau, Mackenzie spent many years in exile in the United States, where his daughter, the mother of Mackenzie King, was born.

52 Ibid., 64–9, 140–3, 218.

53 Carver, "The People and the Times," 15–21; Carver, *Compassionate Landscape*, 37–9.

CHAPTER SEVENTEEN

1 Tunnard and Reed, *American Skyline*, 170–3; Walter Van Nus, "The Fate of City Beautiful Thought in Canada, 1883–1930," in Stelter and Artibise, eds., *The Canadian City*, 162–85; Walter Van Nus, "Towards the City Efficient: The Theory and Practice of Zoning, 1919–1939," in Artibise and Stelter, eds., *The Usable Urban Past*, 226–46.

2 Van Nus, "Towards the City Efficient," 226–46; Van Nus, "The Fate of City Beautiful Thought," 177–9; Donaldson, "Landscape Architecture in Canada," 17–23.

3 Wolfe, "Our Common Past," 18; Sherwood, "Canadian Institute of Planners," 20–1.

4 Girard, *L'écologisme retrouvé*, 188–90.

5 Commission of Conservation, *Civic Improvement League for Canada*, 1916.

6 Armstrong, "Thomas Adams and the Commission of Conservation," 17–35; Oiva Saarinen, "The Influence of Thomas Adams and the British New Towns Movement in the Planning of Canadian Resource Communities," in Artibise and Stelter, *The Usable Urban Past*, 268–92; Simpson, "Thomas Adams in Canada," 1–14; Girard, *L'écologisme retrouvé*, 190–5.

7 *Proceedings of the Sixth National Conference on City Planning*, 27–37. Some disagreed: "In the process [of the march to efficient administration by experts] City Beautiful gradually disappeared"; and "The new efficiency forgot the arts" (Tunnard and Reed, *American Skyline*, 170–3).

8 Delaney, "The Garden Suburb of Lindenlea," 151–64.

9 Pinhey and Klynstra, "Landscape Management Plan," 31–6.

10 Armstrong, "Thomas Adams," 32–5. Adams eventually returned to England following a distinguished career as a professor and author in the United States.

11 G. Hunt, *John M. Lyle*, 82.

12 Saarinen, "The Influence of Thomas Adams," 275–80; Wolfe and Dufaux, *A Topographic Atlas of Montreal*.

13 Paul Trépanier, "Témiscaming: Une cité-jardin du Nord," in R. Fortier, ed., *Villes industrielles planifiées*, 117–52; T. Adams, *Report of the Commission of Conservation, 1919*.

14 T. Adams, *Report of the Commission of Conservation, 1919*, appendix 7.

15 Born in Boston as Arthur Shurcliff, Shurtleff worked for the Olmsted firm before opening his own office in 1904. He designed many planned communities and was the landscape architect for the restoration of colonial Williamsburg in Virginia. Elizabeth Cushing, "Shurcliff, Arthur Asahel (Shurtleff)," in Birnbaum and Karson, eds., *Pioneers*, 351–6.

16 Trépanier, "Témiscaming: Une cité-jardin du Nord," 130–4; Macpherson, "Come to Temiscaming," 22–4, 52, 69; Grimmer, "Gardens in the North," 47, 53, 56–7.

17 Destined for such major companies as Kimberly-Clark (manufacturers of Kleenex) and the New York Times. The prime minister of the province, E.C. Drury, was personally involved in the project. Saarinen, "Provincial Land Use Planning Initiatives," 1–15.

18 Ibid., 1–15; Crawford, "Forgotten Landscape Architectural Firm," 29–35.

19 These three pioneers of landscape architecture in Canada had remained obscure for several decades but were rediscovered by Toronto landscape historian Pleasance Crawford. Crawford, "Forgotten Landscape Architectural Firm," 29–35.

20 Lucie K. Morisset and Luc Noppen, "La ville de l'aluminium," in R. Fortier, ed., *Villes industrielles planifiées*, 175–239. The name of the city of Arvida is based on the first syllables of the name of Alcoa's president, Arthur Vining Davis.

21 Filteau, *L'épopée de Sha8inigan* [sic], 217–19; Robert Fortier and Paul Trépanier, "L'environnement bâti à Shawinigan Falls," in R. Fortier, ed., *Villes industrielles planifiées*, 95–8.

22 Ibid., 97–9; Filteau, *L'épopée de Sha8inigan*, 219.

23 Best, *Thomas Baker McQuesten*, 54–6.

24 This magnificent natatorium was closed in the 1950s but refurbished and reopened in the 1980s.

25 Correspondence between Gordon Culham and H.V. Hubbard of the Olmsted Brothers office, July–August 1930, provided by Peter Jacobs. Filey, *I Remember Sunnyside*, 48.

26 http://www.torontobeach.ca/beaches/history; Greenberg, "Toronto," 37–46; Merrens, "Port Authorities as Urban Land Developers," 92–101.

27 Novak et al, *Reader Rock Garden Management Plan*, 5–17.

28 Graham, "Central (Memorial) Park," 197–201; Barraclough, *Prairie to Park*, 92–3.

29 In Quebec, this role was often played by the Catholic Church; the institutional basis for society was similar in both cases.

30 Paine, "Design of Landscapes," 37–47; P. Crawford, "Grounds of the Old Whitby Psychiatric Hospital, Their Evolution and Significance," in Beck, Moffet, and Smith, eds., *Conserving Ontario's Landscapes*, 45–54.

31 http://www.bcmhas.ca/AboutUs/History.htm. Davidson subsequently pursued a long and distinguished career at UBC as a professor of botany and as director of the university's botanical garden, subsequently relocated to the southwest sector of the campus. The magazine of the garden is named *Davidsonia* in his honour.

32 P. Crawford, "Grounds of the Old Whitby Psychiatric Hospital," 45–8; P. Crawford, "Forgotten Landscape Architectural Firm," 29–35; information provided by Hazel Williams, whose father, Charles Arnott, was the director of horticulture and food production at the Whitby Hospital and subsequently the Hamilton Hospital, 1919–28.

33 Van Nus, "The Fate of City Beautiful Thought," 178.

34 Lachapelle, "La perspective de l'avenue McGill Collège." Rockefeller Center was begun in 1928 and completed in 1937, Raymond Hood, chief architect.

35 Isabelle Gournay, "Gigantism in Downtown Montreal," in Gournay and Vanlaethem, eds., *Montreal Metropolis*, 197–9.

36 The names given to the new avenues and public plazas – Cambrai Avenue, Vimy Circle, St. Julien Place – show that the events of the First World War remained in people's memories more than a decade after the Armistice.

37 Greenberg, "Toronto," 37–46; Lemon, "Plans for Early 20th-Century Toronto," 11–31.

38 DeGrace, "Canada's Capital," 48–51; Hillis, "History of Commissions," 46–60.

39 Cauchon, "Town Planning," 168–70. Several of Cauchon's other ideas mentioned here were also eventually realized, up to sixty years later.

40 Delainey and Sarjeant, *Saskatoon*, 37–8.

41 Bartholomew, *Plan for the City of Vancouver*; Perks, "Idealism, Orchestration and Science," 1–28; Bloomfield, "Ubiquitous Town Planning Missionary," 29–42, http://www.archive.org/stream/vancplnincgen00vanc#page/200/mode/2up.

42 Roger Todhunter's 1983 analysis, based on the criteria of Van Nus, finds that City Beautiful ideals inspired Bartholomew's study. Todhunter, "Vancouver and the City Beautiful Movement," 8–11; Van Nus, "The Fate of City Beautiful Thought."

43 Bartholomew, *Plan for the City of Vancouver*, 19–26, 198–210, 236–56.

44 Ibid., 122–9; Todhunter, "Vancouver and the City Beautiful Movement," 8–11; Berelowitz, *Dream City*, 1–7, 61–3. See chapter 24 with respect to Vancouver's contemporary development.

45 D'Acres and Luxton, *Lions Gate*, 23–8, 30–7, 50–7; Fitzgerald, "The Properties."

46 Dawson, born in Boston and a graduate of Harvard's Bussey Institution (where Rickson Outhet studied), joined the Olmsted firm in 1896 and spent his entire career there. Catherine Joy Johnson, "Dawson, James Frederick, Landscape Architect," in Birnbaum and Karson, eds., *Pioneers,"* 76–9.

47 Dawson had worked on the Uplands project in Oak Bay, BC (see chapter 13), and on the firm's Palos Verdes Estates in suburban Los Angeles, CA. Larry McCann, personal communication, 2012.

48 A familiar "barbell" composition similar to other such boulevards designed by the Olmsted firm, including Midland Way in Uplands; "The Greeting" in Franklin Park, Boston; and the Mall in Central Park, New York.

49 This resembled the village centres built in Palos Verdes Estates in California, on which Dawson also worked and which, according to Larry McCann, served as a model for British Properties (personal communication, 2012).

50 Designed by Stanley F. Thompson; see chapter 18.

51 Fitzgerald, "The Properties."

CHAPTER EIGHTEEN

1 Galbraith, *The Great Crash*, 182–91.

2 Easterbrook and Aitken, *Canadian Economic History*, 490–3; Hamelin and Provencher, *Brève histoire du Québec*, 95. A long period of drought added to the severity of the economic catastrophe on the Prairies.

3 Humphrey Carver, "The People and the Times: The Founding of the CSLA," in Paine, ed., *Fifty Years of Landscape Architecture in Canada,* 13–31; Carver, *Compassionate Landscape*, 28–30, 35–8.

4 Pollock-Ellwand, "Rickson Outhet," 137–83.

5 Ibid., 140, 165–74.

6 As it was in the United States; see Newton, *Design on the Land*, 442–6; von Baeyer, *Garden of Dreams*, 100–1.

7 Bouchard and Hoffman, *Le Jardin botanique de Montréal*, 21.

8 Ibid., 7–12; Dansereau, "Brother Marie-Victorin," ii–viii; Université de Montréal, *Marie-Victorin*.

9 Bouchard and Hoffman, *Le Jardin botanique de Montréal*, 12–20; Lincourt, *Jardin botanique de Montréal*, 9–15; Terry Copp, "Montreal's Municipal Government and the Crisis of the 1930s," in Artibise and Stelter, eds., *The Usable Urban Past,* 117–20. This was the first Union Nationale government under Prime Minister Maurice Duplessis.

10 Bouchard and Hoffman, *Le Jardin botanique de Montréal*, 23–8; Université de Montréal, *Marie-Victorin*; Soderstrom, *Recreating Eden*, 152–64.

11 Best, *Thomas Baker McQuesten*, 56–62; Royal Botanical Gardens, *Garden with a View*; Carver, *Compassionate Landscape*, 45; Laking, "History of the Royal Botanical Gardens (Part 2)," 7–15; Hucker, *Royal Botanical Gardens*, 93–111.

12 McArthur, *A Progressive Traditionalist*, 146–52.

13 Laking, "History of the Royal Botanical Gardens (Part 2)," 7–15; G. Hunt, *John Lyle*, 118–20.

14 Carver, "The People and the Times," 13–31; Carver, *Compassionate Landscape*, 28–30, 35–8.

15 Hucker, *Royal Botanical Gardens*, 96–100, 115, 122–3; Satterthwaite, *Royal Botanical Gardens*, 26–31.

16 Charles H. Thomsen, "A Vision for Peace: The International Peace Garden," in AHLP, *Landscapes of Peace and Commemoration*, 1–12; Thomsen, "A Border Vision," 36–41; John MacLeod, "An Overview of the History of Places for Peace in Canada," in AHLP, *Landscapes of Peace and Commemoration*, 1–13.

17 Thomsen, "A Vision for Peace."

18 Ibid.; C. Macdonald, *Making a Place*, 78–9. The form and character of the International Peace Garden continue to develop. In 1986–87, landscape architects Charlie Thomsen of Winnipeg and Jon Burley of the United States collaborated on an updated master plan for the central Formal Garden; the provisions of this plan are gradually being realized. See C. Macdonald, *Making a Place*, 180–1.

19 The two other gardens so honoured were the Halifax Public Gardens and the Butchart Gardens near Victoria, BC; see chapters 9 and 14.

20 Culham continued his work on the campus until the 1960s; his patron, John Maclean, paid for his services until 1947. See Pollock-Ellwand, "Gordon Culham: Living a 'Useful Life,'" 587–609; http://www.uwo.ca/biology/arboretum/history.htm.

21 Baraness and Richards, *Toronto Places*, 32–3.

22 As early as 1903, Frederick Todd had suggested, in his report on long-term park planning for Ottawa and Hull, that some portions of the experimental farm "may be considered as a public park." See Smith and Bramley, *Ottawa's Farm*, 50–1.

23 Probably for reasons of economy. Ibid., 73–4.

24 Oliver remained at the Farm for the rest of his career, designing landscapes for many stations across Canada and publishing many books and pamphlets. Ibid., 72–4, 112.

25 Filteau, *L'épopée de Sha8inigan* [sic], 245–8; LaRochelle, *Histoires de Shawinigan*, 258–60; Lacoursière, *Shawinigan*, 101–2; "Les 12 travaux des chômeurs," in "L'actualité depuis 1920," S31.

26 LaRochelle, *Histoires de Shawinigan*, 254–7; Filteau, *L'épopée de Sha8inigan* [sic], 245–8; Lacoursière, *Shawinigan*, 102. The construction methods used were described to the author on site by an elderly gentleman, a native of Shawinigan, who had followed the progress of the work as a young boy in the 1930s.

27 It is possible that landscape architect Rickson Outhet, who was involved in much of the work at Shawinigan in this period, was implicated in the design of this attractive promenade, which begins in the Parc Saint-Maurice designed by him.

28 LaRochelle, *Histoires de Shawinigan*, 257.

29 Best, *Thomas Baker McQuesten*, 56–8.

30 Carver, "The People and the Times," 22–3.

31 Both short term (construction jobs) and long term. A principal objective of McQuesten's public works program was the promotion of the tourist industry, targeting a primarily American clientele.

32 Way, "Work of the Niagara Parks Commission," 207–18; Best, *Thomas Baker McQuesten*, 113–17, 134–5; Barnsley and Pierce, *Public Gardens and Parks of Niagara*, 11. Broman completed his career at the Royal Botanical Gardens.

33 Way, "Work of the Niagara Parks Commission," 207–18; Best, *Thomas Baker McQuesten*, 125–9; Carver, *Compassionate Landscape*, 38–9.

34 Again, the work was largely carried out with shovels and hoes so that as much work as possible could be given out to unemployed men, while horses furnished the motive power. Conversation with André Juneau, president of the National Battlefields Commission, March 2008.

35 P. Jacobs, "Frederick Gage Todd," 27–34; P. Jacobs, "Roots 2: The Quiet Vision," 1–4; Versteeg, "Rudolph H.K. Cochius."

36 P. Jacobs, "Frederick Gage Todd," 27–34; P. Jacobs, "Roots 2: The Quiet Vision," 1–4; Jacobs and Foisy, *Les Quatre Saisons du Mont Royal*, 39–40.

37 P. Jacobs, "Frederick G. Todd," 27–34; P. Jacobs, "Roots 2: The Quiet Vision," 1–4; O'Neil and Brunet, *L'île Sainte-Hélène*, 51–2.

38 P. Jacobs, "Frederick G. Todd," 27–34; P. Jacobs, "Roots 2: The Quiet Vision," 1–4.

39 Cornell was well known for its landscape architecture department, established in 1904, and for its expertise in horticulture and plant science. As in most other American landscape programs of the time, Cornell emphasized the large country estate as a main focus of professional endeavour.

40 Perron, "Les Floralies 1980 et l'architecture de paysage au Québec," in Les Floralies internationales de Montréal, *Aménagement paysager*, 89–102; Perron, "Development of the Profession in Quebec," in Paine, ed., *Fifty Years of Landscape Architecture*, 46–9; course notes for "An Introduction to Landscape Architecture," Macdonald College; documents provided by Peter Jacobs; conversations with Louis Perron, 1983, and with Bert Johnstone, president, Town and Country Landscaping, Montreal, 2005.

41 Conversation with Louis Perron, 1983. In 2002, the CCNQ (Commission de la Capitale nationale du Québec) replanted the garden according to Perron's original floral composition.

42 Hunter, *Parkwood*, 43–63; Reford, *The Reford Gardens: Elsie's Paradise*, 106–9.

43 Jacobs and Fortin, *Évolution de l'architecture de paysage*.

44 "Les 12 travaux des chômeurs," in "L'actualité depuis 1920," S31; Lacoursière, *Shawinigan*, 113–14.

45 Dick, "Forgotten Roots," 10–11; Thompson, *Forging the Prairie West*, 126–30. In contrast to the high profile and wide approval such camps enjoyed in the United States, those in Canada were less successful. Complaints and strikes culminated in the Regina Riot of 1935; the camps closed the following year and have received a bad press ever since, despite some excellent completed projects and broad participation. See Cutler, *The Public Landscape of the New Deal*, 90–105; Newton, *Design on the Land*, 576–95, concerning the American program and its accomplishments, of which the lodge and picnic shelters on the North Dakota side of the International Peace Garden are fine examples.

46 Parker, "Cascades of Time," 20–3.

47 Parks Canada, *The Architectural History of Riding Mountain*; C. Macdonald, *Making a Place*, 53; Dick, "Forgotten Roots," 10–11.

48 The Dunington-Grubbs and Carver were active members of the League for Social Reconstruction, a "progressive" political movement of the time.

49 Carver, *Compassionate Landscape*, 39–40.

50 A marvellous description of this sequence of events and the people involved can be found in the proceedings of the CSLA's fiftieth annual meeting, held in Ottawa in July 1984 (Paine, *Fifty Years of Landscape Architecture*). This volume recounts a memorable presentation of the society's creation by CSLA founding member Humphrey Carver, who "introduced" each of his former colleagues, of whom he was the last survivor, as if they were present on the stage beside him. See Carver, "The People and the Times," 13–31; Carver, *Compassionate Landscape*, 39–40; Donaldson, "Landscape Architecture in Canada," 17–23.

51 CSLA Members List 1940–50, provided by Peter Jacobs; D. McDonald, "Planning and Development of the National Capital Region," in Paine, *Fifty Years of Landscape Architecture*, 65–71.

52 Carver, "The People and the Times," 28–9; Sherwood, "Canadian Institute of Planners," 21; J.M. Wolfe, "Our

Common Past," 22. Since its founding in 1919, the TPIC had constantly expanded, reaching a zenith of 367 members in 1930; two years later, it was forced to suspend operations. See "History of CIP," Canadian Institute of Planners webpage, http://www.cip-icu.ca.

53 Laking, "A History of the Royal Botanical Gardens (Part 2)," 7–15; G. Hunt, *John M. Lyle*, 118–20.

54 J.W. Brennan, *Regina*, 135–6; P.H. Brennan, "Thousands of our men," 33–45.

55 Meewasin Valley Authority, *Where City and Water Meet*.

56 D'Acres and Luxton, *Lions Gate*, 65–120. Pratley, a champion of the scientific approach to bridge design, had participated in the design of many previous bridges and in the enquiry concerning the collapse of the first bridge at Quebec City. He later employed the same format as Lions Gate for the Angus Macdonald Bridge (1954) at the Narrows in Halifax Harbour, as did the successor firm Pratley and Dorton for the A. Murray Mackay Bridge (1970) nearby.

57 Passfield, *Philip Louis Pratley*, 1–10, 14–21; Dufresne, *Pont Lions Gate*, 1–18; D'Acres and Luxton, *Lions Gate*, 65–120; Kalman and Roaf, *Exploring Vancouver 2*, 197.

58 Passfield, *Philip Louis Pratley*, 10–14; Marsan, *Montreal in Evolution*, 306.

59 Donovan, *Stanley W. Thompson*, 1–14.

60 Today, the appropriateness of these golf courses within the national parks is being called into question in light of current criteria for ecological integrity (see chapter 12).

61 Kendall, *Northern Links*, 82–90, 248–52; correspondence between S.F. Thompson and the Parks Branch, June 1938 (Stanley Thompson Society Collection, Archival and Special Collections, University of Guelph).

62 At Riding Mountain, a National Parks employee told the author that many golfers undertake a pilgrimage to play all the courses designed by Thompson. The course manager also contributed to the design of this specific course, begun by Thompson in 1928.

63 Kendall, *Northern Links*, 82–90, 248–52.

64 D'Acres and Luxton, *Lions Gate*, 50–1.

65 Carver, *Compassionate Landscape*, 29–30. Thompson also employed sketches and plasticine models to compose his courses and, towards the end of his career, took the measure of his sites by airplane. See "Liberty Profile: Stanley Thompson," 16–17.

66 Williams, "Post-modernism," 9–13.

67 Giedion, *Space, Time, and Architecture*, 68, 425–94.

68 Imbert, *The Modernist Garden*, 27–50. This exhibition lent its name to the Art Deco style of design.

69 Asselin, "Frederick G. Todd," 20–2; Jacobs, "Frederick G. Todd," 27–34. A detailed study of Todd's writings reveals no explicit reference to the modern aesthetic, but he constantly emphasized the social importance of landscape architecture, one of the three ideological pillars of modernism. The inspiration for Todd's design may equally have come from one of many lakes and ponds throughout the Canadian Shield that have a four-lobed amoeba shape similar to that of Beaver Lake; Todd's lake preceded the similarly shaped Tidal Basin in Washington, DC, which did not take its definitive form until 1939.

70 Lance M. Neckar, "Christopher Tunnard: The Garden in the Modern Landscape," in Treib, ed., *Modern Landscape Architecture*, 144–58; J. Brown, *The Modern Garden*, 58–65; J. Brown, *Eminent Gardeners*, 115–38.

71 Both projects were carried out in collaboration with architect Serge Chermayeff.

72 Tunnard, *Gardens in the Modern Landscape*, 65–106.

73 Ibid., 126–33.

74 J. Brown, *The Modern Garden*, 82–5.

75 Carver, *Compassionate Landscape*, 21–2; Carver, "Book Review," 172; Ron Williams, "Courants modernes," 237–8.

CHAPTER NINETEEN

1 Marsan, *Montreal in Evolution*, 320.

2 Ibid., 337–82.

3 As characterized by Carver, *Cities in the Suburbs*, 8–10.

4 According to statistics cited by Marsan, the percentage of Montreal households owning a car increased from 27.8 per cent in 1951 to 68.1 per cent in 1971. *Montreal in Evolution*, 320.

5 Lorimer, *The Developers*, 16–19, 72–3, 121–2. The name of this agency was subsequently changed to Canada Mortgage and Housing Corporation.

6 Ibid., 83–172, 186–215. An engaging description of how these innovations played out in the Calgary metropolitan area is found in Robert Stamp's *Suburban Modern*.

7 Kettle, "Highways as Landscape Architecture," 56–9.

8 Lorimer, *The Developers*, 17–18, 129–31.

9 Carver, *Compassionate Landscape*, 78–125.

10 Ibid., 121. Publications included *Principles of Small House Grouping* (1954), *Choosing a House Design* (1956), and *Small House Designs* (1957). See also Kapelos, "The Small House in Print," 34–45.

11 McBride, *Our Store*, 16–45, 55.

12 Easterbrook and Aitken, *Canadian Economic History*, 548–52.

13 Carver, *Compassionate Landscape*, 77–8.

14 Ron Williams, "Courants modernes," 231–54.

15 Including the Donnell Garden at Sonoma, CA, which is featured on the cover and within the issue. Church, "Transition," 252–4.

16 Eckbo, *The Art of Home Landscaping*, 44–5.

17 Kippax, "Ground Covers," 263.

18 Ibid., 264–5.

19 Stensson, "Approach to Planting," 266–7.

20 Floyd, "The Architect's Garden," 258–9.

21 Floyd, "Garden in Forest Hill Village," 260–2.

22 H. Dunington-Grubb, "Garden of Nineteen-Fifty," 272–3.

23 Nazar, "Design, Utility or Burlesque" and "Garden for a Private Residence in Ottawa, Ontario," 255–7.

24 Eckbo, "What Do We Mean by Modern Landscape Architecture?," 268–71. Eckbo cites Laszlo Moholy-Nagy, Gyorgy Kepes, Frank Lloyd Wright, and Le Corbusier as his personal influences.

25 H. Dunington-Grubb, "Garden of Nineteen-Fifty," 272–3.

26 Ironically, modernism (in the shape of a new state-of-the-art medical centre) would obliterate one of Dunington-Grubb's best works, the Sunken Garden at the entrance to McMaster University, in 1964.

27 Windsor-Liscombe, *The New Spirit.*

28 Laurie, "Thomas Church," 166–79.

29 Marc Treib, "Axioms for a Modern Landscape Architecture," in Treib, *Modern Landscape Architecture*, 51–7.

30 Windsor-Liscombe, "*The New Spirit*," 39–43.

31 Bronson, "Binning Residence," 51–64; Woodworth, "B.C. Binning House," 15–16.

32 Birmingham, "Residential Work," 305–9.

33 Ibid.; Windsor-Liscombe, *The New Spirit*, 111–35; Luxton, "Rise and Fall," 55–61. Other magazines, including *Canadian Homes and Gardens* and the RAIC *Journal*, exerted a similar influence across the country. See Kapelos, "The Small House in Print," 45–57.

34 *Western Homes and Living*, February 1955; Windsor-Liscombe, *The New Spirit*, 127–9; site visit and discussion with Cornelia Hahn Oberlander, November 2000.

35 Manus and Rochon, *Picturing Landscape Architecture*, 27; Stinson, *Love Every Leaf*, 5–23.

36 C.H. Oberlander, *Forging the Way*, 3.

37 LeGeyt, *Changing the Face of Canada, Vol. 1*, 85–8; Rochon, *Up North*, 223–4; Stinson, *Love Every Leaf*, 25–6; H.P. Oberlander, "Making Waves," 17–18.

38 Interview with Clive Justice, Nov. 2000; Windsor-Liscombe, *The New Spirit*, 126–8; Muirhead, "Landscape Design in Western Canada," 235–41.

39 *Western Homes and Living*, August 1955, 16–17.

40 Floyd, "Garden in Forest Hill Village," 261.

41 Nazar, "Garden for a Private Residence in Ottawa," 256–7.

42 Fliess, "The Modern House," 395–6; E.C.S. Cox, "Fitting the House to Its Site," 402.

43 C. Macdonald, *Making a Place*, 94–5.

44 Choko, *Une Cité-jardin à Montréal*, 25–40.

45 Ibid., 39–44. Gitterman brought considerable experience to his task, having served as chief architect for the Wartime Housing program, which had built residences across the country.

46 Ibid., 43–4.

47 Stein, *Toward New Towns for America*, 37–73.

48 Not all the founders' goals were realized. Rapid increases in construction costs in 1945 and 1946 had distorted the financial equation, creating serious obstacles to the completion of the project and leading to the resignation of the management team and the abandonment of the southern sector of the development. Like its inspiration, Radburn, Cité-jardin is an unfinished project. And, even in the early years of the project, the great majority of property owners (including former Montreal mayor Jean Drapeau) came from the professions and the middle class rather than from the ranks of the workers.

49 M.D. Martin, "Returning to Radburn," 160–6, 172; M.D. Martin, "Landscapes of Wildwood Park," 23–6; C. Macdonald, *Making a Place*, 84.

50 M.D. Martin, "Returning to Radburn," 160–1; M.D. Martin, "Landscapes of Wildwood Park," 22–6.

51 Hancock and Lee, "Don Mills New Town," 3–27; Sewell, *Shape of the City*, 79–96; interview with Macklin Hancock, February 2001.

52 With the help of Canadian landscape architect Gordon Culham. Pollock-Elwand, "Gordon Culham: Living a 'Useful Life,'" 594.

53 OALA *Review* 4, no. 1 (March 1978); Macklin Hancock interview, February 2001. Leslie Hancock also served as a member of the Ontario Legislative Assembly.

54 Filler, "Planning for a Better World," 122–7; interview with Gwen Sewell, Director of Community Planning and Development, District of Kitimat, July 2006. Finally, Alcan built only three neighbourhood units, since industrial expansion was less rapid than anticipated. In 2008, the population of the city was about 9,300.

55 Cross-border continuity: Kiley gave the book he bought to learn the plants of the Pacific Northwest (*Trees and Shrubs for Pacific Northwest Gardens*, by J.A. and C.L. Grant) to Cornelia Hahn Oberlander when she moved to Vancouver. Communication from C.H. Oberlander, March 2011.

56 Gwen Sewell interview; District of Kitimat, *Kitimat Townsite Report*; Richardson, "A Tale of Two Cities," 114–20.

57 Developed by the Guinness Company, which built British Properties and the Lions Gate Bridge.

58 Goulding, "Landscape and Plantscape," 331–7.

59 Founded in 1936, the firm of McFadzean and Everley carried out a number of projects in Montreal, including a major restructuring of Westmount Park in the 1960s. They likely maintained a Montreal office during this period.

60 Conrath, *Inattendu/Unforeseen*. The CIBA buildings and site have recently been incorporated within a large condominium development; their original character has been well documented in Gary Conrath's photographic exhibition and accompanying publication of 2008.

61 P. Crawford, "Historical Perspectives: Savery and Blair," 20.

62 P. Jacobs, "Le rôle historique de F. Todd," 1–3; Rolland and Martineau, "The Symbolic Garden," 17–33.

63 H. Dunington-Grubb, "The Garden and the Park Today," 221–5.

64 Williams, "Louis Perron," 32–5.

65 Interview with Bert Johnstone, January 2007; and Louis Perron office documents.

66 Smoke from the wood-industry factories engulfed the whole river valley when the author first visited the capital in 1948.

67 D.L.A. Gordon, "From Noblesse Oblige to Nationalism," 3–34. See chapters 14 and 17.

68 Gréber, *Plan for the National Capital*; D.L.A. Gordon, "Weaving a Modern Plan," 43–61. Gréber's perspectives for the Ottawa report were drawn by Jules Guerin, the well-known artist who had illustrated Gréber's Philadelphia report and the Burnham-Bennett report for Chicago.

69 King willed his Kingsmere domain to the country; it is now a part of Gatineau Park.

70 D.L.A. Gordon, "From Noblesse Oblige to Nationalism," 22–6.

71 "Man of Vision," *Canadian Landscape Architect*, 15; Don Pettit, "Ned Wood and His Impact on the National Capital," in Paine, *Fifty Years of Landscape Architecture*, 72–3.

72 Pettit, "Ned Wood," 73–4; "Man of Vision," *Canadian Landscape Architect*, 15.

73 Graham also contributed to the design of the National Capital Region through two periods of employment with the NCC, in the early years of his career and later in the 1980s.

74 The Town Planning Institute of Canada (TPIC) had reconstituted itself in 1952, following a long hiatus during the Depression and wartime. It grew rapidly throughout the 1950s and founded its own magazine, *Plan Canada*, in 1959. See "History of CIP," http://www.cip-icu.ca.

75 Todd, letter to R.B. Bennett, Prime Minister of Canada, 1934.

76 Blue, "A Short History of the CSLA," 4–7.

77 "Landscape for Leisure," *Canadian Architect*.

CHAPTER TWENTY

1 This paradox was first called to my attention by my colleague Peter Jacobs. See Ron Williams, "Déclin et survie," 11–25; Marsan, *Montréal en evolution*, 356–9, 380–9.

2 Harcourt, Cameron, and Rossiter, *City Making in Paradise*, 51–3.

3 DeLeuw, Cather & Co., *City of Halifax*.

4 Discussions with Gérard Beaudet (2008) and with Blanche Lemco Van Ginkel (2009); Stéphane Baillargeon, "Sandy van Ginkel (1920–2009) – Le sauveur du Vieux-Montréal,"

Le Devoir (Montreal), 11 July 2009; Prochazka, "Entrevue avec Blanche Lemco van Ginkel," 6–11.

5 Greenberg, *Walking Home*, 68–9.

6 Domenico Annese, "Clarke, David Gilmore," in Birnbaum and Karson, eds., *Pioneers*, 56–60; Bradford M. Greene, "Rapuano, Michael," in Birnbaum and Karson, eds., *Pioneers*, 308–11. This office designed many major roads throughout North America, including the Garden State Parkway in New Jersey.

7 Ville de Québec, *Saint-Roch*, 4, 19–20.

8 Some examples: beginning in 1942, the greenhouses closed in Montreal's Westmount Park; a year later, the planting of annuals in flowerbeds was suspended for the duration of the war. The Canadian Army occupied several municipal sports fields as training grounds, and the number of monitors engaged in recreational programs declined in tandem with growing troop strength overseas. See City of Westmount, *Annual Reports*, 1939–1945.

9 Gold, *Urban Recreation Planning*; Soubrier, *Society and Leisure*, 8:1.

10 Gold, *Urban Recreation Planning*, 101–12; J. Jacobs, *Death and Life*, 113–40.

11 C. Macdonald, *Making a Place*, 71–2, 100–4, 123–5.

12 P. Jacobs, "Beyond Parks," 225–35.

13 Giedion, "City Hall and Centre," 49–54; Tyrwhitt, "The City Square," 55–65.

14 Fong, "Toronto," 42–56. Local architects were, respectively, John B. Parkin with Bregman and Hamann, and Page and Steele. Sewell, *Shape of the City*, 119–23, 144–7.

15 Zeidler, "Creating a Livable Winter City," 8–11.

16 Originally the Four Seasons Sheraton Hotel. Adell, "J. Austin Floyd," 26–9; R. Graham, "A Master Landscape Architect," 19–20.

17 Arcop is derived from "Architects in Co-partnership." The firm formally adopted the name Arcop in 1970.

18 This idea, originally proposed by Jacques Gréber in the late 1940s, was enthusiastically elaborated by PVM city planner Vincent Ponte. Marsan, *Montreal in Evolution*, 343–6; Vanlaetham, "A Long-Term Perspective," 12.

19 The PVM plaza welcomed such events as the introduction of Montreal's new baseball team, the Expos, in 1969; a giant political rally for Pierre Trudeau in 1968; and the near-annual Stanley Cup parades of the late 1960s and 1970s.

20 Both projects were revitalized in the 1980s and 1990s to respond to changing needs and wear-and-tear. Landscape architect Sandra Donaldson, with John MacLeod as consultant, designed a major rearrangement of the Place Ville-Marie plaza, while Arbour, Berthiaume and Beauregard carried out a subtle refit of the hotel garden at Place Bonaventure, maintaining the original character while changing much overgrown planting and carrying out a major revision of the swimming-pool area.

21 John Zvonar, "Garden of the Provinces," presentation at 2005 AHLP Meeting. The garden was renamed "Garden of the Provinces and Territories" in 2005.

22 This important urban transformation had also been suggested by Gréber. See Flanders, "Praise," 6.

23 Discussion with John Zvonar, Charlie Thomsen, and Ted McLachlan, June 2002.

24 C. Macdonald, *Making a Place*, 105–6; Thomsen, "Denis R. Wilkinson," 22; Keshavjee, *Winnipeg Modern*, 49.

25 C. Macdonald, *Making a Place*, 152–4.

26 Kalman, *History of Canadian Architecture*, 2:527–31.

27 C.H. Oberlander, "Oasis in the City," 6–15; "Robson Square."

28 Matsushita, "Harry James Webb."

29 Eaton, "Centennial Square, Victoria," 32–4.

30 This project received a Massey Medal for architecture in 1967, as did Trois-Rivières' Champlain Park in 1968. Eaton Centre and Robson Square received the Governor General's Award for architecture in subsequent years.

31 Affleck, Schoenauer, and de Silva, "Fathers of Confederation Memorial Buildings," 39–59.

32 Other design offices, including Project Planning Associates and du Toit Allsopp Hillier, participated in later stages of the work.

33 Rees, "Wascana Centre," 219–32; Riddell, *Origin and Development of Wascana Centre*; Wascana Centre Authority and du Toit Allsopp Hillier, *Wascana Centre Master Plan*, 10–18.

34 Serving food on the sidewalk was illegal in many Canadian cities until the 1960s. In fairness, cold weather and insects (not just social conservatism) might have had some influence on the lack of enthusiasm for sidewalk cafés.

35 J. Jacobs, *Death and Life*, 90.

36 Cooper and Francis, *People Places*.

37 C. Macdonald, *Making a Place*, 129.

38 Linda LeGeyt's *Changing the Face of Canada* (volumes 1 and 2), is the source for much of the information in this section.

39 Including that of the author.

40 E.J. (Jack) Walker, "Development of the Profession in Saskatchewan," in Paine, *Fifty Years of Landscape Architecture*, 59–61.

41 Justice, "John Wesley Neill," 1–3.

42 Chanasyk, "A Tribute," 15.

43 For which the Montreal Alouettes football team was named, at its founding in 1946, by RCAF veteran Lew Hayman. Ouellet was a bombardier; he had seen so much destruction during the war, he later related, that he resolved to spend the rest of his life building things (personal conversation, 1986).

44 Broadfoot, *The Veterans' Years*; Brokaw, *The Greatest Generation*.

45 LeGeyt, *Changing the Face of Canada*, 1:41–8, 85–102, 109–16; 2:15–22, 89–94, 113–22.

46 Ibid., 2:89–94; C. Macdonald, *Making a Place*, 90–5.

47 Daly, "Profile of Sigurd Hoff," 16–17.

48 Kehm, "The Evolution of Landscape Architecture."

49 C. Macdonald, *Making a Place*, 107–13.

50 Ibid., 117–20.

51 The island and peninsula site emerged victorious over many other contenders. Besides the site's obvious physical attractions and its centrality within the city, its status as a federal property made it, in a sense, neutral ground; its selection avoided conflicts among rival urban districts and Montreal real-estate interests. Interview with Andrew Hoffman, July–August 2012.

52 Marcoux, "L'effet des médiations," 27–8.

53 Bernstein and Cawker, *Contemporary Canadian Architecture*, 13–18.

54 It is unlikely that the Expo site, which had been an important bird habitat and nesting ground, would be acceptable today for a project requiring such complete transformation.

55 Fiset had been Jacques Gréber's lieutenant during the preparation of the National Capital Plan of 1950 (see chapter 19).

56 Interviews with Macklin Hancock, February 2001, and Andrew Hoffman, November 2001, July–August 2012, architect and city planner, construction coordinator of the La Ronde amusement area. "Expo 67," *Architecture Canada* 43, no. 7 (1966): 29–62; Prochazka, "Entrevue," 8–10.

57 Interviews with Andrew Hoffman, July–August 2012; Marcoux, "L'effet des médiations," 28–31.

58 Published in 1939, winner of the grand prize for fiction of the Académie française; translated into English as *Wind, Sand and Stars*.

59 Interview with Macklin Hancock, February 2001.

60 This landscape has accommodated many subsequent activities and installations – Olympic rowing basin, beach park, motor racing circuit – while maintaining the integrity of the original design.

61 Johnson, "Robert Gordon Calvert," 3; interview with Andrew Hoffman, July–August 2012.

62 The future director of the Montreal Botanical Garden and mayor of Montreal; see Bourque, *Ma passion pour Montréal*, 13–18.

63 Herrington, "Expo 67 Revisited," 12–14; C.H. Oberlander, *Playgrounds… a Plea for Utopia*.

64 Harper had learned about the profession from his neighbour Louis Perron.

65 Safdie's landmark project was included in the exhibition at the behest of Sandy van Ginkel and Colonel Churchill as a symbol of Expo's lofty goals. Interview with Andrew Hoffman, July 2012; Prochazka, "Entrevue," 10.

66 Ferrabee, "The Shape of Expo 67," 24–31.

67 *IFLA Yearbook 1968*; de Laplante and MacGillivray, *Parks of Montreal 1968–1969*, 16.

68 Interview with Phil Tattersfield, October 2000; Tattersfield, *BCSLA: A History*, 5–17.

69 Blue, *Short History of the CSLA*, 3. Dunington-Grubb had taught courses in landscape at the School of Architecture, University of Toronto, for twenty-five years. Discussions on this subject began even earlier – CSLA representatives met with professors at the University of Toronto's School of Architecture in November 1935. See Pollock-Elwand, "Gordon Culham: Living a 'Useful Life,'" 598–9.

70 The orientations and specialties of these two Ontario schools recall the double origins of the discipline – "land-grant" and "multiversity" – in US schools.

71 Originally situated within the university's architecture school, the program became an autonomous department, the École d'architecture de paysage, in 1978.

72 Later transferred to the Faculty of Agriculture and now a component of the School of Architecture and Landscape Architecture (SALA).

73 C. Macdonald, *Making a Place*, 70–2, 100–4, 123–5.

74 Nelson, "University of Manitoba Campus."

75 Routaboule, "L'Université de Moncton," 24–5.

76 *Architecture-Bâtiment-Construction* 21, no. 246 (October 1966): 30–48; Dubois, *Jean-Marie Roy*, 17–24, 71–85.

77 The Pavillon Louis-Jacques-Casault, designed by architect Ernest Cormier. All other buildings at this and the Cap Rouge campus were resolutely modern in design.

78 Kalman, *A History of Canadian Architecture*, 2:793–8.

79 This space was filled by an enormous crowd at the memorial service for Arthur Erickson after his death in 2009.

80 Cole, *Trent*, 12, 21–3, 69–89.

81 "Massey College, Toronto," 42–3.

CHAPTER TWENTY-ONE

1 American Society of Landscape Architects, http://www.asla.org/MissionStatement.aspx: "The Society's mission is to lead, to educate, and to participate in the careful stewardship, wise planning, and artful design of our cultural and natural environments." Barone, "Growing for Green in the 21st Century," 24–8.

2 Girard, *L'écologisme retrouvé*, 245–73; Armstrong, "Thomas Adams," 32–5.

3 Government of Canada, *Prairie Farm Rehabilitation Administration, Annual Reports 1935–1938*.

4 Anstey, *One Hundred Harvests*, 43–6, 122–6.

5 P. Jacobs, "George Angus Hills," 101–7.

6 Ibid.; Hills, "Landscape Planning," 267–83.

7 Hills, *Developing a Better Environment*, 41–51.

8 Such as Kormondy, *Concepts of Ecology*, 135–6.

9 A model known as the *boule-à-flèches* (ball of arrows). Vaillancourt, "Pierre Dansereau," 191–3.

10 The inventory system was developed under the auspices of both the Department of Regional and Economic Expansion (DREE), 1963–71, and Environment Canada, 1971–94. See historical outline at http://www.geogratis.cgdi.gc.ca/ITC/history.html.

11 McHarg, *Design with Nature*, 1–5.

12 C. Macdonald, *Making a Place*, 96–9.

13 Jacobs and Way, *Visual Analysis of Landscape Development*.

14 Hough did not consider himself a disciple of McHarg, although he recognized McHarg's central contribution to GIS. P. Bélanger, "On Planning," 27.

15 Hough, Stansbury & Associates, "Lakealert, Phase 2."

16 Taylor, Paine, and Fitzgibbon, "From Greenbelt to Greenways," 50–3.

17 Hilderman Feir Witty & Assoc., *Land Use Planning Study*.

18 Todd, Angevine, Solsearch Architects, and Cashman, *Ark for Prince Edward Island*; Mannell, *Atlantic Modern*, 60–3; Lahey, "Headway on the Ark," 36–8.

19 Harcourt, Cameron, and Rossiter, *City Making in Paradise*, 56–75.

20 Berger, *Northern Frontier, Northern Homeland*, vols. 1 and 2.

21 John Ralston Saul argues that this scenario is already a reality at the provincial scale. He suggests that virtually every province consists of a southern metropolitan core and a northern " resource hinterland"; the development of the resources of these hinterlands has historically been carried out for the benefit of those who live in the south, largely excluding those in the North from the benefits of development, although they suffer its inconveniences. Saul, *Reflections of a Siamese Twin*, 464–7.

22 Van Es and Thomas, *Mid-Canada Development Corridor*.

23 Sometimes referred to as "TEK"; increasingly seen as a key contributor to decision-making in northern and other environments. Freeman, "Nature and Utility."

24 Jacobs and Palluq, *People, Resources and the Environment*, 3–5, 26–8; P. Jacobs, "The Lancaster Sound Regional Study."

25 Jacobs and Chatagnier, *Environnement Kativik Environment*.

26 Chagny, "Native Women and Their Homes," 47–64.

27 Lessard and Jutras, *La qualité de l'environnement*, 15–42.

28 The current CBC television series *Arctic Air* faithfully conveys this sense of richness and cosmopolitan complexity.

29 City of Yellowknife Heritage Committee, *Old Town*.

30 City of Yellowknife Heritage Committee, *New Town*.

31 Peters, "Yellowknife – A Town without a Presence," 33–6; confirmed by the author, July 2007.

32 Presentation by Cornelia Hahn Oberlander, University of Montreal, December 2005.

33 Hough, *Cities and Natural Process*, 5–32.

34 Brundtland, *Our Common Future*.

35 http://www.mauricestrong.net/index.php/200806264/
Speeches/Speeches/stockhom.html.

36 Strong, *Where on Earth Are We Going?*

37 P. Jacobs, "Achieving Sustainable Development," 203–9.

38 Lincoln, *Toward New Horizons*, 103–4.

39 With such exceptions as Rachel Carson, Angus Hills, and
Pierre Dansereau.

40 Nerenberg, *Projet-pilote de toit vert.*

41 Manus and Rochon, *Picturing Landscape Architecture*,
108–9.

42 Middleton, "No Net Loss," 11–16.

43 Crombie, *Regeneration*, 11–61.

44 Task Force to Bring Back the Don, *Bringing Back the Don.*

45 Interview with Carolyn Woodland of Hough Woodland
Naylor Dance Leinster, October 2001; site visit with David
Leinster, 2001.

46 Armour and Statham, "City of Toronto Parks and
Recreation Naturalization Program," 14–17; site visit
with David Leinster. The firm continued in practice as
"ENVision – the Hough Group" and subsequently merged
with Dillon Consulting.

47 Kehm, "Wild in the City," 37–8; Carley, "The Leslie Street
Spit," 17–29.

48 Asselin and Williams, "Le Parc Plage, dix ans plus tard,"
24–7.

49 "Practice Profile: EDM," 7–10.

50 See chapter 24 for some recent developments.

CHAPTER TWENTY-TWO

1 Williams, "Post-modernism," 9–14. The term "postmodernism" is subject to widely varying definitions in different
domains, but all agree that what they are defining is
clearly not "modern" in form or philosophy. Robert Stern
has explored the evolving nature of this new movement, as
expressed in architecture, in his twenty-five-year chronicle
Architecture on the Edge of Postmodernism (see particularly
33–7, 107–15, 134–46).

2 Marsan, *Montréal en évolution*, 3rd edn., 384–429.

3 The 1985 design concept was later realized with some
modifications for the city of Montreal's 350th anniversary
celebrations in 1992, under the coordination of Robert
Desjardins of the Montreal Parks Service. Desjardins, "La
réincarnation d'un lieu public," 125–37.

4 CSLA Honour Awards 1986, "Trinity Square Park," 9;
Allsopp, "On Trying to Make a Silk Purse," 5–9.

5 The rediscovery of historic urban design elements was
an international phenomenon. Bodenschatz describes
how "the entire language of the pre-modern city layout
acquired a positive evaluation" in Berlin in the 1980s and
how new projects were carried out with minimum demolition of existing urban fabric through a new process of
"cautious urban renewal" (*Berlin Urban Design*, 70–84).

6 Including the celebration of the Montreal Alouettes' victory in the 2002 Grey Cup game to gain the Canadian football championship. The creation of a broad boulevard in
this location had been proposed in the 1930s (see chapter
17) and was again suggested by Jacques Gréber in the early
postwar years. See Marsan, *Montreal in Evolution*, 346.

7 National Capital Commission, "Confederation Boulevard";
National Capital Commission, *A Capital in the Making*,
38–41; du Toit Associates Ltd., *Ceremonial Routes.*

8 Like many twin cities, Ottawa and Hull had two distinct
personalities: one prosperous, polished, and official, the
other modest, workaday, and polluted. In his 1903 report,
Frederick Todd had urged the removal of Hull's smoky
factories from their site facing Parliament; this was finally
achieved in the last decades of the twentieth century.

9 Paine, "Sparks Street Mall," 6–8.

10 AHLP, "Roots 9," 6–11.

11 Paine, "Reflections on the Third Wave," 21–3.

12 The potential for this project would have been obliterated
if the downtown freeway proposal mentioned in chapter
20 had been built.

13 Annapolis Royal Historic Gardens Society, *Portrait of a
Garden*; Klynstra, "Annapolis Royal Historic Gardens," 5–6.

14 University of Alberta, "Twenty-one Years"; Hickman,
Kurimoto Japanese Garden, 8–21.

15 Forster, *Van Dusen Botanical Garden Guidebook.*

16 Ron Williams, "Floral World's Fair," 408–12.

17 Landscape architect Serge Chateil designed the French
garden, and R.C. Balfour designed that of Great Britain.

18 Reford, *The Reford Gardens: Elsie's Paradise*, 61–6.

19 Reford, *Reford Gardens*, 77; and Reford, *The Reford
Gardens: Elsie's Paradise*, 66–9.

20 Cabot, *The Greater Perfection*, 113–39; Des Gagniers, *Un
jardin extraordinaire*, 88–99.

21 Cabot, *The Greater Perfection*, 140–71; Des Gagniers, *Un
jardin extraordinaire*, 107–17.

22 Cabot, *The Greater Perfection*, 172–239; Des Gagniers, *Un
jardin extraordinaire*, 132–41, 162–79; visits to the garden
in 1987 and 1998 with Francis Cabot.

23 Visit to the garden with Cheryl Cooper, November 2000;
N.B. Simpson, "One Garden," 38–41; McPhedran, "A
Clearing in the Forest," 114–19.

24 Oehmichen, "Ornamental Grasses," 19–22.

25 For a general history of this form of garden art, see Elliott,
"Mosaiculture," 76–98.

26 MacLeod and O'Neill, "Le Vieux Port de Québec," 6–8;
Ron Williams, "Recycling the Expo Islands," 65–9.

27 Bakker, Ball, and Hotson, "Granville Island 'Streetworks,'"
19–22; Bernstein and Cawker, *Contemporary Canadian
Architecture*, 73–6.

28 Messervy, *The Toronto Music Garden.*

29 In fact, as early as 1974 the province of Manitoba and
the federal government had initiated a development

program for the historic waterways of southern Manitoba, engaging landscape architects Hilderman, Feir, Witty and Associates to carry out a study of the heritage and natural resources of the two rivers. Negotiations were formalized in the Canada-Manitoba Agreement for Recreation and Conservation (ARC) in 1978. See Dickson, "The Canada-Manitoba ARC Agreement," 7–10.

30 C. Macdonald, *Making a Place*, 166–8; Cohlmeyer, "Meeting Place in Winnipeg," 5–8; Cohlmeyer, Paterson, and Scatliff, "Le secteur riverain de Winnipeg," 11–17; Emmond, "The Forks," 38–42.

31 CSLA Awards of Excellence 2007, "The Forks Sculpture-Skate Park," 18–19.

32 Such as the "North Portage" site further north along the west bank of the Red River.

33 Dawe and Versteeg, "Grand Concourse Walkway Network," 14–16.

34 G. Carson, "Calgary Rivers," 29.

35 Taylor, Paine, and Fitzgibbon, "From Greenbelt to Greenways," 47–64; D.L. Erickson, "The Relationship of Historic City Form," 199–221.

36 Ville de Montréal, *Plan préliminaire de mise en valeur du mont Royal*.

37 CSLA Professional Awards Program, "Hastings Park Restoration Plan," 16.

38 Fleming, "Fantasyland," 5–8; Mowbray, "Grand Mall," 63–72.

39 These two projects were designed by successive incarnations of the same firm, Toronto landscape architects Strong Moorhead Fleming Corban and Moorhead Fleming Corban and McCarthy. OALA Professional Awards 1981, 5.

40 Designed by City of Montreal landscape architects in collaboration with landscape architects WAA, architects TPL Associates, and special consultant Bob Hartwig from Jacksonville, FL.

41 Girling, "Landscape as Stage Set," 14–19; Eglite, "Planning for the Unpredictable," 6–10.

42 M.J. McKay, "UFO-H2O," 20–1.

43 Taylor, "Calgary Olympic Winter Games," 4; Balls, "Nakiska Ski Area at Mount Allan," 5–7.

44 Architects were Peter Haley and Arcop Thom Associates.

45 G. Carson, "The Canmore Nordic Centre," 8–11.

46 Mooney, "Landscape of Broken Stones," 54–6.

47 Andrighetti, "Village of Yorkville Park," 20–1.

48 Phyllis Lambert, "Design Imperatives," and Melvin Charney, "A Garden for the Canadian Centre for Architecture," in Richards, ed., *Canadian Centre for Architecture*, 64–7, 87–102. The architect of the CCA building was Peter Rose.

49 Architects were Saucier + Perrotte and Menkès Shooner Dagenais of Montreal.

50 CSLA Professional Awards 1998, "Place de la FAO," 13.

51 OALA Professional Awards 1980, 9.

52 ASLA Awards, "Ryerson Community Park," 382–3.

53 Manus and Rochon, *Picturing Landscape Architecture*, 46–51.

54 Sackville, "Ecotourism in Bouctouche," 14–17; Mannell, *Atlantic Modern*, 40–1, 44–6.

55 Bernstein and Cawker, *Contemporary Canadian Architecture*, 145–9. The pond, an essential component of Oberlander's design, was not realized with the original project, but was finally carried out in 2011–12.

56 Crosby, "Wanuskewin Heritage Park," 12–14; Scott, "Tipperary Creek Conservation Area," 5–9.

57 Hilderman Thomas Frank Cram, "Oodena Celebration Circle," http://www.htfc.mb.ca/projects/oodena/html.

CHAPTER TWENTY-THREE

1 R.S., 1985, c. 24 (4th Supp.), C-18.7: *An Act for the preservation and enhancement of multiculturalism in Canada*, assented to 21 July 1988, section 3.

2 Carter et al., "L'immigration et la diversité," i–ii.

3 Only forty-eight years ago, the University of Toronto sociologist John Porter defined Canadian society as consisting of two "charter members" – the British and the French communities, equal in some areas but not in all – who dominated other communities; see Porter, *The Vertical Mosaic*, 60–1. Underlining the central role of the First Nations and Métis peoples in the creation and survival of Canada, John Ralston Saul speaks of "three founding nations" in his *Reflections of a Siamese Twin*.

4 Hayden, *The Power of Place*, 15–18, 46–7.

5 Anctil, *Saint-Laurent*.

6 Ibid., 16–63.

7 Hajjar, "Pratiques vernaculaires," 38–44. Hajjar notes that none of these neighbourhoods was a homogeneous unicultural "ghetto"; for example, the area of highest concentration of people of Portuguese background in the Portuguese district reached only 37.4 per cent of the overall population.

8 Ibid., 80–2.

9 Ibid., 107–8.

10 Ibid., 111–16.

11 Ibid., 118.

12 The second and third generations of the Portuguese community were also clearly less ready to identify with the symbolism and character of the park than the first generation. Hajjar, "Pratiques vernaculaires," 119–21.

13 Anctil, *Saint-Laurent*, 101.

14 Despite its impressive dimensions and splendid décor, it is a parish church; in most other places, it would be a cathedral.

15 Annick Germain, Mabel Contin, Laurent Liégeois, and Martha Radice, "À propos du patrimoine urbaine des communautés culturelles: Nouveaux regards sur l'espace

public," in Jébrak and Julien, eds., *Les temps de l'espace public urbain*, 126–9.

16 Ibid., 129.

17 Also named, like the small Montreal plaza noted above, for the first president of the Chinese Republic. Dr. Sun had lived in Vancouver on three occasions, including a 1911 mission to raise support for the Chinese Revolution, which occurred later that year. See Harcourt, Cameron, and Rossiter, *City Making in Paradise*, 43.

18 Keswick, *The Chinese Garden*, 223–6, 117–20.

19 Joe Wai, "The Development of the Dr. Sun Yat-Sen Classical Chinese Garden," in Keswick, Oberlander, and Wai, *In a Chinese Garden*, 47–57.

20 Suzhou is in climate zone Cfa, Vancouver in Cfb (Koppen system), comparable "warm temperate" zones.

21 Judy Oberlander, "A Walk through the Garden," in Keswick, Oberlander, and Wai, *In a Chinese Garden*, 25–9.

22 Conversation with Ken Nakajima, fall 1987; Nakajima, "The Japanese Garden," 16–18.

23 Desranleau and Jacobs, "From Conception to Reception," 200–16.

24 Tellier, *The Chinese Garden of Montreal*, 2–16.

25 Ibid., 7–12; Bourque, "Un Empire, un Jardin," 23–5.

26 Asselin, "Suivez le Guide!," 4–7.

27 Hoffman, "Aux sources du Jardin des Premières Nations," 8.

28 Manzo Nagano, a carpenter from Yokohama, who landed at New Westminster. K. Adachi, *The Enemy That Never Was*, 9–10; Takata, *Nikkei Legacy*, 74–5.

29 Takata, *Nikkei Legacy*, 59–62.

30 Ibid., 92–102.

31 Ibid., 48–52.

32 Ibid., 44–6; P. Adachi, *Asahi: A Legend in Baseball*.

33 K. Adachi, *The Enemy That Never Was*, 199–249.

34 Ibid., 251–75; Suzuki, *Metamorphosis*, 56–78; Suzuki, *The Autobiography*, 14–23.

35 K. Gordon, *The Slocan*, 178–99; interpretation panels at Nikkei Internment Memorial Centre, New Denver, BC. Also see the children's book *Baseball Saved Us* by Ken Mochizuki.

36 For a discussion of the role of landscapes in reconciliation, see Rev. Canon Albert J. Ogle, "Returning to Places of Wounded Memory: The Role of World Heritage Sites in Reconciliation," in Turgeon, ed., *Spirit of Place*, 261–73.

37 K. Adachi, *The Enemy That Never Was*, 218; Takata, *Nikkei Legacy*, 118–26. Stables were also used as assembly centres in Los Angeles and elsewhere in the United States.

38 John F. Howes and George Oshiro, "Who Was Nitobe?," in Howes, ed., *Nitobe Inazô*, 3–23.

39 Richard Eldridge Copley, "Darkened Lanterns in a Distant Garden," in Howes, ed., *Nitobe Inazô*, 279–83; Neill, "Nitobe Memorial Garden," 10–15.

40 Masuno, *Ten Landscapes*, 62–73.

41 There had been a Japanese community in the farmlands of southern Alberta since the early 1900s. See K. Adachi, *The Enemy That Never Was*, 280–3.

42 Kubo later designed the Kurimoto Japanese Garden in Edmonton; see chapter 22.

43 Van Luven, *Nikka Yuko Centennial Garden*, 15–32.

44 Plants include Colorado spruce, several juniper varieties, Mugho pines, Dolgo and Thunderchild crabapples, lilacs, Russian olive, willows, red pine, Amur maple, red- and yellow-twig dogwood – relatively conventional plants, but expertly pruned, shaped, and juxtaposed. Discussions with guide Brenda Haring and gardener Al White, June 2002.

45 P.E. Roy, "A Tale of Two Cities," 23–47.

46 As explained by Ruby Truly of the Kyowakai Society, New Denver, BC, June 2005.

47 *Vancouver Sun*, 3 November 2000, B7.

48 Chanasyk, "A Tribute," 15.

49 *Nikkei Voice*, July/August 2004, 1, 14; June 2006, 10; Watada, "The J-Town Disappearing Blues."

50 Osborne, *Sleeping Tigers*.

51 For a discussion of "contested landscapes," see Irit Amit-Cohen, "Contested Landscape and Spirit of Place: The Case of the Olive Trees and an Urban Neighborhood in Israel," in Turgeon, ed., *Spirit of Place*, 275–88.

52 Interview with Jeff Cutler, 2 May 2012. See space2place, *(Re)imagining a Social Space*; Kumagai, Iwanaka, and Hanazawa, "Spirit of the Issei Celebrated." One of the park activities is a weekly distribution of food to needy residents by a coalition of charitable organizations, one of many such programs in downtown Vancouver.

53 *Nikkei Voice*, March 2006, 7; December 2003/January 2004, 1, 13; Gill, "Keeping House."

54 http://www.kogawahouse.com; Gill, "Keeping House."

CHAPTER TWENTY-FOUR

1 Paine, "The Third Wave," 21–3.

2 It is, unfortunately, beyond the scope of this book to describe work carried out by Canadian landscape architects outside the country, even though many of these projects are outstanding and make a major contribution to landscapes beyond our borders, as demonstrated, for example, by the prestigious Magnolia Silver Award received by Montreal landscape architect Vincent Asselin in 2001 from the city of Shanghai. In general, the book concentrates on work done in Canada, with the exception of war memorial sites, which may be considered as overseas extensions of Canada.

3 These include Douglas Carlyle of Alberta; Jane Durante, Cornelia Hahn Oberlander, Philip Tattersfield, and Don

Vaughan of British Columbia; and Michael Hough, Brad Johnson, Janet Rosenberg, and Richard A. Strong of Ontario.

4 Reford, *Reford Gardens*, 76–7; Beringer, *Garden Rooms*, 9–13.

5 Beringer, *Garden Rooms*, 40–5, 22–7.

6 Cormier, "Blue Stick Garden," 15–18; Beringer, *Garden Rooms*, 52–7.

7 Poullaouec-Gonidec, "Le projet d'architecture de paysage de Claude Cormier," 16–17.

8 Richer, "La personnalité de la semaine."

9 Cha, "Claude 'Capability' Cormier," 8–13; Meijerink, "Hyper-Nature," 26–8; Valois, "'Faire jardin' par l'installation," 38–40; Herrington, "Claude's Glass," 41–3.

10 Sheppard, "Quebec Pastorale," 49–53.

11 Including administrator Pierre Boucher (who would later become the first chairperson of the Commission de la Capitale nationale du Québec), city planner Serge Filion, and council member Winnie Frohn.

12 The government of Quebec established the CCNQ in 1995 to guide and oversee the environmental quality of the provincial capital, to undertake specific projects to enhance its symbolic and historic sites, and to interpret the capital to the public.

13 Greenberg, *Walking Home*, 263–4.

14 Calta, "Quebec City."

15 In collaboration with the Ministère des Transports du Québec.

16 Collard, "Investissements de 28 M\$"; Ville de Québec, *Québec s'embellit*, 23–5.

17 CSLA Awards of Excellence 2009, "Promenade Samuel-de-Champlain," 14–15.

18 Herzog, "A Legacy of Vision."

19 Communication and interview with Robert Gibbs, Edmonton, 2007.

20 Situated on the old "Hudson Bay Flats," adjacent to the legislative assembly.

21 River Valley Alliance, *A Plan of Action*.

22 City of Edmonton, *Natural Connections Strategic Plan 2007*.

23 Waterfront Toronto, *Report to the Community 2010*, 16.

24 Many of the designs and designers for these projects were selected by competition.

25 CSLA Awards of Excellence 2007. "Innovative Design Competition," 28–9.

26 CSLA Awards of Excellence 2009, "Spadina Wavedeck," 26.

27 The American equivalent is the "Adirondack" chair, also made from lightweight one-inch softwood boards.

28 Cooke, "Open to Negotiation," 37–8; Waldheim, "The Landscape Architect as Camoufleur," 36–7.

29 See http://www.waterfrontoronto.ca/explore_projects2/east_bayfront/canadas_sugar_beach. The overall design of this sector, coordinated by Urban Strategies Inc., was

carried out by Koetter Kim and Associates and Phillips Farevaag Smallenberg, among other firms.

30 http://www.waterfrontoronto.ca/lower_don_lands/lower_don_lands_design_competition.

31 Corner, Kennedy, and Schollen, "Big Nature Park," 13–16.

32 Berelowitz, *Dream City*, 217–20.

33 E. Macdonald, "The Efficacy of Long-Range Physical Planning," 175–213.

34 Girling and Kellett, *Skinny Streets*, 18–21, 57–116; Girling and Kellett, "Green Neighbourhoods at the Edge," 31–4.

35 Condon, *Sustainable Urban Landscapes*; Condon, *Design Charrettes*.

36 Published by Island Press, Washington, DC, 2012.

37 Girling and Kellett, *Skinny Streets*, 118–34.

38 The resources equation has been only temporarily modified by the financial crisis that began in 2008. As the world economy recovers, Canadian resources will once more be under tremendous pressure.

39 Desjardins and Monderie, *L'Erreur boréale/Forest Alert*.

40 Burtynsky, *Manufactured Landscapes*.

41 Denys, *Description and Natural History*.

42 Huck, *Exploring the Fur Trade Routes*, 173; Syncrude Canada, *Syncrude Fact Book*, 9; Regional Municipality of Wood Buffalo, *Fort McMurray Visitors Guide 2007*, 66.

43 Wynn, "The Maritimes," 190–2.

44 Combined with major investments by federal and provincial governments. J.J. Fitzgerald, *Black Gold with Grit*, 159–95.

45 Fondation des communications sur le pétrole, *Les sables pétrolifères*, 6–17; Suncor Energy, *Suncor In-situ*.

46 Wylie, *Coal Culture*, 95–142; Government of Canada, *The History of Coal Mining in Cape Breton*, http://www.collections.ic.gc.ca/coal/history.

47 Including the reconstruction of the Fortress of Louisbourg, the Cape Breton Highlands National Park, the Alexander Graham Bell Museum at Baddeck on Bras d'Or Lake, and the promotion of Acadian handicrafts, all of which provided a great boost to the tourist industry.

48 Sierra Club of Canada, "Sydney Tar Ponds Backgrounder"; Government of Canada, Commissioner of the Environment and Sustainable Development, "Case Study 2.1—The Sydney Tar Ponds." http://www.oag-bvg.gc.ca/.../att_c20021002se01_f_12325.

49 For example, starting salaries at A&W Root Beer in Fort McMurray were \$15.00 per hour in the summer of 2007.

50 These depend on the efficacy of the decontamination process and the resistance to leakage of the decantation basins.

51 S. Macmillan, *Peace-Athabasca Delta Technical Studies*, 5–6, 21–37; Marsden, *Stupid to the Last Drop*, 172–9.

52 Author's impressions, July 2007.

53 It does not appear that the companies involved in oil sands exploitation seek to create new long-term

communities as did those of the period 1899 to 1960, at Shawinigan, Kapuskasing, Kitimat, etc. (see chapters 13, 17, and 19).

54 G. Wright, "Alberta's Booming Oil Sands."

55 Severson-Baker, Grant, and Dyer, *Taking the Wheel*.

56 Government of Alberta, *Responsible Actions*; Suncor Energy, *Over 30 Years*.

57 Syncrude, *Syncrude Fact Book*, 60–2.

58 Referring to the sixtieth parallel of latitude, which is the southern boundary of Yukon, Nunavut, and the Northwest Territories.

59 Saul, *Reflections of a Siamese Twin*, 69, 102–6; Saul, *A Fair Country*, 287–8.

60 Ibid., 104, 115.

61 Peter White, "Out of the Woods," in O'Brian and White, *Beyond Wilderness*, 11–20; McKay, *Picturing the Land*, 227, 242, 277–8.

62 Glickman, *Picturesque and Sublime*, ix.

63 Crnkovich, "Iqaluit Square Project."

64 CSLA Awards of Excellence 2007, "Sylvia Grinnell Park."

65 Average temperature increase in the Arctic is about 2.5 times that for the Earth as a whole. See Caldeira, "The Great Climate Experiment," 83.

66 The territorial government of Nunavut is extremely conscious of the implications of these processes, and has put in place an ambitious plan of research and action in response. See Government of Nunavut, *Nunavut Climate Change Strategy*.

67 Braun, "Pipe Dreams," 18–23.

68 Memorialized as "calm parasols" in Saint-Denys Garneau's 1937 poem "Les Ormes."

69 Domon and Ruiz, *Paysage et multifonctionnnalité*, 15–28.

70 Interview with John MacLeod, June 2010; Laura Rance, "Shelterbelts' Removal Ominous," *Winnipeg Free Press*, 21 November 2009. It should be noted that a significant percentage of corporate farms are managed by family corporations. But these follow the same tendency towards fewer, larger farms.

71 Pawlick, *The War in the Country*. The cooperative movement, another traditional mainstay of the agricultural system in the West, is also in decline, although some larger, well-capitalized communal farms appear to be holding their own. The British historian Niall Ferguson considers the rate of rural property ownership in Canada (which he situates at 87 per cent in 1900) and the United States to have been decisive factors in these countries' economic and political success. See Ferguson, *Civilization*, 125.

72 As estimated by the curé of a parish in the Mauricie region of Quebec, 2001. A chilling scene in Denys Arcand's Oscar-winning film *Les Invasions barbares* (2003) provides a vivid representation of the decline of the Catholic Church in Quebec since the 1960s.

73 American professor Francis Fukuyama has predicted "an increasing homogenization of all human societies, regardless of their historical origins or cultural inheritances" (*The End of History*, xiv).

74 Such as sidewalk cafés (chapter 20) and the environs of industrial canals (chapter 22).

75 City of Edmonton, *Natural Connections Strategic Plan 2007*.

76 Bank of Canada website: http://www.bankofcanada.ca/en/banknotes/general/character/2001–2004.html.

EPILOGUE

1 Clerk, *Framework and Criteria*, 2, 8–10. These criteria had already been outlined as early as 1971, at a Historic Garden Symposium in Fontainebleau, France (see Stewart and Buggey, "The Case for Commemoration," 101–9).

2 Governments have often provided support to such non-profit groups through subsidies and/or tax credits.

3 J. Wright, *Architecture of the Picturesque*, 89–92.

4 Parks Canada, *Bellevue House*.

5 Ibid.

6 Douglas H. Pope, a member of the PEI House of Assembly and editor of the newspaper *The Islander*.

7 Watson, *Ardgowan*, 12, 110–12.

8 Ibid., 111–16.

9 Charlton, *Reader Rock Garden*, CD-ROM; Novak et al., *Reader Rock Garden Management Plan*, 18–24.

10 Government of Canada, *Standards and Guidelines*. The team that planned and carried out the restoration and rehabilitation of Calgary's Reader Rock Garden followed the precepts and methods suggested in this document, and reported on their experience. See M. Reid, "Applying the *Standards and Guidelines*."

11 See Gouvernement du Québec, *Un regard neuf*.

12 As seen in the highly successful series of recent television commercials encouraging tourism in Newfoundland and Labrador, featuring many of the landscapes described in this book.

13 Wassersug, *The Ecology of Point Pleasant Park*; Bigelow and Koblents, "Seeing the Forest, Not the Trees," 18–21; Kheraj, "Restoring Nature," 577–612.

BIBLIOGRAPHY

ABBREVIATIONS

ARQ: Architecture-Quebec	ARQ
British Columbia Society of Landscape Architects	BCSLA
Canada Mortgage and Housing Corporation	CMHC
Canadian Society of Landscape Architects	CSLA
Historic Sites and Monuments Board of Canada	HSMBC
International Council on Monuments and Sites	ICOMOS
International Federation of Landscape Architects	IFLA
Journal of Garden History	JGH
Journal of the Royal Architectural Institute of Canada	JRAIC
Landscape Architectural Review	LAR
Landscape Architecture Canada	LAC
Ontario Association of Landscape Architects	OALA
Society for the Study of Architecture in Canada	SSAC
Studies in the History of Gardens &	SHGDL
Designed Landscapes	
Urban History Review	UHR

Abma, Geoff, and Robert Gibbs. *Frederick G. Todd: Visionary of Valley Park System*. Edmonton: Capital Region River Valley Park 2006

Adachi, Ken. *The Enemy That Never Was: A History of the Japanese Canadians*. Toronto: McClelland & Stewart 1976

Adachi, Pat. *Asahi: A Legend in Baseball*. Etobicoke, ON: Coronex Printing and Publishing 1992

Adams, Annmarie. "Eden Smith and the Canadian Domestic Revival." *UHR* 21, no. 2 (1993): 104–15

Adams, John. *Historic Guide to Ross Bay Cemetery, Victoria, BC, Canada*. 2nd edn. Vancouver: Sono Nis Press 1998 (orig. 1983)

Adams, Thomas. "The British Point of View." In *Proceedings of the Third National Conference on City Planning*, 22–37. Boston: National Conference on City Planning 1911

– *Report of the Commission of Conservation 1919*. Ottawa: Commission of Conservation 1919

– *Rural Planning and Development in Canada*. Ottawa: Commission of Conservation 1917

Adams, Thomas. "Philanthropic Landmarks: The Toronto Trail from a Comparative Perspective, 1870s to the 1930s." *UHR* 30, no. 1 (2001): 3–21

Adamson, Anthony, Alice Alison, Eric Arthur, and William Goulding. *Historic Architecture of Canada*. Ottawa: RAIC 1967

Addison, Ottelyn. *Early Days in Algonquin Park*. Toronto: McGraw-Hill Ryerson 1974

Adell, Jacqueline. "J. Austin Floyd: A Humanistic Landscape Architect." *LAR* 5, no. 2 (1984): 26–9

Affleck, Ray, Norbert Schoenauer, and Walter P. de Silva. "Fathers of Confederation Memorial Buildings, Charlottetown, PEI." *Canadian Architect* 9, no. 11 (1964): 39–59

AHLP (Alliance for Historic Landscape Preservation). *Borderlands: The Shared Canadian and U.S. Experience of Landscape: Proceedings of the 1999 Annual Meeting*. Waterloo, ON: Heritage Resources Centre, University of Waterloo 2002

– *Landscapes of Peace and Commemoration*. Winnipeg: Papers from the Alliance Annual Gathering 2002

– "Roots 9." *LAC* 5, no. 2 (1979): 6–11

Allard, Jean-Pierre, ed. *Documents du Club WOCOP inc. 1948–1973*. Vols. 1, 2, and 3. Parc de la Mauricie, QC, n.d.

Allison, Paul. "Finding Kishida." TV film in the Recreating Eden series. Winnipeg: Merit Motion Pictures 2008

Allsopp, Robert. "On Trying to Make a Silk Purse from a Sow's Ear: Trinity Square Park, Toronto." *LAR* 8, no. 5 (1987): 5–9

Ames, Herbert Brown. *The City below the Hill: A Sociological Study of a Portion of the City of Montreal, Canada*. Montreal: Bishop Printing & Engraving 1897

Anctil, Pierre. *Saint-Laurent: Montreal's Main*. Sillery, QC: Septentrion 2002

Anderson, Dorothy May. *Women, Design, and the Cambridge School*. West Lafayette, IN: PDA Publishers Corporation 1980

– "Women's Breakthrough Via the Cambridge School." *Landscape Architecture* 68 (March 1978): 145–8

Andrighetti, Rick. "Facing the Land: Landscape Design in Canada." *Canadian Architect* 39, no. 8 (1994): 13–19

– "Village of Yorkville Park, Toronto." *Canadian Architect* 39, no. 8 (1994): 20–1

Annapolis Royal Historic Gardens Society. *Portrait of a Garden*: Halifax: The Book Room 1999

Anstey, T.H. *One Hundred Harvests: Research Branch, Agriculture Canada, 1886–1986.* Historical series, no. 27. Ottawa: Supply and Services Canada 1986

Architects in Association and Joseph Daly. *Victoria Park Conceptual Master Plan.* City of Regina 1987

Armour, Garth, and Kim Statham. "City of Toronto Parks and Recreation Naturalization Program." *Landscapes/Paysages* 2, no. 3 (2000): 14–17

Armstrong, Bruce, and John Davis. *Sanctuary: Halifax's Parks & Public Gardens.* Halifax: Nimbus Publishing 1996

Arthur, Eric. *From Front Street to Queen's Park.* Toronto: McClelland & Stewart 1979

– *Toronto, No Mean City.* Toronto: University of Toronto Press 1974

Artibise, Alan. *Winnipeg: An Illustrated History.* Toronto: James Lorimer & Co. and National Museums of Canada 1977

Artibise, Alan F.J., and Gilbert A. Stelter, eds. *The Usable Urban Past: Planning and Politics in the Modern Canadian City.* Toronto: Macmillan 1979

Asano, Jiro. "Kannosuke Mori: The Pioneer of International Cultural Exchange in the Japanese Landscape." *Journal of the Japanese Institute of Landscape Architects* 59, no. 4 (1996): 243–6

ASLA Awards. "Ryerson Community Park." *Landscape Architecture* 69, no. 4 (1979): 382–3

Asselin, Vincent. "Frederick G. Todd, Architecte paysagiste: Une pratique de l'aménagement ancrée dans son époque 1900–1948." Master's thesis, Faculté de l'aménagement, Université de Montréal, May 1995

– "Le Jardin des Premières Nations." *Continuité*, no. 92 (2002): 19–21

– "Suivez le Guide!" *Quatre-Temps* 25, no. 3 (2001): 4–7

Asselin, Vincent, and Ron Williams. "Le Parc Plage, dix ans plus tard: Une cure récréative et environnementale." *Landscapes/Paysages* 2, no. 1 (2000): 24–7

Atwood, Margaret. *Survival: A Thematic Guide to Canadian Literature.* Toronto: Anansi 1972

Aubert de Gaspé, Philippe. *Canadians of Old: An Historical Romance.* Translated by Charles G.D. Roberts. Toronto: Hart 1891 (orig. *Les Anciens Canadiens.* Quebec City: Desbarats & Derbishire 1863)

Audet, Louis Philippe. *Le Frère Marie-Victorin.* Quebec City: Éditions de l'Érable 1942

Awalt, Don. *Camp Hill Cemetery: Recommendations for a General Management Plan.* Halifax: Nova Scotia College of Art and Design 2001

Bacon, Edmund. *Design of Cities.* Rev. edn. New York: Viking Press 1974 (orig. 1967)

Badé, William Frederic. *The Life and Letters of John Muir.* Boston: Houghton Mifflin 1924

Bain, David. "George Allan and the Horticultural Gardens." *Ontario History* 87, no. 3 (1995): 231–52

– "William Mundie and Landscape Gardening in Canada West in the 1850s." *LAR* 7, no. 2 (1986): 19–21

– "William Mundie, Landscape Gardener." *JGH* 5, no. 3 (1985): 298–308

Bain, David, and Mike Leonard. "The Landscape of Dundurn Castle." *JGH* 3, no. 3 (1983): 208–18

Bain Apartments Co-operative Inc. *Bain Apartments Co-operative Inc. Summary Report Rehabilitation Project 1988–1994.* Toronto: CMHC 1994

Baird, George, and Larry Richards. "Halifax: Ten Buildings to See." *Trace* 1, no. 1 (1981): 16–24

Baker, Victoria. *Emanuel Hahn and Elizabeth Wyn Wood: Tradition and Innovation in Canadian Sculpture.* Ottawa: National Gallery of Canada 1997

Baldwin, Alice Sharples. *Metis, Wee Scotland of the Gaspé.* Métis, QC, 1960

Balls, Garth. "Nakiska Ski Area at Mount Allan: Master Planning a Mountain." *LAR* 9, no. 1 (1988): 5–7

Baraness, Marc, and Larry Richards. *Toronto Places: A Context for Urban Design.* Toronto: University of Toronto Press 1992

Barbeau, Marius. *Totem Poles.* 2 vols. Ottawa: National Museum of Canada 1950

Barman, Jean. "Family Life at Fort Langley." *BC Historical News* 32, no. 4 (1999): 16–23

Barnhart, Gordon L. *Building for the Future: A Photo Journal of Saskatchewan's Legislative Building.* Regina: Canadian Plains Research Centre, University of Regina 2002

Barnsley, Roland, and John H. Pierce. *The Public Gardens and Parks of Niagara.* St. Catharines, ON: Vanwell Publishing 1989

Barone, Sandra. "Growing for Green in the 21st Century." *Landscapes/Paysages* 9, no. 2 (2007): 24–6

Barraclough, Morris. *From Prairie to Park: Green Spaces in Calgary.* Calgary: Century Calgary Publications 1975

Barrett, Anthony A., and Rhodri Windsor-Liscombe. *Francis Rattenbury and British Columbia: Architecture and Challenge in the Imperial Age.* Vancouver: University of British Columbia Press 1983

Barrett, Clarence. *Cape Breton Highlands National Park: A Park Lover's Companion.* Wreck Cove, NS: Breton Books 2002

Bartholomew, Harland. *A Plan for the City of Vancouver, British Columbia: Including a General Plan for the Region.* Vancouver: Town Planning Commission 1928

Baskerville, Peter A. *Ontario: Image, Identity and Power.* Toronto: Oxford University Press 2002

Bassnett, Sarah. "Visuality and the Emergence of City Planning in Early Twentieth- Century Toronto and Montreal." *Architecture in/au Canada* 32, no. 1 (2007): 21–38

Basterfield, Brian. "The Otonabee River Trail Project." *Landscapes/Paysages* 4, no. 2 (2002): 14–16

Beard, Geoffrey, and J. Wardman. *Thomas H. Mawson: The Life and Work of a Northern Landscape Architect, 1861–1933.* Lancaster, UK: Visual Arts Centre, University of Lancaster 1978

Beatty, Stephanie, and Susan Gale Hall. *Parkwood.* Erin, ON: Boston Mills Press 1999

Beauchemin-Beaton-Lapointe. *Master Plan, Forillon National Park.* Montreal 1970

Beaulieu, Alain. *Les Autochtones du Québec.* Quebec City: Musée de la civilisation and Éditions Fides 2000

Beck, Julia, William Moffet, and Katherine Smith, eds. *Conserving Ontario's Landscapes: 6th Annual Conference of the Architectural Conservancy of Ontario Inc.* Toronto: Architectural Conservancy of Ontario 1998

Beechwood Cemetery. *Great Canadian Profiles.* Ottawa: Beechwood Cemetery 2001

Bégin, Benoît. "Les jardins de Métis et les Quatre Vents." *Continuité*, special issue no. 1 (1990): 42–6

– "Québec et Montréal: Évolution de l'architecture de paysage." *Continuité*, special issue no. 1 (1990): 9–26

Behr, Sylvia. *Victoria Park, Inventory and Condition Report: Historic and Contemporary.* London, ON: University of Western Ontario 1995

Bélanger, Martin. "Le parc Victoria: Un siècle d'histoire." Student project, Faculté des lettres, Université Laval 1999

Bélanger, Pierre. "On Planning, Preservation, Pedagogy and Public Works: Pierre Bélanger speaks with Michael Hough." *Landscapes/Paysages* 11, no. 4 (2009): 26–8

Bellman, David. "Frederick Law Olmsted and a Plan for Mount Royal Park." *Mount Royal, Montreal.* Montreal: McCord Museum, McGill University/Canadian Art Review, no. 1 (December 1977): S31–S38

Berelowitz, Lance. *Dream City: Vancouver and the Global Imagination.* Vancouver: Douglas & McIntyre 2005

Berger, Thomas R. *Northern Frontier, Northern Homeland: The Report of the Mackenzie Valley Pipeline Inquiry.* Vols. 1 and 2. Ottawa: Minister of Supply and Services Canada 1977

Bergeron, Yves. *Les places et halles de marché au Québec.* Quebec City: Gouvernement du Québec, Ministère des Affaires culturelles 1993

Beringer, Hubert. *Garden Rooms: International Garden Festival/Reford Gardens.* First edition, Summer 2000. Montreal: Jardins de Métis/Musée d'art contemporain de Montréal 2001

Bernier, Lionel. *La bataille de Forillon.* Montreal: Éditions Fides 2001

Bernier, Serge, Jacques Castonguay, André Charbonneau, Yvon Desloges, and Larry Ostola. *Military History of Quebec City, 1608–2008.* Montreal: Les Éditions Art Global 2008

Bernstein, William, and Ruth Cawker. *Contemporary Canadian Architecture: The Mainstream and Beyond.* Markham, ON: Fitzhenry & Whiteside 1988

Berryman, Tom. *Le Mont Royal … au fil des saisons.* Montreal: Centre de la montagne 1997

Berton, Pierre. *The National Dream: The Great Railway, 1871–1881.* Toronto: McClelland & Stewart 1970

Best, John C. *Thomas Baker McQuesten: Public Works, Politics and Imagination.* Hamilton, ON: Corinth Press 1992

Beveridge, Charles E. *Mount Royal in the Works of Frederick Law Olmsted.* Montreal: City of Montreal and Government of Quebec 2011

Beveridge, Charles E., and Carolyn F. Hoffman. *The Master List of Design Projects of the Olmsted Firm, 1857–1950.* Boston: National Association for Olmsted Parks and Massachusetts Association for Olmsted Parks 1987

Beveridge, Charles E., and Paul Rocheleau. *Frederick Law Olmsted: Designing the American Landscape.* New York: Rizzoli 1995

Biagi, Susan. *Louisbourg.* Halifax: Formac Publishing 1997

Bigelow, Peter, and Hanita Koblents. "Seeing the Forest, Not the Trees: Facing Reality in a Post-hurricane Park." *Landscapes/Paysages* 9, no. 4 (2007): 18–21

Bilash, O.S.E., and O.F.G. Sitwell. "Words into Buildings: The University of Alberta, 1906–28." *SSAC Bulletin* 20, no. 1 (1995): 4–20

Bingham, Janet. *More Than a House: The Story of Roedde House and Barclay Heritage Square.* Vancouver: Roedde House Preservation Society 1996

– *Samuel Maclure Architect.* Ganges, BC: Horsdal & Schubart Publishers 1985

Bird, J. Brian. "Settlement Patterns in Maritime Canada, 1687–1786." *Geographical Review* 45, no. 3 (1955): 385–404

Birmingham, W.H. "Residential Work." *RAICJ* 27, no. 9 (1950): 305

Birnbaum, Charles A., and Stephanie S. Foell, eds. *Shaping the American Landscape: New Profiles from the Pioneers of American Landscape Design Project.* Charlottesville: University of Virginia Press 2009

Birnbaum, Charles A., and Robin Karson, eds. *Pioneers of American Landscape Design.* New York: McGraw-Hill 2000

Bisson, Pierre-Richard, Mario Brodeur, and Daniel Drouin. *Cimetière Notre-Dame-des-Neiges.* Montreal: Beaux livres Henri Rivard 2004

Blanchet, Danielle. "Le Parc des Champs de Bataille Nationaux à Québec: Une Histoire Semée d'Embûches." *LAR* 8, no. 1 (1987): 21–6

Bland, John. *Sainte-Anne-de-Bellevue, Heritage Town: An Architect's Perspective.* Sainte-Anne-de-Bellevue, QC: Shoreline Press 2000

Bloomfield, Elizabeth. "'Ubiquitous Town Planning Missionary': The Careers of Horace Seymour, 1882–1940." *Environments* 17, no. 2 (1985): 29–42

Blue, Frances. "A Short History of the Canadian Society of Landscape Architects." Unpublished manuscript. Toronto 1970

Boddy, Trevor. "Regionalism, Nationalism and Modernism: The Ideology of Decoration in the Work of John M. Lyle." *Trace* 1, no. 1 (1981): 8–15

Bodenschatz, Harald. *Berlin Urban Design: A Brief History of a European City.* Berlin: DOM Publishers 2010

Bodson, Gabriel, and Louis-Alain Ferron. "Les Deux Grands Cimetières du Mont Royal." *Continuité*, no. 49 (1991): 19–22

Boissonnault, Charles-Marie, and Lieut.-Col. L. Lamontagne. *Histoire du Royal 22e Régiment.* Quebec City: Éditions du Pélican 1964

Boisvert, André. "Entrevue tenue le 29 septembre 1996 avec Benoît Bégin, urbaniste et architecte paysagiste." *Urbanité* 2, no. 1 (2003): 11–14

Bormke, Diane, ed. *See Saint John.* Saint John, NB, 2001

Bouchard, André, and Francine Hoffman. *Le Jardin botanique de Montréal: Esquisse d'une histoire.* Montreal: Éditions Fides 1998

Boudreau, Daniel, and Anselme Chiasson. *Chansons d'Acadie.* 2nd edn. Moncton, NB: Pères capucins 1979

Bourdages, Jean-Luc, André Bouchard, and Marie-Odile Trépanier. *Les parcs naturels du Canada et du Québec: Politiques, lois et règlements.* Montreal: Université de Montréal 1984

Bourque, Pierre. "Un empire, un jardin." *Quatre-Temps* 15, no. 2 (1991): 23–5

– *Ma passion pour Montréal.* Montreal: Éditions du Méridien 2002

Boyd, Denny. "A Man Who Makes Beauty." *Vancouver Sun*, c. 20 June 1980

Braun, Will. "Pipe Dreams." *United Church Observer* 74, no. 7 (2011): 18–23

Brémault, Lise. *Bienvenue à Saint-Boniface, Manitoba.* St. Boniface: La Société historique de Saint-Boniface and Musée de St-Boniface 1991

Brennan, J. William. *Regina: An Illustrated History.* Toronto: James Lorimer & Co. and Canadian Museum of Civilization 1989

Brennan, Patrick H. "'Thousands of our men are getting practically nothing to do': Public Works Relief Programmes in Regina and Saskatoon, 1929–1940." *UHR* 21, no. 1 (1992): 33–45

Brett, Franklin. "Developing a British Columbian Estate." *American Architect* 109, no. 2099 (1916): 161–6

Brisson, Jacques. "Au coeur de Montréal: L'univers végétal des Autochtones." *Quatre Temps* 25, no. 3 (2001): 9–11

Broadfoot, Barry. *The Veterans' Years: Coming Home from the War.* Vancouver: Douglas & McIntyre 1985

Brokaw, Tom. *The Greatest Generation.* New York: Random House 1998

Bronson, Susan. "Binning Residence, West Vancouver." *SSAC Bulletin* 27, nos. 3 and 4 (2002): 51–64

Brouwers, Tanya. *Canada's Disappearing Farmland.* http://www.organicagcentre.ca/NewspaperArticles/na_disappearing_farmland_tb.asp

Brown, David R. "The University of Saskatchewan, Saskatoon." *RAICJ* 1, no. 4 (1924): 109–17

Brown, Jane. *Eminent Gardeners: Some People of Influence and Their Gardens.* London, UK: Viking 1990

– *The Modern Garden.* Princeton, NJ: Princeton Architectural Press 2000

Brown, Robert D. *Design with Microclimate: The Secret to Comfortable Outdoor Space.* Washington, DC: Island Press 2012

Brown, Ron. *Toronto's Lost Villages.* Toronto: Polar Bear Press 1997

Brumley, John H. *Medicine Wheels on the Northern Plains: A Summary and Appraisal.* Manuscript series, no. 12. Edmonton: Government of Alberta, Culture and Multiculturalism Historical Resources Division, Archaeological Survey of Alberta 1988

Brundtland, Gro Harlem. *Our Common Future: Report of the World Commission on Environment and Development.* Oxford and New York: Oxford University Press 1987

Brunger, Alan G. "Early Settlement in Contrasting Areas of Peterborough County, Ontario." In J.D. Wood, *Perspectives on Landscape,* 117–40

Buck, Frank E. *Planning the Home Lot.* Exhibition Circular No. 9. Ottawa: Agriculture Department, Horticulture Division, June 1915

Buczynski, Michael, and Anne Marceau. *Le Grand Voyage des Continents: La géologie du Parc national du Gros-Morne.* Translated by Michel Tremblay. Ottawa: Ministry of Supply and Services 1990

Buggey, Susan. *An Approach to Aboriginal Cultural Landscapes.* Ottawa: HSMBC 1999

– "Conservation of Landscapes of Historic and Cultural Value: The Emergence of a Movement." *Environments* 26, no. 3 (1999): 17–27

– "Period Gardens in Canada: A Researcher's Resources." Parks Canada Research Bulletin, no. 87 (1978): 1–15

Bumsted, J.M. *The University of Manitoba: An Illustrated History.* Winnipeg: University of Manitoba Press 2001

Bunting, Trudi, and Pierre Filion, eds. *Canadian Cities in Transition.* Toronto/New York/Oxford: Oxford University Press 1991

Burnett, David. *Alex Colville.* Toronto: Art Gallery of Ontario 1983

Burtynsky, Ed. *Manufactured Landscapes.* Film produced by Jennifer Baichwal. 2006

Butts, Edward, and Karl Stensson. *Sheridan Nurseries: One Hundred Years of People, Plans and Plants.* Toronto: Dundurn Press 2012

Cabot, Francis H. "The Element of Surprise, Les Quatre Vents." *Canadian Heritage* 15, no. 4 (1990): 25–30

– *The Greater Perfection: The Story of the Gardens at Les Quatres Vents.* New York and London: Hortus Press and W.W. Norton & Co. 2001

– "Les Quatres Vents: Dans la nature généreuse de Charlevoix, le plus grand jardin privé au Canada." *Continuité,* no. 36 (1987): 30–3

Caldeira, Ken. "The Great Climate Experiment." *Scientific American* 307, no. 3 (2012): 78–83

Caldwell, Wayne. "The Evolving Nature of Agricultural Production." *Plan Canada* 49, no. 4 (2009): 43–7

Calta, Marialisa. "Quebec City: The Redemption of St. Roch." *New York Times,* 26 February 2006

Calvert, R.G. "Plants and Planting for Indoor Gardens." *RAICJ* 37 (1954): 231–4

Cameron, Christina. *Charles Baillairgé: Architect & Engineer.* Montreal & Kingston: McGill-Queen's University Press 1989

– *Index of Houses Featured in Canadian Homes and Gardens from 1925 to 1944.* Ottawa: Parks Canada/Environment Canada 1980

Campbell, Claire Elizabeth, ed. *A Century of Parks Canada, 1911–2011.* Calgary: University of Calgary Press 2011

Campeau, Frère Lucien. *The Beginning of Acadia 1602–1616.* Bridgetown, NS: Gontran Trottier 1999

Canadian Encyclopedia, The. 3 vols. Edmonton: Hurtig Publishers 1985

Cannings, Richard, and Sydney Cannings. *British Columbia: A Natural History.* Vancouver: Greystone Books 1996

Caponigro, Eleanor Morris. *Canadian Centre for Architecture: The First Five Years, 1979–1984.* Montreal: Canadian Centre for Architecture 1988

Carley, Victoria Lister. "The Leslie Street Spit: Let It Be." *LAR* (Convention issue) 6, no. 3 (1985): 17–29

Carson, Garry. "Calgary Rivers – Evolving Perceptions, Changing Public Perceptions Have Made Calgary a More Beautiful and Liveable City." *Landscapes/Paysages* 6, no. 1 (2004): 29

– "The Canmore Nordic Centre: Planning, Design, and Construction." *LAR* 9, no. 1 (1988): 8–11

Carson, Rachel. *Silent Spring.* New York: Crest Books 1962

Carter, Tom, Marc Vachon, John Biles, Erin Tolley, and Jim Zamprelli. "L'immigration et la diversité dans les villes canadiennes – un sujet d'actualité." *Canadian Journal of Urban Research* 15, no. 2 (2006 Supplement), i–x

Cartier, Jacques. *The Voyages of Jacques Cartier.* Introduction by Ramsay Cook. Toronto: University of Toronto Press 1993 (orig. 1545–1600, translated by H.P. Biggar, 1924)

Carver, Humphrey. "Book Review – Gardens in the Modern Landscape." *RAICJ* 16, no. 7 (1939): 172

– *Cities in the Suburbs.* Toronto: University of Toronto Press 1962

– *Compassionate Landscape, Places and People in a Man's Life.* Toronto: University of Toronto Press 1975

Casanova, Jacques-Donat. *Une Amérique française.* Paris/Quebec City: La Documentation Française/l'Éditeur Officiel du Québec 1975

Casid, Jill H. *Sowing Empire: Landscape and Colonization.* Minneapolis: University of Minnesota Press 2005

Casson, A.J., Bernard Cinader, Paul Duval, Dorothy Eber, and Howard Roloff. *A Heritage of Canadian Art: The McMichael Collection.* Toronto and Vancouver: Clarke, Irwin and Company 1979

Castle, Geoffrey, ed. *Hatley Park: An Illustrated Anthology.* Colwood, BC: Friends of Hatley Park Society 1995

Cauchon, Noël. "Town Planning." *RAICJ* 3 (1926): 165–71

Cavett, Mary Ellen, H. John Selwood, and John C. Lehr. "Social Philosophy and the Early Development of Winnipeg's Public Parks." *UHR* 11, no. 1 (1982): 27–39

Central Okanagan Heritage Society. *Guisachan Heritage Park & Benvoulin Heritage Park.* Brochure. Kelowna, BC, c. 2004

Cha, Jonathan. "Claude 'Capability' Cormier." *ARQ,* no. 139 (2007): 8–13

– "Formes et sens des squares victoriens montréalais dans le contexte de développement de la métropole (1801–1914)." Montreal: PhD diss., Université du Québec à Montréal 2012

Chabot, Melanie, and Marc Lescarbeau. *Les Haidas, sculpteurs de cèdres.* Montreal: École d'architecture de paysage, Université de Montréal 2002

Chadwick, George F. *The Park and the Town: Public Landscape in the 19th and 20th Centuries.* London: Architectural Press 1966

Chagny, Maiti. "Native Women and Their Homes: Gender, Housing and Identity, Case Study: Chisasibi, Northern Quebec." Master's thesis, McGill University School of Architecture 1998

Chalmers, Floyd S. *A Gentleman of the Press*. Toronto and New York: Doubleday 1969

Chanasyk, Victor. "A Tribute: George Tanaka." *LAR* 3, no. 3 (1982): 15

Charbonneau, André, Yvon Desloges, and Marc Lafrance. *Québec, ville fortifiée du XVIIe au XIXe siècle*. Quebec City: Éditions du Pélican and Parks Canada 1982

Charlton, Anne. *Reader Rock Garden: Re-rooting to the Future*. CD-ROM. Calgary: City of Calgary 2006

Charney, Melvin. "A Garden for the Canadian Centre for Architecture." In Richards, *Canadian Centre for Architecture: Building and Gardens*, 87–102

Charrett, Doug. *Planners and Planning: The Saskatchewan Experience 1917 to 2005*. Saskatoon: Association of Professional Community Planners of Saskatchewan 2005

Chicoine, Émilia, C.N.D. *La métairie de Marguerite Bourgeoys à la Pointe Saint-Charles*. Montreal: Éditions Fides 1986

Chittenden, Hiram Martin. *The Yellowstone National Park*. Norman: University of Oklahoma Press 1964 (orig. Columbus, OH, 1895)

Chittenden, Newton H. *Official Report of the Exploration of the Queen Charlotte Islands*. Victoria: Government of British Columbia 1884

Choay, François. *L'urbanisme, utopies et réalités, une anthologie*. Paris: Éditions du Seuil 1965

Choko, Marc H. *Une Cité-jardin à Montréal: La Cité-jardin du tricentenaire, 1940–1947*. Montreal: Éditions du Méridien 1989

– *Les grandes places publiques de Montréal*. Montreal: Éditions du Méridien 1987

Christie, Norman M. *For King and Empire*. Vol. 10: *The Newfoundlanders in the Great War: The Western Front, 1916–1918*. Ottawa: CEF Books 2003

Church, Thomas Dolliver. "Transition." *RAICJ* 7, no. 8 (1950): 252

Churchill, Winston. *The World Crisis*. New York/Toronto: Scribners/Macmillan 1923

Cinq-Mars, Irène, Peter Jacobs, and Philippe Poullaouec-Gonidec. "Une profession en mutation." *Continuité*, special issue no. 1 (1990): 74–6

City Improvement League of Montreal. "For a Better Montreal." In *The Second Annual Report for the Year Ending April 30, 1911*. Montreal: City Improvement League 1911

City of Edmonton. *Natural Connections Strategic Plan 2007: City of Edmonton Integrated Natural Areas Conservation Plan*. Edmonton: City of Edmonton, Office of Natural Areas 2007

City of Hamilton. *Hamilton's Heritage*. Vol. 5: *Reasons for Designation under Part IV of the Ontario Heritage Act*. Hamilton, ON: Planning and Development Department 2005

City of Toronto, Department of Arts, Heritage and Culture. *Virtual Collection – John Howard*. http://www.toronto.ca/culture/howard

City of Westmount. *Annual Reports*, 1899, 1902, 1910–19, 1939–58

City of Winnipeg, Department of Parks and Recreation. *Assiniboine Park: History and Development*. Winnipeg 1972

City of Yellowknife Heritage Committee. *New Town: Heritage Walking Tour of Yellowknife*. Yellowknife, NT, 2006

– *Old Town: Heritage Walking Tour of Yellowknife*. Yellowknife, NT, 2005

City Planning Conference. *Proceedings of the Sixth National Conference on City Planning, Toronto, May 25–27, 1914*. Cambridge, MA: University Press 1914

Clark, Douglas. "Memorial Drive – The Landscape of Memory." *Landscapes/Paysages* 8, no. 3 (2006): 14–15

Clark, Jayne. "Anne of Green Gables Still Rules Prince Edward Island." http:// www.islandspiritpei.com/newsandblogs

Clerk, Nathalie. *Framework and Criteria for the Evaluation of Historic Parks and Gardens*. Ottawa. HSMBC Agenda Paper 1994-51

– *Le cimetière Mont-Royal, Outremont et le cimetière Notre-Dame-des-Neiges, Montréal*. HSMBC Agenda Paper 1998-38A

– *Harling Point Cemetery, Oak Bay*. HSMBC Agenda Paper, 1995-18

– *Maison Henry-Stuart, Québec*. HSMBC Agenda Paper 1999-37

– *Mount Pleasant Cemetery, Toronto*. HSMBC Agenda Paper 2000-03

Cleveland, Horace W.S. *Landscape Architecture According to the Wants of the West; with an Essay on Forest Planting on the Great Plains*. Chicago: Jansen, McClurg & Co. 1873

Cloutier, Myriam. *Mount Royal Cemetery since 1852*. Montreal: Mount Royal Cemetery 2002

Cohlmeyer, Stephen. "Meeting Place in Winnipeg, Manitoba: Urban Design and Renewal at the Forks." *LAR* 13, no. 2 (May 1992): 5–8

Cohlmeyer, Stephen, Douglas Paterson, and Michael Scatliff, "Le secteur riverain de Winnipeg." *Landscapes/Paysages* 6, no 1 (2004): 11–17

Cole, A.O.C. *Trent: The Making of a University, 1957–1987*. Peterborough, ON: Trent University Communications Department 1992

Cole, Jean Murray, ed. *This Blessed Wilderness: Archibald McDonald's Fort Langley Letters from the Columbia, 1822–44*. Vancouver: University of British Columbia Press 2001

Coley, G. E. Altree. "A Bit of Nippon on Our Pacific Coast; Clovelly: Sea-laved Garden of Sir Frank Barnard." *Canadian Homes and Gardens* 3, no. 3 (1926): 29–31, 56

– "The Terraced Gardens of Hycroft." *Canadian Homes and Gardens* 4, no. 9 (1927): 31–3

Collard, Marcel. "Investissements de 28 M$ prévus sur trois ans." *Journal Constructo*, 9 April 1999, 3

Collier, Richard, Alanna Morbin, and Colin Jennings. *Invasive Species Management Plan, Uplands Park, Oak Bay, BC*. Victoria: Department of Environmental Studies, University of Victoria 2005

Collins, Janet. "Don Vaughan, Natural Inspiration." *Award* 11, no. 3 (1997): 14–16

Commission of Conservation. *Civic Improvement League for Canada: Report of Preliminary Conference Held under the Auspices of the Commission of Conservation at Ottawa, November 19, 1915*. Ottawa 1916

Condon, Patrick M. *Design Charrettes for Sustainable Communities*. Vancouver: University of British Columbia 2008

– *Sustainable Urban Landscapes: The Surrey Design Charrette*. Vancouver: University of British Columbia 1996

Condon, Patrick, and Jacqueline Teed. *Sustainability by Design: A Vision for a Region of 4 Million*. Vancouver: UBC Design Centre for Sustainability 2007

Conrad, Margaret R., and James K. Hiller. *Atlantic Canada: A Region in the Making*. Toronto: Oxford University Press 2001

Conrath, Gary Michael. *Inattendu/Unforeseen: Considering the Continuum between Architecture and Nature*. Montreal: Indesign Inc. and Musée populaire de la photographie 2008

Conway, Hazel. *People's Parks: The Design and Development of Victorian Parks in Britain*. Cambridge, UK: Cambridge University Press 1991

– *Public Parks*. Princes Risborough, Bucks, UK: Shire Publications 1996

– "The Royal Horticultural Society Bandstand Mystery." *Garden History* 29, no. 2 (2001): 214–16

Cook, Capt. James, and Capt. James King. *A Voyage to the Pacific Ocean, Undertaken by Command of his Majesty.* 4 vols. Dublin: Lords Commissioners of the Admiralty 1784

Cooke, Sandra. "Open to Negotiation." *Landscapes/Paysages* 9, no. 4 (2007): 37–40 (37–8)

Cooper Marcus, Clare, and Carolyn Francis. *People Places: Design Guidelines for Urban Open Space.* New York: John Wiley & Sons 1998

Corbet, Elizabeth A., and Lorne G. Simpson. *Calgary's Mount Royal: A Garden Suburb.* Calgary: City of Calgary, Planning and Building Department and Heritage Advisory Board, September 1994 (reprinted May 2006)

Corboz, André. "La dimension utopique de la grille territoriale américaine." *Architecture in/au Canada* 28, nos. 3 and 4 (2003): 63–8

Cormier, Claude. "Blue Stick Garden, Métis-sur-Mer (Québec)." *Landscapes/Paysages* 3, no. 2 (2001): 15–18

Cormier, Lise. "Schéma régional d'aménagement récréo-touristique de plein air: Critères de performance et critères de sélection des sites naturels." Master's thesis, Faculté de l'aménagement, Université de Montréal 1984

Cormier, Yves. *Les Aboiteaux en Acadie: Hier et aujourd'hui.* Moncton, NB: Chaire d'études acadiennes 1990

Corner, James, Richard Kennedy, and Mark Schollen. "Big Nature Park." *Landscapes/Paysages* 11, no. 4 (2009): 13–16

Cornut, Jacques-Philippe. *Canadensum plantarum, aliarumque nondum editarum historia.* Paris: Simonem Le Moyne 1635

Côté, Renée. *Place-Royale, quatre siècles d'histoire.* Quebec City: Musée de la civilisation and Éditions Fides 2000

Coutts, Sally. "Easeful Death in Toronto: A History of Mount Pleasant Cemetery." *SSAC Bulletin* 11, no. 3 (1986): 8–10

– *Stanley Park, Vancouver, British Columbia.* HSMBC Agenda Paper 1988-37

Cox, Bruce. "John Muir and His Canadian Friends." http://www.johnmuir.org/canada/cox_essay

Cox, E.C.S. "Fitting the House to Its Site." *RAICJ* 27, no. 12 (1950): 402

Craig-Dupont, Olivier. "Hunting, Timber Harvesting, and Precambrian Beauties: The Scientific Reinterpretation of La Mauricie National Park's Landscape History, 1969–1975." In Campbell, *A Century of Parks Canada*, 179–204

Crawford, Bess Hillier. *Rosedale.* Erin, ON: Boston Mills Press 2000

Crawford, Pleasance. "Charles Ernest Woolverton (1879–1934), Ontario Landscape Architect." *LAR* 3, no. 2 (1982): 17–20

– "The Forgotten Landscape Architectural Firm of Harries, Hall and Kruse of Toronto and Buffalo." *Environments* 26, no. 3 (1999): 29–35

– "Frances Verene McLeod Blue, FCSLA, 1914–1992." *CSLA/AAPC Bulletin* 7, no. 3 (1992): 4

– "H.A. Engelhardt (1830–1897): Landscape Designer." *LAR* 5, no. 2 (1984): 30–8

– "H.A. Engelhardt Followup." *LAR* 7, no. 1 (1986): 20–1

– "Historical Perspectives: Bellevue House Garden; RBG Display of 19th Century Vegetables; The Grange Gardens, Toronto." *LAR* 5, no. 1 (1984): 15

– "Historical Perspectives: Notes on Charles Maxson, Max Stolpe and Other Contemporaries of C.E. Woolverton." *LAR* 3, no. 3 (1982): 9–10

– "Historical Perspectives: Notes on Old Nursery Catalogues and Vegetable Varieties; H.A. Engelhardt (1830–1897)." *LAR* 4, no. 2 (1983): 13

– "Historical Perspectives: Robert Savery; John Blair." *LAR* 4, no. 4 (1983): 20–1

– "Of Grounds Tastefully Laid Out: The Landscaping of Public Buildings in 19th Century Ontario." *SSAC Bulletin* 11, no. 3 (1986): 4–7

– "Park and Cemetery Landscape Design in Canada, One Hundred and Fifty Years Ago – The Life and Times of H.A. Engelhardt (1830–1897)." *Green Space* 8, no 12 (1986): 4–10; and 9, no. 1 (1987): 7–9

– "The Roots of the Toronto Horticultural Society." *Ontario History* 89, no. 2 (1997): 125–39

– "Some Early Ontario Nurserymen." *Canadian Horticultural History* 1, no. 1 (1985): 28–64

Crawford, Pleasance, and Sue Donaldson. *The Canadian Landscape and Garden History Directory.* Calgary: Faculty of Environmental Design, University of Calgary 1984

Crawford, Pleasance, and Stephen A. Otto. "André Parmentier's 'Two or Three Places in Upper Canada.'" Unpublished manuscript of a presentation at the CSLA/AAPQ annual congress, Faculté de l'aménagement, Université de Montréal, Montreal, 1998

Critical Wildlife Habitat program. *Manitoba's Mixed-Grass Prairie.* Brochure. Winnipeg, c. 2002

Crnkovich, Mary. "Iqaluit Square Project." Presentation to Dry Stone Walling Association of Canada, Port Hope, ON, October 2007

Crombie, David. *Regeneration: Toronto's Waterfront and the Sustainable City.* Report of the Royal Commission on the Future of the Toronto Waterfront. Toronto: Minister of Supply and Services, Queen's Printer 1992

Crosby, Bob. "Wanuskewin Heritage Park, Saskatchewan: Six Thousand Years of Prairie Culture." *LAR* 13, no. 1 (March 1992): 12–14

Cruickshank, Tom, and John de Visser. *Old Toronto Houses.* Richmond Hill, ON: Firefly Books 2003

CSLA. *Members List 1940–50.* Provided by Peter Jacobs

CSLA Awards of Excellence 2007. "The Forks Sculpture-Skate Park." *Landscapes/Paysages* 9, no. 3 (2007): 18–19

– "Innovative Design Competition – Toronto Central Waterfront." *Landscapes/Paysages* 9, no. 3 (2007): 28–9

– "Sylvia Grinnell Park." *Landscapes/Paysages* 9, no. 3 (2007): 46

CSLA Awards of Excellence 2009. "Promenade Samuel-de-Champlain, Quebec City." *Landscapes/Paysages* 11, no. 3 (2009): 14–15

– "Spadina Wavedeck." *Landscapes/Paysages* 11, no. 3 (2009): 26

CSLA Honour Awards 1986. "Trinity Square Park, Toronto, Ontario." *LAR* 8, no. 4 (1987): 9

CSLA Professional Awards Program. "Hastings Park Restoration Plan." *Landscapes/Paysages* 1, no. 1 (1999): 16

CSLA Professional Awards Program 1998. "Place de la FAO." *LAR* (1999): 13

Culham, Gordon. "The French Style." *Canadian Homes and Gardens* 7, no. 4 (1930): 27–9, 58, 60

– "We Make a Plan for the Estate." *Canadian Homes and Gardens* 7, no. 5 (1930): 28–9, 56, 58

Cullen, Mary K. "The Late Nineteenth Century Development of the Queen Square Gardens, Charlottetown, Prince Edward Island." *APT Bulletin* 9, no. 3 (1977): 1–20

Cumming, Joan. "Charlottetown, Canada's Birthplace." *Plan Canada* 40, no. 3 (2000): 24

Curl, James Stevens. *A Celebration of Death: An Introduction to Some of the Buildings, Monuments and Settings of Funerary Architecture in the Western European Tradition.* London, UK: Constable 1988

– "The Design of the Early British Cemeteries." *JGH* 4, no. 3 (1984): 223–54

– "John Claudius Loudon and the Garden Cemetery Movement." *Garden History* 11, no. 2 (1983): 133–55

Cuthbertson, Brian. *Lunenburg: An Illustrated History*. Halifax: Formac Publishing 1996

Cutler, Phoebe. *The Public Landscape of the New Deal*. New Haven, CT: Yale University Press 1985

Dabbs, Frank. "Hope for the Heartland." *United Church Observer* 73, no. 7 (2010): 22–6

D'Acres, Lilia, and Donald Luxton. *Lions Gate*. Burnaby, BC: Talonbooks 1999

Dale, Bill. "John Blair." In Birnbaum and Karson, *Pioneers*, 27–30

Dalrymple, Anne, and Cathy Van Dusen. "Coal Harbour Plan: Vancouver BC 1912 by Thomas Mawson." Class paper, Landscape Architecture 220, University of British Columbia, March 1985

Daly, Joseph. "Profile of Sigurd Hoff." *LAR* 5, no. 1 (1984): 16–17

Dandavino, Rita Rachele. "Notre-Dame-des-Neiges." *Continuité*, no. 49 (1991): 13–16

Dansereau, Pierre. *Biogeography: An Ecological Perspective*. New York: Ronald Press 1957

– "Brother Marie-Victorin, F.S.C., 1885–1944." Notice of death in *American Midland Naturalist* 33, no. 2 (March 1945): ii–viii

Davis, Derek S. *Natural History Map of Nova Scotia*. Halifax: Nova Scotia Museum 1987

Dawe, Neil, and Edward Versteeg. "Grand Concourse Walkway Network, St. John's, Newfoundland." *Landscapes/Paysages* 5, no. 1 (2003): 14–16

Dean, William R., Conrad E. Heidenreich, Thomas F. McIlwraith, and John Warkentin. *Concise Historical Atlas of Canada*. Toronto: University of Toronto Press 1998

Deffontaines, Pierre. *Le rang, type de peuplement rural du Canada français*. Quebec City: Presses Université de Laval 1953

De Galaup de Lapérouse. *The Journal of Jean-François de Galaup de la Pérouse, 1785–1788*. Vol. 1. Edited and translated by John Dunmore. London: Hakluyt Society 1994

– *Voyage autour du Monde sur l'Astrolabe et la Boussole (1785–1788)*. Paris: La Découverte 1987

DeGrace, William. "Canada's Capital 1900–1950: Five Town Planning Visions." *Environments* 17, no. 2 (1982): 43–57

Delainey, William P., and William A.S. Sarjeant. *Saskatoon: The Growth of a City. Part I: The Formative Years (1882–1960)*. Saskatoon: Saskatoon Environmental Society 1975 (orig. 1974)

Delaney, Jill. "The Garden Suburb of Lindenlea, Ottawa: A Model Project for the First Federal Housing Policy, 1918–24." *UHR* 19, no. 3 (1991): 151–65

Delaney, Paul J., and Andrew D. Nicholls. *After the Fire: Sainte-Marie among the Hurons since 1649*. Elmvale, ON: East Georgian Bay Historical Foundation 1989

De Laplante, Jean. *Les parcs de Montréal des origines à nos jours*. Montreal: Éditions du Méridien 1990

– *Les parcs de Montréal 1968–1969*. English adaptation by Leo MacGillivray. *The Parks of Montreal 1968–1969*. Montreal: City of Montreal 1969

DeLeuw, Cather & Co. of Canada. *City of Halifax – A Functional Planning Report for Harbour Drive*. Halifax: City of Halifax 1965

Demchinsky, Bryan, ed. *Grassroots, Greystones and Glass Towers*. Montreal: Véhicule Press 1989

Dendy, David R.B. "One Huge Orchard." Essay for the BA program, University of Victoria, 1976

Dendy, William. *Lost Toronto*. Toronto/Oxford/New York: Oxford University Press 1978

Denys, Nicholas. *Description and Natural History of the Coasts of North America*. Paris 1672

Déry, Rocray & associés. *Étude sur l'état de santé actuelle du Bois de Coulonge, des causes de sa dégradation et des mesures de conservation et d'amélioration*. Quebec City: Gouvernement du Québec, Ministère de l'Environnement, Direction des réserves écologiques et sites naturels 1980

Deschênes, Gaétan. *L'abbé Leon Provencher, sa contribution scientifique*. HSMBC Agenda Paper 1994-23

– *Histoire de l'horticulture au Québec*. Saint-Laurent, QC: Éditions du Trécarré 1996

Des Gagniers, Jean. *Un jardin extraordinaire: Quatre-Vents, en Charlevoix, Québec*. Cold Spring, NY: Hortus Press 2002

Desjardins, Richard, and Robert Monderie. *L'Erreur boréale/Forest Alert*. Film. National Film Board of Canada/ACPAV Inc. 1999

Desjardins, Robert. "Le réincarnation d'un lieu public: Le nouveau Champ de Mars de Montréal." In *Symposium international*, 125–37

Desloges, Yvon, and Alain Gelly. *The Lachine Canal: Riding the Waves of Industrial and Urban Development 1860–1950*. Translated by Donald Kellough. Sillery, QC: Septentrion 2002

Desranleau, Josée, and Peter Jacobs. "From Conception to Reception: Transforming the Japanese Garden in the Montreal Botanical Garden." *SHGDL* 29, no. 3 (2009): 200–16

Dick, Lyle. *Farmers "Making Good": The Development of Abernethy District, Saskatchewan, 1880–1920*. Ottawa: Minister of Supply and Services Canada, Environment Canada 1989

– "Forgotten Roots: The Gardens of Wasagaming." *NuWest Review* 12, no. 3 (1986): 10–11

– "The Greening of the West: Horticulture on the Canadian Prairies, 1870–1930." *Manitoba History*, no. 31 (1996): 12–17

– *A History of Prairie Settlement Patterns*. Ottawa: HSMBC, Environment Canada 1987

Dickson, I.W. "The Canada-Manitoba ARC Agreement: A Beginning." *LAR* 4, no. 5 (1983): 7–10

Dirschl, H.J. *The Lancaster Sound Region: 1980–2000, Issues and Options on the Use and Management of the Region*. Ottawa: Ministry of Indian Affairs 1982

District of Kitimat. *Kitimat Townsite Report*. Kitimat, BC, March 1969 (orig. 1960)

Domon, Gérald. "De la ferme et de ses bâtiments." *Continuité*, no. 109 (2006): 29–32

Domon, Gérald, and Julie Ruiz. *Paysage et multifonctionnalité des territoires: Enjeux et atouts pour l'agriculture de demain*. Montreal: Chaire en paysage et environnement, Université de Montréal 2007

Donaldson, Sue. "For Beauty and Use: Three Canadians Make Landscapes." *Environments* 17, no. 2 (1985): 75–83

– "Landscape Architecture in Canada." *LAR* 5, no. 2 (1984): 12–24, 39–44

– "Monumental and Other Purposes." *APT Bulletin* 15, no. 4 (1983): 23–6

– "William Pearce: His Vision of Trees." *JGH* 3, no. 3 (1983): 233–44

"Don Mills Shopping Centre." *Canadian Architecture* 4, no. 10 (1959): 72–3

Donovan, Kenneth. *Stanley W. Thompson*. HSMBC Submission Report (Agenda Paper) 2004-74

Doull, Ian. *Motherwell Homestead National Historic Park, Abernethy, Saskatchewan*. Building Report 88-14. Ottawa: Federal Heritage Buildings Review Office 1988

Downing, Andrew Jackson. "The New York Park." *The Horticulturist*, August 1851

– "A Talk about Public Parks and Gardens." *The Horticulturist*, October 1848

- *A Treatise on the Theory and Practice of Landscape Gardening.* Facsimile of George F. Putnam (New York) 1850 edition. Dumbarton Oaks Research Library and Collection, Washington, DC, 1991
Draper, Joan E. *Edward H. Bennett, Architect and City Planner, 1874–1954.* Chicago: Art Institute 1982
Drolet, Georges. "The Mighty Empire of the Past: Lord Dufferin's 1875 Embellishment Proposals for Québec City." *SSAC* 21, no. 1 (1996): 18–24
D.R. Poulton and Associates. *Restoration Master Plan for Victoria Park.* London, ON, c. 2000
Drucker, Philip. *Indians of the Northwest Coast.* Garden City, NY: Natural History Press 1955
Dubé, Philippe. *Charlevoix: Two Centuries at Murray Bay.* Translated by Tony Martin-Sperry. Montreal & Kingston: McGill-Queen's University Press 1990 (orig. 1986)
Dubois, Martin. *Jean-Marie Roy, architecte.* Quebec City: Les Publications du Québec 2012
Dufresne, Judith. *Pont Lions Gate.* HSMBC Agenda Paper 2003-47
Dunington-Grubb, Howard. "The Garden and the Park Today." *RAICJ* 31, no.7 (1954): 221–5
- "The Garden of Nineteen-Fifty." *RAICJ* 27, no. 8 (1950): 272–3
Dunington-Grubb, Lorrie A. "The Allurement of the Rock Garden." *Canadian Homes and Gardens* 3, no. 1 (1926): 18–19, 52, 54
- "The Value of Water as a Garden Feature." *Canadian Homes and Gardens* 3, no. 9 (1926): 26–7, 64, 66
- "When Jack Frost Dips into His Color Pot." *Canadian Homes and Gardens* 2, no. 1 (1925): 16–17, 56
du Prey, Pierre de la Ruffinière, invited curator, and Dorothy Farr, curator. *Ah, Wilderness: Resort Architecture in the Thousand Islands.* Kingston, ON: Agnes Etherington Art Centre, Queen's University 2004
du Toit Associates Ltd. *Ceremonial Routes: The National Capital Core Area.* Toronto: du Toit Associates 1983
Easterbrook, W.T., and Hugh G.J. Aitken. *Canadian Economic History.* Toronto: Macmillan 1961
Eaton, Leonard K. "Centennial Square, Victoria." *AIA Journal*, April 1971, 32–4
Eckbo, Garrett. *The Art of Home Landscaping.* New York: F.W. Dodge 1956
- "What Do We Mean by Modern Landscape Architecture?" *RAICJ* 27, no. 8 (1950): 259
Eglite, Eriks V. "Planning for the Unpredictable: The Design and Development of Expo 86." *LAR* 7, no. 3 (1986): 6–10
Elliott, Brent. "Mosaiculture: Its Origins and Significance." *Garden History* 9, no. 1 (1981): 76–98
- *Victorian Gardens.* London: B.T. Batsford 1986
Ells, A. Dale. *Shaped through Service: An Illustrated History of the Nova Scotia Agricultural College.* Truro, NS: Agrarian Development Services, c. 1999
Ellwand, Nancy. "Motherwell Homestead: Restoration of a Landscape." *APT Bulletin* 15, no. 4 (1983): 67–71
Ellwand, Nancy, and Roman Fodchuk. "Edmonton Restores Its River Valley: A Capital Case for Restoration." *Landscape Architecture* 69, no. 3 (1979): 279–90
Emmond, Ken. "The Forks: A Long-Term Heritage Project for Winnipeg." *Award Magazine*, December 1989–January 1990, 38–42
Engelhardt, H.A. *The Beauties of Nature Combined with Art.* Montreal: John Lovell 1872

Environment Canada, Canadian Park Service. *Le Homestead Motherwell, parc historique national, Saskatchewan.* Publication QS-R098-000-BB-A3, 1988
Environment Canada, Parks Canada. *World Heritage.* Canada: Ministry of Supply and Services 1988
Erickson, Arthur. *The Architecture of Arthur Erickson.* London: Thames and Hudson 1988
Erickson, Donna L. "The Relationship of Historic City Form and Contemporary Greenway Implementation: A Comparison of Milwaukee, Wisconsin (USA) and Ottawa, Ontario (Canada)." *Landscape and Urban Planning*, no. 68 (2004): 199–221
Ermatinger, Edward. *Life of Colonel Talbot and the Talbot Settlement.* Milton, ON: Global Heritage Press 2006 (orig. 1859)
Ethier, Dale. "Un projet de sauvegarde du patrimoine à Québec." *The Archivist* 17, no. 2 (1990): 10–11
- "Quebec City and William Brymner." *The Archivist* 17, no. 2 (1990): 12–13
Etlin, Richard A. *The Architecture of Death: The Transformation of the Cemetery in Eighteenth-Century Paris.* Cambridge, MA: MIT Press 1984
- "Père Lachaise and the Garden Cemetery." *JGH* 4, no. 3 (1984): 211–22
Fardin, Linda Dicaire. "Assessing the Cultural Value of Historic Parks and Gardens." *APT Bulletin* 24, nos. 3 and 4 (1992): 14–24
- "Assessment Strategies for Canada's Historic Sites." *Cultural Resources Magazine* (US National Park Service) 16, no. 4 (1993): 14–16
- "L'esprit du jardin." *Continuité*, no. 36 (1987): 43–5
Fellows, Richard A. *Sir Reginald Blomfield: An Edwardian Architect.* London, UK: A. Zwemmer 1985
Ferguson, Niall. *Civilization: The West and the Rest.* New York: Penguin Press 2011
- *Colossus: The Price of America's Empire.* New York: Penguin Press 2004
Fernet-Beauregard, Carole. "Le Bois de Coulonge, une valeur patrimoniale." *LAR* 6, no. 1 (1985): 11–13
Ferrabee, Lydia. "The Shape of Expo 67." *Design 67 Journal* 217 (1967): 24–31
Fife, Edward. "A Park for the Future." *Landscape Architecture* 8, no. 2 (1990): 34–5
Fife, Edward, Pleasance Crawford, and Ina Elias. "Landscape Architecture." *The Canadian Encyclopedia*, online edition 2012
Filey, Mike. *I Remember Sunnyside.* Toronto: Dundurn Press 1996
- *Mount Pleasant Cemetery: An Illustrated Guide.* 2nd edn. Toronto: Dundurn Press 1999
Filler, Martin. "Planning for a Better World: The Lasting Legacy of Clarence Stein." *Architectural Record*, August 1982, 122–7
Filteau, Gérard. *L'épopée de Sha8nigan [sic].* Shawinigan Falls, QC: Guertin & Gignac 1944
Fischer, Ron. "The Development of the Garden Suburb in Toronto." *JGH* 3, no. 3 (1983): 193–207
Fish Creek Park Management Committee. *Fish Creek Provincial Park, Final Report.* Calgary: Alberta Recreation and Parks 1985
Fitzgerald, Dennis. "The Properties: West Vancouver's High-Altitude Subdivision Is a Peculiar Hybrid of Myth and Money." *Western Living*, November 1985
Fitzgerald, Joseph J. *Black Gold with Grit: The Alberta Oil Sands.* Sidney, BC: Gray's Publishing 1978

Fitzgibbon, Agnes, and Catherine Parr Traill. *Canadian Wild Flowers*. Montreal: John Lovell 1868 (republished Toronto: Coles Publishing 1972)
Flanders, John. "Praise." *Canadian Architect* 12, no. 9 (1967): 6
Fleming, Robert. "Fantasyland, West Edmonton Mall, Edmonton, Alberta." *LAR* 5, no. 1 (1984): 5–8
Fleras, Augie, and Jean Leonard Elliott. *Multiculturalism in Canada: The Challenge of Diversity*. Scarborough, ON: Nelson Canada 1992
Fliess, Henry. "The Modern House: A Brief Critical Analysis." *RAICJ* 27, no. 12 (1950): 395–6
Floyd, J. Austin. "The Architect's Garden versus the Gardener's Garden." *RAICJ* 27, no. 8 (1950): 258–9
– "Garden in Forest Hill Village." *RAICJ* 27, no. 8 (1950): 259–61
– "The Industrial Landscape." *RAICJ* 30, no. 7 (1953): 204–5
– "Landscaping for Winter." *Canadian Architect* 4, no. 8 (1959): 54–7
– "Privacy in the Garden." *RAICJ* 31, no. 7 (1954): 242–3
Flynn, Catherine, and Barbara Huck. "A Continental Crossroads." In Huck, *Crossroads of the Continents*, 46–65
Flynn, Catherine, and E. Leigh Syms. "Manitoba's First Farmers." *Manitoba History* 31 (Spring 1996): 4–11
Foisy, Oswald, and Peter Jacobs. *Les quatres saisons du Mont-Royal*. Montreal: Éditions du Meridien 2000
Fondation des communications sur le pétrole. *Les sables pétrolifères*. Fort MacMurray, n.d.
Fong, Steven. "Toronto: The Modern Squares of Bay Street." In *Metropolitan Mutations: The Architecture of Emerging Public Spaces*, 42–56. Toronto: RAIC 1988
Forbes, Alex, and Bill De Grace. "Two Hundred Years of Planning in Fredericton." *Plan Canada* 40, no. 3 (2000): 25
Forster, Roy. *Van Dusen Botanical Garden Guidebook*. Vancouver: Van Dusen Garden 1993
Fortier, Marie-José. "Deux exemples de jardins civils à Montréal au dix-huitième siècle." *Architecture in/au Canada* 34, no. 1 (2009): 67–74
– "L'intégration d'un jardin historique aux activités du musée: Le jardin du gouverneur au Château Ramezay." Montreal: Master's thesis, Université de Montréal 2000
– *Les jardins d'agrément en Nouvelle-France: Étude historique et cartographique*. Sainte-Foy, QC: Éditions GID 2012
Fortier, Robert, ed. *Villes industrielles planifiées*. Montreal: Canadian Centre for Architecture/Éditions du Boréal 1996
Fortin, Daniel, and Louis Belzile. *Le parc du Bic*. Saint-Laurent, QC: Les Éditions du Trécarré 1996
Foster, Janet. *Working for Wildlife: The Beginnings of Preservation in Canada*. Toronto: University of Toronto Press 1978
Fredericton Heritage Trust. "Walking Tours of Fredericton, the Colonial Capital." Fredericton, May 1977
Freedman, Adele. "A Pioneer Spirit." *Globe and Mail*, 1 February 1992, C-2
Freeman, Milton M.R. "The Nature and Utility of Traditional Ecological Knowledge." *Canadian Arctic Resources Committee*. http://www.carc.org/pubs/v20no1/utility.htm
Friends of the Motherwell Homestead. *Waiting for the Train: Abernethy Area Farming, 1882–1912*. Edited by A.J. Garratt. Regina: Focus Publishing 1988
Fukuyama, Francis. *The End of History and the Last Man*. New York: The Free Press, Macmillan 1992
Fulton, Gordon. *Powell River Townsite Historic District, Powell River, British Columbia*. HSMBC Agenda Paper 1995-17
Fulton, Gordon, and Fern Graham. "Canada's Roads of Remembrance." In *International Symposium*, 164–8

Gagnon-Guimond, Renée. "Le Jardin de Bagatelle." *Continuité*, no. 36 (1987): 36
Gagnon Pratte, France. *L'architecture et la nature à Québec au dix-neuvième siècle: Les villas*. Quebec City: Gouvernement du Québec, Ministère des Affaires culturelles 1980
– *Country Houses for Montrealers, 1892–1924: The Architecture of E. and W.S. Maxwell*. Montreal: Éditions du Méridien 1987
Gagnon Pratte, France, and Line Ouellet. "La Maison Henry." *Continuité*, nos. 32 and 33 (1986): 57–9
Galbraith, John Kenneth. *The Great Crash, 1929*. Sentry edn. Boston: Houghton Mifflin 1972 (orig. 1954)
– *A Life in Our Times*. Boston: Houghton Mifflin 1981
Gamelin, Alain, René Hardy, Jean Roy, Normand Séguin, and Guy Toupin. *Trois-Rivières illustrée*. Trois-Rivières, QC: La Corporation des fêtes du trois cent cinquantième anniversaire 1984
"A Garden Unique in North America." *Canadian Homes and Gardens* 13, no. 10 (October–November 1936): 30–7
Garvin, Alexander. *Parks, Recreation and Open Space: A Twenty-first Century Agenda*. Chicago: American Planning Association 2000
Gazette, The (Montreal). Editorials, 6 June 2006, A18; 7 June 2006, A22
Germain, Annick. *Les Mouvements de réforme urbaine à Montréal au tournant du siècle: Modes de développement, modes d'urbanisation et transformations de la scène politique*, 47–51. Montreal: Université de Montréal, Centre d'information et d'aide à la recherche, Département de sociologie 1984
– "La ville cosmopolite ou la ville des autres?" *Trames* 2–3, no. 3 (1990): 15–22
Germain, Annick, Mabel Contin, Laurent Liégeois, and Martha Radice. "À propos du patrimoine urbaine des communautés culturelles: Nouveaux regards sur l'espace public." In Jébrak and Julien, *Les temps de l'espace public urbain*, 123–43
Gertler, Leonard O., ed. *Planning the Canadian Environment*. Montreal: Harvest House 1968
Gianelli, Adele M. "Almarie." *Canadian Homes and Gardens* 15, nos. 1–2 (1938): 37
Giedion, Sigfried. "City Hall and Centre." *Canadian Architect* 4, no. 4 (1959): 49–54
– *Space, Time, and Architecture: The Growth of a New Tradition*. Cambridge, MA: Harvard University Press, 1941
Gill, Alexandra. "Keeping House for History." *Globe and Mail*, 7 December 2003, R3
Gillies, Marjorie. *Street of Dreams: The Story of Broadway, Western Canada's First Boulevard*. Winnipeg: Heartland Publications 2001
Gilliland, Jason. "The Creative Destruction of Montreal: Street Widenings and Urban (Re)Development in the Nineteenth Century." *UHR* 31, no. 1 (2002): 37–51
Gillmor, R.D. Book review of Anthony A. Barret and Rhodri Windsor Liscombe, *Francis Rattenbury and British Columbia: Architecture and Challenge in the Imperial Age*. *Environments* 17, no. 2 (1985): 109–11
Girard, Michel F. *L'écologisme retrouvé: Essor et déclin de la Commission de la conservation du Canada*. Canada: University of Ottawa Press 1994
Girling, Cynthia. "Landscape as Stage Set." *LAR* 7, no. 3 (1986): 14–19
Girling, Cynthia, and Ronald Kellett. "Green Neighbourhoods at the Edge." *Landscapes/Paysages* 6, no. 1 (2004): 31–4
– *Skinny Streets and Green Neighborhoods: Design for Environment and Community*. Washington, DC: Island Press 2005
Glavin, Terry. *The Last Great Sea: A Voyage through the Human and Natural History of the North Pacific Ocean*. Vancouver: Greystone Books 2000

Glickman, Susan. *The Picturesque and the Sublime: A Poetics of the Canadian Landscape*. Montreal & Kingston: McGill-Queen's University Press 1998
Gold, Seymour. "Nonuse of Neighborhood Parks." *Journal of the American Institute of Planners* 38, no. 6 (1972): 369–78
- *Urban Recreation Planning*. Philadelphia: Lea & Febiger 1973
Goldfarb, Hilliard T., ed. *Expanding Horizons: Painting and Photography of American and Canadian Landscape 1860–1918*, Montreal: Montreal Museum of Fine Arts 2009
Goodspeed, Rhona. *Beechwood Cemetery, Ottawa*. HSMBC Agenda Paper 2000-46, 2279–332
- "Saskatchewan Legislative Buildings and Grounds." *Architecture in/au Canada* 32, no. 1 (2007): 61–88
Gordon, David L.A. "A City Beautiful Plan for Canada's Capital: Edward Bennett and the 1915 Plan for Ottawa and Hull." *Planning Perspectives* 13, no. 3 (1998): 275–300
- "Frederick G. Todd and the Origins of the Park System in Canada's Capital." *Journal of Planning History* 1, no. 1 (2002): 29–57
- "From Noblesse Oblige to Nationalism: Elite Involvement in Planning Canada's Capital." *Journal of Urban History* 28, no. 1 (2001): 3–34
- "Weaving a Modern Plan for Canada's Capital: Jacques Gréber and the 1950 Plan for the National Capital Region." *UHR* 29, no. 2 (2001): 43–61
Gordon, David L.A., and Brian S. Osborne. "Constructing National Identity in Canada's Capital, 1900–2000: Confederation Square and the National War Memorial." *Journal of Historical Geography* 30, no. 4 (2004): 618–42
Gordon, Katherine. *The Slocan: Portrait of a Valley*. Winlaw, BC: Sono Nis Press 2004
Goto, Seiko. "The First Japanese Garden in the Western World: The Garden in the Louisiana Purchase Exposition." *SHGDL* 27, no. 3 (2007): 247–9
- "Maintenance and Restoration of Japanese Gardens in North America: A Case Study of Nitobe Memorial Garden." *SHGDL* 29, no. 4 (2009): 302–13
Goulding, W.S. "Landscape and Plantscape." *RAICJ* 35, no. 9 (1958): 331–7
Gournay, Isabelle, and France Vanlaethem, eds. *Montreal Metropolis, 1880–1930*. Montreal/Toronto: Canadian Centre for Architecture/Stoddart Publishing 1998
Gouvernement du Québec, Commission des Biens Culturels. *Les chemins de la mémoire: Monuments et sites historiques du Québec, Supplément 1987–1999*. Quebec City 2001
- Ministère de la Culture, des Communications et de la Condition féminine. *Un regard neuf sur le patrimoine culturel, Révision de la Loi sur les biens culturels, Document de réflexion*. Quebec City 2007
- Ministère de l'Environnement et de la Faune et Ministère du Tourisme, de la Chasse, et de la Pêche. Brochures and trail guides for the following parks: Bic, Grand-Jardins, Mont-Mégantic, Mont-Orford, Mont-Tremblant, Oka
- Ministère du Loisir, de la Chasse, et de la Pêche. *Les parcs québécois: La politique*. Quebec City 1982
Government of Alberta. *Responsible Actions: A Plan for Alberta's Oil Sands*. Edmonton, 12 February 2009
Government of Alberta, Legislative Assembly Office. *Alberta Legislature Grounds, Self-Guided Tour*. Edmonton 2006
Government of Canada. *Cape Breton Highlands National Park Provisional Master Plan*. Ottawa: Ministry of Indian Affairs and Northern Development 1970

- *Fundy National Park Provisional Master Plan*. Ottawa: Ministry of Indian Affairs and Northern Development 1970
- *National Parks Policy*. Ottawa: Ministry of Indian Affairs and Northern Development 1969
- *Possibilités des terres pour la faune – sauvagine: Inventaire des terres du Canada*. Ottawa: Ministère de l'Expansion économique régionale 1970
- *Prairie Farm Rehabilitation Administration, Annual Reports 1935–1938*. Ottawa: Department of Agriculture 1936–39
- *Prairie Farm Rehabilitation Administration, Annual Report 1990–1991*. Ottawa: Ministry of Supply and Services 1993
Government of Canada, Commissioner of the Environment and Sustainable Development. "Case Study 2.1—The Sydney Tar Ponds." http://www.oag-bvg.gc.ca/.../att_c20021002se01_f_12325
Government of Canada, with governments of provinces and territories. *Standards and Guidelines for the Conservation of Historic Places in Canada*. 2nd edn. Ottawa 2010
Government of Manitoba. *La colonisation par les Mennonites*. Winnipeg: Culture, patrimoine et citoyenneté 1997
- *Guide to the Manitoba Legislative Assembly*. Brochure, Voyage Manitoba 1990
- *The Prehistory of the Lockport Site*. Winnipeg: Manitoba Culture, Heritage and Recreation 1985
Government of Nunavut, Department of Sustainable Development. *Nunavut Climate Change Strategy*. Iqaluit 2003
Gowans, Alan. *Looking at Architecture in Canada*. Toronto: Oxford University Press 1958
Gradidge, Roderick. *Edwin Lutyens, Architect Laureate*. London, UK: George Allen & Unwin 1981
Graham, Donald W. "Degree Courses Begin in Canada." *Canadian Landscape Architect* 6, no. 1 (1965): 6–7
- "Expo '67 Landscape." *Canadian Landscape Architect* 6, no. 1 (1965): 30–1
- "Man of Vision, Edward I. Wood." *Canadian Landscape Architect* 6, no. 1 (1965): 14–15
Graham, Fern. *The Landscape of Dundurn Castle*. HSMBC Agenda Paper 1991-56
Graham, Robert. "J. Austin Floyd MLA: A Master Landscape Architect." *LAR* 2, no. 3 (1981): 16–21
Grant, Rev. George M. *Ocean to Ocean: Sandford Fleming's Expedition through Canada in 1872*. Toronto: Prospero Books 2000 (orig. Toronto: J. Campbell 1873)
- *Picturesque Canada: The Country as It Is and Was*. Toronto: Belden Bros 1882–84
- *Le Québec pittoresque*. Quebec City: Éditions Hurtubise 1991 (partial translation of *Picturesque Canada*)
Gray, Charlotte. *Sisters in the Wilderness: The Lives of Susanna Moodie and Catharine Parr Traill*. Toronto/London: Viking/Penguin Books 1999
Gréber, Jacques. *L'architecture aux États-Unis*. Vol. 2. Paris: Payot et Cie 1920
- *Plan for the National Capital*. 2 vols. Ottawa: King's Printer for the National Planning Service 1950
Greenberg, Ken. "Toronto: The Unknown Grand Tradition." *Trace* 1, no. 2 (1981): 37–46
- *Walking Home: The Life and Lessons of a City Builder*. Toronto: Random House Canada 2011
Gribbin, Thomas, and Judith Tulloch. "Ardgowan – The Restoration of an Island Garden." *APT Bulletin* 18, nos. 1 and 2 (1986): 99–105

Grimmer, A.K. "Gardens in the North." *Canadian Homes and Gardens* 15, no. 3 (1938): 47, 53, 56–7
Grimwood, Paul, Owen R. Scott, and Marilyn Watson. "George Laing – Landscape Gardener, Hamilton, Canada West, 1808–1871." *LAC* 4, no. 1 (1978): 3–14
Gruending, Dennis, ed. *The Middle of Nowhere: Rediscovering Saskatchewan*. Calgary: Fifth House Publishers 1996
Guay, Lorraine. "L'évolution de l'espace de la mort à Québec." *Continuité*, no. 49 (1991): 24–7
Guérard, François, and Guy Trépanier. "Shawinigan, une ville née de l'industrie." *Continuité*, no. 30 (1986): 37–9
Haaf, Angela, and Hilary Meredith. *Frank E. Buck, 1875–1971: An Inventory of His Papers in the Archives of the University of British Columbia*. Vancouver: Archives of University of British Columbia 1981
Habibi-Shandiz, Massoumeh. "L'idée du paradis et les jardins safavides de la fin du XVIe et début du XVIIe siècle." PhD diss., Faculté des Études supérieures (Aménagement), Université de Montréal 2007
Hajjar, Béatrice. "Pratiques vernaculaires et design urbain: Le cas de la communauté portugaise de Montréal." Master's thesis, Faculté des études supérieures, Université de Montréal, April 1999
Hales, Katherine (pseudo. of Amelia Garvin). *Historic Houses of Canada*. Toronto: Ryerson Press 1952 (orig. *Canadian Houses of Romance*. Toronto: Macmillan 1926)
Hall, George D. "The Future Prince Rupert as Conceived by the Landscape Architects." *Architectural Record* 26, no. 2 (1909): 97–106
Hall-Abell, T.S. "The Gardens of Cottesmore Hall, Cobourg, ON." *Canadian Horticulturist* 37 (1914): 14–15
Hallendy, Norman. *Inuksuit: Silent Messengers of the Arctic*. Vancouver/Seattle: Douglas & McIntyre/University of Washington Press 2000
Halmrast, Lawrence. *Story on Stone*. Lethbridge, AB: Archaeological Society of Alberta 1980
Hamelin, Jean, and Jean Provencher. *Brève histoire du Québec*. Montreal: Boréal 1997 (orig. 1981)
Hamelin, Marcel. "Joly De Lotbinière, Sir Henri-Gustave." *Dictionary of Canadian Biography*. Toronto/Quebec City: University of Toronto Press/Presses de l'Université Laval 2000
Hancock, Macklin, and Douglas H. Lee. "Don Mills New Town." *RAICJ* 31, no. 1 (1954): 3–27
Harcourt, Mike, Ken Cameron, and Sean Rossiter. *City Making in Paradise: Nine Decisions That Saved Vancouver*. Vancouver: Douglas & McIntyre 2007
Hardy, W.G. *Alberta, A Natural History*. Edmonton/Vancouver: M.G. Hurtig Publishers/Evergreen Press 1971
Harris, Julie. "Central Exper'l Farm, Ottawa, Ont." HSMBC Agenda Paper 1997-43
– "Lots for Sale, Saskatoon." *Saskatchewan History*, no. 2 (1981–82): 13–15
Harris, Julie, and Jennifer Meuller. "Making Science Beautiful: The Central Experimental Farm." *Ontario History* 89, no. 2 (1997): 103–23
Harris, W.C. "Where Delights of Country and Comforts of City Meet." *Point Grey Gazette*, 2nd progress number (1925): 29–30
Harvey, R.G. *Carving the Western Path*. Vancouver: Heritage House 1998
Harvey, Robert R., and Susan Buggey. "Section 630: Historic Landscapes." *Time-Saver Standards for Landscape Architecture*. Edited by Charles W. Harris and Nicholas T. Dines. New York: McGraw-Hill 1988

Harvey, Sylvain, ed. *The Native Peoples of Québec*. Quebec City: Les Éditions Harvey 1997
"'Hatley Park' at Victoria, B.C. Estate of the Dunsmuirs on Vancouver Island." *Canadian Homes and Gardens* 2, no. 2 (1925): 15–18
Hayden, Dolores. *The Power of Place: Urban Landscape as Public History*. Cambridge, MA, and London, UK: MIT Press 1997 (orig. 1995)
Hayes, Robert M. "Accommodation in and around Kelowna." In Kelowna Museum, *Kelowna: One Hundred Years of History 1905–2005*, 24–8, 33–41
Hémon, Louis. *Maria Chapdelaine*. Montreal: Art Global and Libre Expression 1980 (orig. *Le Temps*. Paris 1914)
Hennessey, Catherine, and Edward MacDonald. "Arthur Newbery and the Greening of Queen Square." *The Island*, no. 28 (1990): 25–9
Herger, Bob, and Brad Nickason. *Pacific Rim National Park*. New Westminster, BC: Natural Color Productions 1990
Herrington, Susan. "Claude's Glass, Cormier's Landscape – Way of Seeing." *ARQ*, no. 139 (2007): 41–3
– *Cornelia Hahn Oberlander: Making the Modern Landscape*. Charlottesville, VA: University of Virginia Press 2014
– "Expo 67 Revisited: Interview with Cornelia Hahn Oberlander." *Landscapes/Paysages* 7, no. 2 (2005): 12–14
Herzog, Lawrence. "A Legacy of Vision." *Real Estate Weekly* (Edmonton), 21 December 2000, 4
Hickman, Michael. *Kurimoto Japanese Garden: A Guide*. Edmonton: Devonian Botanic Garden and Friends of the Garden 2007
Hilderman Feir Witty & Assoc. *Land Use Planning Study: Last Mountain Lake–Flying Creek Area, Qu'Appelle Valley*. Saskatchewan: Department of Municipal Affairs 1977
Hilderman Thomas Frank Cram. "Oodena Celebration Circle." http://www.htfc.mb.ca/projects/oodena/html
Hillis, Ken. "A History of Commissions: Threads of an Ottawa Planning History." *UHR* 21, no. 1 (1992): 46–60
Hills, G. Angus. *Developing a Better Environment: Ecological Land-Use Planning in Ontario*. Toronto: Economic Council, August 1970
– "Landscape Planning – An Overview." *Landscape Planning* 1, no. 1 (1974): 267–83
Hinds, Diane Beverley. "The Evolution of Urban Public Park Design in Europe and America: Vancouver Adaption to 1913." *UHR* 11, no. 1 (1982): 69
Hirano, Robert, Architect. SSAC conference, Lethbridge, AB, June 2005
History Book Committee. *Raymond Remembered, Settlers, Sugar and Stampedes: A History of the Town and People of Raymond*. Raymond, AB: Raymond History Project 1993
Hobsbawm, Eric. *Age of Extremes: A History of the World, 1914–1991*. New York: Pantheon 1995
– *The Age of Revolution: Europe, 1789–1848*. London: Weidenfeld & Nicolson 1962
Hockaday, Joan. *Greenscapes: Olmsted's Pacific Northwest*. Pullman, WA: Washington State University Press 2009
Hodgins, J. Herbert. "An Italian Garden on Île d'Orléans Cliffs." *Canadian Homes and Gardens* 3, no. 12 (1926): 22–5, 106, 108
– "Shadowbrook – Estate of Vibrant Colours." *Canadian Homes and Gardens* 6, no. 1 (1929): 16–20, 50
Hoffman, Francine. "Aux sources du Jardin des Premières Nations." *Quatre-Temps* 25, no. 3 (2001): 8
Homel, Gene Howard. "Sliders and Backsliders: Toronto's Sunday Tobogganing Controversy of 1912." *UHR* 10, no. 2 (1981): 25–34
Horwood, Dennis, and Tom Parkin. *Haida Gwaii: The Queen Charlotte Islands*. Surrey, BC: Heritage House 2000

Hoskins, W.G. *The Making of the English Landscape*. London: Hodder & Stoughton 1955
Hoskins, W.G., and L. Dudley Stamp. *The Common Lands of England & Wales*. London, UK: Collins 1963
Hough, Michael. "Changing Roles of Urban Parks – An Environmental View." *Environments* 17, no. 2 (1985): 84–94
– *Cities and Natural Process*. London and New York: Routledge 1995
– *City Form and Natural Process*. London and New York: Routledge 1989
– "The Urban Landscape – The Hidden Frontier." *APT Bulletin* 15, no. 4 (1983): 9–14
Hough, Stansbury & Associates. "Lakealert, Phase 2 – Methodology." *Landscape Architecture* 69, no. 4 (1979): 408–9
Houlton, Emilia. "Gardening as a Profession for Women." *Canadian Horticulturist* 34, no. 2 (1911): 32–3
Howard, Ebenezer. *Garden Cities of To-Morrow*. Cambridge, MA: MIT Press 1965 (orig. *To-Morrow: A Peaceful Path to Real Reform*, 1898)
Howes, John F., ed. *Nitobe Inazô: Japan's Bridge across the Pacific*. Boulder/San Francisco: Westview Press/Oxford 1995
Huck, Barbara, ed. *Crossroads of the Continents: A History of the Forks of the Red and Assiniboine Rivers*. Winnipeg: Heartland Associates and Forks North Portage Partnership 2003
– *Exploring the Fur Trade Routes of North America*. Winnipeg: Heartland Publications 2000
Huck, Barbara, and Doug Whiteway. *In Search of Ancient Alberta: Seeking the Spirit of the Land*. Winnipeg: Heartland Publications 1998
Hucker, Jacqueline. *Beth Israel Cemetery, Quebec*. HSMBC Agenda Paper OB-1
– *Royal Botanical Gardens, Hamilton, Ontario*. HSMBC Agenda Paper 1993-04
– "Vimy: A Monument for the Modern World." *Architecture in/au Canada* 33, no. 1 (2008): 39–48
Hucker, Jacqueline, and Julian Smith. *Vimy: Canada's Memorial to a Generation*. Ottawa: Sanderling Press 2012
Hugo-Brunt, Michael. "The Origin of Colonial Settlements in the Maritime Provinces." *Plan Canada* 1, no. 2 (1960): 78–114
Hume, Christopher. "Oasis of Urbanity." *Landscape Architecture* 80, no. 2 (1990): 30–3
Hundey, Ian. *Canada: Immigrants and Settlers*. 2nd edn. Toronto: Gage Educational Publishing Co. 1991
Hunt, Geoffrey. *John M. Lyle: Toward a Canadian Architecture*. Kingston, ON: Agnes Etherington Art Centre, Queen's University 1981
Hunt, John Dixon. *Gardens and the Picturesque: Studies in the History of Landscape Architecture*. Cambridge, MA: MIT Press 1992
Hunt, John Dixon, and Peter Willis. *The Genius of the Place: The English Landscape Garden 1620–1820*. London, UK: Elek Books 1975
Hunter, Robert. *Parkwood, Oshawa, Ont*. HSMBC Agenda Paper 1990-21
Hutchison, Bruce. *The Incredible Canadian: A Candid Portrait of Mackenzie King: His Works, His Times, and His Nation*. New York and Toronto: Longmans, Green & Co. 1953
– *The Unknown Country: Canada and Her People*. Toronto: Longmans, Green & Company 1942
Hyams, Edward. *The English Garden*. London: Thames and Hudson 1964
Illustrated Historical Atlas of the County of Brant, ON. Toronto: Page & Smith 1875 (reprint: Belleville, ON: Mika 1972)

Imbert, Dorothée. *The Modernist Garden in France*. New Haven, CT: Yale University Press 1993
International Federation of Landscape Architects (IFLA). *Yearbook 1968*
International Symposium on the Conservation of Urban Squares and Parks – Book of Texts. (CSLA/ICOMOS Congress 1993). Montreal: AAPQ 1993
Irwin, E.H. Rip. *Lighthouses & Lights of Nova Scotia*. Halifax: Nimbus Publishing 2003
Jackson, Anita, and Wayde Brown. "Coming to Light: Two Landscapes in Nova Scotia." *Heritage* 5, no. 3 (2002): 5–9
Jackson, John B. *Discovering the Vernacular Landscape*. New Haven, CT: Yale University Press 1984
– "The Nineteenth Century Rural Landscape: The Courthouse, the Small College, the Mineral Springs, and the Country Store." In Helen Horowitz, ed. *Landscape in Sight*, 139–48. New Haven, CT: Yale University Press 1997
– *A Sense of Place, a Sense of Time*, 3–4. New Haven, CT: Yale University Press 1994
Jacobs, Jane. *The Death and Life of Great American Cities*. New York: Random House 1961
Jacobs, Peter. "Achieving Sustainable Development." *Landscape Planning* 12, no. 3 (1985): 203–9
– "Beyond Parks: Stages in the Innovation and Re-creation of the City of Montreal." *Landscape Planning* (special edition, *Canada: Landscape Planning for People*) 6, no. 2 (1979): 225–36
– *Environmental Strategy and Action*. Vancouver: University of British Columbia Press 1981
– "Folklore and Forest Fragments: Rereading Contemporary Landscape Design in Quebec." *Landscape Journal* 23, no. 2 (2004): 85–101
– "Frederick Gage Todd 1876–1948, Early 20th Century Visions." Unpublished article, 1980
– "Frederick G. Todd and the Creation of Canada's Urban Landscape." *APT Bulletin* 15, no. 4 (1983): 27–34
– "George Angus Hills: A Canadian Tribute." *Landscape Planning* 6, no. 2 (1979): 101–7
– "The Lancaster Sound Regional Study." In Jeffrey A. McNeely and David Pitt, eds., *Culture and Conservation: The Human Dimension in Environmental Planning*. London, UK: Croom Helm 1985
– *People, Resources and the Environment: Perspectives on the Use and Management of the Lancaster Sound Region: Public Review Phase*. Ottawa: Department of Indian Affairs and Northern Resources 1981
– "Preface: Landscape Planning in Canada." *Landscape Planning* 6, no. 3 (1979): 95–100
– "Le rôle historique de Frederick Todd." *Architecture de paysage* 1, no. 4 (1977): 1–3
– "Roots 2: The Quiet Vision of Frederick G. Todd." *LAC* 3, no. 2 (June 1977): 1–4
– "Stories Make Us Human: Verbal Sketches of Canadian Landscapes." *Environments* 26, no. 3 (1999): 7–15
– "A Sustainable Society through Sustainable Development: Towards a Regional Development Strategy for Northern Quebec." *Landscape Planning* 12, no. 3 (1985): 267–83
Jacobs, Peter, Daniel Berrouard, and Mireille Paul. *Nunavik: A Homeland in Transition*. Kuujuaq, Quebec City: Kativik Environmental Quality Commission 2009
Jacobs, Peter, and Susan Buggey, eds. *Environments* (special edition: *Histories of Landscape Architecture in Canada*) 26, no. 3 (1999)

Jacobs, Peter, and Hervé Chatagnier. *Environnement Kativik Environment*. Actes du Colloque sur l'environnement Kativik, Kuujjuaq, Administration régionale Kativik 1985

Jacobs, Peter, and Oswald Foisy. *Les Quatre Saisons du Mont Royal*. Montreal: Éditions du Méridien 2000

Jacobs, Peter, and Lucie Fortin. *Évolution de l'architecture de paysage au Québec*. Montreal: École d'architecture de paysage, Université de Montréal 1982

– "L'histoire du paysage urbain au Québec." *Habitat* 27, no. 3 (1984): 2–7

Jacobs, Peter, and Jonathan Palluq. *Étude de la région du détroit de Lancaster: Les vues du public*. Ottawa: Department of Indian Affairs 1983

Jacobs, Peter, and Douglas Way. *Visual Analysis of Landscape Development*. Cambridge, MA: Department of Landscape Architecture, Harvard University 1969; *Canadian Architect*, May 1969

Jébrak, Yona, and Barbara Julien. "Hydrostone's Heritagization: Garden City of War." *Architecture in/au Canada* 43, no. 1 (2009): 61–6

–, eds. *Les temps de l'espace public urbain: Construction, transformation et utilisation*. Montreal: Éditions Multimondes 2008

Jefferson, Thomas. *Notes on Virginia*. 1782

Jenness, Eileen. *The Indian Tribes of Canada*. Toronto: Ryerson Press 1933

Johnson, Brad. "Robert Gordon Calvert, CSLA Fellow, 1918–93." *CSLA Bulletin* 9, no. 3 (1994): 3

Johnson, Dana. *Historic Marysville (Fredericton), New Brunswick*. HSMBC Agenda Paper 1993-47

Johnson, E. Pauline (Tekahionwake). *Legends of Vancouver*. Vancouver: Douglas & McIntyre 1997 (orig. 1911)

Johnstone, Lesley, ed. *Hybrids: Reshaping the Contemporary Garden in Métis*. Vancouver: Blueimprint 2007

Justice, Clive. "John Wesley Neill, BCSLA." *Sitelines*, October 1999, 1–3

– *Mr. Menzies' Garden Legacy: Plant Collecting on the Northwest Coast*. Vancouver: Cavendish Books 2000

– "The Three Landscape Legacies of Frank Ebenezer Buck: The Record and Personal Encounters." *Davidsonia* 18, no. 3 (2007): 79–104

– "Vancouver's Tree Heritage." *Sitelines*, July 2003, 5–6

Justus, Martha. "Les immigrants dans les villes canadiennes." *Nos diverses cités*, no. 1 (2004): 39–46

Kalm, Pehr. *Travels into North America*. Translated by J.R. Forster. London: T. Lowndes 1772. Barre, MA: Imprint Society 1972 (orig. Sweden 1749)

– *Voyage de Pehr Kalm au Canada en 1749*. Translated by J. Rousseau and G. Béthune. Montreal: Pierre Tisseyre 1977 (orig. Sweden 1749)

Kalman, Harold. *A History of Canadian Architecture*. Vols. 1 and 2. Toronto: Oxford University Press 1994

Kalman, Harold, and John Roaf. *Exploring Vancouver 2: Ten Tours of the City and Its Buildings*. Vancouver: University of British Columbia Press 1978

Kapelos, George Thomas. *Interpretations of Nature, Contemporary Canadian Architecture, Landscape and Urbanism*. Kleinburg, ON: McMichael Canadian Art Collection 1994

– "The Small House in Print: Promoting the Modern Home to Post-war Canadians through Pattern Books, Journals, and Magazines." *Architecture in/au Canada* 43, no. 1 (2009): 33–60

Katz, Elliott. *Great Country Walks around Toronto*. 4th edn. Thornhill, ON: Great North Books 1996

Kavanagh, Basil. "The Historical Research of Bowring Park." Unpublished manuscript, St. John's, NL, 1980

Kay, Edwin. "How and When to Plant Deciduous Shrubs." *Canadian Homes and Gardens* 3, no. 3 (1926): 90, 94, 96

Kehm, Walter. "The Evolution of Landscape Architecture in the Province of Ontario." Paper presented at the Congress of the CSLA, Université de Montréal, 1998

– "Wild in the City." *Landscapes/Paysages* 3, no. 1 (2001): 37–8

Kelowna Museum. *Kelowna: One Hundred Years of History 1905–2005*. Kelowna 2005

Kendall, Brian. *Northern Links: A Duffer's Unforgettable Journey through the World of Canadian Golf*. Toronto: Viking, Penguin Books 2001

Kenyon, Walter A. *Mounds of Sacred Earth: Burial Mounds of Ontario*. Toronto: Royal Ontario Museum 1986

Kerr, Don. *Building the University of Saskatchewan*. Brochure. Saskatoon: University of Saskatchewan, n.d.

Keshavjee, Serena, ed. *Winnipeg Modern, Architecture 1945–1975*. Winnipeg: University of Manitoba Press 2006

Kestenbaum, Joy. "Downing Vaux." In Birnbaum and Karson, *Pioneers*, 409–12

Keswick, Maggie. *The Chinese Garden: History, Art and Architecture*. Rev. edn. Cambridge, MA: Harvard University Press 2003 (orig. Academy Editions, UK, 1978)

Keswick, Maggie, Judy Oberlander, and Joe Wai. *In a Chinese Garden: The Art and Architecture of the Dr. Sun Yat-Sen Classical Chinese Garden*. Vancouver: Dr. Sun Yat-Sen Garden 1990

Kettle, John. "Highways as Landscape Architecture." *Canadian Architect* 4, no. 6 (1959): 56–9

Keynes, John Maynard. *The Economic Consequences of the Peace*. New York: Penguin Books 1988 (orig. London UK 1919)

Kheraj, Sean. "Restoring Nature: Ecology, Memory, and the Storm History of Vancouver's Stanley Park." *Canadian Historical Review* 88, no. 4 (2007): 577–612

Kidd, Kenneth E. "The Architecture of Sainte Marie." *RAICJ* 20, no. 5 (1943): 71–3

Kippax, Helen M. "Ground Covers and Their Uses." *RAICJ* 27, no. 8 (1950): 263–5

Kirk, Ruth. *Wisdom of the Elders: Native Traditions on the Northwest Coast*. Vancouver and Toronto: Douglas & McIntyre 1986

Kirkland, Sheila, ed. *Sheridan Nurseries Ltd*. Oakville, ON, 1988

Kitz, Janet, and Gary Castle. *Point Pleasant Park: An Illustrated History*. Halifax: Pleasant Point Publishing 1999

Klassen, Art, and Jan Teversham. *Exploring the UBC Endowment Lands*. North Vancouver: J.J. Douglas 1977

Klinck, Carl F., Alfred G. Bailey, Claude Bissell, et al., eds. *A Literary History of Canada: Canadian Literature in English*. Toronto: University of Toronto Press 1965

Klynstra, Peter. "Annapolis Royal Historic Gardens." *LAR* 4, no. 3 (1983): 5–6

Knapp, Sandra. *Plant Discoveries: A Botanist's Voyage through Plant Exploration*. Richmond Hill, ON: Firefly Books 2003

Kobayashi, Audrey. *Memories of Our Past: A Brief History & Walking Tour of Powell Street*. Vancouver: NRC Publishing 1992

Kogawa, Joy. *Obasan*. Markham, ON, and Harmondsworth, UK: Penguin Books 1983 (orig. 1981)

Konrad, Victor A. "Distribution, Site and Morphology of Prehistorical Settlements in the Toronto Area." In J.D. Wood, *Perspectives on Landscape*, 6–31

Kormondy, Edward J. *Concepts of Ecology*. New Jersey: Prentice-Hall 1969

Kosydar, Richard. *Hamilton: Images of a City*. Dundas, ON: Tierceron Press 1999

Kowsky, Francis R. *Country, Park and City: The Architecture and Life of Calvert Vaux*. New York: Oxford University Press 1998

Kramer, Pat. *Native Sites in Western Canada*. Vancouver: Altitude Publishing Canada 1998

Kraulis, J.A. *The Canadian Landscape*. Richmond Hill, ON: Firefly Books 2007

Krause, Eric, Carol Corbin, and Williams O'Shea, eds. *Aspects of Louisbourg*. Sydney, NS: University College of Cape Breton Press 1995

Krech, Shepard III. *The Ecological Indian: Myth and History*. New York: W.W. Norton & Co. 1999

Krim, Arthur. "Alexander Wadsworth." In Birnbaum and Karson, *Pioneers*, 420–2

Kuitert, Wybe. "Japonaiserie in London and The Hague: A History of the Japanese Gardens at Shepherd's Bush (1910) and Clingendael (c. 1915)." *Garden History* 30, no. 2 (2002): 221–38

Kumagai, Joji, Derek Iwanaka, and Judy Hanazawa. "Spirit of the Issei Celebrated by Legacy Sakura Coalition." *Nikkei Voice*, March 2009, 1, 9

Kyowakai Society. *A Path of Leaves: A Guided Study to the Nikkei Internment Memorial Centre*. New Denver, BC, 1999

Labbé, Thérèse. "L'objet funéraire: Un imaginaire à explorer." *Continuité*, no. 49 (1991): 28–32

Lachapelle, Jacques. "La perspective de l'avenue McGill Collège." Montreal: Heritage Montréal 1984

Lacoursière, Jacques. *Le champ des batailles: Les plaines d'Abraham 1759–1760*. Sillery, QC: Septentrion 2001

– *Shawinigan, 100 ans d'histoire: De l'effervescence au renouveau*. Shawinigan: Éditions des Glanures 2001

"L'actualité depuis 1920." Historical supplement in the newspaper *Le Nouvelliste* (Trois-Rivières), 28 December 2006

Lafargue, Bernard. "La promenade Olmsted." Unpublished manuscript of lecture presented 30 January 1997 at the Canadian Centre for Architecture, Montreal 1997

Lafleur, Yvon, ed. *Documents du Club Shawinigan 1893–1977*. Vols. 1, 2, and 3. Shawinigan: Service de la conservation des ressources naturelles 1979

Lahey, Don J. "Headway on the Ark." *Canadian Heritage*, February 1981, 36–8

Laking, Leslie. "A History of the Royal Botanical Gardens (Part 2)." *Pappus* 11, no. 1 (1992): 9–11

Lambert, Phyllis. "Canada: Urban Architecture and the Social Contract." Transactions of the Royal Society of Canada, 19 November 2004

– "Design Imperatives." In Richards, *Canadian Centre for Architecture: Building and Gardens*, 64–7

Lambert, Phyllis, Alan Stewart, and Canadian Centre for Architecture. *Opening the Gates of Eighteenth-Century Montreal*. Montreal/Cambridge, MA: Canadian Centre for Architecture/MIT Press 1992

L'amicale Notre-Dame-Du-Vieux-Moulin. *Le moulin de Pointe-Claire*. Pointe-Claire, QC, 1980

Lamonde, Yvan, and Raymond Montpetit. *Le Parc Sohmer de Montréal 1889–1919: Un lieu populaire de culture urbaine*. Quebec City: Institut québécois de recherche sur la culture 1986

Lamontagne, Gaétane. *Beaumont 1672–1972*. Beaumont, QC: Le comité des fêtes du tricentenaire de Beaumont 1972

Lamontagne, Roland. *Jean Talon, agent de Colbert, premier intendant du Canada au temps de Louis XIV*. Paris: Centre de documentation universitaire 1964; also published as *Succès d'intendance de Talon*. Montréal: Éditions Léméac 1964

Landry, Maurice. *Mount Royal: Montréal's Natural Monument*. Montreal: Centre de la montagne inc. 1999

"Landscape for Leisure: The St. Lawrence Seaway Parks." *Canadian Architect* 4, no. 8 (1959): 46–53

Langshaw, Rick. *Geology of the Canadian Rockies*. Banff, AB: Summerthought 1989

Lanthier, Pierre, and Normand Brouillette. "Shawinigan Falls de 1898 à 1930: L'émergence d'une ville industrielle au sein du monde rural." *UHR* 19, no. 1 (1990): 42–7

Lantzius, John. "West Coast Landscape Architecture." *Canadian Architect* 9, no. 4 (1964): 41–8

Larochelle, Fabien. *Histoires de Shawinigan*. Shawinigan, QC: Publicité Pâquet 1988

Larochelle, Pierre. "Le paysage humanisé comme bien culturel." *Continuité*, no. 110 (2006): 20–2

Latremouille, Joann. "The Hydrostone District, Halifax: Canada's Public Housing Began with a Bang." *LAR* 4, no. 4 (1983): 5–7

Laurie, Michael. "Thomas Church, California Gardens, and Public Landscapes." In Treib, ed., *Modern Landscape Architecture: A Critical Review*, 166–79

Lavallée, Madeleine. *Marie-Victorin, un itinéraire exceptionnel*. Saint-Lambert, Quebec City: Les éditions Héritage 1983

Lavoie, Claude. "Pourquoi notre urbanisme est-il Québécois?" *Métropolis* 48/49 (1981): 12–16

Lawrence, R.D. *Canada's National Parks*. Toronto: Collins Publishers 1983

Leacock, Stephen. *Arcadian Adventures with the Idle Rich*. Introduction by Ralph L. Curry. Toronto: McClelland & Stewart 1969 (orig. New York and London: John Lane 1914)

– *Baldwin, Lafontaine, Hincks: Responsible Government*. Toronto: Morang & Co. 1910

– *Canada: The Foundations of Its Future*. Montreal: House of Seagram 1941

– *Social Criticism*. Toronto: University of Toronto Press 1996 (orig. 1907–20)

– *Sunshine Sketches of a Little Town*. Toronto: McClelland & Stewart 2012 (orig. New York and London: John Lane 1912)

Leclerc, Hélène. *Domaine Joly-De Lotbinière*. Quebec City: Éditions Fides 2002

Lee, David. *Skinner's Nursery, Dropmore, Manitoba*. HSMBC Agenda Paper 1997-62

– *William Pearce*. HSMBC Agenda Paper 1973-14

LeGeyt, Linda M. *Changing the Face of Canada: Profiles of Landscape Architects*. Vols. 1 and 2. Ottawa: CSLA 1997, 1998

Leighton, Ann. *American Gardens of the Nineteenth Century*. Amherst: University of Massachusetts Press 1987

Lemelin, André. *Shawinigan, un siècle d'énergie*. Beauport, QC: Publications MNH 2001

LeMoine, James MacPherson. *Picturesque Quebec, a Sequel to Quebec Past and Present*. Montreal: Dawson Brothers 1882

Lemon, James T. "Plans for Early 20th-Century Toronto: Lost in Management." *UHR* 18, no. 1 (1989): 11–31

Lessard, Marie, and Sylvie Jutras. *La qualité de l'environnement perçue par les résidents de Chisasibi*. Montreal: Université de Montréal 1984

Lessard, Michel. *L'art de vivre en banlieue au Québec*. Montreal: Les éditions de l'homme 2001

Lévesque, Évangeline, and Luc Jacques. "Rickson A. Outhet." Student project, École d'architecture de paysage, Université de Montréal 1982

"Liberty Profile: Stanley Thompson." *Liberty Magazine,* 28 September 1948, 16–17

Lightfoot, Gordon. "Canadian Railroad Trilogy." Record album: *The Way I Feel.* 1967

Lincoln, Clifford. *Toward New Horizons.* Sainte-Anne-de-Bellevue, QC: Shoreline Press 2012

Lincourt, Jean-Jacques, with Sylvie Perron. *Jardin botanique de Montréal.* Montreal: Éditions Fides 2001

Lindgren, Edward. "Public Gardens – A Victorian Ideal." *Canadian Heritage* 2, no. 3 (1985): 14–19

Litalien, Raymonde. "Les missions exploratoires du Pacifique nord au XVIIIe siècle, en provenance de la France et du Mexique." In Christian Buchet, ed., *La mer, la France et l'Amérique latine,* 351–68. Paris: Presses de l'Université de Paris-Sorbonne 2006

Lockerby, Earle. "Colonization of Ile St-Jean: Charting Today's Evangeline Region." *The Island,* no. 47 (2000): 20–30

Longfellow, Henry Wadsworth. *Evangeline: A Tale of Acadie.* Halifax: Nimbus Publishing 1951 (orig. 1847)

Lorimer, James. *The Developers.* Toronto: James Lorimer & Co. 1978

Lorne Park Estates Historical Committee. *A Village within a City: The Story of Lorne Park Estates.* Cheltenham, ON: Boston Mills Press 1980

Lothian, W.F. *A Brief History of Canada's National Parks.* One-volume summary of a three-volume series. Ottawa: Ministry of the Environment, Minister of Supply and Services Canada 1976–87

Loudon, John Claudius. *An Encyclopedia of Gardening.* London: Longman, Orme, Brown, Green 1840

–, ed. *The Landscape Gardening and Landscape Architecture of the Late Humphrey Repton, Esq.* London/Edinburgh: Longman & Co./A. & C. Black 1840

– *On the Laying Out, Planting, and Managing of Cemeteries and on the Improvement of Churchyards.* London: Longman, Brown, Green and Longmans 1843

Lovelace, Eldridge. *Harland Bartholomew: His Contributions to American Urban Planning.* Urbana: Board of Trustees, University of Illinois 1993

Lugrin, N. de Bertrand. "December Gardens of Jasmine and Holly." *Canadian Homes and Gardens* 2, no. 3 (1925): 11–13

– "Hatley Park – Estate of Memory and Romance." *Canadian Homes and Gardens* 6, no. 12 (1929)

Luka, Nik. "From Summer Cottage Colony to Metropolitan Suburb: Toronto's Beach District 1889–1929." *UHR* 35, no. 1 (2006): 18–31

Lussier, Patricia. "Not in My Backyard, Yes Please!" In Johnstone, *Hybrids,* 136–8

Luxton, Donald. "The Rise and Fall of West Coast Modernism in Greater Vancouver, British Columbia." *APT Bulletin* 31, nos. 2 and 3 (2000): 55–61

Lynch, Kevin. *The Image of the City.* Cambridge, MA: MIT Press 1960

McAleese, Keven E. *Full Circle: First Contact – Vikings and Skraelings in Newfoundland and Labrador.* St John's: Newfoundland Museum 2000

McAlpine, Mary. "Sculpting with Flowers: He Made Vancouver Blossom City." *Vancouver Sun,* 5 November 1977

McArthur, Glenn. *A Progressive Traditionalist: John M. Lyle, Architect.* Toronto: Coach House Books 2009

McBride, Hugh. *Our Store: 75 Years of Canadians and Canadian Tire.* Toronto: Quantum Book Group 1997

McCann, L.D. "Fragmented Integration: The Nova Scotia Steel and Coal Company and the Anatomy of an Urban-Industrial Landscape, c. 1912." *UHR* 22, no. 2 (1994): 139–58

–, ed. *Heartland and Hinterland: A Geography of Canada.* 2nd edn. Scarborough, ON: Prentice Hall 1987

– *Oak Bay: The Making of a Suburban Landscape.* Oak Bay, BC: Oak Bay Centennial Commission 2006

– "Planning and Building the Corporate Suburb of Mount Royal, 1910–1925." *Planning Perspectives* 11, no. 3 (1996): 259–301

Macdonald, Catherine. *A City at Leisure: An Illustrated History of Parks and Recreation Services in Winnipeg, 1893–1993.* Winnipeg: City of Winnipeg, Parks and Recreation Department 1995

– *Making a Place: A History of Landscape Architects and Landscape Architecture in Manitoba.* CD-ROM. Winnipeg: Manitoba Association of Landscape Architects 2005

Macdonald, Elizabeth. "The Efficacy of Long-Range Physical Planning: The Case of Vancouver." *Journal of Planning History* 7, no. 3 (2008): 175–213

MacDonald, George F. *Ninstints: Haida World Heritage Site.* Vancouver: University of British Columbia Press 1990

MacDonald, Graham. *A Good Solid Comfortable Establishment: An Illustrated History of Lower Fort Garry.* Winnipeg: Watson & Dwyer 1992

Macdonald, Norbert. "C.P.R. Town: The City-Building Process in Vancouver, 1860–1914." In Stelter and Artibise, eds., *Shaping the Urban Landscape,* 382–412

MacEachern, Alan. "The Greening of Green Gables: Establishing Prince Edward Island National Park." *The Island,* no. 45 (1999): 22–31

– *Natural Selections: National Parks in Atlantic Canada, 1935–1970.* Montreal & Kingston: McGill-Queen's University Press 2001

MacEwan, Grant. *French in the West.* St. Boniface, MB: Éditions des Plaines 1986

McGillivray, Leo, and Jean de Laplante. *The Parks of Montreal 1968–69.* Montreal: City of Montreal Parks Department 1969

McHarg, Ian L. *Design with Nature.* Garden City, NY: Natural History Press 1969

McIntyre, William H. *The McIntyre Ranch: A Brief History.* Magrath, AB, 1947 (reprinted 1994)

MacKay, Donald. *Empire of Wood: The McMillan Bloedel Story.* Vancouver: Douglas & McIntyre 1982

– *The Square Mile: Merchant Princes of Montreal.* Vancouver: Douglas & McIntyre 1987

McKay, Mary Jane. "UFO-H2O: A Toy for All Ages." *LAR* 7, no. 3 (1986): 20–1

McKay, Marylin J. *Picturing the Land: Narrating Territories in Canadian Landscape Art, 1500–1950.* Montreal & Kingston: McGill-Queen's University Press 2011

Mckay, Sherry. "Western Living, Western Homes." *SSAC Bulletin* 14, no. 3 (1989): 65–74

McKelvie, B.A. *Fort Langley: Birthplace of British Columbia.* Victoria: Porcépic Books 1991 (orig. 1947)

McKinnon, Kelty, ed. *Grounded: The Work of Phillips Farevaag Smallenberg.* Vancouver: Blueimprint 2010

McLean, Stuart. *Welcome Home: Travels in Smalltown Canada.* Toronto: Penguin Books 1992

McLennan, J.S. *Louisbourg from Its Foundation to Its Fall.* Halifax: Book Room 1979 (orig. London: Macmillan 1918)

MacLeod, John, and Michael O'Neill. "Le Vieux Port de Québec." *LAR* 6, no. 3 (1985): 6–8

McLuhan, Marshall. "Canada: The Borderline Case." In David Staines, ed., *The Canadian Imagination,* 226–48. Cambridge, MA: Harvard University Press 1977

MacMillan, Margaret. "After the Great War." *Images of a Forgotten War: Epilogue, National Film Board of Canada*. http://www3.nfb.ca/ww1

Macmillan, Stuart, Coordinator. *Peace-Athabasca Delta Technical Studies, Final Report*. Fort Chipewyan, AB: Peace-Athabasca Delta Technical Studies 1996

McNally, Kathleen N. "Calgary's Reader Rock Garden: An Historical Landscape Revisited." *LAR* 11, no. 1 (1990): 19–24

Mcphedran, Kerry. "A Clearing in the Forest." *City and Country Home* 11, no. 6 (1992): 114–19

Macpherson, Mary-Etta. "Come to Temiscaming." *Canadian Homes and Gardens* 7, no. 10 (1930): 22–4, 52, 69

Magnuson, Roger. *A Brief History of Quebec Education*. Montreal: Harvest House 1980

Maitland, Leslie. "Architecture for Nation and Empire." *Architecture in/au Canada* 35, no. 1 (2010): 31–46

Mann, Charles C. "1491." *Atlantic Monthly* 289, no. 3 (2002): 41–53

Mannell, Steven, ed. *Atlantic Modern: The Architecture of the Atlantic Provinces 1950–2000*. Halifax: Tuns Press/Faculty of Architecture and Planning, Dalhousie University 2004

Manus, Mechtild, and Lisa Rochon. *Picturing Landscape Architecture: Projects of Cornelia Hahn Oberlander as Seen by Etta Gerdes*. Munich: Édition Topos, Callwey Verlag-Goethe Institut 2006

Marie-Victorin, Frère des Écoles chrétiennes. *Flore laurentienne*. Montreal: Presses de l'Université de Montréal 1964 (orig. Montréal: Imprimerie de la Salle 1935)

Marsan, Jean-Claude. *Montréal en évolution*. 3rd edn. Montreal: Éditions du Méridien 1994

– *Montreal in Evolution*. Montreal & Kingston: McGill-Queen's University Press 1981 (orig. Éditions Fides 1974)

Marsden, William. *Stupid to the Last Drop*. Toronto: Knopf Canada 2007

Martin, Carol. *A History of Canadian Gardening*. Toronto: McArthur & Company 2000

Martin, Linda, and Kerry Segrave. *City Parks of Canada*. Oakville, ON: Mosaic Press 1983

Martin, Michael David. "The Landscapes of Winnipeg's Wildwood Park." *UHR* 30, no. 1 (2001): 22–39

– "Returning to Radburn." *Landscape Journal* 20, no. 2 (2001): 156–75

Martin, Paul-Louis. *Promenades dans les jardins anciens du Québec*. Montreal: Les Éditions du Boréal 1996

"Massey College, Toronto." *Canadian Architect* 9, no. 12 (1964): 42–3

Massie, Robert K. *Dreadnought: Britain, Germany, and the Coming of the Great War*. New York: Ballantine Books 1991

Masuno, Shunmyo. *Ten Landscapes*. Edited by James Grayson Trulove. Rockport, MA: Rockport Publishers 1999

Mathieu, Jacques, and Eugen Kedl, eds. *Les Plaines d'Abraham: Le culte de l'idéal/The Plains of Abraham: The Search for the Ideal*. Translated by Kathe Roth. Quebec City: Septentrion 1993

Matsushita, Dan. "Harry James Webb." Notes dictated to Adrienne Brown. Vancouver 2000

Matthews, Brian R. *A History of Pointe Claire*. Pointe Claire, QC: Brianor 1985

Maumi, Catherine. *Thomas Jefferson et le projet du Nouveau Monde*. Paris: Éditions de la Villette 2007

– *Usonia ou le mythe de la ville-nature américaine*. Paris: Éditions de la Villette 2008

Mawson, David. "Roots 8: The Life and Works of Thomas Hayton Mawson." *LAC* 5, no. 1 (1979): 5–11

Mawson, Thomas H. *The Life and Work of an English Landscape Architect: An Autobiography by Thomas H. Mawson*. London/New York: Richards Press/Charles Scribner's Sons 1927

– "Vancouver: A City of Optimists." *Town Planning Review* 4, no. 1 (1913): 7–13

Meewasin Valley Authority. *Where City and Water Meet: Saskatoon's Riveredge: Walking Tour*. Saskatoon, n.d.

Meijerink, Paula. "Hyper-Nature." *ARQ*, no. 139 (2007): 26–8

Melançon, Yves. *Parcs, espaces verts et dynamique urbaine: Le Parc des champs de bataille à Québec*. Quebec City: Centre de recherches en aménagement et en développement, Université Laval 1988

Mellin, Robert. *Tilting, House Launching, Slide Hauling, Potato Trenching*. New York: Princeton Architectural Press 2003

Merrens, Roy. "Port Authorities as Urban Land Developers: The Case of the Toronto Harbour Commissioners and Their Outer Harbour Project, 1912–1968." *UHR* 17, no. 2 (1988): 92–101

Mertins, Detlef. *Metropolitan Mutations*. Toronto: RAIC 1988

Messervy, Julie Moir. *The Toronto Music Garden: Inspired by Bach*. Saxton Rivers, VT: J.M. Messervy Design Studio 2009

Messier, Denis. *Mackenzie King Estate: Gatineau Park*. Montreal: Éditions Fides 2002

Méthot, Mélanie. "Herbert Brown Ames: Political Reformer and Enforcer." *UHR* 31, no. 2 (2003): 18–31

Michaud, Claude. "Analysis of the Architectural Landscape." *APT Bulletin* 15, no. 4 (1983): 41–53

Michaud, Josette, and Bruno Harel. *Le séminaire de Saint-Sulpice de Montréal*. Quebec City: Gouvernement du Quebec, Ministère des Affaires culturelles 1990

Middleton, Ron. "No Net Loss: The Pine Coulee Project." *Landscapes/Paysages* 3, no. 1 (2001): 11–16

Mika, Nick, and Helma Mika. *Railways of Canada: A Pictorial History*. Toronto: McGraw-Hill Ryerson 1972

Miller, Gifford, Raymond S. Bradley, Peter Schledermann, and Patrick Baird. *The Land That Never Melts: Auyuittuq National Park*. Edited by Roger Wilson. Toronto: Peter Martin Associates 1976

Miller, Orlo. *London 2000: An Illustrated History*. London, ON: London Chamber of Commerce 1988

Miller, Patrick A., and Leonard Diamond, eds. *The Frontier Landscape: Selected Proceedings, IFLA Congress, 1981*. Vancouver: Landscape Architecture Program, University of British Columbia 1982

Mills, Edward, and Nathalie Clerk. *Hatley Park (Royal Roads College), Colwood, BC*. HSMBC Agenda Paper 1982-17

Milovsoroff, Ann. "For the Love of Gardens: A Biography of H.B. and L.A. Dunington-Grubb." *Canadian Horticultural History* 2, no. 3 (1990): 101–33

Milroy, Elizabeth. "A Crowning Feature: The Centennial Exhibition and Philadelphia's Horticultural Hall." *SHGDL* 26, no. 2 (2006): 132–65

Mitchell, Bruce, and James S. Gardner, eds. *River Basin Management: Canadian Experiences*. Waterloo, ON: Department of Geography, Faculty of Environmental Studies, University of Waterloo 1983

Mochizuki, Ken. *Baseball Saved Us*. New York: Lee & Low Books 1993

Montgomery, L.M. *Anne of Avonlea*. Toronto/New York/London: Bantam Books 1976 (orig. Boston: L.C. Page 1909)

– *Anne of the Island*. Toronto/New York/London: Bantam Books 1976 (orig. Boston: L.C. Page 1915)

– "A Garden of Old Delights." *Canadian Magazine*, 1910. Reprinted in von Baeyer and Crawford, *Garden Voices*, 274–9

Montreal Museum of Fine Arts. *The Architecture of Edward & W.S. Maxwell.* Exhibition catalogue. Montreal 1991

Moodie, Susanna. *Life in the Clearings Versus the Bush.* Toronto: Macmillan 1959 (orig. London, UK: Richard Bentley 1853)

– *Roughing It in the Bush, or Forest Life in Canada.* Toronto: McClelland & Stewart 1962 (orig. London, UK: Richard Bentley 1852)

Mooney, Patrick. "Landscape of Broken Stones." *Landscape Architecture* 79, no. 8 (1989): 54–6

Moore, Christopher. *Fortress of Louisbourg.* Guide. Louisbourg, NS: Fortress of Louisbourg Volunteers Association 1981

Moran, P.J. "Some Perceptions of Wascana Centre." *LAR* 5, no. 4 (1984): 18–21

Morell and Nichols, Landscape Architects. *A Report on City Planning for the City of Edmonton, Alberta.* Edmonton, 1 November 1912

Morgan, Keith. "The Emergence of the American Landscape Professional: John Notman and the Design of Rural Cemeteries." *JGH* 4, no. 3 (1984): 269–89

– *Shaping an American Landscape: The Art and Architecture of Charles A. Platt.* Hanover, NH: Hood Museum of Art, Dartmouth College/University Press of New England 1995

Morisset, Lucie K. "Non-fiction Utopia: Arvida, Cité Industrielle Made Real." *Architecture in/au Canada* 36, no. 1 (2011): 3–40

Morisset, Lucie K., Luc Noppen, and Patrick Dieudonné. *Patrimoines modernes: L'architecture du vingtième siècle à Chicoutimi.* Montreal: Presses de l'Université du Québec 2004

Morrow, E. Joyce. *Calgary, Many Years Hence: The Mawson Report in Perspective.* Calgary: City of Calgary and University of Calgary 1979

Morton, Desmond. "Was the Great War Canada's War of Independence?" *Images of a Forgotten War: Epilogue, National Film Board of Canada.* http://www3.nfb.ca/ww1

Mosquin, Alexandra. *The Butchart Gardens, Victoria, British Columbia.* HSMBC Submission Report (Agenda Paper) 2004-30

Mount Royal Cemetery. *The Trees of Mount Royal Cemetery.* Brochure. Montreal: Mount Royal Cemetery 1994

Mowbray, Scott. "Grand Mall." *Western Living,* June 1985, 63–72

Muir, John. *Our National Parks.* San Francisco: Sierra Club Books 1991 (orig. 1901)

Muirhead, Desmond. "Landscape Design in Western Canada." *RAICJ* 31, no. 7 (1954): 235–41

Mumford, Lewis. *The Brown Decades: A Study of the Arts in America 1865–1895.* 2nd edn. New York: Dover Publications 1955

– "Frederick Law Olmsted's Contribution." In *Roots of Contemporary American Architecture,* 101–16. New York: Reinhold Publishing 1952

Murray, A.L. "Frederick Law Olmsted and the Design of Mount Royal Park, Montreal." *Journal of the Society of Architectural Historians* 26, no. 3 (October 1967): 163–71

"My Dream Is of an Island Place Which Distant Seas Keep Lonely." *Canadian Homes and Gardens* 5, no. 5 (1928): 32–3

Nadeau, Hélène. "Granges circulaires: Conserver la forme." *Continuité,* no. 109 (2006): 50–3

Nakajima, Ken. "The Japanese Garden of the Montreal Botanical Garden." *Quatre-Temps* 12, no. 2 (1988): 16–18

National Capital Commission. *A Capital in the Making: Reflections of the Past, Visions of the Future.* Ottawa 1984

– Public Affairs Division. *Major's Hill and Nepean Point.* Ottawa 1983

Naylor, Eha. "Ecologically Based Waterfront Design." *Landscapes/Paysages* 6, no. 1 (2004): 34–5

Nazar, Jack. "Design, Utility or Burlesque" and "Garden for a Private Residence in Ottawa, Ontario." *RAICJ* 27, no. 8 (1950): 255–7

Neill, John. "Nitobe Memorial Garden, History and Development." *Davidsonia* 1, no. 2 (1970): 10–15

Nelson, Carl R., Jr. "University of Manitoba Campus." Unpublished manuscript 1990

Nelson, J.G., ed. *Canadian Parks in Perspective.* Montreal: Harvest House 1970

– *Man's Impact on the Western Canadian Landscape.* Toronto: McClelland & Stewart 1976

Nelson, J.G., and R.E. England. "Some comments on the Causes and Effects of Fire in the Northern Grasslands Area of Canada and the Nearby United States, ca. 1750–1900." *Canadian Geographer* 15, no. 4 (1971): 295–306

Nerenberg, Jacob. *Projet-pilote de toit vert: Démarche d'une construction écologique.* Montreal: Société de développement communautaire de Montréal 2005

Newbury, Robert W. "Return to the Rivers of Discovery of Western Canada." *Landscape Planning* 6, no. 2 (1979): 237–48

Newlands, T.J. "The History and Operations of Hamilton's Parks." *Wentworth Bygones.* Vol. 9. Hamilton: Head-of-the- Lake Historical Society, Walsh Printing Service 1971

Newton, Norman T. *Design on the Land: The Development of Landscape Architecture.* Cambridge, MA: Belknap Press of Harvard University Press 1978

"The Niagara Parks." *Canadian Architect* 4, no. 6 (1959): 67–9

Niagara Parks Commission. *Un monde à découvrir!* Brochure. 1980

Nichols, Frederick Doveton, and Ralph E. Griswold. *Thomas Jefferson, Landscape Architect.* Charlottesville, VA: University Press of Virginia 1978

Nikkei Research and Education Project of Ontario. *Nikkei Voice* (Toronto; monthly newspaper in English and Japanese). Various issues

Nitsitapiisinni: The Story of the Blackfoot People. Toronto: Key Porter Books 2001

Noppen, Luc. "Les archives nationales au Saguenay-Lac-St-Jean: Une vitrine de la mémoire du paysage architectural." *ARQ,* no. 94 (December 1996): 18–22

Noppen, Luc, and Lucie K. Morisset. *L'architecture de Saint-Roch, Guide de Promenade.* Sainte-Foy, QC: Les Publications du Québec 2000

Noppen, Luc, Claude Paulette, and Michel Tremblay. *Québec, trois siècles d'architecture.* Quebec City: Éditions Libre Expression 1979

Norris, John. *Old Silverton, British Columbia 1891–1930.* Silverton Historical Society, c. 1980

Novak, Len. "Canadian Landscape Architecture – Our Past and Future in the Environmental Movement." *LAR* 5, no. 2 (1984): 8–10

Novak, Len, Donna Balzer, Michelle Reid, et al. *Reader Rock Garden Management Plan.* Calgary: City of Calgary Parks 2008

Nova Scotia Museum. *Uniacke Estate Museum Park.* Brochure

Nuffield, Edward W. *The Pacific Northwest: Its Discovery and Early Exploration by Sea, Land, and River.* Surrey, BC: Hancock House 1990

OALA Professional Awards 1980. "Ryerson Community Park – Honours Award." *LAR* 2, no. 1 (1981): 9

OALA Professional Awards 1981. *LAR* 3, no. 1 (1982): 1–20

Oberlander, Cornelia Hahn. *Forging the Way: Landscape Practice in Canada 1953–2011.* Address to IFLA Conference, Zurich, Switzerland, June 2011

- "National Gallery of Canada Landscape Concept." *LAR* 6, no. 5 (1985): 5–7
- "A Need for Green Streets." *Canadian Architect* 19, no. 4 (1974): 34–7
- Notes of an interview with Raoul Robillard. Vancouver, c. 1980
- "An Oasis in the City: Robson Square and the Law Courts." *LAR* 2, no. 2 (1981): 6–15
- *Playgrounds… a Plea for Utopia or the Re-cycled Empty Lot.* 2nd edn. Ottawa: Health and Welfare Canada 1974
- "The Professional Practice of Landscape Architecture." *RAICJ* 31, no. 7 (1954): 243

Oberlander, H. Peter. "Making Waves: The Emergence of the Canadian Planner." *Plan Canada* 42, no. 3 (2002): 17–18

O'Brian, John, and Peter White. *Beyond Wilderness: The Group of Seven, Canadian Identity, and Contemporary Art.* Montreal & Kingston: McGill-Queen's University Press 2007

Oehmichen, Friedrich. "Ornamental Grasses – Why Not?" *LAR* 6, no. 3 (1985): 19–22

Olmsted, Frederick Law. *Mount Royal, Montreal.* New York: G.P. Putnam's Sons 1881
- "Public Parks and the Enlargement of Towns." Paper read to the American Social Science Association, 1870
- *Report of Fred. Law Olmsted on Mount Royal Park, 1874.* Montreal: Archives Municipales, 21 November 1874

Olmsted, Frederick Law, Jr., and Theodora Kimball, eds. *Frederick Law Olmsted Sr, Forty Years of Landscape Architecture: Central Park.* Cambridge, MA: MIT Press 1973

O'Neil, Jean, and Pierre Philippe Burnet. *L'île Sainte-Hélène.* Montreal: Éditions Hurtubise HMH 2001

O'Neill, Anne. "The Gardens of 18th Century Louisbourg." *JGH* 3, no. 3 (1983): 176–8

O'Neill, Michael. "Les parc provinciaux." *Continuité,* special issue no. 1 (Autumn 1990): 35–6

Ontario Parks. Brochures and trail guides for the following parks: Algonquin, Awenda, Long Point, Presqu'ile, Sandbanks, Wasaga Beach
- *Petroglyphs: The Teaching Rocks.* Toronto: Government of Ontario 2001

Opp, James, and John C. Walsh, eds. *Placing Memory and Remembering Place in Canada.* Vancouver: University of British Columbia Press 2010

Osborne, Jari. *Sleeping Tigers: The Asahi Baseball Story.* Film. Montreal: National Film Board of Canada 2003

Ouellet, Fernand. "Louis-Joseph Papineau." *Dictionary of Canadian Biography* 10 (1871–80). Toronto/Quebec City: University of Toronto Press/Presses de l'Université Laval 2000

Ouellet, Karine. "L'importance du paysage dans l'oeuvre de Gabrielle Roy." Master's directed study project, Faculté de l'aménagement, Université de Montréal, April 2004

"Our Cover House, a Lesson in Landscaping." *Western Homes and Living,* August 1955, 16–17

Padover, Saul K. *Jefferson: A Great American's Life and Ideas.* Abridged edn. New York: Mentor Books, New American Library 1952

Paine, Cecelia. "Design of Landscapes in Support of Mental Health: Influences and Practice in Ontario." *Environments* 26, no. 3 (1999): 37–47
- , ed. *Fifty Years of Landscape Architecture in Canada: The Canadian Society of Landscape Architects 1934–1984.* Guelph, ON: University of Guelph 1998
- "Reflections on the Third Wave." *Landscapes/Paysages* 12, no. 2 (2010): 21–3
- "Restoration of the Billings Estate Cemetery." *APT Bulletin* 15, no. 4 (1983): 61–5
- "Sparks Street Mall: Tradition, Elegance and Distinction." *LAR* 9, no. 4 (1988): 6–8

Papineau, Louis-Joseph Amédée. *Journal d'un Fils de la Liberté (1838–1855).* Sillery, QC: Septentrion 1998

Parker, Patricia. "Butcharts' Vision." *Landmark,* February 1991, 33–7
- "Cascades of Time." *Landmark,* August 1991, 20–3

Parkman, Francis. *Montcalm and Wolfe.* NY: Collier-Macmillan 1962 (orig. Boston, 1884)

Parks Canada, *The Architectural History of Riding Mountain National Park.* Technical report. N.d.
- *Bellevue House.* Brochure/Guide. Ottawa 2004
- Brochures and trail guides for the following parks: Banff, Cape Breton Highlands, Georgian Bay Islands, Glacier, Gros-Morne, Jasper, Kootenay, Kouchibouguac, La Mauricie, Pacific Rim, Point Pelée, St. Lawrence Islands, Yoho
- *Grand-Pré National Historic Site.* Brochure/Guide. Ottawa 1999
- *Lanark Place: Memories of an Ontarian West.* Ottawa: Minister of Supply and Services Canada 1983
- *Manoir-Papineau National Historic Site.* Brochure/Guide. Ottawa 2005
- *The Motherwell Homestead National Historic Site.* Brochure/Guide
- "Unimpaired for Future Generations"? Vol. 1: *Protecting Ecological Integrity in Canada's National Parks; Report of the Panel on the Ecological Integrity of Canada's National Parks.* Ottawa: Minister of Public Works and Government Services 2000
- "Unimpaired for Future Generations"? Vol. 2: *Setting a New Direction for Canada's National Parks; Report of the Panel on the Ecological Integrity of Canada's National Parks.* Ottawa: Minister of Public Works and Government Services 2000

Parks Canada, Historical Services Branch. *Central Experimental Farm, Ottawa, Ontario.* HSMBC Agenda Paper 1997-43

Parks Canada, Western Region. *Management Plan: Fort Langley National Historic Park.* Calgary: Environment Canada 1987

Parks Canada and Memramcook Valley Historical Society. *Guide.* Memramcook, NB: n.d.

Passfield, Robert W. *Philip Louis Pratley (1884–1958), Civil Engineer, Montreal.* Ottawa-Hull, HSMBC Agenda Paper 2004-50

Paterson, Douglas D., and Lisa J. Colby. *Heritage Landscapes in British Columbia: A Guide to Their Identification, Documentation and Preservation.* Vancouver: University of British Columbia, Landscape Architecture Program 1989

Paton, J.A. "History of Banner Municipality Shows Many Changes in Five Years." *Point Grey Gazette* (Vancouver), 14 June 1913, 1–3, 5, 9, 11, 13
- "Seventeen Years of Progress." *Point Grey Gazette* (Vancouver), July 1925, 1, 3, 26–7

Paulette, Claude. *Place-Royale c'est…* , Quebec City: Gouvernement du Québec, Ministère des Affaires culturelles, Direction régionale de Québec 1995

Pawlick, Thomas F. *The War in the Country: How the Fight to Save Rural Life Will Shape Our Future.* Vancouver: Greystone Books 2009

Pelletier, Michel, and Roch Samson. *L'ancienne aluminerie de Shawinigan.* HSMBC Agenda Paper 2001-47

Perks, William T. "Idealism, Orchestration and Science in Early Canadian Planning: Calgary and Vancouver Re-visited, 1914–1928." *Environments* 17, no. 2 (1982): 1–28

Perron, Louis. "Les Floralies 1980 et l'architecture de paysage au Québec." Montreal: Floralies 80 and Jardin botanique de Montréal 1980

Peters, Ann. "Yellowknife – A Town without a Presence." *SSAC Bulletin* 13, no. 2 (1988): 33–6

Pinhey, Jeffrey A., and Peter Klynstra. "Landscape Management Plan, Borden-Carleton, PEI." *Plan Canada* 37, no. 2 (1997): 31–6

"Plan for a Remodeled Landscape." *Western Homes and Living*, March 1955, 22–3

"Plan for Leisure Living … The UBC home of Dr and Mrs. Sydney M. Friedman." *Western Homes and Living*, February 1955

Platt, Charles A. *Monograph of the Work of Charles A. Platt*. New York: Architectural Book Publishing Company 1913

Plummer, Christopher. *In Spite of Myself: A Memoir*. New York and Toronto: Alfred E. Knopf 2008

Pollock-Ellwand, Nancy. "Gordon Culham: Living a 'Useful Life' through the Professionalization of Canadian Town Planning and Landscape Architecture." *Planning Perspectives* 27, no. 4 (2012): 587–609

– "A Homestead Restored." *LAR* 7, no. 2 (1986): 10–12

– "The Olmsted Firm in Canada: A Correction of the Record." *Planning Perspectives* 21 (July 2006): 277–310

– "Rickson Outhet: Bringing the Olmsted Legacy to Canada. A Romantic View of Nature in the Metropolis and the Hinterland." *Journal of Canadian Studies* 44, no. 1 (2010): 137–83

Polo, Marco. "Capital Assets." *Canadian Architect* 43, no. 4 (1998): 28–9

Porter, John. *The Vertical Mosaic: An Analysis of Social Class and Power in Canada*. Toronto: University of Toronto Press 1965

"The Porter House." *Canadian Architect* 4, no. 10 (1959): 76–7

Poullaouec-Gonidec, Philippe. "Le projet d'architecture de paysage de Claude Cormier." *ARQ*, no. 139 (May 2007): 16–17

"Practice Profile: EDM Environmental Design and Management Ltd." *Landscapes/Paysages* 3, no. 1 (2001): 7–10

Preston, Isabella. "A Few Lilies for Canadian Gardens." *Canadian Homes and Gardens* 2, no. 3 (1925): 112, 115–16

Pringle, Heather. "The First Americans: Mounting Evidence Prompts Researchers to Reconsider the Peopling of the New World." *Scientific American* 305 (November 2011): 36–45

"Private Golf Course, Toronto." *Canadian Architect* 4, no. 7 (1959): 49–58

Proceedings of the Sixth National Conference on City Planning, 25–27 May 1914, Toronto. Cambridge, MA: The University Press 1914

Prochazka, Alena. "Entrevue avec Blanche Lemco van Ginkel." *ARQ*, no. 160 (August 2012): 6–11

Project Planning Associates Ltd. "Northern Electric Site." *Canadian Landscape Architect* 2, no. 2 (1961–62): 22–5

Provancher, Léon. *Flore canadienne*. Quebec City: Joseph Darveau, imprimeur-éditeur 1862

– *Traité élémentaire de botanique: À l'usage des maisons d'éducation et des amateurs*. Montreal: J.-A. Langlais 1884 (orig. Montreal 1858)

Provencher, Jean. *La station de recherche de Deschambault*. Quebec City: Gouvernement du Québec 2006

Prud'homme, Chantal. "Île d'Orléans: Mutations agricoles." *Continuité*, no. 109 (2006): 36–8

– *Manoir-Papineau, lieu historique national, Montebello, Québec: Etude sur les jardins et le potager*. Quebec City: Public Works and Government Services Canada 1995

Purdy, Sean. "This Is Not a Company: Class, Gender and the Toronto Housing Company, 1912–1920." *UHR* 21, no. 2 (1993): 75–91

Quimby, George Irving. *Indian Life in the Upper Great Lakes, 1100 B.C. to A.D. 1800*. Chicago: University of Chicago Press 1960

Rabinovitch, Victor. "Pragmatic Diversity and National Identity." *Canadian Diversity* 4, no. 1 (2005): 60–5

Raddall, Thomas H. *Halifax: Warden of the North*. Halifax: Nimbus Publishing 1993

Rajotte-LaBrèque, Marie-Paule. "Les Cantons de l'Est: Une région empreinte de traditions britanniques." *Cap-aux-Diamants* 4, no. 3 (1988): 11–14

Ranney, Victoria Post, ed. *Papers of Frederick Law Olmsted*. Vol. 5: *The California Frontier*. Baltimore: Johns Hopkins University Press 1990

Ray, Arthur J. *I Have Lived Here since the World Began: An Illustrated History of Canada's Native People*. Toronto: Lester Publishing and Key Porter Books 1996

Rees, Ronald. *Land of the Loyalists: Their Struggle to Shape the Maritimes*. Halifax: Nimbus Publishing 2000

– "Wascana Centre: A Metaphor for Prairie Settlement." *JGH* 3, no. 3 (1983): 219–32

Reford, Alexander. *Des jardins oubliés 1860–1960*. Sainte-Foy, QC: Les publications du Québec 1999

– *Reford Gardens*. Montreal: Éditions Fides 2001

– *The Reford Gardens: Elsie's Paradise*. Louise Tanguay, photographer. Montreal: Les Éditions de l'Homme 2004

Regional Municipality of Wood Buffalo. *Fort McMurray Visitors Guide 2007*. Fort McMurray, 2007

Reid, Gordon. *Head-Smashed-In Buffalo Jump*. Calgary: Fifth House Publishers 2002

Reid, Michelle. "Applying the *Standards and Guidelines* to the Restoration of the Reader Rock Garden: A Case Study." Presentation to ICOMOS Canada Annual Congress, Ottawa, November 2004

"Renowned Horticulturalist Passes Away." *OALA Review* 4, no. 1 (1978): 7

Reps, John W. *The Making of Urban America: A History of City Planning in the United States*. Princeton, NJ: Princeton University Press 1965

– *Town Planning in Frontier America*. Princeton, NJ: Princeton University Press 1971 (orig. 1965)

Repton, Humphry. *Fragments on the Theory and Practice of Landscape Gardening*. London 1816

– *Observations on the Theory and Practice of Landscape Gardening*. London, UK: T. Bensley, Bolt Court 1803 (republished: Oxford: Phaidon Press 1980)

– *Sketches and Hints on Landscape Gardening*. London, UK: W. Bulmer and Co., Shakespeare Printing Office 1794

"The Residence of Saskatchewan's Lieutenant Governor." *Canadian Homes and Gardens* 2, no. 2 (1925): 22

Richards, Larry, ed. *Canadian Centre for Architecture: Building and Gardens*. Montreal/Cambridge, MA: Canadian Centre for Architecture/MIT Press 1989

Richardson, N.H. "A Tale of Two Cities." *Plan Canada* 4, no. 1 (1963): 110–25

Richer, Anne. "La personnalité de la semaine: Claude Cormier." *La Presse*, 24 February 2008, 10

Riddell, W.A. *The Origin and Development of Wascana Centre*. Regina: Wascana Centre Authority 1994

River Valley Alliance. *A Plan of Action for the Capital Region River Valley Park*. Edmonton 2007

Roberts, Sir Charles G.D. "Tantramar Revisited." In Carole Gerson and Gwendolyn Davies, eds., *Canadian Poetry: From the Beginnings through the First World War*. Toronto: McClelland & Stewart 1994

Robinson, Charles Mulford. *Modern Civic Art or, The City Made Beautiful*. New York: Arno Press 1970 (orig. New York: G.P. Putnam's Sons 1903)

Robson, Robert. "The Central Mortgage and Housing Corporation and the Ontario Resource Town, 1945–1967." *Environments* 17, no. 2 (1985): 66–74

"Robson Square." *Landscape Architecture* 69, no. 4 (July 1979): 377–9

Rochon, Lisa. *Up North: Where Canada's Architecture Meets the Land*. Toronto: Keystone Press 2005

Rock, William, Jr. *A Brief Guide to Landscape Architecture in the Toronto Area*. Toronto: Department of Landscape Architecture, University of Toronto, c. 1980

Rogers, Irene, and R. Tuck. "Charlotte Town: A Walking Tour." Charlottetown, PEI, n.d.

Rolland, Jean-François, and Marie-Claire Martineau. "The Symbolic Garden of the Stations of the Cross at St. Joseph's Oratory in Montreal." *LAC* 4, no. 3 (1978): 17–33

Rompré, Danielle. "Les jardins clos des communautés religieuses." *Continuité*, special issue no. 1 (Autumn 1990): 27–8

Roos, Arnold E. *The McIntosh Apple*. HSMBC Agenda Paper 1999-27

Ross, Alexander M., and Terry Crowley. *The College on the Hill: A New History of the Ontario Agricultural College, 1874–1999*. Toronto: Dundurn Press 1999

Ross, Donald A. "Manitoba Legislative Buildings, Winnipeg." *RAICJ* 1, no. 3 (1924): 75–87

Ross, Sally. *Dykes and Aboiteaux: The Acadians Turned Salt Marshes into Fertile Meadows*. Grand-Pré, NS: Société Promotion Grand-Pré 2002

Ross, Sally, and Alphonse Deveau. *The Acadians of Nova Scotia, Past and Present*. Halifax: Nimbus Publishing 1992

Rotundo, Barbara. "Mount Auburn: Fortunate Coincidences and an Ideal Solution." *JGH* 4, no. 3 (1984): 255–67

Routaboule, Danièle. "L'Université de Moncton." *Architecture Bâtiment Construction*, 1966

Rowe, J.S. *Forest Regions of Canada*. Ottawa: Canadian Forestry Service, Dept. of Fisheries and the Environment 1972

Roy, Gabrielle. *Enchantment and Sorrow: The Autobiography of Gabrielle Roy*. Translated by Patricia Claxton. Toronto: Lester & Orpen Dennys 1987 (orig. 1984)

– *Garden in the Wind*. Translated by Alan Brown. Toronto: McClelland & Stewart 1977 (orig. *Un jardin au bout du monde*, Montreal: Éditions Beauchemin 1975)

Roy, Gilles. "Centre Hospitalier Douglas: Profil historique." *LAR* 6, no. 4 (1985): 11–14

Roy, Patricia E. "A Tale of Two Cities: The Reception of Japanese Evacuees in Kelowna and Kaslo, B.C." *BC Studies*, no. 87 (1990): 23–47

– *Vancouver: An Illustrated History*. Toronto: James Lorimer & Co. 1980

Roy, Patricia E., and John Herd Thompson. *British Columbia: Land of Promises*. Toronto: Oxford University Press 2005

Royal Botanical Gardens. *Garden with a View*. Hamilton: Royal Botanical Gardens, c. 2008

– "Helen M. Kippax Garden: A New Look at Native Plants." Brochure. Hamilton: Royal Botanical Gardens 2007

Royal Commission on the Future of the Toronto Waterfront. *Planning for Sustainability: Towards Integrating Environmental Protection into Land-Use Planning*. Canada: Ministry of Supply and Services 1991

– *Shoreline Regeneration for the Greater Toronto Bioregion*. Canada: Ministry of Supply and Services 1991

Rumilly, Robert. *Papineau*. Montreal: B. Valiquette 1944

Rybczynski, Witold. *A Clearing in the Distance: Frederick Law Olmsted and North America in the Nineteenth Century*. Toronto: HarperCollins/Harper Perennial Canada 1999

– *A Makeshift Metropolis: Ideas about Cities*. New York and Toronto: Scribner 2010

Saarinen, Oiva W. "Provincial Land Use Planning Initiatives in the Town of Kapuskasing." *UHR* 10, no. 1 (1981): 1–15

Sackville, James. "Ecotourism in Bouctouche, New Brunswick." *Landscapes/Paysages* 2, no. 2 (2000): 14–17

– "A River Runs through It." *Landscapes/Paysages* 11, no. 2 (2009): 32–3

St. Andrews Chamber of Commerce. *St. Andrews-by-the-Sea Historic Guide*. 2001

Saint-Pierre, Serge, and Mélodie Lachance. "Le manoir de Philippe Aubert de Gaspé enfin ressuscité." *Histoire Québec* 15, no. 3 (2010): 9–12

Sandalack, Beverly A. "Evolution of the Public Realm: Streets, Squares, Parks and Open Spaces in a Prairie Town." *Environments* 26, no. 3 (1999): 49–58

Sandalack, Beverly A., and Ann Davis, eds. *Excursions into the Cultural Landscapes of Alberta*. Calgary: Nickle Arts Museum 2005

Sandalack, Beverly A., and Andrei Nicolai. *The Calgary Project: Urban Form/Urban Life*. Calgary: University of Calgary Press 2006

Sandercock, Leonie. "Le maintien des villes multiculturelles au Canada." *Nos diverses cites*, no. 1 (Spring 2004): 160–5

Sanders, Harry M. *Calgary's Historic Union Cemetery: A Walking Guide*. Calgary: Fifth House Publishers 2002

"Sarahluff Bond, Garden Architect." *Canadian Homes and Gardens* 3, no. 12 (1926): 37

Sarjeant, Margaret. "Three Million Trees a Year: The Forgotten History of Saskatoon's Forestry Farm Park and Zoo." *Saskatoon History*, no. 8 (1993): 34–41

Satterthwaite, Altona. *Royal Botanical Gardens, Ontario, Canada: A Guide to Five Remarkable Gardens and Four Nature Sanctuaries*. Hamilton, ON: Royal Botanical Gardens 2000

Saul, John Ralston. "The Collapse of Globalism." *Harper's Magazine*, March 2004, 33–43

– *A Fair Country: Telling Truths about Canada*. Toronto: Penguin Group 2008

– *Reflections of a Siamese Twin: Canada at the End of the Twentieth Century/Beginning of the Twenty-first Century*. Toronto: Viking Penguin Canada 1997

Saunders, William, and Auguste Dupuis. *Horticulture au Canada*. Ottawa: Ministère de l'agriculture 1900

Schama, Simon. *Landscape and Memory*. New York: Vintage Books, Random House 1995

Schell, Jonathan. "The Unfinished Twentieth Century." *Harper's Magazine*, January 2000, 41–56

Schneider, Paul. *The Adirondacks: A History of America's First Wilderness*. New York: Henry Holt & Company 1997

School of Architecture, McGill University. *Resolution on the Death of Emeritus Professor Harold Spence-Sales (October 22, 1907 to March 12, 2004)*. http://www.mcgill.ca/architecture/memoriam/spence-sales

Schumann, Ulrich Maximilian. "The Hidden Roots of the Garden City Idea." *Journal of Planning History* 2, no. 4 (2003): 291–310

Schuyler, David. *Apostle of Taste: Andrew Jackson Downing 1815–1852*. Baltimore: Johns Hopkins University Press 1996

- "The Evolution of the Anglo-American Rural Cemetery: Landscape Architecture as Social and Cultural History." *JGH* 4, no. 3 (1984): 291–304
- *The New Urban Landscape: The Redefinition of City Form in Nineteenth-Century America.* Baltimore: Johns Hopkins University Press 1986

Scott, Owen R. "George Laing, Landscape Gardener, Hamilton, Canada West." *APT* 9, no. 3 (1977): 52–64
- "Herman Stensson – 1877–1938." *LAC* 3, no. 3 (1977): 7–9
- "Tipperary Creek Conservation Area, Wanuskewin Heritage Park." *LAR* 7, no. 2 (1986): 5–9
- "Utilizing History to Establish Cultural and Physical Identity in the Landscape." *Landscape Planning* 6, no. 2 (1979): 179–203

Scully, Vincent, Jr. *The Shingle Style and the Stick Style.* Rev. edn. New Haven, UK: Yale University Press 1971 (orig. 1955)

Segger, Martin. *The Buildings of Samuel Maclure: In Search of Appropriate Form.* Victoria: Sono Nis Press 1986
- *Victoria: A Primer for Regional History in Architecture.* Watkins Glen, NY/Victoria: American Life and Foundation and Study Institute/Heritage Architectural Guides 1979

Seibel, George Alfred, and Olive M. Seibel. *Ontario's Niagara Parks: 100 Years, A History.* Niagara Falls, ON: Niagara Parks Commission 1985

Seline, Janice. "Frederick Law Olmsted's Mount Royal Park, Montreal: Design and Context." Master's thesis, Concordia University, Montreal, 1983

SEPAQ. *Le Sault de Montmorency, Guide.* Quebec City, c. 2000

Service d'urbanisme de la Ville de Montréal. *Plan directeur de Montréal: Espaces libres.* Montreal: City of Montreal 1955

Severson-Baker, Chris, Jennifer Grant, and Simon Dyer. *Taking the Wheel: Correcting the Course of Cumulative Environmental Management in the Athabasca Oil Sands.* Calgary: Pembina Institute, August 2008

Sewell, John. *The Shape of the City: Toronto Struggles with Modern Planning.* Toronto: University of Toronto Press 1993

Sharp, Mitchell. *Which Reminds Me…, A Memoir.* Toronto: University of Toronto Press 1994

Shearon, Jim. "The True North: Who Stands on Guard?" *Conservation Canada* (Parks Canada, Ottawa) 4, no. 2 (1978): 10–15

Shelton, Paul. "Places for the Soul: The Role of Environmental Design in the Reconciliation Process." *Canadian Eco-architecture* (Toronto: Ontario Association of Architects) 4 (June 1998): 76–83

Sheppard, Lola. "Quebec Pastorale: The Methods and Approaches of the Next Wave of Quebec Landscape Architects Are Discussed." *Canadian Architect* 52, no. 5 (2007): 49–53

Sherk, Larry. "The Principals, Sven Herman Stensson." In Sheila Kirkland, ed., *The Grape Vine* 2, no. 1 (Oakville, ON, Sheridan Nurseries Ltd., January 1988)

Sherwood, David H. "Canadian Institute of Planners." *Plan Canada*, special issue, July 1994, 20–1

Shipley, Robert. *To Mark Our Place: A History of Canadian War Memorials.* Photos by David Street. Toronto: NC Press 1987

Sierra Club of Canada. "Sydney Tar Ponds Backgrounder." N.d.

Sifton, Clifford. "The Conservation of Canada's Resources." Speech at Empire Club of Canada, Toronto, 20 October 1910
- *Revue du Travail de la Commission de la Conservation.* Montreal: Federated Press 1917

Silversides, Brock V. *Prairie Sentinel: The Story of the Canadian Grain Elevator.* Calgary and Toronto: Fifth House Publishers 1997

Simard, Jean. *L'art religieux des routes du Québec.* Quebec City: Gouvernement du Québec, Ministère des Affaires culturelles et communications 1995

Simpson, Michael. *Thomas Adams and the Modern Planning Movement: Britain, Canada, and the United States, 1900–1940.* London/New York: Mansell 1985
- "Thomas Adams in Canada, 1914–1930." *UHR* 11, no. 2 (1982): 1–15

Simpson, Nan Booth. "One Garden: Hidden Pleasures." *Garden Design* 10, no. 2 (March 1993): 38–41

Singh, Patwant. "Sir Edwin Lutyens and the Building of New Delhi." *Icon World Monuments*, Winter 2002/03, 38–43

Skinner, Helen Ross. "With a Lilac by the Door: Some Research into Early Gardens in Ontario." *APT Bulletin* 15, no. 4 (1983): 35–7

Smith, Carl. *The Plan of Chicago, Daniel Burnham and the Remaking of the American City.* Chicago and London: University of Chicago Press 2006

Smith, Cyndi. *Jasper Park Lodge: In the Heart of the Canadian Rockies.* Canmore, AB: Coyote Books 1985

Smith, Frédéric. *Cataraqui: Histoire d'une villa anglaise à Sillery.* Quebec City: Les Publications du Québec 2001

Smith, Helen, and Mary Bramley. *Ottawa's Farm: A History of the Central Experimental Farm.* Renfrew, ON: General Store Publishing House 1996

Smith, Julian. "Restoring Vimy: The Challenges of Confronting Emerging Modernism." *Architecture in Canada* 33, no. 1 (2008): 49–56

Smyly, Carolyn. "The Maclure Tradition." *Western Living* 8, no. 6 (1978): 6–8

Smyly, John, and Carolyn Smyly. *Those Born at Koona.* Surrey, BC: Hancock House Publishers 1973

Snell, John Ferguson. *Macdonald College of McGill University: A History from 1904–1955.* Montreal: McGill University Press 1963

Société d'histoire et de généalogie du Plateau-Mont-Royal. "Cahier souvenir – Le parc La Fontaine à travers le temps." *Bulletin de la Société d'histoire et de généalogie du Plateau Mont-Royal* 6, no. 3 (2011)

Société du Jardin de Chine de Montréal. *Le Jardin de Chine de Montréal, Guide illustré complet.* Montreal: Éditions Fides 1994

Soderstrom, Mary. *Recreating Eden: A Natural History of Botanical Gardens.* Montreal: Véhicule Press 2001

Sommelier, Christian. *Le Bois-de-Coulonge: Exemple de remise en valeur d'un parc en milieu urbain.* Quebec City: Commission de la capitale nationale du Québec 1999

Sontag, William H., ed. *National Park Service: The First 75 Years.* Fort Washington, PA: Eastern National Park and Monument Association 1990

Soubrier, Robert, invited ed. *Society and Leisure* 8, no. 1 (1985)

space2place. *(Re)imagining a Social Space: Oppenheimer Park, Vancouver BC, 2010.* Vancouver 2010

Spence-Sales, Mary H. *Harold Spence-Sales.* School of City Planning, McGill University, October 2007. http://www.mcgill.ca/urbanplanning/hss100

Spirn, Anne Whiston. *The Granite Garden: Urban Nature and Human Design.* New York: Basic Books 1984

Spry, Irene M. *The Palliser Expedition: An Account of John Palliser's British North American Exploring Expedition 1857–1860.* Toronto: Macmillan 1963

Stamp, Robert M. *Suburban Modern: Postwar Dreams in Calgary.* Calgary: Touch Wood Editions 2004

Steele, Mike. *Vancouver's Famous Stanley Park: The Year-Round Playground*. Vancouver: Heritage House 1993

Steele, Richard M. *The Stanley Park Explorer*. Vancouver: Whitecap Books 1985

Stein, Clarence. *Toward New Towns for America*. Cambridge, MA: MIT Press 1951

Steinberg, Ted. *Down to Earth: Nature's Role in American History*. Oxford and New York: Oxford University Press 2002

Steinhoff Sanders, Frances. "Oasis on the Roof." *Canadian Homes and Gardens*, 1948 (reprinted in von Baeyer and Crawford, *Garden Voices*, 56–7)

Stelter, Gilbert A., and Alan F.J. Artibise, eds. *The Canadian City: Essays in Urban History*. Toronto: McClelland & Stewart 1977

–, eds. *Shaping the Urban Landscape: Aspects of the Canadian City-Building Process*. Ottawa: Carleton University Press 1982

–, eds. *The Usable Urban Past, Planning and Politics in the Modern Canadian City*. Ottawa: Carleton University Press 1980

Stensson, J. Vilhelm. "Approach to Planting." *RAICJ* 27, no. 8 (1950): 266–7

Stern, Robert. *Architecture on the Edge of Postmodernism: Collected Essays, 1964–1988*. New Haven, CT: Yale University Press 2009

Stewart, Hilary. *Looking at Totem Poles*. Vancouver and Toronto: Douglas & McIntyre 1993

Stewart, John J. "Canada's Landscape Heritage." *Landscape Planning* 6, no. 2 (1979): 205–24

– "Historic Gardens in Canada and the United States." *APT Bulletin* 2, no. 3 (1973): 1–22

– "Landscape Archaeologist at Work." *Landscape Architecture* 68 no. 2 (1978): 140–4

– "Landscape Archaeology: Existing Plant Material on Historic Sites as Evidence of Buried Features and as Survivors of Historic Species." *APT Bulletin* 9, no. 3 (1977): 65–70

– "Notes on Calvert Vaux's 1873 Design for the Public Grounds of the Parliament Buildings in Ottawa." *APT Bulletin* 8, no. 1 (1976): 1–27

Stewart, John J., and Susan Buggey. "Canada's Living Past – Historic Landscapes and Gardens." *OALA Review* 2, no. 2 (1976): 6–13

– "The Case for Commemoration of Historic Landscapes and Gardens." *APT Bulletin* 7, no. 2 (1975): 99–123

Stinson, Kathy. *Love Every Leaf: The Life of Landscape Architect Cornelia Hahn Oberlander*. Toronto: Tundra Books 2008

Straley, Gerald B. *Trees of Vancouver*. Vancouver: University of British Columbia Press 1992

Strathdee, Gordon. *Bayfield: Steps to the Sunset*. St. Marys, ON: Stonetown Books 2001

Strickland, Samuel. *Twenty-seven Years in Canada West*. Vols. 1 and 2. Edmonton: M.G. Hurtig 1970 (orig. London: Richard Bentley 1853)

Strong, Maurice. *Where on Earth Are We Going?* Toronto: Alfred A. Knopf Canada 2000

Suncor Energy. *Over 30 Years of Reclaiming the Land*. Fort McMurray, AB, n.d.

– *Suncor In-situ: Growth through Technology*. Fort McMurray, AB, May 2005

Sutow, Mary, and Pauline Murphy. *Worse Than War: The Halifax Explosion*. Tantallon, NS: Four East Publications 1992

Sutton, S.B., ed. *Civilizing American Cities: A Selection of Frederick Law Olmsted's Writings on City Landscapes*. Cambridge, MA: MIT Press 1979

Suzuki, David. *The Autobiography*. Vancouver: Greystone Books 2006

– *The David Suzuki Reader*. Vancouver: Greystone Books 2003

– *Metamorphosis: Stages in a Life*. Toronto: Stoddart Publishing 1987

Symposium International sur la Foresterie Urbaine. *Urban Forestry, Myth or Reality*. Quebec City: Association forestière québécoise inc. 1980

Syncrude Canada Ltd. *Syncrude Fact Book*. Fort McMurray, AB, April 2007

Takata, Toyo. *Nikkei Legacy: The Story of Japanese Canadians from Settlement to Today*. Toronto: NC Press 1983

Tanner, Helen Hornbeck, ed. *The Settling of North America: The Atlas of the Great Migrations into North America from the Ice Age to the Present*. New York: Macmillan 1995

Task Force to Bring Back the Don. *Bringing Back the Don*. Toronto: City of Toronto 1991

Tate, Alan. *Great City Parks*. London: Spon Press 2001

Tattersfield, Philip. *British Columbia Society of Landscape Architects: A History*. Vancouver: BCSLA 1983

Tausky, Nancy Z. *Historical Sketches of London: From Site to City*. Peterborough, ON: Broadview Press 1993

Tausky, Nancy Z., and Lynne D. DiStefano. *Victorian Architecture in London and Southwestern Ontario: Symbols of Aspiration*. Toronto: University of Toronto Press 1986

Taylor, James R. "British and American Influences on Canadian Landscape Architecture." In *Borderlands: The Shared Canadian and U.S. Experience of Landscape: Proceedings of the Alliance for Historic Landscape Preservation*, 105–15. Toronto: AHLP 1999

– "The Calgary Olympic Winter Games." *LAR* 9, no. 1 (1988): 4

– *The Practice of Landscape Architecture in Canada*. Guelph, ON: Landscape Architecture Canada Foundation 2006

Taylor, James R., Cecelia Paine, and John Fitzgibbon. "From Greenbelt to Greenways: Four Canadian Case Studies." *Landscape and Urban Planning*, no. 33 (1995): 47–64

Tchikine, Anatole. "The 'Candelabrum' Fountain Revisited." *SHGDL* 29, no. 4 (2009): 257–69

Tellier, Danielle. *The Chinese Garden of Montreal*. Montreal: Éditions Fides 1994

Tessier, Yves. *An Historical Guide to Quebec*. Quebec City: Société historique de Québec 1984

"This Month's Who's Who." *Canadian Homes and Gardens* 2, no. 3 (1925): 7

Thom, R.J. "Champlain College, Peterborough, Ont." *Canadian Architect* 10, no. 4 (1965): 64–7

Thomas, Nicholas. *Cook: The Extraordinary Voyages of Captain James Cook*. Toronto: Viking Canada 2003

Thomas H. Mawson & Sons. *Calgary: A Preliminary Scheme for Controlling the Economic Growth of the City*. Calgary: City Planning Commission 1914 (also published as *The City of Calgary, Past, Present and Future*. London: B.T. Batsford 1914)

Thompson, Dixon, and Maurice Nelischer. "Oskuna Ka Asusteki: Changing Landscapes and Changing Attitudes." *Landscape Planning* 6, no. 2 (1979): 127–49

Thompson, John Herd. *Forging the Prairie West: The Illustrated History of Canada*. Don Mills, ON: Oxford University Press 1998

Thomsen, Charles H. "A Border Vision: The International Peace Garden." *Manitoba History*, no. 31 (1996): 36–41

– "Denis R. Wilkinson: A Brief but Productive Residency in Manitoba." *LAR* 9, no. 3 (1988): 22

Thomson, Grace Eiko. "New Denver Museum Celebrates Recognition as Nationally Historic." *Nikkei Voice* 24, no. 7 (2010): 1, 7

Thurston, Harry. *Tidal Life: A Natural History of the Bay of Fundy*. Halifax: Nimbus Publishing 1990

Todd, Frederick G. "Character in Park Design." *Canadian Architect and Builder* 18 (1905): 135–7
– *Esthetic Forestry*. Montreal: Witness Printing Co. 1922
– Letter to R. Thomas Orr, Stratford Park Committee, 31 December 1904, Stratford-Perth Archives, Stratford, ON
– Letter to Wm Lyon Mackenzie King, Prime Minister of Canada, 1934, cited in Peter Jacobs, "Frederick Gage Todd 1976–1948." *APT Journal* 15, no. 4 (1983): 27–34
– "Point Grey, BC." *Canadian Municipal Journal* 1, no. 2 (1905): 1–4
– *Preliminary Report to the Ottawa Improvement Commission*. Montreal, 28 August 1903
– *Quebec Battlefields Park Report*. Quebec City: National Battlefields Commission, 15 November 1909
– "Report and Accompanying Plans Showing Recommendations for Parks and Boulevards." Submitted to City of Edmonton on 5 April 1907; parallel document submitted to City of Strathcona on 6 May 1907
– "Where Nature Is Abetted." *Canadian Homes and Gardens* 6, no. 4 (1929): 26–7, 54
Todd, John, Robert Angevine, Solsearch Architects, and Tyrone Cashman. *An Ark for Prince Edward Island: A Report to the Federal Government of Canada*. Little Pond, Souris, PEI, 1976
Todhunter, Rodger. "Banff and the Canadian National Park Idea." *Landscape* 25, no. 2 (1981): 33–9
– "Preservation, Parks and the Vice-Royalty: Lord Dufferin and Lord Grey in Canada." *Landscape Planning* 12 (1985): 141–60
– "The Rockcliffe Park Redevelopment Plan: The Restoration of a Picturesque Pleasure Park." *Environments* 26, no. 3 (1999): 59–72
– "Vancouver and the City Beautiful Movement." *Habitat* 26, no. 3 (1983): 8–11
Toker, Franklin. *The Church of Notre-Dame in Montreal*. 2nd edn. Montreal & Kingston: McGill-Queen's University Press 1991 (orig. 1970)
Tolton, Gordon E. *The Buffalo Legacy*. Lethbridge, AB: Fort Whoop-Up Interpretive Society 1996
Torrance Thakar Associates. *Major's Hill Park and Nepean Point Rehabilitation and Redevelopment Study*. Ottawa: National Capital Commission 1991
Traill, Catharine Parr. *The Backwoods of Canada*. Toronto: McClelland & Stewart 1989 (orig. London: Charles Knight 1836)
– *Studies of Plant Life in Canada, or Gleanings from Forest, Lake and Plain*. Ottawa: A.S. Woodburn 1885
Treggett, Brian. *Le Cimetière Mount-Hermon*. Brochure. Sillery, QC, May 2001
Treib, Marc, ed. *Modern Landscape Architecture: A Critical Review*. Cambridge, MA, and London, UK: MIT Press 1993
Trépanier, Paul. "Les jardins de Métis: Sur la route de la Gaspésie, une promenade haute en couleurs." *Continuité*, no. 36 (1987): 34–5
Trottier, Gontran, and Françoise Lacasse. *Port Royal and Its Inhabitants: 1605–1755*. 2nd edn. Bridgetown, NS: Integrity Printing Inc. 1999
Trudel, Jean. *Un chef-d'œuvre de l'art ancien du Québec, la chapelle des Ursuline*. Quebec City: Les Presses de l'Université de Laval 1972
Trudel, Marcel. *Initiation à la Nouvelle-France*. Montreal 1971 (orig. New York: Holt, Rinehart & Winston 1968)
Tunnard, Christopher. *Gardens in the Modern Landscape*. London, UK: Architectural Press 1938
– "Modern Gardens for Modern Houses: Reflections on Current Trends in Landscape Design." *Landscape Architecture*, January 1942
– "Modern Landscape Design." *RAICJ* 27, no. 8 (1950): 251

Tunnard, Christopher, and Henry Hope Reed. *American Skyline: The Growth and Form of Our Cities and Towns*. New York: Mentor Books, New American Library 1956
Turgeon, Laurier, ed. *The Spirit of Place: Between Tangible and Intangible Heritage*. Quebec City: Presses de l'Université Laval 2009
Turner, Frederick Jackson. "The Significance of the Frontier in American History." Lecture at the World's Columbian Exposition, Chicago, 1893
Tyrwhitt, Jacqueline. "The City Square." *Canadian Architect* 4, no. 4 (1959): 55–65
Université de Montréal, Division des archives. *Marie-Victorin, l'itinéraire d'un botaniste*. Virtual exhibition at http://www.archiv.umontreal.ca/exposition/mv/expomv.htm
University of Alberta, Office of Alumni Affairs. "Twenty-one Years at the Devonian Botanic Garden." Edmonton: University of Alberta 1980
University of Saskatchewan. "Crooked Lake Provincial Park." http://www.interactive/usask.ca/tourism/sask_parks/crooked.html
Unwin, Raymond. *Town Planning in Practice*. Princeton, NJ: Princeton Architectural Press 1994 (orig. London, UK, 1909)
Upton, Dell. *Architecture in the United States*. Oxford and New York: Oxford University Press 1998
Vaillancourt, Jean-Guy. "Pierre Dansereau, écologue, écosociologue et écologiste." *Sociologie et sociétés* 31, no. 2 (1999): 191–3
Valois, Nicole. "'Faire jardin' par l'installation." *ARQ*, no. 139 (2007): 38–40
Vance, Jonathan F. *Death So Noble: Memory, Meaning and the First World War*. Vancouver: University of British Columbia Press 1997
Vandermeulen, Emile G. "Roots 1: Mawson – A Landscape Architect at the Turn of the Century." *LAC* 3, no. 1 (1977): 2, 9–10
Van Dijk, Petronella. *Mount Royal Revisited, Olmsted Trail*. Montreal: Centre de la montagne inc. 1999
Van Es, P.S., and J.B. Thomas. *Mid-Canada Development Corridor … a Concept*. Toronto: Acres Research and Planning, July 1967
Van Ginkel, Blanche Lemco. Book review of Heather Hatch, *Dreams of Development*. *Environments* 17, no. 2 (1985): 102–5
Vanlaetham, France. "A Long-Term Perspective on Place Ville-Marie." *JSSAC* 24, no. 1 (1999): 6–15
– *Patrimoine en devenir: L'architecture moderne au Québec*. Quebec City: Les Publications du Québec 2012
Van Luven, Lynne. *Nikka Yuko Centennial Garden: A History*. Lethbridge, AB: Lethbridge and District Garden Society 1980
Venema, Henry David, Bryan Oborne, and Cynthia Neudoerffer. *The Manitoba Challenge: Linking Water and Land Management for Climate Adaptation*. Winnipeg: International Institute for Sustainable Development/Institut international du développement durable 2010
Vermette, Luce. *L'abbé Léon Provancher, sa contribution scientifique*. HSMBC Agenda Paper 1994-23
Versteeg, Edward. "Rudolph H.K. Cochius and the Creation of Bowring Park: A Preliminary Exploration." Unpublished manuscript of a presentation at the CSLA annual congress, St. John's, June 2004
Ville de Montréal, Service de l'habitation et du développement urbain/Module des parcs, de l'horticulture et des sciences. *Plan préliminaire de mise en valeur du mont Royal*. Montreal, 1990
Ville de Montréal, Service d'urbanisme. *Plan directeur de Montréal: Espaces libres*. Montreal, 1955
Ville de Québec, Service des communications. *Québec s'embellit*. 2nd edn. Quebec City, 2005

Ville de Québec, Service de l'urbanisme. *Saint-Roch, un quartier en constante mutation*. Quebec City, 1987

– *Saint-Sauveur, à l'image du début du siècle*. Quebec City, 1987

Villeneuve, Lynda. *Paysage, mythe et territorialité: Charlevoix au XIXe siècle*. Quebec City: Presses de l'Université Laval 1999

von Baeyer, Edwinna. *Garden of Dreams: Kingsmere and Mackenzie King*. Toronto: Dundurn Press 1990

– *Rhetoric and Roses: A History of Canadian Gardening 1900–1930*. Markham ON: Fitzhenry & Whiteside 1984

– *A Selected Bibliography for Garden History in Canada*. Rev. edn. Ottawa: Parks Canada, Canadian Heritage 1994 (orig. 1987)

von Baeyer, Edwinna, and Pleasance Crawford, eds. *Garden Voices: Two Centuries of Canadian Garden Writing*. Toronto: Random House of Canada 1995

Wade, Jill. "The 'Sting' of Vancouver's Better Housing 'Spree,' 1919–1949." *UHR* 21, no. 2 (1993): 92–8

Wagg, Susan. *Percy Erskine Nobbs: Architect, Artist, Craftsman*. Montreal & Kingston: McGill-Queen's University Press 1982

Waldheim, Charles. "The Landscape Architect as Camoufleur: Observing the Work of Claude Cormier." *ARQ*, no. 139 (2007): 36–7

Wanzel, Grant. *Lunenburg: Memories, Buildings, Places, Events*. Halifax: School of Architecture, Technical University of Nova Scotia 1989

Ward, Barbara, and René Dubos. *Only One Earth: The Care and Maintenance of a Small Planet*. New York: W.W. Norton & Co. 1972

Wascana Centre Authority and du Toit Allsopp Hillier. *1992 Wascana Centre Master Plan*. Regina: WCA 1995

Wassersug, Richard. *The Ecology of Point Pleasant Park: Technical Opinion Report*. Halifax: Point Pleasant Park International Design Competition 2005

Watada, Terry. "The J-Town Disappearing Blues." *Nikkei Voice*, May 2006, 5

Waterfront Toronto. *Report to the Community 2010: Our New Blue Edge*. Toronto: Toronto Waterfront Revitalization Corporation 2010

Waterston, Christina M., and John J. Stewart. "The English Landscape Style and Its Adaptation in Canada." *LAC* 4, no. 4 (1979): 14–23

Watson, Julie V. *Ardgowan: A Journal of House and Garden in Victorian Prince Edward Island*. Charlottetown: Seacroft/Parks and People Association Inc. 2000

Waugh, F.W. *Iroquois Foods and Food Production*. Ohsweken, ON: Iroquois Reprints, Iroqrafts 1991 (orig. Ottawa: Canada Department of Mines 1916)

Way, Ronald. "The Work of the Niagara Parks Commission." *RAICJ* 20, no. 12 (1943): 207–18

Waymark, Janet. *Modern Garden Design*. London: Thames & Hudson 2003

– *Thomas Mawson: Life, Gardens and Landscapes*. London: Frances Lincoln Ltd. 2009

Weaver, John. "Reconstruction of the Richmond District in Halifax: A Canadian Episode in Public Housing and Town Planning, 1918–1921." *Plan Canada* 6, no. 1 (1976): 36–47

"What they are doing – Rickson A. Outhet." *Canadian Municipal Journal* 8, no. 11 (1912): 475

Whistler Village Land Company Ltd. *Whistler Village Design Guidelines*. Vancouver, 1980

Whyte, William H. *The Social Life of Small Urban Spaces*. Washington, DC: Conservation Foundation 1980

Wilks, Brian. *Browsing Science Research at the Federal Level in Canada: History, Research Activities, and Publications*. Toronto: University of Toronto Press 2004

Williams, Robert. "Edwardian Gardens, Old and New." *JGH* 13, nos. 1 and 2 (1993): 90–103

Williams, Ron. "Courants modernes en architecture de paysage au Canada, 1938–1950." *Trames: Architecture et modernité, histoire et enjeux actuels*. Montreal: Faculté de l'aménagement, Université de Montréal, no. 15 (2004): 231–54

– "Floral World's Fair/Transported Frozen Peat-Bog." *Landscape Architecture*, July 1980, 408–12

– "Louis Perron – Master of Floral Orchestration." *Landscapes/Paysages* 9, no. 2 (2007): 32–5

– "Post-modernism: A New Challenge for Landscape Architects." *LAR* 8, no. 1 (1987): 9–14

– "Recycling the Expo Islands and Lachine Canal." In Bryan Demchinsky, ed., *Grassroots, Greystones and Glass Towers: Montreal Urban Issues and Architecture*, 61–9. Montreal: Véhicule Press 1989

Williams, Ron, and Peter Jacobs. "History of Landscape Architecture in Montreal." *Landscape Architecture*, September 2001, 94–7, 135–9

Wilson, Alex. "The Public Gardens of Halifax, Nova Scotia." *JGH* 3, no. 3 (1983): 179–92

Wilson, Alexander. *The Culture of Nature: North American Landscapes from Disney to the Exxon Valdez*. Toronto: Between the Lines 1991

Wilson, D.M. *Cowley, Alberta: History*. http://www.crowsnest-highway.ca

Wilson, Kenneth Wayne. "Irrigating the Okanagan: 1860–1920." MA thesis, University of British Columbia 1989. http://www.livinglandscapes.bc.ca/thomp-ok/irrigating-of-okanagan

Wilson, Lois. "Gardens and Plantings at Wymilwood." *RAICJ* 31, no. 2 (1954): 35–8

Windsor Liscombe, Rhodri, ed. *Architecture and the Canadian Fabric*. Vancouver: University of British Columbia Press 2011

– "The Imperial American Campus: Designing the University of British Columbia, Canada 1912–1914." *Architecture in/au Canada* 35, no. 1 (2010): 47–56

– *"The New Spirit": Modern Architecture in Vancouver 1938–1963*. Montreal/Vancouver: Canadian Centre for Architecture/Douglas & McIntyre 1997

Witty, David. "Brooklands Schoolyard: Discipline Integration." *LAR* 4, no. 5 (1983): 19–22

Wolf, Jim. "Isaburo Kishida: British Columbia's Pioneer Japanese Landscape Designer." *Site Lines*, February 2003

Wolfe, Jeanne M. "Montréal: Des plans d'embellissement." *Continuité*, no. 31 (1986) 24–7

– "Our Common Past: An Interpretation of Canadian Planning History." *Plan Canada*, July 1994, 12–34

Wolfe, Jeanne M., and François Dufaux, eds. *A Topographic Atlas of Montreal*. Montreal: School of Urban Planning, McGill University 1992

Wolfe, Jeanne M., and Grace Strachan. "Practical Idealism: Women in Urban Reform, Julia Drummond and the Montreal Parks and Playgrounds Association." In Caroline Andrew and Beth Moore Milroy, eds., *Life Spaces: Gender, Household, Employment*, 31–64. Vancouver: University of British Columbia Press 1988

Wolfe, Linnie Marsh, and Steven J. Holmes. *Son of the Wilderness: The Life of John Muir*. Madison: University of Wisconsin Press 2003 (orig. 1979)

Wood, Herbert Fairlie, and John Swettenham. *Silent Witnesses*. Toronto: A.M. Hakkert and Department of Veterans Affairs and Canadian War Museum 1974

Wood, J. David. *Making Ontario: Agricultural Colonization and Landscape Re-creation before the Railway*. Montreal & Kingston: McGill-Queen's University Press 2000

–, ed. *Perspectives on Landscape and Settlement in Nineteenth Century Ontario*. Toronto: McClelland & Stewart 1975

Woodcock, George. "Savage and Domestic: The Parks of Vancouver." *JGH* 3, no. 3 (1983): 169–75

Woodworth, John. "The BC Binning House." *Western Homes and Living*, October–November 1950, 15–16

Wright, G. "Alberta's Booming Oil Sands Boast Cold Weather, Hot Market." *Engineering News Record*, 25 February 2008

Wright, J.R. *Urban Parks in Ontario, Part 1: Origins to 1860*. Ottawa: Media Production Services, University of Ottawa 1984

– *Urban Parks in Ontario, Part 2: The Public Park Movement 1860–1914*. Ottawa: Ontario Ministry of Tourism and Recreation and University of Ottawa 1984

– *Urban Parks in Ontario: The Modern Period*. Ottawa: University of Ottawa Press 2000

Wright, J.V. *Ontario Prehistory*. Ottawa: National Museum of Man 1972

Wright, Janet. *Architecture of the Picturesque in Canada*. Ottawa: National Historic Parks and Sites Branch, Parks Canada 1984

Wright, Percy H. "The New Ottawa Roses." *Canadian Homes and Gardens* 13, no. 3 (March 1936): 24, 47, 50

Wuest, Donna Yoshitake. *Coldstream: The Ranch Where It All Began*. Madeira Park, BC: Harbour Publishing 2005

Wylie, William N.T. *Coal Culture: The History and Commemoration of Coal Mining in Nova Scotia*. Ottawa-Hull: Historic Sites and Monuments Board of Canada 1997

Wynn, Graeme. "The Maritimes: The Geography of Fragmentation and Underdevelopment." In McCann, ed., *Heartland and Hinterland*, 156–213

Young, Brian. *Respectable Burial: Montreal's Mount Royal Cemetery*. Montreal & Kingston: McGill-Queen's University Press 2003

Zaitzevsky, Cynthia. *Frederick Law Olmsted and the Boston Park System*. Cambridge, MA: Belknap Press of Harvard University 1982

Zeidler, Eberhard H. "Creating a Livable Winter City." *LAR* 1, no. 3 (1980): 8–11

Zierler, Amy, and Cam Mustard. *Signal Hill: An Illustrated History*. St. John's: Newfoundland Historic Parks Association 1982

Zube, Ervin H., ed. *Landscapes, Selected Writings of J.B. Jackson*. Amherst: University of Massachusetts Press 1970

Zvonar, John. "Garden of the Provinces ... Finally Taking Centre Stage." In *Conserving the Modern in Canada: Buildings, Ensembles, and Sites, 1945–2005*, 151–9. Conference proceedings. Peterborough, ON: Trent University 2005

INDEX

All landscapes, buildings, and projects, with the exception of universities and national and provincial parks, are listed according to the municipalities or rural regions in which they are located.

Aberdeen, Lady, 264, 296
Aberdeen, Lord, 296
Abernethy, SK: Motherwell Homestead (Lanark Place), 124, 140–2
Acres Research and Planning Limited, 461
Adams, Thomas, 314–15, 332, 345–8, 358
Adelaide, Australia
 parklands, 308
 town layout, 304
 Victoria Square, 308
Adirondack Forest Reserve, NY, 245
Affleck, Desbarats, Dimakopoulos, Lebensold, Michaud, Sise, 423. See also Arcop Associates
Affleck, Ray, 424, 440
Aitkin, Alexander, 94
Allan, George William, 178
Allan, William, 166–7
Alliance for Historic Landscape Preservation (AHLP), 481, 559
Allsopp, Robert, 445, 478–9, 538
Allward, Walter, 321
American influence on Canadian landscape design, 215, 237–40, 264–9, 331–2, 334, 384, 394–6, 437–8
Ames, Herbert Brown, 263
Annapolis Valley and Fundy Shore, NS, 42, 87, 149
 Annapolis Royal Historic Gardens, 482
 Bear River Village – Solar Energy Wastewater Project, 473
 Grand-Pré National Historic Site, 44–6
 Port-Royal National Historic Site, 41, 44, 106, 304
 Uniacke House, 100–1
Anne of Green Gables, 85, 251–2
Arcop Associates, 423–5, 431, 440. See also Affleck, Desbarats, Dimakopoulos, Lebensold, Michaud, Sise
Arnoldin, Carmelo, 497
Art Deco, 335–7, 366, 372, 380–2
Arthur, Eric, 368
Arvida, QC: town plan, 347–50, 405
Ashwell, Iris, 334–5
Asselin, Vincent, 230, 469, 528
Association des architectes paysagistes du Québec (AAPQ), 8, 264–6, 444
Association for Preservation Technology (APT), 481, 559
Atchison, J.D., 285
Atelier in situ, 529
Atkinson, Henry, 181–2, 186
Aubertin, Louis, 190
Auyuittuq National Park, NU, 255, 260

Back, Frédéric, 560
Baie-Comeau, QC: town plan, 347
Baillairgé, Charles, 153, 156–8, 204–5, 221–2
Bakker, Joost, 489
Baldwin, Dr. W.W., 155
Balharrie, Watson, 426
Baltzly, Benjamin, 110
Banff National Park (orig. Rocky Mountains Park of Canada), 240–3, 247–8, 260, 377, 383
 Banff Springs Hotel, 240, 382
 Cascades of Time garden, 377
 golf course, 382
 Lake Louise, 242
Baron de Tuyll, 97
Barrie, ON: Queen's Park, 235
Bartholomew, Harland, 358–9, 534. See also Harland Bartholomew and Associates
Batoche, SK: National Historic Site, 106, 115–16, 482, 556
Bayfield, ON: 97
 colonial town plan, 97
 Clan Gregor Square, 97
Beadle, Delos W., 174
Beasley, Larry, 539
Beaumont-Hamel, France: Newfoundland and Labrador War Memorial, 319, 326–7
Beckett, Harold C., 377
Bedell, Paul, 82, 85
Bégin, Benoît, 54, 406, 435–6, 486
Belleville, ON
 Glendale Cemetery, 210
 Institute for the Deaf and Dumb, 168–9
 Veterans' Park, 316
Bell-Smith, Frederic, 239, 247
Bennett, Edward H., 290–1, 410–13
Berger, Thomas R., 460–1
Berwick, Robert A.D., 396, 451
BGH-Planning, 469, 473
Binning, B.C., 389, 396
Bird, Hubert, 403–4
Bishopric, Otis, 256, 441
Blair, John, 223
Blankstein, Coop, Gilmore and Hanna, 401
Blomfield, Sir Reginald, 323
Blouin, André, 440–2
Blue, Frances McLeod, 334
Boissevain, MB: International Peace Garden, 368–9
Bond, Sarahluff, 333

Booth, Percy, 408
Borden Landing, PEI: town plan, 346
Borgstrom, Carl, 364, 380
Borgstrom and Carver, 363–4, 368, 373, 379, 383, 408
Boston, Massachusetts (*incl.* Cambridge, MA)
    Boston Public Gardens 178
    Mount Auburn Cemetery, Cambridge, 202, 215
Boucher, Pierre, 624n11
Bouctouche, NB
    Bouctouche Bay Ecotourism Project, 500, 502
    Irving Eco-Centre, 502
    Pays de la Sagouine tourist complex, 502
Boudreau, N., 379
Bournville, UK: industrial town layout, 315
Bourque, Pierre, 441, 473, 484, 512
Brainerd, Harry Beardslee, 349
Brant, Joseph (Thayendanega), 95–6
Brantford, ON, 91
    colonial town plan, 94
    Ontario Institution for the Education of the Blind, 169
    Victoria Park, 94–5, 97, 308
Brett, Franklin D., 280
Brett and Hall, 280, 301, 302, 313
Brisebois, Inspector Ephrem-A., 127
British Columbia Society of Landscape Architects (BCSLA), 444
Brockville, ON: Fulford Place, 294
Brodie, Neil, 83
Broman, Matt, 373
Brooke, Walter S., 302
Brown, David R., 317
Brown and Vallance, 287
Brundtland, Gro Harlem, 466–7
Buck, Frank Ebenezer, 333
Budrevics, Alexander, 436
Budrevics, Arnis, 436
Buggey, Susan, 257, 481
Bugnet, Georges, 173
Bunnell, A.E.K., 291
Burbidge, Scott, 426
Burnaby, BC: Eagles Estate, Deer Lake, 333
Burnham, Daniel, 264–5, 290
Burton, Harold, 124
Burtynsky, Edward, 543
Burwell, Lewis, 94
Busch, Henry, 177
Butchart, Jennie, 297–8
Butchart, Robert Pim, 297–8
Butler, William Francis, 109
Byng, Lord, 326

Cabot, Francis (grandfather), 339
Cabot, Francis (grandson), 484–7
Cabot, Higginson, 339
Cabot, Maud Bonner, 339
Calgary, AB, 137, 139, 142, 233, 437–8, 542

Central Memorial Park (Central Park), 162–4; Carnegie Library, 163; cenotaph, 323–4
city plan, 128, 162–3, 233, 291
Civic Centre plan, 269–71
Fish Creek Park, 457
founding of the city, 106, 127–8
mall, downtown – Prince's Island Park (Barclay Street), 291, 427
Memorial Drive, 318, 327
Mount Royal district, 275
Prince's Island Park, 233, 269–71, 427
Reader Rock Garden, 353–4, 559
redevelopment plan 1913–1914 (Mawson), 269–71
Riverside pathway and bikeway system, 490
Stephen Avenue Mall (8th Avenue), 427
Union Cemetery, 212–13
Winter Olympic Games 1988, 492–4
California, 126, 244, 492
Blue Tree installation, Sonoma Garden Festival, 530
experimentation with Modernism, 384
influence on Canadian design, 393–4, 397, 486
Calvert, Robert, 441
Cambridge, ON: Victoria Park, 307–8
Cameron, Elaine, 296
Cameron, Roderick, 235
Campbell, Lieutenant Dugald, 82
Canadian archetypes in landscape design, 497–502
Canadian Pacific Railroad Company, 128, 275, 286, 294–5, 356, 360
role in the colonization of the West, 103, 118–19, 137–8, 174–5, 234
role in the creation of the national parks, 239–40, 247
Canadian Society of Landscape Architects (CSLA), 378–80, 410, 444
Canadian Society of Landscape Architects and Town Planners, 379, 415
Canmore, AB: Nordic Skiing Centre 1988, 493
Canneel-Claes, Jean, 386
Cape-Breton Highlands National Park, NS, 251–2, 260, 382–3
    Cabot Trail, 251–2
    Highlands Links Golf Course, Ingonish, 252, 382–3
Cap-Rouge, QC: Campus intercommunautaires de Saint-Augustin, 446–7
Cardinal Hardy et associés, 533
Cardston, AB: Mormon Temple (Church of Jesus Christ of Latter-Day Saints), 123–4
Carling, John, 147–8, 592n59, 594n29
Carlyle, Doug, 535
Carlyle + Associés, 535
Carson, Rachel, 456

Carver, Humphrey, 70, 363, 368, 379, 383, 386, 391, 434
Casavant, Mathieu, 532
Castle, H.J., 160
Catalyse Urbaine, 532
Catlin, George, 238
Cauchon, Noulan, 357, 411
Cautley, Richard W., 252
CBCL Ltd., 438, 482, 545
Cecelia Paine and Associates, 480–1
cemeteries, 33–4, 71–2, 84–5, 113–14, 122, 159–60, 195, 200–15, 315, 322–3
Central Mortgage and Housing Corporation (CMHC), 390–1, 434–5, 441
Champion, George, 230
Champlain, Samuel de, 41, 51, 82
Chanasyk, Victor, 435, 444
Chapman, Alfred H., 352
Charlevoix region, QC, 49, 150–1
    Gil'mont Estate, St-Irénée-Les-Bains, 294
    Les Quatre-Vents Estate, Cap-à-l'aigle, 339, 484
    The Spinney, Pointe-au-Pic, 294
Charlottetown, PEI, 78
    Ardgowan House, 557
    colonial town plan, 7, 80–1, 102, 160–2, 453
    Confederation Centre of the Arts, 430–1
    Connaught Square, 80
    Great George Street, 81–2
    Queen Square, 81–2, 85, 160–1, 431
    Rochford Square, 80
Charney, Melvin, 495–6
Chartrand, André, 435
Chaudière-Appalaches région, QC
    Beaumont, 50, 70, 72, 75
    Domaine Joly-De Lotbinière, Pointe Platon, 188–9
Chaussegros de Léry, Gaspard-Joseph, 54–6, 62–3
Chertsey, Surrey, UK: St. Ann's Hill, 386
Chester, NS: war memorial sculpture, 320
Chicago, IL (*incl.* Riverside, IL), 53, 223, 290–1, 335, 347, 408
    Riverside town plan 1869 (Olmsted), 275, 392
    World's Columbian Exposition 1893, 264–5, 297
Chicoutimi, QC, 245, 347
    Château Dubuc, 611–12n8
    Foyer coopératif neighbourhood, 406
    Plateau du Moulin neighbourhood, 406
    Val-de-Grâce neighbourhood, 406
children's play environments, 277–8, 441–2, 443–4
Childs and Wilson, 212
Chisasibi, QC: village plan, 461–2
Chrétien, Jean, 255
Christchurch, New Zealand
    colonial town plan, 304
    Victoria Park, 308

Victoria Square, 308
Church, Frederic, 244
Church, Thomas D., 385, 432
Churchill, Colonel Edward S., 439
City Beautiful movement, 264–71, 276, 282–91
City of Montreal Parks Service
Clark, Jim, 437
Clarke, Walter F., 369
Clarke and Rapuano, 418, 618n6
Cleveland, Horace W.S., 215, 598n81
Clouard, Micheline, 529
Coalition to Save the Legacy Sakura, 524
Cobb, Henry N., 423
Cochius, Rudolf H.K., 230, 318–19, 375
Cohlmeyer, Hanson and Associates, 489
Cole, Fred, 332–3
Colemen, Richard, 166
colonial town planning, 78–86
Commission de la capitale nationale du Québec (CCNQ), 532–4
Commission of Conservation, 243, 249–50, 332, 345–6, 454
Commonwealth Historic Resource Management Limited, 481
Condon, Patrick, 541
Conseil du paysage québécois, 554
Conservation of heritage landscapes, 481–2, 555–60
Consolidated Garden Research, 512
Constable, John, 150
Cook, Captain James, 109
Cooper Marcus, Clare, 434
Cormier, Claude, 528–9, 532, 538
Cormier, France, 532
Cornell, Frederick James Mott, 196, 212
Cornell, Silas, 212
Cornell University, Ithaca, NY, 302, 333, 348, 375, 411, 413, 435
Corner Brook, NL: industrial town layout, 347, 461
Cornut, Jacques-Philippe, 66
Corush Laroque Sunderland, 438
Cousins, Edward L., 352–3
Couture, Ulric, 435
Crabtree, H.S., 347
Crombie, David, 469, 537
Crooked Lake Provincial Park, SK, 33
Culham, Gordon Joseph, 331–2, 370, 379
Cutler, Jeff, 524
Cynthia Cohlmeyer Landscape Architect, 489

Dalhousie University, Halifax, NS, 592n52, 607n105
Dalibard, Jacques, 481
Daniel Arbour et associés, 462. *See also* Pluram-DAA
Dansereau, Pierre, 454–5
Daoust-Lestage, Groupe, 534
Darling, Frank, 288
Darling and Pearson, 337

Darlingford, MB: Memorial Chapel, 316
Dartmouth, NS: ecological land-use study of North Dartmouth, 473
Daudelin, Georges, 406, 429, 435, 441
Davick, L.A., 605n49
Davidson, John, 355
Dawes, Neil, 490
Dawson, James Frederick, 360
Dawson City, YK, 461; rehabilitation of historic town centre, 482
de Galaup de Lapérouse, Jean-François, 110
de Gaspé, Aubert, 48, 70, 73, 76, 188
de Laval, monseigneur, 61, 145
de La Vérendrye, Pierre, 110
de Lotbinière, Edmond-Gustave Joly, 188–9
de Lotbinière, Sir Henri Gustave Joly, 188–9
Dennis, John Stoughton, 192
Desbarats, Guy, 401
Desjardins, Alphonse, 275
Desjardins, Richard, 543
de Vauban, Sébastien le Prestre, 58
Deville, Édouard Gaston, 314
de Vynck, Alfred, 437
Dicaire, Linda, 481–2
Dockham, Ken, 432
Dollier de Casson, père François, 55–6
Domon, Gérald, 551
Donaldson, Sandra, 477–8
Donald W. Graham and Associates, 256, 413, 425, 438, 441, 449
Don Vaughan and Associates, 437, 446, 450, 489, 492, 494, 497, 512, 519
Dorval, QC: CIBA Complex, 408
Dougall, James, 174
Douglas, David, 109
Douglass, Major David Bates, 203
Doupe, Lonsdale, 275
Downing, Andrew Jackson, 166, 179–80, 183, 187, 191, 215, 217, 220
Drapeau, Jean, 438, 440, 507
Drummond, Lady Julia, 312, 603n6
Drummondville, QC: Parc des Voltigeurs, 410
Dryden, Norm, 379
Dubos, René, 466
Dufferin, Lord, 156, 159, 244
Dufresne, Marius, 275
Dufresne, Oscar, 275
Duke of Kent (Prince Edward Augustus), 99–100, 220
Dunington-Grubb, H.B. and L.A., office, 302, 331, 337, 348, 351, 368
Dunington-Grubb, Howard Burlingham, 302, 328, 348, 373, 379, 394, 409–10, 444
Dunington-Grubb, Lorrie Alfreda, 302, 328, 331, 333–4, 373, 379, 409
Dunington-Grubb and Stensson, 303, 328, 373–4, 408–10, 436, 441
Dunsmuir, James, 299–301
Dunsmuir, Laura, 299–301
Dupuis, Auguste, 173

du Toit Allsopp Hillier (du Toit Associates Ltd.), 478–9, 538

E.D. Smith Company Ltd., 173, 235, 408
Earl Grey, 271, 307
Eastern Townships, QC, 331, 365, 551; land division, 89, 92, 135, 295
Eckbo, Garrett, 385, 393–4, 399–400
eclecticism, 171, 298
École des Beaux-Arts, Paris, 264, 267, 269, 290, 312, 410–11
EDA Collaborative, 438
Edmonton, AB, 114, 124, 127–9, 528
 Alberta Legislative Assembly – forecourt, 283–4, 288, 432
 Capital Region River Valley Park, 453, 534–6, 539
 Devonian Botanic Gardens – Kurimoto Japanese Garden, 484
 Hudson Bay Flats, 232–3
 Louise McKinney Riverfront Park, 534–5
 River Valley Alliance, 554
 Saskatchewan Avenue, 233
 Sir Winston Churchill Square, 291
 urban planning study 1912 (Morell and Nichols), 262–3, 267, 284, 432
 urban planning study of Edmonton and Strathcona 1907 (Todd), 231–2, 288, 528
 Victoria Esplanade, 535–6
 Victoria Park, 233, 288, 308, 535
 West Edmonton Mall, 491
Edmundston, NB: New Brunswick Botanical Garden, 482–4
Edward and William S. Maxwell, 266, 282, 294
EIDOS Consultants Inc., 535, 565–7
Eliot, Charles, 225
Elk Island National Park, AB, 250, 260
Ellis, William, 110,
Emerson, Ralph Waldo, 237
Engelhardt, Henry Adolph, 146,168–9, 174, 210, 220
Environmental Design and Management Ltd. (EDM), 472–3
Erickson, Arthur, 428, 434, 449–50, 486–7
Espace DRAR, 529

Farley Schreiber Williams, 476
Farming and agriculture, 25–6, 42–4, 48, 67–9, 87–93, 107–11, 118–20, 133–51, 354–6, 454, 551–2
Federal District Commission, 291, 357, 413
Feehan, Hugh Vincent, 369
Fellheimer and Wagner, 356
Filion, Serge, 534, 624n11
Fiset, Édouard S., 406, 411, 439, 446
Fleming, Sandford, 239, 478
Fletcher, George, 162
Floyd, J. Austin, 394, 399–400, 410, 420, 441
Fodchuk, Roman, 256, 425, 435
Fondation Héritage Canada, 481

INDEX 655

Forillon National Park, Gaspé Peninsula, QC, 255, 257, 260
Forster, Roy, 484
Forsyth, James Bell, 182
Fort Langley, BC, 106–8, 112, 556
Fort Rouge, MB, 110
Fraser, John, 239
Fredericton, NB, 78, 279, 417, 453
   colonial town plan, 82
   "The Greens," 82
   municipal trail network, 490
   Officers' Square, 82
Frohn, Winnie, 624n11
Frye, Northrop, 18
Fuller, R. Buckminster, 442
Fuller and Jones, 282
Fundy National Park, NB, 253, 260

Gaboury, Étienne, 114, 489
Gagné, Jean, 402
Gagnon, Clarence, 72, 151
Gallant, Brian, 557
Galt, John, 93, 97, 602n60
Garden City principles, 271–2; realizations, 272–7
garden suburbs, 192–3, 272, 277, 302, 360
Garibaldi Provincial Park, BC, 359
Gascon, A. Donat, 402
Gaspésie region, QC, 24, 38, 78, 89, 246, 250, 255, 257, 295, 337, 377, 484, 528
Gatineau (*previously* Hull), QC
   civic centre, 291, 478
   Confederation Boulevard, 291, 410, 478–9, 534
   Gatineau Park, 339–43, 412, 482, 490
   Lac Leamy, 232
   plan for the National Capital 1913–14 (Bennett), 290–1
   plan for the National Capital 1950 (Gréber), 291, 410–13, 425
   plan for the Ottawa Improvement Commission 1903 (Todd), 231–2
Gaultier, Jean-François, 67
Georgian Bay Islands National Park, ON, 250, 260
Gerrard and Mackars, 496
GGLC Architectes, 532
Gibbs, Robert, 535
Gigault, Georges Auguste, 147
Girling, Cynthia, 492, 541
Gitterman, Samuel, 402
Glacier National Park, BC, 242, 260
Goderich, ON: town plan, 97
golf courses, 252–3, 382–4, 551, 616n62
Goshorn, Warner S., 437, 441, 444
Gosselin, Joseph-Auguste, 402
Gotto, Captain Basil, 318–19
Graham, Donald W., 413, 425, 435, 441, 449
Graham, Wendy, 512, 562, 565
grain elevators, 139–40, 551–2

Grant, Alpine, 212, 598n70
Grant, Rev. George Monro, 239
Grasslands National Park, SK, 260
Gréber, Jacques, 291, 410–13, 425
Green, Blankstein and Russell, 404
Greenberg, Ken, 357, 532, 539
Grey Owl (Archie Belaney), 602n55
Gribbin, Thomas, 557
Grimmer, Allan K., 348
Gropius, Walter, 385–6
Gros Morne National Park, NL, 255, 257–8, 260, 318
   Tablelands, 257
   Western Brook Pond, 258
   Woody Point war memorial, 257, 318
Group of Seven, 248, 364
Guelph, ON
   Ontario Agricultural College (OAC), 124, 145–6, 169, 234, 332, 368, 382, 394, 444, 454
   town plan, 97
Gwaii Haanas National Park Reserve, Haida Gwaii, BC, 259

Hageraats, Hans, 437
Hahn, Emanuel, 320
Haida Gwaii, BC (*previously* Queen Charlotte Islands), 104, 127
   Ninstints, 24, 30, 32–3, 36
   Rose Harbour, 459
Haldimand, Sir Frederick, 98–9
Halifax, NS
   Angus Macdonald Bridge, 616n56
   Camp Hill Cemetery, 79, 203
   Citadel – Clock Tower, 79, 100, 320
   colonial town plan, 79–85
   Grand Parade, 79–80, 100; cenotaph, 320
   Halifax Common, 78–9, 177, 203, 305
   Halifax Public Gardens, 6, 79, 170, 173, 176–8, 197, 203, 305, 556
   Historic Properties, Halifax Waterfront, 482, 622n12
   Hydrostone District, 314–15, 345
   Murray Mackay Bridge, 616n56
   Point Pleasant Park, 79, 100, 220–1, 223, 231, 320, 323, 560; Martello Tower, 79, 100, 220, 375; redesign and rehabilitation program, 560; sailors' memorial, 320
   Prince's Lodge and Music Room, 100
   St. George's Church, 79, 100
   St. Paul's Burial Ground, 85
   Sambro Island Lighthouse, 87
Hall, Alfred V., 348
Hall, George Duffield, 280
Halland, Sussex, UK: Bentley Wood, 385–6
Hallandaine, Edward, 212
Halprin, Lawrence, 394, 446
Hamilton, ON
   Dundurn Castle, 184–6
   Gage Park, 351

Gore Park, 161–2, 308; cenotaph, 324
   northwest entrance and High Level Bridge, 380–1
   Ontario Hospital, 354–6
   Royal Botanical Gardens: Cootes Paradise, 368, 373; Helen M. Kippax Garden, 334; Rock Garden, 368
   Woodend Villa, 186
Hancock, Macklin, 404–5, 415, 435, 440–1, 449
Hancock, Marcus Leslie, 404–5
Harkin, James B., 250–3
Harland Bartholomew and Associates, 358–9, 534
Harman, Jack K., 501
Harper, Doug, 441, 445
Harries, William Edward, 348
Harries and Hall, 337, 356
Harries, Hall and Kruse, 348
Harvard University, Cambridge, MA, 438
   American graduates, 437
   Canadian graduates, 329, 332, 373, 394, 398, 404–5, 413, 415, 435, 462, 473, 529
   computer graphics, 456–7, 473
   contribution to modernism, 384–6
Harvey, King, 437
Hébert, François, 497
Hébert, Henri, 325
Hébert, Louis, 66–7, 70
Hébert, Louis-Philippe, 45, 61, 158, 610n39
Henderson, Alexander, 305
Henriquez, Richard, 501
Heritage Canada Foundation, 481, 559
Herrington, Susan, 529
Heubach, Frederick, 277
Heughan, R.G., 325
Hilderman, Garry, 435, 528
Hilderman Crosby Feir Witty, 438
Hilderman Feir Witty and Associates, 458
Hilderman Thomas Frank Cram, 502
Hilderman, Witty, Crosby, Hanna and Associates, 489, 502
Hill, George, 322
Hillier, John, 478
Hills, George Angus, 454
Historic Sites and Monuments Board of Canada (HSMBC), 9, 555, 559
Hodgins, J. Herbert, 331
Hoedeman, Jan, 429, 437
Hoff, Sigurd, 436
Holland, Samuel, 80, 88
Holt, Sir Herbert, 290, 357, 410
Holubowich, Ed, 425, 435
Hopkins, John William, 207
Hosler, Bob, 437
Hotson, Norman, 489
Hough, Michael, 261, 437–8, 444, 450, 457, 465–6
Hough, Stansbury, office, 256, 425, 438
Hough Stansbury Michalski Ltd., 443
Hough Woodland Naylor Dance Leinster, 470

656 INDEX

Houplain, Georges, 436
Howard, Ebenezer, 271–2, 402, 404
Howard, John George, 188, 203, 220
Hucker, Jacqueline, 327
Hudson River Valley, NY: Hyde Park Villa, 166, 191
Hudson's Bay Company, 107–8, 110–11, 113, 118–19, 127–9, 155, 223
Hull, QC. See Gatineau, UK

I.M. Pei and Associates, 423
Ian Martin and Victor Prus, 406
Île d'Orléans, QC, 50, 151, 182
　Les Groisardières Estate, 333
　Île d'Orléans Bridge, 380
　Mauvide-Genest Seigneury, 558
Imperial Order Daughters of the Empire (IODE), 318
Indian Head, SK
　Forest Nursery Station, 148–9
　Indian Head Experimental Farm, 148–9, 151
Infrastructures Alberta, 468
Iqaluit, NU, 461, 549–50
　Iqaluit Square, 550
　Sylvia Grinnell Territorial Park, 550
Iroquois Falls, ON: town plan, 346–7
Iverson, Richard R., 162–3, 212

Jackson, A.Y., 72, 501
Jacobs, Jane, 417, 434
Jacobs, Peter, 230, 247, 435, 456, 462, 467
Japan Landscape Consultants, 519
Jasper National Park, AB, 242–3, 256, 260, 383–4
　golf course, 382
　Jasper Park Lodge, 382
Jeffers, Allan Merrick, 284
Jefferson, Thomas, 119, 189
Jekyll, Gertrude, 330, 337, 376
John B. Parkin and Associates, 406–8, 420
Johnson, Brad, 435, 491
Johnson, Pauline, 225
Johnson Sustronk Weinstein and Associates, 420, 438, 491
Jones, Hugh Griffith, 344–5, 356, 381–2
Justice, Clive, 399, 429–31, 435
Justice and Webb, 429–31, 435, 446

Kalm, Pehr, 67–9, 74
Kalman, Harold, 40, 481
Kananaskis Provincial Park, AB: Nakiska Alpine Ski Centre, 249, 492–3
Kane, Paul, 110, 239
Kapuskasing, ON: town plan, 347–8, 461
Kaslo, BC, 129, 322
Kay, Edwin, 331–2, 370, 379
Kehm, Walter, 437
Kejimkujik National Park, NS, 35, 255, 260
Kellett, Ronald, 541
Kelowna, BC, 106, 468

Guisachan Garden, 144, 296
KLO Orchards, 144
Mission Creek Greenway, 469
Oblate Mission of Father Pandosy, 112–13, 144
Kingston, ON, 90–1, 182, 245
　Bellevue House and Garden, 556–7
　Cataraqui Cemetery, 192, 196, 204, 211–12
　City Park, 196–7
Kinoshita, Masao, 424
Kipawa. See Témiscaming, QC
Kippax, Helen M., 334, 379, 393
Kirkwood, Alexander, 246
Kirouac, Conrad, 365. See also Marie-Victorin, frère
Kishida, Isaburo, 297–302, 515
Kitchen, John M., 411
Kitimat, BC, 461
　Greenway path network, 405
　town layout, 403–6
Kluane National Park, YK, 255, 260
Klynstra, Peter, 437–8, 482
Knowles, Hugh, 435
Kogawa, Joy, 517, 525
Kootenay National Park, BC, 242–3, 260
Kootenay region, BC, 242–3, 260, 279, 516, 520
　Kaslo, 129, 322
　Sandon, 129, 130
　Silverton, 120, 130
　Slocan City, 129, 515–16
Kouchibougouac National Park, NB, 255, 257
Krieghoff, Cornelius, 150
Kruse, Arthur M., 348, 356
Kubo, Dr. Tadashi, 482, 484, 520
Kurelek, William, 133, 151
Kwan, Margaret, 498
Kyowakai Society, 520

Labelle, Josée, 532
Lachance, Claude, 491
Lac-Mégantic, QC: Veterans Park, 316, 491
Lacombe, père Albert, 112, 128
Lafontaine, André, 435
La Haye, Jean-Claude, 406, 425, 438, 448
Laing, George, 186
Laird, John, 550
Lake Simcoe–Georgian Bay Region, ON, 91, 102, 145
　Holland Marsh, 151
　Sainte-Marie among the Hurons (reconstruction), 51–2
L'Allier, Jean-Paul, 532
La Mauricie National Park, QC, 255, 257–60
　Route Promenade, 258–9
Lambert, Phyllis, 496, 560
Lancaster Sound, NU: Regional Study, 461–2
land division
　grid plan of western Canada, 111–16
　Maritimes, 87–9

Quebec and Ontario township system, 89–92, 102
seigneurial system, 67–74
Landplan Collaborative Ltd., 438, 471, 492
Langevin, Michel, 532
Langlois, Michel, 532
Lantzius, John, 437–8, 441, 446, 450
Lapins, Val, 436
large urban parks and park systems, 216–33
Lasserre, Fred, 397–8
Laurentian Region, QC, 50, 70, 75, 364, 470
　Laurentian Autoroute, 391
　Mont Tremblant recreational development, 491–2
　national and provincial parks, 245–6, 257–8
　P'tit train du Nord, 490
Laurier, Sir Wilfrid, 119, 231, 249, 293
Laval University, Quebec City and Sainte-Foy, QC, 59, 145
　campus plan, 446, 448
　transfer to suburbs, 417
Lean, George, 378
Lebensold, Fred, 423, 440
Lebret, SK, 106, 114–15; church precinct – Way of the Cross, 115
Lefèvre, Daniel, 327
Légaré, Joseph, 150
Lemco van Ginkel, Blanche, 417, 440
Lemieux, Denis, 529
Lens, SK: town plan, 314
Le Pennec, Toussaint-Emmanuel, 183
Leslie, Dr. W.R., 316
Lessard, Marie, 462
Letchworth, UK, 271–2, 275, 345
Lethbridge, AB, 243, 453
　City Hall: cenotaph, 325
　Henderson Lake Park, 519
　High Level Bridge, 117, 380
　irrigation, 143
　Nikka Yuko Garden, 519–20
Livingstone, Bill, 333, 401, 484
Lombard North Group Ltd., 426, 438, 457
London, ON, 91–2
　Eldon House, 186
　Victoria Park, 197–8; cenotaph, 324
London, UK, 158, 164, 188
　Battersea Park, 199
　cenotaph, Whitehall, 323
　Hampstead Garden Suburb, 273
　Royal Botanic Gardens at Kew, 109, 170, 200, 230
　Vauxhall Gardens, 199
Lorrain, Claude, 101, 202
Loudon, John Claudius, 179, 202
Louisbourg, NS
　Fortress of Louisbourg, 43–4, 57–8, 62, 87, 481
　lighthouse, 44, 86–7
Low, Judith Eleanor, 334
Lowe, Peter, 181–3, 187

Luis F. Villa and Frank Macioge Associates, 442
Lunenburg, NS: colonial town plan, 80
Lussier, Patricia, 529
Lutyens, Sir Edwin, 323–4, 330, 337
Lyle, John McIntosh, 267–9, 337, 346, 351, 357, 368, 373, 380, 420
Lynn, William H., 156
Lyon, France: *Solange* installation, 530

McCrae, Major John, 326
McDonald, Douglas, 379, 411
Macdonald, Sir John A., 162, 196–7, 556
Macdonald, Sir William, 147
McFadzean and Everley, 408
McGill University, Montreal, QC, 305, 423
McHarg, Ian, 456–7, 473
McIntyre, John, 125
Macioge, Frank, 442
Mackenzie, Dr. C.J., 380
Mackenzie King, William Lyon, 339–43, 357, 410–12, 481–2
Mackenzie Valley and Arctic Shore, NWT, 460, 545
   Mackenzie Valley Highway, 457
   Mackenzie Valley Pipeline project, 460–1, 550
   Maple Leaf Pipeline project, 457
McLarney, Bill, 459
McLaughlin, R. Samuel, 335, 377
MacLean, G.K., 355
Maclean, John Bayne, 332
McLeod, Frances. *See* Blue, Frances McLeod
Maclure, Samuel, 298–300, 312
McMaster University, Hamilton, ON, 372–3; Sunken Garden, 373, 617n26
MacNab, Sir Allan Napier, 184–6
Macoun, William T., 172, 333, 343, 370–1
McQuesten, Thomas Baker, 367–8, 372–3, 380
McTavish, Simon, 201
Magrath, AB: McIntyre Ranch, 125–6
Mahone Bay, NS: "three sisters" (churches), 86
Maisonneuve, QC: Morgan Boulevard, 275, 375
Major, Denis, 256
Man, Cameron, 435, 438
Manning, Warren H., 235, 265, 348
Man Taylor Muret, 427, 438
March, Vernon, 325–6
Marchand, Jean-Omer, 113, 267
Marega, Charles, 381
Marie-Victorin, frère, 364–6, 455
Martin, Frank J., 316
Martin, Ian, 406
Martinez, Carlos, 507
Marysville, NB: industrial town layout, 279
Masuno, Shunmyo, 519
Mather, James R., 212
Mathews, Eddie, 339, 484
Matsuzaki and Wright, 465

Matthews, Marmaduke, 239, 272
Mauricie region, QC
   agriculture, 377, 551
   Calvaire and Way of the Cross, 73–5
   projects to combat unemployment, 371–2
Mawson, Edward P., 269
Mawson, Thomas Hayton, 271, 282–3, 289, 302, 307, 312–13, 331, 334, 348
Maxson, Charles A., 235
Maxwell, Edward, 266, 282–3, 294–5
Maxwell, William S., 266, 282–3, 294–5
Mayer, Albert, 405
Memramcook, NB, 43, 45–7, 327
   Collège St-Joseph, 46–7
   Monument Lefebvre, 47
Menzies, Archibald, 109–10
Merrick, Paul, 478
Messervy, Julie Moir, 489
Metepenagiag (Red Bank), NB: Augustine Mound, 33–4
Métis, Gaspé Peninsula, QC, 50, 78, 89, 295
   Blue Stick Garden, 529–30, 532
   International Garden Festival, 529–32
   "Not in My Back Yard," 529
   Reford Gardens/Jardins de Métis, 337–40, 377, 484, 528–30, 532
   "Surf and Turf," 529
Meyer, David, 495
Middleton, Ron, 468
Mignault, Mélanie, 532
Miller, Charles, 146, 197–8
Miller, George H., 235
modernism, 384–6, 392–401, 406–8, 616n69; problems with modernism, 418–19, 475
Moncton, NB, 43
   Victoria Park, 308
   war memorial sculpture, 320
Montebello, QC: Manoir-Papineau (Montebello Estate), 189–91, 343
Montreal, QC, 16, 21, 50–1, 54–6, 91, 158–9, 205–10, 263–7, 275–7, 365–6, 375, 381–2
   Angrignon Park, 401
   Autoroute du Souvenir/Remembrance Highway, 327
   Beach Park, Île Notre-Dame, 470–1, 473
   Belmont Park, 200
   Biodôme de Montréal, 491
   Canadian Centre for Architecture Garden, 495–6
   Champ-de-Mars, 158, 417–18, 476
   Chinatown/Quartier chinois: Sun Yat-Sen Park, 506–7
   Cité-jardin du tricentenaire, 402–3
   Civic Centre plan, 1913 (Marchand), 267
   community gardens, 377
   Complexe Desjardins, 425
   Complexe environnemental Saint-Michel, 375
   Dominion Park, 200

   Dominion Square (*now* Dorchester Square), 159, 164–5, 356 (*see also* Place du Canada)
   Expo 67, 6, 375, 410, 415–16, 438–45, 484, 507–8, 512; Alcan Aquarium, 441–2; American pavilion, 442; children's creative play area, 441; Cité du Havre, 439; Habitat 67 Housing Complex, 441–2; Île Notre-Dame parks, 438–41; La Ronde Amusement Centre – Children's World, 441; Place des Nations, 442; Rose Garden, 442
   Flora International Exhibition, Old Port of Montreal, 530–2
   Floralies internationales 1980, Île Notre-Dame, 473; Aquatic Garden of the City of Laval, 484; Peat-Bog Garden, 484
   Fort de la Montagne, 66
   geological park project, Plateau Mont Royal, 375
   Governor's Garden, Château Ramezay, 55, 62–3
   Hampstead, garden suburb, 273, 347
   Jacques-Cartier Bridge, 381
   Jeanne-Mance Park, 267, 291
   Lachine Canal, 195, 487, 592n1; bikeway, 490
   Lafontaine Park, 231, 506
   McGill College Avenue, 356, 423, 478
   Maison Saint-Gabriel, 66
   Molson Park, 278
   Montreal Botanical Garden, 364–6, 372, 375, 402, 473, 484, 512–14; Chinese Garden, 512–13; First Nations Garden, 513–14; Japanese Garden, 512–13; master plan, 365–6; Rhododendron Garden, 404–5
   Montreal Congress Centre: "Lipstick Forest," 530
   Mosaiculture Montréal 2000, 487
   Mount Royal Cemetery, 201–12, 206–7, 210
   Mount Royal Park, 217–19, 267, 384, 399, 423, 457, 506; Beaver Lake, 375, 384–5, 399, 401; Beaver Lake Pavilion, 399, 401; Chemin Camillien-Houde, 418; Fletcher's Field Park, 267, 382; McTavish Monument, 201; Remembrance Road, 317–18
   Notre-Dame-des-Neiges Cemetery, 208–10, 215, 315
   Old Montreal freeway proposal, 417
   Olympic Park Project (1930s), 375
   Parc Lahaie, 278, 506, 508
   Parks Department, City of Montreal, 327, 360, 435, 473, 478, 512
   Place Bonaventure: Roof Garden of Hotel Bonaventure, 423–5, 467, 505
   Place d'Armes, 56, 61, 158, 164
   Place de la Cathédrale, 478
   Place du Canada – cenotaph, 324; Windsor Station, 356 (*see also* Dominion Square)

Place Jacques-Cartier, 158
Place Viger, 158
Place Ville-Marie, 420–3, 478, 494
Radio-Canada Headquarters, 418
Royal Montreal Golf Course, 381–2, 408
St. Helen's Island (*now* Parc Jean-Drapeau) 231, 375, 381, 438–9, 442; plan for Beach Peninsula and Swimming Lagoon project (1930s), 375
St. Joseph's Oratory: Way of the Cross, 408–9
St. Lawrence Boulevard, 56, 505–9; Dante Park, 506, 509; Jean-Talon Market, 506, 509; "Little Italy/Petite Italie," 506; Parc des Amériques, 506–7; Parc du Portugal, 506–9; Parc Lahaie, 278, 506, 508; Schwartz's Delicatessen, 507–9
St. Louis Square, 159
Shaar Hashomayim Cemetery, 214
Shearith Israel Cemetery, 214
Sohmer Park, 200
Sulpician Seminary garden, 60–1, 66
"Underground City," 423
urban design for the central area of Montreal 1907–08 (Outhet/PQAA), 266
Victoria Square (Place Victoria), 152, 159, 308
Villa Maria Convent garden, 66
See also Maisonneuve, QC; Outremont, QC; Pointe-Claire, QC; Town of Mount Royal, QC; Verdun, QC; and Westmount, QC
Montreal Urban Ecology Centre (MUEC), 468
Moodie, Susanna, 134, 171–2
Moody, Colonel Richard, 129
Mooney, Estyl, 435
Mooney, Patrick, 541
Moore, Dr. Henry J., 368
Moorhead Fleming Corban McCarthy, 478
Morden, MB: agricultural research station, 150, 316
Morell, Anthony Urbanski, 267
Morell and Nichols, 263, 267, 284, 299, 332, 432
Morgan, Patrick, 339, 484
Mori, Kannosuke, 519
Morris, Charles, 79–80
Morris, Charles Jr., 88
Motherwell, William R., 124, 140–2, 556
Mount Revelstoke National Park, BC, 242–3, 260
Muir, John, 145
Muirhead, Desmond, 399, 431, 437
Mundie, William, 166–8
municipal parks, 196–200, 234–5, 277–8, 418–19
Muret, Claude, 438

Nahanni National Park Reserve, YK, 260
Nakajima, Ken, 512
National Battlefield Commission, 227, 528

National Capital Commission (NCC), 413, 425, 437, 478, 490, 501
national, provincial and territorial parks, 236–61, 377–9, 550
Nazar, Jack, 394, 400
Neff, James P.W., 206–7
Neill, John, 435, 444–5, 519
Neubergthal, MB: street village, 120–1
New Alchemists, 459
Newbery, Arthur, 161–2
New Denver, BC
  Kohan Reflection Garden, 522
  Nikkei Internment Memorial Centre Garden, 520, 523
New Westminster, BC: town plan, 127–9
New York, NY
  Central Park, 168–9, 177
  Fort Tryon Park, 611n16
  Green-Wood Cemetery, Brooklyn, 203
  Regional Plan for New York and Environs, 332, 346, 404
Niagara Falls State Park, NY, 244–5
Niagara Parks, ON, 237, 244–5, 307, 373–4
  historic forts (War of 1812–14), 373
  Niagara Horticultural School, 373
  Niagara Parkway, 373
  Oakes Garden Theatre, 373–4
  Old River Road, 373
  Queen Victoria Park, 245
Nichols, Arthur R., 267–9
Nikkel, Ray, 522
NIP Paysage, 532
Nitobe, Inazo, 518
Nobbs, Percy Erskine, 287–8
North Dakota, US: International Peace Garden, 368–9
North Vancouver, BC
  Grouse Mountain Ski Centre, 359
  Victoria Park – cenotaph/stele, 324
northern Alberta
  Alberta oil sands ("tar sands"), 461, 527, 543–9
  Peace-Athabasca Delta, 545–7
northern Ontario
  Algonquin Park, 245–8, 254
  Lakealert Program, 457
  Manitou Mounds (Kay-Nah-Chi-Wha-Nung), 33
Notman, William, 239

Oak Bay, BC, 332
  Chinese cemetery, Harling Point, 214
  Uplands garden suburb, 276–7, 614n47, 614n48
Oakville, ON
  Ford Motors plant and grounds, 410
  Sheridan Nurseries, 302, 331, 373
Oberlander, Cornelia Hahn, 397–8, 428, 441, 465, 468, 478, 501–2, 528
Oberlander, Peter, 398, 417, 434–5, 487–9

O'Brien, Lucius, 236, 239, 247
Oehmichen, Friedrich, 436, 484
Oleson Worland Architects, 471, 495
Oliver, R. Warren, 370–1
Olmsted, Frederick Law, 217–19, 235, 238, 244, 264, 282, 297, 353, 375, 384–5, 457
Olmsted, Frederick Law Jr., 225, 240, 261, 265
Olmsted, John Charles, 225, 275–6, 277, 294, 360
Olmsted Brothers, 225, 265, 275, 277, 280, 294, 331–2, 349, 352, 359–61, 392
Ontario Agricultural College. *See* Guelph, ON; University of Guelph
Ontario Association of Landscape Architects (OALA), 444
Option Aménagement, 532–4
Oshawa, ON
  Parkwood Estate, 335, 337
  Memorial Park – War Memorial, 326
Ostell, John, 209
Ottawa, ON
  Beechwood Cemetery – National Military Cemetery, 209, 212, 315
  Central Experimental Farm, 148, 151, 172, 174, 232, 343, 370–1; W.T. Macoun Memorial Garden, 371
  Confederation Boulevard, 266–7, 478, 501
  Confederation Square, 291, 357, 410, 425, 478; National War Memorial, 325–6, 430
  Garden of the Provinces, 424–5
  Glebe district, 92
  Greenbelt: La Mer Bleue, 412–13
  Lindenlea residential area, 345–6
  Major's Hill Park, 198–9, 425
  National Arts Centre, 425
  National Gallery, 357, 478, 498–500; Taiga Garden, 498–501
  parkway and boulevard system, 232, 291, 413
  Parliament Hill/Parliament Square, 281–2
  Peacekeeping Monument, 498, 501
  plan for the National Capital 1913–14 (Bennett), 290–1
  Plan for the National Capital 1950 (Gréber), 410–11, 413
  plan for the Ottawa Improvement Commission 1903 (Todd), 231
  Rideau Canal, 198, 232, 290–1, 412, 423, 425, 490
  Rockcliffe Park, 232
  Sparks Street Mall, 425–6, 479–80
  Vimy Way, 357
Our Common Future, 466–7
Outaouais Region, QC
  Gatineau Park/Gatineau Hills, 412–13, 482, 490
  Gatineau Parkway, 232, 413
  Kingsmere, Mackenzie King Estate, 339–43; Moorside Estate, 341–3; Abbey Ruins, 343

INDEX 659

Manoir-Papineau/Montebello Estate, 190–1, 343
Meech Lake, 232
Outhet, Rickson A., 265–7, 275–7, 295, 313, 331, 348–50, 364, 372
Outremont, QC: Vimy Park, 322

Pacific Landplan Collaborative, 438
Pacific Rim National Park Reserve, BC, 254–5, 260
Paine, Cecelia, 8, 437, 480–1, 528
Palliser, John, 104, 109, 123, 140, 151
"Palliser Triangle," AB/SK, 104, 109, 123, 140, 151
Pandosy, père Charles, 112–13, 144
Papineau, Louis-Joseph, 166, 189–91, 343
Papineau, Louis-Joseph Amédée, 191, 312
Parant, Louis, 402
Parc national de la Gaspésie, QC (orig. Réserve de la Gaspésie), 246, 250
Parc national des Cévennes, France, 603n80
Parc national des Laurentides, QC, 245–6
Parc national du Mont-Tremblant, QC (orig. Parc de la Montagne Tremblante), 245, 246, 491–2
Parent, Latreille et associés (PLA), 497
Paris, France: Père Lachaise Cemetery, 202, 208, 215
Parkin, John B., 406, 408, 420
Parks Canada, 9, 58, 114, 186, 256–7, 260, 436, 481–2, 523, 556–60
Parkway Planning Associates, 436, 438
Parmentier, André Joseph Ghislain, 165–6, 191
Paterson, Douglas, 225, 426
Patmore, H.B., 173
Patterson, Juliette, 532
Patterson, Walter, 80
Peace River region, AB/BC: W.A.C. Bennett Dam, 547
Pearce, William, 142–3, 162, 233, 240–2, 601n77, 604n33
Pelham, Peter, 482
Penalosa, Raquel, 532
Penney, George, 183
Perrault, Henri-Maurice, 209–10, 215
Perron, Louis, 375–7, 379, 410, 415, 435, 442, 444
Perry, Clarence, 404
Peterborough, ON, 91–3
  Serpent Mounds Park, 33–4
  Trent-Severn Canal, 34, 482
  war memorial, 321
Petersmann, Reinhart, 256, 436, 446
Pettit, Don, 415, 425, 435
Philadelphia, Pennsylvania, 297, 334, 410
  colonial town plan, 7, 79–81, 304
  Laurel Hill Cemetery, 202, 206
Phillips, Chris, 478
Phillips Farevaag Smallenberg, 327, 491, 511, 539

picturesque, beautiful, and gardenesque, 98, 100–1, 178–80
Pilote, Abbé François, 145
Pin, Gino, 465
Plante, André, 497, 534
Platt, Charles Adams, 280, 331, 337
Pluram-DAA, 534
Pointe-Claire, QC, 74
  Bowling Green neighbourhood, 272–3
  Field of Honour Cemetery, 315
Point Pelée National Park, ON, 249, 260
Pope, Hyrum, 124
Port Colborne, ON: Vimy Park, 322
Port Coquitlam, CB
  Essondale Hospital (later Riverside Hospital), 355
  Veterans' Park, 316
Porter, J.H., 394–6
Port Hope, ON: Union Cemetery, 210
postmodernism, 475–91, 494–6, 621n1
postwar residential communities, 401–6
Poullaouec-Gonidec, Philippe, 528
Poussin, Nicolas, 101, 202, 383
Powell River, BC: town plan, 279
Power, Richard, 177–8
Power, Richard Jr., 178
Pratley, Philip Louis, 380–1
Pratt, C.E. (Ned), 396
Preston, Isabella, 172, 343, 370
Prince Albert National Park, SK, 250, 260, 377–8
Prince Edward Island National Park, PEI, 251–2
  Cavendish Beach, 251–2
  golf course, 382
  Green Gables historic site, 382
Prince Rupert, BC, 461
  hotel and terminal complex, 280
  town plan, 279–301
Proctor, E.M., 380
Project Planning Associates, 256, 406, 415, 438, 441
Provancher, Abbé Léon, 172, 174
Provencher, Évèque Joseph-Norbert, 112–14
Prud'homme, Chantal, 558
Prus, Victor, 406
public squares and plazas, 54–61, 78–85, 90, 94–7, 137, 152, 158–65, 266, 277–8, 304–7, 357, 419–32, 476–8, 494–7
Purdy, Richard, 497

Qu'Appelle River Valley, SK, 105, 114–15, 124
  Last Mountain Lake and Flying Creek, 458
  Moose Lake Burial Mound, 33
Quebec City, QC
  Abitation de Québec, 51, 59
  Avenue and Parc des Braves, 228
  Avenue Honoré-Mercier (previously Autoroute Dufferin-Montmorency), 417, 533

Boulevard Langelier, 153
Boulevard René-Lévesque (previously Boulevard Saint-Cyrille), 417, 533
Chemin du Roy, 68–9
Chutes Montmorency, 98–9
Cimetière Belmont, 204
Cimetière Saint-Charles, 204–5
city gates, 156
Domaine de Maizerets, 64–6
Dufferin Terrace, 155–8
Grande-Allée, 55, 322
Henry-Stuart House, 187, 334
Hôpital général, 66, 153, 222
Hôtel-Dieu Hospital, 61, 63–4, 66
Jardin de l'Intendant (Intendant's Garden), 61–2
Jardin des Gouverneurs (Governors' Garden), 62
Manoir Montmorency (Kent House), Montmorency Falls, 98–9, 186
National Battlefields Park/Plains of Abraham, 116, 226, 322–3, 528; Jardin Jeanne-d'Arc, 374–6; parade ground, 228; war memorial "Cross of Sacrifice," 322
Old Port of Quebec City, 487
Parc de la Francophonie ("Le Pigeonnier"), 429–30
Parc de l'Artillerie, 482
Parliament Hill: Promenade des Premiers Ministres, 533; downtown rebuilding 1990–2000, 532–3
Place d'Armes, 54–5, 59–61
Place de la FAO, 497
Place de l'hôtel de ville (City Hall Square; orig. Place de la Cathédrale), 54–5, 61, 429
Place Royale (orig. Place du Marché), 54–5, 59
Promenade Samuel-de-Champlain, 533–4
Saint-Roch Garden, 153, 532–3
Ursuline monastery, 66
Victoria Park, 221–2, 308, 418
See also Cap Rouge, QC; Sainte-Foy, QC; and Sillery, QC
Queen Charlotte Islands, BC. See Haida Gwaii, BC

Radburn, New Jersey: Garden City town plan, 402–6, 463
Radice, Anna, 529
Rattenbury, Francis Mawson, 280, 286, 428
Rattray, Alex, 435, 445
Raymond, AB: town layout, 129
Reader, William R., 163, 212–13, 318, 353–4, 559
Red River, MB, 106–8, 110–16, 118, 124, 144, 199, 226, 230, 325
Reford, Alexander, 484, 528–9
Reford, Elsie, 337–9, 377, 484
Regina, SK, 106, 127, 269
  Albert Street Bridge, 380

Government House gardens, 296–7
Saskatchewan Legislative Assembly and grounds, 282–4, 380, 432
town plan, 162, 432, 458
Victoria Park, 129, 162, 308, 605n53; war memorial, 324–5
Wascana Centre/Lake Wascana, 282, 380, 432
Reid, William, 185
Repton, Humphrey, 179, 232
resource communities, 278–81, 346–50
resource conservation and sustainable development, 188, 248–50, 260–1, 377–9, 453–73
Revell, Viljo, 420
Rhind, Massey, 320
Richard, Jean-d'Auteuil, 402
Richard Strong and Associates, 256
Richard Strong Steven Moorhead Ltd., 498
Richmond, BC: Steveston Fishing Village, 515
Riding Mountain National Park, MB, 104, 144, 250–2, 260
Clear Lake, 378, 382–3
east entrance gate, 378–9
golf course, 382–3
Wasagaming Village, 378
Robert, Georges, 258, 406, 436, 446
Robillard, Arthur, 299
Robillard, Raoul, 299, 332
Rochester, NY: Mount Hope Cemetery, 212
Rocky Mountains region, AB/BC, 6, 14, 17–18, 20, 33, 50–1, 104–7, 109–10, 118, 125, 142, 236, 269, 322, 492
national parks, 239–43, 246
Rocky Mountains Forest Reserve, 249
Rohmer, Richard, 461
Rose, Peter, 478
Rosenberg, Janet, 538
Ross, Herbert, 174
Ross, J. McPherson, 235
Ross and Macdonald, 315
Routaboule, Danièle, 4, 258, 436, 446
Roy, Gabrielle, 109, 123
Roy, Ormiston, 207, 294, 343
Ruiz, Julie, 551
Ryerson University (Ryerson Polytechnical Institute), Toronto, ON, 445; Devonian Square (Ryerson Community Park), 498, 505

Safdie, Moshe, 440–1, 501
Saint Andrews, NB, 78
colonial town plan, 82, 295
Covenhoven, Minister's Island, 295, 556
Kingsbrae Horticultural Garden, 482
Saint-Arnault, Julie, 529
Saint-Boniface, MB, 106, 113–14
Archbishop's Palace, 114
cathedral, 113–14
cemetery, 113–14
Grey Nuns Convent, 113–14
war memorial, 114
Sainte-Anne-de-Bellevue, QC, 294
Macdonald College, 323, 146–7
Saint-Élie-de-Caxton, QC: *Calvaire* and Way of the Cross, 74–5
Saint-Exupéry, Antoine de, 441
Sainte-Foy, QC, 204, 227–8
Beth Israel Cemetery, 214
southern residential sector (postwar period), 401–2
Saint-Jérôme, QC: cemetery, 504
Saint John, NB
colonial town plan, 82
King's Square, 82–5
market square, 82
Old Burying Ground, 85
Queen Square, 81–2, 85
Rockwood Park, 220–1
Saint John River Valley, NB, 88
St. John's, NL
Bowring Park: Bungalow, 229; *The Caribou* sculpture, 318–20; Duck Pond, 229; *The Fighting Newfoundlander* sculpture, 318
Grand Concourse Authority path system, 490, 534
Newfoundland National War Memorial, 318
original town layout, integration to landscape, 37–40
Quidi Vidi village, 39
streetscape, 39–40
Saint-Laurent, Julie de, 99–100
Saint Lawrence Islands National Park, ON, 250
Saint-Roch-des-Aulnaies, QC
Auguste Dupuis Nursery, 173
Manoir St-Roch-des-Aulnaies, 69
Sakaguchi, Hiroshi, 486
Sanders, Frances Steinhoff. *See* Steinhoff, Frances
Sandon, BC, 129–30
Sarrazin, Michel, 66–7
Sasaki, Hideo, 435, 438, 445
Sasaki, Dawson, Demay, 424
Sasaki, Strong, office, 438, 441, 478
Saskatoon, SK
Broadway Bridge, 380
Kiwanis Memorial Park, 316
Meewasin Valley Greenway, 315–16, 502
Next-of-Kin Memorial Avenue, 317–18
plan for major traffic arteries 1913 (Yorath), 357
plan for park and boulevard system 1911 (Mufflin and Nichols), 267–9
Sutherland Forest Nursery Station, 149, 174
Vimy Memorial, 315–16
Wanuskewin Heritage Park, 28, 502
Woodlawn Cemetery, 317–18
Saunders, Charles, 149
Saunders, Dr. William (Canadian), 148–50, 172, 174, 592n60

Saunders, William (American), 592n60
Sauvé, André, 435
Savannah, Georgia: colonial town plan, 7, 79, 304
Savery, Robert, 408
Scatliff, Miller and Murray, 489
Schlemm, Leonard, 347, 379
Schoch, Gunter, 401, 436
Schoenauer, Norbert, 431
Schreiber, John, 424, 429, 436, 441, 476
Schwartz, Martha, 495, 529
Secord, James E., 441
Selkirk, Lord (Thomas Douglas), 110–11
Selkirk, MB: Lower Fort Garry, 106–8, 556
Senneville, QC, 294
Bois-Briant Estate, 294
Bois-de-la-Roche Estate, 294
Pine Bluff Estate, 294
Sewell Cautley, Marjorie, 402
Seymour, Horace L., 358–9
Shanghai Landscape Architecture Design Institute (SLADI), 512
Sharp, George L., 289
Sharp and Thompson, 289
Shattuck, William, 294
Shawinigan (orig. Shawinigan Falls), QC, 279, 347
Boulevard Saint-Maurice (Promenade du Saint-Maurice), 322, 362, 372
Cascades Inn, 350
community gardens, 377
Monument aux Braves, 322
Parc Saint-Marc, 371
Parc Saint-Maurice, 349, 371–2
Shawinigan Water and Power Company, 279, 349–50
Sherbrooke, QC: war memorial, 322
Sheridan Nurseries, 302, 331, 373
Shipman, Ellen Biddle, 611n8
Shurtleff (Shurcliff), Arthur Asahel, 348
Sidney, James C., 206–7
Sifton, Clifford, 119, 249
Sillery, QC, 180–7, 192, 203
Bois-de-Coulonge Estate (orig. Spencer Wood), 181–2, 192
Cataraqui Estate, 182–4, 192
Mount Hermon Cemetery, 203–5, 207
Saint Patrick Cemetery, 204
Villa Bagatelle (Spencer Cottage), 186–7
Silverton, BC, 129–30, 520
Simcoe, Elizabeth Posthuma, 77, 101, 595n66, 596n72
Simcoe, John Graves, 91–2, 94, 101, 192
Simon, Frank Worthington, 285
Simon Fraser University, Burnaby, BC, 359, 449–50
Siné, Sébastien, 222
Sise, Hazen, 401, 423
Skapsts, Edwin, 436
Skinner, Frank L., 173

INDEX 661

Slater, Norman, 408, 425, 442
Slocan City, BC, 129
Slocan Lake Garden Society (SLUGS), 522
Smith, A.M., 173
Smith, Eden, 272
Smith, Isaac, 81
Smith, Julian, 327
Smith, Ken, 495–6
Society for the Study of Architecture in Canada (SSAC), 559
Solsearch Architects, 459
Somerville, William, 373
Sorel, QC (*orig.* Bourg de William-Henry)
    Carré royal (Royal Square), 90
    Fort William-Henry/Town of William-Henry colonial plan, 90
southern Alberta/Palliser Triangle
    Head-Smashed-In Buffalo Jump, 22–4
    Pine Coulee Irrigation Project, 468
    Sundial Hill, 28
    Writing-on-Stone (Aisinaipi) Provincial Park, 24, 35, 556
southern Manitoba
    East and West Mennonite Reserves, 121
    International Peace Garden, Turtle Mountain, 368–9
southern Ontario
    Highway of Heroes (Macdonald-Cartier Freeway 401), 327, 391
    Queen Elizabeth Way, 373
    Seaway Park, St. Lawrence River, 415
    village of Crieff beautification program, 332
space2place, 524–5
Spence-Sales, Harold, 434
Sproule, George, 88
Spry Point, PEI: The Ark, 458–9, 473
Stansbury, James, 437–8, 457
Stavely, Edward, 182
Stein, Clarence, 402–5
Steinhoff, Frances (*also* Steinhoff Sanders, Frances), 334, 379
Steinitz, Carl, 456, 473
Stensson, Janina Nalesc-Korkuc, 410, 436, 441
Stensson, Sven Herman, 303
Stensson, Vilhelm "Bill," 373, 379, 393, 409–10, 436
Stewart, John, 481
Stewart, Mary, 183, 188, 334
Stirling, AB: town layout – "Plat of Zion," 123–4
Stolpe, Max, 235
Stoughton, Arthur A., 288, 316
Stratford, ON
    Lake Victoria, 234
    North Shore Park, 234
    parks on the Avon River, 234, 292
    Shakespeare Festival site, 234
Strathmore, AB: Canadian Pacific Railway demonstration farms, 137–8
Strickland, Colonel Samuel, 93–4, 134
Strong, Maurice F., 446

Strong, Richard, 437–8, 444, 492
Strong and Moorhead, 498
Stuart, Adele and Mary, 187–8
Sturtevant, Butler S., 299
sublime, 101, 109–10, 549
suburbs, growth and character in postwar period, 390–2
Sugimoto, Mas, 520
Sumi, Roy Tomomichi, 519–20
Summers, G.F., 347
Suncor oil company, 545, 547–8
Sunset Magazine, 394
Sunshine Coast, western mainland, BC
    Lund, 130
    Madeira Park, 130
    Pender Harbour, 130
    See also Powell River, BC
Surrey, BC: design charrettes, 541
Surtees, Robert, 212
Sussex, NB: war memorial, 321
Suzhou garden administration team, 512
Suzuki, Dr. David, 259, 517, 543
Sydenham, Lord, 196
Sydney, NS, 78
    Canadian Coast Guard College, 446
    colonial town plan, 82, 102
    Great George Street, 82
    Sydney Tar Ponds, 545
Sylvia Grinnell Territorial Park, NU, 550
Syncrude oil company, 545

Talon, Jean, 69–70
Tanaka, George, 337, 435, 523
Tanguay et Vallée, 222
Tantramar Marshes (Tintamarre), NB, 43, 47–8
Tattersfield, Philip, 406, 437, 444
Taylor, Alfred J.T. "Fred," 359
Taylor, Edwin P., 168, 178, 404
Taylor, James "Jim," 405, 437–8
Témiscaming (*orig.* Kipawa), QC: Garden City town plan, 347–8
Terra Nova National Park, NL, 253, 260
Teuscher, Henry, 365–6, 484, 514
Thayendanega. *See* Brant, Joseph
Thom, Ron, 434, 451
Thompson, Berwick and Pratt, 451
Thompson, Charles J., 289
Thompson, Stanley F., 252, 382–3, 551
Thomsen, Charlie, 437
Thomson, Tom, 248, 549
Thoreau, Henry David, 237
Thousand Islands – St. Lawrence River, 91, 245, 250
    St. Lawrence Seaway parks, 414–15, 487
    Upper Canada Village, Morrisburg, ON, 415
Thunder Bay, ON: grain elevators, 139
Todd, Frederick Gage, 162
    City Beautiful designs, 282–4
    Garden City projects, 272–7

    later works, 374–5, 384–5, 408–9
    long-term influence and honours, 415, 438–9, 528, 534
    major urban parks and park systems, 225–34, 288, 291
    municipal parks, 234, 307
    private gardens and estates, 294, 331–2
Todd, John, 459
Todd, Nancy Jack, 459
Tolstoi, MB: Saint-Michael's Church and Cemetery, 122
Tonari Gumi, association, 523
Toronto, ON
    Alexander Muir Commemorative Gardens, 370–1
    Allan Gardens, 167, 178
    the Beaches – Kew Gardens, 200
    Canada's Wonderland, 491
    Castle Frank, 77, 95, 101, 167, 192–3
    Clarence Square, 160, 167
    College Street, 154
    Commerce Court, 420–1
    Division of Parks and Recreation, City of Toronto, 471
    Don Mills: Inn on the Park Hotel, 410; new community, 403–10; Ortho Pharmaceuticals site and building, 407–8; shopping centre, 406; Town Plan, 403
    Don River Rehabilitation Study, 452, 469, 537, 539, 542
    Don Valley Brickworks, 452, 471, 536
    Downtown Redevelopment Plan 1929 (Lyle), 356–7
    Eaton Centre, 420–1, 478
    Federal Avenue, project 1911 (Lyle), 267–9, 420–1
    Forest Hill Village garden, 399–400
    Gardiner Expressway, 417, 536
    Harbourfront/Waterfront Projects, 536–9: Canada's Sugar Beach, 537–8; HtO Urban Beach, 537–8; Lake Ontario Park, 539; Lower Don Lands, 539; Music Garden, 489, 536–7; Tommy Thompson Park (Leslie Street Spit), 470–1, 537, 539; "Wavedecks," 537–8; West Don Lands, 537, 539
    High Park, 188, 220; Colborne Lodge, 188, 220; Grenadier Pond, 188, 220
    Humber Bay Shores, renaturalization, 469–71, 536
    Humber Valley Surveys – Old Mill Restaurant, 302
    Lawrence Park Estates, 302
    Leaside residential district, 605n51
    Lorne Park residential district, 200
    Mimico Hospital (Lakeshore Psychiatric Hospital), 354
    Moss Park Estate, 166–7
    Mount Pleasant Cemetery, 210

Nathan Phillips Square/Toronto City Hall, 291, 420–1
Necropolis Cemetery, 210
"New Town" residential and commercial sector, 160
Normal School and Model School grounds, 167–8 (*see also* St. James Square)
Ontario Place, 443, 537
path and trail network (ravines and Belt Line railroad), 491
Queen's Park (*orig.* University Park), 154, 537
Riverdale Courts, 272
Rosedale, garden suburb, 192–3, 203, 210
St. James Cemetery, 203, 220
St. James Square, 167–8
Scarborough College, 450
Shadowbrook Estate, Willowdale, 331
Sheraton Centre Hotel – Interior Garden, 420–1
Spadina Avenue and Crescent, 155, 538
Spadina Expressway, 417
Spruce Court, 272
Sunnyside Beach Park, 351–3
Toronto-Dominion Centre, 420
Toronto Zoo, 491
Trinity Square, 421, 478
University Avenue, 154–5, 356–7, 410
Uplands Estate, 328
Victoria Square, 160, 167
Village of Yorkville Park, 494–6
Wellington Place, 160, 167
Wychwood Village, 272
Tory, Henry Marshall, 288
T. Pringle and Son, 279
Town of Mount Royal, QC
  Garden City town plan, 275–6, 605n53
  Rockland Shopping Centre, 406
Traill, Catharine Parr, 134, 172
Tremblay, William, 366, 374–5
Tremblay, Héroux et associés, 603n86
Trent University, Peterborough, ON, 451
Trois-Rivières, QC
  Champlain Park, 160, 418, 429
  Exhibition Grounds, 371
  old port, 487
  St-Jean-Baptiste de la Salle neighbourhood, 406
  Terrasse Turcotte, 155
Truro, NS: Nova Scotia Agricultural College, 146
Tulloch, Judith, 557–8
Tunnard, Christopher, 385–6, 398, 408
Turner, Frederick Jackson, 133
Turner, J.M.W., 238
Turner, John, 94

Université de Moncton, Moncton, NB, 446
Université de Montréal, Montreal, QC, 448, 496

Université Laval, Québec and Sainte-Foy, QC, 61, 145
  new postwar campus, 417, 446, 448
university and college campus planning, 145–7, 166–9, 287–90, 317, 370, 373, 419, 445–51, 496
University of Alberta, Edmonton, AB, 287–8, 419, 484, 534
University of British Columbia, Vancouver, BC, 333, 335, 359, 385, 445
  campus plan, 299, 333
  Design Centre for Sustainability, 540–1
  Museum of Anthropology, 502
  Nitobe Garden, 517–20
  University Endowment Lands, 333
University of Calgary, Calgary, AB, 291
University of California at Berkeley, CA, 399, 434–5, 437, 438
University of Guelph, Guelph, ON, 444, 449, 529, 541, 562. See also Guelph, ON – Ontario Agricultural College
  Botanic Garden, 405
  master plan, 449
  rhododendron and azalea garden, 404–5
University of Lethbridge, Lethbridge, AB, 6, 450–1
University of Manitoba, Winnipeg, MB, 147, 316, 394, 426, 434, 445
  central avenue, 288, 318
  original site plan, 288
  postwar expansion, 419
University of Massachusetts, Amherst, MA, 225, 435
University of Saskatchewan, Saskatoon, SK, 287, 313, 606n98
  master plan, 287
  Memorial Gates, 317
University of Toronto (*orig.* University of King's College), Toronto, ON, 153–4, 166–8, 178, 305, 368, 391, 444, 529
  Massey College, 451
  Soldiers' Tower, Hart House, 317
  University College, 167
University of Victoria, Victoria, BC, 446
University of Western Ontario, London, ON, 370
Unwin, Raymond, 271, 275–6

Van der Rohe, Mies, 420
Van der Zalm and Associates, 489
Van Ginkel, Blanche Lemco, 417, 440
Van Ginkel, Sandy, 417, 440
Van Horne, Sir William, 295
Van Norman, C.B.K., 399
Vancouver, BC
  Arthur Erickson's garden, 486–7
  Cathedral Place, 478
  Coal Harbour, 269–71
  Dr. Sun Yat-Sen Classical Chinese Garden, 509–12

  Expo 86, 492
  False Creek, residential development, 492
  Friedman Garden, 397–8
  Graham Garden, 399
  Granville Island, 487–9
  Hastings Park, 230, 359, 491, 518; Italian Garden, 511–12; Momiji Garden, 518; rehabilitation (1990s), 491, 511–12; sanctuary, 491
  Joy Kogawa House, Marpole district, 525
  Lions Gate Bridge, 380–2, 474–5
  Marine Drive, 273–4, 332–3, 359, 453–4; Gables Estate, 332–3
  Oppenheimer Park (*orig.* Powell Street Grounds), 514, 523–5
  Park Place, 497
  Point Grey district, town plan, 273–4, 289, 333
  Portland Hotel roof garden, 468
  Powell Street Grounds, 514, 516, 523 (*see also* Oppenheimer Park)
  Queen Elizabeth Park, 359
  Robson Square and law courts, 428–9
  Shaughnessy Heights, 333, 484; The Crescent, 274; Hycroft Estate, 299, 332
  Stanley Park, 6, 216, 223–5, 230–1, 235, 269, 359–60, 380, 475; Lost Lagoon, 225; Seawall, 216, 225
  Urban Design plan 1913 (Mawson), 269–71, 283, 289
  Vancouver Master Plan 1929 (Bartholomew), 358, 359
  Van Dusen Botanical Garden, 484
  See also Burnaby, BC; New Westminster, BC; North Vancouver, BC; Port Coquitlam, BC; Richmond, BC; Surrey, BC; West Vancouver, BC
Vancouver Japanese Gardeners Association, 518
Vandermeulen, Emil, 425–6
Vaughan, Don, 437, 446, 450, 489, 491–2, 494–5, 497, 512, 519
Vaux, Calvert, 217, 281–2
Vaux, Downing, 220–1
Vecsei, Eva, 424
Verdun, QC: Ruisseau des Hérons, Nuns' Island, 468–9
Vernon, BC: Coldstream Ranch, 144
Victoria, BC
  Beacon Hill Park, 223–4
  British Columbia Legislative Assembly and grounds, 285–6
  Butchart Gardens, 297–300, 332, 337, 401, 515
  Centennial Plaza, 429–30
  Clovelly Place, 302
  Empress Hotel, 285–6
  Esquimalt Harbour, 299–300
  Gorge Park (Tramway Park), 200; Takata Tea Gardens, 297

INDEX 663

Government House gardens, 408–9
Hatley Park, Hatley Castle, 299–301
Ross Bay Cemetery, 211–12, 214
St. Ann's Academy, 113
See also Oak Bay, BC
Vigneault, Gilles, 18–19
Villa, Luis F., 442
villa and estate gardens, 98–101, 166, 178–93, 293–302, 328–30, 335–43, 484–6, 556–8
Vimy Ridge, France: Canadian National Vimy Memorial, 321–2
Virginia, US
Monticello, Charlottesville, 189
rebuilding of historic capital, Williamsburg, 413
Vivian, Henry, 271–2
VLAN Paysage, 529

WAA Inc. See Williams, Asselin, Ackaoui et associés
Wai, Joe Y., 512
Walker, Edwin "Jack," 435
Walker, Horatio, 151
Wang, Zu-Xin, 512
Ward, Barbara, 466
Ward, John Wilson
Washington, DC: McMillan Plan for rebuilding the centre of Washington 1901, 265
Waterton Lakes National Park, AB, 242–3, 260, 322
Cameron Lake, 242
townsite, 591n78
Vimy Peak, 322
Watson, Homer, 151
Watt, George, 297
Way, Douglas, 456
Webb, Harry James, 431, 435
Webb and Knapp, 423
Webber, John, 110
Wedd, John, 154
Welland, ON: Welland-Crowland War Memorial, 320
Westby, William H., 299

Western Homes and Living magazine (*Western Living*), 396
Westmount, QC: Westmount Park, 306, 418
West Vancouver, BC
B.C. Binning house and garden, 389, 396
British Pacific Properties, 359–61
Capilano Estates, 359–61
Capilano Golf and Country Club, 383
"Granite Assemblage," Ambleside Village, 474–5, 494–5
J.C.H. Porter house and garden, 394–6
Park Royal Centre, 406
Wetherell, Robert, 185
Wheeler, Seager, 173
Whistler, BC: Olympic Village 2010, 492
Whitby, ON
community gardens, 356
Ontario Hospital (Whitby Psychiatric Hospital), 355–6
war memorial, 326
Whiteshell Provincial Park, MB, 377–8
Whitman, Walt, 237
Whittlesey, Julian, 405–6
Wilkinson, Denis R., 426, 437, 445
Williams, Asselin, Ackaoui et associés (WAA Inc.), 214, 469, 473, 478, 513, 532–4
Wilson, Bunnell and Borgstrom, 363–4, 368, 383
Winnipeg, MB
Assiniboine Park, 226–7, 229–30, 277
Broadway, 154–5, 285, 324
Centennial Library Park, 426
Elm Park, 199–200
The Forks, 489, 490, 501–2
Kildonan Park, 230; Peguis Pavilion, 400–1
Maitland Steinkopf Gardens, 426
Manitoba Agricultural College, 146–7
Manitoba Legislative Assembly and grounds, 285, 324
Memorial Boulevard, 285, 324; cenotaph, 324
Oodena Celebration Circle, 501–2
River Park, 199–200
skate park, 489

Tuxedo Park district, 265–6, 277
Union Station, 155
Upper Fort Garry, 155
Victoria Park, 611n3
Vimy Park, 322, 327
Wildwood Park residential area, 403–4
See also Saint-Boniface, MB
Winona, ON: E.D. Smith Nursery, 173, 235, 408
Wood, Edward I. "Ned," 413
Wood, Elizabeth Wyn, 320, 373
Wood, Percy, 95
Wood Buffalo National Park, AB/NWT, 250, 260
Woodland, Carolyn, 457
Woolverton, Charles Ernest, 234–5
Woolverton, Linus, 173–4, 234
Wordsworth, William, 202, 237
Wright, Henry, 402
Wright, Thomas, 80
Writing-on-Stone (Aisinaipi) Provincial Park, AB, 35, 556
Wylie, Florence, 351
WZMH Architectes, 478

Yamasaki, Minoru, 432
Yarmouth, NS: Mountain Cemetery, 215
Yellowknife, NWT
Bush Pilot's Monument, 463
N'dilo Dene Community, 464
New Town, 464
NWT Legislative Assembly, 464–5
Old Town, 463–4
Yellowstone National Park, Wyoming and Montana, 238–9
Yoho National Park, BC, 242, 260
Yosemite National Park, California, 238
Young, Margot, 473
Yo-Yo Ma, 489

Zeckendorf, William, 423
Zeidler, Eberhard, 443
Zeidler and Roberts, 420
Zhong, Le Wei, 512
Zvonar, John E., 327, 559